SELECTED
PLAYS
OF
BERNARD
SHAW

⫸ ⫷

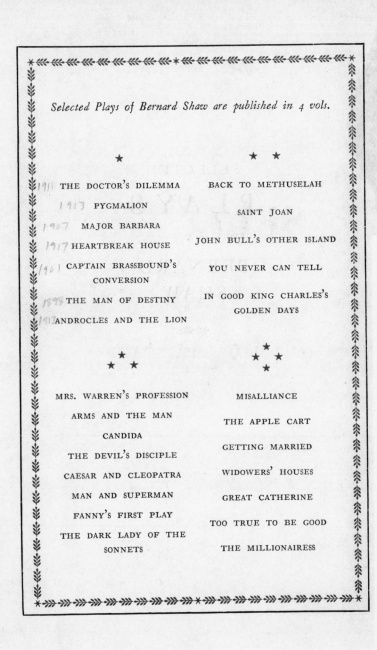

Selected Plays of Bernard Shaw are published in 4 vols.

★

★ ★

1911 THE DOCTOR'S DILEMMA

1913 PYGMALION

1907 MAJOR BARBARA

1917 HEARTBREAK HOUSE

1901 CAPTAIN BRASSBOUND'S
CONVERSION

1898 THE MAN OF DESTINY

1913 ANDROCLES AND THE LION

BACK TO METHUSELAH

SAINT JOAN

JOHN BULL'S OTHER ISLAND

YOU NEVER CAN TELL

IN GOOD KING CHARLES'S
GOLDEN DAYS

★
★ ★

★
★ ★
★

MRS. WARREN'S PROFESSION

ARMS AND THE MAN

CANDIDA

THE DEVIL'S DISCIPLE

CAESAR AND CLEOPATRA

MAN AND SUPERMAN

FANNY'S FIRST PLAY

THE DARK LADY OF THE
SONNETS

MISALLIANCE

THE APPLE CART

GETTING MARRIED

WIDOWERS' HOUSES

GREAT CATHERINE

TOO TRUE TO BE GOOD

THE MILLIONAIRESS

★

BERNARD SHAW

SELECTED
PLAYS

WITH PREFACES

Dodd, Mead & Company

NEW YORK

CONTENTS

PUBLISHER'S NOTE

Readers of these plays will find in some of the Prefaces occasional references to plays which are not included in this volume. It should be explained, for the sake of clarity, that some of these Prefaces were written by Mr. Shaw for volumes containing several plays, and they are printed here without change, in accordance with the wish of the author. The text in this volume is that of the Ayot St. Lawrence Edition, which is the latest revised edition.

PREFACE ON DOCTORS

IT is not the fault of our doctors that the medical service of the community, as at present provided for, is a murderous absurdity. That any sane nation, having observed that you could provide for the supply of bread by giving bakers a pecuniary interest in baking for you, should go on to give a surgeon a pecuniary interest in cutting off your leg, is enough to make one despair of political humanity. But that is precisely what we have done. And the more appalling the mutilation, the more the mutilator is paid. He who corrects the ingrowing toe-nail receives a few shillings: he who cuts your inside out receives hundreds of guineas, except when he does it to a poor person for practice.

Scandalized voices murmur that these operations are necessary. They may be. It may also be necessary to hang a man or pull down a house. But we take good care not to make the hangman and the housebreaker the judges of that. If we did, no man's neck would be safe and no man's house stable. But we do make the doctor the judge, and fine him anything from sixpence to several hundred guineas if he decides in our favor. I cannot knock my shins severely without forcing on some surgeon the difficult question, "Could I not make a better use of a pocketful of guineas than this man is making of his leg? Could he not write as well—or even better—on one leg than on two? And the guineas would make all the difference in the world to me just now. My wife—my pretty ones—the leg may mortify—it is always safer to operate—he will be well in a fortnight—artificial legs are now so well made that they are really better than natural ones—evolution is towards motors and leglessness, &c., &c., &c."

Now there is no calculation that an engineer can make as to the behavior of a girder under a strain, or an astronomer as to the recurrence of a comet, more certain than the calculation that under such circumstances we shall be dismembered unnecessarily in all directions by surgeons who believe the operations to be necessary solely because they want

1

to perform them. The process metaphorically called bleeding the rich man is performed not only metaphorically but literally every day by surgeons who are quite as honest as most of us. After all, what harm is there in it? The surgeon need not take off the rich man's (or woman's) leg or arm: he can remove the appendix or the uvula, and leave the patient none the worse after a fortnight or so in bed, whilst the nurse, the general practitioner, the apothecary, and the surgeon will be the better.

DOUBTFUL CHARACTER BORNE BY THE MEDICAL PROFESSION

Again I hear the voices indignantly muttering old phrases about the high character of a noble profession and the honor and conscience of its members. I must reply that the medical profession has not a high character; it has an infamous character. I do not know a single thoughtful and well-informed person who does not feel that the tragedy of illness at present is that it delivers you helplessly into the hands of a profession which you deeply mistrust, because it not only advocates and practises the most revolting cruelties in the pursuit of knowledge, and justifies them on grounds which would equally justify practising the same cruelties on yourself or your children, or burning down London to test a patent fire extinguisher, but, when it has shocked the public, tries to reassure it with lies of breath-bereaving brazenness. That is the character the medical profession has got just now. It may be deserved or it may not: there it is at all events, and the doctors who have not realized this are living in a fool's paradise. As to the honor and conscience of doctors, they have as much as any other class of men, no more and no less. And what other men dare pretend to be impartial where they have a strong pecuniary interest on one side? Nobody supposes that doctors are less virtuous than judges; but a judge whose salary and reputation depended on whether the verdict was for plaintiff or defendant, prosecutor or prisoner, would be as little trusted as a general in the pay of the enemy. To offer me a doctor as

2

my judge, and then weight his decision with a bribe of a large sum of money and a virtual guarantee that if he makes a mistake it can never be proved against him, is to go wildly beyond the ascertained strain which human nature will bear. It is simply unscientific to allege or believe that doctors do not under existing circumstances perform unnecessary operations and manufacture and prolong lucrative illnesses. The only ones who can claim to be above suspicion are those who are so much sought after that their cured patients are immediately replaced by fresh ones. And there is this curious psychological fact to be remembered: a serious illness or a death advertizes the doctor exactly as a hanging advertizes the barrister who defended the person hanged. Suppose, for example, a royal personage gets something wrong with his throat, or has a pain in his inside. If a doctor effects some trumpery cure with a wet compress or a peppermint lozenge nobody takes the least notice of him. But if he operates on the throat and kills the patient, or extirpates an internal organ and keeps the whole nation palpitating for days whilst the patient hovers in pain and fever between life and death, his fortune is made: every rich man who omits to call him in when the same symptoms appear in his household is held not to have done his utmost duty to the patient. The wonder is that there is a king or queen left alive in Europe.

DOCTORS' CONSCIENCES

There is another difficulty in trusting to the honor and conscience of a doctor. Doctors are just like other Englishmen: most of them have no honor and no conscience: what they commonly mistake for these is sentimentality and an intense dread of doing anything that everybody else does not do, or omitting to do anything that everybody else does. This of course does amount to a sort of working or rule-of-thumb conscience; but it means that you will do anything, good or bad, provided you get enough people to keep you in countenance by doing it also. It is the sort of conscience that makes it possible to keep order on a pirate

3

ship, or in a troop of brigands. It may be said that in the last analysis there is no other sort of honor or conscience in existence—that the assent of the majority is the only sanction known to ethics. No doubt this holds good in political practice. If mankind knew the facts, and agreed with the doctors, then the doctors would be in the right; and any person who thought otherwise would be a lunatic. But mankind does not agree, and does not know the facts. All that can be said for medical popularity is that until there is a practicable alternative to blind trust in the doctor, the truth about the doctor is so terrible that we dare not face it. Molière saw through the doctors; but he had to call them in just the same. Napoleon had no illusions about them; but he had to die under their treatment just as much as the most credulous ignoramus that ever paid sixpence for a bottle of strong medicine. In this predicament most people, to save themselves from unbearable mistrust and misery, or from being driven by their conscience into actual conflict with the law, fall back on the old rule that if you cannot have what you believe in you must believe in what you have. When your child is ill or your wife dying, and you happen to be very fond of them, or even when, if you are not fond of them, you are human enough to forget every personal grudge before the spectacle of a fellow creature in pain or peril, what you want is comfort, reassurance, something to clutch at, were it but a straw. This the doctor brings you. You have a wildly urgent feeling that something must be done; and the doctor does something. Sometimes what he does kills the patient; but you do not know that; and the doctor assures you that all that human skill could do has been done. And nobody has the brutality to say to the newly bereft father, mother, husband, wife, brother, or sister, "You have killed your lost darling by your credulity."

THE PECULIAR PEOPLE

Besides, the calling in of the doctor is now compulsory except in cases where the patient is an adult and not too ill to decide the steps to be taken. We are subject to prosecu-

4

tion for manslaughter or for criminal neglect if the patient dies without the consolations of the medical profession. This menace is kept before the public by the Peculiar People. The Peculiars, as they are called, have gained their name by believing that the Bible is infallible, and taking their belief quite seriously. The Bible is very clear as to the treatment of illness. The Epistle of James, chapter v., contains the following explicit directions:—

> 14. Is any sick among you? let him call for the elders of the Church; and let them pray over him, anointing him with oil in the name of the Lord:

> 15. And the prayer of faith shall save the sick, and the Lord shall raise him up; and if he have committed sins, they shall be forgiven him.

The Peculiars obey these instructions and dispense with doctors. They are therefore prosecuted for manslaughter when their children die.

When I was a young man, the Peculiars were usually acquitted. The prosecution broke down when the doctor in the witness box was asked whether, if the child had had medical attendance, it would have lived. It was, of course, impossible for any man of sense and honor to assume divine omniscience by answering this in the affirmative, or indeed pretending to be able to answer it at all. And on this the judge had to instruct the jury that they must acquit the prisoner. Thus a judge with a keen sense of law (a very rare phenomenon on the Bench, by the way) was spared the possibility of having to sentence one prisoner (under the Blasphemy Laws) for questioning the authority of Scripture, and another for ignorantly and superstitiously accepting it as a guide to conduct. Today all this is changed. The doctor never hesitates to claim divine omniscience, nor to clamor for laws to punish any scepticism on the part of laymen. A modern doctor thinks nothing of signing the death certificate of one of his own diphtheria patients, and then going into the witness box and swearing a Peculiar into prison for six months by assuring the jury, on oath, that

5

if the prisoner's child, dead of diphtheria, had been placed under his treatment instead of that of St James, it would not have died. And he does so not only with impunity, but with public applause, though the logical course would be to prosecute him either for the murder of his own patient, or for perjury in the case of St James. Yet no barrister, apparently, dreams of asking for the statistics of the relative case-mortality in diphtheria among the Peculiars and among the believers in doctors, on which alone any valid opinion could be founded. The barrister is as superstitious as the doctor is infatuated; and the Peculiar goes unpitied to his cell, though nothing whatever has been proved except that his child died without the interference of a doctor as effectually as any of the hundreds of children who die every day of the same diseases in the doctor's care.

RECOIL OF THE DOGMA OF MEDICAL INFALLIBILITY ON THE DOCTOR

On the other hand, when the doctor is in the dock, or is the defendant in an action for malpractice, he has to struggle against the inevitable result of his former pretences to infinite knowledge and unerring skill. He has taught the jury and the judge, and even his own counsel, to believe that every doctor can, with a glance at the tongue, a touch on the pulse, and a reading of the clinical thermometer, diagnose with absolute certainty a patient's complaint, also that on dissecting a dead body he can infallibly put his finger on the cause of death, and, in cases where poisoning is suspected, the nature of the poison used. Now all this supposed exactness and infallibility is imaginary; and to treat a doctor as if his mistakes were necessarily malicious or corrupt malpractices (an inevitable deduction from the postulate that the doctor, being omniscient, cannot make mistakes) is as unjust as to blame the nearest apothecary for not being prepared to supply you with sixpenny-worth of the elixir of life, or the nearest motor garage for not having perpetual motion on sale in gallon tins. But if apothecaries and motor car makers habitually advertized

6

elixir of life and perpetual motion, and succeeded in creating a strong general belief that they could supply it, they would find themselves in an awkward position if they were indicted for allowing a customer to die, or for burning a chauffeur by putting petrol into his car. That is the predicament the doctor finds himself in when he has to defend himself against a charge of malpractice by a plea of ignorance and fallibility. His plea is received with flat incredulity; and he gets little sympathy, even from laymen who know, because he has brought the incredulity on himself. If he escapes, he can only do so by opening the eyes of the jury to the facts that medical science is as yet very imperfectly differentiated from common curemongering witchcraft; that diagnosis, though it means in many instances (including even the identification of pathogenic bacilli under the miscroscope) only a choice among terms so loose that they would not be accepted as definitions in any really exact science, is, even at that, an uncertain and difficult matter on which doctors often differ; and that the very best medical opinion and treatment varies widely from doctor to doctor, one practitioner prescribing six or seven scheduled poisons for so familiar a disease as enteric fever where another will not tolerate drugs at all; one starving a patient whom another would stuff; one urging an operation which another would regard as unnecessary and dangerous; one giving alcohol and meat which another would sternly forbid, &c., &c., &c.: all these discrepancies arising not between the opinion of good doctors and bad ones (the medical contention is, of course, that a bad doctor is an impossibility), but between practitioners of equal eminence and authority. Usually it is impossible to persuade the jury that these facts are facts. Juries seldom notice facts; and they have been taught to regard any doubts of the omniscience and omnipotence of doctors as blasphemy. Even the fact that doctors themselves die of the very diseases they profess to cure passes unnoticed. We do not shoot out our lips and shake our heads, saying, "They save others: themselves they cannot save":

their reputation stands, like an African king's palace, on a foundation of dead bodies; and the result is that the verdict goes against the defendant when the defendant is a doctor accused of malpractice.

Fortunately for the doctors, they very seldom find themselves in this position, because it is so difficult to prove anything against them. The only evidence that can decide a case of malpractice is expert evidence: that is, the evidence of other doctors; and every doctor will allow a colleague to decimate a whole countryside sooner than violate the bond of professional etiquet by giving him away. It is the nurse who gives the doctor away in private, because every nurse has some particular doctor whom she likes; and she usually assures her patients that all the others are disastrous noodles, and soothes the tedium of the sick-bed by gossip about their blunders. She will even give a doctor away for the sake of making the patient believe that she knows more than the doctor. But she dare not, for her livelihood, give the doctor away in public. And the doctors stand by one another at all costs. Now and then some doctor in an unassailable position, like the late Sir William Gull, will go into the witness box and say what he really thinks about the way a patient has been treated; but such behavior is considered little short of infamous by his colleagues.

WHY DOCTORS DO NOT DIFFER

The truth is, there would never be any public agreement among doctors if they did not agree to agree on the main point of the doctor being always in the right. Yet the two guinea man never thinks that the five shilling man is right: if he did, he would be understood as confessing to an overcharge of £1:17s.; and on the same ground the five shilling man cannot encourage the notion that the owner of the six-penny surgery round the corner is quite up to his mark. Thus even the layman has to be taught that infallibility is not quite infallible, because there are two qualities of it to be had at two prices.

But there is no agreement even in the same rank at the

8

same price. During the first great epidemic of influenza towards the end of the nineteenth century a London evening paper sent round a journalist-patient to all the great consultants of that day, and published their advice and prescriptions: a proceeding passionately denounced by the medical papers as a breach of confidence of these eminent physicians. The case was the same; but the prescriptions were different, and so was the advice. Now a doctor cannot think his own treatment right and at the same time think his colleague right in prescribing a different treatment when the patient is the same. Anyone who has ever known doctors well enough to hear medical shop talked without reserve knows that they are full of stories about each other's blunders and errors, and that the theory of their omniscience and omnipotence no more holds good among themselves than it did with Molière and Napoleon. But for this very reason no doctor dare accuse another of malpractice. He is not sure enough of his own opinion to ruin another man by it. He knows that if such conduct were tolerated in his profession no doctor's livelihood or reputation would be worth a year's purchase. I do not blame him: I should do the same myself. But the effect of this state of things is to make the medical profession a conspiracy to hide its own shortcomings. No doubt the same may be said of all professions. They are all conspiracies against the laity; and I do not suggest that the medical conspiracy is either better or worse than the military conspiracy, the legal conspiracy, the sacerdotal conspiracy, the pedagogic conspiracy, the royal and aristocratic conspiracy, the literary and artistic conspiracy, and the innumerable industrial, commercial, and financial conspiracies, from the trade unions to the great exchanges, which make up the huge conflict which we call society. But it is less suspected. The Radicals who used to advocate, as an indispensable preliminary to social reform, the strangling of the last king with the entrails of the last priest, substituted compulsory vaccination for compulsory baptism without a murmur.

9

THE CRAZE FOR OPERATIONS

Thus everything is on the side of the doctor. When men die of disease they are said to die from natural causes. When they recover (and they mostly do) the doctor gets the credit of curing them. In surgery all operations are recorded as successful if the patient can be got out of the hospital or nursing home alive, though the subsequent history of the case may be such as would make an honest surgeon vow never to recommend or perform the operation again. The large range of operations which consist of amputating limbs and extirpating organs admits of no direct verification of their necessity. There is a fashion in operations as there is in sleeves and skirts: the triumph of some surgeon who has at last found out how to make a once desperate operation fairly safe is usually followed by a rage for that operation not only among the doctors, but actually among their patients. There are men and women whom the operating table seems to fascinate: half-alive people who through vanity, or hypochondria, or a craving to be the constant objects of anxious attention or what not, lose such feeble sense as they ever had of the value of their own organs and limbs. They seem to care as little for mutilation as lobsters or lizards, which at least have the excuse that they grow new claws and new tails if they lose the old ones. Whilst this book was being prepared for the press a case was tried in the Courts, of a man who sued a railway company for damages because a train had run over him and amputated both his legs. He lost his case because it was proved that he had deliberately contrived the occurrence himself for the sake of getting an idler's pension at the expense of the railway company, being too dull to realize how much more he had to lose than to gain by the bargain even if he had won his case and received damages above his utmost hopes.

This amazing case makes it possible to say, with some prospect of being believed, that there is in the classes who can afford to pay for fashionable operations a sprinkling of

persons so incapable of appreciating the relative importance
of preserving their bodily integrity (including the capacity
for parentage) and the pleasure of talking about themselves
and hearing themselves talked about as the heroes and
heroines of sensational operations, that they tempt surgeons
to operate on them not only with huge fees, but with personal solicitation. Now it cannot be too often repeated that
when an operation is once performed, nobody can ever
prove that it was unnecessary. If I refuse to allow my leg to
be amputated, its mortification and my death may prove
that I was wrong; but if I let the leg go, nobody can ever
prove that it would not have mortified had I been obstinate.
Operation is therefore the safe side for the surgeon as well
as the lucrative side. The result is that we hear of "conservative surgeons" as a distinct class of practitioners who
make it a rule not to operate if they can possibly help it,
and who are sought after by the people who have vitality
enough to regard an operation as a last resort. But no surgeon is bound to take the conservative view. If he believes
that an organ is at best a useless survival, and that if he
extirpates it the patient will be well and none the worse in a
fortnight, whereas to await the natural cure would mean a
month's illness, then he is clearly justified in recommending
the operation even if the cure without operation is as certain
as anything of the kind ever can be. Thus the conservative
surgeon and the radical or extirpatory surgeon may both be
right as far as the ultimate cure is concerned; so that their
consciences do not help them out of their differences.

CREDULITY AND CHLOROFORM

There is no harder scientific fact in the world than the
fact that belief can be produced in practically unlimited
quantity and intensity, without observation or reasoning,
and even in defiance of both, by the simple desire to believe founded on a strong interest in believing. Everybody
recognizes this in the case of the amatory infatuations of
the adolescents who see angels and heroes in obviously (to
others) commonplace and even objectionable maidens and

youths. But it holds good over the entire field of human activity. The hardest-headed materialist will become a consulter of table-rappers and slate-writers if he loses a child or a wife so beloved that the desire to revive and communicate with them becomes irresistible. The cobbler believes that there is nothing like leather. The Imperialist who regards the conquest of England by a foreign power as the worst of political misfortunes believes that the conquest of a foreign power by England would be a boon to the conquered. Doctors are no more proof against such illusions than other men. Can anyone then doubt that under existing conditions a great deal of unnecessary and mischievous operating is bound to go on, and that patients are encouraged to imagine that modern surgery and anesthesia have made operations much less serious matters than they really are? When doctors write or speak to the public about operations, they imply, and often say in so many words, that chloroform has made surgery painless. People who have been operated on know better. The patient does not feel the knife, and the operation is therefore enormously facilitated for the surgeon; but the patient pays for the anesthesia with hours of wretched sickness; and when that is over there is the pain of the wound made by the surgeon, which has to heal like any other wound. This is why operating surgeons, who are usually out of the house with their fee in their pockets before the patient has recovered consciousness, and who therefore see nothing of the suffering witnessed by the general practitioner and the nurse, occasionally talk of operations very much as the hangman in Barnaby Rudge talked of executions, as if being operated on were a luxury in sensation as well as in price.

MEDICAL POVERTY

To make matters worse, doctors are hideously poor. The Irish gentleman doctor of my boyhood, who took nothing less than a guinea, though he might pay you four visits for it, seems to have no equivalent nowadays in English society. Better be a railway porter than an ordinary

12

PREFACE ON DOCTORS

English general practitioner. A railway porter has from eighteen to twenty-three shillings a week from the Company merely as a retainer; and his additional fees from the public, if we leave the third-class twopenny tip out of account (and I am by no means sure that even this reservation need be made), are equivalent to doctor's fees in the case of second-class passengers, and double doctor's fees in the case of first. Any class of educated men thus treated tends to become a brigand class, and doctors are no exception to the rule. They are offered disgraceful prices for advice and medicine. Their patients are for the most part so poor and so ignorant that good advice would be resented as impracticable and wounding. When you are so poor that you cannot afford to refuse eighteenpence from a man who is too poor to pay you any more, it is useless to tell him that what he or his sick child needs is not medicine, but more leisure, better clothes, better food, and a better drained and ventilated house. It is kinder to give him a bottle of something almost as cheap as water, and tell him to come again with another eighteenpence if it does not cure him. When you have done that over and over again every day for a week, how much scientific conscience have you left? If you are weak-minded enough to cling desperately to your eighteenpence as denoting a certain social superiority to the sixpenny doctor, you will be miserably poor all your life; whilst the sixpenny doctor, with his low prices and quick turnover of patients, visibly makes much more than you do and kills no more people.

A doctor's character can no more stand out against such conditions than the lungs of his patients can stand out against bad ventilation. The only way in which he can preserve his self-respect is by forgetting all he ever learnt of science, and clinging to such help as he can give without cost merely by being less ignorant and more accustomed to sick-beds than his patients. Finally, he acquires a certain skill at nursing cases under poverty-stricken domestic conditions, just as women who have been trained as domestic

13

servants in some huge institution with lifts, vacuum cleaners, electric lighting, steam heating, and machinery that turns the kitchen into a laboratory and engine house combined, manage, when they are sent out into the world to drudge as general servants, to pick up their business in a new way, learning the slatternly habits and wretched makeshifts of homes where even bundles of kindling wood are luxuries to be anxiously economized.

THE SUCCESSFUL DOCTOR

The doctor whose success blinds public opinion to medical poverty is almost as completely demoralized. His promotion means that his practice becomes more and more confined to the idle rich. The proper advice for most of their ailments is typified in Abernethy's "Live on sixpence a day and earn it." But here, as at the other end of the scale, the right advice is neither agreeable nor practicable. And every hypochondriacal rich lady or gentleman who can be persuaded that he or she is a lifelong invalid means anything from fifty to five hundred pounds a year for the doctor. Operations enable a surgeon to earn similar sums in a couple of hours; and if the surgeon also keeps a nursing home, he may make considerable profits at the same time by running what is the most expensive kind of hotel. These gains are so great that they undo much of the moral advantage which the absence of grinding pecuniary anxiety gives the rich doctor over the poor one. It is true that the temptation to prescribe a sham treatment because the real treatment is too dear for either patient or doctor does not exist for the rich doctor. He always has plenty of genuine cases which can afford genuine treatment; and these provide him with enough sincere scientific professional work to save him from the ignorance, obsolescence, and atrophy of scientific conscience into which his poorer colleagues sink. But on the other hand his expenses are enormous. Even as a bachelor, he must, at London west end rates, make over a thousand a year before he can afford even to insure his life. His house,

14

his servants, and his equipage (or autopage) must be on the scale to which his patients are accustomed, though a couple of rooms with a camp bed in one of them might satisfy his own requirements. Above all, the income which provides for these outgoings stops the moment he himself stops working. Unlike the man of business, whose managers, clerks, warehousemen and laborers keep his business going whilst he is in bed or in his club, the doctor cannot earn a farthing by deputy. Though he is exceptionally exposed to infection, and has to face all weathers at all hours of the night and day, often not enjoying a complete night's rest for a week, the money stops coming in the moment he stops going out; and therefore illness has special terrors for him, and success no certain permanence. He dare not stop making hay while the sun shines; for it may set at any time. Men do not resist pressure of this intensity. When they come under it as doctors they pay unnecessary visits; they write prescriptions that are as absurd as the rub of chalk with which an Irish tailor once charmed away a wart from my father's finger; they conspire with surgeons to promote operations; they nurse the delusions of the *malade imaginaire* (who is always really ill because, as there is no such thing as perfect health, nobody is ever really well); they exploit human folly, vanity, and fear of death as ruthlessly as their own health, strength, and patience are exploited by selfish hypochondriacs. They must do all these things or else run pecuniary risks that no man can fairly be asked to run. And the healthier the world becomes, the more they are compelled to live by imposture and the less by that really helpful activity of which all doctors get enough to preserve them from utter corruption. For even the most hardened humbug who ever prescribed ether tonics to ladies whose need for tonics is of precisely the same character as the need of poorer women for a glass of gin, has to help a mother through child-bearing often enough to feel that he is not living wholly in vain.

PREFACE ON DOCTORS
THE PSYCHOLOGY OF SELF-RESPECT IN SURGEONS

The surgeon, though often more unscrupulous than the general practitioner, retains his self-respect more easily. The human conscience can subsist on very questionable food. No man who is occupied in doing a very difficult thing, and doing it very well, ever loses his self-respect. The shirk, the duffer, the malingerer, the coward, the weakling, may be put out of countenance by his own failures and frauds; but the man who does evil skilfully, energetically, masterfully, grows prouder and bolder at every crime. The common man may have to found his self-respect on sobriety, honesty and industry; but a Napoleon needs no such props for his sense of dignity. If Nelson's conscience whispered to him at all in the silent watches of the night, you may depend on it it whispered about the Baltic and the Nile and Cape St Vincent, and not about his unfaithfulness to his wife. A man who robs little children when no one is looking can hardly have much self-respect or even self-esteem; but an accomplished burglar must be proud of himself. In the play to which I am at present preluding I have represented an artist who is so entirely satisfied with his artistic conscience, even to the point of dying like a saint with its support, that he is utterly selfish and unscrupulous in every other relation without feeling at the smallest disadvantage. The same thing may be observed in women who have a genius for personal attractiveness: they expend more thought, labor, skill, inventiveness, taste and endurance on making themselves lovely than would suffice to keep a dozen ugly women honest; and this enables them to maintain a high opinion of themselves, and an angry contempt for unattractive and personally careless women, whilst they lie and cheat and slander and sell themselves without a blush. The truth is, hardly any of us have ethical energy enough for more than one really inflexible point of honor. Andrea del Sarto, like Louis Dubedat in my play, must have expended on the attainment of his great mastery of

16

design and his originality in fresco painting more conscientiousness and industry than go to the making of the reputations of a dozen ordinary mayors and churchwardens; but (if Vasari is to be believed) when the King of France entrusted him with money to buy pictures for him, he stole it to spend on his wife. Such cases are not confined to eminent artists. Unsuccessful, unskilful men are often much more scrupulous than successful ones. In the ranks of ordinary skilled labor many men are to be found who earn good wages and are never out of a job because they are strong, indefatigable, and skilful, and who therefore are bold in a high opinion of themselves; but they are selfish and tyrannical, gluttonous and drunken, as their wives and children know to their cost.

Not only do these talented energetic people retain their self-respect through shameful misconduct: they do not even lose the respect of others, because their talents benefit and interest everybody, whilst their vices affect only a few. An actor, a painter, a composer, an author, may be as selfish as he likes without reproach from the public if only his art is superb; and he cannot fulfil this condition without sufficient effort and sacrifice to make him feel noble and martyred in spite of his selfishness. It may even happen that the selfishness of an artist may be a benefit to the public by enabling him to concentrate himself on their gratification with a recklessness of every other consideration that makes him highly dangerous to those about him. In sacrificing others to himself he is sacrificing them to the public he gratifies; and the public is quite content with that arrangement. The public actually has an interest in the artist's vices.

It has no such interest in the surgeon's vices. The surgeon's art is exercised at its expense, not for its gratification. We do not go to the operating table as we go to the theatre, to the picture gallery, to the concert room, to be entertained and delighted: we go to be tormented and maimed lest a worse thing should befall us. It is of the most extreme importance to us that the experts on whose assurance we face

17

this horror and suffer this mutilation should have no interests but our own to think of; should judge our cases scientifically; and should feel about them kindly. Let us see what guarantees we have: first for the science, and then for the kindness.

ARE DOCTORS MEN OF SCIENCE?

I presume nobody will question the existence of a widely spread popular delusion that every doctor is a man of science. It is escaped only in the very small class which understands by science something more than conjuring with retorts and spirit lamps, magnets and microscopes, and discovering magical cures for disease. To a sufficiently ignorant man every captain of a trading schooner is a Galileo, every organ-grinder a Beethoven, every piano-tuner a Helmholtz, every Old Bailey barrister a Solon, every Seven Dials pigeon-dealer a Darwin, every scrivener a Shakespear, every locomotive engine a miracle, and its driver no less wonderful than George Stephenson. As a matter of fact, the rank and file of doctors are no more scientific than their tailors; or, if you prefer to put it the reverse way, their tailors are no less scientific than they. Doctoring is an art, not a science: any layman who is interested in science sufficiently to take in one of the scientific journals and follow the literature of the scientific movement, knows more about it than those doctors (probably a large majority) who are not interested in it, and practise only to earn their bread. Doctoring is not even the art of keeping people in health (no doctor seems able to advise you what to eat any better than his grandmother or the nearest quack): it is the art of curing illnesses. It does happen exceptionally that a practising doctor makes a contribution to science (my play describes a very notable one); but it happens much oftener that he draws disastrous conclusions from his clinical experience because he has no conception of scientific method, and believes, like any rustic, that the handling of evidence and statistics needs no expertness. The distinction between a quack doctor and a qualified one is mainly that

18

only the qualified one is authorized to sign death certificates, for which both sorts seem to have about equal occasion. Unqualified practitioners now make large incomes as hygienists, and are resorted to as frequently by cultivated amateur scientists who understand quite well what they are doing as by ignorant people who are simply dupes. Bonesetters make fortunes under the very noses of our greatest surgeons from educated and wealthy patients; and some of the most successful doctors on the register use quite heretical methods of treating disease, and have qualified themselves solely for convenience. Leaving out of account the village witches who prescribe spells and sell charms, the humblest professional healers in this country are the herbalists. These men wander through the fields on Sunday seeking for herbs with magic properties of curing disease, preventing childbirth, and the like. Each of them believes that he is on the verge of a great discovery, in which Virginia Snake Root will be an ingredient, heaven knows why! Virginia Snake Root fascinates the imagination of the herbalist as mercury used to fascinate the alchemists. On week days he keeps a shop in which he sells packets of pennyroyal, dandelion, &c., labelled with little lists of the diseases they are supposed to cure, and apparently do cure to the satisfaction of the people who keep on buying them. I have never been able to perceive any distinction between the science of the herbalist and that of the duly registered doctor. A relative of mine recently consulted a doctor about some of the ordinary symptoms which indicate the need for a holiday and a change. The doctor satisfied himself that the patient's heart was a little depressed. Digitalis being a drug labelled as a heart specific by the profession, he promptly administered a stiff dose. Fortunately the patient was a hardy old lady who was not easily killed. She recovered with no worse result than her conversion to Christian Science, which owes its vogue quite as much to public despair of doctors as to superstition. I am not, observe, here concerned with the question as to whether the dose of digitalis was judicious or not: the point is, that a farm laborer consulting a herbalist would have been treated in exactly the same way.

BACTERIOLOGY AS A SUPERSTITION

The smattering of science that all—even doctors—pick up from the ordinary newspapers nowadays only makes the doctor more dangerous than he used to be. Wise men used to take care to consult doctors qualified before 1860, who were usually contemptuous of or indifferent to the germ theory and bacteriological therapeutics; but now that these veterans have mostly retired or died, we are left in the hands of the generations which, having heard of microbes much as St Thomas Aquinas heard of angels, suddenly concluded that the whole art of healing could be summed up in the formula: Find the microbe and kill it. And even that they did not know how to do. The simplest way to kill most microbes is to throw them into an open street or river and let the sun shine on them, which explains the fact that when great cities have recklessly thrown all their sewage into the open river the water has sometimes been cleaner twenty miles below the city than thirty miles above it. But doctors instinctively avoid all facts that are reassuring, and eagerly swallow those that make it a marvel that anyone could possibly survive three days in an atmosphere consisting mainly of countless pathogenic germs. They conceive microbes as immortal until slain by a germicide administered by a duly qualified medical man. All through Europe people are adjured, by public notices and even under legal penalties, not to throw their microbes into the sunshine, but to collect them carefully in a handkerchief; shield the handkerchief from the sun in the darkness and warmth of the pocket; and send it to a laundry to be mixed up with everybody else's handkerchiefs, with results only too familiar to local health authorities.

In the first frenzy of microbe killing, surgical instruments were dipped in carbolic oil, which was a great improvement on not dipping them in anything at all and simply using them dirty; but as microbes are so fond of carbolic oil that they swarm in it, it was not a success from the anti-microbe point of view. Formalin was squirted into the circulation of consumptives until it was discovered that formalin nourishes the tubercle bacillus handsomely and kills men. The popular theory of disease is the common medical theory: namely, that every disease had its microbe duly created in the garden of Eden, and has been steadily propagating itself and producing widening circles of malignant disease ever since. It was plain from the first that if this had been even approximately true, the whole human race would have been wiped out by the plague long ago, and that every epidemic, instead of fading out as mysteriously as it rushed in, would spread over the whole world. It was also evident that the characteristic microbe of a disease might be a symptom instead of a cause. An unpunctual man is always in a hurry; but it does not follow that hurry is the cause of unpunctuality: on the contrary, what is the matter with the patient is sloth. When Florence Nightingale said bluntly that if you overcrowded your soldiers in dirty quarters there would be an outbreak of smallpox among them, she was snubbed as an ignorant female who did not know that smallpox can be produced only by the importation of its specific microbe.

If this was the line taken about smallpox, the microbe of which has never yet been run down and exposed under the microscope by the bacteriologist, what must have been the ardor of conviction as to tuberculosis, tetanus, enteric fever, Maltese fever, diphtheria, and the rest of the diseases in which the characteristic bacillus had been identified! When there was no bacillus it was assumed that, since no disease could exist without a bacillus, it was simply eluding observation. When the bacillus was found, as it frequently was, in persons who were not suffering from the disease, the theory was saved by simply calling the bacillus an impostor, or pseudo-bacillus. The same boundless credulity which the public exhibit as to a doctor's power of diagnosis

21

was shewn by the doctors themselves as to the analytic microbe hunters. These witch finders would give you a certificate of the ultimate constitution of anything from a sample of the water from your well to a scrap of your lungs, for seven-and-sixpence. I do not suggest that the analysts were dishonest. No doubt they carried the analysis as far as they could afford to carry it for the money. No doubt also they could afford to carry it far enough to be of some use. But the fact remains that just as doctors perform for half-a-crown, without the least misgiving, operations which could not be thoroughly and safely performed with due scientific rigor and the requisite apparatus by an unaided private practitioner for less than some thousands of pounds, so did they proceed on the assumption that they could get the last word of science as to the constituents of their pathological samples for a two-hours cab fare.

ECONOMIC DIFFICULTIES OF IMMUNIZATION

I have heard doctors affirm and deny almost every possible proposition as to disease and treatment. I can remember the time when doctors no more dreamt of consumption and pneumonia being infectious than they now dream of sea-sickness being infectious, or than so great a clinical observer as Sydenham dreamt of smallpox being infectious. I have heard doctors deny that there is such a thing as infection. I have heard them deny the existence of hydrophobia as a specific disease differing from tetanus. I have heard them defend prophylactic measures and prophylactic legislation as the sole and certain salvation of mankind from zymotic disease; and I have heard them denounce both as malignant spreaders of cancer and lunacy. But the one objection I have never heard from a doctor is the objection that prophylaxis by the inoculatory methods most in vogue is an economic impossibility under our private practice system. They buy some stuff from somebody for a shilling, and inject a pennyworth of it under their patient's skin for half-a-crown, concluding that, since this primitive rite pays

22

the somebody and pays them, the problem of prophylaxis has been satisfactorily solved. The results are sometimes no worse than the ordinary results of dirt getting into cuts; but neither the doctor nor the patient is quite satisfied unless the inoculation "takes": that is, unless it produces perceptible illness and disablement. Sometimes both doctor and patient get more value in this direction than they bargain for. The results of ordinary private-practice-inoculation at their worst are bad enough to be indistinguishable from those of the most discreditable and dreaded disease known; and doctors, to save the credit of the inoculation, have been driven to accuse their patient or their patient's parents of having contracted this disease independently of the inoculation, an excuse which naturally does not make the family any more resigned, and leads to public recriminations in which the doctors, forgetting everything but the immediate quarrel, naively excuse themselves by admitting, and even claiming as a point in their favor, that it is often impossible to distinguish the disease produced by their inoculation and the disease they have accused the patient of contracting. And both parties assume that what is at issue is the scientific soundness of the prophylaxis. It never occurs to them that the particular pathogenic germ which they intended to introduce into the patient's system may be quite innocent of the catastrophe, and that the casual dirt introduced with it may be at fault. When, as in the case of smallpox or cowpox, the germ has not yet been detected, what you inoculate is simply undefined matter that has been scraped off an anything but chemically clean calf suffering from the disease in question. You take your chance of the germ being in the scrapings, and, lest you should kill it, you take no precautions against other germs being in it as well. Anything may happen as the result of such an inoculation. Yet this is the only stuff of the kind which is prepared and supplied even in State establishments: that is, in the only establishments free from the commercial temptation to adulterate materials and scamp precautionary processes.

23

PREFACE ON DOCTORS

Even if the germ were identified, complete precautions would hardly pay. It is true that microbe farming is not expensive. The cost of breeding and housing two head of cattle would provide for the breeding and housing of enough microbes to inoculate the entire population of the globe since human life first appeared on it. But the precautions necessary to insure that the inoculation shall consist of nothing else but the required germ in the proper state of attenuation are a very different matter from the precautions necessary in the distribution and consumption of beefsteaks. Yet people expect to find vaccines and anti-toxins and the like retailed at "popular prices" in private enterprise shops just as they expect to find ounces of tobacco and papers of pins.

THE PERILS OF INOCULATION

The trouble does not end with the matter to be inoculated. There is the question of the condition of the patient. The discoveries of Sir Almroth Wright have shewn that the appalling results which led to the hasty dropping in 1894 of Koch's tuberculin were not accidents, but perfectly orderly and inevitable phenomena following the injection of dangerously strong "vaccines" at the wrong moment, and reinforcing the disease instead of stimulating the resistance to it. To ascertain the right moment a laboratory and a staff of experts are needed. The general practitioner, having no such laboratory and no such experience, has always chanced it, and insisted, when he was unlucky, that the results were not due to the inoculation, but to some other cause: a favorite and not very tactful one being the drunkenness or licentiousness of the patient. But though a few doctors have now learnt the danger of inoculating without any reference to the patient's "opsonic index" at the moment of inoculation, and though those other doctors who are denouncing the danger as imaginary and opsonin as a craze or a fad, obviously do so because it involves an operation which they have neither the means nor the knowledge to perform, there is still no grasp of the economic change in the situa-

24

tion. They have never been warned that the practicability of any method of extirpating disease depends not only on its efficacy, but on its cost. For example, just at present the world has run raving mad on the subject of radium, which has excited our credulity precisely as the apparitions at Lourdes excited the credulity of Roman Catholics. Suppose it were ascertained that every child in the world could be rendered absolutely immune from all disease during its entire life by taking half an ounce of radium to every pint of its milk. The world would be none the healthier, because not even a Crown Prince—no, not even the son of a Chicago Meat King, could afford the treatment. Yet it is doubtful whether doctors would refrain from prescribing it on that ground. The recklessness with which they now recommend wintering in Egypt or at Davos to people who cannot afford to go to Cornwall, and the orders given for champagne jelly and old port in households where such luxuries must obviously be acquired at the cost of stinting necessaries, often make one wonder whether it is possible for a man to go through a medical training and retain a spark of common sense.

This sort of inconsiderateness gets cured only in the classes where poverty, pretentious as it is even at its worst, cannot pitch its pretences high enough to make it possible for the doctor (himself often no better off than the patient) to assume that the average income of an English family is about £2,000 a year, and that it is quite easy to break up a home, sell an old family seat at a sacrifice, and retire into a foreign sanatorium devoted to some "treatment" that did not exist two years ago and probably will not exist (except as a pretext for keeping an ordinary hotel) two years hence. In a poor practice the doctor must find cheap treatments for cheap people, or humiliate and lose his patients either by prescribing beyond their means or sending them to the public hospitals. When it comes to prophylactic inoculation, the alternative lies between the complete scientific process, which can only be brought down to a reasonable cost by being very highly organized as a public service in a public institution, and such cheap, nasty, dangerous and scientifically spurious imitations as ordinary vaccination, which will probably be ended, like its equally vaunted forerunner, eighteenth century inoculation, by a purely reactionary law making all sorts of vaccination, scientific or not, criminal offences. Naturally, the poor doctor (that is, the average doctor) defends ordinary vaccination frantically, as it means to him the bread of his children. To secure the vehement and practically unanimous support of the rank and file of the medical profession for any sort of treatment or operation, all that is necessary is that it can be easily practised by a rather shabbily dressed man in a surgically dirty room in a surgically dirty house without any assistance, and that the materials for it shall cost, say, a penny, and the charge for it to a patient with £100 a year be half-a-crown. And, on the other hand, a hygienic measure has only to be one of such refinement, difficulty, precision and costliness as to be quite beyond the resources of private practice, to be ignored or angrily denounced as a fad.

TRADE UNIONISM AND SCIENCE

Here we have the explanation of the savage rancor that so amazes people who imagine that the controversy concerning vaccination is a scientific one. It has really nothing to do with science. The medical profession, consisting for the most part of very poor men struggling to keep up appearances beyond their means, find themselves threatened with the extinction of a considerable part of their incomes: a part, too, that is easily and regularly earned, since it is independent of disease, and brings every person born into the nation, healthy or not, to the doctors. To boot, there is the occasional windfall of an epidemic, with its panic and rush for revaccination. Under such circumstances, vaccination would be defended desperately were it twice as dirty, dangerous, and unscientific in method as it actually is. The note of fury in the defence, the feeling that the anti-vaccinator is doing a cruel, ruinous, inconsiderate thing in

26

a mood of malignant folly: all this, so puzzling to the observer who knows nothing of the economic side of the question, and only sees that the anti-vaccinator, having nothing
whatever to gain and a good deal to lose by placing himself
in opposition to the law and to the outcry that adds private
persecution to legal penalties, can have no interest in the
matter except the interest of a reformer in abolishing a
corrupt and mischievous superstition, becomes intelligible
the moment the tragedy of medical poverty and the lucra-
tiveness of cheap vaccination is taken into account.

In the face of such economic pressure as this, it is silly
to expect that medical teaching, any more than medical
practice, can possibly be scientific. The test to which all
methods of treatment are finally brought is whether they
are lucrative to doctors or not. It would be difficult to cite
any proposition less obnoxious to science than that advanced
by Hahnemann: to wit, that drugs which in large doses
produce certain symptoms, counteract them in very small
doses, just as in more modern practice it is found that a sufficiently small inoculation with typhoid rallies our powers
to resist the disease instead of prostrating us with it. But
Hahnemann and his followers were frantically persecuted
for a century by generations of apothecary-doctors whose
incomes depended on the quantity of drugs they could induce their patients to swallow. These two cases of ordinary
vaccination and homeopathy are typical of all the rest. Just
as the object of a trade union under existing conditions must
finally be, not to improve the technical quality of the work
done by its members, but to secure a living wage for them,
so the object of the medical profession today is to secure an
income for the private doctor; and to this consideration all
concern for science and public health must give way when
the two come into conflict. Fortunately they are not always
in conflict. Up to a certain point doctors, like carpenters and
masons, must earn their living by doing the work that the
public wants from them; and as it is not in the nature of
things possible that such public want should be based on

27

unmixed disutility, it may be admitted that doctors have their uses, real as well as imaginary. But just as the best carpenter or mason will resist the introduction of a machine that is likely to throw him out of work, or the public technical education of unskilled laborers' sons to compete with him, so the doctor will resist with all his powers of persecution every advance of science that threatens his income. And as the advance of scientific hygiene tends to make the private doctor's visits rarer, and the public inspector's frequenter, whilst the advance of scientific therapeutics is in the direction of treatments that involve highly organized laboratories, hospitals, and public institutions generally, it unluckily happens that the organization of private practitioners which we call the medical profession is coming more and more to represent, not science, but desperate and embittered anti-science: a statement of things which is likely to get worse until the average doctor either depends upon or hopes for an appointment in the public health service for his livelihood.

So much for our guarantees as to medical science. Let us now deal with the more painful subject of medical kindness.

DOCTORS AND VIVISECTION

The importance to our doctors of a reputation for the tenderest humanity is so obvious, and the quantity of benevolent work actually done by them for nothing (a great deal of it from sheer good nature) so large, that at first sight it seems unaccountable that they should not only throw all their credit away, but deliberately choose to band themselves publicly with outlaws and scoundrels by claiming that in the pursuit of their professional knowledge they should be free from the restraints of law, of honor, of pity, of remorse, of everything that distinguishes an orderly citizen from a South Sea buccaneer, or a philosopher from an inquisitor. For here we look in vain for either an economic or a sentimental motive. In every generation fools and blackguards have made this claim; and honest and reasonable men, led by the strongest contemporary minds,

28

have repudiated it and exposed its crude rascality. From Shakespear and Dr Johnson to Ruskin and Mark Twain, the natural abhorrence of sane mankind for the vivisector's cruelty, and the contempt of able thinkers for his imbecile casuistry, have been expressed by the most popular spokesmen of humanity. If the medical profession were to outdo the Anti-Vivisection Societies in a general professional protest against the practice and principles of the vivisectors, every doctor in the kingdom would gain substantially by the immense relief and reconciliation which would follow such a reassurance of the humanity of the doctor. Not one doctor in a thousand is a vivisector, or has any interest in vivisection, either pecuniary or intellectual, or would treat his dog cruelly or allow anyone else to do it. It is true that the doctor complies with the professional fashion of defending vivisection, and assuring you that people like Shakespear and Dr Johnson and Ruskin and Mark Twain are ignorant sentimentalists, just as he complies with any other silly fashion: the mystery is, how it became the fashion in spite of its being so injurious to those who follow it. Making all possible allowance for the effect of the brazen lying of the few men who bring a rush of despairing patients to their doors by professing in letters to the newspapers to have learnt from vivisection how to cure certain diseases, and the assurances of the sayers of smooth things that the practice is quite painless under the law, it is still difficult to find any civilized motive for an attitude by which the medical profession has everything to lose and nothing to gain.

THE PRIMITIVE SAVAGE MOTIVE

I say civilized motive advisedly; for primitive tribal motives are easy enough to find. Every savage chief who is not a Mahomet learns that if he wishes to strike the imagination of his tribe—and without doing that he cannot rule them—he must terrify or revolt them from time to time by acts of hideous cruelty or disgusting unnaturalness. We are far from being as superior to such tribes as we imagine. It is very doubtful indeed whether Peter the Great could

29

have effected the changes he made in Russia if he had not fascinated and intimidated his people by his monstrous cruelties and grotesque escapades. Had he been a nineteenth-century king of England, he would have had to wait for some huge accidental calamity: a cholera epidemic, a war, or an insurrection, before waking us up sufficiently to get anything done. Vivisection helps the doctor to rule us as Peter ruled the Russians. The notion that the man who does dreadful things is superhuman, and that therefore he can also do wonderful things either as ruler, avenger, healer, or what not, is by no means confined to barbarians. Just as the manifold wickednesses and stupidities of our criminal code are supported, not by any general comprehension of law or study of jurisprudence, not even by simple vindictiveness, but by the superstition that a calamity of any sort must be expiated by a human sacrifice; so the wickednesses and stupidities of our medicine men are rooted in superstitions that have no more to do with science than the traditional ceremony of christening an ironclad has to do with the effectiveness of its armament. We have only to turn to Macaulay's description of the treatment of Charles II in his last illness to see how strongly his physicians felt that their only chance of cheating death was by outraging nature in tormenting and disgusting their unfortunate patient. True, this was more than two centuries ago; but I have heard my own nineteenth-century grandfather describe the cupping and firing and nauseous medicines of his time with perfect credulity as to their beneficial effects; and some more modern treatments appear to me quite as barbarous. It is in this way that vivisection pays the doctor. It appeals to the fear and credulity of the savage in us; and without fear and credulity half the private doctor's occupation and seven-eighths of his influence would be gone.

THE HIGHER MOTIVE. THE TREE OF KNOWLEDGE

But the greatest force of all on the side of vivisection is the mighty and indeed divine force of curiosity. Here we have no decaying tribal instinct which men strive to root out of themselves as they strive to root out the tiger's lust for blood. On the contrary, the curiosity of the ape, or of the child who pulls out the legs and wings of a fly to see what it will do without them, or who, on being told that a cat dropped out of the window will always fall on its legs, immediately tries the experiment on the nearest cat from the highest window in the house (I protest I did it myself from the first floor only), is as nothing compared to the thirst for knowledge of the philosopher, the poet, the biologist, and the naturalist. I have always despised Adam because he had to be tempted by the woman, as she was by the serpent, before he could be induced to pluck the apple from the tree of knowledge. I should have swallowed every apple on the tree the moment the owner's back was turned. When Gray said "Where ignorance is bliss, 'tis folly to be wise," he forgot that it is godlike to be wise; and since nobody wants bliss particularly, or could stand more than a very brief taste of it if it were attainable, and since everybody, by the deepest law of the Life Force, desires to be godlike, it is stupid, and indeed blasphemous and despairing, to hope that the thirst for knowledge will either diminish or consent to be subordinated to any other end whatsoever. We shall see later on that the claim that has arisen in this way for the unconditioned pursuit of knowledge is as idle as all dreams of unconditioned activity; but none the less the right to knowledge must be regarded as a fundamental human right. The fact that men of science have had to fight so hard to secure its recognition, and are still so vigorously persecuted when they discover anything that is not quite palatable to vulgar people, makes them sorely jealous for that right; and when they hear a popular outcry for the suppression of a method of research which has an air of being scientific, their first instinct is to rally to the defence of that method without further consideration, with the result that they sometimes, as in the case of vivisection, presently find themselves fighting on a false issue.

31

THE FLAW IN THE ARGUMENT

I may as well pause here to explain their error. The right to know is like the right to live. It is fundamental and unconditional in its assumption that knowledge, like life, is a desirable thing, though any fool can prove that ignorance is bliss, and that "a little knowledge is a dangerous thing" (a little being the most that any of us can attain), as easily as that the pains of life are more numerous and constant than its pleasures, and that therefore we should all be better dead. The logic is unimpeachable; but its only effect is to make us say that if these are the conclusions logic leads to, so much the worse for logic, after which curt dismissal of Folly, we continue living and learning by instinct: that is, as of right. We legislate on the assumption that no man may be killed on the strength of a demonstration that he would be happier in his grave, not even if he is dying slowly of cancer and begs the doctor to despatch him quickly and mercifully. To get killed lawfully he must violate somebody else's right to live by committing murder. But he is by no means free to live unconditionally. In society he can exercise his right to live only under very stiff conditions. In countries where there is compulsory military service he may even have to throw away his individual life to save the life of the community.

It is just so in the case of the right to knowledge. It is a right that is as yet very imperfectly recognized in practice. But in theory it is admitted that an adult person in pursuit of knowledge must not be refused it on the ground that he would be better or happier without it. Parents and priests may forbid knowledge to those who accept their authority; and social taboo may be made effective by acts of legal persecution under cover of repressing blasphemy, obscenity, and sedition; but no government now openly forbids its subjects to pursue knowledge on the ground that knowledge is in itself a bad thing, or that it is possible for any of us to have too much of it.

32

LIMITATIONS OF THE RIGHT TO KNOWLEDGE

But neither does any government exempt the pursuit of knowledge, any more than the pursuit of life, liberty, and happiness (as the American Constitution puts it), from all social conditions. No man is allowed to put his mother into the stove because he desires to know how long an adult woman will survive at a temperature of 500° Fahrenheit, no matter how important or interesting that particular addition to the store of human knowledge may be. A man who did so would have short work made not only of his right to knowledge, but of his right to live and all his other rights at the same time. The right to knowledge is not the only right; and its exercise must be limited by respect for other rights, and for its own exercise by others. When a man says to Society, "May I torture my mother in pursuit of knowledge?" Society replies "No." If he pleads, "What! Not even if I have a chance of finding out how to cure cancer by doing it?" Society still says, "Not even then." If the scientist, making the best of his disappointment, goes on to ask may he torture a dog, the stupid and callous people who do not realize that a dog is a fellow-creature, and sometimes a good friend, may say Yes, though Shakespear, Dr Johnson and their like may say No. But even those who say "You may torture *a* dog" never say "You may torture *my* dog." And nobody says, "Yes, because in the pursuit of knowledge you may do as you please." Just as even the stupidest people say, in effect, "If you cannot attain to knowledge without burning your mother you must do without knowledge," so the wisest people say, "If you cannot attain to knowledge without torturing a dog, you must do without knowledge."

A FALSE ALTERNATIVE

But in practice you cannot persuade any wise man that this alternative can ever be forced on anyone but a fool, or that a fool can be trusted to learn anything from any experiment, cruel or humane. The Chinaman who burnt down his house to roast his pig was no doubt honestly unable to conceive any less disastrous way of cooking his dinner; and the roast must have been spoiled after all (a perfect type of the average vivisectionist experiment); but this did not prove that the Chinaman was right: it only proved that the Chinaman was an incapable cook and, fundamentally, a fool.

Take another celebrated experiment: one in sanitary reform. In the days of Nero Rome was in the same predicament as London today. If someone would burn down London, and it were rebuilt, as it would now have to be, subject to the sanitary by-laws and Building Act provisions enforced by the London County Council, it would be enormously improved; and the average lifetime of Londoners would be considerably prolonged. Nero argued in the same way about Rome. He employed incendiaries to set it on fire; and he played the harp in scientific raptures whilst it was burning. I am so far of Nero's way of thinking that I have often said, when consulted by despairing sanitary reformers, that what London needs to make her healthy is an earthquake. Why, then, it may be asked, do not I, as a public-spirited man, employ incendiaries to set it on fire, with a heroic disregard of the consequences to myself and others? Any vivisector would, if he had the courage of his opinions. The reasonable answer is that London can be made healthy without burning her down; and that as we have not enough civic virtue to make her healthy in a humane and economical way, we should not have enough to rebuild her in that way. In the old Hebrew legend, God lost patience with the world as Nero did with Rome, and drowned everybody except a single family. But the result was that the progeny of that family reproduced all the vices of their predecessors so exactly that the misery caused by the flood might just as well have been spared: things went on just as they did before. In the same way, the list of

34

diseases which vivisection claims to have cured is long; but the returns of the Registrar-General shew that people still persist in dying of them as if vivisection had never been heard of. Any fool can burn down a city or cut an animal open; and an exceptionally foolish fool is quite likely to promise enormous benefits to the race as the result of such activities. But when the constructive, benevolent part of the business comes to be done, the same want of imagination, the same stupidity and cruelty, the same laziness and want of perseverance that prevented Nero or the vivisector from devising or pushing through humane methods, prevents him from bringing order out of the chaos and happiness out of the misery he has made. At one time it seemed reasonable enough to declare that it was impossible to find whether or not there was a stone inside a man's body except by exploring it with a knife, or to find out what the sun is made of without visiting it in a balloon. Both these impossibilities have been achieved, but not by vivisectors. The Röntgen rays need not hurt the patient; and spectrum analysis involves no destruction. After such triumphs of humane experiment and reasoning, it is useless to assure us that there is no other key to knowledge except cruelty. When the vivisector offers us that assurance, we reply simply and contemptuously, "You mean that you are not clever or humane or energetic enough to find one."

CRUELTY FOR ITS OWN SAKE

It will now, I hope, be clear why the attack on vivisection is not an attack on the right to knowledge: why, indeed, those who have the deepest conviction of the sacredness of that right are the leaders of the attack. No knowledge is finally impossible of human attainment; for even though it may be beyond our present capacity, the needed capacity is not unattainable. Consequently no method of investigation is the only method; and no law forbidding any particular method can cut us off from the knowledge we hope to gain by it. The only knowledge we lose by forbidding cruelty is knowledge at first hand of cruelty itself, which is precisely the knowledge humane people wish to be spared.

But the question remains: Do we all really wish to be spared that knowledge? Are humane methods really to be preferred to cruel ones? Even if the experiments come to nothing, may not their cruelty be enjoyed for its own sake, as a sensational luxury? Let us face these questions boldly, not shrinking from the fact that cruelty is one of the primitive pleasures of mankind, and that the detection of its Protean disguises as law, education, medicine, discipline, sport and so forth, is one of the most difficult of the unending tasks of the legislator.

OUR OWN CRUELTIES

At first blush it may seem not only unnecessary, but even indecent, to discuss such a proposition as the elevation of cruelty to the rank of a human right. Unnecessary, because no vivisector confesses to a love of cruelty for its own sake or claims any general fundamental right to be cruel. Indecent, because there is an accepted convention to repudiate cruelty; and vivisection is only tolerated by the law on condition that, like judicial torture, it shall be done as mercifully as the nature of the practice allows. But the moment the controversy becomes embittered, the recriminations bandied between the opposed parties bring us face-to-face with some very ugly truths. On one occasion I was invited to speak at a large Anti-Vivisection meeting in the Queen's Hall in London. I found myself on the platform with fox hunters, tame stag hunters, men and women whose calendar was divided, not by pay days and quarter days, but by seasons for killing animals for sport: the fox, the hare, the otter, the partridge and the rest having each its appointed date for slaughter. The ladies among us wore hats and cloaks and head-dresses obtained by wholesale massacres, ruthless trappings, callous extermination of our fellow creatures. We insisted on our butchers supplying us with white veal, and were large and constant consumers of *pâté de foie gras:* both comestibles being obtained by revolting methods. We sent our sons to public schools where indecent flogging is a recognized method of taming the young human animal. Yet we were all in hysterics of indignation at the cruelties of the vivisectors. These, if any were present, must have smiled sardonically at such inhuman humanitarians, whose daily habits and fashionable amusements cause more suffering in England in a week than all the vivisectors of Europe do in a year. I made a very effective speech, not exclusively against vivisection, but against cruelty; and I have never been asked to speak since by that Society, nor do I expect to be, as I should probably give such offence to its most affluent subscribers that its attempts to suppress vivisection would be seriously hindered. But that does not prevent the vivisectors from freely using the "youre another" retort, and using it with justice.

We must therefore give ourselves no airs of superiority when denouncing the cruelties of vivisection. We all do just as horrible things, with even less excuse. But in making that admission we are also making short work of the virtuous airs with which we are sometimes referred to the humanity of the medical profession as a guarantee that vivisection is not abused—much as if our burglars should assure us that they are too honest to abuse the practice of burglaring. We are, as a matter of fact, a cruel nation; and our habit of disguising our vices by giving polite names to the offences we are determined to commit, does not, unfortunately for my own comfort, impose on me. Vivisectors can hardly pretend to be better than the classes from which they are drawn, or those above them; and if these classes are capable of sacrificing animals in various cruel ways under cover of sport, fashion, education, discipline, and even, when the cruel sacrifices are human sacrifices, of political economy, it is idle for the vivisector to pretend that he is incapable of practising cruelty for pleasure or profit or both under the cloak of science. We are all tarred with the same brush; and the vivisectors are not slow to remind us of it, and to protest

37

vehemently against being branded as exceptionally cruel and as devisers of horrible instruments of torture by people whose main notion of enjoyment is cruel sport, and whose requirements in the way of villainously cruel traps occupy pages of the catalogue of the Army and Navy Stores.

THE SCIENTIFIC INVESTIGATION OF CRUELTY

There is in man a specific lust for cruelty which infects even his passion of pity and makes it savage. Simple disgust at cruelty is very rare. The people who turn sick and faint and those who gloat are often alike in the pains they take to witness executions, floggings, operations or any other exhibitions of suffering, especially those involving bloodshed, blows, and laceration. A craze for cruelty can be developed just as a craze for drink can; and nobody who attempts to ignore cruelty as a possible factor in the attraction of vivisection and even of anti-vivisection, or in the credulity with which we accept its excuses, can be regarded as a scientific investigator of it. Those who accuse vivisectors of indulging the well-known passion of cruelty under the cloak of research are therefore putting forward a strictly scientific psychological hypothesis, which is also simple, human, obvious, and probable. It may be as wounding to the personal vanity of the vivisector as Darwin's Origin of Species was to the people who could not bear to think that they were cousins to the monkeys (remember Goldsmith's anger when he was told that he could not move his upper jaw); but science has to consider only the truth of the hypothesis, and not whether conceited people will like it or not. In vain do the sentimental champions of vivisection declare themselves the most humane of men, inflicting suffering only to relieve it, scrupulous in the use of anesthetics, and void of all passion except the passion of pity for a disease-ridden world. The really scientific investigator answers that the question cannot be settled by hysterical protestations, and that if the vivisectionist rejects deductive

38

reasoning, he had better clear his character by his own favorite method of experiment.

SUGGESTED LABORATORY TESTS OF THE VIVISECTOR'S EMOTIONS

Take the hackneyed case of the Italian who tortured mice, ostensibly to find out about the effects of pain rather less than the nearest dentist could have told him, and who boasted of the ecstatic sensations (he actually used the word love) with which he carried out his experiments. Or the gentleman who starved sixty dogs to death to establish the fact that a dog deprived of food gets progressively lighter and weaker, becoming remarkably emaciated, and finally dying: an undoubted truth, but ascertainable without laboratory experiments by a simple enquiry addressed to the nearest policeman, or, failing him, to any sane person in Europe. The Italian is diagnosed as a cruel voluptuary: the dog-starver is passed over as such a hopeless fool that it is impossible to take any interest in him. Why not test the diagnosis scientifically? Why not perform a careful series of experiments on persons under the influence of voluptuous ecstasy, so as to ascertain its physiological symptoms? Then perform a second series on persons engaged in mathematical work or machine designing, so as to ascertain the symptoms of cold scientific activity? Then note the symptoms of a vivisector performing a cruel experiment; and compare them with the voluptuary symptoms and the mathematical symptoms? Such experiments would be quite as interesting and important as any yet undertaken by the vivisectors. They might open a line of investigation which would finally make, for instance, the ascertainment of the guilt or innocence of an accused person a much exacter process than the very fallible methods of our criminal courts. But instead of proposing such an investigation, our vivisectors offer us all the pious protestations and all the huffy recriminations that any common unscientific mortal offers when he is accused of unworthy conduct.

39

ROUTINE

Yet most vivisectors would probably come triumphant out of such a series of experiments, because vivisection is now a routine, like butchering or hanging or flogging; and many of the men who practise it do so only because it has been established as part of the profession they have adopted. Far from enjoying it, they have simply overcome their natural repugnance and become indifferent to it, as men inevitably become indifferent to anything they do often enough. It is this dangerous power of custom that makes it so difficult to convince the common sense of mankind that any established commercial or professional practice has its root in passion. Let a routine once spring from passion, and you will presently find thousands of routineers following it passionlessly for a livelihood. Thus it always seems strained to speak of the religious convictions of a clergyman, because nine out of ten clergymen have no religious convictions: they are ordinary officials carrying on a routine of baptizing, marrying, and churching; praying, reciting, and preaching; and, like solicitors or doctors, getting away from their duties with relief to hunt, to garden, to keep bees, to go into society, and the like. In the same way many people do cruel and vile things without being in the least cruel or vile, because the routine to which they have been brought up is superstitiously cruel and vile. To say that every man who beats his children and every schoolmaster who flogs a pupil is a conscious debauchee is absurd: thousands of dull, conscientious people beat their children conscientiously, because they were beaten themselves and think children ought to be beaten. The ill-tempered vulgarity that instinctively strikes at and hurts a thing that annoys it (and all children are annoying), and the simple stupidity that requires from a child perfection beyond the reach of the wisest and best adults (perfect truthfulness coupled with perfect obedience is quite a common condition of leaving a child unwhipped), produce a good deal of flagellation among people who not only do not lust after it, but who hit the harder because they

40

are angry at having to perform an uncomfortable duty. These people will beat merely to assert their authority, or to carry out what they conceive to be a divine order on the strength of the precept of Solomon recorded in the Bible, which carefully adds that Solomon completely spoiled his own son and turned away from the god of his fathers to the sensuous idolatry in which he ended his days.

In the same way we find men and women practising vivisection as senselessly as a humane butcher, who adores his fox terrier, will cut a calf's throat and hang it up by its heels to bleed slowly to death because it is the custom to eat veal and insist on its being white; or as a German purveyor nails a goose to a board and stuffs it with food because fashionable people eat *pâté de foie gras;* or as the crew of a whaler breaks in on a colony of seals and clubs them to death in wholesale massacre because ladies want sealskin jackets; or as fanciers blind singing birds with hot needles, and mutilate the ears and tails of dogs and horses. Let cruelty or kindness or anything else once become customary and it will be practised by people to whom it is not at all natural, but whose rule of life is simply to do only what everybody else does, and who would lose their employment and starve if they indulged in any peculiarity. A respectable man will lie daily, in speech and in print, about the qualities of the article he lives by selling, because it is customary to do so. He will flog his boy for telling a lie, because it is customary to do so. He will also flog him for not telling a lie if the boy tells inconvenient or disrespectful truths, because it is customary to do so. He will give the same boy a present on his birthday, and buy him a spade and bucket at the seaside, because it is customary to do so, being all the time neither particularly mendacious, nor particularly cruel, nor particularly generous, but simply incapable of ethical judgment or independent action.

Just so do we find a crowd of petty vivisectionists daily committing atrocities and stupidities, because it is the custom to do so. Vivisection is customary as part of the routine of

41

preparing lectures in medical schools. For instance, there are two ways of making the action of the heart visible to students. One, a barbarous, ignorant, and thoughtless way, is to stick little flags into a rabbit's heart and let the students see the flags jump. The other, an elegant, ingenious, well-informed, and instructive way, is to put a sphygmograph on the student's wrist and let him see a record of his heart's action traced by a needle on a slip of smoked paper. But it has become the custom for lecturers to teach from the rabbit; and the lecturers are not original enough to get out of their groove. Then there are the demonstrations which are made by cutting up frogs with scissors. The most humane man, however repugnant the operation may be to him at first, cannot do it at lecture after lecture for months without finally—and that very soon—feeling no more for the frog than if he were cutting up pieces of paper. Such clumsy and lazy ways of teaching are based on the cheapness of frogs and rabbits. If machines were as cheap as frogs, engineers would not only be taught the anatomy of machines and the functions of their parts: they would also have machines misused and wrecked before them so that they might learn as much as possible by using their eyes, and as little as possible by using their brains and imaginations. Thus we have, as part of the routine of teaching, a routine of vivisection which soon produces complete indifference to it on the part even of those who are naturally humane. If they pass on from the routine of lecture preparation, not into general practice, but into research work, they carry this acquired indifference with them into the laboratory, where any atrocity is possible, because all atrocities satisfy curiosity. The routine man is in the majority in his profession always: consequently the moment his practice is tracked down to its source in human passion there is a great and quite sincere poohpoohing from himself, from the mass of the profession, and from the mass of the public, which sees that the average doctor is much too commonplace and decent a person to be capable of passionate wickedness of any kind.

Here, then, we have in vivisection, as in all the other tolerated and instituted cruelties, this anti-climax: that only a negligible percentage of those who practise and consequently defend it get any satisfaction out of it. As in Mr Galsworthy's play Justice the useless and detestable torture of solitary imprisonment is shewn at its worst without the introduction of a single cruel person into the drama, so it would be possible to represent all the torments of vivisection dramatically without introducing a single vivisector who had not felt sick at his first experience in the laboratory. Not that this can exonerate any vivisector from suspicion of enjoying his work (or *her* work: a good deal of the vivisection in medical schools is done by women). In every autobiography which records a real experience of school or prison life, we find that here and there among the routineers there is to be found the genuine amateur, the orgiastic flogging schoolmaster or the nagging warder, who has sought out a cruel profession for the sake of its cruelty. But it is the genuine routineer who is the bulwark of the practice, because, though you can excite public fury against a Sade, a Bluebeard, or a Nero, you cannot rouse any feeling against dull Mr Smith doing his duty: that is, doing the usual thing. He is so obviously no better and no worse than anyone else that it is difficult to conceive that the things he does are abominable. If you would see public dislike surging up in a moment against an individual, you must watch one who does something unusual, no matter how sensible it may be. The name of Jonas Hanway lives as that of a brave man because he was the first who dared to appear in the streets of this rainy island with an umbrella.

THE OLD LINE BETWEEN MAN AND BEAST

But there is still a distinction to be clung to by those who dare not tell themselves the truth about the medical profession because they are so helplessly dependent on it when death threatens the household. That distinction is the line that separates the brute from the man in the old classification. Granted, they will plead, that we are all cruel; yet the tame stag hunter does not hunt men; and the sportsman who lets a leash of greyhounds loose on a hare would be horrified at the thought of letting them loose on a human child. The lady who gets her cloak by flaying a sable does not flay a negro; nor does it ever occur to her that her veal cutlet might be improved on by a slice of tender baby.

Now there was a time when some trust could be placed in this distinction. The Roman Catholic Church still maintains, with what it must permit me to call a stupid obstinacy, and in spite of St Francis and St Anthony, that animals have no souls and no rights; so that you cannot sin against an animal, or against God by anything you may choose to do to an animal. Resisting the temptation to enter on an argument as to whether you may not sin against your own soul if you are unjust or cruel to the least of those whom St Francis called his little brothers, I have only to point out here that nothing could be more despicably superstitious in the opinion of a vivisector than the notion that science recognizes any such step in evolution as the step from a physical organism to an immortal soul. That conceit has been taken out of all our men of science, and out of all our doctors, by the evolutionists; and when it is considered how completely obsessed biological science has become in our days, not by the full scope of evolution, but by that particular method of it which has neither sense nor purpose nor life nor anything human, much less godlike, in it: by the method, that is, of so-called Natural Selection (meaning no selection at all, but mere dead accident and luck), the folly of trusting to vivisectors to hold the human animal any more sacred than the other animals becomes so clear that it would be waste of time to insist further on it. As a matter of fact the man who once concedes to the vivisector

44

the right to put a dog outside the laws of honor and fellowship, concedes to him also the right to put himself outside them; for he is nothing to the vivisector but a more highly developed, and consequently more interesting-to-experiment-on vertebrate than the dog.

VIVISECTING THE HUMAN SUBJECT

I have in my hand a printed and published account by a doctor of how he tested his remedy for pulmonary tuberculosis, which was, to inject a powerful germicide directly into the circulation by stabbing a vein with a syringe. He was one of those doctors who are able to command public sympathy by saying, quite truly, that when they discovered that the proposed treatment was dangerous, they experimented thenceforth on themselves. In this case the doctor was devoted enough to carry his experiments to the point of running serious risks, and actually making himself very uncomfortable. But he did not begin with himself. His first experiment was on two hospital patients. On receiving a message from the hospital to the effect that these two martyrs to therapeutic science had all but expired of convulsions, he experimented on a rabbit, which instantly dropped dead. It was then, and not until then, that he began to experiment on himself, with the germicide modified in the direction indicated by the experiments made on the two patients and the rabbit. As a good many people countenance vivisection because they fear that if the experiments are not made on rabbits they will be made on themselves, it is worth noting that in this case, where both rabbits and men were equally available, the men, being of course enormously more instructive and costing nothing, were experimented on first. Once grant the ethics of the vivisectionists and you not only sanction the experiment on the human subject, but make it the first duty of the vivisector. If a guinea pig may be sacrificed for the sake of the very little that can be learnt from it, shall not a man be sacrificed for the sake of the great deal that can be learnt from him? At all events, he *is* sacrificed, as this typical case shows. I may add (not that it touches the argument) that the doctor, the patients, and the rabbit all suffered in vain, as far as the hoped-for rescue of the race from pulmonary consumption is concerned.

"THE LIE IS A EUROPEAN POWER"

Now at the very time when the lectures describing these experiments were being circulated in print and discussed eagerly by the medical profession, the customary denials that patients are experimented on were as loud, as indignant, as high-minded as ever, in spite of the few intelligent doctors who point out rightly that all treatments are experiments on the patient. And this brings us to an obvious but mostly overlooked weakness in the vivisector's position: that is, his inevitable forfeiture of all claim to have his word believed. It is hardly to be expected that a man who does not hesitate to vivisect for the sake of science will hesitate to lie about it afterwards to protect it from what he deems the ignorant sentimentality of the laity. When the public conscience stirs uneasily and threatens suppression, there is never wanting some doctor of eminent position and high character who will sacrifice himself devotedly to the cause of science by coming forward to assure the public on his honor that all experiments on animals are completely painless; although he must know that the very experiments which first provoked the anti-vivisection movement by their atrocity were experiments to ascertain the physiological effects of the sensation of extreme pain (the much more interesting physiology of pleasure remains uninvestigated) and that all experiments in which sensation is a factor are voided by its suppression. Besides, vivisection may be painless in cases where the experiments are very cruel. If a person scratches me with a poisoned dagger so gently that I do not feel the scratch, he has achieved a painless vivisection; but if I presently die in torment I am not likely to consider that his humanity is amply vindicated by his gentleness. A cobra's bite hurts so little that the creature is almost, legally speaking, a vivisector who inflicts no pain. By giving his victims chloroform before biting them he could comply with the law completely.

Here, then, is a pretty deadlock. Public support of vivisection is founded almost wholly on the assurances of the vivisectors that great public benefits may be expected from the practice. Not for a moment do I suggest that such a defence would be valid even if proved. But when the witnesses begin by alleging that in the cause of science all the customary ethical obligations (which include the obligation to tell the truth) are suspended, what weight can any reasonable person give to their testimony? I would rather swear fifty lies than take an animal which had licked my hand in good fellowship and torture it. If I did torture the dog, I should certainly not have the face to turn round and ask how any person dare suspect an honorable man like myself of telling lies. Most sensible and humane people would, I hope, reply flatly that honorable men do not behave dishonorably even to dogs. The murderer who, when asked by the chaplain whether he had any other crimes to confess, replied indignantly "What do you take me for?" reminds us very strongly of the vivisectors who are so deeply hurt when their evidence is set aside as worthless.

AN ARGUMENT WHICH WOULD DEFEND ANY CRIME

The Achilles heel of vivisection, however, is not to be found in the pain it causes, but in the line of argument by which it is justified. The medical code regarding it is simply criminal anarchism at its very worst. Indeed, no criminal has yet had the impudence to argue as every vivisector argues. No burglar contends that as it is admittedly important to have money to spend, and as the object of burglary is to provide the burglar with money to spend, and as in many instances it has achieved this object, therefore the burglar is a public benefactor and the police are ignorant sentimentalists. No highway robber has yet harrowed us with denunciations of the puling moralist who allows his child to suffer all the evils of poverty because certain faddists think it dishonest to garotte an alderman. Thieves and

47

assassins understand quite well that there are paths of acquisition, even of the best things, that are barred to all men of honor. Again, has the silliest burglar ever pretended that to put a stop to burglary is to put a stop to industry? All the vivisections that have been performed since the world began have produced nothing so important as the innocent and honorable discovery of radiography; and one of the reasons why radiography was not discovered sooner was that the men whose business it was to discover new clinical methods were coarsening and stupefying themselves with the sensual villanies and cutthroat's casuistries of vivisection. The law of the conservation of energy holds good in physiology as in other things: every vivisector is a deserter from the army of honorable investigators. But the vivisector does not see this. He not only calls his methods scientific: he contends that there are no other scientific methods. When you express your natural loathing for his cruelty and your natural contempt for his stupidity, he imagines that you are attacking science. Yet he has no inkling of the method and temper of science. The point at issue being plainly whether he is a rascal or not, he not only insists that the real point is whether some hot-headed anti-vivisectionist is a liar (which he proves by ridiculously unscientific assumptions as to the degree of accuracy attainable in human statement), but never dreams of offering any scientific evidence by his own methods.

There are many paths to knowledge already discovered; and no enlightened man doubts that there are many more waiting to be discovered. Indeed, all paths lead to knowledge; because even the vilest and stupidest action teaches us something about vileness and stupidity, and may accidentally teach us a good deal more: for instance, a cutthroat learns (and perhaps teaches) the anatomy of the carotid artery and jugular vein; and there can be no question that the burning of St Joan of Arc must have been a most instructive and interesting experiment to a good observer, and could have been made more so if it had been

48

carried out by skilled physiologists under laboratory conditions. The earthquake in San Francisco proved invaluable as an experiment in the stability of giant steel buildings; and the ramming of the Victoria by the Camperdown settled doubtful points of the greatest importance in naval warfare. According to vivisectionist logic our builders would be justified in producing artificial earthquakes with dynamite, and our admirals in contriving catastrophes at naval manœuvres, in order to follow up the line of research thus accidentally discovered.

The truth is, if the acquisition of knowledge justifies every sort of conduct, it justifies any sort of conduct, from the illumination of Nero's feasts by burning human beings alive (another interesting experiment) to the simplest act of kindness. And in the light of that truth it is clear that the exemption of the pursuit of knowledge from the laws of honor is the most hideous conceivable enlargement of anarchy; worse, by far, than an exemption of the pursuit of money or political power, since these can hardly be attained without some regard for at least the appearances of human welfare, whereas a curious devil might destroy the whole race in torment, acquiring knowledge all the time from his highly interesting experiment. There is more danger in one respectable scientist countenancing such a monstrous claim than in fifty assassins or dynamitards. The man who makes it is ethically imbecile; and whoever imagines that it is a scientific claim has not the faintest conception of what science means. The paths to knowledge are countless. One of these paths is a path through darkness, secrecy, and cruelty. When a man deliberately turns from all other paths and goes down that one, it is scientific to infer that what attracts him is not knowledge, since there are other paths to that, but cruelty. With so strong and scientific a case against him, it is childish for him to stand on his honor and reputation and high character and the credit of a noble profession and so forth: he must clear himself either by reason or by experiment, unless he boldly contends that evolution has retained a passion of cruelty in man just because it is indispensable to the fulness of his knowledge.

THOU ART THE MAN

I shall not be at all surprised if what I have written above has induced in sympathetic readers a transport of virtuous indignation at the expense of the medical profession. I shall not damp so creditable and salutary a sentiment; but I must point out that the guilt is shared by all of us. It is not in his capacity of healer and man of science that the doctor vivisects or defends vivisection, but in his entirely vulgar lay capacity. He is made of the same clay as the ignorant, shallow, credulous, half-miseducated, pecuniarily anxious people who call him in when they have tried in vain every bottle and every pill the advertizing druggist can persuade them to buy. The real remedy for vivisection is the remedy for all the mischief that the medical profession and all the other professions are doing: namely, more knowledge. The juries which send the poor Peculiars to prison, and give vivisectionists heavy damages against humane persons who accuse them of cruelty; the editors and councillors and student-led mobs who are striving to make Vivisection one of the watchwords of our civilization, are not doctors: they are the British public, all so afraid to die that they will cling frantically to any idol which promises to cure all their diseases, and crucify anyone who tells them that they must not only die when their time comes, but die like gentlemen. In their paroxysms of cowardice and selfishness they force the doctors to humor their folly and ignorance. How complete and inconsiderate their ignorance is can only be realized by those who have some knowledge of vital statistics, and of the illusions which beset Public Health legislation.

WHAT THE PUBLIC WANTS AND WILL NOT GET

The demands of this poor public are not reasonable, but they are quite simple. It dreads disease and desires to be protected against it. But it is poor and wants to be protected cheaply. Scientific measures are too hard to understand, too costly, too clearly tending towards a rise in the rates and more public interference with the insanitary, because insufficiently financed, private house. What the public wants, therefore, is a cheap magic charm to prevent, and a cheap pill or potion to cure all disease. It forces all such charms on the doctors.

THE VACCINATION CRAZE

Thus it was really the public and not the medical profession that took up vaccination with irresistible faith, sweeping the invention out of Jenner's hands and establishing it in a form which he himself repudiated. Jenner was not a man of science; but he was not a fool; and when he found that people who had suffered from cowpox either by contagion in the milking shed or by vaccination, were not, as he had supposed, immune from smallpox, he ascribed the cases of immunity which had formerly misled him to a disease of the horse, which, perhaps because we do not drink its milk and eat its flesh, is kept at a greater distance in our imagination than our foster mother the cow. At all events, the public, which had been boundlessly credulous about the cow, would not have the horse on any terms; and to this day the law which prescribes Jennerian vaccination is carried out with an anti-Jennerian inoculation because the public would have it so in spite of Jenner. All the grossest lies and superstitions which have disgraced the vaccination craze were taught to the doctors by the public. It was not the doctors who first began to declare that all our old men remember the time when almost every face they saw in the street was horribly pitted with smallpox, and that all this disfigurement has vanished since the introduction of vaccination. Jenner himself alluded to this imaginary phenomenon before the introduction of vaccination, and attributed it to the older practice of smallpox inoculation, by which Voltaire, Catherine II and Lady Mary Wortley Montagu so confidently expected to see the disease made harmless. It was not Jenner who set people declaring that smallpox, if not abolished by vaccination, had at least been made much milder: on the contrary, he recorded a pre-vaccination epidemic in which none of the persons attacked went to bed or considered themselves as seriously ill. Neither Jenner, nor any other doctor ever, as far as I know, inculcated the popular notion that everybody got smallpox as a matter of course before vaccination was invented. That doctors get infected with these delusions, and are in their unprofessional capacity as members of the public subject to them like other men, is true; but if we had to decide whether vaccination was first forced on the public by the doctors or on the doctors by the public, we should have to decide against the public.

STATISTICAL ILLUSIONS

Public ignorance of the laws of evidence and of statistics can hardly be exaggerated. There may be a doctor here and there who in dealing with the statistics of disease has taken at least the first step towards sanity by grasping the fact that as an attack of even the commonest disease is an exceptional event, apparently overwhelming statistical evidence in favor of any prophylactic can be produced by persuading the public that everybody caught the disease formerly. Thus if a disease is one which normally attacks fifteen per cent of the population, and if the effect of a prophylactic is actually to increase the proportion to twenty per cent, the publication of this figure of twenty per cent will convince the public that the prophylactic has reduced the percentage by eighty per cent instead of increasing it by five, because the public, left to itself and to the old gentlemen who are always ready to remember, on every possible subject, that things used to be much worse than they are now (such old gentlemen greatly outnumber the laudatores tempori acti), will assume that the former percentage was about 100. The vogue of the Pasteur treatment of hydrophobia, for instance, was due to the assumption by the public that every person bitten by a rabid dog necessarily got hydrophobia. I myself heard hydrophobia discussed in my youth by doctors in Dublin before a Pasteur Institute existed, the subject having been brought forward there by the scepticism of an eminent surgeon as to whether hydrophobia is really a specific disease or only ordinary tetanus induced (as tetanus was then supposed to be induced) by a lacerated wound. There were no statistics available as to the proportion of dog bites that ended in hydrophobia; but nobody ever guessed that the cases could be more than two or three per cent of the bites. On me, therefore, the results published by the Pasteur Institute produced no such effect as they did on the ordinary man who thinks that the bite of a mad dog means certain hydrophobia. It seemed to me that the proportion of deaths among the cases treated at the Institute was rather higher, if anything, than might have been expected had there been no Institute in existence. But to the public every Pasteur patient who did not die was miraculously saved from an agonizing death by the beneficent white magic of that most trusty of all wizards, the man of science.

Even trained statisticians often fail to appreciate the extent to which statistics are vitiated by the unrecorded assumptions of their interpreters. Their attention is too much occupied with the cruder tricks of those who make a corrupt use of statistics for advertizing purposes. There is, for example, the percentage dodge. In some hamlet, barely large enough to have a name, two people are attacked during a smallpox epidemic. One dies: the other recovers. One has vaccination marks: the other has none. Immediately either the vaccinists or the anti-vaccinists publish the triumphant news that at such and such a place not a single vaccinated person died of smallpox whilst 100 per cent of the unvaccinated perished miserably; or, as the case may be, that 100 per cent of the unvaccinated recovered whilst the vaccinated succumbed to the last man. Or, to take another common instance, comparisons which are really comparisons between two social classes with different standards of nutrition and education are palmed off as comparisons between the results of a certain medical treatment and its neglect. Thus it is easy to prove that the wearing of tall hats and the carrying of umbrellas enlarges the chest, prolongs life, and confers comparative immunity from disease; for the statistics shew that the classes which use these articles are bigger, healthier, and live longer than the class which never dreams of possessing such things. It does not take much perspicacity to see that what really makes this difference is not the tall hat and the umbrella, but the wealth and nourishment of which they are evidence, and that a gold watch or membership of a club in Pall Mall might be proved in the same way to have the like sovereign virtues. A university degree, a daily bath, the owning of thirty pairs of trousers, a knowledge of Wagner's music, a pew in church, anything, in short, that implies more means and better nurture than the mass of laborers enjoy, can be statistically palmed off as a magic-spell conferring all sorts of privileges.

In the case of a prophylactic enforced by law, this illusion is intensified grotesquely, because only vagrants can evade it. Now vagrants have little power of resisting any disease: their death-rate and their case-mortality rate is always high relatively to that of respectable folk. Nothing is easier, therefore, than to prove that compliance with any public regulation produces the most gratifying results. It would be equally easy even if the regulation actually raised the death-rate, provided it did not raise it sufficiently to make the average householder, who cannot evade regulations, die as early as the average vagrant who can.

THE SURPRISES OF ATTENTION AND NEGLECT

There is another statistical illusion which is independent of class differences. A common complaint of houseowners is that the Public Health Authorities frequently compel them to instal costly sanitary appliances which are condemned a few years later as dangerous to health, and forbidden under penalties. Yet these discarded mistakes are always made in the first instance on the strength of a demonstration that their introduction has reduced the death-rate. The explana-

54

tion is simple. Suppose a law were made that every child in the nation should be compelled to drink a pint of brandy per month, but that the brandy must be administered only when the child was in good health, with its digestion and so forth working normally, and its teeth either naturally or artificially sound. Probably the result would be an immediate and startling reduction in child mortality, leading to further legislation increasing the quantity of brandy to a gallon. Not until the brandy craze had been carried to a point at which the direct harm done by it would outweigh the incidental good, would an anti-brandy party be listened to. That incidental good would be the substitution of attention to the general health of children for the neglect which is now the rule so long as the child is not actually too sick to run about and play as usual. Even if this attention were confined to the children's teeth, there would be an improvement which it would take a good deal of brandy to cancel.

This imaginary case explains the actual case of the sanitary appliances which our local sanitary authorities prescribe today and condemn tomorrow. No sanitary contrivance which the mind of even the very worst plumber can devize could be as disastrous as that total neglect for long periods which gets avenged by pestilences that sweep through whole continents, like the black death and the cholera. If it were proposed at this time of day to discharge all the sewage of London crude and untreated into the Thames, instead of carrying it, after elaborate treatment, far out into the North Sea, there would be a shriek of horror from all our experts. Yet if Cromwell had done that instead of doing nothing, there would probably have been no Great Plague of London. When the Local Health Authority forces every householder to have his sanitary arrangements thought about and attended to by somebody whose special business it is to attend to such things, then it matters not how erroneous or even directly mischievous may be the specific measures taken: the net result at first is sure to be an improvement. Not until attention has been effectually substituted for neglect as the general rule, will the statistics begin to shew the merits of the particular methods of attention adopted. And as we are far from having arrived at this stage, being as to health legislation only at the beginning of things, we have practically no evidence yet as to the value of methods. Simple and obvious as this is, nobody seems as yet to discount the effect of substituting attention for neglect in drawing conclusions from health statistics. Everything is put to the credit of the particular method employed, although it may quite possibly be raising the death-rate by five per thousand whilst the attention incidental to it is reducing the death-rate fifteen per thousand. The net gain to ten per thousand is credited to the method, and made the excuse for enforcing more of it.

STEALING CREDIT FROM CIVILIZATION

There is yet another way in which specifics which have no merits at all, either direct or incidental, may be brought into high repute by statistics. For a century past civilization has been cleaning away the conditions which favor bacterial fevers. Typhus, once rife, has vanished: plague and cholera have been stopped at our frontiers by a sanitary blockade. We still have epidemics of smallpox and typhoid; and diphtheria and scarlet fever are endemic in the slums. Measles, which in my childhood was not regarded as a dangerous disease, has now become so mortal that notices are posted publicly urging parents to take it seriously. But even in these cases the contrast between the death and recovery rates in the rich districts and in the poor ones has led to the general conviction among experts that bacterial diseases are preventible; and they already are to a large extent prevented. The dangers of infection and the way to avoid it are better understood than they used to be. It is barely twenty years since people exposed themselves recklessly to the infection of consumption and pneumonia in the belief that these diseases were not "catching." Nowadays the troubles of consumptive patients are greatly increased by the growing disposition to treat them as lepers. No doubt there is a good

56

deal of ignorant exaggeration and cowardly refusal to face a human and necessary share of the risk. That has always been the case. We now know that the medieval horror of leprosy was out of all proportion to the danger of infection, and was accompanied by apparent blindness to the infectiousness of smallpox, which has since been worked up by our disease terrorists into the position formerly held by leprosy. But the scare of infection, though it sets even doctors talking as if the only really scientific thing to do with a fever patient is to throw him into the nearest ditch and pump carbolic acid on him from a safe distance until he is ready to be cremated on the spot, has led to much greater care and cleanliness. And the net result has been a series of victories over disease.

Now let us suppose that in the early nineteenth century somebody had come forward with a theory that typhus fever always begins at the top joint of the little finger; and that if this joint be amputated immediately after birth, typhus fever will disappear. Had such a suggestion been adopted, the theory would have been triumphantly confirmed; for as a matter of fact, typhus fever *has* disappeared. On the other hand cancer and madness have increased (statistically) to an appalling extent. The opponents of the little finger theory would therefore be pretty sure to allege that the amputations were spreading cancer and lunacy. The vaccination controversy is full of such contentions. So is the controversy as to the docking of horses' tails and the cropping of dogs' ears. So is the less widely known controversy as to circumcision and the declaring certain kinds of flesh unclean by the Jews. To advertize any remedy or operation, you have only to pick out all the most reassuring advances made by civilization, and boldly present the two in the relation of cause and effect: the public will swallow the fallacy without a wry face. It has no idea of the need for what is called a control experiment. In Shakespear's time and for long after it, mummy was a favorite medicament. You took a pinch of the dust of a dead Egyptian in a pint of the hottest water you could bear to drink; and it did you a great deal of good. This, you thought, proved what a sovereign healer mummy was. But if you had tried the control experiment of taking the hot water without the mummy, you might have found the effect exactly the same, and that any hot drink would have done as well.

BIOMETRIKA

Another difficulty about statistics is the technical difficulty of calculation. Before you can even make a mistake in drawing your conclusion from the correlations established by your statistics you must ascertain the correlations. When I turn over the pages of Biometrika, a quarterly journal in which is recorded the work done in the field of biological statistics by Professor Karl Pearson and his colleagues, I am out of my depth at the first line, because mathematics are to me only a concept: I never used a logarithm in my life, and could not undertake to extract the square root of four without misgiving. I am therefore unable to deny that the statistical ascertainment of the correlations between one thing and another must be a very complicated and difficult technical business, not to be tackled successfully except by high mathematicians; and I cannot resist Professor Karl Pearson's immense contempt for, and indignant sense of grave social danger in, the unskilled guesses of the ordinary sociologist.

Now the man in the street knows nothing of Biometrika: all he knows is that "you can prove anything by figures," though he forgets this the moment figures are used to prove anything he wants to believe. If he did take in Biometrika he would probably become abjectly credulous as to all the conclusions drawn in it from the correlations so learnedly worked out; though the mathematician whose correlations would fill a Newton with admiration, may, in collecting and accepting data and drawing conclusions from them, fall into quite crude errors by just such popular oversights as I have been describing.

58

PATIENT-MADE THERAPEUTICS

To all these blunders and ignorances doctors are no less subject than the rest of us. They are not trained in the use of evidence, nor in biometrics, nor in the psychology of human credulity, nor in the incidence of economic pressure. Further, they must believe, on the whole, what their patients believe, just as they must wear the sort of hat their patients wear. The doctor may lay down the law despotically enough to the patient at points where the patient's mind is simply blank; but when the patient has a prejudice the doctor must either keep it in countenance or lose his patient. If people are persuaded that night air is dangerous to health and that fresh air makes them catch cold, it will not be possible for a doctor to make his living in private practice if he prescribes ventilation. We have to go back no further than the days of The Pickwick Papers to find ourselves in a world where people slept in four-post beds with curtains drawn closely round to exclude as much air as possible. Had Mr Pickwick's doctor told him that he would be much healthier if he slept on a camp bed by an open window, Mr Pickwick would have regarded him as a crank and called in another doctor. Had he gone on to forbid Mr Pickwick to drink brandy and water whenever he felt chilly, and assured him that if he were deprived of meat or salt for a whole year, he would not only not die, but would be none the worse, Mr Pickwick would have fled from his presence as from that of a dangerous madman. And in these matters the doctor cannot cheat his patient. If he has no faith in drugs or vaccination, and the patient has, he can cheat him with colored water and pass his lancet through the flame of a spirit lamp before scratching his arm. But he cannot make him change his daily habits without knowing it.

THE REFORMS ALSO COME FROM THE LAITY

In the main, then, the doctor learns that if he gets ahead of the superstitions of his patients he is a ruined man; and the result is that he instinctively takes care not to get ahead of them. That is why all the changes come from the laity. It was not until an agitation had been conducted for many years by laymen, including quacks and faddists of all kinds, that the public was sufficiently impressed to make it possible for the doctors to open their minds and their mouths on the subject of fresh air, cold water, temperance, and the rest of the new fashions in hygiene. At present the tables have been turned on many old prejudices. Plenty of our most popular elderly doctors believe that cold tubs in the morning are unnatural, exhausting, and rheumatic; that fresh air is a fad, and that everybody is the better for a glass or two of port wine every day; but they no longer dare say as much until they know exactly where they are; for many very desirable patients in country houses have lately been persuaded that their first duty is to get up at six in the morning and begin the day by taking a walk barefoot through the dewy grass. He who shews the least scepticism as to this practice is at once suspected of being "an old-fashioned doctor," and dismissed to make room for a younger man.

In short, private medical practice is governed not by science but by supply and demand; and however scientific a treatment may be, it cannot hold its place in the market if there is no demand for it; nor can the grossest quackery be kept off the market if there is a demand for it.

FASHIONS AND EPIDEMICS

A demand, however, can be inculcated. This is thoroughly understood by fashionable tradesmen, who find no difficulty in persuading their customers to renew articles that are not worn out and to buy things they do not want. By making doctors tradesmen, we compel them to learn the tricks of trade; consequently we find that the fashions of the year include treatments, operations, and particular drugs, as well as hats, sleeves, ballads, and games. Tonsils, vermiform appendices, uvulas, even ovaries are sacrificed because it is the fashion to get them cut out, and because the operations are highly profitable. The psychology of

60

fashion becomes a pathology; for the cases have every air of being genuine: fashions, after all, are only induced epidemics, proving that epidemics can be induced by tradesmen, and therefore by doctors.

THE DOCTOR'S VIRTUES

It will be admitted that this is a pretty bad state of things. And the melodramatic instinct of the public, always demanding that every wrong shall have, not its remedy, but its villain to be hissed, will blame, not its own apathy, superstition, and ignorance, but the depravity of the doctors. Nothing could be more unjust or mischievous. Doctors, if no better than other men, are certainly no worse. I was reproached during the performances of The Doctor's Dilemma at the Court Theatre in 1907 because I made the artist a rascal, the journalist an illiterate incapable, and all the doctors "angels." But I did not go beyond the warrant of my own experience. It has been my luck to have doctors among my friends for nearly forty years past (all perfectly aware of my freedom from the usual credulity as to the miraculous powers and knowledge attributed to them); and though I know that there are medical blackguards as well as military, legal, and clerical blackguards (one soon finds that out when one is privileged to hear doctors talking shop among themselves), the fact that I was no more at a loss for private medical advice and attendance when I had not a penny in my pocket than I was later on when I could afford fees on the highest scale, has made it impossible for me to share that hostility to the doctor as a man which exists and is growing as an inevitable result of the present condition of medical practice. Not that the interest in disease and aberrations which turns some men and women to medicine and surgery is not sometimes as morbid as the interest in misery and vice which turns some others to philanthropy and "rescue work." But the true doctor is inspired by a hatred of ill-health, and a divine impatience of any waste of vital forces. Unless a man is led to medicine or surgery through a very exceptional technical aptitude, or because doctoring is a

61

family tradition, or because he regards it unintelligently as a lucrative and gentlemanly profession, his motives in choosing the career of a healer are clearly generous. However actual practice may disillusion and corrupt him, his selection in the first instance is not a selection of a base character.

THE DOCTOR'S HARDSHIPS

A review of the counts in the indictment I have brought against private medical practice will shew that they arise out of the doctor's position as a competitive private tradesman: that is, out of his poverty and dependence. And it should be borne in mind that doctors are expected to treat other people specially well whilst themselves submitting to specially inconsiderate treatment. The butcher and baker are not expected to feed the hungry unless the hungry can pay; but a doctor who allows a fellow-creature to suffer or perish without aid is regarded as a monster. Even if we must dismiss hospital service as really venal, the fact remains that most doctors do a good deal of gratuitous work in private practice all through their careers. And in his paid work the doctor is on a different footing to the tradesman. Although the articles he sells, advice and treatment, are the same for all classes, his fees have to be graduated like the income tax. The successful fashionable doctor may weed his poorer patients out from time to time, and finally use the College of Physicians to place it out of his own power to accept low fees; but the ordinary general practitioner never makes out his bills without considering the taxable capacity of his patients.

Then there is the disregard of his own health and comfort which results from the fact that he is, by the nature of his work, an emergency man. We are polite and considerate to the doctor when there is nothing the matter, and we meet him as a friend or entertain him as a guest; but when the baby is suffering from croup, or its mother has a temperature of 104°, or its grandfather has broken his leg, nobody thinks of the doctor except as a healer and savior. He may

62

be hungry, weary, sleepy, run down by several successive nights disturbed by that instrument of torture, the night bell; but who ever thinks of this in the face of sudden sickness or accident? We think no more of the condition of a doctor attending a case than of the condition of a fireman at a fire. In other occupations night-work is specially recognized and provided for. The worker sleeps all day; has his breakfast in the evening; his lunch or dinner at midnight; his dinner or supper before going to bed in the morning; and he changes to day-work if he cannot stand night-work. But a doctor is expected to work day and night. In practices which consist largely of workmen's clubs, and in which the patients are therefore taken on wholesale terms and very numerous, the unfortunate assistant, or the principal if he has no assistant, often does not undress, knowing that he will be called up before he has snatched an hour's sleep. To the strain of such inhuman conditions must be added the constant risk of infection. One wonders why the impatient doctors do not become savage and unmanageable, and the patient ones imbecile. Perhaps they do, to some extent. And the pay is wretched, and so uncertain that refusal to attend without payment in advance becomes often a necessary measure of self-defence, whilst the County Court has long ago put an end to the tradition that the doctor's fee is an honorarium. Even the most eminent physicians, as such biographies as those of Paget shew, are sometimes miserably, inhumanly poor until they are past their prime.

In short, the doctor needs our help for the moment much more than we often need his. The ridicule of Molière, the death of a well-informed and clever writer like the late Harold Frederic in the hands of Christian Scientists (a sort of sealing with his blood of the contemptuous disbelief in and dislike of doctors he had bitterly expressed in his books), the scathing and quite justifiable exposure of medical practice in the novel by Mr Maarten Maartens entitled The New Religion: all these trouble the doctor very little, and are in any case well set off by the popularity of Sir Luke

63

Fildes' famous picture, and by the verdicts in which juries from time to time express their conviction that the doctor can do no wrong. The real woes of the doctor are the shabby coat, the wolf at the door, the tyranny of ignorant patients, the work-day of 24 hours, and the uselessness of honestly prescribing what most of the patients really need: that is, not medicine, but money.

THE PUBLIC DOCTOR

What then is to be done?

Fortunately we have not to begin absolutely from the beginning: we already have, in the Medical Officer of Health, a sort of doctor who is free from the worst hardships, and consequently from the worst vices, of the private practitioner. His position depends, not on the number of people who are ill, and whom he can keep ill, but on the number of people who are well. He is judged, as all doctors and treatments should be judged, by the vital statistics of his district. When the death-rate goes up his credit goes down. As every increase in his salary depends on the issue of a public debate as to the health of the constituency under his charge, he has every inducement to strive towards the ideal of a clean bill of health. He has a safe, dignified, responsible, independent position based wholly on the public health; whereas the private practitioner has a precarious, shabby-genteel, irresponsible, servile position, based wholly on the prevalence of illness.

It is true, there are grave scandals in the public medical service. The public doctor may be also a private practitioner eking out his earnings by giving a little time to public work for a mean payment. There are cases in which the position is one which no successful practitioner will accept, and where, therefore, incapables or drunkards get automatically selected for the post, *faute de mieux*; but even in these cases the doctor is less disastrous in his public capacity than in his private one: besides, the conditions which produce these bad cases are doomed, as the evil is now recognized and understood. A popular but unstable remedy is to enable local au-

64

thorities, when they are too small to require the undivided time of such men as the Medical Officers of our great municipalities, to combine for public health purposes so that each may share the services of a highly paid official of the best class; but the right remedy is a larger area as the sanitary unit.

MEDICAL ORGANIZATION

Another advantage of public medical work is that it admits of organization, and consequently of the distribution of the work in such a manner as to avoid wasting the time of highly qualified experts on trivial jobs. The individualism of private practice leads to an appalling waste of time on trifles. Men whose dexterity as operators or almost divinatory skill in diagnosis are constantly needed for difficult cases, are poulticing whitlows, vaccinating, changing unimportant dressings, prescribing ether drams for ladies with timid leanings towards dipsomania, and generally wasting their time in the pursuit of private fees. In no other profession is the practitioner expected to do all the work involved in it from the first day of his professional career to the last as the doctor is. The judge passes sentence of death; but he is not expected to hang the criminal with his own hands, as he would be if the legal profession were as unorganized as the medical. The bishop is not expected to blow the organ or wash the baby he baptizes. The general is not asked to plan a campaign or conduct a battle at half-past twelve and to play the drum at half-past two. Even if they were, things would still not be as bad as in the medical profession; for in it not only is the first-class man set to do third-class work, but, what is much more terrifying, the third-class man is expected to do first-class work. Every general practitioner is supposed to be capable of the whole range of medical and surgical work at a moment's notice; and the country doctor, who has not a specialist nor a crack consultant at the end of his telephone, often has to tackle without hesitation cases which no sane practitioner in a town would take in hand without assistance. No doubt this develops the resourcefulness of the country doctor, and makes him a more capable man than his suburban colleague; but it cannot develop the second-class man into a first-class one. If the practice of law not only led to a judge having to hang, but the hangman to judge, or if in the army matters were so arranged that it would be possible for the drummer boy to be in command at Waterloo whilst the Duke of Wellington was playing the drum in Brussels, we should not be consoled by the reflection that our hangmen were thereby made a little more judicial-minded, and our drummers more responsible, than in foreign countries where the legal and military professions recognized the advantages of division of labor.

Under such conditions no statistics as to the graduation of professional ability among doctors are available. Assuming that doctors are normal men and not magicians (and it is unfortunately very hard to persuade people to admit so much and thereby destroy the romance of doctoring) we may guess that the medical profession, like the other professions, consists of a small percentage of highly gifted persons at one end, and a small percentage of altogether disastrous duffers at the other. Between these extremes comes the main body of doctors (also, of course, with a weak and a strong end) who can be trusted to work under regulations with more or less aid from above according to the gravity of the case. Or, to put it in terms of the cases, there are cases that present no difficulties, and can be dealt with by a nurse or student at one end of the scale, and cases that require watching and handling by the very highest existing skill at the other; whilst between come the great mass of cases which need visits from the doctor of ordinary ability and from the chiefs of the profession in the proportion of, say, seven to none, seven to one, three to one, one to one, or, for a day or two, none to one. Such a service is organized at present only in hospitals; though in large towns the practice of calling in the consultant acts, to some extent, as a substitute for it. But in the latter case it is quite unregulated except by professional etiquet, which, as we have seen, has for its object, not the health of the patient or of the community at large, but the protection of the doctor's livelihood and the concealment of his errors. And as the consultant is an expensive luxury, he is a last resource rather than, as he should be, a matter of course in all cases where the general practitioner is not equal to the occasion: a predicament in which a very capable man may find himself at any time through the cropping up of a case of which he has had no clinical experience.

THE SOCIAL SOLUTION OF THE MEDICAL PROBLEM

The social solution of the medical problem, then, depends on that large, slowly advancing, pettishly resisted integration of society called generally Socialism. Until the medical profession becomes a body of men trained and paid by the country to keep the country in health it will remain what it is at present: a conspiracy to exploit popular credulity and human suffering. Already our M.O.H.s (Medical Officers of Health) are in the new position: what is lacking is appreciation of the change, not only by the public but by the private doctors. For, as we have seen, when one of the first-rate posts becomes vacant in one of the great cities, and all the leading M.O.H.s compete for it, they must appeal to the good health of the cities of which they have been in charge, and not to the size of the incomes the local private doctors are making out of the ill-health of their patients. If a competitor can prove that he has utterly ruined every sort of medical private practice in a large city except obstetric practice and the surgery of accidents, his claims are irresistible; and this is the ideal at which every M.O.H. should aim. But the profession at large should none the less welcome him and set its house in order for the social change which will finally be its own salvation. For the M.O.H. as we know him is only the beginning of that army of Public Hygiene which will presently take the place in general interest and honor now occupied by our military and naval

67

forces. It is silly that an Englishman should be more afraid of a German soldier than of a British disease germ, and should clamor for more barracks in the same newspapers that protest against more school clinics, and cry out that if the State fights disease for us it makes us paupers, though they never say that if the State fights the Germans for us it makes us cowards. Fortunately, when a habit of thought is silly it only needs steady treatment by ridicule from sensible and witty people to be put out of countenance and perish. Every year sees an increase in the number of persons employed in the Public Health Service, who would formerly have been mere adventurers in the Private Illness Service. To put it another way, a host of men and women who have now a strong incentive to be mischievous and even murderous rogues will have a much stronger, because a much honester, incentive to be not only good citizens but active benefactors to the community. And they will have no anxiety whatever about their incomes.

THE FUTURE OF PRIVATE PRACTICE

It must not be hastily concluded that this involves the extinction of the private practitioner. What it will really mean for him is release from his present degrading and scientifically corrupting slavery to his patients. As I have already shewn, the doctor who has to live by pleasing his patients in competition with everybody who has walked the hospitals, scraped through the examinations, and bought a brass plate, soon finds himself prescribing water to teetotallers and brandy or champagne jelly to drunkards; beefsteaks and stout in one house, and "uric acid free" vegetarian diet over the way; shut windows, big fires, and heavy overcoats to old Colonels, and open air and as much nakedness as is compatible with decency to young faddists, never once daring to say either "I dont know," or "I dont agree." For the strength of the doctor's, as of every other man's position when the evolution of social organization at last reaches his profession, will be that he will always have open to him the alternative of public employment when the pri-
68

vate employer becomes too tyrannous. And let no one suppose that the words doctor and patient can disguise from the parties the fact that they are employer and employee. No doubt doctors who are in great demand can be as highhanded and independent as employees are in all classes when a dearth in their labor market makes them indispensable; but the average doctor is not in this position: he is struggling for life in an overcrowded profession, and knows well that "a good bedside manner" will carry him to solvency through a morass of illness, whilst the least attempt at plain dealing with people who are eating too much or drinking too much, or frowsting too much (to go no further in the list of intemperances that make up so much of family life) would soon land him in the Bankruptcy Court.

Private practice, thus protected, would itself protect individuals, as far as such protection is possible, against the errors and superstitions of State medicine, which are at worst no worse than the errors and superstitions of private practice, being, indeed, all derived from it. Such monstrosities as vaccination are, as we have seen, founded, not on science, but on half-crowns. If the Vaccination Acts, instead of being wholly repealed as they are already half repealed, were strengthened by compelling every parent to have his child vaccinated by a public officer whose salary was completely independent of the number of vaccinations performed by him, and for whom there was plenty of alternative public health work waiting, vaccination would be dead in two years, as the vaccinator would not only not gain by it, but would lose credit through the depressing effects on the vital statistics of his district of the illness and deaths it causes, whilst it would take from him all the credit of that freedom from smallpox which is the result of good sanitary administration and vigilant prevention of infection. Such absurd panic scandals as that of the last London epidemic, where a fee of half-a-crown per re-vaccination produced raids on houses during the absence of parents, and the forcible seizure and re-vaccination of children left to answer the

69

door, can be prevented simply by abolishing the half-crown
and all similar follies, paying, not for this or that ceremony
of witchcraft, but for immunity from disease, and paying,
too, in a rational way. The officer with a fixed salary saves
himself trouble by doing his business with the least possible
interference with the private citizen. The man paid by the
job loses money by not forcing his job on the public as often
as possible without reference to its results.

THE TECHNICAL PROBLEM

As to any technical medical problem specially involved,
there is none. If there were, I should not be competent to
deal with it, as I am not a technical expert in medicine: I
deal with the subject as an economist, a politician, and a
citizen exercising my common sense. Everything that I
have said applies equally to all the medical techniques, and
will hold good whether public hygiene be based on the
poetic fancies of Christian Science, the tribal superstitions of
the druggist and the vivisector, or the best we can make of
our real knowledge. But I may remind those who confus-
edly imagine that the medical problem is also the scientific
problem, that all problems are finally scientific problems.
The notion that therapeutics or hygiene or surgery is any
more or less scientific than making or cleaning boots is entertained only by people to whom a man of science is still a
magician who can cure diseases, transmute metals, and enable us to live for ever. It may still be necessary for some
time to come to practise on popular credulity, popular love
and dread of the marvellous, and popular idolatry, to induce
the poor to comply with the sanitary regulations they are
too ignorant to understand. As I have elsewhere confessed,
I have myself been responsible for ridiculous incantations
with burning sulphur, experimentally proved to be quite
useless, because poor people are convinced, by the mystical
air of the burning and the horrible smell, that it exorcises
the demons of smallpox and scarlet fever and makes it safe
for them to return to their houses. To assure them that the
real secret is sunshine and soap is only to convince them
70

that you do not care whether they live or die, and wish to save money at their expense. So you perform the incantation; and back they go to their houses, satisfied. A religious ceremony—a poetic blessing of the threshold, for instance—would be much better; but unfortunately our religion is weak on the sanitary side. One of the worst misfortunes of Christendom was that reaction against the voluptuous bathing of the imperial Romans which made dirty habits a part of Christian piety, and in some unlucky places (the Sandwich Islands, for example) made the introduction of Christianity also the introduction of disease, because the formulators of the superseded native religion, like Mahomet, had been enlightened enough to introduce as religious duties such sanitary measures as ablution and the most careful and reverent treatment of everything cast off by the human body, even to nail clippings and hairs; and our missionaries thoughtlessly discredited this godly doctrine without supplying its place, which was promptly taken by laziness and neglect. If the priests of Ireland could only be persuaded to teach their flocks that it is a deadly insult to the Blessed Virgin to place her image in a cottage that is not kept up to that high standard of Sunday cleanliness to which all her worshippers must believe she is accustomed, and to represent her as being especially particular about stables because her son was born in one, they might do more in one year than all the Sanitary Inspectors in Ireland could do in twenty; and they could hardly doubt that Our Lady would be delighted. Perhaps they do nowadays; for Ireland is certainly a transfigured country since my youth as far as clean faces and pinafores can transfigure it. In England, where so many of the inhabitants are too gross to believe in poetic faiths, too respectable to tolerate the notion that the stable at Bethany was a common peasant farmer's stable instead of a first-rate racing one, and too savage to believe that anything can really cast out the devil of disease unless it be some terrifying hoodoo of tortures and stinks, the M.O.H. will no doubt for a long time to come have to preach to

71

fools according to their folly, promising miracles, and threatening hideous personal consequences of neglect of by-laws and the like; therefore it will be important that every M.O.H. shall have, with his (or her) other qualifications, a sense of humor, lest he (or she) should come at last to believe all the nonsense that must needs be talked. But he must, in his capacity of an expert advising the authorities, keep the government itself free of superstition. If Italian peasants are so ignorant that the Church can get no hold of them except by miracles, why, miracles there must be. The blood of St Januarius must liquefy whether the Saint is in the humor or not. To trick a heathen into being a dutiful Christian is no worse than to trick a whitewasher into trusting himself in a room where a smallpox patient has lain, by pretending to exorcise the disease with burning sulphur. But woe to the Church if in deceiving the peasant it also deceives itself; for then the Church is lost, and the peasant too, unless he revolt against it. Unless the Church works the pretended miracle painfully against the grain, and is continually urged by its dislike of the imposture to strive to make the peasant susceptible to the true reasons for behaving well, the Church will become an instrument of his corruption and an exploiter of his ignorance, and will find itself launched upon that persecution of scientific truth of which all priesthoods are accused—and none with more justice than the scientific priesthood.

And here we come to the danger that terrifies so many of us: the danger of having a hygienic orthodoxy imposed on us. But we must face that: in such crowded and poverty ridden civilizations as ours any orthodoxy is better than laisser-faire. If our population ever comes to consist exclusively of well-to-do, highly cultivated, and thoroughly instructed free persons in a position to take care of themselves, no doubt they will make short work of a good deal of official regulation that is now of life-and-death necessity to us; but under existing circumstances, I repeat, almost any sort of attention that democracy will stand is better than

72

neglect. Attention and activity lead to mistakes as well as to successes; but a life spent in making mistakes is not only more honorable but more useful than a life spent doing nothing. The one lesson that comes out of all our theorizing and experimenting is that there is only one really scientific progressive method; and that is the method of trial and error. If you come to that, what is laisser-faire but an orthodoxy? the most tyrannous and disastrous of all the orthodoxies, since it forbids you even to learn.

THE LATEST THEORIES

Medical theories are so much a matter of fashion, and the most fertile of them are modified so rapidly by medical practice and biological research, which are international activities, that the play which furnishes the pretext for this preface is already slightly outmoded, though I believe it may be taken as a faithful record for the year (1906) in which it was begun. I must not expose any professional man to ruin by connecting his name with the entire freedom of criticism which I, as a layman, enjoy; but it will be evident to all experts that my play could not have been written but for the work done by Sir Almroth Wright in the theory and practice of securing immunization from bacterial diseases by the inoculation of "vaccines" made of their own bacteria: a practice incorrectly called vaccinetherapy (there is nothing vaccine about it) apparently because it is what vaccination ought to be and is not. Until Sir Almroth Wright, following up one of Metchnikoff's most suggestive biological romances, discovered that the white corpuscles or phagocytes which attack and devour disease germs for us do their work only when we butter the disease germs appetizingly for them with a natural sauce which Sir Almroth named opsonin, and that our production of this condiment continually rises and falls rhythmically from negligibility to the highest efficiency, nobody had been able even to conjecture why the various serums that were from time to time introduced as having effected marvellous cures, presently made such direful havoc of some unfor-

73

tunate patient that they had to be dropped hastily. The quantity of sturdy lying that was necessary to save the credit of inoculation in those days was prodigious; and had it not been for the devotion shewn by the military authorities throughout Europe, who would order the entire disappearance of some disease from their armies, and bring it about by the simple plan of changing the name under which the cases were reported, or for our own Metropolitan Asylums Board, which carefully suppressed all the medical reports that revealed the sometimes quite appalling effects of epidemics of revaccination, there is no saying what popular reaction might not have taken place against the whole immunization movement in therapeutics.

The situation was saved when Sir Almroth Wright pointed out that if you inoculated a patient with pathogenic germs at a moment when his powers of cooking them for consumption by the phagocytes was receding to its lowest point, you would certainly make him a good deal worse and perhaps kill him, whereas if you made precisely the same inoculation when the cooking power was rising to one of its periodical climaxes, you would stimulate it to still further exertions and produce just the opposite result. And he invented a technique for ascertaining in which phase the patient happened to be at any given moment. The dramatic possibilities of this discovery and invention will be found in my play. But it is one thing to invent a technique: it is quite another to persuade the medical profession to acquire it. Our general practitioners, I gather, simply declined to acquire it, being mostly unable to afford either the acquisition or the practice of it when acquired. Something simple, cheap, and ready at all times for all comers, is, as I have shewn, the only thing that is economically possible in general practice, whatever may be the case in Sir Almroth's famous laboratory in St Mary's Hospital. It would have become necessary to denounce opsonin in the trade papers as a fad and Sir Almroth as a dangerous man if his practice in the laboratory had not led him to the conclusion that the customary inoculations were very much too powerful, and that a comparatively infinitesimal dose would not precipitate a negative phase of cooking activity, and might induce a positive one. And thus it happens that the refusal of our general practitioners to acquire the new technique is no longer quite so dangerous in practice as it was when The Doctor's Dilemma was written: nay, that Sir Ralph Bloomfield Bonington's way of administering inoculations as if they were spoonfuls of squills may sometimes work fairly well. For all that, I find Sir Almroth Wright, on the 23rd May 1910, warning the Royal Society of Medicine that "the clinician has not yet been prevailed upon to reconsider his position," which means that the general practitioner ("the doctor," as he is called in our homes) is going on just as he did before, and could not afford to learn or practise a new technique even if he had ever heard of it. To the patient who does not know about it he will say nothing. To the patient who does, he will ridicule it, and disparage Sir Almroth. What else can he do, except confess his ignorance and starve?

But now please observe how "the whirligig of time brings its revenges." This latest discovery of the remedial virtue of a very very tiny hair of the dog that bit you reminds us, not only of Arndt's law of protoplasmic reaction to stimuli, according to which weak and strong stimuli provoke opposite reactions, but of Hahnemann's homeopathy, which was founded on the fact alleged by Hahnemann that drugs which produce certain symptoms when taken in ordinary perceptible quantities, will, when taken in infinitesimally small quantities, provoke just the opposite symptoms; so that the drug that gives you a headache will also cure a headache if you take little enough of it. I have already explained that the savage opposition which homeopathy encountered from the medical profession was not a scientific oppositon; for nobody seems to deny that some drugs act in the alleged manner. It was opposed simply because doctors and apothecaries lived by selling bottles

75

and boxes of doctor's stuff to be taken in spoonfuls or in pellets as large as peas; and people would not pay as much for drops and globules no bigger than pins' heads. Nowadays, however, the more cultivated folk are beginning to be so suspicious of drugs, and the incorrigibly superstitious people so profusely supplied with patent medicines (the medical advice to take them being wrapped round the bottle and thrown in for nothing) that homeopathy has become a way of rehabilitating the trade of prescription compounding, and is consequently coming into professional credit. At which point the theory of opsonins comes very opportunely to shake hands with it.

Add to the newly triumphant homeopathist and the opsonist that other remarkable innovator, the Swedish masseur, who does not theorize about you, but probes you all over with his powerful thumbs until he finds out your sore spots and rubs them away, besides cheating you into a little wholesome exercise; and you have nearly everything in medical practice today that is not flat witchcraft or pure commercial exploitation of human credulity and fear of death. Add to them a good deal of vegetarian and teetotal controversy raging round a clamor for scientific eating and drinking, and resulting in little so far except calling digestion Metabolism and dividing the public between the eminent doctor who tells us that we do not eat enough fish, and his equally eminent colleague who warns us that a fish diet must end in leprosy, and you have all that opposes with any sort of countenance the rise of Christian Science with its cathedrals and congregations and zealots and miracles and cures: all very silly, no doubt, but sane and sensible, poetic and hopeful, compared to the pseudo science of the commercial general practitioner, who foolishly clamors for the prosecution and even the execution of the Christian Scientists when their patients die, forgetting the long death roll of his own patients.

By the time this preface is in print the kaleidoscope may have had another shake; and opsonin may have gone the

76

way of phlogiston at the hands of its own restless discoverer. I will not say that Hahnemann may have gone the way of Diafoirus; for Diafoirus we have always with us. But we shall still pick up all our knowledge in pursuit of some Will o' the Wisp or other. What is called science has always pursued the Elixir of Life and the Philosopher's Stone, and is just as busy after them today as ever it was in the days of Paracelsus. We call them by different names: Immunization or radiotherapy or what not; but the dreams which lure us into the adventures from which we learn are always at bottom the same. Science becomes dangerous only when it imagines that it has reached its goal. What is wrong with priests and popes is that instead of being apostles and saints, they are nothing but empirics who say "I know" instead of "I am learning," and pray for credulity and inertia as wise men pray for scepticism and activity. Such abominations as the Inquisition and the Vaccination Acts are possible only in the famine years of the soul, when the great vital dogmas of honor, liberty, courage, the kinship of all life, faith that the unknown is greater than the known and is only the As Yet Unknown, and resolution to find a manly highway to it, have been forgotten in a paroxysm of littleness and terror in which nothing is active except concupiscence and the fear of death, playing on which any trader can filch a fortune, any blackguard gratify his cruelty, and any tyrant make us his slaves.

Lest this should seem too rhetorical a conclusion for our professional men of science, who are mostly trained not to believe anything unless it is worded in the jargon of those writers who, because they never really understand what they are trying to say, cannot find familiar words for it, and are therefore compelled to invent a new language of nonsense for every book they write, let me sum up my conclusions as dryly as is consistent with accurate thought and live conviction.

1. Nothing is more dangerous than a poor doctor: not even a poor employer or a poor landlord.

2. Of all the anti-social vested interests the worst is the vested interest in ill-health.

3. Remember that an illness is a misdemeanor; and treat the doctor as an accessory unless he notifies every case to the Public Health Authority.

4. Treat every death as a possible and, under our present system, a probable murder, by making it the subject of a reasonably conducted inquest; and execute the doctor, if necessary, *as* a doctor, by striking him off the register.

5. Make up your mind how many doctors the community needs to keep it well. Do not register more or less than this number; and let registration constitute the doctor a civil servant with a dignified living wage paid out of public funds.

6. Municipalize Harley Street.

7. Treat the private operator exactly as you would treat a private executioner.

8. Treat persons who profess to be able to cure disease as you treat fortune tellers.

9. Keep the public carefully informed, by special statistics and announcements of individual cases, of all illnesses of doctors or in their families.

10. Make it compulsory for a doctor using a brass plate to have inscribed on it, in addition to the letters indicating his qualifications, the words "Remember that I too am mortal."

11. In legislation and social organization, proceed on the principle that invalids, meaning persons who cannot keep themselves alive by their own activities, cannot, beyond reason, expect to be kept alive by the activity of others. There is a point at which the most energetic policeman or doctor, when called upon to deal with an apparently drowned person, gives up artificial respiration, although it is never possible to declare with certainty, at any point short of decomposition, that another five minutes of the exercise would not effect resuscitation. The theory that every individual alive is of infinite value is legislatively

78

impracticable. No doubt the higher the life we secure to the individual by wise social organization, the greater his value is to the community, and the more pains we shall take to pull him through any temporary danger or disablement. But the man who costs more than he is worth is doomed by sound hygiene as inexorably as by sound economics.

12. Do not try to live for ever. You will not succeed.

13. Use your health, even to the point of wearing it out. That is what it is for. Spend all you have before you die; and do not outlive yourself.

14. Take the utmost care to get well born and well brought up. This means that your mother must have a good doctor. Be careful to go to a school where there is what they call a school clinic, where your nutrition and teeth and eyesight and other matters of importance to you will be attended to. Be particularly careful to have all this done at the expense of the nation, as otherwise it will not be done at all, the chances being about forty to one against your being able to pay for it directly yourself, even if you know how to set about it. Otherwise you will be what most people are at present: an unsound citizen of an unsound nation, without sense enough to be ashamed or unhappy about it.

1911.

POSTSCRIPT, 1930. During the years which have elapsed since the foregoing preface was penned, the need for bringing the medical profession under responsible and effective public control has become constantly more pressing as the inevitable collisions between the march of discovery in therapeutic science and the reactionary obsolescence of the General Medical Council have become more frequent and sensational. A later volume in the present edition of my works deals with this development.

G. B. S.

THE DOCTOR'S DILEMMA

A TRAGEDY

1906

I am grateful to Hesba Stretton, the authoress of "Jessica's First Prayer," for permission to use the title of one of her stories for this play.

ACT I

ON the 15th June 1903, *in the early forenoon, a medical student, surname Redpenny, Christian name unknown and of no importance, sits at work in a doctor's consulting-room. He devils for the doctor by answering his letters, acting as his domestic laboratory assistant, and making himself indispensable generally, in return for unspecified advantages involved by intimate intercourse with a leader of his profession, and amounting to an informal apprenticeship and a temporary affiliation. Redpenny is not proud, and will do anything he is asked without reservation of his personal dignity if he is asked in a fellow-creaturely way. He is a wide-open-eyed, ready, credulous, friendly, hasty youth, with his hair and clothes in reluctant transition from the untidy boy to the tidy doctor.*

Redpenny is interrupted by the entrance of an old serving-woman who has never known the cares, the preoccupations, the responsibilities, jealousies, and anxieties of personal beauty. She has the complexion of a never-washed gypsy, incurable by any detergent; and she has, not a regular beard and moustaches, which could at least be trimmed and waxed into a masculine presentableness, but a whole crop of small beards and moustaches, mostly springing from moles all over her face. She carries a duster and toddles about meddlesomely, spying out dust so diligently that whilst she is flicking off one speck she is already looking elsewhere for another. In conversation she has the same trick, hardly ever looking at the person she is addressing except when she is excited. She has only one manner, and that is the manner of an old family nurse to a child just after it has learnt to walk. She has used her ugliness to secure indulgences unattainable by Cleopatra or Fair Rosamund, and has the further great advantage over them that age increases her qualification instead of impairing it. Being an industrious, agreeable, and popular old soul, she is a walking sermon on the vanity of feminine

83

prettiness. Just as Redpenny has no discovered Christian name, she has no discovered surname, and is known throughout the doctors' quarter between Cavendish Square and the Marylebone Road simply as Emmy.

The consulting-room has two windows looking on Queen Anne Street. Between the two is a marble-topped console, with haunched gilt legs ending in sphinx claws. The huge pier-glass which surmounts it is mostly disabled from reflection by elaborate painting on its surface of palms, ferns, lilies, tulips, and sunflowers. The adjoining wall contains the fireplace, with two arm-chairs before it. As we happen to face the corner we see nothing of the other two walls. On the right of the fireplace, or rather on the right of any person facing the fireplace, is the door. On its left is the writing-table at which Redpenny sits. It is an untidy table with a microscope, several test tubes, and a spirit lamp standing up through its litter of papers. There is a couch in the middle of the room, at right angles to the console, and parallel to the fireplace. A chair stands between the couch and the window. Another in the corner. Another at the other end of the windowed wall. The windows have green Venetian blinds and rep curtains; and there is a gasalier; but it is a convert to electric lighting. The wall paper and carpets are mostly green, coeval with the gasalier and the Venetian blinds. The house, in fact, was so well furnished in the middle of the XIXth century that it stands unaltered to this day and is still quite presentable.

EMMY [*entering and immediately beginning to dust the couch*] Theres a lady bothering me to see the doctor.

REDPENNY [*distracted by the interruption*] Well, she cant see the doctor. Look here: whats the use of telling you that the doctor cant take any new patients, when the moment a knock comes to the door, in you bounce to ask whether he can see somebody?

EMMY. Who asked you whether he could see somebody?

84

REDPENNY. You did.

EMMY. I said theres a lady bothering me to see the doctor. That isnt asking. Its telling.

REDPENNY. Well, is the lady bothering you any reason for you to come bothering me when I'm busy?

EMMY. Have you seen the papers?

REDPENNY. No.

EMMY. Not seen the birthday honors?

REDPENNY [beginning to swear] What the—

EMMY. Now, now, ducky!

REDPENNY. What do you suppose I care about the birthday honors? Get out of this with your chattering. Dr Ridgeon will be down before I have these letters ready. Get out.

EMMY. Dr Ridgeon wont never be down any more, young man.

She detects dust on the console and is down on it immediately.

REDPENNY [jumping up and following her] What?

EMMY. He's been made a knight. Mind you dont go Dr Ridgeoning him in them letters. Sir Colenso Ridgeon is to be his name now.

REDPENNY. I'm jolly glad.

EMMY. I never was so taken aback. I always thought his great discoveries was fudge (let alone the mess of them) with his drops of blood and tubes full of Maltese fever and the like. Now he'll have a rare laugh at me.

REDPENNY. Serve you right! It was like your cheek to talk to him about science. [He returns to his table and resumes his writing].

EMMY. Oh, I dont think much of science; and neither will you when youve lived as long with it as I have. Whats on my mind is answering the door. Old Sir Patrick Cullen has been here already and left first congratulations—hadnt time to come up on his way to the hospital, but was determined to be first—coming back, he said. All the rest will

85

THE DOCTOR'S DILEMMA

be here too: the knocker will be going all day. What I'm afraid of is that the doctor'll want a footman like all the rest, now that he's Sir Colenso. Mind: dont you go putting him up to it, ducky; for he'll never have any comfort with anybody but me to answer the door. I know who to let in and who to keep out. And that reminds me of the poor lady. I think he ought to see her. She's just the kind that puts him in a good temper. [*She dusts Redpenny's papers*].

REDPENNY. I tell you he cant see anybody. Do go away, Emmy. How can I work with you dusting all over me like this?

EMMY. I'm not hindering you working—if you call writing letters working. There goes the bell. [*She looks out of the window*]. A doctor's carriage. Thats more congratulations. [*She is going out when Sir Colenso Ridgeon enters*]. Have you finished your two eggs, sonny?

RIDGEON. Yes.

EMMY. Have you put on your clean vest?

RIDGEON. Yes.

EMMY. Thats my ducky diamond! Now keep yourself tidy and dont go messing about and dirtying your hands: the people are coming to congratulate you. [*She goes out*].

Sir Colenso Ridgeon is a man of fifty who has never shaken off his youth. He has the off-handed manner and the little audacities of address which a shy and sensitive man acquires in breaking himself in to intercourse with all sorts and conditions of men. His face is a good deal lined; his movements are slower than, for instance, Redpenny's; and his flaxen hair has lost its lustre; but in figure and manner he is more the young man than the titled physician. Even the lines in his face are those of overwork and restless scepticism, perhaps partly of curiosity and appetite, rather than of age. Just at present the announcement of his knighthood in the morning papers makes him specially self-conscious, and consequently specially off-hand with Redpenny.

RIDGEON. Have you seen the papers? Youll have to

86

alter the name in the letters if you havnt.

REDPENNY. Emmy has just told me. I'm awfully glad. I—

RIDGEON. Enough, young man, enough. You will soon get accustomed to it.

REDPENNY. They ought to have done it years ago.

RIDGEON. They would have; only they couldnt stand Emmy opening the door, I daresay.

EMMY [*at the door, announcing*] Dr Shoemaker. [*She withdraws*].

A middle-aged gentleman, well dressed, comes in with a friendly but propitiatory air, not quite sure of his reception. His combination of soft manners and responsive kindliness, with a certain unseizable reserve and a familiar yet foreign chiselling of feature, reveal the Jew: in this instance the handsome gentlemanly Jew, gone a little pigeonbreasted and stale after thirty, as handsome young Jews often do, but still decidedly good-looking.

THE GENTLEMAN. Do you remember me? Schutzmacher. University College school and Belsize Avenue. Loony Schutzmacher, you know.

RIDGEON. What! Loony! [*He shakes hands cordially*]. Why, man, I thought you were dead long ago. Sit down. [*Schutzmacher sits on the couch: Ridgeon on the chair between it and the window*]. Where have you been these thirty years?

SCHUTZMACHER. In general practice, until a few months ago. I've retired.

RIDGEON. Well done, Loony! I wish *I* could afford to retire. Was your practice in London?

SCHUTZMACHER. No.

RIDGEON. Fashionable coast practice, I suppose.

SCHUTZMACHER. How could I afford to buy a fashionable practice? I hadnt a rap. I set up in a manufacturing town in the midlands in a little surgery at ten shillings a week.

RIDGEON. And made your fortune?

87

SCHUTZMACHER. Well, I'm pretty comfortable. I have a place in Hertfordshire besides our flat in town. If you ever want a quiet Saturday to Monday, I'll take you down in my motor at an hour's notice.

RIDGEON. Just rolling in money! I wish you rich g.p.'s would teach me how to make some. Whats the secret of it?

SCHUTZMACHER. Oh, in my case the secret was simple enough, though I suppose I should have got into trouble if it had attracted any notice. And I'm afraid you'll think it rather infra dig.

RIDGEON. Oh, I have an open mind. What was the secret?

SCHUTZMACHER. Well, the secret was just two words.

RIDGEON. Not Consultation Free, was it?

SCHUTZMACHER [shocked] No, no. Really!

RIDGEON [apologetic] Of course not. I was only joking.

SCHUTZMACHER. My two words were simply Cure Guaranteed.

RIDGEON [admiring] Cure Guaranteed!

SCHUTZMACHER. Guaranteed. After all, thats what everybody wants from a doctor, isn't it?

RIDGEON. My dear Loony, it was an inspiration. Was it on the brass plate?

SCHUTZMACHER. There was no brass plate. It was a shop window: red, you know, with black lettering. Doctor Leo Schutzmacher, L.R.C.P.M.R.C.S. Advice and medicine sixpence. Cure Guaranteed.

RIDGEON. And the guarantee proved sound nine times out of ten, eh?

SCHUTZMACHER [rather hurt at so moderate an estimate] Oh, much oftener than that. You see, most people get well all right if they are careful and you give them a little sensible advice. And the medicine really did them good. Parrish's Chemical Food: phosphates, you know. One tablespoonful to a twelve-ounce bottle of water: nothing better, no matter what the case is.

THE DOCTOR'S DILEMMA

RIDGEON. Redpenny: make a note of Parrish's Chemical Food.

SCHUTZMACHER. I take it myself, you know, when I feel run down. Good-bye. You dont mind my calling, do you? Just to congratulate you.

RIDGEON. Delighted, my dear Loony. Come to lunch on Saturday next week. Bring your motor and take me down to Hertford.

SCHUTZMACHER. I will. We shall be delighted. Thank you. Good-bye. [*He goes out with Ridgeon, who returns immediately*].

REDPENNY. Old Paddy Cullen was here before you were up, to be the first to congratulate you.

RIDGEON. Indeed. Who taught you to speak of Sir Patrick Cullen as old Paddy Cullen, you young ruffian?

REDPENNY. You never call him anything else.

RIDGEON. Not now that I am Sir Colenso. Next thing, you fellows will be calling me old Colly Ridgeon.

REDPENNY. We do, at St Anne's.

RIDGEON. Yach! Thats what makes the medical student the most disgusting figure in modern civilization. No veneration, no manners—no—

EMMY [*at the door, announcing*] Sir Patrick Cullen. [*She retires*].

Sir Patrick Cullen is more than twenty years older than Ridgeon, not yet quite at the end of his tether, but near it and resigned to it. His name, his plain, downright, sometimes rather arid common sense, his large build and stature, the absence of those odd moments of ceremonial servility by which an old English doctor sometimes shews you what the status of the profession was in England in his youth, and an occasional turn of speech, are Irish; but he has lived all his life in England and is thoroughly acclimatized. His manner to Ridgeon, whom he likes, is whimsical and fatherly: to others he is a little gruff and uninviting, apt to substitute more or less expressive grunts for articulate

89

speech, and generally indisposed, at his age, to make much social effort. He shakes Ridgeon's hand and beams at him cordially and jocularly.

SIR PATRICK. Well, young chap. Is your hat too small for you, eh?

RIDGEON. Much too small. I owe it all to you.

SIR PATRICK. Blarney, my boy. Thank you all the same. [*He sits in one of the arm-chairs near the fireplace. Ridgeon sits on the couch*]. Ive come to talk to you a bit. [*To Redpenny*] Young man: get out.

REDPENNY. Certainly, Sir Patrick. [*He collects his papers and makes for the door*].

SIR PATRICK. Thank you. Thats a good lad. [*Redpenny vanishes*]. They all put up with me, these young chaps, because I'm an old man, a real old man, not like you. Youre only beginning to give yourself the airs of age. Did you ever see a boy cultivating a moustache? Well, a middle-aged doctor cultivating a grey head is much the same sort of spectacle.

RIDGEON. Good Lord! yes: I suppose so. And I thought that the days of my vanity were past. Tell me: at what age does a man leave off being a fool?

SIR PATRICK. Remember the Frenchman who asked his grandmother at what age we get free from the temptations of love. The old woman said she didn't know. [*Ridgeon laughs*]. Well, I make you the same answer. But the world's growing very interesting to me now, Colly.

RIDGEON. You keep up your interest in science, do you?

SIR PATRICK. Lord! yes. Modern science is a wonderful thing. Look at your great discovery! Look at all the great discoveries! Where are they leading to? Why, right back to my poor dear old father's ideas and discoveries. He's been dead now over forty years. Oh, it's very interesting.

RIDGEON. Well, theres nothing like progress, is there?

SIR PATRICK. Dont misunderstand me, my boy. I'm not belittling your discovery. Most discoveries are made regularly every fifteen years; and it's fully a hundred and fifty since yours was made last. Thats something to be proud of. But your discovery's not new. It's only inoculation. My father practised inoculation until it was made criminal in eighteen-forty. That broke the poor old man's heart, Colly: he died of it. And now it turns out that my father was right after all. Youve brought us back to inoculation.

RIDGEON. I know nothing about smallpox. My line is tuberculosis and typhoid and plague. But of course the principle of all vaccines is the same.

SIR PATRICK. Tuberculosis? M-m-m-m! You've found out how to cure consumption, eh?

RIDGEON. I believe so.

SIR PATRICK. Ah yes. It's very interesting. What is it the old cardinal says in Browning's play? "I have known four and twenty leaders of revolt." Well, I've known over thirty men that found out how to cure consumption. Why do people go on dying of it, Colly? Devilment, I suppose. There was my father's old friend George Boddington of Sutton Coldfield. He discovered the open-air cure in eighteen-forty. He was ruined and driven out of his practice for only opening the windows; and now we wont let a consumptive patient have as much as a roof over his head. Oh, it's very v e r y interesting to an old man.

RIDGEON. You old cynic, you dont believe a bit in my discovery.

SIR PATRICK. No, no: I dont go quite so far as that, Colly. But still, you remember Jane Marsh?

RIDGEON. Jane Marsh? No.

SIR PATRICK. You dont!

RIDGEON. No.

SIR PATRICK. You mean to tell me you dont remember the woman with the tuberculous ulcer on her arm?

RIDGEON [enlightened] Oh, your washerwoman's daughter. Was her name Jane Marsh? I forgot.

SIR PATRICK. Perhaps youve forgotten also that you undertook to cure her with Koch's tuberculin.

RIDGEON. And instead of curing her, it rotted her arm

91

right off. Yes: I remember. Poor Jane! However, she makes a good living out of that arm now by shewing it at medical lectures.

SIR PATRICK. Still, that wasnt quite what you intended, was it?

RIDGEON. I took my chance of it.

SIR PATRICK. Jane did, you mean.

RIDGEON. Well, it's always the patient who has to take the chance when an experiment is necessary. And we can find out nothing without experiment.

SIR PATRICK. What did you find out from Jane's case?

RIDGEON. I found out that the inoculation that ought to cure sometimes kills.

SIR PATRICK. I could have told you that. Ive tried these modern inoculations a bit myself. Ive killed people with them; and Ive cured people with them; but I gave them up because I never could tell which I was going to do.

RIDGEON [taking a pamphlet from a drawer in the writing-table and handing it to him] Read that the next time you have an hour to spare; and youll find out why.

SIR PATRICK [grumbling and fumbling for his spectacles] Oh, bother your pamphlets. Whats the practice of it? [Looking at the pamphlet] Opsonin? What the devil is opsonin?

RIDGEON. Opsonin is what you butter the disease germs with to make your white blood corpuscles eat them. [He sits down again on the couch].

SIR PATRICK. Thats not new. Ive heard this notion that the white corpuscles—what is it that whats his name?—Metchnikoff—calls them?

RIDGEON. Phagocytes.

SIR PATRICK. Aye, phagocytes: yes, yes, yes. Well, I heard this theory that the phagocytes eat up the disease germs years ago: long before you came into fashion. Besides, they dont always eat them.

RIDGEON. They do when you butter them with opsonin.

SIR PATRICK. Gammon.

RIDGEON. No: it's not gammon. What it comes to in practice is this. The phagocytes wont eat the microbes unless the microbes are nicely buttered for them. Well, the patient manufactures the butter for himself all right; but my discovery is that the manufacture of that butter, which I call opsonin, goes on in the system by ups and downs—Nature being always rhythmical, you know—and that what the inoculation does is to stimulate the ups or downs, as the case may be. If we had inoculated Jane Marsh when her butter factory was on the up-grade, we should have cured her arm. But we got in on the down-grade and lost her arm for her. I call the up-grade the positive phase and the down-grade the negative phase. Everything depends on your inoculating at the right moment. Inoculate when the patient is in the negative phase and you kill: inoculate when the patient is in the positive phase and you cure.

SIR PATRICK. And pray how are you to know whether the patient is in the positive or the negative phase?

RIDGEON. Send a drop of the patient's blood to the laboratory at St Anne's; and in fifteen minutes I'll give you his opsonin index in figures. If the figure is one, inoculate and cure: if it's under point eight, inoculate and kill. Thats my discovery: the most important that has been made since Harvey discovered the circulation of the blood. My tuberculosis patients dont die now.

SIR PATRICK. And mine do when my inoculation catches them in the negative phase, as you call it. Eh?

RIDGEON. Precisely. To inject a vaccine into a patient without first testing his opsonin is as near murder as a respectable practitioner can get. If I wanted to kill a man I should kill him that way.

EMMY [*looking in*] Will you see a lady that wants her husband's lungs cured?

RIDGEON [*impatiently*] No. Havnt I told you I will see nobody? [*To Sir Patrick*] I live in a state of siege ever since it got about that I'm a magician who can cure consumption with a drop of serum. [*To Emmy*] Dont come to me again

93

about people who have no appointments. I tell you I can see nobody.

EMMY. Well, I'll tell her to wait a bit.

RIDGEON [*furious*] Youll tell her I cant see her, and send her away: do you hear?

EMMY [*unmoved*] Well, will you see Mr Cutler Walpole? He dont want a cure: he only wants to congratulate you.

RIDGEON. Of course. Shew him up. [*She turns to go*]. Stop. [*To Sir Patrick*] I want two minutes more with you between ourselves. [*To Emmy*] Emmy: ask Mr. Walpole to wait just two minutes, while I finish a consultation.

EMMY. Oh, he'll wait all right. He's talking to the poor lady. [*She goes out*].

SIR PATRICK. Well? what is it?

RIDGEON. Dont laugh at me. I want your advice.

SIR PATRICK. Professional advice?

RIDGEON. Yes. Theres something the matter with me. I dont know what it is.

SIR PATRICK. Neither do I. I suppose youve been sounded.

RIDGEON. Yes, of course. Theres nothing wrong with any of the organs: nothing special, anyhow. But I have a curious aching: I dont know where: I cant localize it. Sometimes I think it's my heart: sometimes I suspect my spine. It doesn't exactly hurt me; but it unsettles me completely. I feel that something is going to happen. And there are other symptoms. Scraps of tunes come into my head that seem to me very pretty, though theyre quite commonplace.

SIR PATRICK. Do you hear voices?

RIDGEON. No.

SIR PATRICK. I'm glad of that. When my patients tell me that theyve made a greater discovery than Harvey, and that they hear voices, I lock them up.

RIDGEON. You think I'm mad! Thats just the suspicion that has come across me once or twice. Tell me the truth: I can bear it.

SIR PATRICK. Youre sure there are no voices?

RIDGEON. Quite sure.

SIR PATRICK. Then it's only foolishness.

RIDGEON. Have you ever met anything like it before in your practice?

SIR PATRICK. Oh, yes: often. It's very common between the ages of seventeen and twenty-two. It sometimes comes on again at forty or thereabouts. Youre a bachelor, you see. It's not serious—if youre careful.

RIDGEON. About my food?

SIR PATRICK. No: about your behavior. Theres nothing wrong with your spine; and theres nothing wrong with your heart; but theres something wrong with your common sense. Youre not going to die; but you may be going to make a fool of yourself. So be careful.

RIDGEON. I see you dont believe in my discovery. Well, sometimes I dont believe in it myself. Thank you all the same. Shall we have Walpole up?

SIR PATRICK. Oh, have him up. [*Ridgeon rings*]. He's a clever operator, is Walpole, though he's only one of your chloroform surgeons. In my early days, you made your man drunk; and the porters and the students held him down; and you had to set your teeth and finish the job fast. Nowadays you work at your ease; and the pain doesn't come until afterwards, when youve taken your cheque and rolled up your bag and left the house. I tell you, Colly, chloroform has done a lot of mischief. It's enabled every fool to be a surgeon.

RIDGEON [*to Emmy, who answers the bell*] Shew Mr Walpole up.

EMMY. He's talking to the lady.

RIDGEON [*exasperated*] Did I not tell you—

Emmy goes out without heeding him. He gives it up, with a shrug, and plants himself with his back to the console, leaning resignedly against it.

SIR PATRICK. I know your Cutler Walpoles and their like. Theyve found out that a man's body's full of bits and scraps of old organs he has no mortal use for. Thanks to chloroform, you can cut half a dozen of them out without leaving him any the worse, except for the illness and the guineas it costs him. I knew the Walpoles well fifteen years ago. The father used to snip off the ends of people's uvulas for fifty guineas, and paint throats with caustic every day for a year at two guineas a time. His brother-in-law extirpated tonsils for two hundred guineas until he took up women's cases at double the fees. Cutler himself worked hard at anatomy to find something fresh to operate on; and at last he got hold of something he calls the nuciform sac, which he's made quite the fashion. People pay him five hundred guineas to cut it out. They might as well get their hair cut for all the difference it makes; but I suppose they feel important after it. You cant go out to dinner now without your neighbor bragging to you of some useless operation or other.

EMMY [*announcing*] Mr Cutler Walpole. [*She goes out*].

Cutler Walpole is an energetic, unhesitating man of forty, with a cleanly modelled face, very decisive and symmetrical about the shortish, salient, rather pretty nose, and the three trimly turned corners made by his chin and jaws. In comparison with Ridgeon's delicate broken lines, and Sir Patrick's softly rugged aged ones, his face looks machine-made and beeswaxed; but his scrutinizing, daring eyes give it life and force. He seems never at a loss, never in doubt: one feels that if he made a mistake he would make it thoroughly and firmly. He has neat, well-nourished hands, short arms, and is built for strength and compactness rather than for height. He is smartly dressed with a fancy waist-coat, a richly colored scarf secured by a handsome ring, ornaments on his watch chain, spats on his shoes, and a general air of the well-to-do sportsman about him. He goes straight across to Ridgeon and shakes hands with him.

WALPOLE. My dear Ridgeon, best wishes! heartiest congratulations! You deserve it.

THE DOCTOR'S DILEMMA

RIDGEON. Thank you.

WALPOLE. As a man, mind you. You deserve it as a man. The opsonin is simple rot, as any capable surgeon can tell you; but we're all delighted to see your personal qualities officially recognized. Sir Patrick: how are you? I sent you a paper lately about a little thing I invented: a new saw. For shoulder blades.

SIR PATRICK [*meditatively*] Yes: I got it. It's a good saw: a useful, handy instrument.

WALPOLE [*confidently*] I knew youd see its points.

SIR PATRICK. Yes: I remember that saw sixty-five years ago.

WALPOLE. What!

SIR PATRICK. It was called a cabinetmaker's jimmy then.

WALPOLE. Get out! Nonsense! Cabinetmaker be—

RIDGEON. Never mind him, Walpole. He's jealous.

WALPOLE. By the way, I hope I'm not disturbing you two in anything private.

RIDGEON. No, no. Sit down. I was only consulting him. I'm rather out of sorts. Overwork, I suppose.

WALPOLE [*swiftly*] I know whats the matter with you. I can see it in your complexion. I can feel it in the grip of your hand.

RIDGEON. What is it?

WALPOLE. Blood-poisoning.

RIDGEON. Blood-poisoning! Impossible.

WALPOLE. I tell you, blood-poisoning. Ninety-five per cent of the human race suffer from chronic blood-poisoning, and die of it. It's as simple as A.B.C. Your nuciform sac is full of decaying matter—undigested food and waste products—rank ptomaines. Now you take my advice, Ridgeon. Let me cut it out for you. You'll be another man afterwards.

SIR PATRICK. Dont you like him as he is?

WALPOLE. No I dont. I dont like any man who hasnt a healthy circulation. I tell you this: in an intelligently governed country people wouldnt be allowed to go about with nuciform sacs, making themselves centres of infection.

97

The operation ought to be compulsory: it's ten times more important than vaccination.

SIR PATRICK. Have you had your own sac removed, may I ask?

WALPOLE [*triumphantly*] I havnt got one. Look at me! Ive no symptoms. I'm as sound as a bell. About five per cent of the population havnt got any; and I'm one of the five per cent. I'll give you an instance. You know Mrs Jack Foljambe: the smart Mrs Foljambe? I operated at Easter on her sister-in-law, Lady Gorran, and found she had the biggest sac I ever saw: it held about two ounces. Well, Mrs Foljambe had the right spirit—the genuine hygienic instinct. She couldnt stand her sister-in-law being a clean, sound woman, and she simply a whited sepulchre. So she insisted on my operating on her, too. And by George, sir, she hadnt any sac at all. Not a trace! Not a rudiment! ! I was so taken aback—so interested, that I forgot to take the sponges out, and was stitching them up inside her when the nurse missed them. Somehow, I'd made sure she'd have an exceptionally large one. [*He sits down on the couch, squaring his shoulders and shooting his hands out of his cuffs as he sets his knuckles akimbo*].

EMMY [*looking in*] Sir Ralph Bloomfield Bonington. *A long and expectant pause follows this announcement. All look to the door; but there is no Sir Ralph.*

RIDGEON [*at last*] Where is he?

EMMY [*looking back*] Drat him, I thought he was following me. He's stayed down to talk to that lady.

RIDGEON [*exploding*] I told you to tell that lady— [*Emmy vanishes*].

WALPOLE [*jumping up again*] Oh, by the way, Ridgeon, that reminds me. Ive been talking to that poor girl. It's her husband; and she thinks it's a case of consumption: the usual wrong diagnosis: these damned general practitioners ought never to be allowed to touch a patient except under the orders of a consultant. She's been describing his symptoms to me; and the case is as plain as a pikestaff: bad

THE DOCTOR'S DILEMMA

blood-poisoning. Now she's poor. She cant afford to have him operated on. Well, you send him to me: I'll do it for nothing. Theres room for him in my nursing home. I'll put him straight, and feed him up and make her happy. I like making people happy. [*He goes to the chair near the window*].

EMMY [*looking in*] Here he is.

Sir Ralph Bloomfield Bonington wafts himself into the room. He is a tall man, with a head like a tall and slender egg. He has been in his time a slender man; but now, in his sixth decade, his waistcoat has filled out somewhat. His fair eyebrows arch good-naturedly and uncritically. He has a most musical voice; his speech is a perpetual anthem; and he never tires of the sound of it. He radiates an enormous self-satisfaction, cheering, reassuring, healing by the mere incompatibility of disease or anxiety with his welcome presence. Even broken bones, it is said, have been known to unite at the sound of his voice; he is a born healer, as independent of mere treatment and skill as any Christian scientist. When he expands into oratory or scientific exposition, he is as energetic as Walpole; but it is with a bland, voluminous, atmospheric energy, which envelops its subject and its audience, and makes interruption or inattention impossible, and imposes veneration and credulity on all but the strongest minds. He is known in the medical world as B. B.; and the envy roused by his success in practice is softened by the conviction that he is, scientifically considered, a colossal humbug: the fact being that, though he knows just as much (and just as little) as his contemporaries, the qualifications that pass muster in common men reveal their weakness when hung on his egregious personality.

B. B. Aha! Sir Colenso. S i r Colenso, eh? Welcome to the order of knighthood.

RIDGEON [*shaking hands*] Thank you, B. B.

B. B. What! Sir Patrick! And how are we to-day? a little chilly? a little stiff? but hale and still the cleverest of

99

us all. [*Sir Patrick grunts*]. What! Walpole! the absent-minded beggar: eh?

WALPOLE. What does that mean?

B. B. Have you forgotten the lovely opera singer I sent you to have that growth taken off her vocal cords?

WALPOLE [*springing to his feet*] Great heavens, man, you dont mean to say you sent her for a throat operation!

B. B. [*archly*] Aha! Ha ha! Aha! [*trilling like a lark as he shakes his finger at Walpole*]. You removed her nuciform sac. Well, well! force of habit! force of habit! Never mind, ne-e-e-ver mind. She got back her voice after it, and thinks you the greatest surgeon alive; and so you are, so you are, so you are.

WALPOLE [*in a tragic whisper, intensely serious*] Blood-poisoning. I see. I see. [*He sits down again*].

SIR PATRICK. And how is a certain distinguished family getting on under your care, Sir Ralph?

B. B. Our friend Ridgeon will be gratified to hear that I have tried his opsonin treatment on little Prince Henry with complete success.

RIDGEON [*startled and anxious*] But how——

B. B. [*continuing*] I suspected typhoid: the head gardener's boy had it; so I just called at St Anne's one day and got a tube of your very excellent serum. You were out, unfortunately.

RIDGEON. I hope they explained to you carefully——

B. B. [*waving away the absurd suggestion*] Lord bless you, my dear fellow, I didnt need any explanations. I'd left my wife in the carriage at the door; and I'd no time to be taught my business by your young chaps. I know all about it. Ive handled these anti-toxins ever since they first came out.

RIDGEON. But theyre not anti-toxins; and theyre dangerous unless you use them at the right time.

B. B. Of course they are. Everything is dangerous unless you take it at the right time. An apple at breakfast does you good: an apple at bedtime upsets you for a week. There

100

are only two rules for anti-toxins. First, dont be afraid of them: second, inject them a quarter of an hour before meals, three times a day.

RIDGEON [*appalled*] Great heavens, B. B., no, no, no.

B. B. [*sweeping on irresistibly*] Yes, yes, yes, Colly. The proof of the pudding is in the eating, you know. It was an immense success. It acted like magic on the little prince. Up went his temperature; off to bed I packed him; and in a week he was all right again, and absolutely immune from typhoid for the rest of his life. The family were very nice about it: their gratitude was quite touching; but I said they owed it all to you, Ridgeon; and I am glad to think that your knighthood is the result.

RIDGEON. I am deeply obliged to you. [*Overcome, he sits down on the chair near the couch*].

B. B. Not at all, not at all. Your own merit. Come! come! come! dont give way.

RIDGEON. It's nothing. I was a little giddy just now. Overwork, I suppose.

WALPOLE. Blood-poisoning.

B. B. Overwork! Theres no such thing. I do the work of ten men. Am I giddy? No. NO. If youre not well, you have a disease. It may be a slight one; but it's a disease. And what is a disease? The lodgment in the system of a pathogenic germ, and the multiplication of that germ. What is the remedy? A very simple one. Find the germ and kill it.

SIR PATRICK. Suppose theres no germ?

B. B. Impossible, Sir Patrick: there m u s t be a germ: else how could the patient be ill?

SIR PATRICK. Can you shew me the germ of overwork?

B. B. No; but why? Why? Because, my dear Sir Patrick, though the germ is there, it's invisible. Nature has given it no danger signal for us. These germs—these bacilli—are translucent bodies, like glass, like water. To make them visible you must stain them. Well, my dear Paddy, do what you will, some of them wont stain. They wont take cochineal: they wont take methylene blue: they wont take gentian violet: they wont take any coloring matter. Consequently, though we know, as scientific men, that they exist, we cannot see them. But can you disprove their existence? Can you conceive the disease existing without them? Can you, for instance, shew me a case of diphtheria without the bacillus?

SIR PATRICK. No; but I'll shew you the same bacillus, without the disease, in your own throat.

B. B. No, not the same, Sir Patrick. It is an entirely different bacillus; only the two are, unfortunately, so exactly alike that you cannot see the difference. You must understand, my dear Sir Patrick, that every one of these interesting little creatures has an imitator. Just as men imitate each other, germs imitate each other. There is the genuine diphtheria bacillus discovered by Lœffler; and there is the pseudo-bacillus, exactly like it, which you could find, as you say, in my own throat.

SIR PATRICK. And how do you tell one from the other?

B. B. Well, obviously, if the bacillus is the genuine Lœffler, you have diphtheria; and if it's the pseudo-bacillus, youre quite well. Nothing simpler. Science is always simple and always profound. It is only the half-truths that are dangerous. Ignorant faddists pick up some superficial information about germs; and they write to the papers and try to discredit science. They dupe and mislead many honest and worthy people. But science has a perfect answer to them on every point.

> A little learning is a dangerous thing:
> Drink deep; or taste not the Pierian spring.

I mean no disrespect to your generation, Sir Patrick: some of you old stagers did marvels through sheer professional intuition and clinical experience; but when I think of the average men of your day, ignorantly bleeding and cupping and purging, and scattering germs over their patients from their clothes and instruments, and contrast all that with the scientific certainty and simplicity of my treatment of the little prince the other day, I cant help being proud of my own generation: the men who were trained on the germ theory, the veterans of the great struggle over Evolution in the seventies. We may have our faults; but at least we are men of science. That is why I am taking up your treatment, Ridgeon, and pushing it. It's scientific. [*He sits down on the chair near the couch*].

EMMY [*at the door, announcing*] Dr Blenkinsop.

Dr Blenkinsop is in very different case from the others. He is clearly not a prosperous man. He is flabby and shabby, cheaply fed and cheaply clothed. He has the lines made by a conscience between his eyes, and the lines made by continual money worries all over his face, cut all the deeper as he has seen better days, and hails his well-to-do colleagues as their contemporary and old hospital friend, though even in this he has to struggle with the diffidence of poverty and relegation to the poorer middle class.

RIDGEON. How are you, Blenkinsop?

BLENKINSOP. Ive come to offer my humble congratulations. Oh dear! all the great guns are before me.

B. B. [*patronizing, but charming*] How d'ye do, Blenkinsop? How d'ye do?

BLENKINSOP. And Sir Patrick, too! [*Sir Patrick grunts*].

RIDGEON. Youve met Walpole, of course?

WALPOLE. How d'ye do?

BLENKINSOP. It's the first time Ive had that honor. In my poor little practice there are no chances of meeting you great men. I know nobody but the St Anne's men of my own day. [*To Ridgeon*] And so youre Sir Colenso. How does it feel?

RIDGEON. Foolish at first. Dont take any notice of it.

BLENKINSOP. I'm ashamed to say I havnt a notion what your great discovery is; but I congratulate you all the same for the sake of old times.

B. B. [*shocked*] But, my dear Blenkinsop, you used to be rather keen on science.

BLENKINSOP. Ah, I used to be a lot of things. I used to

have two or three decent suits of clothes, and flannels to go up the river on Sundays. Look at me now: this is my best; and it must last till Christmas. What can I do? Ive never opened a book since I was qualified thirty years ago. I used to read the medical papers at first; but you know how soon a man drops that; besides, I cant afford them; and what are they after all but trade papers, full of advertisements? Ive forgotten all my science: whats the use of my pretending I havnt? But I have great experience: clinical experience; and bedside experience is the main thing, isn't it?

B. B. No doubt; always provided, mind you, that you have a sound scientific theory to correlate your observations at the bedside. Mere experience by itself is nothing. If I take my dog to the bedside with me, he sees what I see. But he learns nothing from it. Why? Because he's not a scientific dog.

WALPOLE. It amuses me to hear you physicians and general practitioners talking about clinical experience. What do you see at the bedside but the outside of the patient? Well: it isnt his outside thats wrong, except perhaps in skin cases. What you want is a daily familiarity with people's insides; and that you can only get at the operating table. I know what I'm talking about: Ive been a surgeon and a consultant for twenty years; and Ive never known a general practitioner right in his diagnosis yet. Bring them a perfectly simple case; and they diagnose cancer, and arthritis, and appendicitis, and every other itis, when any really experienced surgeon can see that it's a plain case of blood-poisoning.

BLENKINSOP. Ah, it's easy for you gentlemen to talk; but what would you say if you had my practice? Except for the workmen's clubs, my patients are all clerks and shopmen. They darent be ill: they cant afford it. And when they break down, what can I do for them? Y o u can send your people to St Moritz or to Egypt, or recommend horse exercise or motoring or champagne jelly or complete change and rest for six months. *I* might as well order my people a slice of the moon. And the worst of it is, I'm too poor to keep well myself on the cooking I have to put up with. Ive such a wretched digestion; and I look it. How am I to inspire confidence? [*He sits disconsolately on the couch*].

RIDGEON. [*restlessly*] Dont, Blenkinsop: it's too painful. The most tragic thing in the world is a sick doctor.

WALPOLE. Yes, by George: its like a bald-headed man trying to sell a hair restorer. Thank God I'm a surgeon!

B. B. [*sunnily*] I am never sick. Never had a day's illness in my life. Thats what enables me to sympathize with my patients.

WALPOLE [*interested*] What! youre never ill!

B. B. Never.

WALPOLE. Thats interesting. I believe you have no nuciform sac. If you ever do feel at all queer, I should very much like to have a look.

B. B. Thank you, my dear fellow; but I'm too busy just now.

RIDGEON. I was just telling them when you came in, Blenkinsop, that I have worked myself out of sorts.

BLENKINSOP. Well, it seems presumptuous of me to offer a prescription to a great man like you; but still I have great experience; and if I might recommend a pound of ripe greengages every day half an hour before lunch, I'm sure youd find a benefit. Theyre very cheap.

RIDGEON. What do you say to that, B. B.?

B. B. [*encouragingly*] Very sensible, Blenkinsop: very sensible indeed. I'm delighted to see that you disapprove of drugs.

SIR PATRICK [*grunts*]!

B. B. [*archly*] Aha! Haha! Did I hear from the fireside armchair the bow-wow of the old school defending its drugs? Ah, believe me, Paddy, the world would be healthier if every chemist's shop in England were demolished. Look at the papers! full of scandalous advertisements of patent medicines! a huge commercial system of quackery and poison. Well, whose fault is it? Ours. I say, ours. We set the example. We spread the superstition. We taught the people to believe in bottles of doctor's stuff; and now they buy it at the stores instead of consulting a medical man.

WALPOLE. Quite true. Ive not prescribed a drug for the last fifteen years.

B. B. Drugs can only repress symptoms: they cannot eradicate disease. The true remedy for all diseases is Nature's remedy. Nature and Science are at one, Sir Patrick, believe me; though you were taught differently. Nature has provided, in the white corpuscles as you call them—in the phagocytes as we call them—a natural means of devouring and destroying all disease germs. There is at bottom only one genuinely scientific treatment for all diseases, and that is to stimulate the phagocytes. Stimulate the phagocytes. Drugs are a delusion. Find the germ of the disease; prepare from it a suitable anti-toxin; inject it three times a day quarter of an hour before meals; and what is the result? The phagocytes are stimulated; they devour the disease; and the patient recovers—unless, of course, he's too far gone. That, I take it, is the essence of Ridgeon's discovery.

SIR PATRICK [*dreamily*] As I sit here, I seem to hear my poor old father talking again.

B. B. [*rising in incredulous amazement*] Your father! But, Lord bless my soul, Paddy, your father must have been an older man than you.

SIR PATRICK. Word for word almost, he said what you say. No more drugs. Nothing but inoculation.

B. B. [*almost contemptuously*] Inoculation! Do you mean smallpox inoculation?

SIR PATRICK. Yes. In the privacy of our family circle, sir, my father used to declare his belief that smallpox inoculation was good, not only for smallpox, but for all fevers.

B. B. [*suddenly rising to the new idea with immense interest and excitement*] What! Ridgeon: did you hear that? Sir Patrick: I am more struck by what you have just told me than I can well express. Your father, sir, anticipated a discovery of my own. Listen, Walpole. Blenkinsop: attend one moment. You will all be intensely interested in this. I was put on the track by accident. I had a typhoid case and a tetanus case side by side in the hospital: a beadle and a city missionary. Think of what that meant for them, poor fellows! Can a beadle be dignified with typhoid? Can a missionary be eloquent with lockjaw? No. NO. Well, I got some typhoid anti-toxin from Ridgeon and a tube of Muldooley's anti-tetanus serum. But the missionary jerked all my things off the table in one of his paroxysms; and in replacing them I put Ridgeon's tube where Muldooley's ought to have been. The consequence was that I inoculated the typhoid case for tetanus and the tetanus case for typhoid. [*The doctors look greatly concerned. B. B., undamped, smiles triumphantly*]. Well, they recovered. THEY RECOVERED. Except for a touch of St Vitus's dance the missionary's as well to-day as ever; and the beadle's ten times the man he was.

BLENKINSOP. Ive known things like that happen. They cant be explained.

B. B. [*severely*] Blenkinsop: there is n o t h i n g that cannot be explained by science. What did I do? Did I fold my hands helplessly and say that the case could not be explained? By no means. I sat down and used my brains. I thought the case out on scientific principles. I asked myself why didnt the missionary die of typhoid on top of tetanus, and the beadle of tetanus on top of typhoid? Theres a problem for you, Ridgeon. Think, Sir Patrick. Reflect, Blenkinsop. Look at it without prejudice, Walpole. What is the real work of the anti-toxin? Simply to stimulate the phagocytes. Very well. But so long as you stimulate the phagocytes, what does it matter which particular sort of serum you use for the purpose? Haha! Eh? Do you see? Do you grasp it? Ever since that Ive used all sorts of anti-toxins absolutely indiscriminately, with perfectly satisfactory results. I inoculated the little prince with your stuff, Ridgeon, because I wanted to give you a lift; but two years ago I tried

THE DOCTOR'S DILEMMA

the experiment of treating a scarlet fever case with a sample of hydrophobia serum from the Pasteur Institute, and it answered capitally. It stimulated the phagocytes; and the phagocytes did the rest. That is why Sir Patrick's father found that inoculation cured all fevers. It stimulated the phagocytes. [*He throws himself into his chair, exhausted with the triumph of his demonstration, and beams magnificently on them*].

EMMY [*looking in*]. Mr Walpole: your motor's come for you; and it's frightening Sir Patrick's horses; so come along quick.

WALPOLE [*rising*] Good-bye, Ridgeon.

RIDGEON. Good-bye; and many thanks.

B. B. You see my point, Walpole?

EMMY. He cant wait, Sir Ralph. The carriage will be into the area if he dont come.

WALPOLE. I'm coming. [*To B. B.*] Theres nothing in your point: phagocytosis is pure rot: the cases are all blood-poisoning; and the knife is the real remedy. Bye-bye, Sir Paddy. Happy to have met you, Mr. Blenkinsop. Now, Emmy. [*He goes out, followed by Emmy*].

B. B. [*sadly*] Walpole has no intellect. A mere surgeon. Wonderful operator; but, after all, what is operating? Only manual labor. Brain—BRAIN remains master of the situation. The nuciform sac is utter nonsense: theres no such organ. It's a mere accidental kink in the membrane, occurring in perhaps two-and-a-half per cent of the population. Of course I'm glad for Walpole's sake that the operation is fashionable; for he's a dear good fellow; and after all, as I always tell people, the operation will do them no harm: indeed, Ive known the nervous shake-up and the fortnight in bed do people a lot of good after a hard London season; but still it's a shocking fraud. [*Rising*] Well, I must be toddling. Good-bye, Paddy [*Sir Patrick grunts*] good-bye, good-bye. Good-bye, my dear Blenkinsop, good-bye! Good-bye, Ridgeon. Dont fret about your health: you know what to do: if your liver is sluggish, a little mercury

108

never does any harm. If you feel restless, try bromide. If that doesnt answer, a stimulant, you know: a little phosphorus and strychnine. If you cant sleep, trional, trional, trion—

SIR PATRICK [*drily*] But no drugs, Colly, remember that.

B. B. [*firmly*] Certainly not. Quite right, Sir Patrick. As temporary expedients, of course; but as treatment, no, NO. Keep away from the chemist's shop, my dear Ridgeon, whatever you do.

RIDGEON [*going to the door with him*] I will. And thank you for the knighthood. Good-bye.

B. B. [*stopping at the door, with the beam in his eye twinkling a little*] By the way, who's your patient?

RIDGEON. Who?

B. B. Downstairs. Charming woman. Tuberculous husband.

RIDGEON. Is she there still?

EMMY [*looking in*] Come on, Sir Ralph: your wife's waiting in the carriage.

B. B. [*suddenly sobered*] Oh! Good-bye. [*He goes out almost precipitately*].

RIDGEON. Emmy: is that woman there still? If so, tell her once for all that I cant and wont see her. Do you hear?

EMMY. Oh, she aint in a hurry: she doesnt mind how long she waits. [*She goes out*].

BLENKINSOP. I must be off, too: every half-hour I spend away from my work costs me eighteenpence. Good-bye, Sir Patrick.

SIR PATRICK. Good-bye. Good-bye.

RIDGEON. Come to lunch with me some day this week.

BLENKINSOP. I cant afford it, dear boy; and it would put me off my own food for a week. Thank you all the same.

RIDGEON [*uneasy at Blenkinsop's poverty*] Can I do nothing for you?

BLENKINSOP. Well, if you have an old frock-coat to spare? you see what would be an old one for you would be

109

a new one for me; so remember me the next time you turn out your wardrobe. Good-bye. [*He hurries out*].

RIDGEON [*looking after him*] Poor chap! [*Turning to Sir Patrick*] So thats why they made me a knight! And thats the medical profession!

SIR PATRICK. And a very good profession, too, my lad. When you know as much as I know of the ignorance and superstition of the patients, youll wonder that we're half as good as we are.

RIDGEON. We're not a profession: we're a conspiracy.

SIR PATRICK. All professions are conspiracies against the laity. And we cant all be geniuses like you. Every fool can get ill; but every fool cant be a good doctor: there are not enough good ones to go round. And for all you know, Bloomfield Bonington kills less people than you do.

RIDGEON. Oh, very likely. But he really ought to know the difference between a vaccine and an anti-toxin. Stimulate the phagocytes! The vaccine doesnt affect the phagocytes at all. He's all wrong: hopelessly, dangerously wrong. To put a tube of serum into his hands is murder: simple murder.

EMMY [*returning*] Now, Sir Patrick. How long more are you going to keep them horses standing in the draught?

SIR PATRICK. Whats that to you, you old catamaran?

EMMY. Come, come, now! none of your temper to me. And it's time for Colly to get to his work.

RIDGEON. Behave yourself, Emmy. Get out.

EMMY. Oh, I learnt how to behave myself before I learnt you to do it. I know what doctors are: sitting talking together about themselves when they ought to be with their poor patients. And I know what horses are, Sir Patrick. I was brought up in the country. Now be good; and come along.

SIR PATRICK [*rising*] Very well, very well, very well. Good-bye, Colly. [*He pats Ridgeon on the shoulder and goes out, turning for a moment at the door to look meditatively at Emmy and say, with grave conviction*] You a r e

110

an ugly old devil, and no mistake.

EMMY [*highly indignant, calling after him*] Youre no beauty yourself. [*To Ridgeon, much flustered*] Theyve no manners: they think they can say what they like to me; and you set them on, you do. I'll teach them their places. Here now: are you going to see that poor thing or are you not?

RIDGEON. I tell you for the fiftieth time I wont see anybody. Send her away.

EMMY. Oh, I'm tired of being told to send her away. What good will that do her?

RIDGEON. Must I get angry with you, Emmy?

EMMY [*coaxing*] Come now: just see her for a minute to please me: theres a good boy. She's given me half-a-crown. She thinks it's life and death to her husband for her to see you.

RIDGEON. Values her husband's life at half-a-crown!

EMMY. Well, it's all she can afford, poor lamb. Them others think nothing of half-a-sovereign just to talk about themselves to you, the sluts! Besides, she'll put you in a good temper for the day, because it's a good deed to see her; and she's the sort that gets round you.

RIDGEON. Well, she hasnt done so badly. For half-a-crown she's had a consultation with Sir Ralph Bloomfield Bonington and Cutler Walpole. Thats six guineas' worth to start with. I dare say she's consulted Blenkinsop too: thats another eighteenpence.

EMMY. Then youll see her for me, wont you?

RIDGEON. Oh, send her up and be hanged. [*Emmy trots out, satisfied. Ridgeon calls*] Redpenny!

REDPENNY [*appearing at the door*] What is it?

RIDGEON. Theres a patient coming up. If she hasnt gone in five minutes, come in with an urgent call from the hospital for me. You understand: she's to have a strong hint to go.

REDPENNY. Right O! [*He vanishes*].

Ridgeon goes to the glass, and arranges his tie a little.

EMMY [*announcing*] Mrs Doobidad. [*Ridgeon leaves*

the glass and goes to the writing-table].

The lady comes in. Emmy goes out and shuts the door. Ridgeon, who has put on an impenetrable and rather distant professional manner, turns to the lady, and invites her, by a gesture, to sit down on the couch.

Mrs. Dubedat is beyond all demur an arrestingly good-looking young woman. She has something of the grace and romance of a wild creature, with a good deal of the elegance and dignity of a fine lady. Ridgeon, who is extremely susceptible to the beauty of women, instinctively assumes the defensive at once, and hardens his manner still more. He has an impression that she is very well dressed; but she has a figure on which any dress would look well, and carries herself with the unaffected distinction of a woman who has never in her life suffered from those doubts and fears as to her social position which spoil the manners of most middling people. She is tall, slender, and strong; has dark hair, dressed so as to look like hair and not like a bird's nest or a pantaloon's wig (fashion wavering just then between these two models); has unexpectedly narrow, subtle, dark-fringed eyes that alter her expression disturbingly when she is excited and flashes them wide open; is softly impetuous in her speech and swift in her movements; and is just now in mortal anxiety. She carries a portfolio.

MRS DUBEDAT [*in low urgent tones*] Doctor—

RIDGEON [*curtly*] Wait. Before you begin, let me tell you at once that I can do nothing for you. My hands are full. I sent you that message by my old servant. You would not take that answer.

MRS DUBEDAT. How could I?

RIDGEON. You bribed her.

MRS DUBEDAT. I—

RIDGEON. That doesnt matter. She coaxed me to see you. Well, you must take it from me now that with all the good will in the world, I cannot undertake another case.

MRS DUBEDAT. Doctor: you must save my husband. You must. When I explain to you, you will see that you

112

must. It is not an ordinary case, not like any other case. He is not like anybody else in the world: oh, believe me, he is not. I can prove it to you: [*fingering her portfolio*] I have brought some things to shew you. And you can save him: the papers say you can.

RIDGEON. Whats the matter? Tuberculosis?

MRS DUBEDAT. Yes. His left lung—

RIDGEON. Yes: you neednt tell me about that.

MRS DUBEDAT. You c a n cure him, if only you will. It is true that you can, isnt it? [*In great distress*] Oh, tell me, please.

RIDGEON [*warningly*] You are going to be quiet and self-possessed, arnt you?

MRS. DUBEDAT. Yes. I beg your pardon. I know I shouldnt—[*Giving way again*] Oh, please, say that you c a n; and then I shall be all right.

RIDGEON [*huffily*] I am not a curemonger: if you want cures, you must go to the people who sell them. [*Recovering himself, ashamed of the tone of his own voice*] But I have at the hospital ten tuberculous patients whose lives I believe I can save.

MRS DUBEDAT. Thank God!

RIDGEON. Wait a moment. Try to think of those ten patients as ten shipwrecked men on a raft—a raft that is barely large enough to save them—that will not support one more. Another head bobs up through the waves at the side. Another man begs to be taken aboard. He implores the captain of the raft to save him. But the captain can only do that by pushing one of his ten off the raft and drowning him to make room for the new comer. That is what you are asking me to do.

MRS DUBEDAT. But how can that be? I dont understand. Surely—

RIDGEON. You must take my word for it that it is so. My laboratory, my staff, and myself are working at full pressure. We are doing our utmost. The treatment is a new one. It takes time, means, and skill; and there is not enough for another case. Our ten cases are already chosen cases. Do you understand what I mean by chosen?

MRS DUBEDAT. Chosen. No: I cant understand.

RIDGEON [*sternly*] You m u s t understand. Youve got to understand and to face it. In every single one of those ten cases I have had to consider, not only whether the man could be saved, but whether he was worth saving. There were fifty cases to choose from; and forty had to be condemned to death. Some of the forty had young wives and helpless children. If the hardness of their cases could have saved them they would have been saved ten times over. Ive no doubt your case is a hard one: I can see the tears in your eyes [*she hastily wipes her eyes*]: I know that you have a torrent of entreaties ready for me the moment I stop speaking; but it's no use. You must go to another doctor.

MRS DUBEDAT. But can you give me the name of another doctor who understands your secret?

RIDGEON. I have no secret: I am not a quack.

MRS DUBEDAT. I beg your pardon: I didnt mean to say anything wrong. I dont understand how to speak to you. Oh pray dont be offended.

RIDGEON [*again a little ashamed*] There! there! never mind. [*He relaxes and sits down*]. After all, I'm talking nonsense: I daresay I a m a quack, a quack with a qualification. But my discovery is not patented.

MRS DUBEDAT. Then can any doctor cure my husband? Oh, why dont they do it? I have tried so many: I have spent so much. If only you would give me the name of another doctor.

RIDGEON. Every man in this street is a doctor. But outside myself and the handful of men I am training at St Anne's, there is nobody as yet who has mastered the opsonin treatment. And we are f u l l up. I'm sorry; but that is all I can say. [*Rising*] Good morning.

MRS DUBEDAT [*suddenly and desperately taking some drawings from her portfolio*] Doctor: look at these. You understand drawings: you have good ones in your waiting-room. Look at them. They are his work.

RIDGEON. It's no use my looking. [*He looks, all the same*] Hallo! [*He takes one to the window and studies it*]. Yes: this is the real thing. Yes, yes. [*He looks at another and returns to her*]. These are very clever. Theyre unfinished, arnt they?

MRS DUBEDAT. He gets tired so soon. But you see, dont you, what a genius he is? You see that he is worth saving. Oh, doctor, I married him just to help him to begin: I had money enough to tide him over the hard years at the beginning—to enable him to follow his inspiration until his genius was recognized. And I was useful to him as a model: his drawings of me sold quite quickly.

RIDGEON. Have you got one?

MRS DUBEDAT [*producing another*] Only this one. It was the first.

RIDGEON [*devouring it with his eyes*] Thats a wonderful drawing. Why is it called Jennifer?

MRS DUBEDAT. My name is Jennifer.

RIDGEON. A strange name.

MRS DUBEDAT. Not in Cornwall. I am Cornish. It's only what you call Guinevere.

RIDGEON [*repeating the names with a certain pleasure in them*] Guinevere. Jennifer. [*Looking again at the drawing*] Yes: it's really a wonderful drawing. Excuse me; but may I ask is it for sale? I'll buy it.

MRS DUBEDAT. Oh, take it. It's my own: he gave it to me. Take it. Take them all. Take everything; ask anything; but save him. You can: you will: you must.

REDPENNY [*entering with every sign of alarm*]. Theyve just telephoned from the hospital that youre to come instantly—a patient on the point of death. The carriage is waiting.

RIDGEON [*intolerantly*] Oh, nonsense: get out. [*Greatly annoyed*] What do you mean by interrupting me like this?

REDPENNY. But—

RIDGEON. Chut! cant you see I'm engaged? Be off.

Redpenny, bewildered, vanishes.

MRS DUBEDAT [*rising*] Doctor: one instant only before you go—

RIDGEON. Sit down. It's nothing.

MRS DUBEDAT. But the patient. He said he was dying.

RIDGEON. Oh, he's dead by this time. Never mind. Sit down.

MRS DUBEDAT [*sitting down and breaking down*] Oh, you none of you care. You see people die every day.

RIDGEON [*petting her*] Nonsense! it's nothing: I told him to come in and say that. I thought I should want to get rid of you.

MRS DUBEDAT [*shocked at the falsehood*] Oh!

RIDGEON [*continuing*] Dont look so bewildered: theres nobody dying.

MRS DUBEDAT. My husband is.

RIDGEON [*pulling himself together*] Ah, yes: I had forgotten your husband. Mrs Dubedat: you are asking me to do a very serious thing.

MRS DUBEDAT. I am asking you to save the life of a great man.

RIDGEON. You are asking me to kill another man for his sake; for as surely as I undertake another case, I shall have to hand back one of the old ones to the ordinary treatment. Well, I dont shrink from that. I have had to do it before; and I will do it again if you can convince me that his life is more important than the worst life I am now saving. But you must convince me first.

MRS DUBEDAT. He made those drawings; and they are not the best—nothing like the best; only I did not bring the really best: so few people like them. He is twenty-three: his whole life is before him. Wont you let me bring him to you? wont you speak to him? wont you see for yourself?

RIDGEON. Is he well enough to come to a dinner at the Star and Garter at Richmond?

MRS DUBEDAT. Oh yes. Why?

RIDGEON. I'll tell you. I am inviting all my old friends to a dinner to celebrate my knighthood—youve seen about it in the papers, havnt you?

MRS DUBEDAT. Yes, oh yes. That was how I found out about you.

RIDGEON. It will be a doctors' dinner; and it was to have been a bachelors' dinner. I'm a bachelor. Now if you will entertain for me, and bring your husband, he will meet me; and he will meet some of the most eminent men in my profession: Sir Patrick Cullen, Sir Ralph Bloomfield Bonington, Cutler Walpole, and others. I can put the case to them; and your husband will have to stand or fall by what we think of him. Will you come?

MRS DUBEDAT. Yes, of course I will come. Oh, thank you, thank you. And may I bring some of his drawings—the really good ones?

RIDGEON. Yes. I will let you know the date in the course of to-morrow. Leave me your address.

MRS DUBEDAT. Thank you again and again. You have made me so happy: I know you will admire him and like him. This is my address. [*She gives him her card*].

RIDGEON. Thank you. [*He rings*].

MRS DUBEDAT [*embarrassed*] May I—is there—should I—I mean— [*She blushes and stops in confusion*].

RIDGEON. Whats the matter?

MRS DUBEDAT. Your fee for this consultation?

RIDGEON. Oh, I forgot that. Shall we say a beautiful drawing of his favorite model for the whole treatment, including the cure?

MRS DUBEDAT. You are very generous. Thank you. I know you will cure him. Good-bye.

RIDGEON. I will. Good-bye. [*They shake hands*]. By the way, you know, dont you, that tuberculosis is catching. You take every precaution, I hope.

MRS DUBEDAT. I am not likely to forget it. They treat us

117

THE DOCTOR'S DILEMMA

like lepers at the hotels.

EMMY [*at the door*] Well, deary: have you got round him?

RIDGEON. Yes. Attend to the door and hold your tongue.

EMMY. Thats a good boy. [*She goes out with Mrs Dubedat*].

RIDGEON [*alone*] Consultation free. Cure guaranteed. [*He heaves a great sigh*].

118

ACT II

AFTER dinner on the terrace at the Star and Garter, Richmond. Cloudless summer night; nothing disturbs the stillness except from time to time the long trajectory of a distant train and the measured clucking of oars coming up from the Thames in the valley below. The dinner is over; and three of the eight chairs are empty. Sir Patrick, with his back to the view, is at the head of the square table with Ridgeon. The two chairs opposite them are empty. On their right come, first, a vacant chair, and then one very fully occupied by B. B., who basks blissfully in the moonbeams. On their left, Schutzmacher and Walpole. The entrance to the hotel is on their right, behind B. B. The five men are silently enjoying their coffee and cigarets, full of food, and not altogether void of wine.

Mrs Dubedat, wrapped up for departure, comes in. They rise, except Sir Patrick; but she takes one of the vacant places at the foot of the table, next B. B.; and they sit down again.

MRS DUBEDAT [as she enters] Louis will be here presently. He is shewing Dr Blenkinsop how to work the telephone. [She sits.] Oh, I am so sorry we have to go. It seems such a shame, this beautiful night. And we have enjoyed ourselves so much.

RIDGEON. I dont believe another half-hour would do Mr Dubedat a bit of harm.

SIR PATRICK. Come now, Colly, come! come! none of that. You take your man home, Mrs Dubedat; and get him to bed before eleven.

B. B. Yes, yes. Bed before eleven. Quite right, quite right. Sorry to lose you, my dear lady; but Sir Patrick's orders are the laws of—er—of Tyre and Sidon.

WALPOLE. Let me take you home in my motor.

SIR PATRICK. No. You ought to be ashamed of yourself, Walpole. Your motor will take Mr and Mrs Dubedat to

119

the station, and quite far enough too for an open carriage at night.

MRS DUBEDAT. Oh, I am sure the train is best.

RIDGEON. Well, Mrs Dubedat, we have had a most enjoyable evening.

WALPOLE. { Most enjoyable.

B. B. { Delightful. Charming. Unforgettable.

MRS DUBEDAT [*with a touch of shy anxiety*] What did you think of Louis? Or am I wrong to ask?

RIDGEON. Wrong! Why, we are all charmed with him.

WALPOLE. Delighted.

B. B. Most happy to have met him. A privilege, a real privilege.

SIR PATRICK [*grunts*]!

MRS DUBEDAT [*quickly*] Sir Patrick: are y o u uneasy about him?

SIR PATRICK [*discreetly*] I admire his drawings greatly, maam.

MRS DUBEDAT. Yes; but I meant—

RIDGEON. You shall go away quite happy. He's worth saving. He must and shall be saved.

Mrs Dubedat rises and gasps with delight, relief, and gratitude. They all rise except Sir Patrick and Schutzmacher, and come reassuringly to her.

B. B. Certainly, c e r-tainly.

WALPOLE. Theres no real difficulty, if only you know what to do.

MRS DUBEDAT. Oh, how can I ever thank you! From this night I can begin to be happy at last. You dont know what I feel.

She sits down in tears. They crowd about her to console her.

B. B. My dear lady: come come! come come! [*very persuasively*] c o m e come!

WALPOLE. Dont mind us. Have a good cry.

RIDGEON. No: dont cry. Your husband had better not

know that weve been talking about him.

MRS DUBEDAT [*quickly pulling herself together*] No, of course not. Please dont mind me. What a glorious thing it must be to be a doctor! [*They laugh*]. Dont laugh. You dont know what youve done for me. I never knew until now how deadly afraid I was—how I had come to dread the worst. I never dared let myself know. But now the relief has come: now I know.

Louis Dubedat comes from the hotel, in his overcoat, his throat wrapped in a shawl. He is a slim young man of 23, physically still a stripling, and pretty, though not effeminate. He has turquoise blue eyes, and a trick of looking you straight in the face with them, which, combined with a frank smile, is very engaging. Although he is all nerves, and very observant and quick of apprehension, he is not in the least shy. He is younger than Jennifer; but he patronizes her as a matter of course. The doctors do not put him out in the least: neither Sir Patrick's years nor Bloomfield Bonington's majesty have the smallest apparent effect on him: he is as natural as a cat: he moves among men as most men move among things, though he is intentionally making himself agreeable to them on this occasion. Like all people who can be depended on to take care of themselves, he is welcome company; and his artist's power of appealing to the imagination gains him credit for all sorts of qualities and powers, whether he possesses them or not.

LOUIS [*pulling on his gloves behind Ridgeon's chair*] Now, Jinny-Gwinny: the motor has come round.

RIDGEON. Why do you let him spoil your beautiful name like that, Mrs Dubedat?

MRS DUBEDAT. Oh, on grand occasions I am Jennifer.

B. B. You are a bachelor: you do not understand these things, Ridgeon. Look at me. [*They look*]. I also have two names. In moments of domestic worry, I am simple Ralph. When the sun shines in the home, I am Beedle-Deedle-Dumkins. Such is married life! Mr Dubedat: may I ask you to do me a favor before you go. Will you sign your name to this menu card, under the sketch you have made of me?

WALPOLE. Yes; and mine too, if you will be so good.

LOUIS. Certainly. [*He sits down and signs the cards*].

MRS DUBEDAT. Wont you sign Dr Schutzmacher's for him, Louis?

LOUIS. I dont think Dr Schutzmacher is pleased with his portrait. I'll tear it up. [*He reaches across the table for Schutzmacher's menu card, and is about to tear it. Schutzmacher makes no sign*].

RIDGEON. No, no: if Loony doesnt want it, I do.

LOUIS. I'll sign it for you with pleasure. [*He signs and hands it to Ridgeon*]. Ive just been making a little note of the river to-night: it will work up into something good [*he shews a pocket sketch-book*]. I think I'll call it the Silver Danube.

B. B. Ah, charming, charming.

WALPOLE. Very sweet. Youre a nailer at pastel.

Louis coughs, first out of modesty, then from tuberculosis.

SIR PATRICK. Now then, Mr Dubedat: youve had enough of the night air. Take him home, maam.

MRS DUBEDAT. Yes. Come, Louis.

RIDGEON. Never fear. Never mind. I'll make that cough all right.

B. B. We will stimulate the phagocytes. [*With tender effusion, shaking her hand*] G o o d-night, Mrs Dubedat. Good-night. Good-night.

WALPOLE. If the phagocytes fail, come to me. I'll put you right.

LOUIS. Good-night, Sir Patrick. Happy to have met you.

SIR PATRICK. 'Night [*half a grunt*].

MRS DUBEDAT. Good-night, Sir Patrick.

SIR PATRICK. Cover yourself well up. Dont think your

122

lungs are made of iron because theyre better than his. Good-night.

MRS DUBEDAT. Thank you. Thank you. Nothing hurts me. Good-night.

Louis goes out through the hotel without noticing Schutzmacher. Mrs Dubedat hesitates, then bows to him. Schutzmacher rises and bows formally, German fashion. She goes out, attended by Ridgeon. The rest resume their seats, ruminating or smoking quietly.

B. B. [*harmoniously*] Dee-lightful couple! Charming woman! Gifted lad! Remarkable talent! Graceful out-lines! Perfect evening! **Great** success! Interesting case! Glorious night! Exquisite scenery! Capital dinner! Stimu-lating conversation! Restful outing! Good wine! Happy ending! Touching gratitude! Lucky Ridgeon——

RIDGEON [*returning*] Whats that? Calling me, B. B.? [*He goes back to his seat next Sir Patrick*].

B. B. No, no. Only congratulating you on a most success-ful evening! Enchanting woman! Thorough breeding! Gentle nature! Refined——

Blenkinsop comes from the hotel and takes the empty chair next Ridgeon.

BLENKINSOP. I'm so sorry to have left you like this, Ridgeon; but it was a telephone message from the police. Theyve found half a milkman at our level crossing with a prescription of mine in its pocket. Wheres Mr Dubedat?

RIDGEON. Gone.

BLENKINSOP [*rising, very pale*] Gone!

RIDGEON. Just this moment——

BLENKINSOP. Perhaps I could overtake him——[*he rushes into the hotel*].

WALPOLE [*calling after him*] He's in the motor, man, miles off. You cant—— [*Giving it up*]. No use.

RIDGEON. Theyre really very nice people. I confess I was afraid the husband would turn out an appalling bounder. But he's almost as charming in his way as she is in

123

THE DOCTOR'S DILEMMA

hers. And theres no mistake about his being a genius. It's something to have got a case really worth saving. Somebody else will have to go; but at all events it will be easy to find a worse man.

SIR PATRICK. How do you know?

RIDGEON. Come now, Sir Paddy, no growling. Have something more to drink.

SIR PATRICK. No, thank you.

WALPOLE. Do y o u see anything wrong with Dubedat, B. B.?

B. B. Oh, a charming young fellow. Besides, after all, what c o u l d be wrong with him? L o o k at him. What c o u l d be wrong with him?

SIR PATRICK. There are two things that can be wrong with any man. One of them is a cheque. The other is a woman. Until you know that a man's sound on these two points, you know nothing about him.

B. B. Ah, cynic, cynic!

WALPOLE. He's all right as to the cheque, for a while at all events. He talked to me quite frankly before dinner as to the pressure of money difficulties on an artist. He says he has no vices and is very economical, but that theres one extravagance he cant afford and yet cant resist; and that is dressing his wife prettily. So I said, bang plump out, "Let me lend you twenty pounds, and pay me when your ship comes home." He was really very nice about it. He took it like a man; and it was a pleasure to see how happy it made him, poor chap.

B. B. [who has listened to Walpole with growing perturbation] But—but—but—when was this, may I ask?

WALPOLE. When I joined you that time down by the river.

B. B. But, my dear Walpole, he had just borrowed ten pounds from me.

WALPOLE. What!

SIR PATRICK [grunts]!

124

B. B. [*indulgently*] Well, well, it was really hardly borrowing; for he said heaven only knew when he could pay me. I couldnt refuse. It appears that Mrs Dubedat has taken a sort of fancy to me—

WALPOLE [*quickly*] No: it was to me.

B. B. Certainly not. Your name was never mentioned between us. He is so wrapped up in his work that he has to leave her a good deal alone; and the poor innocent young fellow—he has of course no idea of my position or how busy I am—actually wanted me to call occasionally and talk to her.

WALPOLE. Exactly what he said to me!

B. B. Pooh! Pooh pooh! Really, I must say. [*Much disturbed, he rises and goes up to the balustrade, contemplating the landscape vexedly*].

WALPOLE. Look here, Ridgeon! this is beginning to look serious.

Blenkinsop, very anxious and wretched, but trying to look unconcerned, comes back.

RIDGEON. Well, did you catch him?

BLENKINSOP. No. Excuse my running away like that. [*He sits down at the foot of the table, next Bloomfield Bonington's chair*].

WALPOLE. Anything the matter?

BLENKINSOP. Oh no. A trifle—something ridiculous. It cant be helped. Never mind.

RIDGEON. Was it anything about Dubedat?

BLENKINSOP [*almost breaking down*] I ought to keep it to myself, I know. I cant tell you, Ridgeon, how ashamed I am of dragging my miserable poverty to your dinner after all your kindness. It's not that you wont ask me again; but it's so humiliating. And I did so look forward to one evening in my dress clothes (t h e y r e still presentable, you see) with all my troubles left behind, just like old times.

RIDGEON. But what has happened?

BLENKINSOP. Oh, nothing. It's too ridiculous. I had just scraped up four shillings for this little outing; and it

125

cost me one-and-fourpence to get here. Well, Dubedat asked me to lend him half-a-crown to tip the chambermaid of the room his wife left her wraps in, and for the cloakroom. He said he only wanted it for five minutes, as she had his purse. So of course I lent it to him. And he's forgotten to pay me. I've just tuppence to get back with.

RIDGEON. Oh, never mind that—

BLENKINSOP [*stopping him resolutely*] No: I know what youre going to say; but I wont take it. Ive never borrowed a penny; and I never will. Ive nothing left but my friends; and I wont sell them. If none of you were to be able to meet me without being afraid that my civility was leading up to the loan of five shillings, there would be an end of everything for me. I'll take your old clothes, Colly, sooner than disgrace you by talking to you in the street in my own; but I wont borrow money. I'll train it as far as the twopence will take me; and I'll tramp the rest.

WALPOLE. Youll do the whole distance in my motor. [*They are all greatly relieved; and Walpole hastens to get away from the painful subject by adding*] Did he get anything out of y o u, Mr Schutzmacher?

SCHUTZMACHER [*shakes his head in a most expressive negative*].

WALPOLE. You didnt appreciate his drawing, I think.

SCHUTZMACHER. Oh yes I did. I should have liked very much to have kept the sketch and got it autographed.

B. B. But why didnt you?

SCHUTZMACHER. Well, the fact is, when I joined Dubedat after his conversation with Mr Walpole, he said the Jews were the only people who knew anything about art, and that though he had to put up with your Philistine twaddle, as he called it, it was what I said about the drawings that really pleased him. He also said that his wife was greatly struck with my knowledge, and that she always admired Jews. Then he asked me to advance him £50 on the security of the drawings.

B. B.		No, no. Positively! Seriously!
WALPOLE	[*All exclaiming together*]	What! Another fifty!
BLENKINSOP		Think of that!
SIR PATRICK		[*grunts*]!

SCHUTZMACHER. Of course I couldnt lend money to a stranger like that.

B. B. I envy you the power to say No, Mr Schutzmacher. Of course, I knew I oughtnt to lend money to a young fellow in that way; but I simply hadnt the nerve to refuse. I couldnt very well, you know, could I?

SCHUTZMACHER. I dont understand that. *I* felt that I couldnt very well lend it.

WALPOLE. What did he say?

SCHUTZMACHER. Well, he made a very uncalled-for remark about a Jew not understanding the feelings of a gentleman. I must say you Gentiles are very hard to please. You say we are no gentlemen when we lend money; and when we refuse to lend it you say just the same. I didnt mean to behave badly. As I told him, I might have lent it to him if he had been a Jew himself.

SIR PATRICK [*with a grunt*]. And what did he say to that?

SCHUTZMACHER. Oh, he began trying to persuade me that he was one of the chosen people—that his artistic faculty shewed it, and that his name was as foreign as my own. He said he didnt really want £50; that he was only joking; that all he wanted was a couple of sovereigns.

B. B. No, no, Mr Schutzmacher. You invented that last touch. Seriously, now?

SCHUTZMACHER. No. You cant improve on Nature in telling stories about gentlemen like Mr Dubedat.

BLENKINSOP. You certainly do stand by one another, you chosen people, Mr Schutzmacher.

SCHUTZMACHER. Not at all. Personally, I like Englishmen better than Jews, and always associate with them.

Thats only natural, because, as I am a Jew, theres nothing interesting in a Jew to me, whereas there is always something interesting and foreign in an Englishman. But in money matters it's quite different. You see, when an Englishman borrows, all he knows or cares is that he wants money; and he'll sign anything to get it, without in the least understanding it, or intending to carry out the agreement if it turns out badly for him. In fact, he thinks you a cad if you ask him to carry it out under such circumstances. Just like the Merchant of Venice, you know. But if a Jew makes an agreement, he means to keep it and expects you to keep it. If he wants money for a time, he borrows it and knows he must pay it at the end of the time. If he knows he cant pay, he begs it as a gift.

RIDGEON. Come, Loony! do you mean to say that Jews are never rogues and thieves?

SCHUTZMACHER. Oh, not at all. But I was not talking of criminals. I was comparing honest Englishmen with honest Jews.

One of the hotel maids, a pretty, fair-haired woman of about 25, comes from the hotel, rather furtively. She accosts Ridgeon.

THE MAID. I beg your pardon, sir—

RIDGEON. Eh?

THE MAID. I beg pardon, sir. It's not about the hotel. I'm not allowed to be on the terrace; and I should be discharged if I were seen speaking to you, unless you were kind enough to say you called me to ask whether the motor has come back from the station yet.

WALPOLE. Has it?

THE MAID. Yes, sir.

RIDGEON. Well, what do you want?

THE MAID. Would you mind, sir, giving me the address of the gentleman that was with you at dinner?

RIDGEON [*sharply*] Yes, of course I should mind very much. You have no right to ask.

128

THE DOCTOR'S DILEMMA

THE MAID. Yes, sir, I know it looks like that. But what am I to do?

SIR PATRICK. Whats the matter with you?

THE MAID. Nothing, sir. I want the address: thats all.

B. B. You mean the young gentleman?

THE MAID. Yes, sir: that went to catch the train with the woman he brought with him.

RIDGEON. The woman! Do you mean the l a d y who dined here? the gentleman's wife?

THE MAID. Dont believe them, sir. She cant be his wife. I'm his wife.

B. B.		[*in amazed remonstrance*] My good girl!
RIDGEON		You his wife!
WALPOLE		What! whats that? Oh, this is getting perfectly fascinating, Ridgeon.

THE MAID. I could run upstairs and get you my marriage lines in a minute, sir, if you doubt my word. He's Mr Louis Dubedat, isnt he?

RIDGEON. Yes.

THE MAID. Well, sir, you may believe me or not; but I'm the lawful Mrs Dubedat.

SIR PATRICK. And why arnt you living with your husband?

THE MAID. We couldnt afford it, sir. I had thirty pounds saved; and we spent it all on our honeymoon in three weeks, and a lot more that he borrowed. Then I had to go back into service, and he went to London to get work at his drawing; and he never wrote me a line or sent me an address. I never saw nor heard of him again until I caught sight of him from the window going off in the motor with that woman.

SIR PATRICK. Well, thats two wives to start with.

B. B. Now upon my soul I dont want to be uncharitable; but really I'm beginning to suspect that our young friend is rather careless.

THE DOCTOR'S DILEMMA

SIR PATRICK. Beginning to think! How long will it take you, man, to find out that he's a damned young blackguard?

BLENKINSOP. Oh, thats severe, Sir Patrick, very severe. Of course it's bigamy; but still he's very young; and she's very pretty. Mr Walpole: may I spunge on you for another of those nice cigarets of yours? [*He changes his seat for the one next Walpole*].

WALPOLE. Certainly. [*He feels in his pockets*]. Oh bother! Where—? [*Suddenly remembering*] I say: I recollect now: I passed my cigaret case to Dubedat and he didnt return it. It was a gold one.

THE MAID. He didnt mean any harm: he never thinks about things like that, sir. I'll get it back for you, sir, if youll tell me where to find him.

RIDGEON. What am I to do? Shall I give her the address or not?

SIR PATRICK. Give her your own address; and then we'll see. [*To the maid*] Youll have to be content with that for the present, my girl. [*Ridgeon gives her his card*]. Whats your name?

THE MAID. Minnie Tinwell, sir.

SIR PATRICK. Well, you write him a letter to care of this gentleman; and it will be sent on. Now be off with you.

THE MAID. Thank you, sir. I'm sure you wouldnt see me wronged. Thank you all, gentlemen; and excuse the liberty.

She goes into the hotel. They watch her in silence.

RIDGEON [*when she is gone*] Do you realize, you chaps, that we have promised Mrs Dubedat to save this fellow's life?

BLENKINSOP. Whats the matter with him?

RIDGEON. Tuberculosis.

BLENKINSOP [*interested*] And can you cure that?

RIDGEON. I believe so.

BLENKINSOP. Then I wish youd cure me. My right lung is touched, I'm sorry to say.

130

RIDGEON		What! y o u r lung is going!
B. B.		My dear Blenkinsop, what do you tell me? [*full of concern for Blenkinsop, he comes back from the balustrade*].
	[*all together*]	
SIR PATRICK		Eh? Eh? whats that?
WALPOLE		Hullo! you mustnt neglect this, you know.

BLENKINSOP [*putting his fingers in his ears*] No, no: it's no use. I know what youre going to say: Ive said it often to others. I cant afford to take care of myself; and theres an end of it. If a fortnight's holiday would save my life, I'd have to die. I shall get on as others have to get on. We cant all go to St Moritz or to Egypt, you know, Sir Ralph. Dont talk about it.

Embarrassed silence.

SIR PATRICK [*grunts and looks hard at Ridgeon*]!

SCHUTZMACHER [*looking at his watch and rising*] I must go. It's been a very pleasant evening, Colly. You might let me have my portrait if you dont mind. I'll send Mr Dubedat that couple of sovereigns for it.

RIDGEON [*giving him the menu card*] Oh dont do that, Loony. I dont think he'd like that.

SCHUTZMACHER. Well, of course I shant if you feel that way about it. But I dont think you understand Dubedat. However, perhaps thats because I'm a Jew. Good-night, Dr Blenkinsop [*shaking hands*].

BLENKINSOP. Good-night, sir—I mean—Good-night.

SCHUTZMACHER [*waving his hand to the rest*] Good-night, everybody.

WALPOLE	
B. B.	Good-night.
SIR PATRICK	
RIDGEON	

THE DOCTOR'S DILEMMA

B. B. repeats the salutation several times, in varied musical tones. Schutzmacher goes out.

SIR PATRICK. It's time for us all to move. [*He rises and comes between Blenkinsop and Walpole. Ridgeon also rises*]. Mr. Walpole: take Blenkinsop home: he's had enough of the open air cure for to-night. Have you a thick overcoat to wear in the motor, Dr Blenkinsop?

BLENKINSOP. Oh, theyll give me some brown paper in the hotel; and a few thicknesses of brown paper across the chest are better than any fur coat.

WALPOLE. Well, come along. Good-night, Colly. Youre coming with us, arnt you, B. B.?

B. B. Yes: I'm coming. [*Walpole and Blenkinsop go into the hotel*]. Good-night, my dear Ridgeon [*shaking hands affectionately*]. Dont let us lose sight of your interesting patient and his very charming wife. We must not judge him too hastily, you know. [*With unction*] G o o o o o o o o d-night, Paddy. Bless you, dear old chap. [*Sir Patrick utters a formidable grunt. B. B. laughs and pats him indulgently on the shoulder*] Good-night. Good-night. Good-night. Good-night. [*He good-nights himself into the hotel*].

The others have meanwhile gone without ceremony. Ridgeon and Sir Patrick are left alone together. Ridgeon, deep in thought, comes down to Sir Patrick.

SIR PATRICK. Well, Mr Savior of Lives: which is it to be? that honest decent man Blenkinsop, or that rotten blackguard of an artist, eh?

RIDGEON. It's not an easy case to judge, is it? Blenkinsop's an honest decent man; but is he any use? Dubedat's a rotten blackguard; but he's a genuine source of pretty and pleasant and good things.

SIR PATRICK. What will he be a source of for that poor innocent wife of his, when she finds him out?

RIDGEON. Thats true. Her life will be a hell.

SIR PATRICK. And tell me this. Suppose you had this choice put before you: either to go through life and find all the pictures bad but all the men and women good, or to go through life and find all the pictures good and all the men and women rotten. Which would you choose?

RIDGEON. Thats a devilishly difficult question, Paddy. The pictures are so agreeable, and the good people so infernally disagreeable and mischievous, that I really cant undertake to say offhand which I should prefer to do without.

SIR PATRICK. Come come! none of your cleverness with me: I'm too old for it. Blenkinsop isnt that sort of good man; and you know it.

RIDGEON. It would be simpler if Blenkinsop could paint Dubedat's pictures.

SIR PATRICK. It would be simpler still if Dubedat had some of Blenkinsop's honesty. The world isnt going to be made simple for you, my lad: you must take it as it is. Youve to hold the scales between Blenkinsop and Dubedat. Hold them fairly.

RIDGEON. Well, I'll be as fair as I can. I'll put into one scale all the pounds Dubedat has borrowed, and into the other all the half-crowns that Blenkinsop hasnt borrowed.

SIR PATRICK. And youll take out of Dubedat's scale all the faith he has destroyed and the honor he has lost, and youll put into Blenkinsop's scale all the faith he has justified and the honor he has created.

RIDGEON. Come come, Paddy! none of your claptrap with me: I'm too sceptical for it. I'm not at all convinced that the world wouldnt be a better world if everybody behaved as Dubedat does than it is now that everybody behaves as Blenkinsop does.

SIR PATRICK. Then why dont y o u behave as Dubedat does?

RIDGEON. Ah, that beats me. Thats the experimental test. Still, it's a dilemma. It's a dilemma. You see theres a complication we havnt mentioned.

SIR PATRICK. Whats that?

RIDGEON. Well, if I let Blenkinsop die, at least nobody

133

can say I did it because I wanted to marry his widow.

SIR PATRICK. Eh? Whats that?

RIDGEON. Now if I let Dubedat die, I'll marry his widow.

SIR PATRICK. Perhaps she wont have you, you know.

RIDGEON [*with a self-assured shake of the head*] Ive a pretty good flair for that sort of thing. I know when a woman is interested in me. She is.

SIR PATRICK. Well, sometimes a man knows best; and sometimes he knows worst. Youd much better cure them both.

RIDGEON. I cant. I'm at my limit. I can squeeze in one more case, but not two. I must choose.

SIR PATRICK. Well, you must choose as if she didn't exist: thats clear.

RIDGEON. Is that clear to you? Mind: it's not clear to me. She troubles my judgment.

SIR PATRICK. To me, it's a plain choice between a man and a lot of pictures.

RIDGEON. It's easier to replace a dead man than a good picture.

SIR PATRICK. Colly: when you live in an age that runs to pictures and statues and plays and brass bands because its men and women are not good enough to comfort its poor aching soul, you should thank Providence that you belong to a profession which is a high and great profession because its business is to heal and mend men and women.

RIDGEON. In short, as a member of a high and great profession, I'm to kill my patient.

SIR PATRICK. Dont talk wicked nonsense. You cant kill him. But you can leave him in other hands.

RIDGEON. In B. B.'s, for instance: eh? [*looking at him significantly*].

SIR PATRICK [*demurely facing his look*] Sir Ralph Bloomfield Bonington is a very eminent physician.

RIDGEON. He is.

SIR PATRICK. I'm going for my hat.

*Ridgeon strikes the bell as Sir Patrick makes for the
hotel. A waiter comes.*

RIDGEON [*to the waiter*] My bill, please.

WAITER. Yes, sir.

He goes for it.

ACT III

IN Dubedat's studio. Viewed from the large window the outer door is in the wall on the left at the near end. The door leading to the inner rooms is in the opposite wall, at the far end. The facing wall has neither window nor door. The plaster on all the walls is uncovered and undecorated, except by scrawlings of charcoal sketches and memoranda. There is a studio throne (a chair on a dais) a little to the left, opposite the inner door, and an easel to the right, opposite the outer door, with a dilapidated chair at it. Near the easel and against the wall is a bare wooden table with bottles and jars of oil and medium, paint-smudged rags, tubes of color, brushes, charcoal, a small lay figure, a kettle and spirit-lamp, and other odds and ends. By the table is a sofa, littered with drawing blocks, sketch-books, loose sheets of paper, newspapers, books, and more smudged rags. Next the outer door is an umbrella and hat stand, occupied partly by Louis' hats and cloak and muffler, and partly by odds and ends of costumes. There is an old piano stool on the near side of this door. In the corner near the inner door is a little tea-table. A lay figure, in a cardinal's robe and hat, with an hour-glass in one hand and a scythe slung on its back, smiles with inane malice at Louis, who, in a milkman's smock much smudged with colors, is painting a piece of brocade which he has draped about his wife. She is sitting on the throne, not interested in the painting, and appealing to him very anxiously about another matter.

MRS DUBEDAT. Promise.

LOUIS [putting on a touch of paint with notable skill and care and answering quite perfunctorily] I promise, my darling.

MRS DUBEDAT. When you want money, you will always come to me.

LOUIS. But it's so sordid, dearest. I hate money. I cant keep always bothering you for money, money, money. Thats what drives me sometimes to ask other people,

136

though I hate doing it.

MRS DUBEDAT. It is far better to ask me, dear. It gives people a wrong idea of you.

LOUIS. But I want to spare your little fortune, and raise money on my own work. Dont be unhappy, love: I can easily earn enough to pay it all back. I shall have a one-man-show next season; and then there will be no more money troubles. [*Putting down his palette*] There! I mustnt do any more on that until it's bone-dry; so you may come down.

MRS DUBEDAT [*throwing off the drapery as she steps down, and revealing a plain frock of tussore silk*] But you have promised, remember, seriously and faithfully, never to borrow again until you have first asked me.

LOUIS. Seriously and faithfully. [*Embracing her*] Ah, my love, how right you are! how much it means to me to have you by me to guard me against living too much in the skies. On my solemn oath, from this moment forth I will never borrow another penny.

MRS DUBEDAT [*delighted*] Ah, thats right. Does his wicked worrying wife torment him and drag him down from the clouds? [*She kisses him*]. And now, dear, wont you finish those drawings for Maclean?

LOUIS. Oh, they dont matter. Ive got nearly all the money from him in advance.

MRS DUBEDAT. But, dearest, that is just the reason why you should finish them. He asked me the other day whether you really intended to finish them.

LOUIS. Confound his impudence! What the devil does he take me for? Now that just destroys all my interest in the beastly job. Ive a good mind to throw up the commission, and pay him back his money.

MRS DUBEDAT. We cant afford that, dear. You had better finish the drawings and have done with them. I think it is a mistake to accept money in advance.

LOUIS. But how are we to live?

MRS DUBEDAT. Well, Louis, it is getting hard enough

137

THE DOCTOR'S DILEMMA

as it is, now that they are all refusing to pay except on delivery.

LOUIS. Damn those fellows! they think of nothing and care for nothing but their wretched money.

MRS DUBEDAT. Still, if they pay us, they ought to have what they pay for.

LOUIS [coaxing] There now: thats enough lecturing for to-day. Ive promised to be good, havnt I?

MRS DUBEDAT [putting her arms round his neck] You know that I hate lecturing, and that I dont for a moment misunderstand you, dear, dont you?

LOUIS [fondly] I know. I know. I'm a wretch; and youre an angel. Oh, if only I were strong enough to work steadily, I'd make my darling's house a temple, and her shrine a chapel more beautiful than was ever imagined. I cant pass the shops without wrestling with the temptation to go in and order all the really good things they have for you.

MRS DUBEDAT. I want nothing but you, dear. [She gives him a caress, to which he responds so passionately that she disengages herself]. There! be good now: remember that the doctors are coming this morning. Isnt it extraordinarily kind of them, Louis, to insist on coming? all of them, to consult about you?

LOUIS [coolly] Oh, I daresay they think it will be a feather in their cap to cure a rising artist. They wouldnt come if it didnt amuse them, anyhow. [Someone knocks at the door]. I say: it's not time yet, is it?

MRS DUBEDAT. No, not quite yet.

LOUIS [opening the door and finding RIDGEON there] Hello, Ridgeon. Delighted to see you. Come in.

MRS DUBEDAT [shaking hands] It's so good of you to come, doctor.

LOUIS. Excuse this place, wont you? It's only a studio, you know: theres no real convenience for living here. But we pig along somehow, thanks to Jennifer.

MRS DUBEDAT. Now I'll run away. Perhaps later on,

138

when youre finished with Louis, I may come in and hear the verdict. [*Ridgeon bows rather constrainedly*]. Would you rather I didnt?

RIDGEON. Not at all. Not at all.

Mrs Dubedat looks at him, a little puzzled by his formal manner; then goes into the inner room.

LOUIS [*flippantly*] I say: dont look so grave. Theres nothing awful going to happen, is there?

RIDGEON. No.

LOUIS. Thats all right. Poor Jennifer has been looking forward to your visit more than you can imagine. Shes taken quite a fancy to you, Ridgeon. The poor girl has nobody to talk to: I'm always painting. [*Taking up a sketch*] Theres a little sketch I made of her yesterday.

RIDGEON. She shewed it to me a fortnight ago when she first called on me.

LOUIS [*quite unabashed*] Oh! did she? Good Lord! how time does fly! I could have sworn I'd only just finished it. It's hard for her here, seeing me piling up drawings and nothing coming in for them. Of course I shall sell them next year fast enough, after my one-man-show; but while the grass grows the steed starves. I hate to have her coming to me for money, and having none to give her. But what can I do?

RIDGEON. I understood that Mrs Dubedat had some property of her own.

LOUIS. Oh yes, a little; but how could a man with any decency of feeling touch that? Suppose I did, what would she have to live on if I died? I'm not insured: cant afford the premiums. [*Picking out another drawing*] How do you like that?

RIDGEON [*putting it aside*] I have not come here today to look at your drawings. I have more serious and pressing business with you.

LOUIS. You want to sound my wretched lung. [*With impulsive candor*] My dear Ridgeon: I'll be frank with you. Whats the matter in this house isnt lungs but bills. It

139

THE DOCTOR'S DILEMMA

doesnt matter about me; but Jennifer has actually to economize in the matter of food. Youve made us feel that we can treat you as a friend. Will you lend us a hundred and fifty pounds?

RIDGEON. No.

LOUIS [*surprised*] Why not?

RIDGEON. I am not a rich man; and I want every penny I can spare and more for my researches.

LOUIS. You mean youd want the money back again.

RIDGEON. I presume people sometimes have that in view when they lend money.

LOUIS [*after a moment's reflection*] Well, I can manage that for you. I'll give you a cheque—or see here: theres no reason why you shouldnt have your bit too: I'll give you a cheque for two hundred.

RIDGEON. Why not cash the cheque at once without troubling me?

LOUIS. Bless you! they wouldnt cash it: I'm overdrawn as it is. No: the way to work it is this. I'll post-date the cheque next October. In October Jennifer's dividends come in. Well, you present the cheque. It will be returned marked "refer to drawer" or some rubbish of that sort. Then you can take it to Jennifer, and hint that if the cheque isnt taken up at once I shall be put in prison. She'll pay you like a shot. Youll clear £50; and youll do me a real service; for I do want the money very badly, old chap, I assure you.

RIDGEON [*staring at him*] You see no objection to the transaction; and you anticipate none from me!

LOUIS. Well, what objection can there be? It's quite safe. I can convince you about the dividends.

RIDGEON. I mean on the score of its being—shall I say dishonorable?

LOUIS. Well, of course I shouldnt suggest it if I didnt want the money.

RIDGEON. Indeed! Well, you will have to find some other means of getting it.

LOUIS. Do you mean that you refuse?

140

RIDGEON. Do I mean—! [*letting his indignation loose*] Of course I refuse, man. What do you take me for? How dare you make such a proposal to me?

LOUIS. Why not?

RIDGEON. Faugh! You would not understand me if I tried to explain. Now, once for all, I will not lend you a farthing. I should be glad to help your wife; but lending you money is no service to her.

LOUIS. Oh well, if youre in earnest about helping her, I'll tell you what you might do. You might get your patients to buy some of my things, or to give me a few portrait commissions.

RIDGEON. My patients call me in as a physician, not as a commercial traveller.

A knock at the door. Louis goes unconcernedly to open it, pursuing the subject as he goes.

LOUIS. But you must have great influence with them. You must know such lots of things about them—private things that they wouldnt like to have known. They wouldnt dare to refuse you.

RIDGEON [*exploding*] Well, upon my—

Louis opens the door, and admits Sir Patrick, Sir Ralph, and Walpole.

RIDGEON [*proceeding furiously*] Walpole: Ive been here hardly ten minutes; and already he's tried to borrow £150 from me. Then he proposed that I should get the money for him by blackmailing his wife; and youve just interrupted him in the act of suggesting that I should blackmail my patients into sitting to him for their portraits.

LOUIS. Well, Ridgeon, if that is what you call being an honorable man! I spoke to you in confidence.

SIR PATRICK. We're all going to speak to you in confidence, young man.

WALPOLE [*hanging his hat on the only peg left vacant on the hat-stand*] We shall make ourselves at home for half an hour, Dubedat. Dont be alarmed: youre a most fascinating chap; and we love you.

LOUIS. Oh, all right, all right. Sit down—anywhere you can. Take this chair, Sir Patrick [*indicating the one on the throne*]. Up-z-z-z! [*helping him up: Sir Patrick grunts and enthrones himself*]. Here you are, B. B. [*Sir Ralph glares at the familiarity; but Louis, quite undisturbed, puts a big book and a sofa cushion on the dais, on Sir Patrick's right; and B. B. sits down, under protest*]. Let me take your hat. [*He takes B. B.'s hat unceremoniously, and substitutes it for the cardinal's hat on the head of the lay figure, thereby ingeniously destroying the dignity of the conclave. He then draws the piano stool from the wall and offers it to Walpole*]. You dont mind this, Walpole, do you? [*Walpole accepts the stool, and puts his hand into his pocket for his cigaret case. Missing it, he is reminded of his loss*].

WALPOLE. By the way, I'll trouble you for my cigaret case, if you dont mind?

LOUIS. What cigaret case?

WALPOLE. The gold one I lent you at the Star and Garter.

LOUIS [*surprised*] Was that yours?

WALPOLE. Yes.

LOUIS. I'm awfully sorry, old chap. I wondered whose it was. I'm sorry to say this is all thats left of it. [*He hitches up his smock; produces a card from his waistcoat pocket; and hands it to Walpole*].

WALPOLE. A pawn ticket!

LOUIS [*reassuringly*] It's quite safe: he cant sell it for a year, you know. I say, my dear Walpole, I am sorry. [*He places his hand ingenuously on Walpole's shoulder and looks frankly at him*].

WALPOLE [*sinking on the stool with a gasp*] Dont mention it. It adds to your fascination.

RIDGEON [*who has been standing near the easel*] Before we go any further, you have a debt to pay, Mr Dubedat.

LOUIS. I have a precious lot of debts to pay, Ridgeon. I'll fetch you a chair. [*He makes for the inner door*].

RIDGEON [*stopping him*] You shall not leave the room

until you pay it. It's a small one; and pay it you must and shall. I dont so much mind your borrowing £10 from one of my guests and £20 from the other—

WALPOLE. I walked into it, you know. I offered it.

RIDGEON. —they could afford it. But to clean poor Blenkinsop out of his last half-crown was damnable. I intend to give him that half-crown and to be in a position to pledge him my word that you paid it. I'll have that out of you, at all events.

B. B. Quite right, Ridgeon. Quite right. Come, young man! down with the dust. Pay up.

LOUIS. Oh, you neednt make such a fuss about it. Of course I'll pay it. I had no idea the poor fellow was hard up. I'm as shocked as any of you about it. [*Putting his hand into his pocket*] Here you are. [*Finding his pocket empty*] Oh, I say, I havnt any money on me just at present. Walpole: would you mind lending me half-a-crown just to settle this.

WALPOLE. Lend you half— [*his voice faints away*].

LOUIS. Well, if you dont, Blenkinsop wont get it; for I havnt a rap: you may search my pockets if you like.

WALPOLE. Thats conclusive. [*He produces half-a-crown*].

LOUIS [*passing it to Ridgeon*] There! I'm really glad thats settled: it was the only thing that was on my conscience. Now I hope youre all satisfied.

SIR PATRICK. Not quite, Mr Dubedat. Do you happen to know a young woman named Minnie Tinwell?

LOUIS. Minnie! I should think I do; and Minnie knows me too. She's a really nice good girl, considering her station. Whats become of her?

WALPOLE. It's no use b l u ffi n g, Dubedat. Weve seen Minnie's marriage lines.

LOUIS [*coolly*] Indeed? Have you seen Jennifer's?

RIDGEON [*rising in irrepressible rage*] Do you dare insinuate that Mrs Dubedat is living with you without being married to you?

LOUIS. Why not?

B. B.		*[echoing him in*		Why not!
SIR PATRICK		*various tones of*		Why not!
RIDGEON		*scandalized*		Why not!
WALPOLE		*amazement]*		Why not!

LOUIS. Yes, why not? Lots of people do it: just as good people as you. Why dont you learn to think, instead of bleating and baahing like a lot of sheep when you come up against anything youre not accustomed to? [*Contemplating their amazed faces with a chuckle*] I say: I should like to draw the lot of you now: you do look jolly foolish. Especially you, Ridgeon. I had you that time, you know.

RIDGEON. How, pray?

LOUIS. Well, you set up to appreciate Jennifer, you know. And you despise me, dont you?

RIDGEON [*curtly*] I loathe you. [*He sits down again on the sofa*].

LOUIS. Just so. And yet you believe that Jennifer is a bad lot because you think I told you so.

RIDGEON. Were you lying?

LOUIS. No; but you were smelling out a scandal instead of keeping your mind clean and wholesome. I can just play with people like you. I only asked you had you seen Jennifer's marriage lines; and you concluded straight away that she hadnt got any. You dont know a lady when you see one.

B. B. [*majestically*] What do you mean by that, may I ask?

LOUIS. Now, I'm only an immoral artist; but if youd told me that Jennifer wasnt married, I'd have had the gentlemanly feeling and artistic instinct to say that she carried her marriage certificate in her face and in her character. But y o u are all moral men; and Jennifer is only an artist's wife —probably a model; and morality consists in suspecting other people of not being legally married. Arnt you ashamed of yourselves? Can one of you look me in the face after it?

144

WALPOLE. It's very hard to look you in the face, Dubedat; you have such a dazzling cheek. What about Minnie Tinwell, eh?

LOUIS. Minnie Tinwell is a young woman who has had three weeks of glorious happiness in her poor little life, which is more than most girls in her position get, I can tell you. Ask her whether she'd take it back if she could. She's got her name into history, that girl. My little sketches of her will be fought for by collectors at Christie's. She'll have a page in my biography. Pretty good, that, for a still-room maid at a seaside hotel, I think. What have you fellows done for her to compare with that?

RIDGEON. We havnt trapped her into a mock marriage and deserted her.

LOUIS. No: you wouldnt have the pluck. But dont fuss yourselves. *I* didnt desert little Minnie. We spent all our money—

WALPOLE. All h e r money. Thirty pounds.

LOUIS. I said all o u r money: hers and mine too. Her thirty pounds didnt last three days. I had to borrow four times as much to spend on her. But I didnt grudge it; and she didnt grudge her few pounds either, the brave little lassie. When we were cleaned out, we'd had enough of it: you can hardly suppose that we were fit company for longer than that: I an artist, and she quite out of art and literature and refined living and everything else. There was no desertion, no misunderstanding, no police court or divorce court sensation for you moral chaps to lick your lips over at breakfast. We just said, Well, the money's gone: weve had a good time that can never be taken from us; so kiss; part good friends; and she back to service, and I back to my studio and my Jennifer, both the better and happier for our holiday.

WALPOLE. Quite a little poem, by George!

B. B. If you had been scientifically trained, Mr. Dubedat, you would know how very seldom an actual case bears out a principle. In medical practice a man may die when, scientifically speaking, he ought to have lived. I have actually known a man die of a disease from which he was, scientifically speaking, immune. But that does not affect the fundamental truth of science. In just the same way, in moral cases, a man's behavior may be quite harmless and even beneficial, when he is morally behaving like a scoundrel. And he may do great harm when he is morally acting on the highest principles. But that does not affect the fundamental truth of morality.

SIR PATRICK. And it doesn't affect the criminal law on the subject of bigamy.

LOUIS. Oh bigamy! bigamy! bigamy! What a fascination anything connected with the police has for you all, you moralists! Ive proved to you that you were utterly wrong on the moral point: now I'm going to shew you that youre utterly wrong on the legal point; and I hope it will be a lesson to you not to be so jolly cocksure next time.

WALPOLE. Rot! You were married already when you married her; and that settles it.

LOUIS. Does it! Why cant you think? How do you know she wasnt married already too?

B. B.		Walpole! Ridgeon!
RIDGEON	*[all crying out together]*	This is beyond everything!
WALPOLE		Well, damn me!
SIR PATRICK		You young rascal.

LOUIS [*ignoring their outcry*] She was married to the steward of a liner. He cleared out and left her; and she thought, poor girl, that it was the law that if you hadnt heard of your husband for three years you might marry again. So as she was a thoroughly respectable girl and refused to have anything to say to me unless we were married I went through the ceremony to please her and to preserve her self-respect.

RIDGEON. Did you tell her you were already married?

LOUIS. Of course not. Dont you see that if she had known, she wouldnt have considered herself my wife? You dont seem to understand, somehow.

SIR PATRICK. You let her risk imprisonment in her ignorance of the law?

LOUIS. Well, *I* risked imprisonment for her sake, I could have been had up for it just as much as she. But when a man makes a sacrifice of that sort for a woman, he doesnt go and brag about it to her; at least, not if he's a gentleman.

WALPOLE. What a r e we to do with this daisy!

LOUIS [*impatiently*] Oh, go and do whatever the devil you please. Put Minnie in prison. Put me in prison. Kill Jennifer with the disgrace of it all. And then, when youve done all the mischief you can, go to church and feel good about it. [*He sits down pettishly on the old chair at the easel, and takes up a sketching block, on which he begins to draw*].

WALPOLE. He's got us.

SIR PATRICK [*grimly*] He has.

B. B. But is he to be allowed to defy the criminal law of the land?

SIR PATRICK. The criminal law is no use to decent people. It only helps blackguards to blackmail their families. What are we family doctors doing half our time but conspiring with the family solicitor to keep some rascal out of jail and some family out of disgrace?

B. B. But at least it will punish him.

SIR PATRICK. Oh, yes: itll punish him. Itll punish not only him but everybody connected with him, innocent and guilty alike. Itll throw his board and lodging on our rates and taxes for a couple of years, and then turn him loose on us a more dangerous blackguard than ever. Itll put the girl in prison and ruin her: itll lay his wife's life waste. You may put the criminal law out of your head once for all: it's only fit for fools and savages.

LOUIS. Would you mind turning your face a little more this way, Sir Patrick. [*Sir Patrick turns indignantly and glares at him*]. Oh, thats too much.

SIR PATRICK. Put down your foolish pencil, man; and

147

think of your position. You can defy the laws made by men; but there are other laws to reckon with. Do you know that youre going to die?

LOUIS. We're all going to die, arnt we?

WALPOLE. We're not all going to die in six months.

LOUIS. How do you know?

This for B. B. is the last straw. He completely loses his temper and begins to walk excitedly about.

B. B. Upon my soul, I will not stand this. It is in questionable taste under any circumstances or in any company to harp on the subject of death; but it is a dastardly advantage to take of a medical man. [*Thundering at Dubedat*] I will not allow it, do you hear?

LOUIS. Well, I didn't begin it: you chaps did. It's always the way with the inartistic professions: when theyre beaten in argument they fall back on intimidation. I never knew a lawyer yet who didnt threaten to put me in prison sooner or later. I never knew a parson who didnt threaten me with damnation. And now you threaten me with death. With all your tall talk youve only one real trump in your hand, and thats Intimidation. Well, I'm not a coward; so it's no use with me.

B. B. [*advancing upon him*] I'll tell you what you are, sir. Youre a scoundrel.

LOUIS. Oh, I don't mind you calling me a scoundrel a bit. It's only a word: a word that you dont know the meaning of. What is a scoundrel?

B. B. You are a scoundrel, sir.

LOUIS. Just so. What is a scoundrel? I am. What am I? A scoundrel. It's just arguing in a circle. And you imagine youre a man of science!

B. B. I—I—I—I have a good mind to take you by the scruff of your neck, you infamous rascal, and give you a sound thrashing.

LOUIS. I wish you would. Youd pay me something handsome to keep it out of court afterwards. [*B. B., baffled, flings away from him with a snort*]. Have you any more

148

civilities to address to me in my own house? I should like
to get them over before my wife comes back. [*He resumes
his sketching*].

RIDGEON. My mind's made up. When the law breaks
down, honest men must find a remedy for themselves. I will
not lift a finger to save this reptile.

B. B. That is the word I was trying to remember. Reptile.

WALPOLE. I cant help rather liking you, Dubedat. But
you certainly are a thoroughgoing specimen.

SIR PATRICK. You know our opinion of you now, at all
events.

LOUIS [*patiently putting down his pencil*] Look here.
All this is no good. You dont understand. You imagine that
I'm simply an ordinary criminal.

WALPOLE. Not an ordinary one, Dubedat. Do yourself
justice.

LOUIS. Well, youre on the wrong tack altogether. I'm
not a criminal. All your moralizings have no value for me.
I don't believe in morality. I'm a disciple of Bernard Shaw.

ȘIR PATRICK   } { [*puzzled*] Eh?
B. B.   } { [*waving his hand as if the subject
               } {   were now disposed of*] Thats
               } {   enough: I wish to hear no more.

LOUIS. Of course I havnt the ridiculous vanity to set up
to be exactly a Superman; but still, it's an ideal that I strive
towards just as any other man strives towards his ideal.

B. B. [*intolerant*] Dont trouble to explain. I now understand you perfectly. Say no more, please. When a man pretends to discuss science, morals, and religion, and then
avows himself a follower of a notorious and avowed anti-vaccinationist, there is nothing more to be said. [*Suddenly
putting in an effusive saving clause in parenthesis to Ridgeon*] Not, my dear Ridgeon, that I believe in vaccination
in the popular sense any more than you do: I neednt tell
you that. But there are things that place a man socially;
and anti-vaccination is one of them. [*He resumes his seat*

149

on the dais].

SIR PATRICK. Bernard Shaw? I never heard of him. He's a Methodist preacher, I suppose.

LOUIS [*scandalized*] No, no. He's the most advanced man now living: he isn't anything.

SIR PATRICK. I assure you, young man, my father learnt the doctrine of deliverance from sin from John Wesley's own lips before you or Mr. Shaw were born. It used to be very popular as an excuse for putting sand in sugar and water in milk. Youre a sound Methodist, my lad; only you don't know it.

LOUIS [*seriously annoyed for the first time*] It's an intellectual insult. I don't believe theres such a thing as sin.

SIR PATRICK. Well, sir, there are people who dont believe theres such a thing as disease either. They call themselves Christian Scientists, I believe. Theyll just suit your complaint. We can do nothing for you. [*He rises*]. Good afternoon to you.

LOUIS [*running to him piteously*] Oh dont get up, Sir Patrick. Don't go. Please dont. I didnt mean to shock you, on my word. Do sit down again. Give me another chance. Two minutes more: thats all I ask.

SIR PATRICK [*surprised by this sign of grace, and a little touched*] Well— [*He sits down*]—

LOUIS [*gracefully*] Thanks awfully.

SIR PATRICK [*continuing*] —I don't mind giving you two minutes more. But dont address yourself to me; for Ive retired from practice; and I dont pretend to be able to cure your complaint. Your life is in the hands of these gentlemen.

RIDGEON. Not in mine. My hands are full. I have no time and no means available for this case.

SIR PATRICK. What do you say, Mr. Walpole?

WALPOLE. Oh, I'll take him in hand: I dont mind. I feel perfectly convinced that this is not a moral case at all: it's a physical one. Theres something abnormal about his brain. That means, probably, some morbid condition af-

150

fecting the spinal cord. And that means the circulation. In short, it's clear to me that he's suffering from an obscure form of blood-poisoning, which is almost certainly due to an accumulation of ptomaines in the nuciform sac. I'll remove the sac—

LOUIS [*changing color*] Do you mean, operate on me? Ugh! No, thank you.

WALPOLE. Never fear: you wont feel anything. Youll be under an anæsthetic, of course. And it will be extraordinarily interesting.

LOUIS. Oh, well, if it would interest you, and if it wont hurt, thats another matter. How much will you give me to let you do it?

WALPOLE [*rising indignantly*] How much! What do you mean?

LOUIS. Well, you don't expect me to let you cut me up for nothing, do you?

WALPOLE. Will you paint my portrait for nothing?

LOUIS. No; but I'll give you the portrait when it's painted; and you can sell it afterwards for perhaps double the money. But I cant sell my nuciform sac when youve cut it out.

WALPOLE. Ridgeon: did you ever hear anything like this! [*To Louis*] Well, you can keep your nuciform sac, and your tubercular lung, and your diseased brain: Ive done with you. One would think I was not conferring a favor on the fellow! [*He returns to his stool in high dudgeon*].

SIR PATRICK. That leaves only one medical man who has not withdrawn from your case, Mr Dubedat. You have nobody left to appeal to now but Sir Ralph Bloomfield Bonington.

WALPOLE. If I were you, B. B., I shouldnt touch him with a pair of tongs. Let him take his lungs to the Brompton Hospital. They wont cure him; but theyll teach him manners.

B. B. My weakness is that I have never been able to say

No, even to the most thoroughly undeserving people. Besides, I am bound to say that I dont think it is possible in medical practice to go into the question of the value of the lives we save. Just consider, Ridgeon. Let me put it to you, Paddy. Clear your mind of cant, Walpole.

WALPOLE [*indignantly*] My mind is perfectly clear of cant.

B. B. Quite so. Well now, look at my practice. It is what I suppose you would call a fashionable practice, a smart practice, a practice among the best people. You ask me to go into the question of whether my patients are of any use either to themselves or anyone else. Well, if you apply any scientific test known to me, you will achieve a reductio ad absurdum. You will be driven to the conclusion that the majority of them would be, as my friend Mr J. M. Barrie has tersely phrased it, better dead. Better dead. There are exceptions, no doubt. For instance, there is the court, an essentially social-democratic institution, supported out of public funds by the public because the public wants it and likes it. My court patients are hard-working people who give satisfaction, undoubtedly. Then I have a duke or two whose estates are probably better managed than they would be in public hands. But as to most of the rest, if I once began to argue about them, unquestionably the verdict would be, Better dead. When they actually do die, I sometimes have to offer that consolation, thinly disguised, to the family. [*Lulled by the cadences of his own voice, he becomes drowsier and drowsier*]. The fact that they spend money so extravagantly on medical attendance really would not justify me in wasting my talents—such as they are—in keeping them alive. After all, if my fees are high, I have to spend heavily. My own tastes are simple: a camp bed, a couple of rooms, a crust, a bottle of wine; and I am happy and contented. My wife's tastes are perhaps more luxurious; but even she deplores an expenditure the sole object of which is to maintain the state my patients require from their medical attendant. The—er—er—er— [*suddenly waking up*] I have lost the thread of these remarks. What was I talking about, Ridgeon?

RIDGEON. About Dubedat.

B. B. Ah yes. Precisely. Thank you. Dubedat, of course. Well, what is our friend Dubedat? A vicious and ignorant young man with a talent for drawing.

LOUIS. Thank you. Dont mind me.

B. B. But then, what are many of my patients? Vicious and ignorant young men without a talent for anything. If I were to stop to argue about their merits I should have to give up three-quarters of my practice. Therefore I have made it a rule not so to argue. Now, as an honorable man, having made that rule as to paying patients, can I make an exception as to a patient who, far from being a paying patient, may more fitly be described as a borrowing patient? No. I say No. Mr Dubedat: your moral character is nothing to me. I look at you from a purely scientific point of view. To me you are simply a field of battle in which an invading army of tubercle bacilli struggles with a patriotic force of phagocytes. Having made a promise to your wife, which my principles will not allow me to break, to stimulate those phagocytes, I will stimulate them. And I take no further responsibility. [*He flings himself back in his seat exhausted*].

SIR PATRICK. Well, Mr Dubedat, as Sir Ralph has very kindly offered to take charge of your case, and as the two minutes I promised you are up, I must ask you to excuse me. [*He rises*].

LOUIS. Oh, certainly. Ive quite done with you. [*Rising and holding up the sketch block*] There! While youve been talking, Ive been doing. What is there left of your moralizing? Only a little carbonic acid gas which makes the room unhealthy. What is there left of my work? That. Look at it [*Ridgeon rises to look at it*].

SIR PATRICK [*who has come down to him from the throne*] You young rascal, was it drawing me you were?

LOUIS. Of course. What else?

SIR PATRICK [*takes the drawing from him and grunts approvingly*] Thats rather good. Dont you think so, Colly?

153

RIDGEON. Yes. So good that I should like to have it.

SIR PATRICK. Thank you; but I should like to have it myself. What d'ye think, Walpole?

WALPOLE [*rising and coming over to look*] No, by Jove: *I* must have this.

LOUIS. I wish I could afford to give it to you, Sir Patrick. But I'd pay five guineas sooner than part with it.

RIDGEON. Oh, for that matter, I will give you six for it.

WALPOLE. Ten.

LOUIS. I think Sir Patrick is morally entitled to it, as he sat for it. May I send it to your house, Sir Patrick, for twelve guineas?

SIR PATRICK. Twelve guineas! Not if you were President of the Royal Academy, young man. [*He gives him back the drawing decisively and turns away, taking up his hat*].

LOUIS [*to B. B.*] Would you like to take it at twelve, Sir Ralph?

B. B. [*coming between Louis and Walpole*] Twelve guineas? Thank you: I'll take it at that. [*He takes it and presents it to Sir Patrick*]. Accept it from me, Paddy; and may you long be spared to contemplate it.

SIR PATRICK. Thank you. [*He puts the drawing into his hat*].

B. B. I neednt settle with you now, Mr Dubedat: my fees will come to more than that. [*He also retrieves his hat*].

LOUIS [*indignantly*] Well, of all the mean—[*words fail him*]! I'd let myself be shot sooner than do a thing like that. I consider youve stolen that drawing.

SIR PATRICK [*drily*] So weve converted you to a belief in morality after all, eh?

LOUIS. Yah! [*To Walpole*] I'll do another one for you, Walpole, if youll let me have the ten you promised.

WALPOLE. Very good. I'll pay on delivery.

LOUIS. Oh! What do you take me for? Have you no confidence in my honor?

WALPOLE. None whatever.

LOUIS. Oh well, of course if you feel that way, you cant help it. Before you go, Sir Patrick, let me fetch Jennifer. I know she'd like to see you, if you dont mind. [*He goes to the inner door*]. And now, before she comes in, one word. Youve all been talking here pretty freely about me—in my own house too. *I* dont mind that: I'm a man and can take care of myself. But when Jennifer comes in, please remember that she's a lady, and that you are supposed to be gentlemen. [*He goes out*].

WALPOLE. Well!!! [*He gives the situation up as indescribable, and goes for his hat*].

RIDGEON. Damn his impudence!

B. B. I shouldnt be at all surprised to learn that he's well connected. Whenever I meet dignity and self-possession without any discoverable basis, I diagnose good family.

RIDGEON. Diagnose artistic genius, B. B. Thats what saves his self-respect.

SIR PATRICK. The world is made like that. The decent fellows are always being lectured and put out of countenance by the snobs.

B. B. [*altogether refusing to accept this*] I am not out of countenance. I should like, by Jupiter, to see the man who could put me out of countenance. [*Jennifer comes in*]. Ah, Mrs Dubedat! And how are we to-day?

MRS DUBEDAT [*shaking hands with him*] Thank you all so much for coming. [*She shakes Walpole's hand*]. Thank you, Sir Patrick [*she shakes Sir Patrick's*]. Oh, life has been worth living since I have known you. Since Richmond I have not known a moment's fear. And it used to be nothing but fear. Wont you sit down and tell me the result of the consultation?

WALPOLE. I'll go, if you dont mind, Mrs Dubedat. I have an appointment. Before I go, let me say that I am quite agreed with my colleagues here as to the character of the case. As to the cause and the remedy, thats not my business: I'm only a surgeon; and these gentlemen are physicians and will advise you. I may have my own views: in fact

155

THE DOCTOR'S DILEMMA

I h a v e them; and they are perfectly well known to my colleagues. If I am needed—and needed I shall be finally —they know where to find me; and I am always at your service. So for to-day, good-bye. [*He goes out, leaving Jennifer much puzzled by his unexpected withdrawal and formal manner*].

SIR PATRICK. I also will ask you to excuse me, Mrs Dubedat.

RIDGEON [*anxiously*] Are you going?

SIR PATRICK. Yes: I can be of no use here; and I must be getting back. As you know, maam, I'm not in practice now; and I shall not be in charge of the case. It rests between Sir Colenso Ridgeon and Sir Ralph Bloomfield Bonington. They know my opinion. Good afternoon to you, maam. [*He bows and makes for the door*].

MRS DUBEDAT [*detaining him*] Theres nothing wrong, is there? You dont think Louis is worse, do you?

SIR PATRICK. No: he's not worse. Just the same as at Richmond.

MRS DUBEDAT. Oh, thank you: you frightened me. Excuse me.

SIR PATRICK. Dont mention it, maam. [*He goes out*].

B. B. Now, Mrs Dubedat, if I am to take the patient in hand—

MRS DUBEDAT [*apprehensively, with a glance at Ridgeon*] You! But I thought that Sir Colenso—

B. B. [*beaming with the conviction that he is giving her a most gratifying surprise*] My dear lady, your husband shall have Me.

MRS DUBEDAT. But—

B. B. Not a word: it is a pleasure to me, for your sake. Sir Colenso Ridgeon will be in his proper place, in the bacteriological laboratory. *I* shall be in my proper place, at the bedside. Your husband shall be treated exactly as if he were a member of the royal family. [*Mrs Dubedat uneasy, again is about to protest*]. No gratitude: it would embarrass me, I assure you. Now, may I ask whether you are particularly
156

tied to these apartments. Of course, the motor has annihilated distance; but I confess that if you were rather nearer to me, it would be a l i t t l e more convenient.

MRS DUBEDAT. You see, this studio and flat are self-contained. I have suffered so much in lodgings. The servants are so frightfully dishonest.

B. B. Ah! Are they? Are they? Dear me!

MRS DUBEDAT. I was never accustomed to lock things up. And I missed so many small sums. At last a dreadful thing happened. I missed a five-pound note. It was traced to the housemaid; and she actually said Louis had given it to her. And he wouldnt let me do anything: he is so sensitive that these things drive him mad.

B. B. Ah—hm—ha—yes—say no more, Mrs Dubedat: you shall not move. If the mountain will not come to Mahomet, Mahomet must come to the mountain. Now I must be off. I will write and make an appointment. We shall begin stimulating the phagocytes on—on—probably on Tuesday next; but I will let you know. Depend on me; dont fret; eat regularly; sleep well; keep your spirits up; keep the patient cheerful; hope for the best; no tonic like a charming woman; no medicine like cheerfulness; no resource like science; good-bye, good-bye, good-bye. [*Having shaken hands—she being too overwhelmed to speak— he goes out, stopping to say to Ridgeon*] On Tuesday morning send me down a tube of some really stiff anti-toxin. Any kind will do. Dont forget. Good-bye, Colly. [*He goes out*].

RIDGEON. You look quite discouraged again. [*She is almost in tears*]. What's the matter? Are you disappointed?

MRS DUBEDAT. I know I ought to be very grateful. Believe me, I am very grateful. But—but—

RIDGEON. Well?

MRS DUBEDAT. I had set my heart on y o u r curing Louis.

RIDGEON. Well, Sir Ralph Bloomfield Bonington—

MRS DUBEDAT. Yes, I know, I know. It is a great privilege to have him. But oh, I wish it had been you. I know it's unreasonable; I cant explain; but I had such a strong instinct that you would cure him. I dont—I cant feel the same about Sir Ralph. You promised me. Why did you give Louis up?

RIDGEON. I explained to you. I cannot take another case.

MRS DUBEDAT. But at Richmond?

RIDGEON. At Richmond I thought I could make room for one more case. But my old friend Dr Blenkinsop claimed that place. His lung is attacked.

MRS DUBEDAT [*attaching no importance whatever to Blenkinsop*] Do you mean that elderly man—that rather silly—

RIDGEON [*sternly*] I mean the gentleman that dined with us: an excellent and honest man, whose life is as valuable as anyone else's. I have arranged that I shall take his case, and that Sir Ralph Bloomfield Bonington shall take Mr Dubedat's.

MRS DUBEDAT [*turning indignantly on him*] I see what it is. Oh! it is envious, mean, cruel. And I thought that you would be above such a thing.

RIDGEON. What do you mean?

MRS DUBEDAT. Oh, do you think I dont know? do you think it has never happened before? Why does everybody turn against him? Can you not forgive him for being superior to you? for being cleverer? for being braver? for being a great artist?

RIDGEON. Yes: I can forgive him for all that.

MRS DUBEDAT. Well, have you anything to say against him? I have challenged everyone who has turned against him—challenged them face to face to tell me any wrong thing he has done, any ignoble thought he has uttered. They have always confessed that they could not tell me one. I challenge you now. What do you accuse him of?

RIDGEON. I am like all the rest. Face to face, I cannot tell you one thing against him.

MRS DUBEDAT [*not satisfied*] But your manner is changed. And you have broken your promise to me to make

158

room for him as your patient.

RIDGEON. I think you are a little unreasonable. You have
had the very best medical advice in London for him; and
his case has been taken in hand by a leader of the profession.
Surely—

MRS DUBEDAT. Oh, it is so cruel to keep telling me that.
It seems all right; and it puts me in the wrong. But I am
not in the wrong. I have faith in you; and I have no faith
in the others. We have seen so many doctors: I have come to
know at last when they are only talking and can do nothing.
It is different with you. I feel that you know. You must
listen to me, doctor. [*With sudden misgiving*] Am I of-
fending you by calling you doctor instead of remembering
your title?

RIDGEON. Nonsense. I a m a doctor. But mind you, dont
call Walpole one.

MRS DUBEDAT. I dont care about Mr Walpole: it is you
who must befriend me. Oh, will you please sit down and
listen to me just for a few minutes. [*He assents with a grave
inclination, and sits on the sofa. She sits on the easel chair*].
Thank you. I wont keep you long; but I must tell you the
whole truth. Listen. I know Louis as nobody else in the
world knows him or ever can know him. I am his wife. I
know he has little faults: impatience, sensitiveness, even
little selfishnesses that are too trivial for him to notice. I
know that he sometimes shocks people about money because
he is so utterly above it, and cant understand the value ordinary people set on it. Tell me: did he—did he borrow
any money from you?

RIDGEON. He asked me for some—once.

MRS DUBEDAT [*tears again in her eyes*] Oh, I am so
sorry—so sorry. But he will never do it again: I pledge
you my word for that. He has given me his promise: here
in this room just before you came; and he is incapable of
breaking his word. That was his only real weakness; and
now it is conquered and done with for ever.

RIDGEON. Was that really his only weakness?

159

MRS DUBEDAT. He is perhaps sometimes weak about women, because they adore him so, and are always laying traps for him. And of course when he says he doesnt believe in morality, ordinary pious people think he must be wicked. You can understand, cant you, how all this starts a great deal of gossip about him, and gets repeated until even good friends get set against him?

RIDGEON. Yes: I understand.

MRS DUBEDAT. Oh, if you only knew the other side of him as I do! Do you know, doctor, that if Louis dishonored himself by a really bad action, I should kill myself.

RIDGEON. Come! dont exaggerate.

MRS DUBEDAT. I should. You dont understand that, you east country people.

RIDGEON. You did not see much of the world in Cornwall, did you?

MRS DUBEDAT [*naïvely*] Oh yes. I saw a great deal every day of the beauty of the world—more than you ever see here in London. But I saw very few people, if that is what you mean. I was an only child.

RIDGEON. That explains a good deal.

MRS DUBEDAT. I had a great many dreams; but at last they all came to one dream.

RIDGEON [*with half a sigh*] Yes, the usual dream.

MRS DUBEDAT [*surprised*] Is it usual?

RIDGEON. As I guess. You havnt yet told me what it was.

MRS DUBEDAT. I didn't want to waste myself. I could do nothing myself; but I had a little property and I could help with it. I had even a little beauty: dont think me vain for knowing it. I knew that men of genius always had a terrible struggle with poverty and neglect at first. My dream was to save one of them from that, and bring some charm and happiness into his life. I prayed Heaven to send me one. I firmly believe that Louis was guided to me in answer to my prayer. He was no more like the other men I had met than the Thames Embankment is like our Cornish coasts.

He saw everything that I saw, and drew it for me. He understood everything. He came to me like a child. Only fancy, doctor: he never even wanted to marry me: he never thought of the things other men think of! I had to propose it myself. Then he said he had no money. When I told him I had some, he said "Oh, all right," just like a boy. He is still like that, quite unspoiled, a man in his thoughts, a great poet and artist in his dreams, and a child in his ways. I gave him myself and all that I had that he might grow to his full height with plenty of sunshine. If I lost faith in him, it would mean the wreck and failure of my life. I should go back to Cornwall and die. I could show you the very cliff I should jump off. You must cure him: you must make him quite well again for me. I know that you can do it and that nobody else can. I implore you not to refuse what I am going to ask you to do. Take Louis yourself; and let Sir Ralph cure Dr Blenkinsop.

RIDGEON [*slowly*] Mrs Dubedat: do you really believe in my knowledge and skill as you say you do?

MRS DUBEDAT. Absolutely. I do not give my trust by halves.

RIDGEON. I know that. Well, I am going to test you— hard. Will you believe me when I tell you that I understand what you have just told me; that I have no desire but to serve you in the most faithful friendship; and that your hero must be preserved to you.

MRS DUBEDAT. Oh forgive me. Forgive what I said. You will preserve him to me.

RIDGEON. At all hazards. [*She kisses his hand. He rises hastily*]. N o: you have not heard the rest. [*She rises too*]. You must believe me when I tell you that the one chance of preserving the hero lies in Louis being in the care of Sir Ralph.

MRS DUBEDAT [*firmly*] You say so: I have no more doubt: I believe you. Thank you.

RIDGEON. Good-bye. [*She takes his hand*]. I hope this

THE DOCTOR'S DILEMMA

will be a lasting friendship.

MRS DUBEDAT. It will. My friendships end only with death.

RIDGEON. Death ends everything, doesnt it? Good-bye. *With a sigh and a look of pity at her which she does not understand, he goes.*

ACT IV

THE studio. The easel is pushed back to the wall. Cardinal Death, holding his scythe and hour-glass like a sceptre and globe, sits on the throne. On the hat-stand hang the hats of Sir Patrick and Bloomfield Bonington. Walpole, just come in, is hanging up his beside them. There is a knock. He opens the door and finds Ridgeon there.

WALPOLE. Hallo, Ridgeon!
They come into the middle of the room together, taking off their gloves.

RIDGEON. Whats the matter! Have you been sent for, too?

WALPOLE. Weve all been sent for. Ive only just come: I havnt seen him yet. The charwoman says that old Paddy Cullen has been here with B. B. for the last half-hour. [*Sir Patrick, with bad news in his face, enters from the inner room*]. Well: whats up?

SIR PATRICK. Go in and see. B. B. is in there with him.
Walpole goes. Ridgeon is about to follow him; but Sir Patrick stops him with a look.

RIDGEON. What has happened?

SIR PATRICK. Do you remember Jane Marsh's arm?

RIDGEON. Is that whats happened?

SIR PATRICK. Thats whats happened. His lung has gone like Jane's arm. I never saw such a case. He has got through three months galloping consumption in three days.

RIDGEON. B. B. got in on the negative phase.

SIR PATRICK. Negative or positive, the lad's done for. He wont last out the afternoon. He'll go suddenly: Ive often seen it.

RIDGEON. So long as he goes before his wife finds him out, *I* don't care. I fully expected this.

SIR PATRICK [*drily*] It's a little hard on a lad to be killed because his wife has too high an opinion of him. Fortunately few of us are in any danger of that.

163

THE DOCTOR'S DILEMMA

Sir Ralph comes from the inner room and hastens between them, humanely concerned, but professionally elate and communicative.

B. B. Ah, here you are, Ridgeon. Paddy's told you, of course.

RIDGEON. Yes.

B. B. It's an enormously interesting case. You know, Colly, by Jupiter, if I didnt know as a matter of scientific fact that I'd been stimulating the phagocytes, I should say I'd been stimulating the other things. What is the explanation of it, Sir Patrick? How do you account for it, Ridgeon? Have we over-stimulated the phagocytes? Have they not only eaten up the bacilli, but attacked and destroyed the red corpuscles as well? a possibility suggested by the patient's pallor. Nay, have they finally begun to prey on the lungs themselves? Or on one another? I shall write a paper about this case.

Walpole comes back, very serious, even shocked. He comes between B. B. and Ridgeon.

WALPOLE. Whew! B. B.: youve done it this time.

B. B. What do you mean?

WALPOLE. Killed him. The worst case of neglected blood-poisoning I ever saw. It's too late now to do anything. He'd die under the anæsthetic.

B. B. [*offended*] Killed! Really, Walpole, if your monomania were not well known, I should take such an expression very seriously.

SIR PATRICK. Come come! When youve both killed as many people as I have in my time youll feel humble enough about it. Come and look at him, Colly.

Ridgeon and Sir Patrick go into the inner room.

WALPOLE. I apologize, B. B. But it's blood-poisoning.

B. B. [*recovering his irresistible good nature*] My dear Walpole, e v e r y t h i n g is blood-poisoning. But upon my soul, I shall not use any of that stuff of Ridgeon's again. What made me so sensitive about what you said just now is that, strictly between ourselves, Ridgeon has cooked our
164

THE DOCTOR'S DILEMMA

young friend's goose.

Jennifer, worried and distressed, but always gentle, comes between them from the inner room. She wears a nurse's apron.

MRS DUBEDAT. Sir Ralph: what am I to do? That man who insisted on seeing me, and sent in word that his business was important to Louis, is a newspaper man. A paragraph appeared in the paper this morning saying that Louis is seriously ill; and this man wants to interview him about it. How can people be so brutally callous?

WALPOLE [*moving vengefully towards the door*] You just leave me to deal with him!

MRS DUBEDAT [*stopping him*] But Louis insists on seeing him: he almost began to cry about it. And he says he cant bear his room any longer. He says he wants to [*she struggles with a sob*]—to die in his studio. Sir Patrick says let him have his way: it can do no harm. What shall we do?

B. B. [*encouragingly*] Why, follow Sir Patrick's excellent advice, of course. As he says, it can do him no harm; and it will no doubt do him good—a great deal of good. He will be much the better for it.

MRS DUBEDAT [*a little cheered*] Will you bring the man up here, Mr Walpole, and tell him that he may see Louis, but that he mustnt exhaust him by talking? [*Walpole nods and goes out by the outer door*]. Sir Ralph, dont be angry with me; but Louis will die if he stays here. I must take him to Cornwall. He will recover there.

B. B. [*brightening wonderfully, as if Dubedat were already saved*] Cornwall! The very place for him! Wonderful for the lungs. Stupid of me not to think of it before. You are his best physician after all, dear lady. An inspiration! Cornwall: of course, yes, yes, yes.

MRS DUBEDAT [*comforted and touched*] You are so kind, Sir Ralph. But dont give me m u c h hope or I shall cry; and Louis cant bear that.

B. B. [*gently putting his protecting arm round her shoulders*] Then let us come back to him and help to carry

165

him in. Cornwall! of course, of course. The very thing! [*They go together into the bedroom*].

Walpole returns with The Newspaper Man, a cheerful, affable young man who is disabled for ordinary business pursuits by a congenital erroneousness which renders him incapable of describing accurately anything he sees, or understanding or reporting accurately anything he hears. As the only employment in which these defects do not matter is journalism (for a newspaper, not having to act on its descriptions and reports, but only to sell them to idly curious people, has nothing but honor to lose by inaccuracy and unveracity), he has perforce become a journalist, and has to keep up an air of high spirits through a daily struggle with his own illiteracy and the precariousness of his employment. He has a note-book, and occasionally attempts to make a note; but as he cannot write shorthand, and does not write with ease in any hand, he generally gives it up as a bad job before he succeeds in finishing a sentence.

THE NEWSPAPER MAN [*looking round and making indecisive attempts at notes*] This is the studio, I suppose.

WALPOLE. Yes.

THE NEWSPAPER MAN [*wittily*] Where he has his models, eh?

WALPOLE [*grimly irresponsive*] No doubt.

THE NEWSPAPER MAN. Cubicle, you said it was?

WALPOLE. Yes, tubercle.

THE NEWSPAPER MAN. Which way do you spell it: is it c-u-b-i-c-a-l or c-l-e?

WALPOLE. Tubercle, man, not cubical. [*Spelling it for him*] T-u-b-e-r-c-l-e.

THE NEWSPAPER MAN. Oh! tubercle. Some disease, I suppose. I thought he had consumption. Are you one of the family or the doctor?

WALPOLE. I'm neither one nor the other. I am M i s t e r Cutler Walpole. Put that down. Then put down Sir Colenso Ridgeon.

THE NEWSPAPER MAN. Pigeon?

WALPOLE. Ridgeon. [*Contemptuously snatching his book*] Here: youd better let me write the names down for you: youre sure to get them wrong. That comes of belonging to an illiterate profession, with no qualifications and no public register. [*He writes the particulars*].

THE NEWSPAPER MAN. Oh, I say: you h a v e got your knife into us, havnt you?

WALPOLE [*vindictively*] I wish I had: I'd make a better man of you. Now attend. [*Shewing him the book*] These are the names of the three doctors. This is the patient. This is the address. This is the name of the disease. [*He shuts the book with a snap which makes the journalist blink, and returns it to him*]. Mr Dubedat will be brought in here presently. He wants to see you because he doesnt know how bad he is. We'll allow you to wait a few minutes to humor him; but if you talk to him, out you go. He may die at any moment.

THE NEWSPAPER MAN [*interested*] Is he as bad as that? I say: I a m in luck to-day. Would you mind letting me photograph you? [*He produces a camera*]. Could you have a lancet or something in your hand?

WALPOLE. Put it up. If you want my photograph you can get it in Baker Street in any of the series of celebrities.

THE NEWSPAPER MAN. But theyll want to be paid. If you wouldnt mind [*fingering the camera*]—?

WALPOLE. I would. Put it up, I tell you. Sit down there and be quiet.

The Newspaper Man quickly sits down on the piano stool as Dubedat, in an invalid's chair, is wheeled in by Mrs Dubedat and Sir Ralph. They place the chair between the dais and the sofa, where the easel stood before. Louis is not changed as a robust man would be; and he is not scared. His eyes look larger; and he is so weak physically that he can hardly move, lying on his cushions with complete languor; but his mind is active; it is making the most of his condition, finding voluptuousness in languor and drama in death. They are all impressed, in spite of themselves, except

167

Ridgeon, who is implacable. B. B. is entirely sympathetic and forgiving. Ridgeon follows the chair with a tray of milk and stimulants. Sir Patrick, who accompanies him, takes the tea-table from the corner and places it behind the chair for the tray. B. B. takes the easel chair and places it for Jennifer at Dubedat's side, next the dais, from which the lay figure ogles the dying artist. B. B. then returns to Dubedat's left. Jennifer sits. Walpole sits down on the edge of the dais. Ridgeon stands near him.

LOUIS [*blissfully*] Thats happiness. To be in a studio! Happiness!

MRS DUBEDAT. Yes, dear. Sir Patrick says you may stay here as long as you like.

LOUIS. Jennifer.

MRS DUBEDAT. Yes, my darling.

LOUIS. Is the newspaper man here?

THE NEWSPAPER MAN [*glibly*] Yes, Mr Dubedat: I'm here, at your service. I represent the press. I thought you might like to let us have a few words about—about—er—well, a few words on your illness, and your plans for the season.

LOUIS. My plans for the season are very simple. I'm going to die.

MRS DUBEDAT [*tortured*] Louis—dearest—

LOUIS. My darling: I'm very weak and tired. Dont put on me the horrible strain of pretending that I dont know. Ive been lying there listening to the doctors—laughing to myself. They know. Dearest: dont cry. It makes you ugly; and I cant bear that. [*She dries her eyes and recovers herself with a proud effort*]. I want you to promise me something.

MRS DUBEDAT. Yes, yes: you know I will. [*Imploringly*] Only, my love, my love, dont talk: it will waste your strength.

LOUIS. No: it will only use it up. Ridgeon: give me something to keep me going for a few minutes—not one of your confounded anti-toxins, if you dont mind. I have some things to say before I go.

RIDGEON [*looking at Sir Patrick*] I suppose it can do no harm? [*He pours out some spirit, and is about to add soda water when Sir Patrick corrects him*].

SIR PATRICK. In milk. Dont set him coughing.

LOUIS [*after drinking*] Jennifer.

MRS DUBEDAT. Yes, dear.

LOUIS. If theres one thing I hate more than another, it's a widow. Promise me that youll never be a widow.

MRS DUBEDAT. My dear, what do you mean?

LOUIS. I want you to look beautiful. I want people to see in your eyes that you were married to me. The people in Italy used to point at Dante and say "There goes the man who has been in hell." I want them to point at you and say "There goes a woman who has been in heaven." It h a s been heaven, darling, hasnt it—sometimes?

MRS DUBEDAT. Oh yes, yes. Always, always.

LOUIS. If you wear black and cry, people will say "Look at that miserable woman: her husband made her miserable."

MRS DUBEDAT. No, never. You are the light and the blessing of my life. I never lived until I knew you.

LOUIS [*his eyes glistening*] Then you must always wear beautiful dresses and splendid magic jewels. Think of all the wonderful pictures I shall never paint. [*She wins a terrible victory over a sob*] Well, you must be transfigured with all the beauty of those pictures. Men must get such dreams from seeing you as they never could get from any daubing with paints and brushes. Painters must paint you as they never painted any mortal woman before. There must be a great tradition of beauty, a great atmosphere of wonder and romance. That is what men must always think of when they think of me. That is the sort of immortality I want. You can make that for me, Jennifer. There are lots of things you dont understand that every woman in the street understands; but you can understand that and do it as nobody else can. Promise me that immortality. Promise me you will not make a little hell of crape and crying and

THE DOCTOR'S DILEMMA

undertaker's horrors and withering flowers and all that vulgar rubbish.

MRS DUBEDAT. I promise. But all that is far off, dear. You are to come to Cornwall with me and get well. Sir Ralph says so.

LOUIS. Poor old B. B.!

B. B. [*affected to tears, turns away and whispers to Sir Patrick*] Poor fellow! Brain going.

LOUIS. Sir Patrick's there, isnt he?

SIR PATRICK. Yes, yes. I'm here.

LOUIS. Sit down, wont you? It's a shame to keep you standing about.

SIR PATRICK. Yes, yes. Thank you. All right.

LOUIS. Jennifer.

MRS DUBEDAT. Yes, dear.

LOUIS [*with a strange look of delight*] Do you remember the burning bush?

MRS DUBEDAT. Yes, yes. Oh, my dear, how it strains my heart to remember it now!

LOUIS. Does it? It fills me with joy. Tell them about it.

MRS DUBEDAT. It was nothing—only that once in my old Cornish home we lit the first fire of the winter; and when we looked through the window we saw the flames dancing in a bush in the garden.

LOUIS. Such a color! Garnet color. Waving like silk. Liquid lovely flame flowing up through the bay leaves, and not burning them. Well, I shall be a flame like that. I'm sorry to disappoint the poor little worms; but the last of me shall be the flame in the burning bush. Whenever you see the flame, Jennifer, that will be me. Promise me that I shall be burnt.

MRS DUBEDAT. Oh, if I might be with you, Louis!

LOUIS. No: you must always be in the garden when the bush flames. You are my hold on the world: you are my immortality. Promise.

MRS DUBEDAT. I'm listening. I shall not forget. You know that I promise.

170

LOUIS. Well, thats about all; except that you are to hang my pictures at the one-man-show. I can trust your eye. You wont let anyone else touch them.

MRS DUBEDAT. You can trust me.

LOUIS. Then theres nothing more to worry about, is there? Give me some more of that milk. I'm fearfully tired; but if I stop talking I shant begin again. [*Sir Ralph gives him a drink. He takes it and looks up quaintly*]. I say, B. B., do you think anything would stop y o u talking?

B. B. [*almost unmanned*] He confuses me with you, Paddy. Poor fellow! Poor fellow!

LOUIS [*musing*] I used to be awfully afraid of death; but now it's come I have no fear; and I'm perfectly happy. Jennifer.

MRS DUBEDAT. Yes, dear?

LOUIS. I'll tell you a secret. I used to think that our marriage was all an affectation, and that I'd break loose and run away some day. But now that I'm going to be broken loose whether I like it or not, I'm perfectly fond of you, and perfectly satisfied because I'm going to live as part of you and not as my troublesome self.

MRS DUBEDAT [*heartbroken*] Stay with me, Louis. Oh. dont leave me, dearest.

LOUIS. Not that I'm selfish. With all my faults I dont think Ive ever been really selfish. No artist can: Art is too large for that. You will marry again, Jennifer.

MRS DUBEDAT. Oh, how c a n you, Louis?

LOUIS [*insisting childishly*] Yes, because people who have found marriage happy always marry again. Ah, *I* shant be jealous. [*Slyly.*] But dont talk to the other fellow too much about me: he wont like it. [*Almost chuckling*] *I* shall be your lover all the time; but it will be a secret from him, poor devil!

SIR PATRICK. Come! youve talked enough. Try to rest awhile.

LOUIS [*wearily*] Yes: I'm fearfully tired; but I shall have a long rest presently. I have something to say to you fellows. Youre all there, arnt you? I'm too weak to see anything but Jennifer's bosom. That promises rest.

RIDGEON. We are all here.

LOUIS [*startled*] That voice sounded devilish. Take care, Ridgeon: my ears hear things that other people's ears cant. Ive been thinking—thinking. I'm cleverer than you imagine.

SIR PATRICK [*whispering to Ridgeon*] Youve got on his nerves, Colly. Slip out quietly.

RIDGEON [*apart to Sir Patrick*] Would you deprive the dying actor of his audience?

LOUIS [*his face lighting up faintly with mischievous glee*] I heard that, Ridgeon. That was good. Jennifer, dear: be kind to Ridgeon always; because he was the last man who amused me.

RIDGEON [*relentless*] Was I?

LOUIS. But it's not true. It's you who are still on the stage. I'm half way home already.

MRS DUBEDAT [*to Ridgeon*] What did you say?

LOUIS [*answering for him*] Nothing, dear. Only one of those little secrets that men keep among themselves. Well, all you chaps have thought pretty hard things of me, and said them.

B. B. [*quite overcome*] No, no, Dubedat. Not at all.

LOUIS. Yes, you have. I know what you all think of me. Dont imagine I'm sore about it. I forgive you.

WALPOLE [*involuntarily*] Well, damn me! [*Ashamed*] I beg your pardon.

LOUIS. That was old Walpole, I know. Dont grieve, Walpole. I'm perfectly happy. I'm not in pain. I dont want to live. I've escaped from myself. I'm in heaven, immortal in the heart of my beautiful Jennifer. I'm not afraid, and not ashamed. [*Reflectively, puzzling it out for himself weakly*] I know that in an accidental sort of way, struggling through the unreal part of life, I havnt always been able to live up to my ideal. But in my own real world I have never done anything wrong, never denied my faith, never

172

been untrue to myself. Ive been threatened and blackmailed and insulted and starved. But Ive played the game. Ive fought the good fight. And now it's all over, theres an indescribable peace. [*He feebly folds his hands and utters his creed*] I believe in Michael Angelo, Velasquez, and Rembrandt; in the might of design, the mystery of color, the redemption of all things by Beauty everlasting, and the message of Art that has made these hands blessed. Amen. Amen. [*He closes his eyes and lies still*].

MRS DUBEDAT [*breathless*] Louis: are you—
Walpole rises and comes quickly to see whether he is dead.

LOUIS. Not yet, dear. Very nearly, but not yet. I should like to rest my head on your bosom; only it would tire you.

MRS DUBEDAT. No, no, no, darling: how could you tire me? [*She lifts him so that he lies in her bosom*].

LOUIS. Thats good. Thats real.

MRS DUBEDAT. Dont spare me, dear. Indeed, i n d e e d you will not tire me. Lean on me with all your weight.

LOUIS [*with a sudden half return of his normal strength and comfort*] Jinny Gwinny: I think I shall recover after all. [*Sir Patrick looks significantly at Ridgeon, mutely warning him that this is the end*].

MRS DUBEDAT [*hopefully*] Yes, yes: you shall.

LOUIS. Because I suddenly want to sleep. Just an ordinary sleep.

MRS DUBEDAT [*rocking him*] Yes, dear. Sleep. [*He seems to go to sleep. Walpole makes another movement. She protests*]. Sh-sh: please dont disturb him. [*His lips move*]. What did you say, dear? [*In great distress*] I cant listen without moving him. [*His lips move again: Walpole bends down and listens*].

WALPOLE. He wants to know is the newspaper man here.

THE NEWSPAPER MAN [*excited; for he has been enjoying himself enormously*] Yes, Mr Dubedat. Here I am.
Walpole raises his hand warningly to silence him. Sir

Ralph sits down quietly on the sofa and frankly buries his face in his handkerchief.

MRS DUBEDAT [*with great relief*] Oh thats right, dear: dont spare me: lean with all your weight on me. Now you are really resting.

Sir Patrick quickly comes forward and feels Louis's pulse; then takes him by the shoulders.

SIR PATRICK. Let me put him back on the pillow, maam. He will be better so.

MRS DUBEDAT [*piteously*], Oh no, please, p l e a s e, doctor. He is not tiring me; and he will be so hurt when he wakes if he finds I have put him away.

SIR PATRICK. He will never wake again. [*He takes the body from her and replaces it in the chair. Ridgeon, unmoved, lets down the back and makes a bier of it*].

MRS DUBEDAT [*who has unexpectedly sprung to her feet, and stands dry-eyed and stately*] Was that death?

WALPOLE. Yes.

MRS DUBEDAT [*with complete dignity*] Will you wait for me a moment? I will come back. [*She goes out*].

WALPOLE. Ought we to follow her? Is she in her right senses?

SIR PATRICK [*with quiet conviction*] Yes. She's all right. Leave her alone. She'll come back.

RIDGEON [*callously*] Let us get this thing out of the way before she comes.

B. B. [*rising, shocked*] My dear Colly! The poor lad! He died splendidly.

SIR PATRICK. Aye! that is how the wicked die.

> For there are no bands in their death;
> But their strength is firm:
> They are not in trouble as other men.

No matter: it's not for us to judge. He's in another world now.

WALPOLE. Borrowing his first five-pound note there, probably.

RIDGEON. I said the other day that the most tragic thing in the world is a sick doctor. I was wrong. The most tragic thing in the world is a man of genius who is not also a man of honor.

Ridgeon and Walpole wheel the chair into the recess.

THE NEWSPAPER MAN [*to Sir Ralph*] I thought it shewed a very nice feeling, his being so particular about his wife going into proper mourning for him and making her promise never to marry again.

B. B. [*impressively*] Mrs Dubedat is not in a position to carry the interview any further. Neither are we.

SIR PATRICK. Good afternoon to you.

THE NEWSPAPER MAN. Mrs Dubedat said she was coming back.

B. B. After you have gone.

THE NEWSPAPER MAN. Do you think she would give me a few words on How It Feels to be a Widow? Rather a good title for an article, isnt it?

B. B. Young man: if you wait until Mrs Dubedat comes back, you will be able to write an article on How It Feels to be Turned Out of the House.

THE NEWSPAPER MAN [*unconvinced*] You think she'd rather not—

B. B. [*cutting him short*] Good day to you. [*Giving him a visiting-card*] Mind you get my name correctly. Good day.

THE NEWSPAPER MAN. Good day. Thank you. [*Vaguely trying to read the card*] Mr—

B. B. No, not Mister. This is your hat, I think [*giving it to him*]. Gloves? No, of course: no gloves. Good day to you. [*He edges him out at last; shuts the door on him; and returns to Sir Patrick as Ridgeon and Walpole come back from the recess, Walpole crossing the room to the hatstand, and Ridgeon coming between Sir Ralph and Sir Patrick*]. Poor fellow! Poor young fellow! How well he died! I feel a better man, really.

SIR PATRICK. When youre as old as I am, youll know

THE DOCTOR'S DILEMMA

that it matters very little how a man dies. What matters is, how he lives. Every fool that runs his nose against a bullet is a hero nowadays, because he dies for his country. Why dont he live for it to some purpose?

B. B. No, please, Paddy: dont be hard on the poor lad. Not now, not now. After all, was he so bad? He had only two failings: money and women. Well, let us be honest. Tell the truth, Paddy. Dont be hypocritical, Ridgeon. Throw off the mask, Walpole. Are these two matters so well arranged at present that a disregard of the usual arrangements indicates real depravity?

WALPOLE. I dont mind his disregarding the usual arrangements. Confound the usual arrangements! To a man of science theyre beneath contempt both as to money and women. What I mind is his disregarding everything except his own pocket and his own fancy. He didnt disregard the usual arrangements when they paid him. Did he give us his pictures for nothing? Do you suppose he'd have hesitated to blackmail me if I'd compromised myself with his wife? Not he.

SIR PATRICK. Dont waste your time wrangling over him. A blackguard's a blackguard; an honest man's an honest man; and neither of them will ever be at a loss for a religion or a morality to prove that their ways are the right ways. It's the same with nations, the same with professions, the same all the world over and always will be.

B. B. Ah, well, perhaps, perhaps, perhaps. Still, d e m o r t u i s n i l n i s i b o n u m. He died extremely well, remarkably well. He has set us an example: let us endeavor to follow it rather than harp on the weaknesses that have perished with him. I think it is Shakespear who says that the good that most men do lives after them: the evil lies interréd with their bones. Yes: interréd with their bones. Believe me, Paddy, we are all mortal. It is the common lot, Ridgeon. Say what you will, Walpole, Nature's debt must be paid. If tis not to-day, twill be to-morrow.

176

THE DOCTOR'S DILEMMA

To-morrow and to-morrow and to-morrow
After life's fitful fever they sleep well
And like this insubstantial bourne from which
No traveller returns
Leave not a wrack behind.

Walpole is about to speak, but B. B., suddenly and vehemently proceeding, extinguishes him.

Out, out, brief candle:
For nothing canst thou to damnation add;
The readiness is all.

WALPOLE [*gently; for B. B.'s feeling, absurdly expressed as it is, is too sincere and humane to be ridiculed*] Yes, B. B. Death makes people go on like that. I dont know why it should; but it does. By the way, what are we going to do? Ought we to clear out; or had we better wait and see whether Mrs Dubedat will come back?

SIR PATRICK. I think we'd better go. We can tell the charwoman what to do.

They take their hats and go to the door.

MRS DUBEDAT [*coming from the inner room wonderfully and beautifully dressed, and radiant, carrying a great piece of purple silk, handsomely embroidered, over her arm*] I'm so sorry to have kept you waiting.

SIR PATRICK	[*amazed, all together in a confused murmur*]	Dont mention it, madam.
B. B.		Not at all, not at all.
RIDGEON		By no means.
WALPOLE		It doesnt matter in the least.

MRS DUBEDAT [*coming to them*] I felt that I must shake hands with his friends once before we part to-day. We have shared together a great privilege and a great happiness. I dont think we can ever think of ourselves as ordinary people again. We have had a wonderful experience; and that gives us a common faith, a common ideal, that nobody else can quite have. Life will always be beautiful to us: death will always be beautiful to us. May we shake hands on that?

SIR PATRICK [*shaking hands*] Remember: all letters had better be left to your solicitor. Let him open everything and settle everything. Thats the law, you know.

MRS DUBEDAT. Oh, thank you: I didnt know. [*Sir Patrick goes*].

WALPOLE. Good-bye. I blame myself: I should have insisted on operating. [*He goes*].

B. B. I will send the proper people: they will know what to do: you shall have no trouble. G o o d-bye, my dear lady. [*He goes*].

RIDGEON. Good-bye. [*He offers his hand*].

MRS DUBEDAT [*drawing back with gentle majesty*] I said his f r i e n d s, Sir Colenso. [*He bows and goes*].

She unfolds the great piece of silk, and goes into the recess to cover her dead.

ACT V

ONE of the smaller Bond Street Picture Galleries. The entrance is from a picture shop. Nearly in the middle of the gallery there is a writing-table, at which the Secretary, fashionably dressed, sits with his back to the entrance, correcting catalogue proofs. Some copies of a new book are on the desk, also the Secretary's shining hat and a couple of magnifying glasses. At the side, on his left, a little behind him, is a small door marked PRIVATE. Near the same side is a cushioned bench parallel to the walls, which are covered with Dubedat's works. Two screens, also covered with drawings, stand near the corners right and left of the entrance.

Jennifer, beautifully dressed and apparently very happy and prosperous, comes into the gallery through the private door.

JENNIFER. Have the catalogues come yet, Mr Danby?

THE SECRETARY. Not yet.

JENNIFER. What a shame! It's a quarter past: the private view will begin in less than half an hour.

THE SECRETARY. I think I'd better run over to the printers to hurry them up.

JENNIFER. Oh, if you would be so good, Mr Danby. I'll take your place while youre away.

THE SECRETARY. If anyone should come before the time dont take any notice. The commissionaire wont let anyone through unless he knows him. We have a few people who like to come before the crowd—people who really buy; and of course we're glad to see them. Have you seen the notices in Brush and Crayon and in The Easel?

JENNIFER [indignantly] Yes: most disgraceful. They write quite patronizingly, as if they were Mr Dubedat's superiors. After all the cigars and sandwiches they had from us on the press day, and all they drank, I really think it is infamous that they should write like that. I hope you have not sent them tickets for to-day.

179

THE SECRETARY. Oh, they wont come again: theres no lunch to-day. The advance copies of your book have come. [*He indicates the new books*].

JENNIFER [*pouncing on a copy, wildly excited*] Give it to me. Oh! excuse me a moment [*she runs away with it through the private door*].

The Secretary takes a mirror from his drawer and smartens himself before going out. Ridgeon comes in.

RIDGEON. Good morning. May I look round, as usual, before the doors open?

THE SECRETARY. Certainly, Sir Colenso. I'm sorry the catalogues have not come: I'm just going to see about them. Heres my own list, if you dont mind.

RIDGEON. Thanks. Whats this? [*He takes up one of the new books*].

THE SECRETARY. Thats just come in. An advance copy of Mrs Dubedat's Life of her late husband.

RIDGEON [*reading the title*] The Story of a King of Men. By His Wife. [*He looks at the portrait frontispiece*]. Ay: there he is. You knew him here, I suppose.

THE SECRETARY. Oh, we knew him. Better than she did, Sir Colenso, in some ways, perhaps.

RIDGEON. So did I. [*They look significantly at one another*]. I'll take a look round.

The Secretary puts on the shining hat and goes out. Ridgeon begins looking at the pictures. Presently he comes back to the table for a magnifying glass, and scrutinizes a drawing very closely. He sighs; shakes his head, as if constrained to admit the extraordinary fascination and merit of the work; then marks the Secretary's list. Proceeding with his survey, he disappears behind the screen. Jennifer comes back with her book. A look round satisfies her that she is alone. She seats herself at the table and admires the memoir—her first printed book—to her heart's content. Ridgeon re-appears, face to the wall, scrutinizing the drawings. After using his glass again, he steps back to get a more distant view of one of the larger pictures. She hastily closes the book at the sound; looks round; recognizes him; and stares, petrified. He takes a further step back which brings him nearer to her.

RIDGEON [*shaking his head as before, ejaculates*] Clever brute! [*She flushes as though he had struck her. He turns to put the glass down on the desk, and finds himself face to face with her intent gaze*]. I beg your pardon. I thought I was alone.

JENNIFER [*controlling herself, and speaking steadily and meaningly*] I am glad we have met, Sir Colenso Ridgeon. I met Dr Blenkinsop yesterday. I congratulate you on a wonderful cure.

RIDGEON [*can find no words: makes an embarrassed gesture of assent after a moment's silence, and puts down the glass and the Secretary's list on the table*].

JENNIFER. He looked the picture of health and strength and prosperity. [*She looks for a moment at the walls, contrasting Blenkinsop's fortune with the artist's fate*].

RIDGEON [*in low tones, still embarrassed*] He has been fortunate.

JENNIFER. V e r y fortunate. His life has been spared.

RIDGEON. I mean that he has been made a Medical Officer of Health. He cured the Chairman of the Borough Council very successfully.

JENNIFER. With y o u r medicines?

RIDGEON. No. I believe it was with a pound of ripe greengages.

JENNIFER [*with deep gravity*] Funny!

RIDGEON. Yes. Life does not cease to be funny when people die any more than it ceases to be serious when people laugh.

JENNIFER. Dr Blenkinsop said one very strange thing to me.

RIDGEON. What was that?

JENNIFER. He said that private practice in medicine ought to be put down by law. When I asked him why, he said that private doctors were ignorant licensed murderers.

RIDGEON. That is what the public doctor always thinks of the private doctor. Well, Blenkinsop ought to know. He was a private doctor long enough himself. Come! you have talked at me long enough. Talk to me. You have something to reproach me with. There is reproach in your face, in your voice: you are full of it. Out with it.

JENNIFER. It is too late for reproaches now. When I turned and saw you just now, I wondered how you could come here coolly to look at his pictures. You answered the question. To you, he was only a clever brute.

RIDGEON [*quivering*] Oh, dont. You know I did not know you were here.

JENNIFER [*raising her head a little with a quite gentle impulse of pride*] You think it only mattered because I heard it. As if it could touch me, or touch him! Dont you see that what is really dreadful is that to you living things have no souls.

RIDGEON [*with a sceptical shrug*] The soul is an organ I have not come across in the course of my anatomical work.

JENNIFER. You know you would not dare to say such a silly thing as that to anybody but a woman whose mind you despise. If you dissected me you could not find my conscience. Do you think I have got none?

RIDGEON. I have met people who had none.

JENNIFER. Clever brutes? Do you know, doctor, that some of the dearest and most faithful friends I ever had were only brutes! You would have vivisected them. The dearest and greatest of all my friends had a sort of beauty and affectionateness that only animals have. I hope you may never feel what I felt when I had to put him into the hands of men who defend the torture of animals because they are only brutes.

RIDGEON. Well, did you find us so very cruel, after all? They tell me that though you have dropped me, you stay for weeks with the Bloomfield Boningtons and the Walpoles. I think it must be true, because they never mention you to me now.

THE DOCTOR'S DILEMMA

JENNIFER. The animals in Sir Ralph's house are like spoiled children. When Mr Walpole had to take a splinter out of the mastiff's paw, I had to hold the poor dog myself; and Mr Walpole had to turn Sir Ralph out of the room. And Mrs Walpole has to tell the gardener not to kill wasps when Mr Walpole is looking. But there are doctors who are naturally cruel; and there are others who get used to cruelty and are callous about it. They blind themselves to the souls of animals; and that blinds them to the souls of men and women. You made a dreadful mistake about Louis; but you would not have made it if you had not trained yourself to make the same mistake about dogs. You saw nothing in them but dumb brutes; and so you could see nothing in him but a clever brute.

RIDGEON [*with sudden resolution*] I made no mistake whatever about him.

JENNIFER. Oh, doctor!

RIDGEON [*obstinately*] I made no mistake whatever about him.

JENNIFER. Have you forgotten that he died?

RIDGEON [*with a sweep of his hand towards the pictures*] He is not dead. He is there. [*Taking up the book*] And there.

JENNIFER. [*springing up with blazing eyes*] Put that down. How dare you touch it?

Ridgeon, amazed at the fierceness of the outburst, puts it down with a deprecatory shrug. She takes it up and looks at it as if he had profaned a relic.

RIDGEON. I am very sorry. I see I had better go.

JENNIFER [*putting the book down*] I beg your pardon. I—I forgot myself. But it is not yet—it is a private copy.

RIDGEON. But for me it would have been a very different book.

JENNIFER. But for you it would have been a longer one.

RIDGEON. You know then that I killed him?

JENNIFER [*suddenly moved and softened*] Oh, doctor, if you acknowledge that—if you have confessed it to your-

183

self—if you realize what you have done, then there is forgiveness. I trusted in your strength instinctively at first; then I thought I had mistaken callousness for strength. Can you blame me? But if it was really strength—if it was only such a mistake as we all make sometimes—it will make me so happy to be friends with you again.

RIDGEON. I tell you I made no mistake. I cured Blenkinsop: was there any mistake there?

JENNIFER. He recovered. Oh, dont be foolishly proud, doctor. Confess to a failure, and save our friendship. Remember, Sir Ralph gave Louis your medicine; and it made him worse.

RIDGEON. I cant be your friend on false pretences. Something has got me by the throat: the truth must come out. I used that medicine myself on Blenkinsop. It did not make him worse. It is a dangerous medicine: it cured Blenkinsop: it killed Louis Dubedat. When I handle it, it cures. When another man handles it, it kills—sometimes.

JENNIFER [naïvely: not yet taking it all in] Then why did you let Sir Ralph give it to Louis?

RIDGEON. I'm going to tell you. I did it because I was in love with you.

JENNIFER [innocently surprised] In lo— You! an elderly man!

RIDGEON [thunderstruck, raising his fists to heaven] Dubedat: thou art avenged! [He drops his hands and collapses on the bench]. I never thought of that. I suppose I appear to you a ridiculous old fogey.

JENNIFER. But surely—I did not mean to offend you, indeed—but you must be at least twenty years older than I am.

RIDGEON. Oh, quite. More, perhaps. In twenty years you will understand how little difference that makes.

JENNIFER. But even so, how could you think that I— his wife—could ever think of y o u—

RIDGEON [stopping her with a nervous waving of his

184

fingers] Yes, yes, yes, yes: I quite understand: you neednt rub it in.

JENNIFER. But—oh, it is only dawning on me now— I was so surprised at first—do you dare to tell me that it was to gratify a miserable jealousy that you deliberately— oh! oh! you murdered him.

RIDGEON. I think I did. It really comes to that.

> Thou shalt not kill, but needst not strive
> Officiously to keep alive.

I suppose—yes: I killed him.

JENNIFER. And you tell me that! to my face! callously! You are not afraid!

RIDGEON. I am a doctor: I have nothing to fear. It is not an indictable offence to call in B. B. Perhaps it ought to be; but it isnt.

JENNIFER. I did not mean that. I meant afraid of my taking the law into my own hands, and killing you.

RIDGEON. I am so hopelessly idiotic about you that I should not mind it a bit. You would always remember me if you did that.

JENNIFER. I shall remember you always as a little man who tried to kill a great one.

RIDGEON. Pardon me. I succeeded.

JENNIFER [*with quiet conviction*] No. Doctors think they hold the keys of life and death; but it is not their will that is fulfilled. I dont believe you made any difference at all.

RIDGEON. Perhaps not. But I intended to.

JENNIFER [*looking at him amazedly: not without pity*] And you tried to destroy that wonderful and beautiful life merely because you grudged him a woman whom you could never have expected to care for you!

RIDGEON. Who kissed my hands. Who believed in me. Who told me her friendship lasted until death.

JENNIFER. And whom you were betraying.

185

RIDGEON. No. Whom I was saving.

JENNIFER [*gently*] Pray, doctor, from what?

RIDGEON. From making a terrible discovery. From having your life laid waste.

JENNIFER. How?

RIDGEON. No matter. I h a v e saved you. I have been the best friend you ever had. You are happy. You are well. His works are an imperishable joy and pride for you.

JENNIFER. And you think that is y o u r doing. Oh doctor, doctor! Sir Patrick is right: you do think you are a little god. How can you be so silly? Y o u did not paint those pictures which are my imperishable joy and pride: y o u did not speak the words that will always be heavenly music in my ears. I listen to them now whenever I am tired or sad. That is why I am always happy.

RIDGEON. Yes, now that he is dead. Were you always happy when he was alive?

JENNIFER [*wounded*] Oh, you are cruel, cruel. When he was alive I did not know the greatness of my blessing. I worried meanly about little things. I was unkind to him. I was unworthy of him.

RIDGEON [*laughing bitterly*] Ha!

JENNIFER. Dont insult me: dont blaspheme. [*She snatches up the book and presses it to her heart in a paroxysm of remorse, exclaiming*] Oh, my King of Men!

RIDGEON. King of Men! Oh, this is too monstrous, too grotesque. We cruel doctors have kept the secret from you faithfully; but it is like all secrets: it will not keep itself. The buried truth germinates and breaks through to the light.

JENNIFER. What truth?

RIDGEON. What truth! Why, that Louis Dubedat, King of Men, was the most entire and perfect scoundrel, the most miraculously mean rascal, the most callously selfish blackguard that ever made a wife miserable.

JENNIFER [*unshaken: calm and lovely*] He made his wife the happiest woman in the world, doctor.

186

THE DOCTOR'S DILEMMA

RIDGEON. No: by all thats true on earth, he made his
w i d o w the happiest woman in the world; but it was I
who made her a widow. And her happiness is my justification and my reward. Now you know what I did and what
I thought of him. Be as angry with me as you like: at least
you know me as I really am. If you ever come to care for
an elderly man, you will know what you are caring for.

JENNIFER [*kind and quiet*] I am not angry with you any
more, Sir Colenso. I knew quite well that you did not like
Louis; but it is not your fault: you dont understand: that
is all. You never could have believed in him. It is just like
your not believing in my religion: it is a sort of sixth sense
that you have not got. And [*with a gentle reassuring movement towards him*] dont think that you have shocked me
so dreadfully. I know quite well what you mean by his
selfishness. He sacrificed everything for his art. In a certain
sense he had even to sacrifice everybody—

RIDGEON. Everybody except himself. By keeping that
back he lost the right to sacrifice you, and gave me the
right to sacrifice him. Which I did.

JENNIFER [*shaking her head, pitying his error*] He was
one of the men who know what women know: that self-
sacrifice is vain and cowardly.

RIDGEON. Yes, when the sacrifice is rejected and thrown
away. Not when it becomes the food of godhead.

JENNIFER. I dont understand that. And I cant argue
with you: you are clever enough to puzzle me, but not to
shake me. You are so utterly, so wildly wrong; so incapable
of appreciating Louis—

RIDGEON. Oh! [*taking up the Secretary's list*] I have
marked five pictures as sold to me.

JENNIFER. They will not be sold to you. Louis' creditors
insisted on selling them; but this is my birthday; and they
were all bought in for me this morning by my husband.

RIDGEON. By whom? ! ! !

JENNIFER. By my husband.

RIDGEON [*gabbling and stuttering*] What husband?

187

THE DOCTOR'S DILEMMA

Whose husband? Which husband? Whom? how? what? Do you mean to say that you have married again?

JENNIFER. Do you forget that Louis disliked widows, and that people who have married happily once always marry again?

RIDGEON. Then I have committed a purely disinterested murder!

The Secretary returns with a pile of catalogues.

THE SECRETARY. Just got the first batch of catalogues in time. The doors are open.

JENNIFER [*to Ridgeon, politely*] So glad you like the pictures, Sir Colenso. Good morning.

RIDGEON. Good morning. [*He goes towards the door; hesitates; turns to say something more; gives it up as a bad job; and goes*].

PYGMALION

A ROMANCE IN FIVE ACTS

1912

PREFACE TO PYGMALION
A PROFESSOR OF PHONETICS

AS will be seen later on, Pygmalion needs, not a preface, but a sequel, which I have supplied in its due place. The English have no respect for their language, and will not teach their children to speak it. They spell it so abominably that no man can teach himself what it sounds like. It is impossible for an Englishman to open his mouth without making some other Englishman hate or despise him. German and Spanish are accessible to foreigners: English is not accessible even to Englishmen. The reformer England needs today is an energetic phonetic enthusiast: that is why I have made such a one the hero of a popular play. There have been heroes of that kind crying in the wilderness for many years past. When I became interested in the subject towards the end of the eighteen-seventies, the illustrious Alexander Melville Bell, the inventor of Visible Speech, had emigrated to Canada, where his son invented the telephone; but Alexander J. Ellis was still a London patriarch, with an impressive head always covered by a velvet skull cap, for which he would apologize to public meetings in a very courtly manner. He and Tito Pagliardini, another phonetic veteran, were men whom it was impossible to dislike. Henry Sweet, then a young man, lacked their sweetness of character: he was about as conciliatory to conventional mortals as Ibsen or Samuel Butler. His great ability as a phonetician (he was, I think, the best of them all at his job) would have entitled him to high official recognition, and perhaps enabled him to popularize his subject, but for his Satanic contempt for all academic dignitaries and persons in general who thought more of Greek than of phonetics. Once, in the days when the Imperial Institute rose in South Kensington, and Joseph Chamberlain was booming the Empire, I induced the editor of a leading monthly review to commission an article from Sweet on the imperial importance of his subject. When it arrived, it contained nothing but a savagely derisive attack on a professor

191

of language and literature whose chair Sweet regarded as proper to a phonetic expert only. The article, being libellous, had to be returned as impossible; and I had to renounce my dream of dragging its author into the limelight. When I met him afterwards, for the first time for many years, I found to my astonishment that he, who had been a quite tolerably presentable young man, had actually managed by sheer scorn to alter his personal appearance until he had become a sort of walking repudiation of Oxford and all its traditions. It must have been largely in his own despite that he was squeezed into something called a Readership of phonetics there. The future of phonetics rests probably with his pupils, who all swore by him; but nothing could bring the man himself into any sort of compliance with the university to which he nevertheless clung by divine right in an intensely Oxonian way. I daresay his papers, if he has left any, include some satires that may be published without too destructive results fifty years hence. He was, I believe, not in the least an illnatured man: very much the opposite, I should say; but he would not suffer fools gladly.

Those who knew him will recognize in my third act the allusion to the patent shorthand in which he used to write postcards, and which may be acquired from a four and six-penny manual published by the Clarendon Press. The post-cards which Mrs Higgins describes are such as I have received from Sweet. I would decipher a sound which a cockney would represent by *zerr*, and a Frenchman by *seu*, and then write demanding with some heat what on earth it meant. Sweet, with boundless contempt for my stupidity, would reply that it not only meant but obviously was the word Result, as no other word containing that sound, and capable of making sense with the context, existed in any language spoken on earth. That less expert mortals should require fuller indications was beyond Sweet's patience. Therefore, though the whole point of his Current Short-hand is that it can express every sound in the language perfectly, vowels as well as consonants, and that your hand has to make no stroke except the easy and current ones with which you write m, n, and u, l, p, and q, scribbling them at whatever angle comes easiest to you, his unfortunate determination to make this remarkable and quite legible script serve also as a shorthand reduced it in his own practice to the most inscrutable of cryptograms. His true objective was the provision of a full, accurate, legible script for our noble but ill-dressed language; but he was led past that by his contempt for the popular Pitman system of shorthand, which he called the Pitfall system. The triumph of Pitman was a triumph of business organization: there was a weekly paper to persuade you to learn Pitman: there were cheap textbooks and exercise books and transcripts of speeches for you to copy, and schools where experienced teachers coached you up to the necessary proficiency. Sweet could not organize his market in that fashion. He might as well have been the Sybil who tore up the leaves of prophecy that nobody would attend to. The four and sixpenny manual, mostly in his lithographed handwriting, that was never vulgarly advertized, may perhaps some day be taken up by a syndicate and pushed upon the public as The Times pushed the Encyclopædia Britannica; but until then it will certainly not prevail against Pitman. I have bought three copies of it during my lifetime; and I am informed by the publishers that its cloistered existence is still a steady and healthy one. I actually learned the system two several times; and yet the shorthand in which I am writing these lines is Pitman's. And the reason is, that my secretary cannot transcribe Sweet, having been perforce taught in the schools of Pitman. Therefore, Sweet railed at Pitman as vainly as Thersites railed at Ajax: his raillery, however it may have eased his soul, gave no popular vogue to Current Shorthand.

Pygmalion Higgins is not a portrait of Sweet, to whom the adventure of Eliza Doolittle would have been impossible; still, as will be seen, there are touches of Sweet in the play. With Higgins's physique and temperament Sweet might have set the Thames on fire. As it was, he impressed himself professionally on Europe to an extent that made his comparative personal obscurity, and the failure of Oxford to do justice to his eminence, a puzzle to foreign specialists in his subject. I do not blame Oxford, because I think Oxford is quite right in demanding a certain social amenity from its nurslings (heaven knows it is not exorbitant in its requirements!); for although I well know how hard it is for a man of genius with a seriously underrated subject to maintain serene and kindly relations with the men who underrate it, and who keep all the best places for less important subjects which they profess without originality and sometimes without much capacity for them, still, if he overwhelms them with wrath and disdain, he cannot expect them to heap honors on him.

Of the later generations of phoneticians I know little. Among them towers the Poet Laureate, to whom perhaps Higgins may owe his Miltonic sympathies, though here again I must disclaim all portraiture. But if the play makes the public aware that there are such people as phoneticians, and that they are among the most important people in England at present, it will serve its turn.

I wish to boast that Pygmalion has been an extremely successful play all over Europe and North America as well as at home. It is so intensely and deliberately didactic, and its subject is esteemed so dry, that I delight in throwing it at the heads of the wiseacres who repeat the parrot cry that art should never be didactic. It goes to prove my contention that art should never be anything else.

Finally, and for the encouragement of people troubled with accents that cut them off from all high employment, I may add that the change wrought by Professor Higgins in the flower-girl is neither impossible nor uncommon. The modern concierge's daughter who fulfils her ambition by playing the Queen of Spain in Ruy Blas at the Théâtre Français is only one of many thousands of men and women who have sloughed off their native dialects and acquired a new tongue. But the thing has to be done scientifically, or

194

the last state of the aspirant may be worse than the first. An honest and natural slum dialect is more tolerable than the attempt of a phonetically untaught person to imitate the vulgar dialect of the golf club; and I am sorry to say that in spite of the efforts of our Royal Academy of Dramatic Art, there is still too much sham golfing English on our stage, and too little of the noble English of Forbes Robertson.

PYGMALION

ACT I

COVENT *Garden at 11.15 p.m. Torrents of heavy summer rain. Cab whistles blowing frantically in all directions. Pedestrians running for shelter into the market and under the portico of St Paul's Church, where there are already several people, among them a lady and her daughter in evening dress. They are all peering out gloomily at the rain, except one man with his back turned to the rest, who seems wholly preoccupied with a notebook in which he is writing busily.*

The church clock strikes the first quarter.

THE DAUGHTER [*in the space between the central pillars, close to the one on her left*] I'm getting chilled to the bone. What can Freddy be doing all this time? He's been gone twenty minutes.

THE MOTHER [*on her daughter's right*] Not so long. But he ought to have got us a cab by this.

A BYSTANDER [*on the lady's right*] He wont get no cab not until half-past eleven, missus, when they come back after dropping their theatre fares.

THE MOTHER. But we must have a cab. We cant stand here until half-past eleven. It's too bad.

THE BYSTANDER. Well, it aint my fault, missus.

THE DAUGHTER. If Freddy had a bit of gumption, he would have got one at the theatre door.

THE MOTHER. What could he have done, poor boy?

THE DAUGHTER. Other people got cabs. Why couldnt he?

Freddy rushes in out of the rain from the Southampton Street side, and comes between them closing a dripping umbrella. He is a young man of twenty, in evening dress, very wet round the ankles.

THE DAUGHTER. Well, havnt you got a cab?

FREDDY. Theres not one to be had for love or money.

THE MOTHER. Oh, Freddy, there must be one. You cant have tried.

THE DAUGHTER. It's too tiresome. Do you expect us to go and get one ourselves?

FREDDY. I tell you theyre all engaged. The rain was so

sudden: nobody was prepared; and everybody had to take a cab. Ive been to Charing Cross one way and nearly to Ludgate Circus the other; and they were all engaged.

THE MOTHER. Did you try Trafalgar Square?

FREDDY. There wasnt one at Trafalgar Square.

THE DAUGHTER. Did you try?

FREDDY. I tried as far as Charing Cross Station. Did you expect me to walk to Hammersmith?

THE DAUGHTER. You havnt tried at all.

THE MOTHER. You really are very helpless, Freddy. Go again; and dont come back until you have found a cab.

FREDDY. I shall simply get soaked for nothing.

THE DAUGHTER. And what about us? Are we to stay here all night in this draught, with next to nothing on? You selfish pig——

FREDDY. Oh, very well: I'll go, I'll go. [*He opens his umbrella and dashes off Strandwards, but comes into collision with a flower girl, who is hurrying in for shelter, knocking her basket out of her hands. A blinding flash of lightning, followed instantly by a rattling peal of thunder, orchestrates the incident*].

THE FLOWER GIRL. Nah then, Freddy: look wh' y' gowin, deah.

FREDDY. Sorry [*he rushes off*].

THE FLOWER GIRL [*picking up her scattered flowers and replacing them in the basket*] Theres menners f' yer! Te-oo banches o voylets trod into the mad. [*She sits down on the plinth of the column, sorting her flowers, on the lady's right. She is not at all an attractive person. She is perhaps eighteen, perhaps twenty, hardly older. She wears a little sailor hat of black straw that has long been exposed to the dust and soot of London and has seldom if ever been brushed. Her hair needs washing rather badly: its mousy color can hardly be natural. She wears a shoddy black coat that reaches nearly to her knees and is shaped to her waist. She has a brown skirt with a coarse apron. Her boots are much the worse for wear. She is no doubt as clean as she can afford to be; but compared to the ladies she is very dirty. Her features are no worse than theirs; but their condition leaves some-*]

198

PYGMALION

thing to be desired; and she needs the services of a dentist].

THE MOTHER. How do you know that my son's name is Freddy, pray?

THE FLOWER GIRL. Ow, eez ye-ooa san, is e? Wal, fewd dan y' de-ooty bawmz a mather should, eed now bettern to spawl a pore gel's flahrzn than ran awy athaht pyin. Will ye-oo py me f'them? [*Here, with apologies, this desperate attempt to represent her dialect without a phonetic alphabet must be abandoned as unintelligible outside London*].

THE DAUGHTER. Do nothing of the sort, mother. The idea!

THE MOTHER. Please allow me, Clara. Have you any pennies?

THE DAUGHTER. No. Ive nothing smaller than sixpence.

THE FLOWER GIRL [*hopefully*] I can give you change for a tanner, kind lady.

THE MOTHER [*to Clara*] Give it to me. [*Clara parts reluctantly*]. Now [*to the girl*] this is for your flowers.

THE FLOWER GIRL. Thank you kindly, lady.

THE DAUGHTER. Make her give you the change. These things are only a penny a bunch.

THE MOTHER. Do hold your tongue, Clara. [*To the girl*] You can keep the change.

THE FLOWER GIRL. Oh, thank you, lady.

THE MOTHER. Now tell me how you know that young gentleman's name.

THE FLOWER GIRL. I didnt.

THE MOTHER. I heard you call him by it. Dont try to deceive me.

THE FLOWER GIRL [*protesting*] Who's trying to deceive you? I called him Freddy or Charlie same as you might yourself if you was talking to a stranger and wished to be pleasant. [*She sits down beside her basket*].

THE DAUGHTER. Sixpence thrown away! Really, mamma, you might have spared Freddy that. [*She retreats in disgust behind the pillar*].

An elderly gentleman of the amiable military type rushes into

199

the shelter, and closes a dripping umbrella. He is in the same plight as Freddy, very wet about the ankles. He is in evening dress, with a light overcoat. He takes the place left vacant by the daughter's retirement.

THE GENTLEMAN. Phew!

THE MOTHER [*to the gentleman*] Oh, sir, is there any sign of its stopping?

THE GENTLEMAN. I'm afraid not. It started worse than ever about two minutes ago [*he goes to the plinth beside the flower girl; puts up his foot on it; and stoops to turn down his trouser ends*].

THE MOTHER. Oh dear! [*She retires sadly and joins her daughter*].

THE FLOWER GIRL [*taking advantage of the military gentleman's proximity to establish friendly relations with him*] If it's worse, it's a sign it's nearly over. So cheer up, Captain; and buy a flower off a poor girl.

THE GENTLEMAN. I'm sorry. I havnt any change.

THE FLOWER GIRL. I can give you change, Captain.

THE GENTLEMAN. For a sovereign? Ive nothing less.

THE FLOWER GIRL. Garn! Oh do buy a flower off me, Captain. I can change half-a-crown. Take this for tuppence.

THE GENTLEMAN. Now dont be troublesome: theres a good girl. [*Trying his pockets*] I really havnt any change— Stop: heres three hapence, if thats any use to you [*he retreats to the other pillar*].

THE FLOWER GIRL [*disappointed, but thinking three half-pence better than nothing*] Thank you, sir.

THE BYSTANDER [*to the girl*] You be careful: give him a flower for it. Theres a bloke here behind taking down every blessed word youre saying. [*All turn to the man who is taking notes*].

THE FLOWER GIRL [*springing up terrified*] I aint done nothing wrong by speaking to the gentleman. Ive a right to sell flowers if I keep off the kerb. [*Hysterically*] I'm a respectable girl: so help me, I never spoke to him except to ask him to buy a flower off me. [*General hubbub, mostly sympathetic to*

PYGMALION

the flower girl, but deprecating her excessive sensibility. Cries of Dont start hollerin. Who's hurting you? Nobody's going to touch you. Whats the good of fussing? Steady on. Easy easy, etc., *come from the elderly staid spectators, who pat her comfortingly. Less patient ones bid her shut her head, or ask her roughly what is wrong with her. A remoter group, not knowing what the matter is, crowd in and increase the noise with question and answer:* Whats the row? Whatshe do? Where is he? A tec taking her down. What! him? Yes: him over there: Took money off the gentleman, etc. *The flower girl, distraught and mobbed, breaks through them to the gentleman, crying wildly*] Oh, sir, dont let him charge me. You dunno what it means to me. Theyll take away my character and drive me on the streets for speaking to gentlemen. They—

THE NOTE TAKER [*coming forward on her right, the rest crowding after him*] There, there, there, there! who's hurting you, you silly girl? What do you take me for?

THE BYSTANDER. It's all right: he's a gentleman: look at his boots. [*Explaining to the note taker*] She thought you was a copper's nark, sir.

THE NOTE TAKER [*with quick interest*] Whats a copper's nark?

THE BYSTANDER [*inapt at definition*] It's a—well, it's a copper's nark, as you might say. What else would you call it? A sort of informer.

THE FLOWER GIRL [*still hysterical*] I take my Bible oath I never said a word—

THE NOTE TAKER [*overbearing but good-humored*] Oh, shut up, shut up. Do I look like a policeman?

THE FLOWER GIRL [*far from reassured*] Then what did you take down my words for? How do I know whether you took me down right? You just shew me what youve wrote about me. [*The note taker opens his book and holds it steadily under her nose, though the pressure of the mob trying to read it over his shoulders would upset a weaker man*]. Whats that? That aint proper writing. I cant read that.

THE NOTE TAKER. I can. [*Reads, reproducing her pronuncia-*

tion exactly] "Cheer ap, Keptin; n' baw ya flahr orf a pore gel."

THE FLOWER GIRL [*much distressed*] It's because I called him Captain. I meant no harm. [*To the gentleman*] Oh, sir, dont let him lay a charge agen me for a word like that. You—

THE GENTLEMAN. Charge! I make no charge. [*To the note taker*] Really, sir, if you are a detective, you need not begin protecting me against molestation by young women until I ask you. Anybody could see that the girl meant no harm.

THE BYSTANDERS GENERALLY [*demonstrating against police espionage*] Course they could. What business is it of yours? You mind your own affairs. He wants promotion, he does. Taking down people's words! Girl never said a word to him. What harm if she did? Nice thing a girl cant shelter from the rain without being insulted, etc., etc., etc. [*She is conducted by the more sympathetic demonstrators back to her plinth, where she resumes her seat and struggles with her emotion*].

THE BYSTANDER. He aint a tec. He's a blooming busy-body: thats what he is. I tell you, look at his boots.

THE NOTE TAKER [*turning on him genially*] And how are all your people down at Selsey?

THE BYSTANDER [*suspiciously*] Who told you my people come from Selsey?

THE NOTE TAKER. Never you mind. They did. [*To the girl*] How do you come to be up so far east? You were born in Lisson Grove.

THE FLOWER GIRL [*appalled*] Oh, what harm is there in my leaving Lisson Grove? It wasnt fit for a pig to live in; and I had to pay four-and-six a week. [*In tears*] Oh, boo—hoo—oo—

THE NOTE TAKER. Live where you like; but stop that noise.

THE GENTLEMAN [*to the girl*] Come, come! he cant touch you: you have a right to live where you please.

A SARCASTIC BYSTANDER [*thrusting himself between the note taker and the gentleman*] Park Lane, for instance. I'd like to go into the Housing Question with you, I would.

THE FLOWER GIRL [*subsiding into a brooding melancholy over her basket, and talking very low-spiritedly to herself*] I'm a good girl, I am.

THE SARCASTIC BYSTANDER [*not attending to her*] Do you know where *I* come from?

THE NOTE TAKER [*promptly*] Hoxton.

Titterings. Popular interest in the note taker's performance increases.

THE SARCASTIC ONE [*amazed*] Well, who said I didnt? Bly me! You know everything, you do.

THE FLOWER GIRL [*still nursing her sense of injury*] Aint no call to meddle with me, he aint.

THE BYSTANDER [*to her*] Of course he aint. Dont you stand it from him. [*To the note taker*] See here: what call have you to know about people what never offered to meddle with you? Wheres your warrant?

SEVERAL BYSTANDERS [*encouraged by this seeming point of law*] Yes: wheres your warrant?

THE FLOWER GIRL. Let him say what he likes. I dont want to have no truck with him.

THE BYSTANDER. You take us for dirt under your feet, dont you? Catch you taking liberties with a gentleman!

THE SARCASTIC BYSTANDER. Yes: tell him where he come from if you want to go fortune-telling.

THE NOTE TAKER. Cheltenham, Harrow, Cambridge, and India.

THE GENTLEMAN. Quite right. [*Great laughter. Reaction in the note taker's favor. Exclamations of* He knows all about it. Told him proper. Hear him tell the toff where he come from? *etc.*]. May I ask, sir, do you do this for your living at a music hall?

THE NOTE TAKER. Ive thought of that. Perhaps I shall some day.

The rain has stopped; and the persons on the outside of the crowd begin to drop off.

THE FLOWER GIRL [*resenting the reaction*] He's no gentleman, he aint, to interfere with a poor girl.

THE DAUGHTER [*out of patience, pushing her way rudely to the front and displacing the gentleman, who politely retires to the other side of the pillar*] What on earth is Freddy doing? I shall get pneumonia if I stay in this draught any longer.

THE NOTE TAKER [*to himself, hastily making a note of her pronunciation of "monia"*] Earlscourt.

THE DAUGHTER [*violently*] Will you please keep your impertinent remarks to yourself.

THE NOTE TAKER. Did I say that out loud? I didnt mean to. I beg your pardon. Your mother's Epsom, unmistakeably.

THE MOTHER [*advancing between her daughter and the note taker*] How very curious! I was brought up in Largelady Park, near Epsom.

THE NOTE TAKER [*uproariously amused*] Ha! ha! What a devil of a name! Excuse me. [*To the daughter*] You want a cab, do you?

THE DAUGHTER. Dont dare speak to me.

THE MOTHER. Oh please, please, Clara. [*Her daughter repudiates her with an angry shrug and retires haughtily*]. We should be so grateful to you, sir, if you found us a cab. [*The note taker produces a whistle*]. Oh, thank you. [*She joins her daughter*].

The note taker blows a piercing blast.

THE SARCASTIC BYSTANDER. There! I knowed he was a plain-clothes copper.

THE BYSTANDER. That aint a police whistle: thats a sporting whistle.

THE FLOWER GIRL [*still preoccupied with her wounded feelings*] He's no right to take away my character. My character is the same to me as any lady's.

THE NOTE TAKER. I dont know whether youve noticed it; but the rain stopped about two minutes ago.

THE BYSTANDER. So it has. Why didnt you say so before? and us losing our time listening to your silliness! [*He walks off towards the Strand*].

THE SARCASTIC BYSTANDER. I can tell where y o u come from. You come from Anwell. Go back there.

THE NOTE TAKER [*helpfully*] *H*anwell.

THE SARCASTIC BYSTANDER [*affecting great distinction of speech*] Thenk you, teacher. Haw haw! So long [*he touches his hat with mock respect and strolls off*].

THE FLOWER GIRL. Frightening people like that! How would he like it himself?

THE MOTHER. It's quite fine now, Clara. We can walk to a motor bus. Come. [*She gathers her skirts above her ankles and hurries off towards the Strand*].

THE DAUGHTER. But the cab—[*her mother is out of hearing*]. Oh, how tiresome! [*She follows angrily*].

All the rest have gone except the note taker, the gentleman, and the flower girl, who sits arranging her basket and still pitying herself in murmurs.

THE FLOWER GIRL. Poor girl! Hard enough for her to live without being worrited and chivied.

THE GENTLEMAN [*returning to his former place on the note taker's left*] How do you do it, if I may ask?

THE NOTE TAKER. Simply phonetics. The science of speech. Thats my profession: also my hobby. Happy is the man who can make a living by his hobby! Y o u can spot an Irishman or a Yorkshireman by his brogue. *I* can place any man within six miles. I can place him within two miles in London. Sometimes within two streets.

THE FLOWER GIRL. Ought to be ashamed of himself, unmanly coward!

THE GENTLEMAN. But is there a living in that?

THE NOTE TAKER. Oh yes. Quite a fat one. This is an age of upstarts. Men begin in Kentish Town with £80 a year, and end in Park Lane with a hundred thousand. They want to drop Kentish Town; but they give themselves away every time they open their mouths. Now I can teach them—

THE FLOWER GIRL. Let him mind his own business and leave a poor girl—

THE NOTE TAKER [*explosively*] Woman: cease this detest-

PYGMALION

able boohooing instantly; or else seek the shelter of some other place of worship.

THE FLOWER GIRL [*with feeble defiance*] Ive a right to be here if I like, same as you.

THE NOTE TAKER. A woman who utters such depressing and disgusting sounds has no right to be anywhere—no right to live. Remember that you are a human being with a soul and the divine gift of articulate speech: that your native language is the language of Shakespear and Milton and The Bible: and dont sit there crooning like a bilious pigeon.

THE FLOWER GIRL [*quite overwhelmed, looking up at him in mingled wonder and deprecation without daring to raise her head*] Ah-ah-ah-ow-ow-ow-oo!

THE NOTE TAKER [*whipping out his book*] Heavens! what a sound! [*He writes; then holds out the book and reads, reproducing her vowels exactly*] Ah-ah-ah-ow-ow-ow-oo!

THE FLOWER GIRL [*tickled by the performance, and laughing in spite of herself*] Garn!

THE NOTE TAKER. You see this creature with her kerbstone English: the English that will keep her in the gutter to the end of her days. Well, sir, in three months I could pass that girl off as a duchess at an ambassador's garden party. I could even get her a place as lady's maid or shop assistant, which requires better English. Thats the sort of thing I do for commercial millionaires. And on the profits of it I do genuine scientific work in phonetics, and a little as a poet on Miltonic lines.

THE GENTLEMAN. I am myself a student of Indian dialects; and—

THE NOTE TAKER [*eagerly*] Are you? Do you know Colonel Pickering, the author of Spoken Sanscrit?

THE GENTLEMAN. I am Colonel Pickering. Who are you?

THE NOTE TAKER. Henry Higgins, author of Higgins's Universal Alphabet.

PICKERING [*with enthusiasm*] I came from India to meet you.

HIGGINS. I was going to India to meet you.

206

PICKERING. Where do you live?

HIGGINS. 27A Wimpole Street. Come and see me to-morrow.

PICKERING. I'm at the Carlton. Come with me now and lets have a jaw over some supper.

HIGGINS. Right you are.

THE FLOWER GIRL [*to Pickering, as he passes her*] Buy a flower, kind gentleman. I'm short for my lodging.

PICKERING. I really havnt any change. I'm sorry [*he goes away*].

HIGGINS [*shocked at the girl's mendacity*] Liar. You said you could change half-a-crown.

THE FLOWER GIRL [*rising in desperation*] You ought to be stuffed with nails, you ought. [*Flinging the basket at his feet*] Take the whole blooming basket for sixpence.

The church clock strikes the second quarter.

HIGGINS [*hearing in it the voice of God, rebuking him for his Pharisaic want of charity to the poor girl*] A reminder. [*He raises his hat solemnly; then throws a handful of money into the basket and follows Pickering*].

THE FLOWER GIRL [*picking up a half-crown*] Ah-ow-ooh! [*Picking up a couple of florins*] Aaah-ow-ooh! [*Picking up several coins*] Aaaaaah-ow-ooh! [*Picking up a half-sovereign*] Aaaaaaaaaaaah-ow-ooh!!!

FREDDY [*springing out of a taxicab*] Got one at last. Hallo! [*To the girl*] Where are the two ladies that were here?

THE FLOWER GIRL. They walked to the bus when the rain stopped.

FREDDY. And left me with a cab on my hands! Damnation!

THE FLOWER GIRL [*with grandeur*] Never mind, young man. I'm going home in a taxi. [*She sails off to the cab. The driver puts his hand behind him and holds the door firmly shut against her. Quite understanding his mistrust, she shews him her handful of money*]. Eightpence aint no object to me, Charlie. [*He grins and opens the door*]. Angel Court, Drury Lane, round the corner of Micklejohn's oil shop. Lets see how fast you can make her hop it. [*She gets in and pulls the door to with a slam as the taxicab starts*].

FREDDY. Well, I'm dashed!

ACT II

NEXT *day at* 11 *a.m. Higgins's laboratory in Wimpole Street. It is a room on the first floor, looking on the street, and was meant for the drawing room. The double doors are in the middle of the back wall; and persons entering find in the corner to their right two tall file cabinets at right angles to one another against the walls. In this corner stands a flat writing-table, on which are a phonograph, a laryngoscope, a row of tiny organ pipes with bellows, a set of lamp chimneys for singing flames with burners attached to a gas plug in the wall by an indiarubber tube, several tuning-forks of different sizes, a life-size image of half a human head, shewing in section the vocal organs, and a box containing a supply of wax cylinders for the phonograph.*

Further down the room, on the same side, is a fireplace, with a comfortable leather-covered easy-chair at the side of the hearth nearest the door, and a coal-scuttle. There is a clock on the mantel-piece. Between the fireplace and the phonograph table is a stand for newspapers.

On the other side of the central door, to the left of the visitor, is a cabinet of shallow drawers. On it is a telephone and the telephone directory. The corner beyond, and most of the side wall, is occupied by a grand piano, with the keyboard at the end furthest from the door, and a bench for the player extending the full length of the keyboard. On the piano is a dessert dish heaped with fruit and sweets, mostly chocolates.

The middle of the room is clear. Besides the easy-chair, the piano bench, and two chairs at the phonograph table, there is one stray chair. It stands near the fireplace. On the walls, engravings: mostly Piranesis and mezzotint portraits. No paintings.

Pickering is seated at the table, putting down some cards and a tuning-fork which he has been using. Higgins is standing up near him, closing two or three file drawers which are hanging out. He appears in the morning light as a robust, vital, appetizing sort of man of forty or thereabouts, dressed in a professional-looking black frock-coat with a white linen collar and black silk tie. He is of the energetic, scientific type, heartily, even violently

209

PYGMALION

interested in everything that can be studied as a scientific subject, and careless about himself and other people, including their feelings. He is, in fact, but for his years and size, rather like a very impetuous baby "taking notice" eagerly and loudly, and requiring almost as much watching to keep him out of unintended mischief. His manner varies from genial bullying when he is in a good humor to stormy petulance when anything goes wrong; but he is so entirely frank and void of malice that he remains likeable even in his least reasonable moments.

HIGGINS [*as he shuts the last drawer*] Well, I think thats the whole show.

PICKERING. It's really amazing. I havnt taken half of it in, you know.

HIGGINS. Would you like to go over any of it again?

PICKERING [*rising and coming to the fireplace, where he plants himself with his back to the fire*] No, thank you; not now. I'm quite done up for this morning.

HIGGINS [*following him, and standing beside him on his left*] Tired of listening to sounds?

PICKERING. Yes. It's a fearful strain. I rather fancied myself because I can pronounce twenty-four distinct vowel sounds; but your hundred and thirty beat me. I cant hear a bit of difference between most of them.

HIGGINS [*chuckling, and going over to the piano to eat sweets*] Oh, that comes with practice. You hear no difference at first; but you keep on listening, and presently you find theyre all as different as A from B. [*Mrs Pearce looks in: she is Higgins's housekeeper*]. Whats the matter?

MRS PEARCE [*hesitating, evidently perplexed*] A young woman wants to see you sir.

HIGGINS. A young woman! What does she want?

MRS PEARCE. Well, sir, she says youll be glad to see her when you know what she's come about. She's quite a common girl, sir. Very common indeed. I should have sent her away, only I thought perhaps you wanted her to talk into your machines. I hope Ive not done wrong; but really you see such queer people sometimes—youll excuse me, I'm sure, sir—

HIGGINS. Oh, thats all right, Mrs Pearce. Has she an interesting accent?

MRS PEARCE. Oh, something dreadful, sir, really. I dont know how you can take an interest in it.

HIGGINS [to Pickering] Lets have her up. Shew her up, Mrs Pearce [he rushes across to his working table and picks out a cylinder to use on the phonograph].

MRS PEARCE [only half resigned to it] Very well, sir. It's for you to say. [She goes downstairs].

HIGGINS. This is rather a bit of luck. I'll shew you how I make records. We'll set her talking; and I'll take it down first in Bell's visible Speech; then in broad Romic; and then we'll get her on the phonograph so that you can turn her on as often as you like with the written transcript before you.

MRS PEARCE [returning] This is the young woman, sir.

The flower girl enters in state. She has a hat with three ostrich feathers, orange, sky-blue, and red. She has a nearly clean apron, and the shoddy coat has been tidied a little. The pathos of this deplorable figure, with its innocent vanity and consequential air, touches Pickering, who has already straightened himself in the presence of Mrs Pearce. But as to Higgins, the only distinction he makes between men and women is that when he is neither bullying nor exclaiming to the heavens against some feather-weight cross, he coaxes women as a child coaxes its nurse when it wants to get anything out of her.

HIGGINS [brusquely, recognizing her with unconcealed disappointment, and at once, babylike, making an intolerable grievance of it] Why, this is the girl I jotted down last night. She's no use: Ive got all the records I want of the Lisson Grove lingo; and I'm not going to waste another cylinder on it. [To the girl] Be off with you: I dont want you.

THE FLOWER GIRL. Dont you be so saucy. You aint heard what I come for yet. [To Mrs Pearce, who is waiting at the door for further instructions] Did you tell him I come in a taxi?

MRS PEARCE. Nonsense, girl! what do you think a gentleman like Mr Higgins cares what you came in?

THE FLOWER GIRL. Oh, we are proud! He aint above giving lessons, not him: I heard him say so. Well, I aint come here to ask for any compliment; and if my money's not good enough I can go elsewhere.

HIGGINS. Good enough for what?

THE FLOWER GIRL. Good enough for ye-oo. Now you know, dont you? I'm come to have lessons, I am. And to pay for em too: make no mistake.

HIGGINS [*stupent*] Well!!! [*Recovering his breath with a gasp*] What do you expect me to say to you?

THE FLOWER GIRL. Well, if you was a gentleman, you might ask me to sit down, I think. Dont I tell you I'm bringing you business?

HIGGINS. Pickering: shall we ask this baggage to sit down, or shall we throw her out of the window?

THE FLOWER GIRL [*running away in terror to the piano, where she turns at bay*] Ah-ah-oh-ow-ow-ow-oo! [*Wounded and whimpering*] I wont be called a baggage when Ive offered to pay like any lady.

Motionless, the two men stare at her from the other side of the room, amazed.

PICKERING [*gently*] What is it you want, my girl?

THE FLOWER GIRL. I want to be a lady in a flower shop stead of selling at the corner of Tottenham Court Road. But they wont take me unless I can talk more genteel. He said he could teach me. Well, here I am ready to pay him— not asking any favor—and he treats me as if I was dirt.

MRS PEARCE. How can you be such a foolish ignorant girl as to think you could afford to pay Mr Higgins?

THE FLOWER GIRL. Why shouldnt I? I know what lessons cost as well as you do; and I'm ready to pay.

HIGGINS. How much?

THE FLOWER GIRL [*coming back to him, triumphant*] Now youre talking! I thought youd come off it when you saw a chance of getting back a bit of what you chucked at me last night. [*Confidentially*] Youd had a drop in, hadnt you?

PYGMALION

HIGGINS [*peremptorily*] Sit down.

THE FLOWER GIRL. Oh, if youre going to make a compliment of it—

HIGGINS [*thundering at her*] Sit down.

MRS PEARCE [*severely*] Sit down, girl. Do as youre told. [*She places the stray chair near the hearthrug between Higgins and Pickering, and stands behind it waiting for the girl to sit down*].

THE FLOWER GIRL. Ah-ah-ah-ow-ow-oo! [*She stands, half rebellious, half bewildered*].

PICKERING [*very courteous*] Wont you sit down?

LIZA [*coyly*] Dont mind if I do. [*She sits down. Pickering returns to the hearthrug*].

HIGGINS. Whats your name?

THE FLOWER GIRL. Liza Doolittle.

HIGGINS [*declaiming gravely*]

    Eliza, Elizabeth, Betsy and Bess,
    They went to the woods to get a bird's nes':

PICKERING. They found a nest with four eggs in it:

HIGGINS. They took one apiece, and left three in it.

They laugh heartily at their own wit.

LIZA. Oh, dont be silly.

MRS PEARCE. You mustnt speak to the gentleman like that.

LIZA. Well, why wont he speak sensible to me?

HIGGINS. Come back to business. How much do you propose to pay me for the lessons?

LIZA. Oh, I know whats right. A lady friend of mine gets French lessons for eighteenpence an hour from a real French gentleman. Well, you wouldnt have the face to ask me the same for teaching me my own language as you would for French; so I wont give more than a shilling. Take it or leave it.

HIGGINS [*walking up and down the room, rattling his keys and his cash in his pockets*] You know, Pickering, if you consider a shilling, not as a simple shilling, but as a percentage of this girl's income, it works out as fully equivalent to sixty

213

PYGMALION

or seventy guineas from a millionaire.

PICKERING. How so?

HIGGINS. Figure it out. A millionaire has about £150 a day. She earns about half-a-crown.

LIZA [*haughtily*] Who told you I only—

HIGGINS [*continuing*] She offers me two-fifths of her day's income for a lesson. Two-fifths of a millionaire's income for a day would be somewhere about £60. It's handsome. By George, it's enormous! it's the biggest offer I ever had.

LIZA [*rising, terrified*] Sixty pounds! What are you talking about? I never offered you sixty pounds. Where would I get—

HIGGINS. Hold your tongue.

LIZA [*weeping*] But I aint got sixty pounds. Oh—

MRS PEARCE. Dont cry, you silly girl. Sit down. Nobody is going to touch your money.

HIGGINS. Somebody is going to touch you, with a broomstick, if you dont stop snivelling. Sit down.

LIZA [*obeying slowly*] Ah-ah-ah-ow-oo-o! One would think you was my father.

HIGGINS. If I decide to teach you, I'll be worse than two fathers to you. Here [*he offers her his silk handkerchief*]!

LIZA. Whats this for?

HIGGINS. To wipe your eyes. To wipe any part of your face that feels moist. Remember: thats your handkerchief; and thats your sleeve. Dont mistake the one for the other if you wish to become a lady in a shop.

Liza, utterly bewildered, stares helplessly at him.

MRS PEARCE. It's no use talking to her like that, Mr Higgins: she doesnt understand you. Besides, youre quite wrong: she doesnt do it that way at all [*she takes the handkerchief*].

LIZA [*snatching it*] Here! You give me that handkerchief. He give it to me, not to you.

PICKERING [*laughing*] He did. I think it must be regarded as her property, Mrs Pearce.

MRS PEARCE [*resigning herself*] Serve you right, Mr

214

Higgins.

PICKERING. Higgins: I'm interested. What about the ambassador's garden party? I'll say youre the greatest teacher alive if you make that good. I'll bet you all the expenses of the experiment you cant do it. And I'll pay for the lessons.

LIZA. Oh, you are real good. Thank you, Captain.

HIGGINS [*tempted, looking at her*] It's almost irresistible. She's so deliciously low—so horribly dirty—

LIZA [*protesting extremely*] Ah-ah-ah-ah-ow-ow-oo-oo!!! I aint dirty: I washed my face and hands afore I come, I did.

PICKERING. Youre certainly not going to turn her head with flattery, Higgins.

MRS PEARCE [*uneasy*] Oh, dont say that, sir: theres more ways than one of turning a girl's head; and nobody can do it better than Mr Higgins, though he may not always mean it. I do hope, sir, you wont encourage him to do anything foolish.

HIGGINS [*becoming excited as the idea grows on him*] What is life but a series of inspired follies? The difficulty is to find them to do. Never lose a chance: it doesnt come every day. I shall make a duchess of this draggletailed guttersnipe.

LIZA [*strongly deprecating this view of her*] Ah-ah-ah-ow-ow-oo!

HIGGINS [*carried away*] Yes: in six months—in three if she has a good ear and a quick tongue—I'll take her anywhere and pass her off as anything. We'll start today: now! this moment! Take her away and clean her, Mrs Pearce. Monkey Brand, if it wont come off any other way. Is there a good fire in the kitchen?

MRS PEARCE [*protesting*] Yes; but—

HIGGINS [*storming on*] Take all her clothes off and burn them. Ring up Whiteley or somebody for new ones. Wrap her up in brown paper til they come.

LIZA. Youre no gentleman, youre not, to talk of such things. I'm a good girl, I am; and I know what the like of you are, I do.

HIGGINS. We want none of your Lisson Grove prudery here, young woman. Youve got to learn to behave like a duchess. Take her away, Mrs Pearce. If she gives you any trouble, wallop her.

LIZA [*springing up and running between Pickering and Mrs Pearce for protection*] No! I'll call the police, I will.

MRS PEARCE. But Ive no place to put her.

HIGGINS. Put her in the dustbin.

LIZA. Ah-ah-ah-ow-ow-oo!

PICKERING. Oh come, Higgins! be reasonable.

MRS PEARCE [*resolutely*] You must be reasonable, Mr Higgins: really you must. You cant walk over everybody like this.

Higgins, thus scolded, subsides. The hurricane is succeeded by a zephyr of amiable surprise.

HIGGINS [*with professional exquisiteness of modulation*] I walk over everybody! My dear Mrs Pearce, my dear Pickering, I never had the slightest intention of walking over anyone. All I propose is that we should be kind to this poor girl. We must help her to prepare and fit herself for her new station in life. If I did not express myself clearly it was because I did not wish to hurt her delicacy, or yours.

Liza, reassured, steals back to her chair.

MRS PEARCE [*to Pickering*] Well, did you ever hear anything like that, sir?

PICKERING [*laughing heartily*] Never, Mrs Pearce: never.

HIGGINS [*patiently*] Whats the matter?

MRS PEARCE. Well, the matter is, sir, that you cant take a girl up like that as if you were picking up a pebble on the beach.

HIGGINS. Why not?

MRS PEARCE. Why not! But you dont know anything about her. What about her parents? She may be married.

LIZA. Garn!

HIGGINS. There! As the girl very properly says, Garn! Married indeed! Dont you know that a woman of that class looks a worn out drudge of fifty a year after she's married?

PYGMALION

LIZA. Whood marry me?

HIGGINS [*suddenly resorting to the most thrillingly beautiful low tones in his best elocutionary style*] By George, Eliza, the streets will be strewn with the bodies of men shooting themselves for your sake before Ive done with you.

MRS PEARCE. Nonsense, sir. You mustnt talk like that to her.

LIZA [*rising and squaring herself determinedly*] I'm going away. He's off his chump, he is. I dont want no balmies teaching me.

HIGGINS [*wounded in his tenderest point by her insensibility to his elocution*] Oh, indeed! I'm mad, am I? Very well, Mrs Pearce: you neednt order the new clothes for her. Throw her out.

LIZA [*whimpering*] Nah-ow. You got no right to touch me.

MRS PEARCE. You see now what comes of being saucy. [*Indicating the door*] This way, please.

LIZA [*almost in tears*] I didnt want no clothes. I wouldnt have taken them [*she throws away the handkerchief*]. I can buy my own clothes.

HIGGINS [*deftly retrieving the handkerchief and intercepting her on her reluctant way to the door*] Youre an ungrateful wicked girl. This is my return for offering to take you out of the gutter and dress you beautifully and make a lady of you.

MRS PEARCE. Stop, Mr Higgins. I wont allow it. It's you that are wicked. Go home to your parents, girl; and tell them to take better care of you.

LIZA. I aint got no parents. They told me I was big enough to earn my own living and turned me out.

MRS PEARCE. Wheres your mother?

LIZA. I aint got no mother. Her that turned me out was my sixth stepmother. But I done without them. And I'm a good girl, I am.

HIGGINS. Very well, then, what on earth is all this fuss about? The girl doesnt belong to anybody—is no use to anybody but me. [*He goes to Mrs Pearce and begins coaxing*]. You can adopt her, Mrs Pearce: I'm sure a daughter would

217

be a great amusement to you. Now dont make any more fuss. Take her downstairs; and—

MRS PEARCE. But whats to become of her? Is she to be paid anything? Do be sensible, sir.

HIGGINS. Oh, pay her whatever is necessary: put it down in the housekeeping book. [*Impatiently*] What on earth will she want with money? She'll have her food and her clothes. She'll only drink if you give her money.

LIZA [*turning on him*] Oh you a r e a brute. It's a lie: nobody ever saw the sign of liquor on me. [*She goes back to her chair and plants herself there defiantly*].

PICKERING [*in good-humored remonstrance*] Does it occur to you, Higgins, that the girl has some feelings?

HIGGINS [*looking critically at her*] Oh no, I dont think so. Not any feelings that we need bother about. [*Cheerily*] Have you, Eliza?

LIZA. I got my feelings same as anyone else.

HIGGINS [*to Pickering, reflectively*] You see the difficulty?

PICKERING. Eh? What difficulty?

HIGGINS. To get her to talk grammar. The mere pronunciation is easy enough.

LIZA. I dont want to talk grammar. I want to talk like a lady.

MRS PEARCE. Will you please keep to the point, Mr Higgins? I want to know on what terms the girl is to be here. Is she to have any wages? And what is to become of her when youve finished your teaching? You must look ahead a little.

HIGGINS [*impatiently*] Whats to become of her if I leave her in the gutter? Tell me that, Mrs Pearce.

MRS PEARCE. Thats her own business, not yours, Mr Higgins.

HIGGINS. Well, when Ive done with her, we can throw her back into the gutter; and then it will be her own business again; so thats all right.

LIZA. Oh, youve no feeling heart in you: you dont care for nothing but yourself [*she rises and takes the floor resolutely*]. Here! Ive had enough of this. I'm going [*making for the door*]. You ought to be ashamed of yourself, you ought.

HIGGINS [*snatching a chocolate cream from the piano, his eyes suddenly beginning to twinkle with mischief*] Have some chocolates, Eliza.

LIZA [*halting, tempted*] How do I know what might be in them? Ive heard of girls being drugged by the like of you.

Higgins whips out his penknife; cuts a chocolate in two; puts one half into his mouth and bolts it; and offers her the other half.

HIGGINS. Pledge of good faith, Eliza. I eat one half: you eat the other. [*Liza opens her mouth to retort: he pops the half chocolate into it*]. You shall have boxes of them, barrels of them, every day. You shall live on them. Eh?

LIZA [*who has disposed of the chocolate after being nearly choked by it*] I wouldnt have ate it, only I'm too ladylike to take it out of my mouth.

HIGGINS. Listen, Eliza. I think you said you came in a taxi.

LIZA. Well, what if I did? Ive as good a right to take a taxi as anyone else.

HIGGINS. You have, Eliza; and in future you shall have as many taxis as you want. You shall go up and down and round the town in a taxi every day. Think of that, Eliza.

MRS PEARCE. Mr Higgins: youre tempting the girl. It's not right. She should think of the future.

HIGGINS. At her age! Nonsense! Time enough to think of the future when you havnt any future to think of. No, Eliza: do as this lady does: think of other people's futures; but never think of your own. Think of chocolates, and taxis, and gold, and diamonds.

LIZA. No: I dont want no gold and no diamonds. I'm a good girl, I am. [*She sits down again, with an attempt at dignity*].

HIGGINS. You shall remain so, Eliza, under the care of Mrs Pearce. And you shall marry an officer in the Guards, with a beautiful moustache: the son of a marquis, who will disinherit him for marrying you, but will relent when he sees your beauty and goodness—

PICKERING. Excuse me, Higgins; but I really must interfere. Mrs Pearce is quite right. If this girl is to put herself in your hands for six months for an experiment in teaching, she must understand thoroughly what she's doing.

HIGGINS. How can she? She's incapable of understanding anything. Besides, do any of us understand what we are doing? If we did, would we ever do it?

PICKERING. Very clever, Higgins; but not sound sense. [*To Eliza*] Miss Doolittle—

LIZA [*overwhelmed*] Ah-ah-ow-oo!

HIGGINS. There! Thats all youll get out of Eliza. Ah-ah-ow-oo! No use explaining. As a military man you ought to know that. Give her her orders: thats what she wants. Eliza: you are to live here for the next six months, learning how to speak beautifully, like a lady in a florist's shop. If youre good and do whatever youre told, you shall sleep in a proper bedroom, and have lots to eat, and money to buy chocolates and take rides in taxis. If youre naughty and idle you will sleep in the back kitchen among the black beetles, and be walloped by Mrs Pearce with a broomstick. At the end of six months you shall go to Buckingham Palace in a carriage, beautifully dressed. If the King finds out youre not a lady, you will be taken by the police to the Tower of London, where your head will be cut off as a warning to other presumptuous flower girls. If you are not found out, you shall have a present of seven-and-sixpence to start life with as a lady in a shop. If you refuse this offer you will be a most ungrateful and wicked girl; and the angels will weep for you. [*To Pickering*] Now are you satisfied, Pickering? [*To Mrs Pearce*] Can I put it more plainly and fairly, Mrs Pearce?

MRS PEARCE [*patiently*] I think youd better let me speak to the girl properly in private. I dont know that I can take charge of her or consent to the arrangement at all. Of course I know you dont mean her any harm; but when you get what you call interested in people's accents, you never think or care what may happen to them or you. Come with me, Eliza.

PYGMALION

HIGGINS. Thats all right. Thank you, Mrs Pearce. Bundle her off to the bath-room.

LIZA [*rising reluctantly and suspiciously*] Youre a great bully, you are. I wont stay here if I dont like. I wont let nobody wallop me. I never asked to go to Bucknam Palace, I didnt. I was never in trouble with the police, not me. I'm a good girl—

MRS PEARCE. Dont answer back, girl. You dont understand the gentleman. Come with me. [*She leads the way to the door, and holds it open for Eliza*].

LIZA [*as she goes out*] Well, what I say is right. I wont go near the King, not if I'm going to have my head cut off. If I'd known what I was letting myself in for, I wouldnt have come here. I always been a good girl; and I never offered to say a word to him; and I dont owe him nothing; and I dont care; and I wont be put upon; and I have my feelings the same as anyone else—

Mrs Pearce shuts the door; and Eliza's plaints are no longer audible. Pickering comes from the hearth to the chair and sits astride it with his arms on the back.

PICKERING. Excuse the straight question, Higgins. Are you a man of good character where women are concerned?

HIGGINS [*moodily*] Have you ever met a man of good character where women are concerned?

PICKERING. Yes: very frequently.

HIGGINS [*dogmatically, lifting himself on his hands to the level of the piano, and sitting on it with a bounce*] Well, I havnt. I find that the moment I let a woman make friends with me, she becomes jealous, exacting, suspicious, and a damned nuisance. I find that the moment I let myself make friends with a woman, I become selfish and tyrannical. Women upset everything. When you let them into your life, you find that the woman is driving at one thing and youre driving at another.

PICKERING. At what, for example?

HIGGINS [*coming off the piano restlessly*] Oh, Lord knows! I suppose the woman wants to live her own life; and the man

PYGMALION

wants to live his; and each tries to drag the other on to the wrong track. One wants to go north and the other south; and the result is that both have to go east, though they both hate the east wind. [*He sits down on the bench at the keyboard*]. So here I am, a confirmed old bachelor, and likely to remain so.

PICKERING [*rising and standing over him gravely*] Come, Higgins! You know what I mean. If I'm to be in this business I shall feel responsible for that girl. I hope it's understood that no advantage is to be taken of her position.

HIGGINS. What! That thing! Sacred, I assure you. [*Rising to explain*] You see, she'll be a pupil; and teaching would be impossible unless pupils were sacred. Ive taught scores of American millionairesses how to speak English: the best looking women in the world. I'm seasoned. They might as well be blocks of wood. *I* might as well be a block of wood. It's—

Mrs Pearce opens the door. She has Eliza's hat in her hand. Pickering retires to the easy-chair at the hearth and sits down.

HIGGINS [*eagerly*] Well, Mrs Pearce: is it all right?

MRS PEARCE [*at the door*] I just wish to trouble you with a word, if I may, Mr Higgins.

HIGGINS. Yes, certainly. Come in. [*She comes forward*]. Dont burn that, Mrs Pearce. I'll keep it as a curiosity. [*He takes the hat*].

MRS PEARCE. Handle it carefully, sir, please. I had to promise her not to burn it; but I had better put it in the oven for a while.

HIGGINS [*putting it down hastily on the piano*] Oh! thank you. Well, what have you to say to me?

PICKERING. Am I in the way?

MRS PEARCE. Not at all, sir. Mr Higgins: will you please be very particular what you say before the girl?

HIGGINS [*sternly*] Of course. I'm always particular about what I say. Why do you say this to me?

MRS PEARCE [*unmoved*] No, sir: youre not at all particular when youve mislaid anything or when you get a little im-

222

patient. Now it doesnt matter before me: I'm used to it. But you really must not swear before the girl.

HIGGINS [*indignantly*] *I* swear! [*Most emphatically*] I never swear. I detest the habit. What the devil do you mean?

MRS PEARCE [*stolidly*] Thats what I mean, sir. You swear a great deal too much. I dont mind your damning and blasting, and w h a t the devil and w h e r e the devil and w h o the devil—

HIGGINS. Mrs Pearce: this language from your lips! Really!

MRS PEARCE [*not to be put off*]—but there is a certain word I must ask you not to use. The girl has just used it herself because the bath was too hot. It begins with the same letter as bath. She knows no better: she learnt it at her mother's knee. But she must not hear it from your lips.

HIGGINS [*loftily*] I cannot charge myself with having ever uttered it, Mrs Pearce. [*She looks at him steadfastly. He adds, hiding an uneasy conscience with a judicial air*] Except perhaps in a moment of extreme and justifiable excitement.

MRS PEARCE. Only this morning, sir, you applied it to your boots, to the butter, and to the brown bread.

HIGGINS. Oh, that! Mere alliteration, Mrs Pearce, natural to a poet.

MRS PEARCE. Well, sir, whatever you choose to call it, I beg you not to let the girl hear you repeat it.

HIGGINS. Oh, very well, very well. Is that all?

MRS PEARCE. No, sir. We shall have to be very particular with this girl as to personal cleanliness.

HIGGINS. Certainly. Quite right. Most important.

MRS PEARCE. I mean not to be slovenly about her dress or untidy in leaving things about.

HIGGINS [*going to her solemnly*] Just so. I intended to call your attention to that. [*He passes on to Pickering, who is enjoying the conversation immensely*]. It is these little things that matter, Pickering. Take care of the pence and the pounds will take care of themselves is as true of personal habits as of money. [*He comes to anchor on the hearthrug, with the air of a*

223

man in an unassailable position].

MRS PEARCE. Yes, sir. Then might I ask you not to come down to breakfast in your dressing-gown, or at any rate not to use it as a napkin to the extent you do, sir. And if you would be so good as not to eat everything off the same plate, and to remember not to put the porridge saucepan out of your hand on the clean tablecloth, it would be a better example to the girl. You know you nearly choked yourself with a fishbone in the jam only last week.

HIGGINS [*routed from the hearthrug and drifting back to the piano*] I may do these things sometimes in absence of mind; but surely I dont do them habitually. [*Angrily*] By the way: my dressing-gown smells most damnably of benzine.

MRS PEARCE. No doubt it does, Mr Higgins. But if you will wipe your fingers—

HIGGINS [*yelling*] Oh very well, very well: I'll wipe them in my hair in future.

MRS PEARCE. I hope youre not offended, Mr Higgins.

HIGGINS [*shocked at finding himself thought capable of an unamiable sentiment*] Not at all, not at all. Youre quite right, Mrs Pearce: I shall be particularly careful before the girl. Is that all?

MRS PEARCE. No, sir. Might she use some of those Japanese dresses you brought from abroad? I really cant put her back into her old things.

HIGGINS. Certainly. Anything you like. Is that all?

MRS PEARCE. Thank you, sir. Thats all. [*She goes out*].

HIGGINS. You know, Pickering, that woman has the most extraordinary ideas about me. Here I am, a shy, diffident sort of man. Ive never been able to feel really grown-up and tremendous, like other chaps. And yet she's firmly persuaded that I'm an arbitrary overbearing bossing kind of person. I cant account for it.

Mrs Pearce returns.

MRS PEARCE. If you please, sir, the trouble's beginning already. Theres a dustman downstairs, Alfred Doolittle, wants to see you. He says you have his daughter here.

PICKERING [*rising*] Phew! I say! [*He retreats to the hearth-rug*].

HIGGINS [*promptly*] Send the blackguard up.

MRS PEARCE. Oh, very well, sir. [*She goes out*].

PICKERING. He may not be a blackguard, Higgins.

HIGGINS. Nonsense. Of course he's a blackguard.

PICKERING. Whether he is or not, I'm afraid we shall have some trouble with him.

HIGGINS [*confidently*] Oh no: I think not. If theres any trouble he shall have it with me, not I with him. And we are sure to get something interesting out of him.

PICKERING. About the girl?

HIGGINS. No. I mean his dialect.

PICKERING. Oh!

MRS PEARCE [*at the door*] Doolittle, sir. [*She admits Doo-little and retires*].

Alfred Doolittle is an elderly but vigorous dustman, clad in the costume of his profession, including a hat with a back brim covering his neck and shoulders. He has well marked and rather interesting features, and seems equally free from fear and con-science. He has a remarkably expressive voice, the result of a habit of giving vent to his feelings without reserve. His present pose is that of wounded honor and stern resolution.

DOOLITTLE [*at the door, uncertain which of the two gentle-men is his man*] Professor Higgins?

HIGGINS. Here. Good morning. Sit down.

DOOLITTLE. Morning, Governor. [*He sits down magisteri-ally*] I come about a very serious matter, Governor.

HIGGINS [*to Pickering*] Brought up in Hounslow. Mother Welsh, I should think. [*Doolittle opens his mouth, amazed. Higgins continues*] What do you want, Doolittle?

DOOLITTLE [*menacingly*] I want my daughter: thats what I want. See?

HIGGINS. Of course you do. Youre her father, arnt you? You dont suppose anyone else wants her, do you? I'm glad to see you have some spark of family feeling left. She's up-stairs. Take her away at once.

PYGMALION

DOOLITTLE [*rising, fearfully taken aback*] What!

HIGGINS. Take her away. Do you suppose I'm going to keep your daughter for you?

DOOLITTLE [*remonstrating*] Now, now, look here, Governor. Is this reasonable? Is it fairity to take advantage of a man like this? The girl belongs to me. You got her. Where do I come in? [*He sits down again*].

HIGGINS. Your daughter had the audacity to come to my house and ask me to teach her how to speak properly so that she could get a place in a flower-shop. This gentleman and my housekeeper have been here all the time. [*Bullying him*] How dare you come here and attempt to blackmail me? You sent her here on purpose.

DOOLITTLE [*protesting*] No, Governor.

HIGGINS. You must have. How else could you possibly know that she is here?

DOOLITTLE. Dont take a man up like that, Governor.

HIGGINS. The police shall take you up. This is a plant—a plot to extort money by threats. I shall telephone for the police. [*He goes resolutely to the telephone and opens the directory*].

DOOLITTLE. Have I asked you for a brass farthing? I leave it to the gentleman here: have I said a word about money?

HIGGINS [*throwing the book aside and marching down on Doolittle with a poser*] What else did you come for?

DOOLITTLE [*sweetly*] Well, what would a man come for? Be human, Governor.

HIGGINS [*disarmed*] Alfred: did you put her up to it?

DOOLITTLE. So help me, Governor, I never did. I take my Bible oath I aint seen the girl these two months past.

HIGGINS. Then how did you know she was here?

DOOLITTLE ["*most musical, most melancholy*"] I'll tell you, Governor, if youll only let me get a word in. I'm willing to tell you. I'm wanting to tell you. I'm waiting to tell you.

HIGGINS. Pickering: this chap has a certain natural gift of rhetoric. Observe the rhythm of his native woodnotes wild. "I'm willing to tell you: I'm wanting to tell you: I'm

226

waiting to tell you." Sentimental rhetoric! thats the Welsh strain in him. It also accounts for his mendacity and dishonesty.

PICKERING. Oh, p l e a s e , Higgins: I'm west country myself. [*To Doolittle*] How did you know the girl was here if you didnt send her?

DOOLITTLE. It was like this, Governor. The girl took a boy in the taxi to give him a jaunt. Son of her landlady, he is. He hung about on the chance of her giving him another ride home. Well, she sent him back for her luggage when she heard you was willing for her to stop here. I met the boy at the corner of Long Acre and Endell Street.

HIGGINS. Public house. Yes?

DOOLITTLE. The poor man's club, Governor: why shouldnt I?

PICKERING. Do let him tell his story, Higgins.

DOOLITTLE. He told me what was up. And I ask you, what was my feelings and my duty as a father? I says to the boy, "You bring me the luggage," I says—

PICKERING. Why didnt you go for it yourself?

DOOLITTLE. Landlady wouldnt have trusted me with it, Governor. She's that kind of woman: you know. I had to give the boy a penny afore he trusted me with it, the little swine. I brought it to her just to oblige you like, and make myself agreeable. Thats all.

HIGGINS. How much luggage?

DOOLITTLE. Musical instrument, Governor. A few pictures, a trifle of jewelry, and a bird-cage. She said she didnt want no clothes. What was I to think from that, Governor? I ask you as a parent what was I to think?

HIGGINS. So you came to rescue her from worse than death, eh?

DOOLITTLE [*appreciatively: relieved at being so well understood*] Just so, Governor. Thats right.

PICKERING. But why did you bring her luggage if you intended to take her away?

DOOLITTLE. Have I said a word about taking her away?

Have I now?

HIGGINS [*determinedly*] Youre going to take her away, double quick. [*He crosses to the hearth and rings the bell*].

DOOLITTLE [*rising*] No, Governor. Dont say that. I'm not the man to stand in my girl's light. Heres a career opening for her, as you might say; and—

Mrs Pearce opens the door and awaits orders.

HIGGINS. Mrs Pearce: this is Eliza's father. He has come to take her away. Give her to him. [*He goes back to the piano, with an air of washing his hands of the whole affair*].

DOOLITTLE. No. This is a misunderstanding. Listen here—

MRS PEARCE. He cant take her away, Mr Higgins: how can he? You told me to burn her clothes.

DOOLITTLE. Thats right. I cant carry the girl through the streets like a blooming monkey, can I? I put it to you.

HIGGINS. You have put it to me that you want your daughter. Take your daughter. If she has no clothes go out and buy her some.

DOOLITTLE [*desperate*] Wheres the clothes she come in? Did I burn them or did your missus here?

MRS PEARCE. I am the housekeeper, if you please. I have sent for some clothes for your girl. When they come you can take her away. You can wait in the kitchen. This way, please.

Doolittle, much troubled, accompanies her to the door; then hesitates; finally turns confidentially to Higgins.

DOOLITTLE. Listen here, Governor. You and me is men of the world, aint we?

HIGGINS. Oh! Men of the world, are we? Youd better go, Mrs Pearce.

MRS PEARCE. I think so, indeed, sir. [*She goes, with dignity*].

PICKERING. The floor is yours, Mr Doolittle.

DOOLITTLE [*to Pickering*] I thank you, Governor. [*To Higgins, who takes refuge on the piano bench, a little overwhelmed by the proximity of his visitor; for Doolittle has a pro-*

fessional flavor of dust about him]. Well, the truth is, Ive taken a sort of fancy to you, Governor; and if you want the girl, I'm not so set on having her back home again but what I might be open to an arrangement. Regarded in the light of a young woman, she's a fine handsome girl. As a daughter she's not worth her keep; and so I tell you straight. All I ask is my rights as a father; and youre the last man alive to expect me to let her go for nothing; for I can see youre one of the straight sort, Governor. Well, whats a five-pound note to you? And whats Eliza to me? [*He returns to his chair and sits down judicially*].

PICKERING. I think you ought to know, Doolittle, that Mr Higgins's intentions are entirely honorable.

DOOLITTLE. Course they are, Governor. If I thought they wasnt, I'd ask fifty.

HIGGINS [*revolted*] Do you mean to say, you callous rascal, that you would sell your daughter for £50?

DOOLITTLE. Not in a general way I wouldnt; but to oblige a gentleman like you I'd do a good deal, I do assure you.

PICKERING. Have you no morals, man?

DOOLITTLE [*unabashed*] Cant afford them, Governor. Neither could you if you was as poor as me. Not that I mean any harm, you know. But if Liza is going to have a bit out of this, why not me too?

HIGGINS [*troubled*] I dont know what to do, Pickering. There can be no question that as a matter of morals it's a positive crime to give this chap a farthing. And yet I feel a sort of rough justice in his claim.

DOOLITTLE. Thats it, Governor. Thats all I say. A father's heart, as it were.

PICKERING. Well, I know the feeling; but really it seems hardly right—

DOOLITTLE. Dont say that, Governor. Dont look at it that way. What am I, Governors both? I ask you, what am I? I'm one of the undeserving poor: thats what I am. Think of what that means to a man. It means that he's up agen middle class morality all the time. If theres anything going,

229

and I put in for a bit of it, it's always the same story: "Youre undeserving; so you cant have it." But my needs is as great as the most deserving widow's that ever got money out of six different charities in one week for the death of the same husband. I dont need less than a deserving man: I need more. I dont eat less hearty than him; and I drink a lot more. I want a bit of amusement, cause I'm a thinking man. I want cheerfulness and a song and a band when I feel low. Well, they charge me just the same for everything as they charge the deserving. What is middle class morality? Just an excuse for never giving me anything. Therefore, I ask you, as two gentlemen, not to play that game on me. I'm playing straight with you. I aint pretending to be deserving. I'm undeserving; and I mean to go on being undeserving. I like it; and thats the truth. Will you take advantage of a man's nature to do him out of the price of his own daughter what he's brought up and fed and clothed by the sweat of his brow until she's growed big enough to be interesting to you two gentlemen? Is five pounds unreasonable? I put it to you; and I leave it to you.

HIGGINS [*rising, and going over to Pickering*] Pickering: if we were to take this man in hand for three months, he could choose between a seat in the Cabinet and a popular pulpit in Wales.

PICKERING. What do you say to that, Doolittle?

DOOLITTLE. Not me, Governor, thank you kindly. Ive heard all the preachers and all the prime ministers—for I'm a thinking man and game for politics or religion or social reform same as all the other amusements—and I tell you it's a dog's life any way you look at it. Undeserving poverty is my line. Taking one station in society with another, it's —it's—well, it's the only one that has any ginger in it, to my taste.

HIGGINS. I suppose we must give him a fiver.

PICKERING. He'll make a bad use of it, I'm afraid.

DOOLITTLE. Not me, Governor, so help me I wont. Dont you be afraid that I'll save it and spare it and live idle on it.

230

There wont be a penny of it left by Monday: I'll have to go to work same as if I'd never had it. It wont pauperize me, you bet. Just one good spree for myself and the missus, giving pleasure to ourselves and employment to others, and satisfaction to you to think it's not been throwed away. You couldnt spend it better.

HIGGINS [*taking out his pocket book and coming between Doolittle and the piano*] This is irresistible. Lets give him ten. [*He offers two notes to the dustman*].

DOOLITTLE. No, Governor. She wouldnt have the heart to spend ten; and perhaps I shouldnt neither. Ten pounds is a lot of money: it makes a man feel prudent like; and then goodbye to happiness. You give me what I ask you, Governor: not a penny more, and not a penny less.

PICKERING. Why dont you marry that missus of yours? I rather draw the line at encouraging that sort of immorality.

DOOLITTLE. Tell her so, Governor: tell her so. *I'm* willing. It's me that suffers by it. Ive no hold on her. I got to be agreeable to her. I got to give her presents. I got to buy her clothes something sinful. I'm a slave to that woman, Governor, just because I'm not her lawful husband. And she knows it too. Catch her marrying me! Take my advice, Governor: marry Eliza while she's young and dont know no better. If you dont youll be sorry for it after. If you do, she'll be sorry for it after; but better her than you, because youre a man, and she's only a woman and dont know how to be happy anyhow.

HIGGINS. Pickering: if we listen to this man another minute, we shall have no convictions left. [*To Doolittle*] Five pounds I think you said.

DOOLITTLE. Thank you kindly, Governor.

HIGGINS. Youre sure you wont take ten?

DOOLITTLE. Not now. Another time, Governor.

HIGGINS [*handing him a five-pound note*] Here you are.

DOOLITTLE. Thank you, Governor. Good morning. [*He hurries to the door, anxious to get away with his booty. When he opens it he is confronted with a dainty and exquisitely clean young Japanese lady in a simple blue cotton kimono printed cunningly with small white jasmine blossoms. Mrs Pearce is with her. He gets out of her way deferentially and apologizes].* Beg pardon, miss.

THE JAPANESE LADY. Garn! Dont you know your own daughter?

DOOLITTLE	*exclaiming*	Bly me! it's Eliza!
HIGGINS	*simul-*	Whats that! This!
PICKERING	*taneously*	By Jove!

LIZA. Dont I look silly?

HIGGINS. Silly?

MRS PEARCE [*at the door*] Now, Mr Higgins, please dont say anything to make the girl conceited about herself.

HIGGINS [*conscientiously*] Oh! Quite right, Mrs Pearce. [*To Eliza*] Yes: damned silly.

MRS PEARCE. Please, sir.

HIGGINS [*correcting himself*] I mean extremely silly.

LIZA. I should look all right with my hat on. [*She takes up her hat; puts it on; and walks across the room to the fireplace with a fashionable air*].

HIGGINS. A new fashion, by George! And it ought to look horrible!

DOOLITTLE [*with fatherly pride*] Well, I never thought she'd clean up as good looking as that, Governor. She's a credit to me, aint she?

LIZA. I tell you, it's easy to clean up here. Hot and cold water on tap, just as much as you like, there is. Woolly towels, there is; and a towel horse so hot, it burns your fingers. Soft brushes to scrub yourself, and a wooden bowl of soap smelling like primroses. Now I know why ladies is so clean. Washing's a treat for them. Wish they saw what it is for the like of me!

HIGGINS. I'm glad the bathroom met with your approval.

LIZA. It didnt: not all of it; and I dont care who hears me say it. Mrs Pearce knows.

PYGMALION

HIGGINS. What was wrong, Mrs Pearce?

MRS PEARCE [*blandly*] Oh, nothing, sir. It doesnt matter.

LIZA. I had a good mind to break it. I didnt know which way to look. But I hung a towel over it, I did.

HIGGINS. Over what?

MRS PEARCE. Over the looking-glass, sir.

HIGGINS. Doolittle: you have brought your daughter up too strictly.

DOOLITTLE. Me! I never brought her up at all, except to give her a lick of a strap now and again. Dont put it on me, Governor. She aint accustomed to it, you see: thats all. But she'll soon pick up your free-and-easy ways.

LIZA. I'm a good girl, I am; and I wont pick up no free-and-easy ways.

HIGGINS. Eliza: if you say again that youre a good girl, your father shall take you home.

LIZA. Not him. You dont know my father. All he come here for was to touch you for some money to get drunk on.

DOOLITTLE. Well, what else would I want money for? To put into the plate in church, I suppose. [*She puts out her tongue at him. He is so incensed by this that Pickering presently finds it necessary to step between them*]. Dont you give me none of your lip; and dont let me hear you giving this gentleman any of it neither, or youll hear from me about it. See?

HIGGINS. Have you any further advice to give her before you go, Doolittle? Your blessing, for instance.

DOOLITTLE. No, Governor: I aint such a mug as to put up my children to all I know myself. Hard enough to hold them in without that. If you want Eliza's mind improved, Governor, you do it yourself with a strap. So long, gentlemen. [*He turns to go*].

HIGGINS [*impressively*] Stop. Youll come regularly to see your daughter. It's your duty, you know. My brother is a clergyman; and he could help you in your talks with her.

DOOLITTLE [*evasively*] Certainly. I'll come, Governor. Not just this week, because I have a job at a distance. But later on you may depend on me. Afternoon, gentlemen.

233

PYGMALION

Afternoon, maam. [*He takes off his hat to Mrs Pearce, who disdains the salutation and goes out. He winks at Higgins, thinking him probably a fellow-sufferer from Mrs Pearce's difficult disposition, and follows her*].

LIZA. Dont you believe the old liar. He'd as soon you set a bull-dog on him as a clergyman. You wont see him again in a hurry.

HIGGINS. I dont want to, Eliza. Do you?

LIZA. Not me. I dont want never to see him again, I dont. He's a disgrace to me, he is, collecting dust, instead of working at his trade.

PICKERING. What is his trade, Eliza?

LIZA. Taking money out of other people's pockets into his own. His proper trade's a navvy; and he works at it sometimes too—for exercise—and earns good money at it. Aint you going to call me Miss Doolittle any more?

PICKERING. I beg your pardon, Miss Doolittle. It was a slip of the tongue.

LIZA. Oh, I dont mind; only it sounded so genteel. I should just like to take a taxi to the corner of Tottenham Court Road and get out there and tell it to wait for me, just to put the girls in their place a bit. I wouldnt speak to them, you know.

PICKERING. Better wait til we get you something really fashionable.

HIGGINS. Besides, you shouldnt cut your old friends now that you have risen in the world. Thats what we call snobbery.

LIZA. You dont call the like of them my friends now, I should hope. Theyve took it out of me often enough with their ridicule when they had the chance; and now I mean to get a bit of my own back. But if I'm to have fashionable clothes, I'll wait. I should like to have some. Mrs Pearce says youre going to give me some to wear in bed at night different to what I wear in the daytime; but it do seem a waste of money when you could get something to shew. Besides, I never could fancy changing into cold things on

234

a winter night.

MRS PEARCE [*coming back*] Now, Eliza. The new things have come for you to try on.

LIZA. Ah-ow-oo-ooh! [*She rushes out*].

MRS PEARCE [*following her*] Oh, dont rush about like that, girl. [*She shuts the door behind her*].

HIGGINS. Pickering: we have taken on a stiff job.

PICKERING [*with conviction*] Higgins: we have.

ACT III

IT is Mrs Higgins's at-home day. Nobody has yet arrived. Her drawing room, in a flat on Chelsea Embankment, has three windows looking on the river; and the ceiling is not so lofty as it would be in an older house of the same pretension. The windows are open, giving access to a balcony with flowers in pots. If you stand with your face to the windows, you have the fireplace on your left and the door in the right-hand wall close to the corner nearest the windows.

Mrs Higgins was brought up on Morris and Burne Jones; and her room, which is very unlike her son's room in Wimpole Street, is not crowded with furniture and little tables and nicknacks. In the middle of the room there is a big ottoman; and this, with the carpet, the Morris wall-papers, and the Morris chintz window curtains and brocade covers of the ottoman and its cushions, supply all the ornament, and are much too handsome to be hidden by odds and ends of useless things. A few good oil-paintings from the exhibitions in the Grosvenor Gallery thirty years ago (the Burne Jones, not the Whistler side of them) are on the walls. The only landscape is a Cecil Lawson on the scale of a Rubens. There is a portrait of Mrs Higgins as she was when she defied fashion in her youth in one of the beautiful Rossettian costumes which, when caricatured by people who did not understand, led to the absurdities of popular estheticism in the eighteen-seventies.

In the corner diagonally opposite the door Mrs Higgins, now over sixty and long past taking the trouble to dress out of the fashion, sits writing at an elegantly simple writing-table with a bell button within reach of her hand. There is a Chippendale chair further back in the room between her and the window nearest her side. At the other side of the room, further forward, is an Elizabethan chair roughly carved in the taste of Inigo Jones. On the same side a piano in a decorated case. The corner between the fireplace and the window is occupied by a divan cushioned in Morris chintz.

It is between four and five in the afternoon.

The door is opened violently; and Higgins enters with his hat on.

236

PYGMALION

MRS HIGGINS [*dismayed*] Henry [*scolding him*]! What are you doing here to-day? It is my at-home day: you promised not to come. [*As he bends to kiss her, she takes his hat off, and presents it to him*].

HIGGINS. Oh bother! [*He throws the hat down on the table*].

MRS HIGGINS. Go home at once.

HIGGINS [*kissing her*] I know, mother. I came on purpose.

MRS HIGGINS. But you mustnt. I'm serious, Henry. You offend all my friends: they stop coming whenever they meet you.

HIGGINS. Nonsense! I know I have no small talk; but people dont mind. [*He sits on the settee*].

MRS HIGGINS. Oh! dont they? Small talk indeed! What about your large talk? Really, dear, you mustnt stay.

HIGGINS. I must. Ive a job for you. A phonetic job.

MRS HIGGINS. No use, dear. I'm sorry; but I cant get round your vowels; and though I like to get pretty postcards in your patent shorthand, I always have to read the copies in ordinary writing you so thoughtfully send me.

HIGGINS. Well, this isnt a phonetic job.

MRS HIGGINS. You said it was.

HIGGINS. Not your part of it. Ive picked up a girl.

MRS HIGGINS. Does that mean that some girl has picked you up?

HIGGINS. Not at all. I dont mean a love affair.

MRS HIGGINS. What a pity!

HIGGINS. Why?

MRS HIGGINS. Well, you never fall in love with anyone under forty-five. When will you discover that there are some rather nice-looking young women about?

HIGGINS. Oh, I cant be bothered with young women. My idea of a lovable woman is something as like you as possible. I shall never get into the way of seriously liking young women: some habits lie too deep to be changed. [*Rising abruptly and walking about, jingling his money and his keys in his trouser pockets*] Besides, theyre all idiots.

MRS HIGGINS. Do you know what you would do if you

237

really loved me, Henry?

HIGGINS. Oh bother! What? Marry, I suppose?

MRS HIGGINS. No. Stop fidgeting and take your hands out of your pockets. [*With a gesture of despair, he obeys and sits down again.*] Thats a good boy. Now tell me about the girl.

HIGGINS. She's coming to see you.

MRS HIGGINS. I dont remember asking her.

HIGGINS. You didnt. *I* asked her. If youd known her you wouldnt have asked her.

MRS HIGGINS. Indeed! Why?

HIGGINS. Well, it's like this. She's a common flower girl. I picked her off the kerbstone.

MRS HIGGINS. And invited her to my at-home!

HIGGINS [*rising and coming to her to coax her*] Oh, thatll be all right. Ive taught her to speak properly; and she has strict orders as to her behavior. She's to keep to two subjects: the weather and everybody's health—Fine day and How do you do, you know—and not to let herself go on things in general. That will be safe.

MRS HIGGINS. Safe! To talk about our health! about our insides! perhaps about our outsides! How could you be so silly, Henry?

HIGGINS [*impatiently*] Well, she must talk about something. [*He controls himself and sits down again*]. Oh, she'll be all right: dont you fuss. Pickering is in it with me. Ive a sort of bet on that I'll pass her off as a duchess in six months. I started on her some months ago; and she's getting on like a house on fire. I shall win my bet. She has a quick ear; and she's been easier to teach than my middle-class pupils because she's had to learn a complete new language. She talks English almost as you talk French.

MRS HIGGINS. Thats satisfactory, at all events.

HIGGINS. Well, it is and it isnt.

MRS HIGGINS. What does that mean?

HIGGINS. You see, Ive got her pronunciation all right; but you have to consider not only h o w a girl pronounces, but

238

wh a t she pronounces; and thats where—

They are interrupted by the parlor-maid, announcing guests.

THE PARLOR-MAID. Mrs and Miss Eynsford Hill. [*She withdraws*].

HIGGINS. Oh Lord! [*He rises; snatches his hat from the table; and makes for the door; but before he reaches it his mother introduces him*].

Mrs and Miss Eynsford Hill are the mother and daughter who sheltered from the rain in Covent Garden. The mother is well bred, quiet, and has the habitual anxiety of straitened means. The daughter has acquired a gay air of being very much at home in society: the bravado of genteel poverty.

MRS EYNSFORD HILL [*to Mrs Higgins*] How do you do? [*They shake hands*].

MISS EYNSFORD HILL. How d'you do? [*She shakes*].

MRS HIGGINS [*introducing*] My son Henry.

MRS EYNSFORD HILL. Your celebrated son! I have so longed to meet you, Professor Higgins.

HIGGINS [*glumly, making no movement in her direction*] Delighted. [*He backs against the piano and bows brusquely*].

MISS EYNSFORD HILL [*going to him with confident familiarity*] How do you do?

HIGGINS [*staring at her*] Ive seen you before somewhere. I havnt the ghost of a notion where; but Ive heard your voice. [*Drearily*] It doesnt matter. Youd better sit down.

MRS HIGGINS. I'm sorry to say that my celebrated son has no manners. You mustnt mind him.

MISS EYNSFORD HILL [*gaily*] I dont. [*She sits in the Elizabethan chair*].

MRS EYNSFORD HILL [*a little bewildered*] Not at all. [*She sits on the ottoman between her daughter and Mrs Higgins, who has turned her chair away from the writing-table*].

HIGGINS. Oh, have I been rude? I didnt mean to be.

He goes to the central window, through which, with his back to the company, he contemplates the river and the flowers in Battersea Park on the opposite bank as if they were a frozen desert.

239

PYGMALION

The parlor-maid returns, ushering in Pickering.

THE PARLOR-MAID. Colonel Pickering. [*She withdraws*].

PICKERING. How do you do, Mrs Higgins?

MRS HIGGINS. So glad youve come. Do you know Mrs Eynsford Hill—Miss Eynsford Hill? [*Exchange of bows. The Colonel brings the Chippendale chair a little forward between Mrs Hill and Mrs Higgins, and sits down*].

PICKERING. Has Henry told you what weve come for?

HIGGINS [*over his shoulder*] We were interrupted: damn it!

MRS HIGGINS. Oh Henry, Henry, really!

MRS EYNSFORD HILL [*half rising*] Are we in the way?

MRS HIGGINS [*rising and making her sit down again*] No, no. You couldnt have come more fortunately: we want you to meet a friend of ours.

HIGGINS [*turning hopefully*] Yes, by George! We want two or three people. Youll do as well as anybody else.

The parlor-maid returns, ushering Freddy.

THE PARLOR-MAID. Mr Eynsford Hill.

HIGGINS [*almost audibly, past endurance*] God of Heaven! another of them.

FREDDY [*shaking hands with Mrs Higgins*] Ahdedo?

MRS HIGGINS. Very good of you to come. [*Introducing*] Colonel Pickering.

FREDDY [*bowing*] Ahdedo?

MRS HIGGINS. I dont think you know my son, Professor Higgins.

FREDDY [*going to Higgins*] Ahdedo?

HIGGINS [*looking at him much as if he were a pickpocket*] I'll take my oath Ive met y o u before somewhere. Where was it?

FREDDY. I dont think so.

HIGGINS [*resignedly*] It dont matter, anyhow. Sit down.

He shakes Freddy's hand, and almost slings him on to the ottoman with his face to the windows; then comes round to the other side of it.

HIGGINS. Well, here we are, anyhow! [*He sits down on the ottoman next Mrs Eynsford Hill, on her left*]. And now, what the devil are we going to talk about until Eliza comes?

MRS HIGGINS. Henry: you are the life and soul of the Royal Society's soirées; but really youre rather trying on more commonplace occasions.

HIGGINS. Am I? Very sorry. [*Beaming suddenly*] I suppose I am, you know. [*Uproariously*] Ha, ha!

MISS EYNSFORD HILL [*who considers Higgins quite eligible matrimonially*] I sympathize. *I* havnt any small talk. If people would only be frank and say what they really think!

HIGGINS [*relapsing into gloom*] Lord forbid!

MRS EYNSFORD HILL [*taking up her daughter's cue*] But why?

HIGGINS. What they think they ought to think is bad enough, Lord knows; but what they really think would break up the whole show. Do you suppose it would be really agreeable if I were to come out now with what *I* really think?

MISS EYNSFORD HILL [*gaily*] Is it so very cynical?

HIGGINS. Cynical! Who the dickens said it was cynical? I mean it wouldnt be decent.

MRS EYNSFORD HILL [*seriously*] Oh! I'm sure you dont mean that, Mr Higgins.

HIGGINS. You see, we're all savages, more or less. We're supposed to be civilized and cultured—to know all about poetry and philosophy and art and science, and so on; but how many of us know even the meanings of these names? [*To Miss Hill*] What do you know of poetry? [*To Mrs Hill*] What do you know of science? [*Indicating Freddy*] What does he know of art or science or anything else? What the devil do you imagine I know of philosophy?

MRS HIGGINS [*warningly*] Or of manners, Henry?

THE PARLOR-MAID [*opening the door*] Miss Doolittle. [*She withdraws*].

HIGGINS [*rising hastily and running to Mrs Higgins*] Here she is, mother. [*He stands on tiptoe and makes signs over his mother's head to Eliza to indicate to her which lady is her hostess*].

Eliza, who is exquisitely dressed, produces an impression of

PYGMALION

such remarkable distinction and beauty as she enters that they all rise, quite fluttered. Guided by Higgins's signals, she comes to Mrs Higgins with studied grace.

LIZA [*speaking with pedantic correctness of pronunciation and great beauty of tone*] How do you do, Mrs Higgins? [*She gasps slightly in making sure of the H in Higgins, but is quite successful*]. Mr Higgins told me I might come.

MRS HIGGINS [*cordially*] Quite right: I'm very glad indeed to see you.

PICKERING. How do you do, Miss Doolittle?

LIZA [*shaking hands with him*] Colonel Pickering, is it not?

MRS EYNSFORD HILL. I feel sure we have met before, Miss Doolittle. I remember your eyes.

LIZA. How do you do? [*She sits down on the ottoman gracefully in the place just left vacant by Higgins*].

MRS EYNSFORD HILL [*introducing*] My daughter Clara.

LIZA. How do you do?

CLARA [*impulsively*] How do you do? [*She sits down on the ottoman beside Eliza, devouring her with her eyes*].

FREDDY [*coming to their side of the ottoman*] Ive certainly had the pleasure.

MRS EYNSFORD HILL [*introducing*] My son Freddy.

LIZA. How do you do?

Freddy bows and sits down in the Elizabethan chair, infatuated.

HIGGINS [*suddenly*] By George, yes: it all comes back to me! [*They stare at him*]. Covent Garden! [*Lamentably*] What a damned thing!

MRS HIGGINS. Henry, please! [*He is about to sit on the edge of the table*] Dont sit on my writing-table: youll break it.

HIGGINS [*sulkily*] Sorry.

He goes to the divan, stumbling into the fender and over the fire-irons on his way; extricating himself with muttered imprecations; and finishing his disastrous journey by throwing himself so impatiently on the divan that he almost breaks it. Mrs Higgins looks at him, but controls herself and says nothing.

A long and painful pause ensues.

MRS HIGGINS [*at last, conversationally*] Will it rain, do you think?

LIZA. The shallow depression in the west of these islands is likely to move slowly in an easterly direction. There are no indications of any great change in the barometrical situation.

FREDDY. Ha! ha! how awfully funny!

LIZA. What is wrong with that, young man? I bet I got it right.

FREDDY. Killing!

MRS EYNSFORD HILL. I'm sure I hope it wont turn cold. Theres so much influenza about. It runs right through our whole family regularly every spring.

LIZA [*darkly*] My aunt died of influenza: so they said.

MRS EYNSFORD HILL [*clicks her tongue sympathetically*]!!!

LIZA [*in the same tragic tone*] But it's my belief they done the old woman in.

MRS HIGGINS [*puzzled*] Done her in?

LIZA. Y-e-e-e-es, Lord love you! Why should she die of influenza? She come through diphtheria right enough the year before. I saw her with my own eyes. Fairly blue with it, she was. They all thought she was dead; but my father he kept ladling gin down her throat til she came to so sudden that she bit the bowl off the spoon.

MRS EYNSFORD HILL [*startled*] Dear me!

LIZA [*piling up the indictment*] What call would a woman with that strength in her have to die of influenza? What become of her new straw hat that should have come to me? Somebody pinched it; and what I say is, them as pinched it done her in.

MRS EYNSFORD HILL. What does doing her in mean?

HIGGINS [*hastily*] Oh, thats the new small talk. To do a person in means to kill them.

MRS EYNSFORD HILL [*to Eliza, horrified*] You surely dont believe that your aunt was killed?

LIZA. Do I not! Them she lived with would have killed

243

her for a hat-pin, let alone a hat.

MRS EYNSFORD HILL. But it cant have been right for your father to pour spirits down her throat like that. It might have killed her.

LIZA. Not her. Gin was mother's milk to her. Besides, he'd poured so much down his own throat that he knew the good of it.

MRS EYNSFORD HILL. Do you mean that he drank?

LIZA. Drank! My word! Something chronic.

MRS EYNSFORD HILL. How dreadful for you!

LIZA. Not a bit. It never did him no harm what I could see. But then he did not keep it up regular. [*Cheerfully*] On the burst, as you might say, from time to time. And always more agreeable when he had a drop in. When he was out of work, my mother used to give him fourpence and tell him to go out and not come back until he'd drunk himself cheerful and loving-like. Theres lots of women has to make their husbands drunk to make them fit to live with. [*Now quite at her ease*] You see, it's like this. If a man has a bit of a conscience, it always takes him when he's sober; and then it makes him low-spirited. A drop of booze just takes that off and makes him happy. [*To Freddy, who is in convulsions of suppressed laughter*] Here! what are you sniggering at?

FREDDY. The new small talk. You do it so awfully well.

LIZA. If I was doing it proper, what was you laughing at? [*To Higgins*] Have I said anything I oughtnt?

MRS HIGGINS [*interposing*] Not at all, Miss Doolittle.

LIZA. Well, thats a mercy, anyhow. [*Expansively*] What I always say is—

HIGGINS [*rising and looking at his watch*] Ahem!

LIZA [*looking round at him; taking the hint; and rising*] Well: I must go. [*They all rise. Freddy goes to the door*]. So pleased to have met you. Goodbye. [*She shakes hands with Mrs Higgins*].

MRS HIGGINS. Goodbye.

LIZA. Goodbye, Colonel Pickering.

PICKERING. Goodbye, Miss Doolittle. [*They shake hands*].

PYGMALION

LIZA [*nodding to the others*] Goodbye, all.

FREDDY [*opening the door for her*] Are you walking across the Park, Miss Doolittle? If so—

LIZA. Walk! Not bloody likely. [*Sensation*]. I am going in a taxi. [*She goes out*].

Pickering gasps and sits down. Freddy goes out on the balcony to catch another glimpse of Eliza.

MRS EYNSFORD HILL [*suffering from shock*] Well, I really cant get used to the new ways.

CLARA [*throwing herself discontentedly into the Elizabethan chair*] Oh, it's all right, mamma, quite right. People will think we never go anywhere or see anybody if you are so old-fashioned.

MRS EYNSFORD HILL. I daresay I am very old-fashioned; but I do hope you wont begin using that expression, Clara. I have got accustomed to hear you talking about men as rotters, and calling everything filthy and beastly; though I do think it horrible and unladylike. But this last is really too much. Dont you think so, Colonel Pickering?

PICKERING. Dont ask me. Ive been away in India for several years; and manners have changed so much that I sometimes dont know whether I'm at a respectable dinner-table or in a ship's forecastle.

CLARA. It's all a matter of habit. Theres no right or wrong in it. Nobody means anything by it. And it's so quaint, and gives such a smart emphasis to things that are not in themselves very witty. I find the new small talk delightful and quite innocent.

MRS EYNSFORD HILL [*rising*] Well, after that, I think it's time for us to go.

Pickering and Higgins rise.

CLARA [*rising*] Oh yes: we have three at-homes to go to still. Goodbye, Mrs Higgins. Goodbye, Colonel Pickering. Goodbye, Professor Higgins.

HIGGINS [*coming grimly at her from the divan, and accompanying her to the door*] Goodbye. Be sure you try on that small talk at the three at-homes. Dont be nervous about it.

Pitch it in strong.

CLARA [*all smiles*] I will. Goodbye. Such nonsense, all this early Victorian prudery!

HIGGINS [*tempting her*] Such damned nonsense!

CLARA. Such bloody nonsense!

MRS EYNSFORD HILL [*convulsively*] Clara!

CLARA. Ha! ha! [*She goes out radiant, conscious of being thoroughly up to date, and is heard descending the stairs in a stream of silvery laughter*].

FREDDY [*to the heavens at large*] Well, I ask you— [*He gives it up, and comes to Mrs Higgins*]. Goodbye.

MRS HIGGINS [*shaking hands*] Goodbye. Would you like to meet Miss Doolittle again?

FREDDY [*eagerly*] Yes, I should, most awfully.

MRS HIGGINS. Well, you know my days.

FREDDY. Yes. Thanks awfully. Goodbye. [*He goes out*].

MRS EYNSFORD HILL. Goodbye, Mr Higgins.

HIGGINS. Goodbye. Goodbye.

MRS EYNSFORD HILL [*to Pickering*] It's no use. I shall never be able to bring myself to use that word.

PICKERING. Dont. It's not compulsory, you know. Youll get on quite well without it.

MRS EYNSFORD HILL. Only, Clara is so down on me if I am not positively reeking with the latest slang. Goodbye.

PICKERING. Goodbye [*They shake hands*].

MRS EYNSFORD HILL [*to Mrs Higgins*] You mustnt mind Clara. [*Pickering, catching from her lowered tone that this is not meant for him to hear, discreetly joins Higgins at the window*]. We're so poor! and she gets so few parties, poor child! She doesnt quite know. [*Mrs Higgins, seeing that her eyes are moist, takes her hand sympathetically and goes with her to the door*]. But the boy is nice. Dont you think so?

MRS HIGGINS. Oh, quite nice. I shall always be delighted to see him.

MRS EYNSFORD HILL. Thank you, dear. Goodbye. [*She goes out*].

HIGGINS [*eagerly*] Well? Is Eliza presentable? [*He swoops*

PYGMALION

on his mother and drags her to the ottoman, where she sits down in Eliza's place with her son on her left].

Pickering returns to his chair on her right.

MRS HIGGINS. You silly boy, of course she's not presentable. She's a triumph of your art and of her dressmaker's; but if you suppose for a moment that she doesnt give herself away in every sentence she utters, you must be perfectly cracked about her.

PICKERING. But dont you think something might be done? I mean something to eliminate the sanguinary element from her conversation.

MRS HIGGINS. Not as long as she is in Henry's hands.

HIGGINS [*aggrieved*] Do you mean that my language is improper?

MRS HIGGINS. No, dearest: it would be quite proper— say on a canal barge; but it would not be proper for her at a garden party.

HIGGINS [*deeply injured*] Well I must say—

PICKERING [*interrupting him*] Come, Higgins: you must learn to know yourself. I havnt heard such language as yours since we used to review the volunteers in Hyde Park twenty years ago.

HIGGINS [*sulkily*] Oh, well, if you say so, I suppose I dont always talk like a bishop.

MRS HIGGINS [*quieting Henry with a touch*] Colonel Pickering: will you tell me what is the exact state of things in Wimpole Street?

PICKERING [*cheerfully: as if this completely changed the subject*] Well, I have come to live there with Henry. We work together at my Indian Dialects; and we think it more convenient—

MRS HIGGINS. Quite so. I know all about that: it's an excellent arrangement. But where does this girl live?

HIGGINS. With us, of course. Where should she live?

MRS HIGGINS. But on what terms? Is she a servant? If not, what is she?

PICKERING [*slowly*] I think I know what you mean, Mrs

247

Higgins.

HIGGINS. Well, dash me if *I* do! Ive had to work at the girl every day for months to get her to her present pitch. Besides, she's useful. She knows where my things are, and remembers my appointments and so forth.

MRS HIGGINS. How does your housekeeper get on with her?

HIGGINS. Mrs Pearce? Oh, she's jolly glad to get so much taken off her hands; for before Eliza came, she used to have to find things and remind me of my appointments. But she's got some silly bee in her bonnet about Eliza. She keeps saying "You dont think, sir": doesnt she, Pick?

PICKERING. Yes: thats the formula. "You dont think, sir." Thats the end of every conversation about Eliza.

HIGGINS. As if I ever stop thinking about the girl and her confounded vowels and consonants. I'm worn out, thinking about her, and watching her lips and her teeth and her tongue, not to mention her soul, which is the quaintest of the lot.

MRS HIGGINS. You certainly are a pretty pair of babies, playing with your live doll.

HIGGINS. Playing! The hardest job I ever tackled: make no mistake about that, mother. But you have no idea how frightfully interesting it is to take a human being and change her into a quite different human being by creating a new speech for her. It's filling up the deepest gulf that separates class from class and soul from soul.

PICKERING [*drawing his chair closer to Mrs Higgins and bending over to her eagerly*] Yes: it's enormously interesting. I assure you, Mrs Higgins, we take Eliza very seriously. Every week—every day almost—there is some new change. [*Closer again*] We keep records of every stage—dozens of gramophone disks and photographs—

HIGGINS [*assailing her at the other ear*] Yes, by George: it's the most absorbing experiment I ever tackled. She regularly fills our lives up: doesnt she, Pick?

PICKERING. We're always talking Eliza.

248

HIGGINS. Teaching Eliza.

PICKERING. Dressing Eliza.

MRS HIGGINS. What!

HIGGINS. Inventing new Elizas.

HIGGINS.	*[speaking together]*	You know, she has the most extraordinary quickness of ear:
PICKERING.		I assure you, my dear Mrs Higgins, that girl
HIGGINS.		just like a parrot. Ive tried her with every
PICKERING.		is a genius. She can play the piano quite beautifully.
HIGGINS.		possible sort of sound that a human being can make—
PICKERING.		We have taken her to classical concerts and to music
HIGGINS.		Continental dialects, African dialects, Hottentot
PICKERING.		halls; and it's all the same to her: she plays everything
HIGGINS.		clicks, things it took me years to get hold of; and
PICKERING.		she hears right off when she comes home, whether it's
HIGGINS.		she picks them up like a shot, right away, as if she had
PICKERING.		Beethoven and Brahms or Lehar and Lionel Monckton;
HIGGINS.		been at it all her life.
PICKERING.		though six months ago, she'd never as much as touched a piano—

MRS HIGGINS [*putting her fingers in her ears, as they are by this time shouting one another down with an intolerable noise*] Sh-sh-sh—sh! [*They stop*].

PICKERING. I beg your pardon. [*He draws his chair back apologetically*].

PYGMALION

HIGGINS. Sorry. When Pickering starts shouting nobody can get a word in edgeways.

MRS HIGGINS. Be quiet, Henry. Colonel Pickering: dont you realize that when Eliza walked into Wimpole Street, something walked in with her?

PICKERING. Her father did. But Henry soon got rid of him.

MRS HIGGINS. It would have been more to the point if her mother had. But as her mother didnt something else did.

PICKERING. But what?

MRS HIGGINS [*unconsciously dating herself by the word*] A problem.

PICKERING. Oh, I see. The problem of how to pass her off as a lady.

HIGGINS. I'll solve that problem. Ive half solved it already.

MRS HIGGINS. No, you two infinitely stupid male creatures: the problem of what is to be done with her afterwards.

HIGGINS. I dont see anything in that. She can go her own way, with all the advantages I have given her.

MRS HIGGINS. The advantages of that poor woman who was here just now! The manners and habits that disqualify a fine lady from earning her own living without giving her a fine lady's income! Is that what you mean?

PICKERING [*indulgently, being rather bored*] Oh, that will be all right, Mrs Higgins. [*He rises to go*].

HIGGINS [*rising also*] We'll find her some light employment.

PICKERING. She's happy enough. Dont you worry about her. Goodbye. [*He shakes hands as if he were consoling a frightened child, and makes for the door*].

HIGGINS. Anyhow, theres no good bothering now. The thing's done. Goodbye, mother. [*He kisses her, and follows Pickering*].

PICKERING [*turning for a final consolation*] There are plenty of openings. We'll do whats right. Goodbye.

HIGGINS [*to Pickering as they go out together*] Let's take

PYGMALION

her to the Shakespear exhibition at Earls Court.

PICKERING. Yes: lets. Her remarks will be delicious.

HIGGINS. She'll mimic all the people for us when we get home.

PICKERING. Ripping. [*Both are heard laughing as they go downstairs*].

MRS HIGGINS [*rises with an impatient bounce, and returns to her work at the writing-table. She sweeps a litter of disarranged papers out of her way; snatches a sheet of paper from her stationery case; and tries resolutely to write. At the third line she gives it up; flings down her pen; grips the table angrily and exclaims*] Oh, men! men!! men!!!

ACT IV

THE *Wimpole Street laboratory. Midnight. Nobody in the room. The clock on the mantelpiece strikes twelve. The fire is not alight: it is a summer night.*

Presently Higgins and Pickering are heard on the stairs.

HIGGINS [*calling down to Pickering*] I say, Pick: lock up, will you? I shant be going out again.

PICKERING. Right. Can Mrs Pearce go to bed? We dont want anything more, do we?

HIGGINS. Lord, no!

Eliza opens the door and is seen on the lighted landing in opera cloak, brilliant evening dress, and diamonds, with fan, flowers, and all accessories. She comes to the hearth, and switches on the electric lights there. She is tired: her pallor contrasts strongly with her dark eyes and hair; and her expression is almost tragic. She takes off her cloak; puts her fan and flowers on the piano; and sits down on the bench, brooding and silent. Higgins, in evening dress, with overcoat and hat, comes in, carrying a smoking jacket which he has picked up downstairs. He takes off the hat and overcoat; throws them carelessly on the newspaper stand; disposes of his coat in the same way; puts on the smoking jacket; and throws himself wearily into the easy-chair at the hearth. Pickering, similarly attired, comes in. He also takes off his hat and overcoat, and is about to throw them on Higgins's when he hesitates.

PICKERING. I say: Mrs Pearce will row if we leave these things lying about in the drawing room.

HIGGINS. Oh, chuck them over the bannisters into the hall. She'll find them there in the morning and put them away all right. She'll think we were drunk.

PICKERING. We are, slightly. Are there any letters?

HIGGINS. I didnt look. [*Pickering takes the overcoats and hats and goes downstairs. Higgins begins half singing half yawning an air from La Fanciulla del Golden West. Suddenly he stops and exclaims*] I wonder where the devil my slippers are!

Eliza looks at him darkly; then rises suddenly and leaves the room.

252

PYGMALION

Higgins yawns again, and resumes his song.

Pickering returns, with the contents of the letter-box in his hand.

PICKERING. Only circulars, and this coroneted billet-doux for you. [*He throws the circulars into the fender, and posts himself on the hearthrug, with his back to the grate*].

HIGGINS [*glancing at the billet-doux*] Money-lender. [*He throws the letter after the circulars*].

Eliza returns with a pair of large down-at-heel slippers. She places them on the carpet before Higgins, and sits as before without a word.

HIGGINS [*yawning again*] Oh Lord! What an evening! What a crew! What a silly tomfoolery! [*He raises his shoe to unlace it, and catches sight of the slippers. He stops unlacing and looks at them as if they had appeared there of their own accord*]. Oh! theyre there, are they?

PICKERING [*stretching himself*] Well, I feel a bit tired. It's been a long day. The garden party, a dinner party, and the opera! Rather too much of a good thing. But youve won your bet, Higgins. Eliza did the trick, and something to spare, eh?

HIGGINS [*fervently*] Thank God it's over!

Eliza flinches violently; but they take no notice of her; and she recovers herself and sits stonily as before.

PICKERING. Were you nervous at the garden party? *I* was. Eliza didnt seem a bit nervous.

HIGGINS. Oh, s h e wasnt nervous. I knew she'd be all right. No: it's the strain of putting the job through all these months that has told on me. It was interesting enough at first, while we were at the phonetics; but after that I got deadly sick of it. If I hadnt backed myself to do it I should have chucked the whole thing up two months ago. It was a silly notion: the whole thing has been a bore.

PICKERING. Oh come! the garden party was frightfully exciting. My heart began beating like anything.

HIGGINS. Yes, for the first three minutes. But when I saw we were going to win hands down, I felt like a bear in a cage, hanging about doing nothing. The dinner was worse: sitting gorging there for over an hour, with nobody but a damned fool of a fashionable woman to talk to! I tell you, Pickering, never again for me. No more artificial duchesses. The whole thing has been simple purgatory.

PICKERING. Youve never been broken in properly to the social routine. [*Strolling over to the piano*] I rather enjoy dipping into it occasionally myself: it makes me feel young again. Anyhow, it was a great success: an immense success. I was quite frightened once or twice because Eliza was doing it so well. You see, lots of the real people cant do it at all: theyre such fools that they think style comes by nature to people in their position; and so they never learn. Theres always something professional about doing a thing superlatively well.

HIGGINS. Yes: thats what drives me mad: the silly people dont know their own silly business. [*Rising*] However, it's over and done with; and now I can go to bed at last without dreading tomorrow.

Eliza's beauty becomes murderous.

PICKERING. I think I shall turn in too. Still, it's been a great occasion: a triumph for you. Goodnight. [*He goes*].

HIGGINS [*following him*] Goodnight. [*Over his shoulder, at the door*] Put out the lights, Eliza; and tell Mrs Pearce not to make coffee for me in the morning: I'll take tea. [*He goes out*].

Eliza tries to control herself and feel indifferent as she rises and walks across to the hearth to switch off the lights. By the time she gets there she is on the point of screaming. She sits down in Higgins's chair and holds on hard to the arms. Finally she gives way and flings herself furiously on the floor, raging.

HIGGINS [*in despairing wrath outside*] What the devil have I done with my slippers? [*He appears at the door*].

LIZA [*snatching up the slippers, and hurling them at him one after the other with all her force*] There are your slippers. And there. Take your slippers; and may you never have a day's luck with them!

HIGGINS [*astounded*] What on earth—! [*He comes to her*]. Whats the matter? Get up. [*He pulls her up*]. Anything wrong?

LIZA [*breathless*] Nothing wrong—with you. Ive won your bet for you, havnt I? Thats enough for you. *I* dont matter, I suppose.

HIGGINS. Y o u won my bet! You! Presumptuous insect! *I* won it. What did you throw those slippers at me for?

LIZA. Because I wanted to smash your face. I'd like to kill you, you selfish brute. Why didnt you leave me where you picked me out of—in the gutter? You thank God it's all over, and that now you can throw me back again there, do you? [*She crisps her fingers frantically*].

HIGGINS [*looking at her in cool wonder*] The creature is nervous, after all.

LIZA [*gives a suffocated scream of fury, and instinctively darts her nails at his face*]! !

HIGGINS [*catching her wrists*] Ah! would you? Claws in, you cat. How dare you shew your temper to me? Sit down and be quiet. [*He throws her roughly into the easy-chair*].

LIZA [*crushed by superior strength and weight*] Whats to become of me? Whats to become of me?

HIGGINS. How the devil do I know whats to become of you? What does it matter what becomes of you?

LIZA. You dont care. I know you dont care. You wouldnt care if I was dead. I'm nothing to you—not so much as them slippers.

HIGGINS [*thundering*] T h o s e slippers.

LIZA [*with bitter submission*] Those slippers. I didnt think it made any difference now.

A pause. Eliza hopeless and crushed. Higgins a little uneasy.

HIGGINS [*in his loftiest manner*] Why have you begun going on like this? May I ask whether you complain of your treatment here?

LIZA. No.

HIGGINS. Has anybody behaved badly to you? Colonel Pickering? Mrs Pearce? Any of the servants?

LIZA. No.

HIGGINS. I presume you dont pretend that *I* have treated you badly?

LIZA. No.

HIGGINS. I am glad to hear it. [*He moderates his tone*]. Perhaps youre tired after the strain of the day. Will you have a glass of champagne? [*He moves towards the door*].

LIZA. No. [*Recollecting her manners*] Thank you.

HIGGINS [*good-humored again*] This has been coming on you for some days. I suppose it was natural for you to be anxious about the garden party. But thats all over now. [*He pats her kindly on the shoulder. She writhes*]. Theres nothing more to worry about.

LIZA. No. Nothing more for y o u to worry about. [*She suddenly rises and gets away from him by going to the piano bench, where she sits and hides her face*]. Oh God! I wish I was dead.

HIGGINS [*staring after her in sincere surprise*] Why? In heaven's name, why? [*Reasonably, going to her*] Listen to me, Eliza. All this irritation is purely subjective.

LIZA. I dont understand. I'm too ignorant.

HIGGINS. It's only imagination. Low spirits and nothing else. Nobody's hurting you. Nothing's wrong. You go to bed like a good girl and sleep it off. Have a little cry and say your prayers: that will make you comfortable.

LIZA. I heard your prayers. "Thank God it's all over!"

HIGGINS [*impatiently*] Well, d o n t you thank God it's all over? Now you are free and can do what you like.

LIZA [*pulling herself together in desperation*] What am I fit for? What have you left me fit for? Where am I to go? What am I to do? Whats to become of me?

HIGGINS [*enlightened, but not at all impressed*] Oh t h a t s whats worrying you, is it? [*He thrusts his hands into his pockets, and walks about in his usual manner, rattling the contents of his pockets, as if condescending to a trivial subject out of pure kindness*]. I shouldnt bother about it if I were you. I should imagine you wont have much difficulty in settling yourself somewhere or other, though I hadnt quite realized that you were going away. [*She looks quickly at him: he does not look at her, but examines the dessert stand on the piano and decides that he will eat an apple*]. You might marry, you know. [*He bites a large piece out of the apple and munches it noisily*]. You see, Eliza, all men are not confirmed old bachelors like me and the Colonel. Most men are the marrying sort (poor devils!); and youre not bad-looking: it's quite a pleasure to look at you sometimes—not now, of course, because youre crying and looking as ugly as the very devil; but when youre all right and quite yourself, youre what I should call attractive. That is, to the people in the marrying line, you understand. You go to bed and have a good nice rest; and then get up and look at yourself in the glass; and you wont feel so cheap.

Eliza again looks at him, speechless, and does not stir.

The look is quite lost on him: he eats his apple with a dreamy expression of happiness, as it is quite a good one.

HIGGINS [*a genial afterthought occurring to him*] I daresay my mother could find some chap or other who would do very well.

LIZA. We were above that at the corner of Tottenham Court Road.

HIGGINS [*waking up*] What do you mean?

LIZA. I sold flowers. I didnt sell myself. Now youve made a lady of me I'm not fit to sell anything else. I wish youd left me where you found me.

HIGGINS [*slinging the core of the apple decisively into the grate*] Tosh, Eliza. Dont you insult human relations by dragging all this cant about buying and selling into it. You neednt marry the fellow if you dont like him.

LIZA. What else am I to do?

HIGGINS. Oh, lots of things. What about your old idea of a florist's shop? Pickering could set you up in one: he's lots of money. [*Chuckling*] He'll have to pay for all those togs you have been wearing today; and that, with the hire of the jewellery, will make a big hole in two hundred pounds. Why, six months ago you would have thought it the millennium to have a flower shop of your own. Come! youll be all right. I must clear off to bed: I'm devilish sleepy. By the way, I came down for something: I forget what it was.

LIZA. Your slippers.

HIGGINS. Oh yes, of course. You shied them at me. [*He picks them up, and is going out when she rises and speaks to him*].

LIZA. Before you go, sir—

HIGGINS [*dropping the slippers in his surprise at her calling him Sir*] Eh?

LIZA. Do my clothes belong to me or to Colonel Pickering?

HIGGINS [*coming back into the room as if her question were the very climax of unreason*] What the devil use would they be to Pickering?

LIZA. He might want them for the next girl you pick up to experiment on.

HIGGINS [*shocked and hurt*] Is that the way you feel towards us?

LIZA. I dont want to hear anything more about that. All I want to know is whether anything belongs to me. My own clothes were burnt.

HIGGINS. But what does it matter? Why need you start bothering about that in the middle of the night?

LIZA. I want to know what I may take away with me. I dont want to be accused of stealing.

HIGGINS [*now deeply wounded*] Stealing! You shouldnt have said that, Eliza. That shews a want of feeling.

LIZA. I'm sorry. I'm only a common ignorant girl; and in my station I have to be careful. There cant be any feelings between the like of you and the like of me. Please will you tell me what belongs to me and what doesnt?

HIGGINS [*very sulky*] You may take the whole damned houseful if you like. Except the jewels. Theyre hired. Will that satisfy you? [*He turns on his heel and is about to go in extreme dudgeon*].

LIZA [*drinking in his emotion like nectar, and nagging him to provoke a further supply*] Stop, please. [*She takes off her jewels*]. Will you take these to your room and keep them safe? I dont want to run the risk of their being missing.

HIGGINS [*furious*] Hand them over. [*She puts them into his hands*]. If these belonged to me instead of to the jeweller, I'd ram them down your ungrateful throat. [*He perfunctorily thrusts them into his pockets, unconsciously decorating himself with the protruding ends of the chains*].

LIZA [*taking a ring off*] This ring isnt the jeweller's: it's the one you bought me in Brighton. I dont want it now. [*Higgins dashes the ring violently into the fireplace, and turns on her so threateningly that she crouches over the piano with her hands over her face, and exclaims*] Dont you hit me.

HIGGINS. Hit you! You infamous creature, how dare you accuse me of such a thing? It is you who have hit me. You have wounded me to the heart.

LIZA [*thrilling with hidden joy*] I'm glad. Ive got a little of my own back, anyhow.

HIGGINS [*with dignity, in his finest professional style*] You have caused me to lose my temper: a thing that has hardly ever happened to me before. I prefer to say nothing more tonight. I am going to bed.

LIZA [*pertly*] Youd better leave a note for Mrs Pearce about the coffee; for she wont be told by me.

HIGGINS [*formally*] Damn Mrs Pearce; and damn the coffee; and damn you; and damn my own folly in having lavished hard-earned knowledge and the treasure of my regard and intimacy on a heartless guttersnipe. [*He goes out with impressive decorum, and spoils it by slamming the door savagely*].

Eliza smiles for the first time; expresses her feelings by a wild pantomime in which an imitation of Higgins's exit is confused with her own triumph; and finally goes down on her knees on the hearthrug to look for the ring.

ACT V

MRS HIGGINS'S *drawing room. She is at her writing-table as before. The parlor-maid comes in.*

THE PARLOR-MAID [*at the door*] Mr Henry, maam, is downstairs with Colonel Pickering.

MRS HIGGINS. Well, shew them up.

THE PARLOR-MAID. Theyre using the telephone, maam. Telephoning to the police, I think.

MRS HIGGINS. What!

THE PARLOR-MAID [*coming further in and lowering her voice*] Mr Henry is in a state, maam. I thought I'd better tell you.

MRS HIGGINS. If you had told me that Mr Henry was not in a state it would have been more surprising. Tell them to come up when theyve finished with the police. I suppose he's lost something.

THE PARLOR-MAID. Yes, maam [*going*].

MRS HIGGINS. Go upstairs and tell Miss Doolittle that Mr Henry and the Colonel are here. Ask her not to come down til I send for her.

THE PARLOR-MAID. Yes, maam.

Higgins bursts in. He is, as the parlor-maid has said, in a state.

HIGGINS. Look here, mother: heres a confounded thing!

MRS HIGGINS. Yes, dear. Good morning. [*He checks his impatience and kisses her, whilst the parlor-maid goes out*]. What is it?

HIGGINS. Eliza's bolted.

MRS HIGGINS [*calmly continuing her writing*] You must have frightened her.

HIGGINS. Frightened her! nonsense! She was left last night, as usual, to turn out the lights and all that; and instead of going to bed she changed her clothes and went right off: her bed wasnt slept in. She came in a cab for her things before seven this morning; and that fool Mrs Pearce let her have them without telling me a word about it. What am I to do?

MRS HIGGINS. Do without, I'm afraid, Henry. The girl has a perfect right to leave if she chooses.

HIGGINS [*wandering distractedly across the room*] But I cant find anything. I dont know what appointments Ive got. I'm—[*Pickering comes in. Mrs Higgins puts down her pen and turns away from the writing-table*].

PICKERING [*shaking hands*] Good morning, Mrs Higgins. Has Henry told you? [*He sits down on the ottoman*].

HIGGINS. What does that ass of an inspector say? Have you offered a reward?

MRS HIGGINS [*rising in indignant amazement*] You dont mean to say you have set the police after Eliza.

HIGGINS. Of course. What are the police for? What else could we do? [*He sits in the Elizabethan chair*].

PICKERING. The inspector made a lot of difficulties. I really think he suspected us of some improper purpose.

MRS HIGGINS. Well, of course he did. What right have you to go to the police and give the girl's name as if she were a thief, or a lost umbrella, or something? Really! [*She sits down again, deeply vexed*].

HIGGINS. But we want to find her.

PICKERING. We cant let her go like this, you know, Mrs Higgins. What were we to do?

MRS HIGGINS. You have no more sense, either of you, than two children. Why—

The parlor-maid comes in and breaks off the conversation.

THE PARLOR-MAID. Mr Henry: a gentleman wants to see you very particular. He's been sent on from Wimpole Street.

HIGGINS. Oh, bother! I cant see anyone now. Who is it?

THE PARLOR-MAID. A Mr Doolittle, sir.

PICKERING. Doolittle! Do you mean the dustman?

THE PARLOR-MAID. Dustman! Oh no, sir: a gentleman.

HIGGINS [*springing up excitedly*] By George, Pick, it's some relative of hers that she's gone to. Somebody we know nothing about. [*To the parlor-maid*] Send him up, quick.

261

PYGMALION

THE PARLOR-MAID. Yes, sir. [*She goes*].

HIGGINS [*eagerly, going to his mother*] Genteel relatives! now we shall hear something. [*He sits down in the Chippendale chair*].

MRS HIGGINS. Do you know any of her people?

PICKERING. Only her father: the fellow we told you about.

THE PARLOR-MAID [*announcing*] Mr Doolittle. [*She withdraws*].

Doolittle enters. He is brilliantly dressed in a new fashionable frock-coat, with white waistcoat and grey trousers. A flower in his buttonhole, a dazzling silk hat, and patent leather shoes complete the effect. He is too concerned with the business he has come on to notice Mrs Higgins. He walks straight to Higgins, and accosts him with vehement reproach.

DOOLITTLE [*indicating his own person*] See here! Do you see this? You done this.

HIGGINS. Done what, man?

DOOLITTLE. This, I tell you. Look at it. Look at this hat. Look at this coat.

PICKERING. Has Eliza been buying you clothes?

DOOLITTLE. Eliza! not she. Not half. Why would she buy me clothes?

MRS HIGGINS. Good morning, Mr Doolittle. Wont you sit down?

DOOLITTLE [*taken aback as he becomes conscious that he has forgotten his hostess*] Asking your pardon, maam. [*He approaches her and shakes her proffered hand*]. Thank you. [*He sits down on the ottoman, on Pickering's right*]. I am that full of what has happened to me that I cant think of anything else.

HIGGINS. What the dickens has happened to you?

DOOLITTLE. I shouldnt mind if it had only happened to me: anything might happen to anybody and nobody to blame but Providence, as you might say. But this is something that you done to me: yes, you, Henry Higgins.

HIGGINS. Have you found Eliza? Thats the point.

DOOLITTLE. Have you lost her?

HIGGINS. Yes.

DOOLITTLE. You have all the luck, you have. I aint found her; but she'll find me quick enough now after what you done to me.

MRS HIGGINS. But what has my son done to you, Mr Doolittle?

DOOLITTLE. Done to me! Ruined me. Destroyed my happiness. Tied me up and delivered me into the hands of middle class morality.

HIGGINS [*rising intolerantly and standing over Doolittle*] Youre raving. Youre drunk. Youre mad. I gave you five pounds. After that I had two conversations with you, at half-a-crown an hour. Ive never seen you since.

DOOLITTLE. Oh! Drunk! am I? Mad! am I? Tell me this. Did you or did you not write a letter to an old blighter in America that was giving five millions to found Moral Reform Societies all over the world, and that wanted you to invent a universal language for him?

HIGGINS. What! Ezra D. Wannafeller! He's dead. [*He sits down again carelessly*].

DOOLITTLE. Yes: he's dead; and I'm done for. Now did you or did you not write a letter to him to say that the most original moralist at present in England, to the best of your knowledge, was Alfred Doolittle, a common dustman.

HIGGINS. Oh, after your last visit I remember making some silly joke of the kind.

DOOLITTLE. Ah! you may well call it a silly joke. It put the lid on me right enough. Just give him the chance he wanted to shew that Americans is not like us: that they recognize and respect merit in every class of life, however humble. Them words is in his blooming will, in which, Henry Higgins, thanks to your silly joking, he leaves me a share in his Pre-digested Cheese Trust worth three thousand a year on condition that I lecture for his Wannafeller Moral Reform World League as often as they ask me up to six times a year.

HIGGINS. The devil he does! Whew! [*Brightening suddenly*] What a lark!

PICKERING. A safe thing for you, Doolittle. They wont ask you twice.

DOOLITTLE. It aint the lecturing I mind. I'll lecture them blue in the face, I will, and not turn a hair. It's making a gentleman of me that I object to. Who asked him to make a gentleman of me? I was happy. I was free. I touched pretty nigh everybody for money when I wanted it, same as I touched you, Henry Higgins. Now I am worrited; tied neck and heels; and everybody touches me for money. It's a fine thing for you, says my solicitor. Is it? says I. You mean it's a good thing for you, I says. When I was a poor man and had a solicitor once when they found a pram in the dust cart, he got me off, and got shut of me and got me shut of him as quick as he could. Same with the doctors: used to shove me out of the hospital before I could hardly stand on my legs, and nothing to pay. Now they finds out that I'm not a healthy man and cant live unless they looks after me twice a day. In the house I'm not let do a hand's turn for myself: somebody else must do it and touch me for it. A year ago I hadnt a relative in the world except two or three that wouldnt speak to me. Now Ive fifty, and not a decent week's wages among the lot of them. I have to live for others and not for myself: thats middle class morality. You talk of losing Eliza. Dont you be anxious: I bet she's on my doorstep by this: she that could support herself easy by selling flowers if I wasnt respectable. And the next one to touch me will be you, Henry Higgins. I'll have to learn to speak middle class language from you, instead of speaking proper English. Thats where youll come in; and I daresay thats what you done it for.

MRS HIGGINS. But, my dear Mr Doolittle, you need not suffer all this if you are really in earnest. Nobody can force you to accept this bequest. You can repudiate it. Isnt that so, Colonel Pickering?

PICKERING. I believe so.

DOOLITTLE [*softening his manner in deference to her sex*] Thats the tragedy of it, maam. It's easy to say chuck it; but I havnt the nerve. Which of us has? We're all intimidated. Intimidated, maam: thats what we are. What is there for me if I chuck it but the workhouse in my old age? I have to dye my hair already to keep my job as a dustman. If I was one of the deserving poor, and had put by a bit, I could chuck it; but then why should I, acause the deserving poor might as well be millionaires for all the happiness they ever has. They dont know what happiness is. But I, as one of the undeserving poor, have nothing between me and the pauper's uniform but this here blasted three thousand a year that shoves me into the middle class. (Excuse the expression, maam: youd use it yourself if you had my provocation.) Theyve got you every way you turn: it's a choice between the Skilly of the workhouse and the Char Bydis of the middle class; and I havnt the nerve for the workhouse. Intimidated: thats what I am. Broke. Bought up. Happier men than me will call for my dust, and touch me for their tip; and I'll look on helpless, and envy them. And thats what your son has brought me to. [*He is overcome by emotion*].

MRS HIGGINS. Well, I'm very glad youre not going to do anything foolish, Mr Doolittle. For this solves the problem of Eliza's future. You can provide for her now.

DOOLITTLE [*with melancholy resignation*] Yes, maam: I'm expected to provide for everyone now, out of three thousand a year.

HIGGINS [*jumping up*] Nonsense! he cant provide for her. He shant provide for her. She doesnt belong to him. I paid him five pounds for her. Doolittle: either youre an honest man or a rogue.

DOOLITTLE [*tolerantly*] A little of both, Henry, like the rest of us: a little of both.

HIGGINS. Well, you took that money for the girl; and you have no right to take her as well.

MRS HIGGINS. Henry: dont be absurd. If you want to know where Eliza is, she is upstairs.

PYGMALION

HIGGINS [*amazed*] Upstairs!!! Then I shall jolly soon fetch her downstairs. [*He makes resolutely for the door*].

MRS HIGGINS [*rising and following him*] Be quiet, Henry. Sit down.

HIGGINS. I—

MRS HIGGINS. Sit down, dear; and listen to me.

HIGGINS. Oh very well, very well, very well. [*He throws himself ungraciously on the ottoman, with his face towards the windows*]. But I think you might have told us this half an hour ago.

MRS HIGGINS. Eliza came to me this morning. She passed the night partly walking about in a rage, partly trying to throw herself into the river and being afraid to, and partly in the Carlton Hotel. She told me of the brutal way you two treated her.

HIGGINS [*bounding up again*] What!

PICKERING [*rising also*] My dear Mrs Higgins, she's been telling you stories. We didnt treat her brutally. We hardly said a word to her; and we parted on particularly good terms. [*Turning on Higgins*]. Higgins: did you bully her after I went to bed?

HIGGINS. Just the other way about. She threw my slippers in my face. She behaved in the most outrageous way. I never gave her the slightest provocation. The slippers came bang into my face the moment I entered the room—before I had uttered a word. And used perfectly awful language.

PICKERING [*astonished*] But why? What did we do to her?

MRS HIGGINS. I think I know pretty well what you did. The girl is naturally rather affectionate, I think. Isnt she, Mr Doolittle?

DOOLITTLE. Very tender-hearted, maam. Takes after me.

MRS HIGGINS. Just so. She had become attached to you both. She worked very hard for you, Henry! I dont think you quite realize what anything in the nature of brain work means to a girl like that. Well, it seems that when the great day of trial came, and she did this wonderful thing for you without making a single mistake, you two sat there and never said a word to her, but talked together of how glad you were that it was all over and how you had been bored with the whole thing. And then you were surprised because she threw your slippers at you! *I* should have thrown the fire-irons at you.

HIGGINS. We said nothing except that we were tired and wanted to go to bed. Did we, Pick?

PICKERING [*shrugging his shoulders*] That was all.

MRS HIGGINS [*ironically*] Quite sure?

PICKERING. Absolutely. Really, that was all.

MRS HIGGINS. You didnt thank her, or pet her, or admire her, or tell her how splendid she'd been.

HIGGINS [*impatiently*] But she knew all about that. We didnt make speeches to her, if thats what you mean.

PICKERING [*conscience stricken*] Perhaps we were a little inconsiderate. Is she very angry?

MRS HIGGINS [*returning to her place at the writing-table*] Well, I'm afraid she wont go back to Wimpole Street, especially now that Mr Doolittle is able to keep up the position you have thrust on her; but she says she is quite willing to meet you on friendly terms and to let bygones be bygones.

HIGGINS [*furious*] Is she, by George? Ho!

MRS HIGGINS. If you promise to behave yourself, Henry, I'll ask her to come down. If not, go home; for you have taken up quite enough of my time.

HIGGINS. Oh, all right. Very well. Pick: you behave yourself. Let us put on our best Sunday manners for this creature that we picked out of the mud. [*He flings himself sulkily into the Elizabethan chair*].

DOOLITTLE [*remonstrating*] Now, now, Henry Higgins! have some consideration for my feelings as a middle class man.

MRS HIGGINS. Remember your promise, Henry. [*She presses the bell-button on the writing-table*]. Mr Doolittle: will you be so good as to step out on the balcony for a moment. I dont want Eliza to have the shock of your news until she has made it up with these two gentlemen. Would you mind?

PYGMALION

DOOLITTLE. As you wish, lady. Anything to help Henry to keep her off my hands. [*He disappears through the window*].

The parlor-maid answers the bell. Pickering sits down in Doolittle's place.

MRS HIGGINS. Ask Miss Doolittle to come down, please.

THE PARLOR-MAID. Yes, maam. [*She goes out*].

MRS HIGGINS. Now, Henry: be good.

HIGGINS. I am behaving myself perfectly.

PICKERING. He is doing his best, Mrs Higgins.

A pause. Higgins throws back his head; stretches out his legs; and begins to whistle.

MRS HIGGINS. Henry, dearest, you dont look at all nice in that attitude.

HIGGINS [*pulling himself together*] I was not trying to look nice, mother.

MRS HIGGINS. It doesnt matter, dear. I only wanted to make you speak.

HIGGINS. Why?

MRS HIGGINS. Because you cant speak and whistle at the same time.

Higgins groans. Another very trying pause.

HIGGINS [*springing up, out of patience*] Where the devil is that girl? Are we to wait here all day?

Eliza enters, sunny, self-possessed, and giving a staggeringly convincing exhibition of ease of manner. She carries a little work-basket, and is very much at home. Pickering is too much taken aback to rise.

LIZA. How do you do, Professor Higgins? Are you quite well?

HIGGINS [*choking*] Am I—[*He can say no more*].

LIZA. But of course you are: you are never ill. So glad to see you again, Colonel Pickering. [*He rises hastily; and they shake hands*]. Quite chilly this morning, isnt it? [*She sits down on his left. He sits beside her*].

HIGGINS. Dont you dare try this game on me. I taught it to you; and it doesnt take me in. Get up and come home; and dont be a fool.

268

PYGMALION

Eliza takes a piece of needlework from her basket, and begins to stitch at it, without taking the least notice of this outburst.

MRS HIGGINS. Very nicely put, indeed, Henry. No woman could resist such an invitation.

HIGGINS. You let her alone, mother. Let her speak for herself. You will jolly soon see whether she has an idea that I havnt put into her head or a word that I havnt put into her mouth. I tell you I have created this thing out of the squashed cabbage leaves of Covent Garden; and now she pretends to play the fine lady with me.

MRS HIGGINS [*placidly*] Yes, dear; but youll sit down, wont you?

Higgins sits down again, savagely.

LIZA [*to Pickering, taking no apparent notice of Higgins, and working away deftly*] Will you drop me altogether now that the experiment is over, Colonel Pickering?

PICKERING. Oh dont. You mustnt think of it as an experiment. It shocks me, somehow.

LIZA. Oh, I'm only a squashed cabbage leaf—

PICKERING [*impulsively*] No.

LIZA [*continuing quietly*]—but I owe so much to you that I should be very unhappy if you forgot me.

PICKERING. It's very kind of you to say so, Miss Doolittle.

LIZA. It's not because you paid for my dresses. I know you are generous to everybody with money. But it was from you that I learnt really nice manners; and that is what makes one a lady, isnt it? You see it was so very difficult for me with the example of Professor Higgins always before me. I was brought up to be just like him, unable to control myself, and using bad language on the slightest provocation. And I should never have known that ladies and gentlemen didnt behave like that if you hadnt been there.

HIGGINS. Well!!

PICKERING. Oh, thats only his way, you know. He doesnt mean it.

LIZA. Oh, *I* didnt mean it either, when I was a flower girl. It was only my way. But you see I did it; and thats what

269

makes the difference after all.

PICKERING. No doubt. Still, he taught you to speak; and I couldnt have done that, you know.

LIZA [*trivially*] Of course: that is his profession.

HIGGINS. Damnation!

LIZA [*continuing*] It was just like learning to dance in the fashionable way: there was nothing more than that in it. But do you know what began my real education?

PICKERING. What?

LIZA [*stopping her work for a moment*] Your calling me Miss Doolittle that day when I first came to Wimpole Street. That was the beginning of self-respect for me. [*She resumes her stitching*]. And there were a hundred little things you never noticed, because they came naturally to you. Things about standing up and taking off your hat and opening doors—

PICKERING. Oh, that was nothing.

LIZA. Yes: things that shewed you thought and felt about me as if I were something better than a scullery-maid; though of course I know you would have been just the same to a scullery-maid if she had been let into the drawing room. You never took off your boots in the dining room when I was there.

PICKERING. You mustnt mind that. Higgins takes off his boots all over the place.

LIZA. I know. I am not blaming him. It is his way, isnt it? But it made s u c h a difference to me that you didnt do it. You see, really and truly, apart from the things anyone can pick up (the dressing and the proper way of speaking, and so on), the difference between a lady and a flower girl is not how she behaves, but how she's treated. I shall always be a flower girl to Professor Higgins, because he always treats me as a flower girl, and always will; but I know I can be a lady to you, because you always treat me as a lady, and always will.

MRS HIGGINS. Please dont grind your teeth, Henry.

PICKERING. Well, this is really very nice of you, Miss Doolittle.

LIZA. I should like you to call me Eliza, now, if you would.

PICKERING. Thank you. Eliza, of course.

LIZA. And I should like Professor Higgins to call me Miss Doolittle.

HIGGINS. I'll see you damned first.

MRS HIGGINS. Henry! Henry!

PICKERING [*laughing*] Why dont you slang back at him? Dont stand it. It would do him a lot of good.

LIZA. I cant. I could have done it once; but now I cant go back to it. Last night, when I was wandering about, a girl spoke to me; and I tried to get back into the old way with her; but it was no use. You told me, you know, that when a child is brought to a foreign country, it picks up the language in a few weeks, and forgets its own. Well, I am a child in your country. I have forgotten my own language, and can speak nothing but yours. Thats the real break-off with the corner of Tottenham Court Road. Leaving Wimpole Street finishes it.

PICKERING [*much alarmed*] Oh! but youre coming back to Wimpole Street, arnt you? Youll forgive Higgins?

HIGGINS [*rising*] Forgive! Will she, by George! Let her go. Let her find out how she can get on without us. She will relapse into the gutter in three weeks without me at her elbow.

Doolittle appears at the centre window. With a look of dignified reproach at Higgins, he comes slowly and silently to his daughter, who, with her back to the window, is unconscious of his approach.

PICKERING. He's incorrigible, Eliza. You wont relapse, will you?

LIZA. No: not now. Never again. I have learnt my lesson. I dont believe I could utter one of the old sounds if I tried. [*Doolittle touches her on her left shoulder. She drops her work, losing her self-possession utterly at the spectacle of her father's splendor*] A-a-a-a-a-ah-ow-ooh!

HIGGINS [*with a crow of triumph*] Aha! Just so. A-a-a-a-ahowooh! A-a-a-a-ahowooh! A-a-a-a-ahowooh! Victory!

Victory! [*He throws himself on the divan, folding his arms, and spraddling arrogantly*].

DOOLITTLE. Can you blame the girl? Dont look at me like that, Eliza. It aint my fault. Ive come into some money.

LIZA. You must have touched a millionaire this time, dad.

DOOLITTLE. I have. But I'm dressed something special today. I'm going to St George's, Hanover Square. Your stepmother is going to marry me.

LIZA [*angrily*] Youre going to let yourself down to marry that low common woman!

PICKERING [*quietly*] He ought to, Eliza. [*To Doolittle*] Why has she changed her mind?

DOOLITTLE [*sadly*] Intimidated, Governor. Intimidated. Middle class morality claims its victim. Wont you put on your hat, Liza, and come and see me turned off?

LIZA. If the Colonel says I must, I—I'll [*almost sobbing*] I'll demean myself. And get insulted for my pains, like enough.

DOOLITTLE. Dont be afraid: she never comes to words with anyone now, poor woman! respectability has broke all the spirit out of her.

PICKERING [*squeezing Eliza's elbow gently*] Be kind to them, Eliza. Make the best of it.

LIZA [*forcing a little smile for him through her vexation*] Oh well, just to shew theres no ill feeling. I'll be back in a moment. [*She goes out*].

DOOLITTLE [*sitting down beside Pickering*] I feel uncommon nervous about the ceremony, Colonel. I wish youd come and see me through it.

PICKERING. But youve been through it before, man. You were married to Eliza's mother.

DOOLITTLE. Who told you that, Colonel?

PICKERING. Well, nobody told me. But I concluded—naturally—

DOOLITTLE. No: that aint the natural way, Colonel: it's only the middle class way. My way was always the un-

PYGMALION

deserving way. But dont say nothing to Eliza. She dont know: I always had a delicacy about telling her.

PICKERING. Quite right. We'll leave it so, if you dont mind.

DOOLITTLE. And youll come to the church, Colonel, and put me through straight?

PICKERING. With pleasure. As far as a bachelor can.

MRS HIGGINS. May I come, Mr Doolittle? I should be very sorry to miss your wedding.

DOOLITTLE. I should indeed be honored by your condescension, maam; and my poor old woman would take it as a tremenjous compliment. She's been very low, thinking of the happy days that are no more.

MRS HIGGINS [*rising*] I'll order the carriage and get ready. [*The men rise, except Higgins*]. I shant be more than fifteen minutes. [*As she goes to the door Eliza comes in, hatted and buttoning her gloves*]. I'm going to the church to see your father married, Eliza. You had better come in the brougham with me. Colonel Pickering can go on with the bridegroom.

Mrs Higgins goes out. Eliza comes to the middle of the room between the centre window and the ottoman. Pickering joins her.

DOOLITTLE. Bridegroom! What a word! It makes a man realize his position, somehow. [*He takes up his hat and goes towards the door*].

PICKERING. Before I go, Eliza, do forgive him and come back to us.

LIZA. I dont think papa would allow me. Would you, dad?

DOOLITTLE [*sad but magnanimous*] They played you off very cunning, Eliza, them two sportsmen. If it had been only one of them, you could have nailed him. But you see, there was two; and one of them chaperoned the other, as you might say. [*To Pickering*] It was artful of you, Colonel; but I bear no malice: I should have done the same myself. I been the victim of one woman after another all my life; and I dont grudge you two getting the better of Eliza. I shant interfere. It's time for us to go, Colonel. So long, Henry. See you in St George's, Eliza. [*He goes out*].

PICKERING [*coaxing*] Do stay with us, Eliza. [*He follows Doolittle*].

Eliza goes out on the balcony to avoid being alone with Higgins. He rises and joins her there. She immediately comes back into the room and makes for the door; but he goes along the balcony quickly and gets his back to the door before she reaches it.

HIGGINS. Well, Eliza, youve had a bit of your own back, as you call it. Have you had enough? and are you going to be reasonable? Or do you want any more?

LIZA. You want me back only to pick up your slippers and put up with your tempers and fetch and carry for you.

HIGGINS. I havnt said I wanted you back at all.

LIZA. Oh, indeed. Then what are we talking about?

HIGGINS. About you, not about me. If you come back I shall treat you just as I have always treated you. I cant change my nature; and I dont intend to change my manners. My manners are exactly the same as Colonel Pickering's.

LIZA. Thats not true. He treats a flower girl as if she was a duchess.

HIGGINS. And I treat a duchess as if she was a flower girl.

LIZA. I see. [*She turns away composedly, and sits on the ottoman, facing the window*]. The same to everybody.

HIGGINS. Just so.

LIZA. Like father.

HIGGINS [*grinning, a little taken down*] Without accepting the comparison at all points, Eliza, it's quite true that your father is not a snob, and that he will be quite at home in any station of life to which his eccentric destiny may call him. [*Seriously*] The great secret, Eliza, is not having bad manners or good manners or any other particular sort of manners, but having the same manner for all human souls: in short, behaving as if you were in Heaven, where there are no third-class carriages, and one soul is as good as another.

LIZA. Amen. You are a born preacher.

HIGGINS [*irritated*] The question is not whether I treat you rudely, but whether you ever heard me treat anyone else better.

PYGMALION

LIZA [*with sudden sincerity*] I dont care how you treat me. I dont mind your swearing at me. I dont mind a black eye: Ive had one before this. But [*standing up and facing him*] I wont be passed over.

HIGGINS. Then get out of my way; for I wont stop for you. You talk about me as if I were a motor bus.

LIZA. So you are a motor bus: all bounce and go, and no consideration for anyone. But I can do without you: dont think I cant.

HIGGINS. I know you can. I told you you could.

LIZA [*wounded, getting away from him to the other side of the ottoman with her face to the hearth*] I know you did, you brute. You wanted to get rid of me.

HIGGINS. Liar.

LIZA. Thank you. [*She sits down with dignity*].

HIGGINS. You never asked yourself, I suppose, whether *I* could do without you.

LIZA [*earnestly*] Dont you try to get round me. Youll have to do without me.

HIGGINS [*arrogant*] I can do without anybody. I have my own soul: my own spark of divine fire. But [*with sudden humility*] I shall miss you, Eliza. [*He sits down near her on the ottoman*]. I have learnt something from your idiotic notions: I confess that humbly and gratefully. And I have grown accustomed to your voice and appearance. I like them, rather.

LIZA. Well, you have both of them on your gramophone and in your book of photographs. When you feel lonely without me, you can turn the machine on. It's got no feelings to hurt.

HIGGINS. I cant turn your soul on. Leave me those feelings; and you can take away the voice and the face. They are not you.

LIZA. Oh, you a re a devil. You can twist the heart in a girl as easy as some could twist her arms to hurt her. Mrs Pearce warned me. Time and again she has wanted to leave you; and you always got round her at the last minute. And you dont care a bit for her. And you dont care a bit for me.

HIGGINS. I care for life, for humanity; and you are a part of it that has come my way and been built into my house. What more can you or anyone ask?

LIZA. I wont care for anybody that doesnt care for me.

HIGGINS. Commercial principles, Eliza. Like [*reproducing her Covent Garden pronunciation with professional exactness*] s'yollin voylets [selling violets], isnt it?

LIZA. Dont sneer at me. It's mean to sneer at me.

HIGGINS. I have never sneered in my life. Sneering doesnt become either the human face or the human soul. I am expressing my righteous contempt for Commercialism. I dont and wont trade in affection. You call me a brute because you couldnt buy a claim on me by fetching my slippers and finding my spectacles. You were a fool: I think a woman fetching a man's slippers is a disgusting sight: did I ever fetch your slippers? I think a good deal more of you for throwing them in my face. No use slaving for me and then saying you want to be cared for: who cares for a slave? If you come back, come back for the sake of good fellowship; for youll get nothing else. Youve had a thousand times as much out of me as I have out of you; and if you dare to set up your little dog's tricks of fetching and carrying slippers against my creation of a Duchess Eliza, I'll slam the door in your silly face.

LIZA. What did you do it for if you didnt care for me?

HIGGINS [*heartily*] Why, because it was my job.

LIZA. You never thought of the trouble it would make for me.

HIGGINS. Would the world ever have been made if its maker had been afraid of making trouble? Making life means making trouble. Theres only one way of escaping trouble; and thats killing things. Cowards, you notice, are always shrieking to have troublesome people killed.

LIZA. I'm no preacher: I dont notice things like that. I notice that you dont notice me.

HIGGINS [*jumping up and walking about intolerantly*] Eliza: youre an idiot. I waste the treasures of my Miltonic mind by spreading them before you. Once for all, understand that I go my way and do my work without caring two-pence what happens to either of us. I am not intimidated, like your father and your stepmother. So you can come back or go to the devil: which you please.

LIZA. What am I to come back for?

HIGGINS [*bouncing up on his knees on the ottoman and leaning over it to her*] For the fun of it. Thats why I took you on.

LIZA [*with averted face*] And you may throw me out to-morrow if I dont do everything you want me to?

HIGGINS. Yes; and you may walk out tomorrow if I dont do everything you want me to.

LIZA. And live with my stepmother?

HIGGINS. Yes, or sell flowers.

LIZA. Oh! if I only c o u l d go back to my flower basket! I should be independent of both you and father and all the world! Why did you take my independence from me? Why did I give it up? I'm a slave now, for all my fine clothes.

HIGGINS. Not a bit. I'll adopt you as my daughter and settle money on you if you like. Or would you rather marry Pickering?

LIZA [*looking fiercely round at him*] I wouldnt marry y o u if you asked me; and youre nearer my age than what he is.

HIGGINS [*gently*] Than he is: not "than what he is."

LIZA [*losing her temper and rising*] I'll talk as I like. Youre not my teacher now.

HIGGINS [*reflectively*] I dont suppose Pickering would, though. He's as confirmed an old bachelor as I am.

LIZA. Thats not what I want; and dont you think it. Ive always had chaps enough wanting me that way. Freddy Hill writes to me twice and three times a day, sheets and sheets.

HIGGINS [*disagreeably surprised*] Damn his impudence! [*He recoils and finds himself sitting on his heels*].

LIZA. He has a right to if he likes, poor lad. And he does love me.

HIGGINS [*getting off the ottoman*] You have no right to en-courage him.

LIZA. Every girl has a right to be loved.

HIGGINS. What! By fools like that?

LIZA. Freddy's not a fool. And if he's weak and poor and wants me, may be he'd make me happier than my betters that bully me and dont want me.

HIGGINS. Can he m a k e anything of you? Thats the point.

LIZA. Perhaps I could make something of him. But I never thought of us making anything of one another; and you never think of anything else. I only want to be natural.

HIGGINS. In short, you want me to be as infatuated about you as Freddy? Is that it?

LIZA. No I dont. Thats not the sort of feeling I want from you. And dont you be too sure of yourself or of me. I could have been a bad girl if I'd liked. Ive seen more of some things than you, for all your learning. Girls like me can drag gentlemen down to make love to them easy enough. And they wish each other dead the next minute.

HIGGINS. Of course they do. Then what in thunder are we quarrelling about?

LIZA [much troubled] I want a little kindness. I know I'm a common ignorant girl, and you a book-learned gentleman; but I'm not dirt under your feet. What I done [correcting herself] what I did was not for the dresses and the taxis: I did it because we were pleasant together and I come—came—to care for you; not to want you to make love to me, and not forgetting the difference between us, but more friendly like.

HIGGINS. Well, of course. Thats just how I feel. And how Pickering feels. Eliza: youre a fool.

LIZA. Thats not a proper answer to give me [she sinks on the chair at the writing-table in tears].

HIGGINS. It's all youll get until you stop being a common idiot. If youre going to be a lady, youll have to give up feeling neglected if the men you know dont spend half their time snivelling over you and the other half giving you black eyes. If you cant stand the coldness of my sort of life, and the strain of it, go back to the gutter. Work til you are more a brute than a human being; and then cuddle and squabble and drink til you fall asleep. Oh, it's a fine life, the life of the gutter. It's real: it's warm: it's violent: you can feel it through the thickest skin: you can taste it and smell it without any training or any work. Not like Science and Literature and Classical Music and Philosophy and Art. You find me cold, unfeeling, selfish, dont you? Very well: be off with you to the sort of people you like. Marry some sentimental hog or other with lots of money, and a thick pair of lips to kiss you with and a thick pair of boots to kick you with. If you cant appreciate what youve got, youd better get what you can appreciate.

LIZA [*desperate*] Oh, you are a cruel tyrant. I cant talk to you: you turn everything against me: I'm always in the wrong. But you know very well all the time that youre nothing but a bully. You know I cant go back to the gutter, as you call it, and that I have no real friends in the world but you and the Colonel. You know well I couldnt bear to live with a low common man after you two; and it's wicked and cruel of you to insult me by pretending I could. You think I must go back to Wimpole Street because I have nowhere else to go but father's. But dont you be too sure that you have me under your feet to be trampled on and talked down. I'll marry Freddy, I will, as soon as he's able to support me.

HIGGINS [*sitting down beside her*] Rubbish! you shall marry an ambassador. You shall marry the Governor-General of India or the Lord-Lieutenant of Ireland, or somebody who wants a deputy-queen. I'm not going to have my masterpiece thrown away on Freddy.

LIZA. You think I like you to say that. But I havnt forgot what you said a minute ago; and I wont be coaxed round as if I was a baby or a puppy. If I cant have kindness, I'll have independence.

HIGGINS. Independence? Thats middle class blasphemy. We are all dependent on one another, every soul of us on earth.

LIZA [*rising determinedly*] I'll let you see whether I'm dependent on you. If you can preach, I can teach. I'll go and be a teacher.

PYGMALION

HIGGINS. Whatll you teach, in heaven's name?

LIZA. What you taught me. I'll teach phonetics.

HIGGINS. Ha! ha! ha!

LIZA. I'll offer myself as an assistant to Professor Nepean.

HIGGINS [*rising in a fury*] What! That impostor! that humbug! that toadying ignoramus! Teach him my methods! my discoveries! You take one step in his direction and I'll wring your neck. [*He lays hands on her*]. Do you hear?

LIZA [*defiantly non-resistant*] Wring away. What do I care? I knew youd strike me some day. [*He lets her go, stamping with rage at having forgotten himself, and recoils so hastily that he stumbles back into his seat on the ottoman*]. Aha! Now I know how to deal with you. What a fool I was not to think of it before! You cant take away the knowledge you gave me. You said I had a finer ear than you. And I can be civil and kind to people, which is more than you can. Aha! Thats done you, Henry Higgins, it has. Now I dont care that [*snapping her fingers*] for your bullying and your big talk. I'll advertize it in the papers that your duchess is only a flower girl that you taught, and that she'll teach anybody to be a duchess just the same in six months for a thousand guineas. Oh, when I think of myself crawling under your feet and being trampled on and called names, when all the time I had only to lift up my finger to be as good as you, I could just kick myself.

HIGGINS [*wondering at her*] You damned impudent slut, you! But it's better than snivelling; better than fetching slippers and finding spectacles, isnt it? [*Rising*] By George, Eliza, I said I'd make a woman of you; and I have. I like you like this.

LIZA. Yes: you turn round and make up to me now that I'm not afraid of you, and can do without you.

HIGGINS. Of course I do, you little fool. Five minutes ago you were like a millstone round my neck. Now youre a tower of strength: a consort battleship. You and I and Pickering will be three old bachelors together instead of only two men and a silly girl.

PYGMALION

Mrs Higgins returns, dressed for the wedding. Eliza instantly becomes cool and elegant.

MRS HIGGINS. The carriage is waiting, Eliza. Are you ready?

LIZA. Quite. Is the Professor coming?

MRS HIGGINS. Certainly not. He cant behave himself in church. He makes remarks out loud all the time on the clergyman's pronunciation.

LIZA. Then I shall not see you again, Professor. Goodbye. [*She goes to the door*].

MRS HIGGINS [*coming to Higgins*] Goodbye, dear.

HIGGINS. Goodbye, mother. [*He is about to kiss her, when he recollects something*]. Oh, by the way, Eliza, order a ham and a Stilton cheese, will you? And buy me a pair of reindeer gloves, number eights, and a tie to match that new suit of mine, at Eale & Binman's. You can choose the color. [*His cheerful, careless, vigorous voice shows that he is incorrigible*].

LIZA [*disdainfully*] Buy them yourself. [*She sweeps out*].

MRS HIGGINS. I'm afraid youve spoiled that girl, Henry. But never mind, dear: I'll buy you the tie and gloves.

HIGGINS [*sunnily*] Oh, dont bother. She'll buy em all right enough. Goodbye.

They kiss. Mrs Higgins runs out. Higgins, left alone, rattles his cash in his pocket; chuckles; and disports himself in a highly self-satisfied manner.

*　　　*　　　*　　　*　　　*

The rest of the story need not be shewn in action, and indeed, would hardly need telling if our imaginations were not so enfeebled by their lazy dependence on the ready-mades and reach-me-downs of the ragshop in which Romance keeps its stock of "happy endings" to misfit all stories. Now, the history of Eliza Doolittle, though called a romance because the transfiguration it records seems exceedingly improbable, is common enough. Such transfigurations have been achieved by hundreds of resolutely ambitious young women since Nell Gwynne set them the example by playing queens and fascinating kings in the theatre in which she began by selling oranges. Nevertheless, people in all directions have assumed, for no other reason than that she became the heroine of a romance, that she must have married the hero of it. This is unbearable, not only because her little drama, if acted on such a thoughtless assumption, must be spoiled, but because the true sequel is patent to anyone with a sense of human nature in general, and of feminine instinct in particular.

Eliza, in telling Higgins she would not marry him if he asked her, was not coquetting: she was announcing a well-considered decision. When a bachelor interests, and dominates, and teaches, and becomes important to a spinster, as Higgins with Eliza, she always, if she has character enough to be capable of it, considers very seriously indeed whether she will play for becoming that bachelor's wife, especially if he is so little interested in marriage that a determined and devoted woman might capture him if she set herself resolutely to do it. Her decision will depend a good deal on whether she is really free to choose; and that, again, will depend on her age and income. If she is at the end of her youth, and has no security for her livelihood, she will marry him because she must marry anybody who will provide for her. But at Eliza's age a good-looking girl does not feel that pressure: she feels free to pick and choose. She is therefore guided by her instinct in the matter. Eliza's instinct tells her not to marry Higgins. It does not tell her to give him up. It is not in the slightest doubt as to his remaining one of the strongest personal interests in her life. It would be very sorely strained if there was another woman likely to supplant her with him. But as she feels sure of him on that last point, she has no doubt at all as to her course, and would not have any, even if the difference of twenty years in age, which seems so great to youth, did not exist between them.

As our own instincts are not appealed to by her conclusion, let us see whether we cannot discover some reason in it. When Higgins excused his indifference to young women on the ground that they had an irresistible rival in his mother, he gave the clue to his inveterate old-bachelordom. The case is uncommon only to the extent that remarkable mothers are uncommon. If an imaginative boy has a sufficiently rich mother who has intelligence, personal grace, dignity of character without harshness, and a cultivated sense of the best art of her time to enable her to make her house beautiful, she sets a standard for him against which very few women can struggle, besides effecting for him a disengagement of his affections, his sense of beauty, and his idealism from his specifically sexual impulses. This makes him a standing puzzle to the huge number of uncultivated people who have been brought up in tasteless homes by commonplace or disagreeable parents, and to whom, consequently, literature, painting, sculpture, music, and affectionate personal relations come as modes of sex if they come at all. The word passion means nothing else to them; and that Higgins could have a passion for phonetics and idealize his mother instead of Eliza, would seem to them absurd and unnatural. Nevertheless, when we look round and see that hardly anyone is too ugly or disagreeable to find a wife or a husband if he or she wants one, whilst many old maids and bachelors are above the average in quality and culture, we cannot help suspecting that the disentanglement of sex from the associations with which it is so commonly confused, a disentanglement which persons of genius achieve by sheer intellectual analysis, is sometimes produced or aided by parental fascination.

Now, though Eliza was incapable of thus explaining to herself Higgins's formidable powers of resistance to the charm that prostrated Freddy at the first glance, she was instinctively aware that she could never obtain a complete grip of him, or come between him and his mother (the first necessity of the married woman). To put it shortly, she knew that for some mysterious reason he had not the makings of a married man in him, according to her conception of a husband as one to whom she would be his nearest and fondest and warmest interest. Even had there been no mother-rival,

PYGMALION

she would still have refused to accept an interest in herself that was secondary to philosophic interests. Had Mrs Higgins died, there would still have been Milton and the Universal Alphabet. Landor's remark that to those who have the greatest power of loving, love is a secondary affair, would not have recommended Landor to Eliza. Put that along with her resentment of Higgins's domineering superiority, and her mistrust of his coaxing cleverness in getting round her and evading her wrath when he had gone too far with his impetuous bullying, and you will see that Eliza's instinct had good grounds for warning her not to marry her Pygmalion.

And now, whom did Eliza marry? For if Higgins was a predestinate old bachelor, she was most certainly not a predestinate old maid. Well, that can be told very shortly to those who have not guessed it from the indications she has herself given them.

Almost immediately after Eliza is stung into proclaiming her considered determination not to marry Higgins, she mentions the fact that young Mr Frederick Eynsford Hill is pouring out his love for her daily through the post. Now Freddy is young, practically twenty years younger than Higgins: he is a gentleman (or, as Eliza would qualify him, a toff), and speaks like one; he is nicely dressed, is treated by the Colonel as an equal, loves her unaffectedly, and is not her master, nor ever likely to dominate her in spite of his advantage of social standing. Eliza has no use for the foolish romantic tradition that all women love to be mastered, if not actually bullied and beaten. "When you go to women," says Nietzsche, "take your whip with you." Sensible despots have never confined that precaution to women: they have taken their whips with them when they have dealt with men, and been slavishly idealized by the men over whom they have flourished the whip much more than by women. No doubt there are slavish women as well as slavish men: and women, like men, admire those that are stronger than themselves. But to admire a strong person and to live under that

284

strong person's thumb are two different things. The weak may not be admired and hero-worshipped; but they are by no means disliked or shunned; and they never seem to have the least difficulty in marrying people who are too good for them. They may fail in emergencies; but life is not one long emergency: it is mostly a string of situations for which no exceptional strength is needed, and with which even rather weak people can cope if they have a stronger partner to help them out. Accordingly, it is a truth everywhere in evidence that strong people, masculine or feminine, not only do not marry stronger people, but do not shew any preference for them in selecting their friends. When a lion meets another with a louder roar "the first lion thinks the last a bore." The man or woman who feels strong enough for two, seeks for every other quality in a partner than strength.

The converse is also true. Weak people want to marry strong people who do not frighten them too much; and this often leads them to make the mistake we describe metaphorically as "biting off more than they can chew." They want too much for too little; and when the bargain is unreasonable beyond all bearing, the union becomes impossible: it ends in the weaker party being either discarded or borne as a cross, which is worse. People who are not only weak, but silly or obtuse as well, are often in these difficulties.

This being the state of human affairs, what is Eliza fairly sure to do when she is placed between Freddy and Higgins? Will she look forward to a lifetime of fetching Higgins's slippers or to a lifetime of Freddy fetching hers? There can be no doubt about the answer. Unless Freddy is biologically repulsive to her, and Higgins biologically attractive to a degree that overwhelms all her other instincts, she will, if she marries either of them, marry Freddy.

And that is just what Eliza did.

Complications ensued; but they were economic, not romantic. Freddy had no money and no occupation. His mother's jointure, a last relic of the opulence of Largelady

Park, had enabled her to struggle along in Earlscourt with
an air of gentility, but not to procure any serious secondary
education for her children, much less give the boy a profession. A clerkship at thirty shillings a week was beneath
Freddy's dignity, and extremely distasteful to him besides.
His prospects consisted of a hope that if he kept up appearances somebody would do something for him. The something appeared vaguely to his imagination as a private
secretaryship or a sinecure of some sort. To his mother it
perhaps appeared as a marriage to some lady of means who
could not resist her boy's niceness. Fancy her feelings when
he married a flower girl who had become déclassée under
extraordinary circumstances which were now notorious!

It is true that Eliza's situation did not seem wholly in-
elegible. Her father, though formerly a dustman, and now
fantastically disclassed, had become extremely popular in
the smartest society by a social talent which triumphed over
every prejudice and every disadvantage. Rejected by the
middle class, which he loathed, he had shot up at once into
the highest circles by his wit, his dustmanship (which he
carried like a banner), and his Nietzschean transcendence
of good and evil. At intimate ducal dinners he sat on the
right hand of the Duchess; and in country houses he smoked
in the pantry and was made much of by the butler when he
was not feeding in the dining room and being consulted by
cabinet ministers. But he found it almost as hard to do all
this on four thousand a year as Mrs Eynsford Hill to live
in Earlscourt on an income so pitiably smaller that I have
not the heart to disclose its exact figure. He absolutely
refused to add the last straw to his burden by contributing
to Eliza's support.

Thus Freddy and Eliza, now Mr and Mrs Eynsford
Hill, would have spent a penniless honeymoon but for a
wedding present of £500 from the Colonel to Eliza. It lasted
a long time because Freddy did not know how to spend
money, never having had any to spend, and Eliza, socially
trained by a pair of old bachelors, wore her clothes as long

as they held together and looked pretty, without the least regard to their being many months out of fashion. Still, £500 will not last two young people for ever; and they both knew, and Eliza felt as well, that they must shift for themselves in the end. She could quarter herself on Wimpole Street because it had come to be her home; but she was quite aware that she ought not to quarter Freddy there, and that it would not be good for his character if she did.

Not that the Wimpole Street bachelors objected. When she consulted them, Higgins declined to be bothered about her housing problem when that solution was so simple. Eliza's desire to have Freddy in the house with her seemed of no more importance than if she had wanted an extra piece of bedroom furniture. Pleas as to Freddy's character, and the moral obligation on him to earn his own living, were lost on Higgins. He denied that Freddy had any character, and declared that if he tried to do any useful work some competent person would have the trouble of undoing it: a procedure involving a net loss to the community, and great unhappiness to Freddy himself, who was obviously intended by Nature for such light work as amusing Eliza, which, Higgins declared, was a much more useful and honorable occupation than working in the city. When Eliza referred again to her project of teaching phonetics, Higgins abated not a jot of his violent opposition to it. He said she was not within ten years of being qualified to meddle with his pet subject; and as it was evident that the Colonel agreed with him, she felt she could not go against them in this grave matter, and that she had no right, without Higgins's consent, to exploit the knowledge he had given her; for his knowledge seemed to her as much his private property as his watch: Eliza was no communist. Besides, she was superstitiously devoted to them both, more entirely and frankly after her marriage than before it.

It was the Colonel who finally solved the problem, which had cost him much perplexed cogitation. He one day asked Eliza, rather shyly, whether she had quite given up her notion of keeping a flower shop. She replied that she had thought of it, but had put it out of her head, because the Colonel had said, that day at Mrs Higgins's, that it would never do. The Colonel confessed that when he said that, he had not quite recovered from the dazzling impression of the day before. They broke the matter to Higgins that evening. The sole comment vouchsafed by him very nearly led to a serious quarrel with Eliza. It was to the effect that she would have in Freddy an ideal errand boy.

Freddy himself was next sounded on the subject. He said he had been thinking of a shop himself; though it had presented itself to his pennilessness as a small place in which Eliza should sell tobacco at one counter whilst he sold newspapers at the opposite one. But he agreed that it would be extraordinarily jolly to go early every morning with Eliza to Covent Garden and buy flowers on the scene of their first meeting: a sentiment which earned him many kisses from his wife. He added that he had always been afraid to propose anything of the sort, because Clara would make an awful row about a step that must damage her matrimonial chances, and his mother could not be expected to like it after clinging for so many years to that step of the social ladder on which retail trade is impossible.

This difficulty was removed by an event highly unexpected by Freddy's mother. Clara, in the course of her incursions into those artistic circles which were the highest within her reach, discovered that her conversational qualifications were expected to include a grounding in the novels of Mr H. G. Wells. She borrowed them in various directions so energetically that she swallowed them all within two months. The result was a conversion of a kind quite common today. A modern Acts of the Apostles would fill fifty whole Bibles if anyone were capable of writing it.

Poor Clara, who appeared to Higgins and his mother as a disagreeable and ridiculous person, and to her own mother as in some inexplicable way a social failure, had never seen herself in either light; for, though to some extent ridiculed

PYGMALION

and mimicked in West Kensington like everybody else there, she was accepted as a rational and normal—or shall we say inevitable?—sort of human being. At worst they called her The Pusher; but to them no more than to herself had it ever occurred that she was pushing the air, and pushing it in a wrong direction. Still, she was not happy. She was growing desperate. Her one asset, the fact that her mother was what the Epsom greengrocer called a carriage lady, had no exchange value, apparently. It had prevented her from getting educated, because the only education she could have afforded was education with the Earlscourt greengrocer's daughter. It had led her to seek the society of her mother's class; and that class simply would not have her, because she was much poorer than the greengrocer, and, far from being able to afford a maid, could not afford even a housemaid, and had to scrape along at home with an illiberally treated general servant. Under such circumstances nothing could give her an air of being a genuine product of Largelady Park. And yet its tradition made her regard a marriage with anyone within her reach as an unbearable humiliation. Commercial people and professional people in a small way were odious to her. She ran after painters and novelists; but she did not charm them; and her bold attempts to pick up and practice artistic and literary talk irritated them. She was, in short, an utter failure, an ignorant, incompetent, pretentious, unwelcome, penniless, useless little snob; and though she did not admit these disqualifications (for nobody ever faces unpleasant truths of this kind until the possibility of a way out dawns on them) she felt their effects too keenly to be satisfied with her position.

Clara had a startling eyeopener when, on being suddenly wakened to enthusiasm by a girl of her own age who dazzled her and produced in her a gushing desire to take her for a model, and gain her friendship, she discovered that this exquisite apparition had graduated from the gutter in a few months time. It shook her so violently, that when Mr H. G. Wells lifted her on the point of his puissant pen, and placed

289

her at the angle of view from which the life she was leading
and the society to which she clung appeared in its true relation to real human needs and worthy social structure, he
effected a conversion and a conviction of sin comparable to
the most sensational feats of General Booth or Gypsy Smith.
Clara's snobbery went bang. Life suddenly began to move
with her. Without knowing how or why, she began to make
friends and enemies. Some of the acquaintances to whom
she had been a tedious or indifferent or ridiculous affliction,
dropped her: others became cordial. To her amazement she
found that some "quite nice" people were saturated with
Wells, and that this accessibility to ideas was the secret of
their niceness. People she had thought deeply religious, and
had tried to conciliate on that tack with disastrous results,
suddenly took an interest in her, and revealed a hostility to
conventional religion which she had never conceived possible except among the most desperate characters. They
made her read Galsworthy; and Galsworthy exposed the
vanity of Largelady Park and finished her. It exasperated
her to think that the dungeon in which she had languished
for so many unhappy years had been unlocked all the time,
and that the impulses she had so carefully struggled with
and stifled for the sake of keeping well with society, were
precisely those by which alone she could have come into any
sort of sincere human contact. In the radiance of these discoveries, and the tumult of their reaction, she made a fool of
herself as freely and conspicuously as when she so rashly
adopted Eliza's expletive in Mrs Higgins's drawing room;
for the new-born Wellsian had to find her bearings almost
as ridiculously as a baby; but nobody hates a baby for its in-
eptitudes, or thinks the worse of it for trying to eat the
matches; and Clara lost no friends by her follies. They
laughed at her to her face this time; and she had to defend
herself and fight it out as best she could.

When Freddy paid a visit to Earlscourt (which he never
did when he could possibly help it) to make the desolating
announcement that he and his Eliza were thinking of black-

ening the Largelady scutcheon by opening a shop, he found the little household already convulsed by a prior announcement from Clara that she also was going to work in an old furniture shop in Dover Street, which had been started by a fellow Wellsian. This appointment Clara owed, after all, to her old social accomplishment of Push. She had made up her mind that, cost what it might, she would see Mr Wells in the flesh; and she had achieved her end at a garden party. She had better luck than so rash an enterprise deserved. Mr Wells came up to her expectations. Age had not withered him, nor could custom stale his infinite variety in half an hour. His pleasant neatness and compactness, his small hands and feet, his teeming ready brain, his unaffected accessibility, and a certain fine apprehensiveness which stamped him as susceptible from his topmost hair to his tipmost toe, proved irresistible. Clara talked of nothing else for weeks and weeks afterwards. And as she happened to talk to the lady of the furniture shop, and that lady also desired above all things to know Mr Wells and sell pretty things to him, she offered Clara a job on the chance of achieving that end through her.

And so it came about that Eliza's luck held, and the expected opposition to the flower shop melted away. The shop is in the arcade of a railway station not very far from the Victoria and Albert Museum; and if you live in that neighborhood you may go there any day and buy a buttonhole from Eliza.

Now here is a last opportunity for romance. Would you not like to be assured that the shop was an immense success, thanks to Eliza's charms and her early business experience in Covent Garden? Alas! the truth is the truth: the shop did not pay for a long time, simply because Eliza and her Freddy did not know how to keep it. True, Eliza had not to begin at the very beginning: she knew the names and prices of the cheaper flowers; and her elation was unbounded when she found that Freddy, like all youths educated at cheap, pretentious, and thoroughly inefficient schools, knew a little

Latin. It was very little, but enough to make him appear to her a Porson or Bentley, and to put him at his ease with botanical nomenclature. Unfortunately he knew nothing else; and Eliza, though she could count money up to eighteen shillings or so, and had acquired a certain familiarity with the language of Milton from her struggles to qualify herself for winning Higgins's bet, could not write out a bill without utterly disgracing the establishment. Freddy's power of stating in Latin that Balbus built a wall and that Gaul was divided into three parts did not carry with it the slightest knowledge of accounts or business: Colonel Pickering had to explain to him what a cheque book and a bank account meant. And the pair were by no means easily teachable. Freddy backed up Eliza in her obstinate refusal to believe that they could save money by engaging a bookkeeper with some knowledge of the business. How, they argued, could you possibly save money by going to extra expense when you already could not make both ends meet? But the Colonel, after making the ends meet over and over again, at last gently insisted; and Eliza, humbled to the dust by having to beg from him so often, and stung by the uproarious derision of Higgins, to whom the notion of Freddy succeeding at anything was a joke that never palled, grasped the fact that business, like phonetics, has to be learned.

On the piteous spectacle of the pair spending their evenings in shorthand schools and polytechnic classes, learning bookkeeping and typewriting with incipient junior clerks, male and female, from the elementary schools, let me not dwell. There were even classes at the London School of Economics, and a humble personal appeal to the director of that institution to recommend a course bearing on the flower business. He, being a humorist, explained to them the method of the celebrated Dickensian essay on Chinese Metaphysics by the gentleman who read an article on China and an article on Metaphysics and combined the information. He suggested that they should combine the London

School with Kew Gardens. Eliza, to whom the procedure of the Dickensian gentleman seemed perfectly correct (as in fact it was) and not in the least funny(which was only her ignorance), took his advice with entire gravity. But the effort that cost her the deepest humiliation was a request to Higgins, whose pet artistic fancy, next to Milton's verse, was caligraphy, and who himself wrote a most beautiful Italian hand, that he would teach her to write. He declared that she was congenitally incapable of forming a single letter worthy of the least of Milton's words; but she persisted; and again he suddenly threw himself into the task of teaching her with a combination of stormy intensity, concentrated patience, and occasional bursts of interesting disquisition on the beauty and nobility, the august mission and destiny, of human handwriting. Eliza ended by acquiring an extremely uncommercial script which was a positive extension of her personal beauty, and spending three times as much on stationery as anyone else because certain qualities and shapes of paper became indispensable to her. She could not even address an envelope in the usual way because it made the margins all wrong.

Their commercial schooldays were a period of disgrace and despair for the young couple. They seemed to be learning nothing about flower shops. At last they gave it up as hopeless, and shook the dust of the shorthand schools, and the polytechnics, and the London School of Economics from their feet for ever. Besides, the business was in some mysterious way beginning to take care of itself. They had somehow forgotten their objections to employing other people. They came to the conclusion that their own way was the best, and that they had really a remarkable talent for business. The Colonel, who had been compelled for some years to keep a sufficient sum on current account at his bankers to make up their deficits, found that the provision was unnecessary: the young people were prospering. It is true that there was not quite fair play between them and their competitors in trade. Their week-ends in the country cost them nothing, and saved them the price of their Sunday dinners; for the motor car was the Colonel's; and he and Higgins paid the hotel bills. Mr F. Hill, florist and greengrocer (they soon discovered that there was money in asparagus; and asparagus led to other vegetables), had an air which stamped the business as classy; and in private life he was still Frederick Eynsford Hill, Esquire. Not that there was any swank about him: nobody but Eliza knew that he had been christened Frederick Challoner. Eliza herself swanked like anything.

That is all. That is how it has turned out. It is astonishing how much Eliza still manages to meddle in the housekeeping at Wimpole Street in spite of the shop and her own family. And it is notable that though she never nags her husband, and frankly loves the Colonel as if she were his favorite daughter, she has never got out of the habit of nagging Higgins that was established on the fatal night when she won his bet for him. She snaps his head off on the faintest provocation, or on none. He no longer dares to tease her by assuming an abysmal inferiority of Freddy's mind to his own. He storms and bullies and derides: but she stands up to him so ruthlessly that the Colonel has to ask her from time to time to be kinder to Higgins; and it is the only request of his that brings a mulish expression into her face. Nothing but some emergency or calamity great enough to break down all likes and dislikes, and throw them both back on their common humanity—and may they be spared any such trial!—will ever alter this. She knows that Higgins does not need her, just as her father did not need her. The very scrupulousness with which he told her that day that he had become used to having her there, and dependent on her for all sorts of little services, and that he should miss her if she went away (it would never have occurred to Freddy or the Colonel to say anything of the sort) deepens her inner certainty that she is "no more to him than them slippers"; yet she has a sense, too, that his indifference is deeper than the infatuation of commoner souls. She is immensely interested in him. She has even secret mischievous moments in which she wishes she could get him alone, on a desert island, away from all ties and with nobody else in the world to consider, and just drag him off his pedestal and see him making love like any common man. We all have private imaginations of that sort. But when it comes to business, to the life that she really leads as distinguished from the life of dreams and fancies, she likes Freddy and she likes the Colonel; and she does not like Higgins and Mr Doolittle. Galatea never does quite like Pygmalion: his relation to her is too godlike to be altogether agreeable.

MAJOR BARBARA

1905

PREFACE TO MAJOR BARBARA
FIRST AID TO CRITICS

BEFORE dealing with the deeper aspects of Major Barbara, let me, for the credit of English literature, make a protest against an unpatriotic habit into which many of my critics have fallen. Whenever my view strikes them as being at all outside the range of, say, an ordinary suburban churchwarden, they conclude that I am echoing Schopenhauer, Nietzsche, Ibsen, Strindberg, Tolstoy, or some other heresiarch in northern or eastern Europe.

I confess there is something flattering in this simple faith in my accomplishment as a linguist and my erudition as a philosopher. But I cannot countenance the assumption that life and literature are so poor in these islands that we must go abroad for all dramatic material that is not common and all ideas that are not superficial. I therefore venture to put my critics in possession of certain facts concerning my contact with modern ideas.

About half a century ago, an Irish novelist, Charles Lever, wrote a story entitled A Day's Ride: A Life's Romance. It was published by Charles Dickens in Household Words, and proved so strange to the public taste that Dickens pressed Lever to make short work of it. I read scraps of this novel when I was a child; and it made an enduring impression on me. The hero was a very romantic hero, trying to live bravely, chivalrously, and powerfully by dint of mere romance-fed imagination, without courage, without means, without knowledge, without skill, without anything real except his bodily appetites. Even in my childhood I found in this poor devil's unsuccessful encounters with the facts of life, a poignant quality that romantic fiction lacked. The book, in spite of its first failure, is not dead: I saw its title the other day in the catalogue of Tauchnitz.

Now why is it that when I also deal in the tragi-comic irony of the conflict between real life and the romantic imagination, critics never affiliate me to my countryman and immediate forerunner, Charles Lever, whilst they confi-

PREFACE TO MAJOR BARBARA

dently derive me from a Norwegian author of whose language I do not know three words, and of whom I knew nothing until years after the Shavian *Anschauung* was already unequivocally declared in books full of what came, ten years later, to be perfunctorily labelled Ibsenism? I was not Ibsenist even at second hand; for Lever, though he may have read Henri Beyle, *alias* Stendhal, certainly never read Ibsen. Of the books that made Lever popular, such as Charles O'Malley and Harry Lorrequer, I know nothing but the names and some of the illustrations. But the story of the day's ride and life's romance of Potts (claiming alliance with Pozzo di Borgo) caught me and fascinated me as something strange and significant, though I already knew all about Alnaschar and Don Quixote and Simon Tappertit and many another romantic hero mocked by reality. From the plays of Aristophanes to the tales of Stevenson that mockery has been made familiar to all who are properly saturated with letters.

Where, then, was the novelty in Lever's tale? Partly, I think, in a new seriousness in dealing with Potts's disease. Formerly, the contrast between madness and sanity was deemed comic: Hogarth shews us how fashionable people went in parties to Bedlam to laugh at the lunatics. I myself have had a village idiot exhibited to me as something irresistibly funny. On the stage the madman was once a regular comic figure: that was how Hamlet got his opportunity before Shakespear touched him. The originality of Shakespear's version lay in his taking the lunatic sympathetically and seriously, and thereby making an advance towards the eastern consciousness of the fact that lunacy may be inspiration in disguise, since a man who has more brains than his fellows necessarily appears as mad to them as one who has less. But Shakespear did not do for Pistol and Parolles what he did for Hamlet. The particular sort of madman they represented, the romantic make-believer, lay outside the pale of sympathy in literature: he was pitilessly despised and ridiculed here as he was in the east under the name of

300

Alnaschar, and was doomed to be, centuries later, under the name of Simon Tappertit. When Cervantes relented over Don Quixote, and Dickens relented over Pickwick, they did not become impartial: they simply changed sides, and became friends and apologists where they had formerly been mockers.

In Lever's story there is a real change of attitude. There is no relenting towards Potts: he never gains our affections like Don Quixote and Pickwick: he has not even the infatuate courage of Tappertit. But we dare not laugh at him, because, somehow, we recognize ourselves in Potts. We may, some of us, have enough nerve, enough muscle, enough luck, enough tact or skill or address or knowledge to carry things off better than he did; to impose on the people who saw through him; to fascinate Katinka (who cut Potts so ruthlessly at the end of the story); but for all that, we know that Potts plays an enormous part in ourselves and in the world, and that the social problem is not a problem of story-book heroes of the older pattern, but a problem of Pottses, and of how to make men of them. To fall back on my old phrase, we have the feeling—one that Alnaschar, Pistol, Parolles, and Tappertit never gave us—that Potts is a piece of really scientific natural history as distinguished from funny story telling. His author is not throwing a stone at a creature of another and inferior order, but making a confession, with the effect that the stone hits each of us full in the conscience and causes our self-esteem to smart very sorely. Hence the failure of Lever's book to please the readers of Household Words. That pain in the self-esteem nowadays causes critics to raise a cry of Ibsenism. I therefore assure them that the sensation first came to me from Lever and may have come to him from Beyle, or at least out of the Stendhalian atmosphere. I exclude the hypothesis of complete originality on Lever's part, because a man can no more be completely original in that sense than a tree can grow out of air.

Another mistake as to my literary ancestry is made

whenever I violate the romantic convention that all women
are angels when they are not devils; that they are better
looking than men; that their part in courtship is entirely
passive; and that the human female form is the most beautiful object in nature. Schopenhauer wrote a splenetic essay
which, as it is neither polite nor profound, was probably
intended to knock this nonsense violently on the head. A
sentence denouncing the idolized form as ugly has been
largely quoted. The English critics have read that sentence;
and I must here affirm, with as much gentleness as the implication will bear, that it has yet to be proved that they have
dipped any deeper. At all events, whenever an English
playwright represents a young and marriageable woman as
being anything but a romantic heroine, he is disposed of
without further thought as an echo of Schopenhauer. My
own case is a specially hard one, because, when I implore
the critics who are obsessed with the Schopenhauerian formula to remember that playwrights, like sculptors, study
their figures from life, and not from philosophic essays, they
reply passionately that I am not a playwright and that my
stage figures do not live. But even so, I may and do ask
them why, if they must give the credit of my plays to a philosopher, they do not give it to an English philosopher?
Long before I ever read a word by Schopenhauer, or even
knew whether he was a philosopher or a chemist, the Socialist revival of the eighteen-eighties brought me into contact,
both literary and personal, with Ernest Belfort Bax, an
English Socialist and philosophic essayist, whose handling
of modern feminism would provoke romantic protests from
Schopenhauer himself, or even Strindberg. As a matter of
fact I hardly noticed Schopenhauer's disparagements of
women when they came under my notice later on, so thoroughly had Bax familiarized me with the homoist attitude,
and forced me to recognize the extent to which public opinion, and consequently legislation and jurisprudence, is cor-
rupted by feminist sentiment.

Belfort Bax's essays were not confined to the Feminist

question. He was a ruthless critic of current morality. Other writers have gained sympathy for dramatic criminals by eliciting the alleged "soul of goodness in things evil"; but Bax would propound some quite undramatic and apparently shabby violation of our commercial law and morality, and not merely defend it with the most disconcerting ingenuity, but actually prove it to be a positive duty that nothing but the certainty of police persecution should prevent every right-minded man from at once doing on principle. The Socialists were naturally shocked, being for the most part morbidly moral people; but at all events they were saved later on from the delusion that nobody but Nietzsche had ever challenged our mercanto-Christian morality. I first heard the name of Nietzsche from a German mathematician, Miss Borchardt, who had read my Quintessence of Ibsenism, and told me that she saw what I had been reading: namely, Nietzsche's Jenseits von Gut und Böse. Which I protest I had never seen, and could not have read with any comfort, for want of the necessary German, if I had seen it.

Nietzsche, like Schopenhauer, is the victim in England of a single much quoted sentence containing the phrase "big blonde beast." On the strength of this alliteration it is assumed that Nietzsche gained his European reputation by a senseless glorification of selfish bullying as the rule of life, just as it is assumed, on the strength of the single word Superman (Übermensch) borrowed by me from Nietzsche, that I look for the salvation of society to the despotism of a single Napoleonic Superman, in spite of my careful demonstration of the folly of that outworn infatuation. But even the less recklessly superficial critics seem to believe that the modern objection to Christianity as a pernicious slave-morality was first put forward by Nietzsche. It was familiar to me before I ever heard of Nietzsche. The late Captain Wilson, author of several queer pamphlets, propagandist of a metaphysical system called Comprehensionism, and inventor of the term "Crosstianity" to distinguish the retrograde element in Christendom, was wont thirty years ago, in the discussions of the Dialectical Society, to protest earnestly against the beatitudes of the Sermon on the Mount as excuses for cowardice and servility, as destructive of our will, and consequently of our honor and manhood. Now it is true that Captain Wilson's moral criticism of Christianity was not a historical theory of it, like Nietzsche's; but this objection cannot be made to Stuart-Glennie, the successor of Buckle as a philosophic historian, who devoted his life to the elaboration and propagation of his theory that Christianity is part of an epoch (or rather an aberration, since it began as recently as 6000 B.C. and is already collapsing) produced by the necessity in which the numerically inferior white races found themselves to impose their domination on the colored races by priestcraft, making a virtue and a popular religion of drudgery and submissiveness in this world not only as a means of achieving saintliness of character but of securing a reward in heaven. Here was the slave-morality view formulated by a Scotch philosopher of my acquaintance long before we all began chattering about Nietzsche.

As Stuart-Glennie traced the evolution of society to the conflict of races, his theory made some sensation among Socialists—that is, among the only people who were seriously thinking about historical evolution at all—by its collision with the class-conflict theory of Karl Marx. Nietzsche, as I gather, regarded the slave-morality as having been invented and imposed on the world by slaves making a virtue of necessity and a religion of their servitude. Stuart-Glennie regarded the slave-morality as an invention of the superior white race to subjugate the minds of the inferior races whom they wished to exploit, and who would have destroyed them by force of numbers if their minds had not been subjugated. As this process is in operation still, and can be studied at first hand not only in our Church schools and in the struggle between our modern proprietary classes and the proletariat, but in the part played by Christian mission-

304

aries in reconciling the black races of Africa to their subjugation by European Capitalism, we can judge for ourselves whether the initiative came from above or below. My object here is not to argue the historical point, but simply to make our theatre critics ashamed of their habit of treating Britain as an intellectual void, and assuming that every philosophical idea, every historic theory, every criticism of our moral, religious and juridical institutions, must necessarily be either a foreign import, or else a fantastic sally (in rather questionable taste) totally unrelated to the existing body of thought. I urge them to remember that this body of thought is the slowest of growths and the rarest of blossomings, and that if there is such a thing on the philosophic plane as a matter of course, it is that no individual can make more than a minute contribution to it. In fact, their conception of clever persons parthenogenetically bringing forth complete original cosmogonies by dint of sheer "brilliancy" is part of that ignorant credulity which is the despair of the honest philosopher, and the opportunity of the religious impostor.

THE GOSPEL OF ST ANDREW UNDER-SHAFT

It is this credulity that drives me to help my critics out with Major Barbara by telling them what to say about it. In the millionaire Undershaft I have represented a man who has become intellectually and spiritually as well as practically conscious of the irresistible natural truth which we all abhor and repudiate: to wit, that the greatest of our evils, and the worst of our crimes is poverty, and that our first duty, to which every other consideration should be sacrificed, is not to be poor. "Poor but honest," "the respectable poor," and such phrases are as intolerable and as immoral as "drunken but amiable," "fraudulent but a good after-dinner speaker," "splendidly criminal," or the like. Security, the chief pretence of civilization, cannot exist where the worst of dangers, the danger of poverty, hangs over everyone's head, and where the alleged protection of our persons from violence is only an accidental result of the

305

existence of a police force whose real business is to force the poor man to see his children starve whilst idle people over-feed pet dogs with the money that might feed and clothe them.

It is exceedingly difficult to make people realize that an evil is an evil. For instance, we seize a man and deliberately do him a malicious injury: say, imprison him for years. One would not suppose that it needed any exceptional clearness of wit to recognize in this an act of diabolical cruelty. But in England such a recognition provokes a stare of surprise, followed by an explanation that the outrage is punishment or justice or something else that is all right, or perhaps by a heated attempt to argue that we should all be robbed and murdered in our beds if such stupid villainies as sentences of imprisonment were not committed daily. It is useless to argue that even if this were true, which it is not, the alternative to adding crimes of our own to the crimes from which we suffer is not helpless submission. Chickenpox is an evil; but if I were to declare that we must either submit to it or else repress it sternly by seizing everyone who suffers from it and punishing them by inoculation with smallpox, I should be laughed at; for though nobody could deny that the result would be to prevent chickenpox to some extent by making people avoid it much more carefully, and to effect a further apparent prevention by making them conceal it very anxiously, yet people would have sense enough to see that the deliberate propagation of smallpox was a creation of evil, and must therefore be ruled out in favor of purely humane and hygienic measures. Yet in the precisely parallel case of a man breaking into my house and stealing my wife's diamonds I am expected as a matter of course to steal ten years of his life, torturing him all the time. If he tries to defeat that monstrous retaliation by shooting me, my survivors hang him. The net result suggested by the police statistics is that we inflict atrocious injuries on the burglars we catch in order to make the rest take effectual precautions against detection; so that instead of saving our wives' diamonds from burglary we only greatly decrease our chances of ever getting them back, and increase our chances of being shot by the robber if we are unlucky enough to disturb him at his work.

But the thoughtless wickedness with which we scatter sentences of imprisonment, torture in the solitary cell and on the plank bed, and flogging, on moral invalids and energetic rebels, is as nothing compared to the silly levity with which we tolerate poverty as if it were either a wholesome tonic for lazy people or else a virtue to be embraced as St Francis embraced it. If a man is indolent, let him be poor. If he is drunken, let him be poor. If he is not a gentleman, let him be poor. If he is addicted to the fine arts or to pure science instead of to trade and finance, let him be poor. If he chooses to spend his urban eighteen shillings a week or his agricultural thirteen shillings a week on his beer and his family instead of saving it up for his old age, let him be poor. Let nothing be done for "the undeserving": let him be poor. Serve him right! Also—somewhat inconsistently—blessed are the poor!

Now what does this Let Him Be Poor mean? It means let him be weak. Let him be ignorant. Let him become a nucleus of disease. Let him be a standing exhibition and example of ugliness and dirt. Let him have rickety children. Let him be cheap and let him drag his fellows down to his own price by selling himself to do their work. Let his habitations turn our cities into poisonous congeries of slums. Let his daughters infect our young men with the diseases of the streets, and his sons revenge him by turning the nation's manhood into scrofula, cowardice, cruelty, hypocrisy, political imbecility, and all the other fruits of oppression and malnutrition. Let the undeserving become still less deserving; and let the deserving lay up for himself, not treasures in heaven, but horrors in hell upon earth. This being so, is it really wise to let him be poor? Would he not do ten times less harm as a prosperous burglar, incendiary, ravisher or murderer, to the utmost limits of humanity's comparatively

307

negligible impulses in these directions? Suppose we were to abolish all penalties for such activities, and decide that poverty is the one thing we will not tolerate—that every adult with less than, say, £365 a year, shall be painlessly but inexorably killed, and every hungry half naked child forcibly fattened and clothed, would not that be an enormous improvement on our existing system, which has already destroyed so many civilizations, and is visibly destroying ours in the same way?

Is there any radicle of such legislation in our parliamentary system? Well, there are two measures just sprouting in the political soil, which may conceivably grow to something valuable. One is the institution of a Legal Minimum Wage. The other, Old Age Pensions. But there is a better plan than either of these. Some time ago I mentioned the subject of Universal Old Age Pensions to my fellow Socialist Cobden-Sanderson, famous as an artist-craftsman in bookbinding and printing. "Why not Universal Pensions for Life?" said Cobden-Sanderson. In saying this, he solved the industrial problem at a stroke. At present we say callously to each citizen "If you want money, earn it" as if his having or not having it were a matter that concerned himself alone. We do not even secure for him the opportunity of earning it: on the contrary, we allow our industry to be organized in open dependence on the maintenance of "a reserve army of unemployed" for the sake of "elasticity." The sensible course would be Cobden-Sanderson's: that is, to give every man enough to live well on, so as to guarantee the community against the possibility of a case of the malignant disease of poverty, and then (necessarily) to see that he earned it.

Undershaft, the hero of Major Barbara, is simply a man who, having grasped the fact that poverty is a crime, knows that when society offered him the alternative of poverty or a lucrative trade in death and destruction, it offered him, not a choice between opulent villainy and humble virtue, but between energetic enterprise and cowardly infamy. His

308

conduct stands the Kantian test, which Peter Shirley's does not. Peter Shirley is what we call the honest poor man. Undershaft is what we call the wicked rich one: Shirley is Lazarus, Undershaft Dives. Well, the misery of the world is due to the fact that the great mass of men act and believe as Peter Shirley acts and believes. If they acted and believed as Undershaft acts and believes, the immediate result would be a revolution of incalculable beneficence. To be wealthy, says Undershaft, is with me a point of honor for which I am prepared to kill at the risk of my own life. This preparedness is, as he says, the final test of sincerity. Like Froissart's medieval hero, who saw that "to rob and pill was a good life" he is not the dupe of that public sentiment against killing which is propagated and endowed by people who would otherwise be killed themselves, or of the mouth-honor paid to poverty and obedience by rich and insubordinate donothings who want to rob the poor without courage and command them without superiority. Froissart's knight, in placing the achievement of a good life before all the other duties—which indeed are not duties at all when they conflict with it, but plain wickednesses—behaved bravely, admirably, and, in the final analysis, public-spiritedly. Medieval society, on the other hand, behaved very badly indeed in organizing itself so stupidly that a good life could be achieved by robbing and pilling. If the knight's contemporaries had been all as resolute as he, robbing and pilling would have been the shortest way to the gallows, just as, if we were all as resolute and clearsighted as Undershaft, an attempt to live by means of what is called "an independent income" would be the shortest way to the lethal chamber. But as, thanks to our political imbecility and personal cowardice (fruits of poverty, both), the best imitation of a good life now procurable is life on an independent income, all sensible people aim at securing such an income, and are, of course, careful to legalize and moralize both it and all the actions and sentiments which lead to it and support it as an institution. What else can they do? They know, of course, that they are rich because others are poor. But they cannot help that: it is for the poor to repudiate poverty when they have had enough of it. The thing can be done easily enough: the demonstrations to the contrary made by the economists, jurists, moralists and sentimentalists hired by the rich to defend them, or even doing the work gratuitously out of sheer folly and abjectness, impose only on those who want to be imposed on.

The reason why the independent income-tax payers are not solid in defence of their position is that since we are not medieval rovers through a sparsely populated country, the poverty of those we rob prevents our having the good life for which we sacrifice them. Rich men or aristocrats with a developed sense of life—men like Ruskin and William Morris and Kropotkin—have enormous social appetites and very fastidious personal ones. They are not content with handsome houses: they want handsome cities. They are not content with bediamonded wives and blooming daughters: they complain because the charwoman is badly dressed, because the laundress smells of gin, because the sempstress is anemic, because every man they meet is not a friend and every woman not a romance. They turn up their noses at their neighbors' drains, and are made ill by the architecture of their neighbors' houses. Trade patterns made to suit vulgar people do not please them (and they can get nothing else): they cannot sleep nor sit at ease upon "slaughtered" cabinet makers' furniture. The very air is not good enough for them: there is too much factory smoke in it. They even demand abstract conditions: justice, honor, a noble moral atmosphere, a mystic nexus to replace the cash nexus. Finally they declare that though to rob and pill with your own hand on horseback and in steel coat may have been a good life, to rob and pill by the hands of the policeman, the bailiff, and the soldier, and to underpay them meanly for doing it, is not a good life, but rather fatal to all possibility of even a tolerable one. They call on the poor to revolt, and, finding the poor shocked at their ungentlemanliness, despairingly revile the proletariat for its "damned wantlessness" (*verdammte Bedürfnislosigkeit*).

So far, however, their attack on society has lacked simplicity. The poor do not share their tastes nor understand their art-criticisms. They do not want the simple life, nor the esthetic life; on the contrary, they want very much to wallow in all the costly vulgarities from which the elect souls among the rich turn away with loathing. It is by surfeit and not by abstinence that they will be cured of their hankering after unwholesome sweets. What they do dislike and despise and are ashamed of is poverty. To ask them to fight for the difference between the Christmas number of the Illustrated London News and the Kelmscott Chaucer is silly: they prefer the News. The difference between a stockbroker's cheap and dirty starched white shirt and collar and the comparatively costly and carefully dyed blue shirt of William Morris is a difference so disgraceful to Morris in their eyes that if they fought on the subject at all, they would fight in defence of the starch. "Cease to be slaves, in order that you may become cranks" is not a very inspiring call to arms; nor is it really improved by substituting saints for cranks. Both terms denote men of genius; and the common man does not want to live the life of a man of genius: he would much rather live the life of a pet collie if that were the only alternative. But he does want more money. Whatever else he may be vague about, he is clear about that. He may or may not prefer Major Barbara to the Drury Lane pantomime; but he always prefers five hundred pounds to five hundred shillings.

Now to deplore this preference as sordid, and teach children that it is sinful to desire money, is to strain towards the extreme possible limit of impudence in lying and corruption in hypocrisy. The universal regard for money is the one hopeful fact in our civilization, the one sound spot in our social conscience. Money is the most important thing in the world. It represents health, strength, honor, generosity and beauty as conspicuously and undeniably as the want of it represents illness, weakness, disgrace, meanness and ugliness. Not the least of its virtues is that it destroys base people as certainly as it fortifies and dignifies noble people. It is only when it is cheapened to worthlessness for some and made impossibly dear to others, that it becomes a curse. In short, it is a curse only in such foolish social conditions that life itself is a curse. For the two things are inseparable: money is the counter that enables life to be distributed socially: it *is* life as truly as sovereigns and bank notes are money. The first duty of every citizen is to insist on having money on reasonable terms; and this demand is not complied with by giving four men three shillings each for ten or twelve hours' drudgery and one man a thousand pounds for nothing. The crying need of the nation is not for better morals, cheaper bread, temperance, liberty, culture, redemption of fallen sisters and erring brothers, nor the grace, love and fellowship of the Trinity, but simply for enough money. And the evil to be attacked is not sin, suffering, greed, priestcraft, kingcraft, demagogy, monopoly, ignorance, drink, war, pestilence, nor any other of the scapegoats which reformers sacrifice, but simply poverty.

Once take your eyes from the ends of the earth and fix them on this truth just under your nose; and Andrew Undershaft's views will not perplex you in the least. Unless indeed his constant sense that he is only the instrument of a Will or Life Force which uses him for purposes wider than his own, may puzzle you. If so, that is because you are walking either in artificial Darwinian darkness, or in mere stupidity. All genuinely religious people have that consciousness. To them Undershaft the Mystic will be quite intelligible, and his perfect comprehension of his daughter the Salvationist and her lover the Euripidean republican natural and inevitable. That, however, is not new, even on the stage. What is new, as far as I know, is that article in Undershaft's religion which recognizes in Money the first need and in poverty the vilest sin of man and society.

This dramatic conception has not, of course, been attained *per saltum*. Nor has it been borrowed from Nietzsche or from any man born beyond the Channel. The late Samuel Butler, in his own department the greatest English writer of the latter half of the XIX century, steadily inculcated the necessity and morality of a conscientious Laodiceanism in religion and of an earnest and constant sense of the importance of money. It drives one almost to despair of English literature when one sees so extraordinary a study of English life as Butler's posthumous Way of All Flesh making so little impression that when, some years later, I produce plays in which Butler's extraordinarily fresh, free and future-piercing suggestions have an obvious share, I am met with nothing but vague cacklings about Ibsen and Nietzsche, and am only too thankful that they are not about Alfred de Musset and Georges Sand. Really, the English do not deserve to have great men. They allowed Butler to die practically unknown, whilst I, a comparatively insignificant Irish journalist, was leading them by the nose into an advertisement of me which has made my own life a burden. In Sicily there is a Via Samuele Butler. When an English tourist sees it, he either asks "Who the devil was Samuele Butler?" or wonders why the Sicilians should perpetuate the memory of the author of Hudibras.

Well, it cannot be denied that the English are only too anxious to recognize a man of genius if somebody will kindly point him out to them. Having pointed myself out in this manner with some success, I now point out Samuel Butler, and trust that in consequence I shall hear a little less in future of the novelty and foreign origin of the ideas which are now making their way into the English theatre through plays written by Socialists. There are living men whose originality and power are as obvious as Butler's and when they die that fact will be discovered. Meanwhile I recommend them to insist on their own merits as an important part of their own business.

313

PREFACE TO MAJOR BARBARA
THE SALVATION ARMY

When Major Barbara was produced in London, the second act was reported in an important northern newspaper as a withering attack on the Salvation Army, and the despairing ejaculation of Barbara deplored by a London daily as a tasteless blasphemy. And they were set right, not by the professed critics of the theatre, but by religious and philosophical publicists like Sir Oliver Lodge and Dr Stanton Coit, and strenuous Nonconformist journalists like William Stead, who not only understood the act as well as the Salvationists themselves, but also saw it in its relation to the religious life of the nation, a life which seems to lie not only outside the sympathy of many of our theatre critics, but actually outside their knowledge of society. Indeed nothing could be more ironically curious than the confrontation Major Barbara effected of the theatre enthusiasts with the religious enthusiasts. On the one hand was the playgoer, always seeking pleasure, paying exorbitantly for it, suffering unbearable discomforts for it, and hardly ever getting it. On the other hand was the Salvationist, repudiating gaiety and courting effort and sacrifice, yet always in the wildest spirits, laughing, joking, singing, rejoicing, drumming, and tambourining: his life flying by in a flash of excitement, and his death arriving as a climax of triumph. And, if you please, the playgoer despising the Salvationist as a joyless person, shut out from the heaven of the theatre, self-condemned to a life of hideous gloom; and the Salvationist mourning over the playgoer as over a prodigal with vine leaves in his hair, careering outrageously to hell amid the popping of champagne corks and the ribald laughter of sirens! Could misunderstanding be more complete, or sympathy worse misplaced?

Fortunately, the Salvationists are more accessible to the religious character of the drama than the playgoers to the gay energy and artistic fertility of religion. They can see, when it is pointed out to them, that a theatre, as a place where two or three are gathered together, takes from that

314

PREFACE TO MAJOR BARBARA

divine presence an inalienable sanctity of which the grossest and profanest farce can no more deprive it than a hypocritical sermon by a snobbish bishop can desecrate Westminster Abbey. But in our professional playgoers this indispensable preliminary conception of sanctity seems wanting. They talk of actors as mimes and mummers, and, I fear, think of dramatic authors as liars and pandars, whose main business is the voluptuous soothing of the tired city speculator when what he calls the serious business of the day is over. Passion, the life of drama, means nothing to them but primitive sexual excitement: such phrases as "impassioned poetry" or "passionate love of truth" have fallen quite out of their vocabulary and been replaced by "passional crime" and the like. They assume, as far as I can gather, that people in whom passion has a larger scope are passionless and therefore uninteresting. Consequently they come to think of religious people as people who are not interesting and not amusing. And so, when Barbara cuts the regular Salvation Army jokes, and snatches a kiss from her lover across his drum, the devotees of the theatre think they ought to appear shocked, and conclude that the whole play is an elaborate mockery of the Army. And then either hypocritically rebuke me for mocking, or foolishly take part in the supposed mockery!

Even the handful of mentally competent critics got into difficulties over my demonstration of the economic deadlock in which the Salvation Army finds itself. Some of them thought that the Army would not have taken money from a distiller and a cannon founder: others thought it should not have taken it: all assumed more or less definitely that it reduced itself to absurdity or hypocrisy by taking it. On the first point the reply of the Army itself was prompt and conclusive. As one of its officers said, they would take money from the devil himself and be only too glad to get it out of his hands and into God's. They gratefully acknowledged that publicans not only give them money but allow them to collect it in the bar—sometimes even when there is a Salvation meeting outside preaching teetotalism. In fact, they questioned the verisimilitude of the play, not because Mrs Baines took the money, but because Barbara refused it.

On the point that the Army ought not to take such money, its justification is obvious. It must take the money because it cannot exist without money, and there is no other money to be had. Practically all the spare money in the country consists of a mass of rent, interest, and profit, every penny of which is bound up with crime, drink, prostitution, disease, and all the evil fruits of poverty, as inextricably as with enterprise, wealth, commercial probity, and national prosperity. The notion that you can earmark certain coins as tainted is an unpractical individualist superstition. None the less the fact that all our money is tainted gives a very severe shock to earnest young souls when some dramatic instance of the taint first makes them conscious of it. When an enthusiastic young clergyman of the Established Church first realizes that the Ecclesiastical Commissioners receive the rents of sporting public houses, brothels, and sweating dens; or that the most generous contributor at his last charity sermon was an employer trading in female labor cheapened by prostitution as unscrupulously as a hotel keeper trades in waiters' labor cheapened by tips, or commissionaires' labor cheapened by pensions; or that the only patron who can afford to rebuild his church or his schools or give his boys' brigade a gymnasium or a library is the son-in-law of a Chicago meat King, that young clergyman has, like Barbara, a very bad quarter hour. But he cannot help himself by refusing to accept money from anybody except sweet old ladies with independent incomes and gentle and lovely ways of life. He has only to follow up the income of the sweet ladies to its industrial source, and there he will find Mrs Warren's profession and the poisonous canned meat and all the rest of it. His own stipend has the same root. He must either share the world's guilt or go to another planet. He must save the world's honor if he is to save his own. This is what all the Churches find just as the Salvation Army and Barbara find it in the play. Her discovery that she is her father's accomplice; that the Salvation Army is the accomplice of the distiller and the dynamite maker; that they can no more escape one another than they can escape the air they breathe; that there is no salvation for them through personal righteousness, but only through the redemption of the whole nation from its vicious, lazy, competitive anarchy: this discovery has been made by everyone except the Pharisees and (apparently) the professional playgoers, who still wear their Tom Hood shirts and underpay their washerwomen without the slightest misgiving as to the elevation of their private characters, the purity of their private atmospheres, and their right to repudiate as foreign to themselves the coarse depravity of the garret and the slum. Not that they mean any harm: they only desire to be, in their little private way, what they call gentlemen. They do not understand Barbara's lesson because they have not, like her, learnt it by taking their part in the larger life of the nation.

BARBARA'S RETURN TO THE COLORS

Barbara's return to the colors may yet provide a subject for the dramatic historian of the future. To go back to the Salvation Army with the knowledge that even the Salvationists themselves are not saved yet; that poverty is not blessed, but a most damnable sin; and that when General Booth chose Blood and Fire for the emblem of Salvation instead of the Cross, he was perhaps better inspired than he knew: such knowledge, for the daughter of Andrew Undershaft, will clearly lead to something hopefuller than distributing bread and treacle at the expense of Bodger.

It is a very significant thing, this instinctive choice of the military form of organization, this substitution of the drum for the organ, by the Salvation Army. Does it not suggest that the Salvationists divine that they must actually fight the devil instead of merely praying at him? At present, it is true, they have not quite ascertained his correct address. When they do, they may give a very rude shock to that sense of security which he has gained from his experience of

317

PREFACE TO MAJOR BARBARA

the fact that hard words, even when uttered by eloquent essayists and lecturers, or carried unanimously at enthusiastic public meetings on the motion of eminent reformers, break no bones. It has been said that the French Revolution was the work of Voltaire, Rousseau and the Encyclopedists. It seems to me to have been the work of men who had observed that virtuous indignation, caustic criticism, conclusive argument and instructive pamphleteering, even when done by the most earnest and witty literary geniuses, were as useless as praying, things going steadily from bad to worse whilst the Social Contract and the pamphlets of Voltaire were at the height of their vogue. Eventually, as we know, perfectly respectable citizens and earnest philanthropists connived at the September massacres because hard experience had convinced them that if they contented themselves with appeals to humanity and patriotism, the aristocracy, though it would read their appeals with the greatest enjoyment and appreciation, flattering and admiring the writers, would none the less continue to conspire with foreign monarchists to undo the revolution and restore the old system with every circumstance of savage vengeance and ruthless repression of popular liberties.

The nineteenth century saw the same lesson repeated in England. It had its Utilitarians, its Christian Socialists, its Fabians (still extant): it had Bentham, Mill, Dickens, Ruskin, Carlyle, Butler, Henry George, and Morris. And the end of all their efforts is the Chicago described by Mr Upton Sinclair, and the London in which the people who pay to be amused by my dramatic representation of Peter Shirley turned out to starve at forty because there are younger slaves to be had for his wages, do not take, and have not the slightest intention of taking, any effective step to organize society in such a way as to make that everyday infamy impossible. I, who have preached and pamphleteered like any Encyclopedist, have to confess that my methods are no use, and would be no use if I were Voltaire, Rousseau,

318

PREFACE TO MAJOR BARBARA

Bentham, Marx, Mill, Dickens, Carlyle, Ruskin, Butler, and Morris all rolled into one, with Euripides, More, Montaigne, Molière, Beaumarchais, Swift, Goethe, Ibsen, Tolstoy, Jesus and the prophets all thrown in (as indeed in some sort I actually am, standing as I do on all their shoulders). The problem being to make heroes out of cowards, we paper apostles and artist-magicians have succeeded only in giving cowards all the sensations of heroes whilst they tolerate every abomination, accept every plunder, and submit to every oppression. Christianity, in making a merit of such submission, has marked only that depth in the abyss at which the very sense of shame is lost. The Christian has been like Dickens' doctor in the debtor's prison, who tells the newcomer of its ineffable peace and security: no duns; no tyrannical collectors of rates, taxes, and rent; no importunate hopes nor exacting duties; nothing but the rest and safety of having no farther to fall.

Yet in the poorest corner of this soul-destroying Christendom vitality suddenly begins to germinate again. Joyousness, a sacred gift long dethroned by the hellish laughter of derision and obscenity, rises like a flood miraculously out of the fetid dust and mud of the slums; rousing marches and impetuous dithyrambs rise to the heavens from people among whom the depressing noise called "sacred music" is a standing joke; a flag with Blood and Fire on it is unfurled, not in murderous rancor, but because fire is beautiful and blood a vital and splendid red; Fear, which we flatter by calling Self, vanishes; and transfigured men and women carry their gospel through a transfigured world, calling their leader General, themselves captains and brigadiers, and their whole body an Army: praying, but praying only for refreshment, for strength to fight, and for needful Money (a notable sign, that); preaching, but not preaching submission; daring ill-usage and abuse, but not putting up with more of it than is inevitable; and practising what the world will let them practise, including soap and water,

319

PREFACE TO MAJOR BARBARA

color and music. There is danger in such activity; and where there is danger there is hope. Our present security is nothing, and can be nothing, but evil made irresistible.

WEAKNESSES OF THE SALVATION ARMY

For the present, however, it is not my business to flatter the Salvation Army. Rather must I point out to it that it has almost as many weaknesses as the Church of England itself. It is building up a business organization which will compel it eventually to see that its present staff of enthusiast-commanders shall be succeeded by a bureaucracy of men of business who will be no better than bishops, and perhaps a good deal more unscrupulous. That has always happened sooner or later to great orders founded by saints; and the order founded by St William Booth is not exempt from the same danger. It is even more dependent than the Church on rich people who would cut off supplies at once if it began to preach that indispensable revolt against poverty which must also be a revolt against riches. It is hampered by a heavy contingent of pious elders who are not really Salvationists at all, but Evangelicals of the old school. It still, as Commissioner Howard affirms, "sticks to Moses," which is flat nonsense at this time of day if the Commissioner means, as I am afraid he does, that the Book of Genesis contains a trustworthy scientific account of the origin of species, and that the god to whom Jephthah sacrificed his daughter is any less obviously a tribal idol than Dagon or Chemosh.

Further, there is still too much other-worldliness about the Army. Like Frederick's grenadier, the Salvationist wants to live for ever (the most monstrous way of crying for the moon); and though it is evident to anyone who has ever heard General Booth and his best officers that they would work as hard for human salvation as they do at present if they believed that death would be the end of them individually, they and their followers have a bad habit of talking as if the Salvationists were heroically enduring a very bad time on earth as an investment which will bring them in dividends later on in the form, not of a better life to

320

come for the whole world, but of an eternity spent by themselves personally in a sort of bliss which would bore any active person to a second death. Surely the truth is that the Salvationists are unusually happy people. And is it not the very diagnostic of true salvation that it shall overcome the fear of death? Now the man who has come to believe that there is no such thing as death, the change so called being merely the transition to an exquisitely happy and utterly careless life, has not overcome the fear of death at all: on the contrary, it has overcome him so completely that he refuses to die on any terms whatever. I do not call a Salvationist really saved until he is ready to lie down cheerfully on the scrap heap, having paid scot and lot and something over, and let his eternal life pass on to renew its youth in the battalions of the future.

Then there is the nasty lying habit called confession, which the Army encourages because it lends itself to dramatic oratory, with plenty of thrilling incident. For my part, when I hear a convert relating the violences and oaths and blasphemies he was guilty of before he was saved, making out that he was a very terrible fellow then and is the most contrite and chastened of Christians now, I believe him no more than I believe the millionaire who says he came up to London or Chicago as a boy with only three halfpence in his pocket. Salvationists have said to me that Barbara in my play would never have been taken in by so transparent a humbug as Snobby Price; and certainly I do not think Snobby could have taken in any experienced Salvationist on a point on which the Salvationist did not wish to be taken in. But on the point of conversion all Salvationists wish to be taken in; for the more obvious the sinner the more obvious the miracle of his conversion. When you advertize a converted burglar or reclaimed drunkard as one of the attractions at an experience meeting, your burglar can hardly have been too burglarious or your drunkard too drunken. As long as such attractions are relied on, you will have your Snobbies claiming to have beaten their mothers when they were as a matter of prosaic fact habitually beaten by them, and your Rummies of the tamest respectability pretending to a past of reckless and dazzling vice. Even when confessions are sincerely autobiographic we should beware of assuming that the impulse to make them is pious or the interest of the hearers is wholesome. As well might we assume that the poor people who insist on shewing disgusting ulcers to district visitors are convinced hygienists, or that the curiosity which sometimes welcomes such exhibitions is a pleasant and creditable one. One is often tempted to suggest that those who pester our police superintendents with confessions of murder might very wisely be taken at their word and executed, except in the few cases in which a real murderer is seeking to be relieved of his guilt by confession and expiation. For though I am not, I hope, an unmerciful person, I do not think that the inexorability of the deed once done should be disguised by any ritual, whether in the confessional or on the scaffold.

And here my disagreement with the Salvation Army, and with all propagandists of the Cross (which I loathe as I loathe all gibbets) becomes deep indeed. Forgiveness, absolution, atonement, are figments: punishment is only a pretence of cancelling one crime by another; and you can no more have forgiveness without vindictiveness than you can have a cure without a disease. You will never get a high morality from people who conceive that their misdeeds are revocable and pardonable, or in a society where absolution and expiation are officially provided for us all. The demand may be very real; but the supply is spurious. Thus Bill Walker, in my play, having assaulted the Salvation Lass, presently finds himself overwhelmed with an intolerable conviction of sin under the skilled treatment of Barbara. Straightway he begins to try to unassault the lass and deruffianize his deed, first by getting punished for it in kind, and, when that relief is denied him, by fining himself a pound to compensate the girl. He is foiled both ways. He finds the Salvation Army as inexorable as fact

322

itself. It will not punish him: it will not take his money. It will not tolerate a redeemed ruffian: it leaves him no means of salvation except ceasing to be a ruffian. In doing this, the Salvation Army instinctively grasps the central truth of Christianity and discards its central superstition: that central truth being the vanity of revenge and punishment, and that central superstition the salvation of the world by the gibbet.

For, be it noted, Bill has assaulted an old and starving woman also; and for this worse offence he feels no remorse whatever, because she makes it clear that her malice is as great as his own. "Let her have the law of me, as she said she would," says Bill: "what I done to her is no more on what you might call my conscience than sticking a pig." This shews a perfectly natural and wholesome state of mind on his part. The old woman, like the law she threatens him with, is perfectly ready to play the game of retaliation with him: to rob him if he steals, to flog him if he strikes, to murder him if he kills. By example and precept the law and public opinion teach him to impose his will on others by anger, violence, and cruelty, and to wipe off the moral score by punishment. That is sound Crosstianity. But this Crosstianity has got entangled with something which Barbara calls Christianity, and which unexpectedly causes her to refuse to play the hangman's game of Satan casting out Satan. She refuses to prosecute a drunken ruffian; she converses on equal terms with a blackguard to whom no lady should be seen speaking in the public street: in short, she imitates Christ. Bill's conscience reacts to this just as naturally as it does to the old woman's threats. He is placed in a position of unbearable moral inferiority, and strives by every means in his power to escape from it, whilst he is still quite ready to meet the abuse of the old woman by attempting to smash a mug on her face. And that is the triumphant justification of Barbara's Christianity as against our system of judicial punishment and the vindictive villain-thrashings and "poetic justice" of the romantic stage.

323

PREFACE TO MAJOR BARBARA

For the credit of literature it must be pointed out that the situation is only partly novel. Victor Hugo long ago gave us the epic of the convict and the bishop's candlesticks, of the Crosstian policeman annihilated by his encounter with the Christian Valjean. But Bill Walker is not, like Valjean, romantically changed from a demon into an angel. There are millions of Bill Walkers in all classes of society today; and the point which I, as a professor of natural psychology, desire to demonstrate, is that Bill, without any change in his character or circumstances whatsoever, will react one way to one sort of treatment and another way to another.

In proof I might point to the sensational object lesson provided by our commercial millionaires today. They begin as brigands: merciless, unscrupulous, dealing out ruin and death and slavery to their competitors and employees, and facing desperately the worst that their competitors can do to them. The history of the English factories, the American Trusts, the exploitation of African gold, diamonds, ivory and rubber, outdoes in villainy the worst that has ever been imagined of the buccaneers of the Spanish Main. Captain Kidd would have marooned a modern Trust magnate for conduct unworthy of a gentleman of fortune. The law every day seizes on unsuccessful scoundrels of this type and punishes them with a cruelty worse than their own, with the result that they come out of the torture house more dangerous than they went in, and renew their evil doing (nobody will employ them at anything else) until they are again seized, again tormented, and again let loose, with the same result.

But the successful scoundrel is dealt with very differently, and very Christianly. He is not only forgiven: he is idolized, respected, made much of, all but worshipped. Society returns him good for evil in the most extravagant overmeasure. And with what result? He begins to idolize himself, to respect himself, to live up to the treatment he receives. He preaches sermons; he writes books of the most

324

edifying advice to young men, and actually persuades himself that he got on by taking his own advice; he endows educational institutions; he supports charities; he dies finally in the odor of sanctity, leaving a will which is a monument of public spirit and bounty. And all this without any change in his character. The spots of the leopard and the stripes of the tiger are as brilliant as ever; but the conduct of the world towards him has changed; and his conduct has changed accordingly. You have only to reverse your attitude towards him—to lay hands on his property, revile him, assault him, and he will be a brigand again in a moment, as ready to crush you as you are to crush him, and quite as full of pretentious moral reasons for doing it.

In short, when Major Barbara says that there are no scoundrels, she is right: there are no absolute scoundrels, though there are impracticable people of whom I shall treat presently. Every reasonable man (and woman) is a potential scoundrel and a potential good citizen. What a man is depends on his character; but what he does, and what we think of what he does, depends on his circumstances. The characteristics that ruin a man in one class make him eminent in another. The characters that behave differently in different circumstances behave alike in similar circumstances. Take a common English character like that of Bill Walker. We meet Bill everywhere: on the judicial bench, on the episcopal bench, in the Privy Council, at the War Office and Admiralty, as well as in the Old Bailey dock or in the ranks of casual unskilled labor. And the morality of Bill's characteristics varies with these various circumstances. The faults of the burglar are the qualities of the financier: the manners and habits of a duke would cost a city clerk his situation. In short, though character is independent of circumstances, conduct is not; and our moral judgments of character are not: both are circumstantial. Take any condition of life in which the circumstances are for a mass of men practically alike: felony, the House of Lords, the factory, the stables, the gipsy encampment or where you please! In spite of diversity of character and temperament, the conduct and morals of the individuals in each group are as predicable and as alike in the main as if they were a flock of sheep, morals being mostly only social habits and circumstantial necessities. Strong people know this and count upon it. In nothing have the master-minds of the world been distinguished from the ordinary suburban season-ticket holder more than in their straightforward perception of the fact that mankind is practically a single species, and not a menagerie of gentlemen and bounders, villains and heroes, cowards and daredevils, peers and peasants, grocers and aristocrats, artisans and laborers, washerwomen and duchesses, in which all the grades of income and caste represent distinct animals who must not be introduced to one another or intermarry. Napoleon constructing a galaxy of generals and courtiers, and even of monarchs, out of his collection of social nobodies; Julius Caesar appointing as governor of Egypt the son of a freedman—one who but a short time before would have been legally disqualified for the post even of a private soldier in the Roman army; Louis XI making his barber his privy councillor: all these had in their different ways a firm hold of the scientific fact of human equality, expressed by Barbara in the Christian formula that all men are children of one father. A man who believes that men are naturally divided into upper and lower and middle classes morally is making exactly the same mistake as the man who believes that they are naturally divided in the same way socially. And just as our persistent attempts to found political institutions on a basis of social inequality have always produced long periods of destructive friction relieved from time to time by violent explosions of revolution; so the attempt —will Americans please note—to found moral institutions on a basis of moral inequality can lead to nothing but unnatural Reigns of the Saints relieved by licentious Restorations; to Americans who have made divorce a public institution turning the face of Europe into one huge sardonic

326

smile by refusing to stay in the same hotel with a Russian man of genius who has changed wives without the sanction of South Dakota; to grotesque hypocrisy, cruel persecution, and final utter confusion of conventions and compliances with benevolence and respectability. It is quite useless to declare that all men are born free if you deny that they are born good. Guarantee a man's goodness and his liberty will take care of itself. To guarantee his freedom on condition that you approve of his moral character is formally to abolish all freedom whatsoever, as every man's liberty is at the mercy of a moral indictment which any fool can trump up against everyone who violates custom, whether as a prophet or as a rascal. This is the lesson Democracy has to learn before it can become anything but the most oppressive of all the priesthoods.

Let us now return to Bill Walker and his case of conscience against the Salvation Army. Major Barbara, not being a modern Tetzel, or the treasurer of a hospital, refuses to sell absolution to Bill for a sovereign. Unfortunately, what the Army can afford to refuse in the case of Bill Walker, it cannot refuse in the case of Bodger. Bodger is master of the situation because he holds the purse strings. "Strive as you will," says Bodger, in effect: "me you cannot do without. You cannot save Bill Walker without my money." And the Army answers, quite rightly under the circumstances, "We will take money from the devil himself sooner than abandon the work of Salvation." So Bodger pays his conscience-money and gets the absolution that is refused to Bill. In real life Bill would perhaps never know this. But I, the dramatist whose business it is to shew the connexion between things that seem apart and unrelated in the haphazard order of events in real life, have contrived to make it known to Bill, with the result that the Salvation Army loses its hold of him at once.

But Bill may not be lost, for all that. He is still in the grip of the facts and of his own conscience, and may find his taste for blackguardism permanently spoiled. Still, I

327

cannot guarantee that happy ending. Walk through the poorer quarters of our cities on Sunday when the men are not working, but resting and chewing the cud of their reflections. You will find one expression common to every mature face: the expression of cynicism. The discovery made by Bill Walker about the Salvation Army has been made by everyone there. They have found that every man has his price; and they have been foolishly or corruptly taught to mistrust and despise him for that necessary and salutary condition of social existence. When they learn that General Booth, too, has his price, they do not admire him because it is a high one, and admit the need of organizing society so that he shall get it in an honorable way: they conclude that his character is unsound and that all religious men are hypocrites and allies of their sweaters and oppressors. They know that the large subscriptions which help to support the Army are endowments, not of religion, but of the wicked doctrine of docility in poverty and humility under oppression; and they are rent by the most agonizing of all the doubts of the soul, the doubt whether their true salvation must not come from their most abhorrent passions, from murder, envy, greed, stubbornness, rage, and terrorism, rather than from public spirit, reasonableness, humanity, generosity, tenderness, delicacy, pity and kindness. The confirmation of that doubt, at which our newspapers have been working so hard for years past, is the morality of militarism; and the justification of militarism is that circumstances may at any time make it the true morality of the moment. It is by producing such moments that we produce violent and sanguinary revolutions, such as the one now in progress in Russia and the one which Capitalism in England and America is daily and diligently provoking.

At such moments it becomes the duty of the Churches to evoke all the powers of destruction against the existing order. But if they do this, the existing order must forcibly suppress them. Churches are suffered to exist only on condition that they preach submission to the State as at present capitalistically organized. The Church of England itself is compelled to add to the thirtysix articles in which it formulates its religious tenets, three more in which it apologetically protests that the moment any of these articles comes in conflict with the State it is to be entirely renounced, abjured, violated, abrogated and abhorred, the policeman being a much more important person than any of the Persons of the Trinity. And this is why no tolerated Church nor Salvation Army can ever win the entire confidence of the poor. It must be on the side of the police and the military, no matter what it believes or disbelieves; and as the police and the military are the instruments by which the rich rob and oppress the poor (on legal and moral principles made for the purpose), it is not possible to be on the side of the poor and of the police at the same time. Indeed the religious bodies, as the almoners of the rich, become a sort of auxiliary police, taking off the insurrectionary edge of poverty with coals and blankets, bread and treacle, and soothing and cheering the victims with hopes of immense and inexpensive happiness in another world when the process of working them to premature death in the service of the rich is complete in this.

CHRISTIANITY AND ANARCHISM

Such is the false position from which neither the Salvation Army nor the Church of England nor any other religious organization whatever can escape except through a reconstitution of society. Nor can they merely endure the State passively, washing their hands of its sins. The State is constantly forcing the consciences of men by violence and cruelty. Not content with exacting money from us for the maintenance of its soldiers and policemen, its gaolers and executioners, it forces us to take an active personal part in its proceedings on pain of becoming ourselves the victims of its violence. As I write these lines, a sensational example is given to the world. A royal marriage has been celebrated, first by sacrament in a cathedral, and then by a

PREFACE TO MAJOR BARBARA

bullfight having for its main amusement the spectacle of horses gored and disembowelled by the bull, after which, when the bull is so exhausted as to be no longer dangerous, he is killed by a cautious matador. But the ironic contrast between the bullfight and the sacrament of marriage does not move anyone. Another contrast—that between the splendor, the happiness, the atmosphere of kindly admiration surrounding the young couple, and the price paid for it under our abominable social arrangements in the misery, squalor and degradation of millions of other young couples —is drawn at the same moment by a novelist, Mr Upton Sinclair, who chips a corner of the veneering from the huge meat packing industries of Chicago, and shews it to us as a sample of what is going on all over the world underneath the top layer of prosperous plutocracy. One man is sufficiently moved by that contrast to pay his own life as the price of one terrible blow at the responsible parties. His poverty has left him ignorant enough to be duped by the pretence that the innocent young bride and bridegroom, put forth and crowned by plutocracy as the heads of a State in which they have less personal power than any policeman, and less influence than any Chairman of a Trust, are responsible. At them accordingly he launches his sixpennorth of fulminate, missing his mark, but scattering the bowels of as many horses as any bull in the arena, and slaying twentythree persons, besides wounding ninety-nine. And of all these, the horses alone are innocent of the guilt he is avenging: had he blown all Madrid to atoms with every adult person in it, not one could have escaped the charge of being an accessory, before, at, and after the fact, to poverty and prostitution, to such wholesale massacre of infants as Herod never dreamt of, to plague, pestilence and famine, battle, murder and lingering death—perhaps not one who had not helped, through example, precept, connivance, and even clamor, to teach the dynamiter his well-learnt gospel of hatred and vengeance, by approving every day of sentences of years of imprisonment so infernal

330

in their unnatural stupidity and panic-stricken cruelty, that their advocates can disavow neither the dagger nor the bomb without stripping the mask of justice and humanity from themselves also.

Be it noted that at this very moment there appears the biography of one of our dukes, who, being a Scot, could argue about politics, and therefore stood out as a great brain among our aristocrats. And what, if you please, was his grace's favorite historical episode, which he declared he never read without intense satisfaction? Why, the young General Bonapart's pounding of the Paris mob to pieces in 1795, called in playful approval by our respectable classes "the whiff of grapeshot," though Napoleon, to do him justice, took a deeper view of it, and would fain have had it forgotten. And since the Duke of Argyll was not a demon, but a man of like passions with ourselves, by no means rancorous or cruel as men go, who can doubt that all over the world proletarians of the ducal kidney are now revelling in "the whiff of dynamite" (the flavor of the joke seems to evaporate a little, does it not?) because it was aimed at the class they hate even as our argute duke hated what he called the mob.

In such an atmosphere there can be only one sequel to the Madrid explosion. All Europe burns to emulate it. Vengeance! More blood! Tear "the Anarchist beast" to shreds. Drag him to the scaffold. Imprison him for life. Let all civilized States band together to drive his like off the face of the earth; and if any State refuses to join, make war on it. This time the leading London newspaper, anti-Liberal and therefore anti-Russian in politics, does not say "Serve you right" to the victims, as it did, in effect, when Bobrikoff, and De Plehve, and Grand Duke Sergius, were in the same manner unofficially fulminated into fragments. No: fulminate our rivals in Asia by all means, ye brave Russian revolutionaries; but to aim at an English princess! monstrous! hideous! hound down the wretch to his doom: and observe, please, that we are a civilized and merciful people, and, however much we may regret it, must not treat him as Ravaillac and Damiens were treated. And meanwhile, since we have not yet caught him, let us soothe our quivering nerves with the bullfight, and comment in a courtly way on the unfailing tact and good taste of the ladies of our royal houses, who, though presumably of full normal natural tenderness, have been so effectually broken in to fashionable routine that they can be taken to see the horses slaughtered as helplessly as they could no doubt be taken to a gladiator show, if that happened to be the mode just now.

Strangely enough, in the midst of this raging fire of malice, the one man who still has faith in the kindness and intelligence of human nature is the fulminator, now a hunted wretch, with nothing, apparently, to secure his triumph over all the prisons and scaffolds of infuriate Europe except the revolver in his pocket and his readiness to discharge it at a moment's notice into his own or any other head. Think of him setting out to find a gentleman and a Christian in the multitude of human wolves howling for his blood. Think also of this: that at the very first essay he finds what he seeks, a veritable grandee of Spain, a noble, high-thinking, unterrified, malice-void soul, in the guise—of all masquerades in the world!—of a modern editor. The Anarchist wolf, flying from the wolves of plutocracy, throws himself on the honor of the man. The man, not being a wolf (nor a London editor), and therefore not having enough sympathy with his exploit to be made blood-thirsty by it, does not throw him back to the pursuing wolves—gives him, instead, what help he can to escape, and sends him off acquainted at last with a force that goes deeper than dynamite, though you cannot buy so much of it for sixpence. That righteous and honorable high human deed is not wasted on Europe, let us hope, though it benefits the fugitive wolf only for a moment. The pluto-cratic wolves presently smell him out. The fugitive shoots the unlucky wolf whose nose is nearest; shoots himself;

332

and then convinces the world, by his photograph, that he was no monstrous freak of reversion to the tiger, but a good looking young man with nothing abnormal about him except his appalling courage and resolution (that is why the terrified shriek Coward at him): one to whom murdering a happy young couple on their wedding morning would have been an unthinkably unnatural abomination under rational and kindly human circumstances.

Then comes the climax of irony and blind stupidity. The wolves, balked of their meal of fellow-wolf, turn on the man, and proceed to torture him, after their manner, by imprisonment, for refusing to fasten his teeth in the throat of the dynamiter and hold him down until they came to finish him.

Thus, you see, a man may not be a gentleman nowadays even if he wishes to. As to being a Christian, he is allowed some latitude in that matter, because, I repeat, Christianity has two faces. Popular Christianity has for its emblem a gibbet, for its chief sensation a sanguinary execution after torture, for its central mystery an insane vengeance bought off by a trumpery expiation. But there is a nobler and profounder Christianity which affirms the sacred mystery of Equality, and forbids the glaring futility and folly of vengeance, often politely called punishment or justice. The gibbet part of Christianity is tolerated. The other is criminal felony. Connoisseurs in irony are well aware of the fact that the only editor in England who denounces punishment as radically wrong, also repudiates Christianity; calls his paper The Freethinker; and has been imprisoned for "bad taste" under the law against blasphemy.

SANE CONCLUSIONS

And now I must ask the excited reader not to lose his head on one side or the other, but to draw a sane moral from these grim absurdities. It is not good sense to propose that laws against crime should apply to principals only and not to accessories whose consent, counsel, or silence may secure impunity to the principal. If you institute

333

punishment as part of the law, you must punish people for refusing to punish. If you have a police, part of its duty must be to compel everybody to assist the police. No doubt if your laws are unjust, and your policemen agents of oppression, the result will be an unbearable violation of the private consciences of citizens. But that cannot be helped: the remedy is, not to license everybody to thwart the law if they please, but to make laws that will command the public assent, and not to deal cruelly and stupidly with lawbreakers. Everybody disapproves of burglars; but the modern burglar, when caught and overpowered by a householder, usually appeals, and often, let us hope, with success, to his captor not to deliver him over to the useless horrors of penal servitude. In other cases the lawbreaker escapes because those who could give him up do not consider his breach of the law a guilty action. Sometimes, even, private tribunals are formed in opposition to the official tribunals; and these private tribunals employ assassins as executioners, as was done, for example, by Mahomet before he had established his power officially, and by the Ribbon lodges of Ireland in their long struggle with the landlords. Under such circumstances, the assassin goes free although everybody in the district knows who he is and what he has done. They do not betray him, partly because they justify him exactly as the regular Government justifies its official executioner, and partly because they would themselves be assassinated if they betrayed him: another method learnt from the official government. Given a tribunal, employing a slayer who has no personal quarrel with the slain; and there is clearly no moral difference between official and unofficial killing.

In short, all men are anarchists with regard to laws which are against their consciences, either in the preamble or in the penalty. In London our worst anarchists are the magistrates, because many of them are so old and ignorant that when they are called upon to administer any law that is based on ideas or knowledge less than half a century old, they disagree with it, and being mere ordinary homebred private Englishmen without any respect for law in the abstract, naïvely set the example of violating it. In this instance the man lags behind the law; but when the law lags behind the man, he becomes equally an anarchist. When some huge change in social conditions, such as the industrial revolution of the eighteenth and nineteenth centuries, throws our legal and industrial institutions out of date, Anarchism becomes almost a religion. The whole force of the most energetic geniuses of the time in philosophy, economics, and art, concentrates itself on demonstrations and reminders that morality and law are only conventions, fallible and continually obsolescing. Tragedies in which the heroes are bandits, and comedies in which law-abiding and conventionally moral folk are compelled to satirize themselves by outraging the conscience of the spectators every time they do their duty, appear simultaneously with economic treatises entitled "What is Property? Theft!" and with histories of "The Conflict between Religion and Science."

Now this is not a healthy state of things. The advantages of living in society are proportionate, not to the freedom of the individual from a code, but to the complexity and subtlety of the code he is prepared not only to accept but to uphold as a matter of such vital importance that a lawbreaker at large is hardly to be tolerated on any plea. Such an attitude becomes impossible when the only men who can make themselves heard and remembered throughout the world spend all their energy in raising our gorge against current law, current morality, current respectability, and legal property. The ordinary man, uneducated in social theory even when he is schooled in Latin verse, cannot be set against all the laws of his country and yet persuaded to regard law in the abstract as vitally necessary to society. Once he is brought to repudiate the laws and institutions he knows, he will repudiate the very conception of law and the very groundwork of institutions, ridiculing human rights, extolling brainless methods as "historical," and tolerating nothing except pure empiricism in conduct, with dynamite as the basis of politics and vivisection as the basis of science. That is hideous; but what is to be done? Here am I, for instance, by class a respectable man, by common sense a hater of waste and disorder, by intellectual constitution legally minded to the verge of pedantry, and by temperament apprehensive and economically disposed to the limit of old-maidishness; yet I am, and have always been, and shall now always be, a revolutionary writer, because our laws make law impossible; our liberties destroy all freedom; our property is organized robbery; our morality is an impudent hypocrisy; our wisdom is administered by inexperienced or malexperienced dupes, our power wielded by cowards and weaklings, and our honor false in all its points. I am an enemy of the existing order for good reasons; but that does not make my attacks any less encouraging or helpful to people who are its enemies for bad reasons. The existing order may shriek that if I tell the truth about it, some foolish person may drive it to become still worse by trying to assassinate it. I cannot help that, even if I could see what worse it could do than it is already doing. And the disadvantage of that worst even from its own point of view is that society, with all its prisons and bayonets and whips and ostracisms and starvations, is powerless in the face of the Anarchist who is prepared to sacrifice his own life in the battle with it. Our natural safety from the cheap and devastating explosives which every Russian student can make, and every Russian grenadier has learnt to handle in Manchuria, lies in the fact that brave and resolute men, when they are rascals, will not risk their skins for the good of humanity, and, when they are not, are sympathetic enough to care for humanity, abhorring murder, and never committing it until their consciences are outraged beyond endurance. The remedy is, then, simply not to outrage their consciences.

Do not be afraid that they will not make allowances.

336

PREFACE TO MAJOR BARBARA

All men make very large allowances indeed before they stake their own lives in a war to the death with society. Nobody demands or expects the millennium. But there are two things that must be set right, or we shall perish, like Rome, of soul atrophy disguised as empire.

The first is, that the daily ceremony of dividing the wealth of the country among its inhabitants shall be so conducted that no crumb shall, save as a criminal's ration, go to any able-bodied adults who are not producing by their personal exertions not only a full equivalent for what they take, but a surplus sufficient to provide for their superannuation and pay back the debt due for their nurture.

The second is that the deliberate infliction of malicious injuries which now goes on under the name of punishment be abandoned; so that the thief, the ruffian, the gambler, and the beggar, may without inhumanity be handed over to the law, and made to understand that a State which is too humane to punish will also be too thrifty to waste the life of honest men in watching or restraining dishonest ones. That is why we do not imprison dogs. We even take our chance of their first bite. But if a dog delights to bark and bite, it goes to the lethal chamber. That seems to me sensible. To allow the dog to expiate his bite by a period of torment, and then let him loose in a much more savage condition (for the chain makes a dog savage) to bite again and expiate again, having meanwhile spent a great deal of human life and happiness in the task of chaining and feeding and tormenting him, seems to me idiotic and superstitious. Yet that is what we do to men who bark and bite and steal. It would be far more sensible to put up with their vices, as we put up with their illnesses, until they give more trouble than they are worth, at which point we should, with many apologies and expressions of sympathy, and some generosity in complying with their last wishes, place them in the lethal chamber and get rid of them. Under no circumstances should they be allowed to expiate their misdeeds by a manufactured penalty, to subscribe to a charity, or to compensate the victims. If there is to be no punishment there can be no forgiveness. We shall never have real moral responsibility until everyone knows that his deeds are ir-revocable, and that his life depends on his usefulness. Hitherto, alas! humanity has never dared face these hard facts. We frantically scatter conscience money and invent systems of conscience banking, with expiatory penalties, atonements, redemptions, salvations, hospital subscription lists and what not, to enable us to contract-out of the moral code. Not content with the old scapegoat and sacrificial lamb, we deify human saviors, and pray to miraculous virgin intercessors. We attribute mercy to the inexorable; soothe our consciences after committing murder by throw-ing ourselves on the bosom of divine love; and shrink even from our own gallows because we are forced to admit that it, at least, is irrevocable—as if one hour of imprisonment were not as irrevocable as any execution!

If a man cannot look evil in the face without illusion, he will never know what it really is, or combat it effectually. The few men who have been able (relatively) to do this have been called cynics, and have sometimes had an ab-normal share of evil in themselves, corresponding to the abnormal strength of their minds; but they have never done mischief unless they intended to do it. That is why great scoundrels have been beneficent rulers whilst amiable and privately harmless monarchs have ruined their coun-tries by trusting to the hocus-pocus of innocence and guilt, reward and punishment, virtuous indignation and pardon, instead of standing up to the facts without either malice or mercy. Major Barbara stands up to Bill Walker in that way, with the result that the ruffian who cannot get hated, has to hate himself. To relieve this agony he tries to get punished; but the Salvationist whom he tries to provoke is as merciless as Barbara, and only prays for him. Then he tries to pay, but can get nobody to take his money. His doom is the doom of Cain, who, failing to find either a savior, a policeman, or an almoner to help him to pretend that his brother's blood no longer cried from the ground, had to live and die a murderer. Cain took care not to commit another murder, unlike our railway shareholders (I am one) who kill and maim shunters by hundreds to save the cost of automatic couplings, and make atonement by annual subscriptions to deserving charities. Had Cain been allowed to pay off his score, he might possibly have killed Adam and Eve for the mere sake of a second luxurious reconciliation with God afterwards. Bodger, you may depend on it, will go on to the end of his life poisoning people with bad whisky, because he can always depend on the Salvation Army or the Church of England to negotiate a redemption for him in consideration of a trifling percentage of his profits.

There is a third condition too, which must be fulfilled before the great teachers of the world will cease to scoff at its religions. Creeds must become intellectually honest. At present there is not a single credible established religion in the world. That is perhaps the most stupendous fact in the whole world-situation. This play of mine, Major Barbara, is, I hope, both true and inspired; but whoever says that it all happened, and that faith in it and understanding of it consist in believing that it is a record of an actual occurrence, is, to speak according to Scripture, a fool and a liar, and is hereby solemnly denounced and cursed as such by me, the author, to all posterity.

London, June 1906.

N.B. The Euripidean verses in the second act of Major Barbara are not by me, nor even directly by Euripides. They are by Professor Gilbert Murray, whose English version of The Bacchæ came into our dramatic literature with all the impulsive power of an original work shortly before Major Barbara was begun. The play, indeed, stands indebted to him in more ways than one.

G. B. S.

ACT I

IT is after dinner in January 1906, in the library in Lady Britomart Undershaft's house in Wilton Crescent. A large and comfortable settee is in the middle of the room, upholstered in dark leather. A person sitting on it (it is vacant at present) would have, on his right, Lady Britomart's writing-table, with the lady herself busy at it; a smaller writing-table behind him on his left; the door behind him on Lady Britomart's side; and a window with a window-seat directly on his left. Near the window is an armchair.

Lady Britomart is a woman of fifty or thereabouts, well dressed and yet careless of her dress, well bred and quite reckless of her breeding, well mannered and yet appallingly outspoken and indifferent to the opinion of her interlocutors, amiable and yet peremptory, arbitrary, and high-tempered to the last bearable degree, and withal a very typical managing matron of the upper class, treated as a naughty child until she grew into a scolding mother, and finally settling down with plenty of practical ability and worldly experience, limited in the oddest way with domestic and class limitations, conceiving the universe exactly as if it were a large house in Wilton Crescent, though handling her corner of it very effectively on that assumption, and being quite enlightened and liberal as to the books in the library, the pictures on the walls, the music in the portfolios, and the articles in the papers.

Her son, Stephen, comes in. He is a gravely correct young man under 25, taking himself very seriously, but still in some awe of his mother, from childish habit and bachelor shyness rather than from any weakness of character.

STEPHEN. Whats the matter?

LADY BRITOMART. Presently, Stephen.

Stephen submissively walks to the settee and sits down. He takes up a Liberal weekly called The Speaker.

LADY BRITOMART. Dont begin to read, Stephen. I shall

341

require all your attention.

STEPHEN. It was only while I was waiting—

LADY BRITOMART. Dont make excuses, Stephen. [*He puts down The Speaker*]. Now! [*She finishes her writing; rises; and comes to the settee*]. I have not kept you waiting v e r y long, I think.

STEPHEN. Not at all, mother.

LADY BRITOMART. Bring me my cushion. [*He takes the cushion from the chair at the desk and arranges it for her as she sits down on the settee*]. Sit down. [*He sits down and fingers his tie nervously*]. Dont fiddle with your tie, Stephen: there is nothing the matter with it.

STEPHEN. I beg your pardon. [*He fiddles with his watch chain instead*].

LADY BRITOMART. Now are you attending to me, Stephen?

STEPHEN. Of course, mother.

LADY BRITOMART. No: it's n o t of course. I want something much more than your everyday matter-of-course attention. I am going to speak to you very seriously, Stephen. I wish you would let that chain alone.

STEPHEN [*hastily relinquishing the chain*] Have I done anything to annoy you, mother? If so, it was quite unintentional.

LADY BRITOMART [*astonished*] Nonsense! [*With some remorse*] My poor boy, did you think I was angry with you?

STEPHEN. What is it, then, mother? You are making me very uneasy.

LADY BRITOMART [*squaring herself at him rather aggressively*] Stephen: may I ask how soon you intend to realize that you are a grown-up man, and that I am only a woman?

STEPHEN [*amazed*] Only a—

LADY BRITOMART. Dont repeat my words, please: it is a most aggravating habit. You must learn to face life seriously, Stephen. I really cannot bear the whole burden of our family affairs any longer. You must advise me: you must assume the responsibility.

STEPHEN. I!

LADY BRITOMART. Yes, you, of course. You were 24 last June. Youve been at Harrow and Cambridge. Youve been to India and Japan. You must know a lot of things, now; unless you have wasted your time most scandalously. Well, a d v i s e me.

STEPHEN [much perplexed] You know I have never interfered in the household—

LADY BRITOMART. No: I should think not. I dont want you to order the dinner.

STEPHEN. I mean in our family affairs.

LADY BRITOMART. Well, you must interfere now; for they are getting quite beyond me.

STEPHEN [troubled] I have thought sometimes that perhaps I ought; but really, mother, I know so little about them; and what I do know is so painful—it is so impossible to mention some things to you— [He stops, ashamed].

LADY BRITOMART. I suppose you mean your father.

STEPHEN [almost inaudibly] Yes.

LADY BRITOMART. My dear: we cant go on all our lives not mentioning him. Of course you were quite right not to open the subject until I asked you to; but you are old enough now to be taken into my confidence, and to help me to deal with him about the girls.

STEPHEN. But the girls are all right. They are engaged.

LADY BRITOMART [complacently] Yes: I have made a very good match for Sarah. Charles Lomax will be a millionaire at 35. But that is ten years ahead; and in the meantime his trustees cannot under the terms of his father's will allow him more than £800 a year.

STEPHEN. But the will says also that if he increases his income by his own exertions, they may double the increase.

LADY BRITOMART. Charles Lomax's exertions are much more likely to decrease his income than to increase it. Sarah will have to find at least another £800 a year for the next

343

ten years; and even then they will be as poor as church mice. And what about Barbara? I thought Barbara was going to make the most brilliant career of all of you. And what does she do? Joins the Salvation Army; discharges her maid; lives on a pound a week; and walks in one evening with a professor of Greek whom she has picked up in the street, and who pretends to be a Salvationist, and actually plays the big drum for her in public because he has fallen head over ears in love with her.

STEPHEN. I was certainly rather taken aback when I heard they were engaged. Cusins is a very nice fellow, certainly: nobody would ever guess that he was born in Australia; but—

LADY BRITOMART. Oh, Adolphus Cusins will make a very good husband. After all, nobody can say a word against Greek: it stamps a man at once as an educated gentleman. And my family, thank Heaven, is not a pigheaded Tory one. We are Whigs, and believe in liberty. Let snobbish people say what they please: Barbara shall marry, not the man they like, but the man *I* like.

STEPHEN. Of course I was thinking only of his income. However, he is not likely to be extravagant.

LADY BRITOMART. Dont be too sure of that, Stephen. I know your quiet, simple, refined, poetic people like Adolphus—quite content with the best of everything! They cost more than your extravagant people, who are always as mean as they are second rate. No: Barbara will need at least £2000 a year. You see it means two additional households. Besides, my dear, y o u must marry soon. I dont approve of the present fashion of philandering bachelors and late marriages; and I am trying to arrange something for you.

STEPHEN. It's very good of you, mother; but perhaps I had better arrange that for myself.

LADY BRITOMART. Nonsense! you are much too young to begin matchmaking: you would be taken in by some pretty little nobody. Of course I dont mean that you are not to be consulted: you know that as well as I do. [*Stephen closes his lips and is silent*]. Now don't sulk, Stephen.

STEPHEN. I am not sulking, mother. What has all this got to do with—with—with my father?

LADY BRITOMART. My dear Stephen: where is the money to come from? It is easy enough for you and the other children to live on my income as long as we are in the same house; but I cant keep four families in four separate houses. You know how poor my father is: he has barely seven thousand a year now; and really, if he were not the Earl of Stevenage, he would have to give up society. He can do nothing for us. He says, naturally enough, that it is absurd that he should be asked to provide for the children of a man who is rolling in money. You see, Stephen, your father must be fabulously wealthy, because there is always a war going on somewhere.

STEPHEN. You need not remind me of that, mother. I have hardly ever opened a newspaper in my life without seeing our name in it. The Undershaft torpedo! The Undershaft quick firers! The Undershaft ten inch! The Undershaft disappearing rampart gun! The Undershaft submarine! and now the Undershaft aerial battleship! At Harrow they called me the Woolwich Infant. At Cambridge it was the same. A little brute at King's who was always trying to get up revivals, spoilt my Bible—your first birthday present to me—by writing under my name, "Son and heir to Undershaft and Lazarus, Death and Destruction Dealers: address, Christendom and Judea." But that was not so bad as the way I was kowtowed to everywhere because my father was making millions by selling cannons.

LADY BRITOMART. It is not only the cannons, but the war loans that Lazarus arranges under cover of giving credit for the cannons. You know, Stephen, it's perfectly scandalous. Those two men, Andrew Undershaft and Lazarus, positively have Europe under their thumbs. That is why your father is able to behave as he does. He is above the law. Do you think Bismarck or Gladstone or Disraeli could have openly defied every social and moral obligation all their lives as your father has? They simply wouldnt have dared. I asked Gladstone to take it up. I asked The Times to take it up. I asked the Lord Chamberlain to take it up. But it was just like asking them to declare war on the Sultan. They w o u l d n t. They said they couldnt touch him. I believe they were afraid.

STEPHEN. What could they do? He does not actually break the law.

LADY BRITOMART. Not break the law! He is always breaking the law. He broke the law when he was born: his parents were not married.

STEPHEN. Mother! Is that true?

LADY BRITOMART. Of course it's true: that was why we separated.

STEPHEN. He married without letting you know this!

LADY BRITOMART [*rather taken aback by this inference*] Oh no. To do Andrew justice, that was not the sort of thing he did. Besides, you know the Undershaft motto: Unashamed. Everybody knew.

STEPHEN. But you said that was why you separated.

LADY BRITOMART. Yes, because he was not content with being a foundling himself: he wanted to disinherit you for another foundling. That was what I couldnt stand.

STEPHEN [*ashamed*] Do you mean for—for—for—

LADY BRITOMART. Dont stammer, Stephen. Speak distinctly.

STEPHEN. But this so frightful to me, mother. To have to speak to you about such things!

LADY BRITOMART. It's not pleasant for me, either, especially if you are still so childish that you must make it worse by a display of embarrassment. It is only in the middle classes, Stephen, that people get into a state of dumb helpless horror when they find that there are wicked people in the world. In our class, we have to decide what is to be done with wicked people; and nothing should disturb our self-possession. Now ask your question properly.

STEPHEN. Mother: you have no consideration for me. For Heaven's sake either treat me as a child, as you always do, and tell me nothing at all; or tell me everything and let me take it as best I can.

LADY BRITOMART. Treat you as a child! What do you mean? It is most unkind and ungrateful of you to say such a thing. You know I have never treated any of you as children. I have always made you my companions and friends, and allowed you perfect freedom to do and say whatever you liked, so long as you liked what I could approve of.

STEPHEN [*desperately*] I daresay we have been the very imperfect children of a very perfect mother; but I do beg you to let me alone for once, and tell me about this horrible business of my father wanting to set me aside for another son.

LADY BRITOMART [*amazed*] Another son! I never said anything of the kind. I never dreamt of such a thing. This is what comes of interrupting me.

STEPHEN. But you said—

LADY BRITOMART [*cutting him short*] Now be a good boy, Stephen, and listen to me patiently. The Undershafts are descended from a foundling in the parish of St Andrew Undershaft in the city. That was long ago, in the reign of James the First. Well, this foundling was adopted by an armorer and gun-maker. In the course of time the foundling succeeded to the business; and from some notion of gratitude, or some vow or something, he adopted another foundling, and left the business to him. And that foundling did the same. Ever since that, the cannon business has always been left to an adopted foundling named Andrew Undershaft.

STEPHEN. But did they never marry? Were there no legitimate sons?

LADY BRITOMART. Oh yes: they married just as your father did; and they were rich enough to buy land for their

347

own children and leave them well provided for. But they always adopted and trained some foundling to succeed them in the business; and of course they always quarrelled with their wives furiously over it. Your father was adopted in that way; and he pretends to consider himself bound to keep up the tradition and adopt somebody to leave the business to. Of course I was not going to stand that. There may have been some reason for it when the Undershafts could only marry women in their own class, whose sons were not fit to govern great estates. But there could be no excuse for passing over m y son.

STEPHEN [*dubiously*] I am afraid I should make a poor hand of managing a cannon foundry.

LADY BRITOMART. Nonsense! you could easily get a manager and pay him a salary.

STEPHEN. My father evidently had no great opinion of my capacity.

LADY BRITOMART. Stuff, child! you were only a baby: it had nothing to do with your capacity. Andrew did it on principle, just as he did every perverse and wicked thing on principle. When my father remonstrated, Andrew actually told him to his face that history tells us of only two successful institutions: one the Undershaft firm, and the other the Roman Empire under the Antonines. That was because the Antonine emperors all adopted their successors. Such rubbish! The Stevenages are as good as the Antonines, I hope; and you are a Stevenage. But that was Andrew all over. There you have the man! Always clever and unanswerable when he was defending nonsense and wickedness: always awkward and sullen when he had to behave sensibly and decently!

STEPHEN. Then it was on my account that your home life was broken up, mother. I am sorry.

LADY BRITOMART. Well, dear, there were other differences. I really cannot bear an immoral man. I am not a Pharisee, I hope; and I should not have minded his merely d o i n g wrong things: we are none of us perfect.

348

But your father didnt exactly d o wrong things: he said them and thought them: that was what was so dreadful. He really had a sort of religion of wrongness. Just as one doesnt mind men practising immorality so long as they own that they are in the wrong by preaching morality; so I couldnt forgive Andrew for preaching immorality while he practised morality. You would all have grown up without principles, without any knowledge of right and wrong, if he had been in the house. You know, my dear, your father was a very attractive man in some ways. Children did not dislike him; and he took advantage of it to put the wickedest ideas into their heads, and make them quite unmanageable. I did not dislike him myself: very far from it; but nothing can bridge over moral disagreement.

STEPHEN. All this simply bewilders me, mother. People may differ about matters of opinion, or even about religion; but how can they differ about right and wrong? Right is right; and wrong is wrong; and if a man cannot distinguish them properly, he is either a fool or a rascal: thats all.

LADY BRITOMART [touched] Thats my own boy [She pats his cheek]! Your father never could answer that: he used to laugh and get out of it under cover of some affectionate nonsense. And now that you understand the situation, what do you advise me to do?

STEPHEN. Well, what c a n you do?

LADY BRITOMART. I must get the money somehow.

STEPHEN. We cannot take money from him. I had rather go and live in some cheap place like Bedford Square or even Hampstead than take a farthing of his money.

LADY BRITOMART. But after all, Stephen, our present income comes from Andrew.

STEPHEN [shocked] I never knew that.

LADY BRITOMART. Well, you surely didnt suppose your grandfather had anything to give me. The Stevenages could not do everything for you. We gave you social position. Andrew had to contribute s o m e t h i n g. He had a

349

very good bargain, I think.

STEPHEN [*bitterly*] We are utterly dependent on him and his cannons, then?

LADY BRITOMART. Certainly not: the money is settled. But he provided it. So you see it is not a question of taking money from him or not: it is simply a question of how much. I dont want any more for myself.

STEPHEN. Nor do I.

LADY BRITOMART. But Sarah does; and Barbara does. That is, Charles Lomax and Adolphus Cusins will cost them more. So I must put my pride in my pocket and ask for it, I suppose. That is your advice, Stephen, is it not?

STEPHEN. No.

LADY BRITOMART [*sharply*] Stephen!

STEPHEN. Of course if you are determined—

LADY BRITOMART. I am not determined: I ask your advice; and I am waiting for it. I will not have all the responsibility thrown on my shoulders.

STEPHEN [*obstinately*] I would die sooner than ask him for another penny.

LADY BRITOMART [*resignedly*] You mean that *I* must ask him. Very well, Stephen: it shall be as you wish. You will be glad to know that your grandfather concurs. But he thinks I ought to ask Andrew to come here and see the girls. After all, he must have some natural affection for them.

STEPHEN. Ask him here!!!

LADY BRITOMART. Do n o t repeat my words, Stephen. Where else can I ask him?

STEPHEN. I never expected you to ask him at all.

LADY BRITOMART. Now dont tease, Stephen. Come! you see that it is necessary that he should pay us a visit, dont you?

STEPHEN [*reluctantly*] I suppose so, if the girls cannot do without his money.

LADY BRITOMART. Thank you, Stephen: I knew you would give me the right advice when it was properly explained to you. I have asked your father to come this evening. [*Stephen bounds from his seat*]. Dont jump, Stephen: it fidgets me.

STEPHEN [*in utter consternation*] Do you mean to say that my father is coming here to-night—that he may be here at any moment?

LADY BRITOMART [*looking at her watch*] I said nine. [*He gasps. She rises*]. Ring the bell, please. [*Stephen goes to the smaller writing table; presses a button on it; and sits at it with his elbows on the table and his head in his hands, outwitted and overwhelmed*]. It is ten minutes to nine yet; and I have to prepare the girls. I asked Charles Lomax and Adolphus to dinner on purpose that they might be here. Andrew had better see them in case he should cherish any delusions as to their being capable of supporting their wives. [*The butler enters: Lady Britomart goes behind the settee to speak to him*]. Morrison: go up to the drawing-room and tell everybody to come down here at once. [*Morrison withdraws. Lady Britomart turns to Stephen*]. Now remember, Stephen: I shall need all your countenance and authority. [*He rises and tries to recover some vestige of these attributes*]. Give me a chair, dear. [*He pushes a chair forward from the wall to where she stands, near the smaller writing table. She sits down; and he goes to the arm-chair, into which he throws himself*]. I dont know how Barbara will take it. Ever since they made her a major in the Salvation Army she has developed a propensity to have her own way and order people about which quite cows me sometimes. It's not ladylike: I'm sure I dont know where she picked it up. Anyhow, Barbara shant bully m e; but still it's just as well that your father should be here before she has time to refuse to meet him or make a fuss. Dont look nervous, Stephen: it will only encourage Barbara to make difficulties. *I* am nervous enough, goodness knows; but I dont shew it.

Sarah and Barbara come in with their respective young men, Charles Lomax and Adolphus Cusins. Sarah is slender,

MAJOR BARBARA

bored, and mundane. Barbara is robuster, jollier, much more energetic. Sarah is fashionably dressed: Barbara is in Salvation Army uniform. Lomax, a young man about town, is like many other young men about town. He is afflicted with a frivolous sense of humor which plunges him at the most inopportune moments into paroxysms of imperfectly suppressed laughter. Cusins is a spectacled student, slight, thin haired, and sweet voiced, with a more complex form of Lomax's complaint. His sense of humor is intellectual and subtle, and is complicated by an appalling temper. The life-long struggle of a benevolent temperament and a high conscience against impulses of inhuman ridicule and fierce impatience has set up a chronic strain which has visibly wrecked his constitution. He is a most implacable, determined, tenacious, intolerant person who by mere force of character presents himself as—and indeed actually is—considerate, gentle, explanatory, even mild and apologetic, capable possibly of murder, but not of cruelty or coarseness. By the operation of some instinct which is not merciful enough to blind him with the illusions of love, he is obstinately bent on marrying Barbara. Lomax likes Sarah and thinks it will be rather a lark to marry her. Consequently he has not attempted to resist Lady Britomart's arrangements to that end.

All four look as if they had been having a good deal of fun in the drawing room. The girls enter first, leaving the swains outside. Sarah comes to the settee. Barbara comes in after her and stops at the door.

BARBARA. Are Cholly and Dolly to come in?

LADY BRITOMART [*forcibly*] Barbara: I will not have Charles called Cholly: the vulgarity of it positively makes me ill.

BARBARA. It's all right, mother: Cholly is quite correct nowadays. Are they to come in?

LADY BRITOMART. Yes, if they will behave themselves.

BARBARA [*through the door*] Come in, Dolly; and behave yourself.

Barbara comes to her mother's writing table. Cusins

352

MAJOR BARBARA

enters smiling, and wanders towards Lady Britomart.

SARAH [*calling*] Come in, Cholly. [*Lomax enters, controlling his features very imperfectly, and places himself vaguely between Sarah and Barbara*].

LADY BRITOMART [*peremptorily*] Sit down, all of you. [*They sit. Cusins crosses to the window and seats himself there. Lomax takes a chair. Barbara sits at the writing table and Sarah on the settee*]. I dont in the least know what you are laughing at, Adolphus. I am surprised at you, though I expected nothing better from Charles Lomax.

CUSINS [*in a remarkably gentle voice*] Barbara has been trying to teach me the West Ham Salvation March.

LADY BRITOMART. I see nothing to laugh at in that; nor should you if you are really converted.

CUSINS [*sweetly*] You were not present. It was really funny, I believe.

LOMAX. Ripping.

LADY BRITOMART. Be quiet, Charles. Now listen to me, children. Your father is coming here this evening.

General stupefaction. Lomax, Sarah, and Barbara rise: Sarah scared, and Barbara amused and expectant.

LOMAX [*remonstrating*] Oh I say!

LADY BRITOMART. You are not called on to say anything, Charles.

SARAH. Are you serious, mother?

LADY BRITOMART. Of course I am serious. It is on your account, Sarah, and also on Charles's. [*Silence. Sarah sits, with a shrug. Charles looks painfully unworthy*]. I hope you are not going to object, Barbara.

BARBARA. I! why should I? My father has a soul to be saved like anybody else. He's quite welcome as far as I am concerned. [*She sits on the table, and softly whistles 'Onward, Christian Soldiers'*].

LOMAX [*still remonstrant*] But really, dont you know! Oh I say!

LADY BRITOMART [*frigidly*] What do you wish to convey, Charles?

LOMAX. Well, you must admit that this is a bit thick.

353

LADY BRITOMART [*turning with ominous suavity to Cusins*] Adolphus: you are a professor of Greek. Can you translate Charles Lomax's remarks into reputable English for us?

CUSINS [*cautiously*] If I may say so, Lady Brit, I think Charles has rather happily expressed what we all feel. Homer, speaking of Autolycus, uses the same phrase. πυκινὸν δόμον ἐλθεῖν means a bit thick.

LOMAX [*handsomely*] Not that I mind, you know, if Sarah dont. [*He sits*].

LADY BRITOMART [*crushingly*] Thank you. Have I y o u r permission, Adolphus, to invite my own husband to my own house?

CUSINS [*gallantly*] You have my unhesitating support in everything you do.

LADY BRITOMART. Tush! Sarah: have you nothing to say?

SARAH. Do you mean that he is coming regularly to live here?

LADY BRITOMART. Certainly not. The spare room is ready for him if he likes to stay for a day or two and see a little more of you; but there are limits.

SARAH. Well, he cant eat us, I suppose. *I* dont mind.

LOMAX [*chuckling*] I wonder how the old man will take it.

LADY BRITOMART. Much as the old woman will, no doubt, Charles.

LOMAX [*abashed*] I didnt mean—at least—

LADY BRITOMART. You didnt t h i n k, Charles. You never do; and the result is, you never mean anything. And now please attend to me, children. Your father will be quite a stranger to us.

LOMAX. I suppose he hasnt seen Sarah since she was a little kid.

LADY BRITOMART. Not since she was a little kid, Charles, as you express it with that elegance of diction and refinement of thought that seem never to desert you. Accordingly—er— [*Impatiently*] Now I have forgotten what I was going to say. That comes of your provoking me to be sarcastic, Charles. Adolphus: will you kindly tell me where I was.

CUSINS [*sweetly*] You were saying that as Mr Undershaft has not seen his children since they were babies, he will form his opinion of the way you have brought them up from their behavior to-night, and that therefore you wish us all to be particularly careful to conduct ourselves well, especially Charles.

LADY BRITOMART [*with emphatic approval*] Precisely.

LOMAX. Look here, Dolly: Lady Brit didnt say that.

LADY BRITOMART [*vehemently*] I did, Charles. Adolphus's recollection is perfectly correct. It is most important that you should be good; and I do beg you for once not to pair off into opposite corners and giggle and whisper while I am speaking to your father.

BARBARA. All right, mother. We'll do you credit. [*She comes off the table, and sits in her chair with ladylike elegance*].

LADY BRITOMART. Remember, Charles, that Sarah will want to feel proud of you instead of ashamed of you.

LOMAX. Oh I say! theres nothing to be exactly proud of, dont you know.

LADY BRITOMART. Well, try and look as if there was.

Morrison, pale and dismayed, breaks into the room in unconcealed disorder.

MORRISON. Might I speak a word to you, my lady?

LADY BRITOMART. Nonsense! Shew him up.

MORRISON. Yes, my lady. [*He goes*].

LOMAX. Does Morrison know who it is?

LADY BRITOMART. Of course. Morrison has always been with us.

LOMAX. It must be a regular corker for him, dont you know.

LADY BRITOMART. Is this a moment to get on my nerves, Charles, with your outrageous expressions?

LOMAX. But this is something out of the ordinary, really—

MORRISON [*at the door*] The—er—Mr Undershaft. [*He retreats in confusion*].

Andrew Undershaft comes in. All rise. Lady Britomart meets him in the middle of the room behind the settee.

Andrew is, on the surface, a stoutish, easygoing elderly man, with kindly patient manners, and an engaging simplicity of character. But he has a watchful, deliberate, waiting, listening face, and formidable reserves of power, both bodily and mental, in his capacious chest and long head. His gentleness is partly that of a strong man who has learnt by experience that his natural grip hurts ordinary people unless he handles them very carefully, and partly the mellowness of age and success. He is also a little shy in his present very delicate situation.

LADY BRITOMART. Good evening, Andrew.

UNDERSHAFT. How d'ye do, my dear.

LADY BRITOMART. You look a good deal older.

UNDERSHAFT [*apologetically*] I am somewhat older. [*Taking her hand with a touch of courtship*] Time has stood still with you.

LADY BRITOMART [*throwing away his hand*] Rubbish! This is your family.

UNDERSHAFT [*surprised*] Is it so large? I am sorry to say my memory is failing very badly in some things. [*He offers his hand with paternal kindness to Lomax*].

LOMAX [*jerkily shaking his hand*] Ahdedoo.

UNDERSHAFT. I can see you are my eldest. I am very glad to meet you again, my boy.

LOMAX [*remonstrating*] No, but look here dont you know— [*Overcome*] Oh I say!

LADY BRITOMART [*recovering from momentary speechlessness*] Andrew: do you mean to say that you dont remember how many children you have?

UNDERSHAFT. Well, I am afraid I—. They have grown so much—er. Am I making any ridiculous mistake? I may as well confess: I recollect only one son. But so many things have happened since, of course—er—

LADY BRITOMART [*decisively*] Andrew: you are talking nonsense. Of course you have only one son.

UNDERSHAFT. Perhaps you will be good enough to introduce me, my dear.

LADY BRITOMART. That is Charles Lomax, who is engaged to Sarah.

UNDERSHAFT. My dear sir, I beg your pardon.

LOMAX. Notatall. Delighted, I assure you.

LADY BRITOMART. This is Stephen.

UNDERSHAFT [*bowing*] Happy to make your acquaintance, Mr Stephen. Then [*going to Cusins*] y o u must be my son. [*Taking Cusins' hands in his*] How are you, my young friend? [*To Lady Britomart*] He is very like you, my love.

CUSINS. You flatter me, Mr. Undershaft. My name is Cusins: engaged to Barbara. [*Very explicitly*] That is Major Barbara Undershaft, of the Salvation Army. That is Sarah, your second daughter. This is Stephen Undershaft, your son.

UNDERSHAFT. My dear Stephen, I b e g your pardon.

STEPHEN. Not at all.

UNDERSHAFT. Mr Cusins: I am much indebted to you for explaining so precisely. [*Turning to Sarah*] Barbara, my dear—

SARAH [*prompting him*] Sarah.

UNDERSHAFT. Sarah, of course. [*They shake hands. He goes over to Barbara*]. Barbara—I am right this time, I hope.

BARBARA. Quite right. [*They shake hands*].

LADY BRITOMART [*resuming command*] Sit down, all of you. Sit down, Andrew. [*She comes forward and sits on the settee. Cusins also brings his chair forward on her left. Barbara and Stephen resume their seats. Lomax gives his chair to Sarah and goes for another*].

UNDERSHAFT. Thank you, my love.

LOMAX [*conversationally, as he brings a chair forward between the writing table and the settee, and offers it to Undershaft*] Takes you some time to find out exactly where you are, dont it?

UNDERSHAFT [*accepting the chair, but remaining stand-*

357

ing] That is not what embarrasses me, Mr Lomax. My difficulty is that if I play the part of a father, I shall produce the effect of an intrusive stranger; and if I play the part of a discreet stranger, I may appear a callous father.

LADY BRITOMART. There is no need for you to play any part at all, Andrew. You had much better be sincere and natural.

UNDERSHAFT [*submissively*] Yes, my dear: I daresay that will be best. [*He sits down comfortably*]. Well, here I am. Now what can I do for you all?

LADY BRITOMART. You need not do anything, Andrew. You are one of the family. You can sit with us and enjoy yourself.

A painfully conscious pause. Barbara makes a face at Lomax, whose too long suppressed mirth immediately explodes in agonized neighings.

LADY BRITOMART [*outraged*] Charles Lomax: if you can behave yourself, behave yourself. If not, leave the room.

LOMAX. I'm awfully sorry, Lady Brit; but really, you know, upon my soul! [*He sits on the settee between Lady Britomart and Undershaft, quite overcome*].

BARBARA. Why dont you laugh if you want to, Cholly? It's good for your inside.

LADY BRITOMART. Barbara: you have had the education of a lady. Please let your father see that; and dont talk like a street girl.

UNDERSHAFT. Never mind me, my dear. As you know, I am not a gentleman; and I was never educated.

LOMAX [*encouragingly*] Nobody'd know it, I assure you. You look all right, you know.

CUSINS. Let me advise you to study Greek, Mr Undershaft. Greek scholars are privileged men. Few of them know Greek; and none of them know anything else; but their position is unchallengeable. Other languages are the qualifications of waiters and commercial travellers: Greek is to a man of position what the hallmark is to silver.

BARBARA. Dolly: dont be insincere. Cholly: fetch your concertina and play something for us.

LOMAX [*jumps up eagerly, but checks himself to remark doubtfully to Undershaft*] Perhaps that sort of thing isnt in your line, eh?

UNDERSHAFT. I am particularly fond of music.

LOMAX [*delighted*] Are you? Then I'll get it. [*He goes upstairs for the instrument*].

UNDERSHAFT. Do you play, Barbara?

BARBARA. Only the tambourine. But Cholly's teaching me the concertina.

UNDERSHAFT. Is Cholly also a member of the Salvation Army?

BARBARA. No: he says it's bad form to be a dissenter. But I dont despair of Cholly. I made him come yesterday to a meeting at the dock gates, and take the collection in his hat.

UNDERSHAFT [*looks whimsically at his wife*]!!

LADY BRITOMART. It is not my doing, Andrew. Barbara is old enough to take her own way. She has no father to advise her.

BARBARA. Oh yes she has. There are no orphans in the Salvation Army.

UNDERSHAFT. Your father there has a great many children and plenty of experience, eh?

BARBARA [*looking at him with quick interest and nodding*] Just so. How did y o u come to understand that? [*Lomax is heard at the door trying the concertina*].

LADY BRITOMART. Come in, Charles. Play us something at once.

LOMAX. Righto! [*He sits down in his former place, and preludes*].

UNDERSHAFT. One moment, Mr Lomax. I am rather interested in the Salvation Army. Its motto might be my own: Blood and Fire.

LOMAX [*shocked*] But not your sort of blood and fire, you know.

UNDERSHAFT. My sort of blood cleanses: my sort of fire purifies.

BARBARA. So do ours. Come down to-morrow to my

359

MAJOR BARBARA

shelter—the West Ham shelter—and see what we're doing. We're going to march to a great meeting in the Assembly Hall at Mile End. Come and see the shelter and then march with us: it will do you a lot of good. Can you play anything?

UNDERSHAFT. In my youth I earned pennies, and even shillings occasionally, in the streets and in public house parlors by my natural talent for stepdancing. Later on, I became a member of the Undershaft orchestral society, and performed passably on the tenor trombone.

LOMAX [*scandalized—putting down the concertina*] Oh I say!

BARBARA. Many a sinner has played himself into heaven on the trombone, thanks to the Army.

LOMAX [*to Barbara, still rather shocked*] Yes; but what about the cannon business, dont you know? [*To Undershaft*] Getting into heaven is not exactly in your line, is it?

LADY BRITOMART. Charles!!!

LOMAX. Well; but it stands to reason, dont it? The cannon business may be necessary and all that: we cant get on without cannons; but it isnt right, you know. On the other hand, there may be a certain amount of tosh about the Salvation Army—I belong to the Established Church myself—but still you cant deny that it's religion; and you cant go against religion, can you? At least unless youre downright immoral, dont you know.

UNDERSHAFT. You hardly appreciate my position, Mr Lomax—

LOMAX [*hastily*] I'm not saying anything against you personally—

UNDERSHAFT. Quite so, quite so. But consider for a moment. Here I am, a profiteer in mutilation and murder. I find myself in a specially amiable humor just now because, this morning, down at the foundry, we blew twenty-seven dummy soldiers into fragments with a gun which formerly destroyed only thirteen.

LOMAX [*leniently*] Well, the more destructive war becomes, the sooner it will be abolished, eh?

360

MAJOR BARBARA

UNDERSHAFT. Not at all. The more destructive war becomes the more fascinating we find it. No, Mr Lomax: I am obliged to you for making the usual excuse for my trade; but I am not ashamed of it. I am not one of those men who keep their morals and their business in watertight compartments. All the spare money my trade rivals spend on hospitals, cathedrals, and other receptacles for conscience money, I devote to experiments and researches in improved methods of destroying life and property. I have always done so; and I always shall. Therefore your Christmas card moralities of peace on earth and goodwill among men are of no use to me. Your Christianity, which enjoins you to resist not evil, and to turn the other cheek, would make me a bankrupt. M y morality—m y religion—must have a place for cannons and torpedoes in it.

STEPHEN [*coldly—almost sullenly*] You speak as if there were half a dozen moralities and religions to choose from, instead of one true morality and one true religion.

UNDERSHAFT. For me there is only one true morality; but it might not fit you, as you do not manufacture aerial battleships. There is only one true morality for every man; but every man has not the same true morality.

LOMAX [*overtaxed*] Would you mind saying that again? I didnt quite follow it.

CUSINS. It's quite simple. As Euripides says, one man's meat is another man's poison morally as well as physically.

UNDERSHAFT. Precisely.

LOMAX. Oh, t h a t. Yes, yes, yes. True. True.

STEPHEN. In other words, some men are honest and some are scoundrels.

BARBARA. Bosh. There are no scoundrels.

UNDERSHAFT. Indeed? Are there any good men?

BARBARA. No. Not one. There are neither good men nor scoundrels: there are just children of one Father; and the sooner they stop calling one another names the better. You neednt talk to me: I know them. Ive had scores of them through my hands: scoundrels, criminals, infidels,

361

MAJOR BARBARA

philanthropists, missionaries, county councillors, all sorts. Theyre all just the same sort of sinner; and theres the same salvation ready for them all.

UNDERSHAFT. May I ask have you ever saved a maker of cannons?

BARBARA. No. Will you let me try?

UNDERSHAFT. Well, I will make a bargain with you. If I go to see you to-morrow in your Salvation Shelter, will you come the day after to see me in my cannon works?

BARBARA. Take care. It may end in your giving up the cannons for the sake of the Salvation Army.

UNDERSHAFT. Are you sure it will not end in your giving up the Salvation Army for the sake of the cannons?

BARBARA. I will take my chance of that.

UNDERSHAFT. And I will take my chance of the other. [*They shake hands on it*]. Where is your shelter?

BARBARA. In West Ham. At the sign of the cross. Ask anybody in Canning Town. Where are your works?

UNDERSHAFT. In Perivale St Andrews. At the sign of the sword. Ask anybody in Europe.

LOMAX. Hadnt I better play something?

BARBARA. Yes. Give us Onward, Christian Soldiers.

LOMAX. Well, thats rather a strong order to begin with, dont you know. Suppose I sing Thourt passing hence, my brother. It's much the same tune.

BARBARA. It's too melancholy. You get saved, Cholly; and youll pass hence, my brother, without making such a fuss about it.

LADY BRITOMART. Really, Barbara, you go on as if religion were a pleasant subject. Do have some sense of propriety.

UNDERSHAFT. I do not find it an unpleasant subject, my dear. It is the only one that capable people really care for.

LADY BRITOMART [*looking at her watch*] Well, if you are determined to have it, I insist on having it in a proper and respectable way. Charles: ring for prayers. [*General*
362

amazement. Stephen rises in dismay].

LOMAX [*rising*] Oh I say!

UNDERSHAFT [*rising*] I am afraid I must be going.

LADY BRITOMART. You cannot go now, Andrew: it would be most improper. Sit down. What will the servants think?

UNDERSHAFT. My dear: I have conscientious scruples. May I suggest a compromise? If Barbara will conduct a little service in the drawing room, with Mr Lomax as organist, I will attend it willingly. I will even take part, if a trombone can be procured.

LADY BRITOMART. Dont mock, Andrew.

UNDERSHAFT [*shocked—to Barbara*] You dont think I am mocking, my love, I hope.

BARBARA. No, of course not; and it wouldnt matter if you were: half the Army came to their first meeting for a lark. [*Rising*] Come along. [*She throws her arm round her father and sweeps him out, calling to the others from the threshold*]. Come, Dolly. Come, Cholly.

Cusins rises.

LADY BRITOMART. I will not be disobeyed by everybody. Adolphus: sit down. [*He does not*]. Charles: you may go. You are not fit for prayers: you cannot keep your countenance.

LOMAX. Oh I say! [*He goes out*].

LADY BRITOMART [*continuing*] But you, Adolphus, can behave yourself if you choose to. I insist on your staying.

CUSINS. My dear Lady Brit: there are things in the family prayer book that I couldnt bear to hear you say.

LADY BRITOMART. What things, pray?

CUSINS. Well, you would have to say before all the servants that we have done things we ought not to have done, and left undone things we ought to have done, and that there is no health in us. I cannot bear to hear you doing yourself such an injustice, and Barbara such an injustice. As for myself, I flatly deny it: I have done my best. I

363

shouldnt dare to marry Barbara—I couldnt look you in the face—if it were true. So I must go to the drawing room.

LADY BRITOMART [*offended*] Well, go. [*He starts for the door*]. And remember this, Adolphus [*he turns to listen*]: I have a very strong suspicion that you went to the Salvation Army to worship Barbara and nothing else. And I quite appreciate the very clever way in which you systematically humbug me. I have found you out. Take care Barbara doesnt. Thats all.

CUSINS [*with unruffled sweetness*] Dont tell on me. [*He steals out*].

LADY BRITOMART. Sarah: if you want to go, go. Anything's better than to sit there as if you wished you were a thousand miles away.

SARAH [*languidly*] Very well, mamma. [*She goes*].

Lady Britomart, with a sudden flounce, gives way to a little gust of tears.

STEPHEN [*going to her*] Mother: whats the matter?

LADY BRITOMART [*swishing away her tears with her handkerchief*] Nothing. Foolishness. You can go with him, too, if you like, and leave me with the servants.

STEPHEN. Oh, you mustnt think that, mother. I—I dont like him.

LADY BRITOMART. The others do. That is the injustice of a woman's lot. A woman has to bring up her children; and that means to restrain them, to deny them things they want, to set them tasks, to punish them when they do wrong, to do all the unpleasant things. And then the father, who has nothing to do but pet them and spoil them, comes in when all her work is done and steals their affection from her.

STEPHEN. He has not stolen our affection from you. It is only curiosity.

LADY BRITOMART [*violently*] I wont be consoled, Stephen. There is nothing the matter with me. [*She rises and goes towards the door*].

STEPHEN. Where are you going, mother?

MAJOR BARBARA

LADY BRITOMART. To the drawing room, of course. [*She goes out. Onward, Christian Soldiers, on the concertina, with tambourine accompaniment, is heard when the door opens*]. Are you coming, Stephen?

STEPHEN. No. Certainly not. [*She goes. He sits down on the settee, with compressed lips and an expression of strong dislike*].

END OF ACT I

ACT II

THE yard of the West Ham shelter of the Salvation Army is a cold place on a January morning. The building itself, an old warehouse, is newly whitewashed. Its gabled end projects into the yard in the middle, with a door on the ground floor, and another in the loft above it without any balcony or ladder, but with a pulley rigged over it for hoisting sacks. Those who come from this central gable end into the yard have the gateway leading to the street on their left, with a stone horse-trough just beyond it, and, on the right, a penthouse shielding a table from the weather. There are forms at the table; and on them are seated a man and a woman, both much down on their luck, finishing a meal of bread (one thick slice each, with margarine and golden syrup) and diluted milk.

The man, a workman out of employment, is young, agile, a talker, a poser, sharp enough to be capable of anything in reason except honesty or altruistic considerations of any kind. The woman is a commonplace old bundle of poverty and hard-worn humanity. She looks sixty and probably is forty-five. If they were rich people, gloved and muffed and well wrapped up in furs and overcoats, they would be numbed and miserable; for it is a grindingly cold, raw, January day; and a glance at the background of grimy warehouses and leaden sky visible over the whitewashed walls of the yard would drive any idle rich person straight to the Mediterranean. But these two, being no more troubled with visions of the Mediterranean than of the moon, and being compelled to keep more of their clothes in the pawnshop, and less on their persons, in winter than in summer, are not depressed by the cold: rather are they stung into vivacity, to which their meal has just now given an almost jolly turn. The man takes a pull at his mug, and then gets up and moves about the yard with his hands deep in his pockets, occasionally breaking into a stepdance.

THE WOMAN. Feel better arter your meal, sir?

THE MAN. No. Call that a meal! Good enough for you,

366

praps; but wot is it to me, an intelligent workin man.

THE WOMAN. Workin man! Wot are you?

THE MAN. Painter.

THE WOMAN [*sceptically*] Yus, I dessay.

THE MAN. Yus, you dessay! I know. Every loafer that cant do nothink calls isself a painter. Well, I'm a real painter: grainer, finisher, thirty-eight bob a week when I can get it.

THE WOMAN. Then why dont you go and get it?

THE MAN. I'll tell you why. Fust: I'm intelligent—fffff! it's rotten cold here [*he dances a step or two*]—yes: intelligent beyond the station o life into which it has pleased the capitalists to call me; and they dont like a man that sees through em. Second, an intelligent bein needs a doo share of appiness; so I drink somethink cruel when I get the chawnce. Third, I stand by my class and do as little as I can so's to leave arf the job for me fellow workers. Fourth, I'm fly enough to know wots inside the law and wots outside it; and inside it I do as the capitalists do: pinch wot I can lay me ands on. In a proper state of society I am sober, industrious and honest: in Rome, so to speak, I do as the Romans do. Wots the consequence? When trade is bad—and it's rotten bad just now—and the employers az to sack arf their men, they generally start on me.

THE WOMAN. Whats your name?

THE MAN. Price. Bronterre O'Brien Price. Usually called Snobby Price, for short.

THE WOMAN. Snobby's a carpenter, aint it? You said you was a painter.

PRICE. Not that kind of snob, but the genteel sort. I'm too uppish, owing to my intelligence, and my father being a Chartist and a reading, thinking man: a stationer, too. I'm none of your common hewers of wood and drawers of water; and dont you forget it. [*He returns to his seat at the table, and takes up his mug*]. Wots y o u r name?

THE WOMAN. Rummy Mitchens, sir.

PRICE [*quaffing the remains of his milk to her*] Your

367

elth, Miss Mitchens.

RUMMY [*correcting him*] Missis Mitchens.

PRICE. Wot! Oh Rummy, Rummy! Respectable married woman, Rummy, gittin rescued by the Salvation Army by pretendin to be a bad un. Same old game!

RUMMY. What am I to do? I cant starve. Them Salvation lasses is dear good girls; but the better you are, the worse they likes to think you were before they rescued you. Why shouldnt they av a bit o credit, poor loves? theyre worn to rags by their work. And where would they get the money to rescue us if we was to let on we're no worse than other people? You know what ladies and gentlemen are.

PRICE. Thievin swine! Wish I ad their job, Rummy, all the same. Wot does Rummy stand for? Pet name praps?

RUMMY. Short for Romola.

PRICE. For wot!?

RUMMY. Romola. It was out of a new book. Somebody me mother wanted me to grow up like.

PRICE. We're companions in misfortune, Rummy. Both on us got names that nobody cawnt pronounce. Consequently I'm Snobby and youre Rummy because Bill and Sally wasnt good enough for our parents. Such is life!

RUMMY. Who saved you, Mr Price? Was it Major Barbara?

PRICE. No: I come here on my own. I'm goin to be Bronterre O'Brien Price, the converted painter. I know wot they like. I'll tell em how I blasphemed and gambled and wopped my poor old mother—

RUMMY [*shocked*] Used you to beat your mother?

PRICE. Not likely. She used to beat me. No matter: you come and listen to the converted painter, and youll hear how she was a pious woman that taught me me prayers at er knee, an how I used to come home drunk and drag her out o bed be er snow white airs, an lam into er with the poker.

RUMMY. Thats whats so unfair to us women. Your confessions is just as big lies as ours: you dont tell what you really done no more than us; but you men can tell your lies right out at the meetins and be made much of for it; while the sort o confessions we az to make az to be whispered to one lady at a time. It aint right, spite of all their piety.

PRICE. Right! Do you spose the Army 'd be allowed if it went and did right? Not much. It combs our air and makes us good little blokes to be robbed and put upon. But I'll play the game as good as any of em. I'll see somebody struck by lightnin, or hear a voice sayin "Snobby Price: where will you spend eternity?" I'll ave a time of it, I tell you.

RUMMY. You wont be let drink, though.

PRICE. I'll take it out in gorspellin, then. I dont want to drink if I can get fun enough any other way.

Jenny Hill, a pale, overwrought, pretty Salvation lass of 18, comes in through the yard gate, leading Peter Shirley, a half hardened, half worn-out elderly man, weak with hunger.

JENNY [*supporting him*] Come! pluck up. I'll get you something to eat. Youll be all right then.

PRICE [*rising and hurrying officiously to take the old man off Jenny's hands*] Poor old man! Cheer up, brother: youll find rest and peace and appiness ere. Hurry up with the food, miss: e's fair done. [*Jenny hurries into the shelter*]. Ere, buck up, daddy! shes fetchin y'a thick slice o breadn treacle, an a mug o skyblue. [*He seats him at the corner of the table*].

RUMMY [*gaily*] Keep up your old art! Never say die!

SHIRLEY. I'm not an old man. I'm ony 46. I'm as good as ever I was. The grey patch come in my hair before I was thirty. All it wants is three pennorth o hair dye: am I to be turned on the streets to starve for it? Holy God! Ive worked ten to twelve hours a day since I was thirteen, and paid my way all through; and now am I to be thrown into the gutter and my job given to a young man that can do it no better than me because I've black hair that goes white at the first change?

PRICE [*cheerfully*] No good jawrin about it. Youre ony a jumped-up, jerked-off, orspittle-turned-out incurable of an ole workin man: who cares about you? Eh? Make the thievin swine give you a meal: theyve stole many a one from you. Get a bit o your own back. [*Jenny returns with the usual meal*]. There you are, brother. Awsk a blessin an tuck that into you.

SHIRLEY [*looking at it ravenously but not touching it, and crying like a child*] I never took anything before.

JENNY [*petting him*] Come, come! the Lord sends it to you: he wasnt above taking bread from his friends; and why should you be? Besides, when we find you a job you can pay us for it if you like.

SHIRLEY [*eagerly*] Yes, yes: thats true. I can pay you back: its only a loan. [*Shivering*] Oh Lord! oh Lord! [*He turns to the table and attacks the meal ravenously*].

JENNY. Well, Rummy, are you more comfortable now?

RUMMY. God bless you, lovey! youve fed my body and saved my soul, havent you? [*Jenny, touched, kisses her*]. Sit down and rest a bit: you must be ready to drop.

JENNY. Ive been going hard since morning. But theres more work than we can do. I mustnt stop.

RUMMY. Try a prayer for just two minutes. Youll work all the better after.

JENNY [*her eyes lighting up*] Oh isnt it wonderful how a few minutes prayer revives you! I was quite light-headed at twelve o'clock, I was so tired; but Major Barbara just sent me to pray for five minutes; and I was able to go on as if I had only just begun. [*To Price*] Did you have a piece of bread?

PRICE [*with unction*] Yes, miss; but Ive got the piece that I value more; and thats the peace that passeth hall hannerstennin.

RUMMY [*fervently*] Glory Hallelujah!

Bill Walker, a rough customer of about 25, appears at the yard gate and looks malevolently at Jenny.

JENNY. That makes me so happy. When you say that,

I feel wicked for loitering here. I must get to work again.

She is hurrying to the shelter, when the new-comer moves quickly up to the door and intercepts her. His manner is so threatening that she retreats as he comes at her truculently, driving her down the yard.

BILL. Aw knaow you. Youre the one that took awy maw girl. Youre the one that set er agen me. Well, I'm gowin to ev er aht. Not that Aw care a carse for er or you: see? Bat Aw'll let er knaow; and Aw'll let y o u knaow. Aw'm gowing to give her a doin thatll teach er to cat awy from me. Nah in wiv you and tell er to cam aht afore Aw cam in and kick er aht. Tell er Bill Walker wants er. She'll knaow wot thet means; and if she keeps me witin itll be worse. You stop to jawr beck at me; and Aw'll stawt on you: d'ye eah? Theres your wy. In you gow. [*He takes her by the arm and slings her towards the door of the shelter. She falls on her hand and knee. Rummy helps her up again*].

PRICE [*rising, and venturing irresolutely towards Bill*] Easy there, mate. She aint doin you no arm.

BILL. Oo are you callin mite? [*Standing over him threateningly*] Youre gowin to stend ap for er, aw yer? Put ap your ends.

RUMMY [*running indignantly to him to scold him*] Oh, you great brute— [*He instantly swings his left hand back against her face. She screams and reels back to the trough, where she sits down, covering her bruised face with her hands and rocking herself and moaning with pain*].

JENNY [*going to her*] Oh, God forgive you! How could you strike an old woman like that?

BILL [*seizing her by the hair so violently that she also screams, and tearing her away from the old woman*] You Gawd forgimme again and Aw'll Gawd forgive you one on the jawr thetll stop you pryin for a week. [*Holding her and turning fiercely on Price*] Ev you ennything to sy agen it?

PRICE [*intimidated*] No, matey: she aint anything to do with me.

371

BILL. Good job for you! Aw'd pat two meals into you and fawt you with one finger arter, you stawved cur. [*To Jenny*] Nah are you gowin to fetch aht Mog Ebbijem; or em Aw to knock your fice off you and fetch her meself?

JENNY [*writhing in his grasp*] Oh please someone go in and tell Major Barbara— [*She screams again as he wrenches her head down; and Price and Rummy flee into the shelter*].

BILL. You want to gow in and tell your Mijor of me, do you?

JENNY. Oh please dont drag my hair. Let me go.

BILL. Do you or downt you? [*She stifles a scream*]. Yus or nao?

JENNY. God give me strength—

BILL. [*striking her with his fist in the face*] Gow an shaow her thet, and tell her if she wants one lawk it to cam and interfere with me. [*Jenny, crying with pain, goes into the shed. He goes to the form and addresses the old man*]. Eah: finish your mess; and git aht o maw wy.

SHIRLEY [*springing up and facing him fiercely, with the mug in his hand*] You take a liberty with me, and I'll smash you over the face with the mug and cut your eye out. Aint you satisfied—young whelps like you—with takin the bread out o the mouths of your elders that have brought you up and slaved for you, but you must come shovin and cheekin and bullyin in here, where the bread o charity is sickenin in our stummicks?

BILL [*contemptuously, but backing a little*] Wot good are you, you aold palsy mag? Wot good are you?

SHIRLEY. As good as you and better. I'll do a day's work agen you or any fat young soaker of your age. Go and take my job at Horrockses, where I worked for ten year. They want young men there: they cant afford to keep men over forty-five. Theyre very sorry—give you a character and happy to help you to get anything suited to your years— sure a steady man wont be long out of a job. Well, let em try y o u. Theyll find the differ. What do y o u know? Not as much as how to beeyave yourself—layin your dirty fist across the mouth of a respectable woman!

BILL. Downt provowk me to ly it acrost yours: d'ye eah?

SHIRLEY [*with blighting contempt*] Yes: you like an old man to hit, dont you, when youve finished with the women. I aint seen you hit a young one yet.

BILL [*stung*] You loy, you aold soupkitchener, you. There was a yang menn eah. Did Aw offer to itt him or did Aw not?

SHIRLEY. Was he starvin or was he not? Was he a man or only a crosseyed thief an a loafer? Would you hit my son-in-law's brother?

BILL. Oo's ee?

SHIRLEY. Todger Fairmile o Balls Pond. Him that won £20 off the Japanese wrastler at the music hall by standin out 17 minutes 4 seconds agen him.

BILL [*sullenly*] Aw'm nao music awl wrastler. Ken he box?

SHIRLEY. Yes: an you cant.

BILL. Wot! Aw cawnt, cawnt Aw? Wots thet you sy [*threatening him*]?

SHIRLEY [*not budging an inch*] Will you box Todger Fairmile if I put him on to you? Say the word.

BILL [*subsiding with a slouch*] Aw'll stend ap to enny menn alawv, if he was ten Todger Fairmawls. But Aw dont set ap to be a perfeshnal.

SHIRLEY [*looking down on him with unfathomable disdain*] Y o u box! Slap an old woman with the back o your hand! You hadnt even the sense to hit her where a magistrate couldnt see the mark of it, you silly young lump of conceit and ignorance. Hit a girl in the jaw and ony make her cry! If Todger Fairmile'd done it, she wouldnt a got up inside o ten minutes, no more than you would if he got on to you. Yah! I'd set about you myself if I had a week's feedin in me instead o two months' starvation. [*He turns his back on him and sits down moodily at the table*].

BILL [*following him and stooping over him to drive*

the taunt in] You loy! youve the bread and treacle in you that you cam eah to beg.

SHIRLEY [*bursting into tears*] Oh God! it's true: I'm only an old pauper on the scrap heap. [*Furiously*] But youll come to it yourself; and then youll know. Youll come to it sooner than a teetotaller like me, fillin yourself with gin at this hour o the mornin!

BILL. Aw'm nao gin drinker, you oald lawr; bat wen Aw want to give my girl a bloomin good awdin Aw lawk to ev a bit o devil in me: see? An eah Aw emm, talkin to a rotten aold blawter like you sted o given er wot for. [*Working himself into a rage*] Aw'm gowin in there to fetch her aht. [*He makes vengefully for the shelter door*].

SHIRLEY. Youre goin to the station on a stretcher, more likely; and theyll take the gin and the devil out of you there when they get you inside. You mind what youre about: the major here is the Earl o Stevenage's granddaughter.

BILL [*checked*] Garn!

SHIRLEY. Youll see.

BILL [*his resolution oozing*] Well, Aw aint dan nathin to er.

SHIRLEY. Spose she said you did! who'd believe you?

BILL [*very uneasy, skulking back to the corner of the penthouse*] Gawd! theres no jastice in this cantry. To think wot them people can do! Aw'm as good as er.

SHIRLEY. Tell her so. Its just what a fool like you would do.

Barbara, brisk and businesslike, comes from the shelter with a note book, and addresses herself to Shirley. Bill, cowed, sits down in the corner on a form, and turns his back on them.

BARBARA. Good morning.

SHIRLEY [*standing up and taking off his hat*] Good morning, miss.

BARBARA. Sit down: make yourself at home. [*He hesitates; but she puts a friendly hand on his shoulder and makes him obey*]. Now then! since youve made friends with

374

us, we want to know all about you. Names and addresses and trades.

SHIRLEY. Peter Shirley. Fitter. Chucked out two months ago because I was too old.

BARBARA [*not at all surprised*] Youd pass still. Why didnt you dye your hair?

SHIRLEY. I did. Me age come out at a coroner's inquest on me daughter.

BARBARA. Steady?

SHIRLEY. Teetotaller. Never out of a job before. Good worker. And sent to the knackers like an old horse!

BARBARA. No matter: if you did your part God will do his.

SHIRLEY [*suddenly stubborn*] My religion's no concern of anybody but myself.

BARBARA [*guessing*] I know. Secularist?

SHIRLEY [*hotly*] Did I offer to deny it?

BARBARA. Why should you? My own father's a Secularist, I think. Our Father—yours and mine—fulfils himself in many ways; and I daresay he knew what he was about when he made a Secularist of you. So buck up, Peter! we can always find a job for a steady man like you. [*Shirley, disarmed and a little bewildered, touches his hat. She turns from him to Bill*]. Whats y o u r name?

BILL [*insolently*] Wots thet to you?

BARBARA [*calmly making a note*] Afraid to give his name. Any trade?

BILL. Oo's afride to give is nime? [*Doggedly, with a sense of heroically defying the House of Lords in the person of Lord Stevenage*] If you want to bring a chawge agen me, bring it. [*She waits, unruffled*]. Moy nime's Bill Walker.

BARBARA [*as if the name were familiar: trying to remember how*] Bill Walker? [*Recollecting*] Oh, I know: youre the man that Jenny Hill was praying for inside just now. [*She enters his name in her note book*].

BILL. Oo's Jenny Ill? And wot call as she to pry for me?

375

BARBARA. I dont know. Perhaps it was you that cut her lip.

BILL [*defiantly*] Yus, it w a s me that cat her lip. Aw aint afride o y o u.

BARBARA. How could you be, since youre not afraid of God? Youre a brave man, Mr Walker. It takes some pluck to do o u r work here; but none of us dare lift our hand against a girl like that, for fear of her father in heaven.

BILL [*sullenly*] I want nan o your kentin jawr. I spowse you think Aw cam eah to beg from you, like this demmiged lot eah. Not me. Aw downt want your bread and scripe and ketlep. Aw dont blieve in your Gawd, no more than you do yourself.

BARBARA [*sunnily apologetic and ladylike, as on a new footing with him*] Oh, I beg your pardon for putting your name down, Mr Walker. I didnt understand. I'll strike it out.

BILL [*taking this as a slight, and deeply wounded by it*] Eah! you let maw nime alown. Aint it good enaff to be in your book?

BARBARA [*considering*] Well, you see, theres no use putting down your name unless I can do something for you, is there? Whats your trade?

BILL [*still smarting*] Thets nao concern o yours.

BARBARA. Just so. [*Very businesslike*] I'll put you down as [*writing*] the man who—struck—poor little Jenny Hill —in the mouth.

BILL [*rising threateningly*] See eah. Awve ed enaff o this.

BARBARA [*quite sunny and fearless*] What did you come to us for?

BILL. Aw cam for maw gel, see? Aw cam to tike her aht o this and to brike er jawr for er.

BARBARA [*complacently*] You see I was right about your trade. [*Bill, on the point of retorting furiously, finds himself, to his great shame and terror, in danger of crying instead. He sits down again suddenly*]. Whats her name?

376

BILL [*dogged*] Er nime's Mog Ebbijem: thets wot her nime is.

BARBARA. Mog Habbijam! Oh, she's gone to Canning Town, to our barracks there.

BILL [*fortified by his resentment of Mog's perfidy*] Is she? [*Vindictively*] Then Aw'm gowin to Kennintahn arter her. [*He crosses to the gate; hesitates; finally comes back at Barbara*]. Are you loyin to me to git shat o me?

BARBARA. I dont want to get shut of you. I want to keep you here and save your soul. Youd better stay: youre going to have a bad time today, Bill.

BILL. Oo's gowin to give it to me? Y o u, preps?

BARBARA. Someone you dont believe in. But youll be glad afterwards.

BILL [*slinking off*] Aw'll gow to Kennintahn to be aht o reach o your tangue. [*Suddenly turning on her with intense malice*] And if Aw downt fawnd Mog there, Aw'll cam beck and do two years for you, selp me Gawd if Aw downt!

BARBARA [*a shade kindlier, if possible*] It's no use, Bill. She's got another bloke.

BILL. Wot!

BARBARA. One of her own converts. He fell in love with her when he saw her with her soul saved, and her face clean, and her hair washed.

BILL [*surprised*] Wottud she wash it for, the carroty slat? It's red.

BARBARA. It's quite lovely now, because she wears a new look in her eyes with it. It's a pity youre too late. The new bloke has put your nose out of joint, Bill.

BILL. Aw'll put his nowse aht o joint for him. Not that Aw care a carse for er, mawnd thet. But Aw'll teach her to drop me as if Aw was dirt. And Aw'll teach him to meddle with maw judy. Wots iz bleedin nime?

BARBARA. Sergeant Todger Fairmile.

SHIRLEY [*rising with grim joy*] I'll go with him, miss. I want to see them two meet. I'll take him to the infirmary when it's over.

BILL [*to Shirley, with undissembled misgiving*] Is thet im you was speakin on?

SHIRLEY. Thats him.

BILL. Im that wrastled in the music awl?

SHIRLEY. The competitions at the National Sportin Club was worth nigh a hundred a year to him. He's gev em up now for religion; so he's a bit fresh for want of the exercise he was accustomed to. He'll be glad to see you. Come along.

BILL. Wots is wight?

SHIRLEY. Thirteen four. [*Bill's last hope expires*].

BARBARA. Go and talk to him, Bill. He'll convert you.

SHIRLEY. He'll convert your head into a mashed potato.

BILL [*sullenly*] Aw aint afride of im. Aw aint afride of ennybody. Bat e can lick me. She's dan me. [*He sits down moodily on the edge of the horse trough*].

SHIRLEY. You aint goin. I thought not. [*He resumes his seat*].

BARBARA [*calling*] Jenny!

JENNY [*appearing at the shelter door with a plaster on the corner of her mouth*] Yes, Major.

BARBARA. Send Rummy Mitchens out to clear away here.

JENNY. I think she's afraid.

BARBARA [*her resemblance to her mother flashing out for a moment*] Nonsense! she must do as she's told.

JENNY [*calling into the shelter*] Rummy: the Major says you must come.

Jenny comes to Barbara, purposely keeping on the side next Bill, lest he should suppose that she shrank from him or bore malice.

BARBARA. Poor little Jenny! Are you tired? [*Looking at the wounded cheek*] Does it hurt?

JENNY. No: it's all right now. It was nothing.

BARBARA [*critically*] It was as hard as he could hit, I expect. Poor Bill! You dont feel angry with him, do you?

378

JENNY. Oh no, no, no: indeed I dont, Major, bless his poor heart! [*Barbara kisses her; and she runs away merrily into the shelter. Bill writhes with an agonizing return of his new and alarming symptoms, but says nothing. Rummy Mitchens comes from the shelter*].

BARBARA [*going to meet Rummy*] Now Rummy, bustle. Take in those mugs and plates to be washed; and throw the crumbs about for the birds.

Rummy takes the three plates and mugs; but Shirley takes back his mug from her, as there is still some milk left in it.

RUMMY. There aint any crumbs. This aint a time to waste good bread on birds.

PRICE [*appearing at the shelter door*] Gentleman come to see the shelter, Major. Says he's your father.

BARBARA. All right. Coming. [*Snobby goes back into the shelter, followed by Barbara*].

RUMMY [*stealing across to Bill and addressing him in a subdued voice, but with intense conviction*] I'd av the lor of you, you flat eared pignosed potwalloper, if she'd let me. Youre no gentleman, to hit a lady in the face. [*Bill, with greater things moving in him, takes no notice*].

SHIRLEY [*following her*] Here! in with you and dont get yourself into more trouble by talking.

RUMMY [*with hauteur*] I aint ad the pleasure o being hintroduced to you, as I can remember. [*She goes into the shelter with the plates*].

SHIRLEY. Thats the—

BILL [*savagely*] Downt you talk to me, d'ye eah? You lea me alown, or Aw'll do you a mischief. Aw'm not dirt under y o u r feet, ennywy.

SHIRLEY [*calmly*] Dont you be afeerd. You aint such prime company that you need expect to be sought after. [*He is about to go into the shelter when Barbara comes out, with Undershaft on her right*].

BARBARA. Oh, there you are, Mr Shirley! [*Between them*] This is my father: I told you he was a Secularist, didnt I? Perhaps youll be able to comfort one another.

UNDERSHAFT [*startled*] A Secularist! Not the least in the world: on the contrary, a confirmed mystic.

BARBARA. Sorry, I'm sure. By the way, papa, what i s your religion? in case I have to introduce you again.

UNDERSHAFT. My religion? Well, my dear, I am a Millionaire. That is my religion.

BARBARA. Then I'm afraid you and Mr Shirley wont be able to comfort one another after all. Youre not a Millionaire, are you, Peter?

SHIRLEY. No; and proud of it.

UNDERSHAFT [*gravely*] Poverty, my friend, is not a thing to be proud of.

SHIRLEY [*angrily*] Who made your millions for you? Me and my like. Whats kep us poor? Keepin you rich. I wouldnt have your conscience, not for all your income.

UNDERSHAFT. I wouldnt have your income, not for all your conscience, Mr Shirley. [*He goes to the penthouse and sits down on a form*].

BARBARA [*stopping Shirley adroitly as he is about to retort*] You wouldnt think he was my father, would you, Peter? Will you go into the shelter and lend the lasses a hand for a while: we're worked off our feet.

SHIRLEY [*bitterly*] Yes: I'm in their debt for a meal, aint I?

BARBARA. Oh, not because youre in their debt, but for love of them, Peter, for love of them. [*He cannot understand, and is rather scandalized*]. There! dont stare at me. In with you; and give that conscience of yours a holiday. [*Bustling him into the shelter*].

SHIRLEY [*as he goes in*] Ah! it's a pity you never was trained to use your reason, miss. Youd have been a very taking lecturer on Secularism.

Barbara turns to her father.

UNDERSHAFT. Never mind me, my dear. Go about your work; and let me watch it for a while.

BARBARA. All right.

MAJOR BARBARA

UNDERSHAFT. For instance, whats the matter with that out-patient over there?

BARBARA [*looking at Bill, whose attitude has never changed, and whose expression of brooding wrath has deepened*] Oh, we shall cure him in no time. Just watch. [*She goes over to Bill and waits. He glances up at her and casts his eyes down again, uneasy, but grimmer than ever*]. It w o u l d be nice to just stamp on Mog Habbijam's face, wouldnt it, Bill?

BILL [*starting up from the trough in consternation*] It's a loy: Aw never said so. [*She shakes her head*]. Oo taold you wot was in moy mawnd?

BARBARA. Only your new friend.

BILL. Wot new friend?

BARBARA. The devil, Bill. When he gets round people they get miserable, just like you.

BILL [*with a heartbreaking attempt at devil-may-care cheerfulness*] Aw aint miserable. [*He sits down again, and stretches his legs in an attempt to seem indifferent*].

BARBARA. Well, if youre happy, why dont you look happy, as we do?

BILL [*his legs curling back in spite of him*] Aw'm eppy enaff, Aw tell you. Woy cawnt you lea me alown? Wot ev I dan to y o u? Aw aint smashed y o u r fice, ev Aw?

BARBARA [*softly: wooing his soul*] It's not me thats getting at you, Bill.

BILL. Oo else is it?

BARBARA. Somebody that doesnt intend you to smash women's faces, I suppose. Somebody or something that wants to make a man of you.

BILL [*blustering*] Mike a menn o m e! Aint Aw a menn? eh? Oo sez Aw'm not a menn?

BARBARA. Theres a man in you somewhere, I suppose. But why did he let you hit poor little Jenny Hill? That wasnt very manly of him, was it?

BILL [*tormented*] Ev dan wiv it, Aw tell you. Chack it. Aw'm sick o your Jenny Ill and er silly little fice.

BARBARA. Then why do you keep thinking about it? Why does it keep coming up against you in your mind? Youre not getting converted, are you?

BILL [*with conviction*] Not ME. Not lawkly.

BARBARA. Thats right, Bill. Hold out against it. Put out your strength. Dont lets get you cheap. Todger Fairmile said he wrestled for three nights against his salvation harder than he ever wrestled with the Jap at the music hall. He gave in to the Jap when his arm was going to break. But he didnt give in to his salvation until his heart was going to break. Perhaps youll escape that. You havnt any heart, have you?

BILL. Wot d'ye mean? Woy aint Aw got a awt the sime as ennybody else?

BARBARA. A man with a heart wouldnt have bashed poor little Jenny's face, would he?

BILL [*almost crying*] Ow, w i l l you lea me alown? Ev Aw ever offered to meddle with y o u, that you cam neggin and provowkin me lawk this? [*He writhes convulsively from his eyes to his toes*].

BARBARA [*with a steady soothing hand on his arm and a gentle voice that never lets him go*] It's your soul thats hurting you, Bill, and not me. Weve been through it all ourselves. Come with us, Bill. [*He looks wildly round*]. To brave manhood on earth and eternal glory in heaven. [*He is on the point of breaking down*]. Come. [*A drum is heard in the shelter; and Bill, with a gasp, escapes from the spell as Barbara turns quickly. Adolphus enters from the shelter with a big drum*]. Oh! there you are, Dolly. Let me introduce a new friend of mine, Mr Bill Walker. This is my bloke, Bill: Mr Cusins. [*Cusins salutes with his drumstick*].

BILL. Gowin to merry im?

BARBARA. Yes.

BILL [*fervently*] Gawd elp im! Gaw-aw-aw-awd elp im!

BARBARA. Why? Do you think he wont be happy with me?

382

BILL. Awve aony ed to stend it for a mawnin: e'll ev to stend it for a lawftawm.

CUSINS. That is a frightful reflection, Mr Walker. But I cant tear myself away from her.

BILL. Well, Aw ken. [*To Barbara*] Eah! do you knaow where Aw'm gowin to, and wot Aw'm gowin to do?

BARBARA. Yes: youre going to heaven; and youre coming back here before the week's out to tell me so.

BILL. You loy. Aw'm gowin to Kennintahn, to spit in Todger Fairmawl's eye. Aw beshed Jenny Ill's fice; an nar Aw'll git me aown fice beshed and cam beck and shaow it to er. Ee'll itt me ardern Aw itt er. Thatll mike us square. [*To Adolphus*] Is thet fair or is it not? Youre a genlmn: you oughter knaow.

BARBARA. Two black eyes wont make one white one, Bill.

BILL. Aw didnt awst y o u. Cawnt you never keep your mahth shat? Oy awst the genlmn.

CUSINS [*reflectively*] Yes: I think youre right, Mr Walker. Yes: I should do it. It's curious: it's exactly what an ancient Greek would have done.

BARBARA. But what good will it do?

CUSINS. Well, it will give Mr Fairmile some exercise; and it will satisfy Mr Walker's soul.

BILL. Rot! there aint nao sach a thing as a saoul. Ah kin you tell wevver Awve a saoul or not? You never seen it.

BARBARA. Ive seen it hurting you when you went against it.

BILL [*with compressed aggravation*] If you was maw gel and took the word aht o me mahth lawk thet, Aw'd give you sathink youd feel urtin, Aw would. [*To Adolphus*] You tike maw tip, mite. Stop er jawr; or youll doy afoah your tawm. [*With intense expression*] Wore aht: thets wot youll be: wore aht. [*He goes away through the gate*].

CUSINS [*looking after him*] I wonder!

BARBARA. Dolly! [*Indignant, in her mother's manner*].

CUSINS. Yes, my dear, it's very wearing to be in love with you. If it lasts, I quite think I shall die young.

383

BARBARA. Should you mind?

CUSINS. Not at all. [*He is suddenly softened, and kisses her over the drum, evidently not for the first time, as people cannot kiss over a big drum without practice. Undershaft coughs*].

BARBARA. It's all right, papa, weve not forgotten you. Dolly: explain the place to papa: I havnt time. [*She goes busily into the shelter*].

Undershaft and Adolphus now have the yard to themselves. Undershaft, seated on a form, and still keenly attentive, looks hard at Adolphus. Adolphus looks hard at him.

UNDERSHAFT. I fancy you guess something of what is in my mind, Mr Cusins. [*Cusins flourishes his drumsticks as if in the act of beating a lively rataplan, but makes no sound*]. Exactly so. But suppose Barbara finds you out!

CUSINS. You know, I do not admit that I am imposing on Barbara. I am quite genuinely interested in the views of the Salvation Army. The fact is, I am a sort of collector of religions; and the curious thing is that I find I can believe them all. By the way, have you any religion?

UNDERSHAFT. Yes.

CUSINS. Anything out of the common?

UNDERSHAFT. Only that there are two things necessary to Salvation.

CUSINS [*disappointed, but polite*] Ah, the Church Catechism. Charles Lomax also belongs to the Established Church.

UNDERSHAFT. The two things are—

CUSINS. Baptism and—

UNDERSHAFT. No. Money and gunpowder.

CUSINS [*surprised, but interested*] That is the general opinion of our governing classes. The novelty is in hearing any man confess it.

UNDERSHAFT. Just so.

CUSINS. Excuse me: is there any place in your religion for honor, justice, truth, love, mercy and so forth?

384

UNDERSHAFT. Yes: they are the graces and luxuries of a rich, strong, and safe life.

CUSINS. Suppose one is forced to choose between them and money or gunpowder?

UNDERSHAFT. Choose money a n d gunpowder; for without enough of both you cannot afford the others.

CUSINS. That is your religion?

UNDERSHAFT. Yes.

The cadence of this reply makes a full close in the conversation. Cusins twists his face dubiously and contemplates Undershaft. Undershaft contemplates him.

CUSINS. Barbara wont stand that. You will have to choose between your religion and Barbara.

UNDERSHAFT. So will you, my friend. She will find out that that drum of yours is hollow.

CUSINS. Father Undershaft: you are mistaken: I am a sincere Salvationist. You do not understand the Salvation Army. It is the army of joy, of love, of courage: it has banished the fear and remorse and despair of the old hell-ridden evangelical sects: it marches to fight the devil with trumpet and drum, with music and dancing, with banner and palm, as becomes a sally from heaven by its happy garrison. It picks the waster out of the public house and makes a man of him: it finds a worm wriggling in a back kitchen, and lo! a woman! Men and women of rank too, sons and daughters of the Highest. It takes the poor professor of Greek, the most artificial and self-suppressed of human creatures, from his meal of roots, and lets loose the rhapsodist in him; reveals the true worship of Dionysos to him; sends him down the public street drumming dithyrambs [*he plays a thundering flourish on the drum*].

UNDERSHAFT. You will alarm the shelter.

CUSINS. Oh, they are accustomed to these sudden ecstasies of piety. However, if the drum worries you— [*He pockets the drumsticks; unhooks the drum; and stands it on the ground opposite the gateway*].

UNDERSHAFT. Thank you.

385

CUSINS. You remember what Euripides says about your money and gunpowder?

UNDERSHAFT. No.

CUSINS [*declaiming*]

> One and another
> In money and guns may outpass his brother;
> And men in their millions float and flow
> And seethe with a million hopes as leaven;
> And they win their will; or they miss their will;
> And their hopes are dead or are pined for still;
> But whoe'er can know
> As the long days go
> That to live is happy, has found h i s heaven.

My translation: what do you think of it?

UNDERSHAFT. I think, my friend, that if you wish to know, as the long days go, that to live is happy, you must first acquire money enough for a decent life, and power enough to be your own master.

CUSINS. You are damnably discouraging. [*He resumes his declamation*].

> Is it so hard a thing to see
> That the spirit of God——whate'er it be——
> The law that abides and changes not, ages long,
> The Eternal and Nature-born: t h e s e things be strong?
> What else is Wisdom? What of Man's endeavor,
> Or God's high grace so lovely and so great?
> To stand from fear set free? to breathe and wait?
> To hold a hand uplifted over Fate?
> And shall not Barbara be loved for ever?

UNDERSHAFT. Euripides mentions Barbara, does he?

CUSINS. It is a fair translation. The word means Loveliness.

UNDERSHAFT. May I ask——as Barbara's father——how much a year she is to be loved for ever on?

CUSINS. As Barbara's father, that is more your affair than mine. I can feed her by teaching Greek: that is about all.

386

MAJOR BARBARA

UNDERSHAFT. Do you consider it a good match for her?

CUSINS [*with polite obstinacy*] Mr Undershaft: I am in many ways a weak, timid, ineffectual person; and my health is far from satisfactory. But whenever I feel that I must have anything, I get it, sooner or later. I feel that way about Barbara. I dont like marriage: I feel intensely afraid of it; and I dont know what I shall do with Barbara or what she will do with me. But I feel that I and nobody else must marry her. Please regard that as settled.—Not that I wish to be arbitrary; but why should I waste your time in discussing what is inevitable?

UNDERSHAFT. You mean that you will stick at nothing: not even the conversion of the Salvation Army to the worship of Dionysos.

CUSINS. The business of the Salvation Army is to save, not to wrangle about the name of the pathfinder. Dionysos or another: what does it matter?

UNDERSHAFT [*rising and approaching him*] Professor Cusins: you are a young man after my own heart.

CUSINS. Mr Undershaft: you are, as far as I am able to gather, a most infernal old rascal; but you appeal very strongly to my sense of ironic humor.

Undershaft mutely offers his hand. They shake.

UNDERSHAFT [*suddenly concentrating himself*] And now to business.

CUSINS. Pardon me. We were discussing religion. Why go back to such an uninteresting and unimportant subject as business?

UNDERSHAFT. Religion is our business at present, because it is through religion alone that we can win Barbara.

CUSINS. Have you, too, fallen in love with Barbara?

UNDERSHAFT. Yes, with a father's love.

CUSINS. A father's love for a grown-up daughter is the most dangerous of all infatuations. I apologize for mentioning my own pale, coy, mistrustful fancy in the same breath with it.

UNDERSHAFT. Keep to the point. We have to win her;

and we are neither of us Methodists.

CUSINS. That doesnt matter. The power Barbara wields here—the power that wields Barbara herself—is not Calvinism, not Presbyterianism, not Methodism—

UNDERSHAFT. Not Greek Paganism either, eh?

CUSINS. I admit that. Barbara is quite original in her religion.

UNDERSHAFT [*triumphantly*] Aha! Barbara Undershaft would be. Her inspiration comes from within herself.

CUSINS. How do you suppose it got there?

UNDERSHAFT [*in towering excitement*] It is the Undershaft inheritance. I shall hand on my torch to my daughter. She shall make my converts and preach my gospel—

CUSINS. What! Money and gunpowder!

UNDERSHAFT. Yes, money and gunpowder; freedom and power; command of life and command of death.

CUSINS [*urbanely: trying to bring him down to earth*] This is extremely interesting, Mr Undershaft. Of course you know that you are mad.

UNDERSHAFT [*with redoubled force*] And you?

CUSINS. Oh, mad as a hatter. You are welcome to my secret since I have discovered yours. But I am astonished. Can a madman make cannons?

UNDERSHAFT. Would anyone else than a madman make them? And now [*With surging energy*] question for question. Can a sane man translate Euripides?

CUSINS. No.

UNDERSHAFT [*seizing him by the shoulder*] Can a sane woman make a man of a waster or a woman of a worm?

CUSINS [*reeling before the storm*] Father Colossus—Mammoth Millionaire—

UNDERSHAFT [*pressing him*] Are there two mad people or three in this Salvation shelter to-day?

CUSINS. You mean Barbara is as mad as we are?

UNDERSHAFT [*pushing him lightly off and resuming his equanimity suddenly and completely*] Pooh, Professor! let us call things by their proper names. I am a millionaire; you

388

are a poet; Barbara is a savior of souls. What have we three to do with the common mob of slaves and idolaters? [*He sits down again with a shrug of contempt for the mob*].

CUSINS. Take care! Barbara is in love with the common people. So am I. Have you never felt the romance of that love?

UNDERSHAFT [*cold and sardonic*] Have you ever been in love with Poverty, like St Francis? Have you ever been in love with Dirt, like St Simeon? Have you ever been in love with disease and suffering, like our nurses and philanthropists? Such passions are not virtues, but the most unnatural of all the vices. This love of the common people may please an earl's granddaughter and a university professor; but I have been a common man and a poor man; and it has no romance for me. Leave it to the poor to pretend that poverty is a blessing: leave it to the coward to make a religion of his cowardice by preaching humility: we know better than that. We three must stand together above the common people: how else can we help their children to climb up beside us? Barbara must belong to us, not to the Salvation Army.

CUSINS. Well, I can only say that if you think you will get her away from the Salvation Army by talking to her as you have been talking to me, you dont know Barbara.

UNDERSHAFT. My friend: I never ask for what I can buy.

CUSINS [*in a white fury*] Do I understand you to imply that you can buy Barbara?

UNDERSHAFT. No; but I can buy the Salvation Army.

CUSINS. Quite impossible.

UNDERSHAFT. You shall see. All religious organizations exist by selling themselves to the rich.

CUSINS. Not the Army. That is the Church of the poor.

UNDERSHAFT. All the more reason for buying it.

CUSINS. I dont think you quite know what the Army does for the poor.

UNDERSHAFT. Oh yes I do. It draws their teeth: that is

389

enough for me—as a man of business—

CUSINS. Nonsense! It makes them sober—

UNDERSHAFT. I prefer sober workmen. The profits are larger.

CUSINS. —honest—

UNDERSHAFT. Honest workmen are the most economical.

CUSINS. —attached to their homes—

UNDERSHAFT. So much the better: they will put up with anything sooner than change their shop.

CUSINS. —happy—

UNDERSHAFT. An invaluable safeguard against revolution.

CUSINS. —unselfish—

UNDERSHAFT. Indifferent to their own interests, which suits me exactly.

CUSINS. —with their thoughts on heavenly things—

UNDERSHAFT [rising] And not on Trade Unionism nor Socialism. Excellent.

CUSINS [revolted] You really are an infernal old rascal.

UNDERSHAFT [indicating Peter Shirley, who has just come from the shelter and strolled dejectedly down the yard between them] And this is an honest man!

SHIRLEY. Yes; and what av I got by it? [He passes on bitterly and sits on the form, in the corner of the penthouse].

Snobby Price, beaming sanctimoniously, and Jenny Hill, with a tambourine full of coppers, come from the shelter and go to the drum, on which Jenny begins to count the money.

UNDERSHAFT [replying to Shirley] Oh, your employers must have got a good deal by it from first to last. [He sits on the table, with one foot on the side form, Cusins, overwhelmed, sits down on the same form nearer the shelter. Barbara comes from the shelter to the middle of the yard. She is excited and a little overwrought].

BARBARA. Weve just had a splendid experience meeting at the other gate in Cripps's lane. Ive hardly ever seen them so much moved as they were by your confession, Mr Price.

PRICE. I could almost be glad of my past wickedness if I could believe that it would elp to keep hathers stright.

BARBARA. So it will, Snobby. How much, Jenny?

JENNY. Four and tenpence, Major.

BARBARA. Oh Snobby, if you had given your poor mother just one more kick, we should have got the whole five shillings!

PRICE. If she heard you say that, miss, she'd be sorry I didnt. But I'm glad. Oh what a joy it will be to her when she hears I'm saved!

UNDERSHAFT. Shall I contribute the odd twopence, Barbara? The millionaire's mite, eh? [*He takes a couple of pennies from his pocket*].

BARBARA. How did you make that twopence?

UNDERSHAFT. As usual. By selling cannons, torpedoes, submarines, and my new patent Grand Duke hand grenade.

BARBARA. Put it back in your pocket. You cant buy your Salvation here for twopence: you must work it out.

UNDERSHAFT. Is twopence not enough? I can afford a little more, if you press me.

BARBARA. Two million millions would not be enough. There is bad blood on your hands; and nothing but good blood can cleanse them. Money is no use. Take it away. [*She turns to Cusins*]. Dolly: you must write another letter for me to the papers. [*He makes a wry face*]. Yes: I know you dont like it; but it must be done. The starvation this winter is beating us: everybody is unemployed. The General says we must close this shelter if we cant get more money. I force the collections at the meetings until I am ashamed: dont I, Snobby?

PRICE. It's a fair treat to see you work it, Miss. The way you got them up from three-and-six to four-and-ten with that hymn, penny by penny and verse by verse, was a caution. Not a Cheap Jack on Mile End Waste could touch you at it.

BARBARA. Yes; but I wish we could do without it. I am getting at last to think more of the collection than of the

MAJOR BARBARA

people's souls. And what are those hatfuls of pence and halfpence? We want thousands! tens of thousands! hundreds of thousands! I want to convert people, not to be always begging for the Army in a way I'd die sooner than beg for myself.

UNDERSHAFT [*in profound irony*] Genuine unselfishness is capable of anything, my dear.

BARBARA [*unsuspectingly, as she turns away to take the money from the drum and put it in a cash bag she carries*] Yes, isnt it? [*Undershaft looks sardonically at Cusins*].

CUSINS [*aside to Undershaft*] Mephistopheles! Machiavelli!

BARBARA [*tears coming into her eyes as she ties the bag and pockets it*] How are we to feed them? I cant talk religion to a man with bodily hunger in his eyes. [*Almost breaking down*] It's frightful.

JENNY [*running to her*] Major, dear—

BARBARA [*rebounding*] No: dont comfort me. It will be all right. We shall get the money.

UNDERSHAFT. How?

JENNY. By praying for it, of course. Mrs Baines says she prayed for it last night; and she has never prayed for it in vain: never once. [*She goes to the gate and looks out into the street*].

BARBARA [*who has dried her eyes and regained her composure*] By the way, dad, Mrs Baines has come to march with us to our big meeting this afternoon; and she is very anxious to meet you, for some reason or other. Perhaps she'll convert you.

UNDERSHAFT. I shall be delighted, my dear.

JENNY [*at the gate: excitedly*] Major! Major! heres that man back again.

BARBARA. What man?

JENNY. The man that hit me. Oh, I hope he's coming back to join us.

Bill Walker, with frost on his jacket, comes through the gate, his hands deep in his pockets and his chin sunk
392

between his shoulders, like a cleaned-out gambler. He halts between Barbara and the drum.

BARBARA. Hullo, Bill! Back already!

BILL [*nagging at her*] Bin talkin ever sence, ev you?

BARBARA. Pretty nearly. Well, has Todger paid you out for poor Jenny's jaw?

BILL. Nao e aint.

BARBARA. I thought your jacket looked a bit snowy.

BILL. Sao it is snaowy. You want to knaow where the snaow cam from, downt you?

BARBARA. Yes.

BILL. Well, it cam from orf the grahnd in Pawkinses Corner in Kennintahn. It got rabbed orf be maw shaoulders: see?

BARBARA. Pity you didnt rub some off with your knees, Bill! That would have done you a lot of good.

BILL [*with sour mirthless humor*] Aw was sivin another menn's knees at the tawm. E was kneelin on moy ed, e was.

JENNY. Who was kneeling on your head?

BILL. Todger was. E was pryin for me: pryin camfortable wiv me as a cawpet. Sow was Mog. Sao was the aol bloomin meetin. Mog she sez "Ow Lawd brike is stabborn sperrit; bat downt urt is dear art." Thet was wot she said. "Downt urt is dear art"! An er blowk—thirteen stun four! —kneelin wiv all is wight on me. Fanny, aint it?

JENNY. Oh no. We're so sorry, Mr Walker.

BARBARA [*enjoying it frankly*] Nonsense! of course it's funny. Served you right, Bill! You must have done something to him first.

BILL [*doggedly*] Aw did wot Aw said Aw'd do. Aw spit in is eye. E looks ap at the skoy and sez, "Ow that Aw should be fahnd worthy to be spit upon for the gospel's sike!" e sez; an Mog sez "Glaory Allelloolier!"; an then e called me Braddher, an dahned me as if Aw was a kid and e was me mather worshin me a Setterda nawt. Aw ednt jast nao shaow wiv im at all. Arf the street pryed; an the tather arf larfed fit to split theirselves. [*To Barbara*] There! are you settisfawd nah?

BARBARA [*her eyes dancing*] Wish I'd been there, Bill.

BILL. Yus: youd a got in a hextra bit o talk on me, wouldnt you?

JENNY. I'm so sorry, Mr Walker.

BILL [*fiercely*] Downt you gow bein sorry for me: youve no call. Listen eah. Aw browk your jawr.

JENNY. No, it didnt hurt me: indeed it didnt, except for a moment. It was only that I was frightened.

BILL. Aw downt want to be forgive be you, or be ennybody. Wot Aw did Aw'll py for. Aw trawd to gat me aown jawr browk to settisfaw you—

JENNY [*distressed*] Oh no—

BILL [*impatiently*] Tell y' Aw did: cawnt you listen to wots bein taold you? All Aw got be it was bein mide a sawt of in the pablic street for me pines. Well, if Aw cawnt settisfaw you one wy, Aw ken anather. Listen eah! Aw ed two quid sived agen the frost; an Awve a pahnd of it left. A mite o mawn last week ed words with the judy e's gowin to merry. E give er wot-for; an e's bin fawnd fifteen bob. E ed a rawt to itt er cause they was gowin to be merrid; but Aw ednt nao rawt to itt you; sao put anather fawv bob on an call it a pahnd's worth. [*He produces a sovereign*]. Eahs the manney. Tike it; and lets ev no more o your forgivin an pryin and your Mijor jawrin me. Let wot Aw dan be dan an pide for; and let there be a end of it.

JENNY. Oh, I couldnt take it, Mr Walker. But if you would give a shilling or two to poor Rummy Mitchens! you really did hurt her; and she's old.

BILL [*contemptuously*] Not lawkly. Aw'd give her anather as soon as look at er. Let her ev the lawr o me as she threatened! S h e aint forgiven me: not mach. Wot Aw dan to er is not on me mawnd—wot she [*indicating Barbara*] mawt call on me conscience—no more than stickin a pig. It's this Christian gime o yours that Aw wownt ev plyed agen me: this bloomin forgivin an neggin an jawrin that mikes a menn thet sore that iz lawf's a burdn to im. Aw

394

wownt ev it, Aw tell you; sao tike your manney and stop thraowin your silly beshed fice hap agen me.

JENNY. Major: may I take a little of it for the Army?

BARBARA. No: the Army is not to be bought. We want your soul, Bill; and we'll take nothing less.

BILL [*bitterly*] Aw knaow. Me an maw few shillins is not good enaff for you. Youre a earl's grendorter, you are. Nathink less than a anderd pahnd for you.

UNDERSHAFT. Come, Barbara! you could do a great deal of good with a hundred pounds. If you will set this gentleman's mind at ease by taking his pound, I will give the other ninety-nine.

Bill, dazed by such opulence, instinctively touches his cap.

BARBARA. Oh, youre too extravagant, papa. Bill offers twenty pieces of silver. All you need offer is the other ten. That will make the standard price to buy anybody who's for sale. I'm not; and the Army's not. [*To Bill*] Youll never have another quiet moment, Bill, until you come round to us. You cant stand out against your salvation.

BILL [*sullenly*] Aw cawnt stend aht agen music awl wrastlers and awtful tangued women. Awve offered to py. Aw can do no more. Tike it or leave it. There it is. [*He throws the sovereign on the drum, and sits down on the horse-trough. The coin fascinates Snobby Price, who takes an early opportunity of dropping his cap on it*].

Mrs Baines comes from the shelter. She is dressed as a Salvation Army Commissioner. She is an earnest looking woman of about 40, with a caressing, urgent voice, and an appealing manner.

BARBARA. This is my father, Mrs Baines. [*Undershaft comes from the table, taking his hat off with marked civility*]. Try what you can do with him. He wont listen to me, because he remembers what a fool I was when I was a baby. [*She leaves them together and chats with Jenny*].

MRS BAINES. Have you been shewn over the shelter, Mr Undershaft? You know the work we're doing, of course.

UNDERSHAFT [*very civilly*] The whole nation knows it,

Mrs Baines.

MRS BAINES. No, sir: the whole nation does not know it, or we should not be crippled as we are for want of money to carry our work through the length and breadth of the land. Let me tell you that there would have been rioting this winter in London but for us.

UNDERSHAFT. You really think so?

MRS BAINES. I know it. I remember 1886, when you rich gentlemen hardened your hearts against the cry of the poor. They broke the windows of your clubs in Pall Mall.

UNDERSHAFT [*gleaming with approval of their method*] And the Mansion House Fund went up next day from thirty thousand pounds to seventy-nine thousand! I remember quite well.

MRS BAINES. Well, wont you help me to get at the people? They wont break windows then. Come here, Price. Let me shew you to this gentleman. [*Price comes to be inspected*]. Do you remember the window breaking?

PRICE. My ole father thought it was the revolution, maam.

MRS BAINES. Would you break windows now?

PRICE. Oh no maam. The windows of eaven av bin opened to me. I know now that the rich man is a sinner like myself.

RUMMY [*appearing above at the loft door*] Snobby Price!

SNOBBY. Wot is it?

RUMMY. Your mother's askin for you at the other gate in Crippses Lane. She's heard about your confession. [*Price turns pale*].

MRS BAINES. Go, Mr Price; and pray with her.

JENNY. You can go through the shelter, Snobby.

PRICE [*to Mrs Baines*] I couldnt face her now, maam, with all the weight of my sins fresh on me. Tell her she'll find her son at ome, waitin for her in prayer. [*He skulks off through the gate, incidentally stealing the sovereign on*

MAJOR BARBARA

his way out by picking up his cap from the drum].

MRS BAINES [*with swimming eyes*] You see how we take the anger and the bitterness against you out of their hearts, Mr Undershaft.

UNDERSHAFT. It is certainly most convenient and gratifying to all large employers of labor, Mrs Baines.

MRS BAINES. Barbara: Jenny: I have good news: most wonderful news. [*Jenny runs to her*]. My prayers have been answered. I told you they would, Jenny, didnt I?

JENNY. Yes, yes.

BARBARA [*moving nearer to the drum*] Have we got money enough to keep the shelter open?

MRS BAINES. I hope we shall have enough to keep all the shelters open. Lord Saxmundham has promised us five thousand pounds—

BARBARA. Hooray!

JENNY. Glory!

MRS BAINES. —if—

BARBARA. "If!" If what?

MRS BAINES. —if five other gentlemen will give a thousand each to make it up to ten thousand.

BARBARA. Who is Lord Saxmundham? I never heard of him.

UNDERSHAFT [*who has pricked up his ears at the peer's name, and is now watching Barbara curiously*] A new creation, my dear. You have heard of Sir Horace Bodger?

BARBARA. Bodger! Do you mean the distiller? Bodger's whisky!

UNDERSHAFT. That is the man. He is one of the greatest of our public benefactors. He restored the cathedral at Hakington. They made him a baronet for that. He gave half a million to the funds of his party: they made him a baron for that.

SHIRLEY. What will they give him for the five thousand?

UNDERSHAFT. There is nothing left to give him. So the five thousand, I should think, is to save his soul.

397

MAJOR BARBARA

MRS BAINES. Heaven grant it may! Oh Mr Undershaft, you have some very rich friends. Cant you help us towards the other five thousand? We are going to hold a great meeting this afternoon at the Assembly Hall in the Mile End Road. If I could only announce that one gentleman had come forward to support Lord Saxmundham, others would follow. Dont you know somebody? couldnt you? wouldnt you? [*her eyes fill with tears*] oh, think of those poor people, Mr Undershaft: think of how much it means to them, and how little to a great man like you.

UNDERSHAFT [*sardonically gallant*] Mrs Baines: you are irresistible. I cant disappoint you; and I cant deny myself the satisfaction of making Bodger pay up. You shall have your five thousand pounds.

MRS BAINES. Thank God!

UNDERSHAFT. You dont thank m e?

MRS BAINES. Oh sir, dont try to be cynical: dont be ashamed of being a good man. The Lord will bless you abundantly; and our prayers will be like a strong fortification round you all the days of your life. [*With a touch of caution*] You will let me have the cheque to shew at the meeting, wont you? Jenny: go in and fetch a pen and ink. [*Jenny runs to the shelter door*].

UNDERSHAFT. Do not disturb Miss Hill: I have a fountain pen. [*Jenny halts. He sits at the table and writes the cheque. Cusins rises to make room for him. They all watch him silently*].

BILL [*cynically, aside to Barbara, his voice and accent horribly debased*] Wot prawce Selvytion nah?

BARBARA. Stop. [*Undershaft stops writing: they all turn to her in surprise*]. Mrs Baines: are you really going to take this money?

MRS BAINES [*astonished*] Why not, dear?

BARBARA. Why not! Do you know what my father is? Have you forgotten that Lord Saxmundham is Bodger the whisky man? Do you remember how we implored the County Council to stop him from writing Bodger's Whisky
398

in letters of fire against the sky; so that the poor drink-ruined creatures on the Embankment could not wake up from their snatches of sleep without being reminded of their deadly thirst by that wicked sky sign? Do you know that the worst thing I have had to fight here is not the devil, but Bodger, Bodger, Bodger, with his whisky, his distilleries, and his tied houses? Are you going to make our shelter another tied house for him, and ask me to keep it?

BILL. Rotten dranken whisky it is too.

MRS BAINES. Dear Barbara: Lord Saxmundham has a soul to be saved like any of us. If heaven has found the way to make a good use of his money, are we to set ourselves up against the answer to our prayers?

BARBARA. I know he has a soul to be saved. Let him come down here; and I'll do my best to help him to his salvation. But he wants to send his cheque down to buy us, and go on being as wicked as ever.

UNDERSHAFT [*with a reasonableness which Cusins alone perceives to be ironical*] My dear Barbara: alcohol is a very necessary article. It heals the sick—

BARBARA. It does nothing of the sort.

UNDERSHAFT. Well, it assists the doctor: that is perhaps a less questionable way of putting it. It makes life bearable to millions of people who could not endure their existence if they were quite sober. It enables Parliament to do things at eleven at night that no sane person would do at eleven in the morning. Is it Bodger's fault that this inestimable gift is deplorably abused by less than one per cent of the poor? [*He turns again to the table; signs the cheque; and crosses it*].

MRS BAINES. Barbara: will there be less drinking or more if all those poor souls we are saving come tomorrow and find the doors of our shelters shut in their faces? Lord Saxmundham gives us the money to stop drinking—to take his own business from him.

CUSINS [*impishly*] Pure self-sacrifice on Bodger's part, clearly! Bless dear Bodger! [*Barbara almost breaks down*

399

as Adolphus, too, fails her].

UNDERSHAFT [*tearing out the cheque and pocketing the book as he rises and goes past Cusins to Mrs Baines*] I also, Mrs Baines, may claim a little disinterestedness. Think of my business! think of the widows and orphans! the men and lads torn to pieces with shrapnel and poisoned with lyddite [*Mrs Baines shrinks; but he goes on remorsely*]! the oceans of blood, not one drop of which is shed in a really just cause! the ravaged crops! the peaceful peasants forced, women and men, to till their fields under the fire of opposing armies on pain of starvation! the bad blood of the fierce little cowards at home who egg on others to fight for the gratification of their national vanity! All this makes money for me: I am never richer, never busier than when the papers are full of it. Well, it is your work to preach peace on earth and goodwill to men. [*Mrs Baines's face lights up again*]. Every convert you make is a vote against war. [*Her lips move in prayer*]. Yet I give you this money to help you to hasten my own commercial ruin. [*He gives her the cheque*].

CUSINS [*mounting the form in an ecstasy of mischief*] The millennium will be inaugurated by the unselfishness of Undershaft and Bodger. Oh be joyful! [*He takes the drum-sticks from his pocket and flourishes them*].

MRS BAINES [*taking the cheque*] The longer I live the more proof I see that there is an Infinite Goodness that turns everything to the work of salvation sooner or later. Who would have thought that any good could have come out of war and drink? And yet their profits are brought today to the feet of salvation to do its blessed work. [*She is affected to tears*].

JENNY [*running to Mrs Baines and throwing her arms round her*] Oh dear! how blessed, how glorious it all is!

CUSINS [*in a convulsion of irony*] Let us seize this unspeakable moment. Let us march to the great meeting at once. Excuse me just an instant. [*He rushes into the shelter. Jenny takes her tambourine from the drum head*].

MRS BAINES. Mr Undershaft: have you ever seen a thousand people fall on their knees with one impulse and pray? Come with us to the meeting. Barbara shall tell them that the Army is saved, and saved through you.

CUSINS [*returning impetuously from the shelter with a flag and a trombone, and coming between Mrs Baines and Undershaft*] You shall carry the flag down the first street, Mrs Baines. [*He gives her the flag*]. Mr Undershaft is a gifted trombonist: he shall intone an Olympian diapason to the West Ham Salvation March. [*Aside to Undershaft, as he forces the trombone on him*]. Blow, Machiavelli, blow.

UNDERSHAFT [*aside to him, as he takes the trombone*] The trumpet in Zion! [*Cusins rushes to the drum, which he takes up and puts on. Undershaft continues, aloud*] I will do my best. I could vamp a bass if I knew the tune.

CUSINS. It is a wedding chorus from one of Donizetti's operas; but we have converted it. We convert everything to good here, including Bodger. You remember the chorus. "For thee immense rejoicing—immenso giubilo—immenso giubilo." [*With drum obbligato*] Rum tum ti tum tum, tum tum ti ta—

BARBARA. Dolly: you are breaking my heart.

CUSINS. What is a broken heart more or less here? Dionysos Undershaft has descended. I am possessed.

MRS BAINES. Come, Barbara: I must have my dear Major to carry the flag with me.

JENNY. Yes, yes, Major darling.

Cusins snatches the tambourine out of Jenny's hand and mutely offers it to Barbara.

BARBARA [*coming forward a little as she puts the offer behind her with a shudder, whilst Cusins recklessly tosses the tambourine back to Jenny and goes to the gate*] I cant come.

JENNY. Not come!

MRS BAINES [*with tears in her eyes*] Barbara: do you think I am wrong to take the money?

BARBARA [*impulsively going to her and kissing her*] No, no: God help you, dear, you must: you are saving the Army. Go; and may you have a great meeting!

JENNY. But arnt you coming?

BARBARA. No. [*She begins taking off the silver S brooch from her collar*].

MRS BAINES. Barbara: what are you doing?

JENNY. Why are you taking your badge off? You cant be going to leave us, Major.

BARBARA [*quietly*] Father: come here.

UNDERSHAFT [*coming to her*] My dear! [*Seeing that she is going to pin the badge on his collar, he retreats to the penthouse in some alarm*].

BARBARA [*following him*] Dont be frightened. [*She pins the badge on and steps back towards the table, shewing him to the others*]. There! It's not much for £5000, is it?

MRS. BAINES. Barbara: if you wont come and pray w i t h us, promise me you will pray f o r us.

BARBARA. I cant pray now. Perhaps I shall never pray again.

MRS BAINES. Barbara!

JENNY. Major!

BARBARA [*almost delirious*] I cant bear any more. Quick march!

CUSINS [*calling to the procession in the street outside*] Off we go. Play up, there! I m m e n s o g i u b i l o. [*He gives the time with his drum; and the band strikes up the march, which rapidly becomes more distant as the procession moves briskly away*].

MRS BAINES. I must go, dear. Youre overworked: you will be all right tomorrow. We'll never lose you. Now Jenny: step out with the old flag. Blood and Fire! [*She marches out through the gate with her flag*].

JENNY. Glory Hallelujah! [*Flourishing her tambourine and marching*].

UNDERSHAFT [*to Cusins, as he marches out past him easing the slide of his trombone*] "My ducats and my daughter"!

CUSINS [*following him out*] Money and gunpowder!

BARBARA. Drunkenness and Murder! My God: why hast thou forsaken me?

She sinks on the form with her face buried in her hands. The march passes away into silence. Bill Walker steals across to her.

BILL [*taunting*] Wot prawce selvytion nah?

SHIRLEY. Dont you hit her when she's down.

BILL. She itt me wen aw wiz dahn. Waw shouldnt Aw git a bit o me aown beck?

BARBARA [*raising her head*] I didnt take y o u r money, Bill. [*She crosses the yard to the gate and turns her back on the two men to hide her face from them*].

BILL [*sneering after her*] Naow, it warnt enaff for you. [*Turning to the drum, he misses the money*] Ellow! If you aint took it sammun else ez. Weres it gorn? Bly me if Jenny Ill didnt tike it arter all!

RUMMY [*screaming at him from the loft*] You lie, you dirty blackguard! Snobby Price pinched it off the drum when he took up his cap. I was up here all the time an see im do it.

BILL. Wot! Stowl maw manney! Waw didnt you call thief on him, you silly aold macker you?

RUMMY. To serve you aht for ittin me acrost the fice. It's cost y'pahnd, that az. [*Raising a pæan of squalid triumph*] I done you. I'm even with you. Ive.ad it aht o y— [*Bill snatches up Shirley's mug and hurls it at her. She slams the loft door and vanishes. The mug smashes against the door and falls in fragments*].

BILL [*beginning to chuckle*] Tell us, aol menn, wot o'clock this mawnin was it wen im as they call Snobby Prawce was sived?

BARBARA [*turning to him more composedly, and with unspoiled sweetness*] About half past twelve, Bill. And he pinched your pound at a quarter to two. *I* know. Well, you cant afford to lose it. I'll send it to you.

BILL [*his voice and accent suddenly improving*] Not

403

if Aw wiz to stawve for it. Aw aint to be bought.

SHIRLEY. Aint you? Youd sell yourself to the devil for a pint o beer; ony there aint no devil to make the offer.

BILL [*unshamed*] Sao Aw would, mite, and often ev, cheerful. But she cawnt baw me. [*Approaching Barbara*] You wanted maw saoul, did you? Well, you aint got it.

BARBARA. I nearly got it, Bill. But weve sold it back to you for ten thousand pounds.

SHIRLEY. And dear at the money!

BARBARA. No, Peter: it was worth more than money.

BILL [*salvationproof*] It's nao good: you cawnt get rahnd me nah. Aw downt blieve in it; and Awve seen tody that Aw was rawt. [*Going*] Sao long, aol soupkitchener! Ta, ta, Mijor Earl's Grendorter! [*Turning at the gate*] Wot prawce selvytion nah? Snobby Prawce! Ha! ha!

BARBARA [*offering her hand*] Goodbye, Bill.

BILL [*taken aback, half plucks his cap off; then shoves it on again defiantly*] Git aht. [*Barbara drops her hand, discouraged. He has a twinge of remorse*]. But thets aw rawt, you knaow. Nathink pasnl. Naow mellice. Sao long, Judy. [*He goes*].

BARBARA. No malice. So long, Bill.

SHIRLEY [*shaking his head*] You make too much of him, miss, in your innocence.

BARBARA [*going to him*] Peter: I'm like you now. Cleaned out, and lost my job.

SHIRLEY. Youve youth an hope. Thats two better than me.

BARBARA. I'll get you a job, Peter. Thats hope for you: the youth will have to be enough for me. [*She counts her money*]. I have just enough left for two teas at Lockharts, a Rowton doss for you, and my tram and bus home. [*He frowns and rises with offended pride. She takes his arm*]. Dont be proud, Peter: it's sharing between friends. And promise me youll talk to me and not let me cry. [*She draws him towards the gate*].

404

SHIRLEY. Well, I'm not accustomed to talk to the like of you—

BARBARA [*urgently*] Yes, yes: you must talk to me. Tell me about Tom Paine's books and Bradlaugh's lectures. Come along.

SHIRLEY. Ah, if you would only read Tom Paine in the proper spirit, Miss! [*They go out through the gate together*].

END OF ACT II

ACT III

NEXT *day after lunch Lady Britomart is writing in the library in Wilton Crescent. Sarah is reading in the armchair near the window. Barbara, in ordinary fashionable dress, pale and brooding, is on the settee. Charles Lomax enters. He starts on seeing Barbara fashionably attired and in low spirits.*

LOMAX. Youve left off your uniform!

Barbara says nothing; but an expression of pain passes over her face.

LADY BRITOMART [*warning him in low tones to be careful*] Charles!

LOMAX [*much concerned, coming behind the settee and bending sympathetically over Barbara*] I'm awfully sorry, Barbara. You know I helped you all I could with the concertina and so forth. [*Momentously*] Still, I have never shut my eyes to the fact that there is a certain amount of tosh about the Salvation Army. Now the claims of the Church of England—

LADY BRITOMART. Thats enough, Charles. Speak of something suited to your mental capacity.

LOMAX. But surely the Church of England is suited to all our capacities.

BARBARA [*pressing his hand*] Thank you for your sympathy, Cholly. Now go and spoon with Sarah.

LOMAX [*dragging a chair from the writing table and seating himself affectionately by Sarah's side*] How is my ownest today?

SARAH. I wish you wouldnt tell Cholly to do things, Barbara. He always comes straight and does them. Cholly: we're going to the works this afternoon.

LOMAX. What works?

SARAH. The cannon works.

LOMAX. What? your governor's shop!

SARAH. Yes.

LOMAX. Oh I say!

Cusins enters in poor condition. He also starts visibly when he sees Barbara without her uniform.

BARBARA. I expected you this morning, Dolly. Didnt you guess that?

CUSINS [*sitting down beside her*] I'm sorry. I have only just breakfasted.

SARAH. But weve just finished lunch.

BARBARA. Have you had one of your bad nights?

CUSINS. No: I had rather a good night: in fact, one of the most remarkable nights I have ever passed.

BARBARA. The meeting?

CUSINS. No: after the meeting.

LADY BRITOMART. You should have gone to bed after the meeting. What were you doing?

CUSINS. Drinking.

LADY BRITOMART.	Adolphus!
SARAH.	Dolly!
BARBARA.	Dolly!
LOMAX.	Oh I say!

LADY BRITOMART. What were you drinking, may I ask?

CUSINS. A most devilish kind of Spanish burgundy, warranted free from added alcohol: a Temperance burgundy in fact. Its richness in natural alcohol made any addition superfluous.

BARBARA. Are you joking, Dolly?

CUSINS [*patiently*] No. I have been making a night of it with the nominal head of this household: that is all.

LADY BRITOMART. Andrew made you drunk!

CUSINS. No: he only provided the wine. I think it was Dionysos who made me drunk. [*To Barbara*] I told you I was possessed.

LADY BRITOMART. Youre not sober yet. Go home to bed at once.

CUSINS. I have never before ventured to reproach you, Lady Brit; but how could you marry the Prince of Darkness?

LADY BRITOMART. It was much more excusable to marry

407

him than to get drunk with him. That is a new accomplishment of Andrew's, by the way. He usent to drink.

CUSINS. He doesnt now. He only sat there and completed the wreck of my moral basis, the rout of my convictions, the purchase of my soul. He cares for you, Barbara. That is what makes him so dangerous to me.

BARBARA. That has nothing to do with it, Dolly. There are larger loves and diviner dreams than the fireside ones. You know that, dont you?

CUSINS. Yes: that is our understanding. I know it. I hold to it. Unless he can win me on that holier ground he may amuse me for a while; but he can get no deeper hold, strong as he is.

BARBARA. Keep to that; and the end will be right. Now tell me what happened at the meeting?

CUSINS. It was an amazing meeting. Mrs Baines almost died of emotion. Jenny Hill simply gibbered with hysteria. The Prince of Darkness played his trombone like a madman: its brazen roarings were like the laughter of the damned. 117 conversions took place then and there. They prayed with the most touching sincerity and gratitude for Bodger, and for the anonymous donor of the £5000. Your father would not let his name be given.

LOMAX. That was rather fine of the old man, you know. Most chaps would have wanted the advertisement.

CUSINS. He said all the charitable institutions would be down on him like kites on a battle field if he gave his name.

LADY BRITOMART. Thats Andrew all over. He never does a proper thing without giving an improper reason for it.

CUSINS. He convinced me that I have all my life been doing improper things for proper reasons.

LADY BRITOMART. Adolphus: now that Barbara has left the Salvation Army, you had better leave it too. I will not have you playing that drum in the streets.

CUSINS. Your orders are already obeyed, Lady Brit.

BARBARA. Dolly: were you ever really in earnest about

it? Would you have joined if you had never seen me?

CUSINS [*disingenuously*] Well—er—well, possibly, as a collector of religions—

LOMAX [*cunningly*] Not as a drummer, though, you know. You are a very clearheaded brainy chap, Dolly; and it must have been apparent to you that there is a certain amount of tosh about—

LADY BRITOMART. Charles: if you must drivel, drivel like a grown-up man and not like a schoolboy.

LOMAX [*out of countenance*] Well, drivel is drivel, dont you know, whatever a man's age.

LADY BRITOMART. In good society in England, Charles, men drivel at all ages by repeating silly formulas with an air of wisdom. Schoolboys make their own formulas out of slang, like you. When they reach your age, and get political private secretaryships and things of that sort, they drop slang and get their formulas out of The Spectator or The Times. Y o u had better confine yourself to The Times. You will find that there is a certain amount of tosh about The Times; but at least its language is reputable.

LOMAX [*overwhelmed*] You are so awfully strong-minded, Lady Brit—

LADY BRITOMART. Rubbish! [*Morrison comes in*]. What is it?

MORRISON. If you please, my lady, Mr Undershaft has just drove up to the door.

LADY BRITOMART. Well, let him in. [*Morrison hesitates*]. Whats the matter with you?

MORRISON. Shall I announce him, my lady; or is he at home here, so to speak, my lady?

LADY BRITOMART. Announce him.

MORRISON. Thank you, my lady. You wont mind my asking, I hope. The occasion is in a manner of speaking new to me.

LADY BRITOMART. Quite right. Go and let him in.

MORRISON. Thank you, my lady. [*He withdraws*].

LADY BRITOMART. Children: go and get ready. [*Sarah*

and Barbara go upstairs for their out-of-door wraps].
Charles: go and tell Stephen to come down here in five
minutes: you will find him in the drawing room. [*Charles
goes*]. Adolphus: tell them to send round the carriage in
about fifteen minutes. [*Adolphus goes*].

MORRISON [*at the door*] Mr Undershaft.

Undershaft comes in. Morrison goes out.

UNDERSHAFT. Alone! How fortunate!

LADY BRITOMART [*rising*] Dont be sentimental, Andrew. Sit down. [*She sits on the settee: he sits beside her,
on her left. She comes to the point before he has time to
breathe*]. Sarah must have £800 a year until Charles Lomax
comes into his property. Barbara will need more, and need
it permanently, because Adolphus hasnt any property.

UNDERSHAFT [*resignedly*] Yes, my dear: I will see to
it. Anything else? for yourself, for instance?

LADY BRITOMART. I want to talk to you about Stephen.

UNDERSHAFT [*rather wearily*] Dont, my dear. Stephen
doesnt interest me.

LADY BRITOMART. He does interest me. He is our son.

UNDERSHAFT. Do you really think so? He has induced
us to bring him into the world; but he chose his parents very
incongruously, I think. I see nothing of myself in him, and
less of you.

LADY BRITOMART. Andrew: Stephen is an excellent son,
and a most steady, capable, highminded young man. You
are simply trying to find an excuse for disinheriting him.

UNDERSHAFT. My dear Biddy: the Undershaft tradition disinherits him. It would be dishonest of me to leave
the cannon foundry to my son.

LADY BRITOMART. It would be most unnatural and improper of you to leave it to anyone else, Andrew. Do you
suppose this wicked and immoral tradition can be kept up
for ever? Do you pretend that Stephen could not carry on
the foundry just as well as all the other sons of the big
business houses?

UNDERSHAFT. Yes: he could learn the office routine

without understanding the business, like all the other sons; and the firm would go on by its own momentum until the real Undershaft—probably an Italian or a German—would invent a new method and cut him out.

LADY BRITOMART. There is nothing that any Italian or German could do that Stephen could not do. And Stephen at least has breeding.

UNDERSHAFT. The son of a foundling! Nonsense!

LADY BRITOMART. My son, Andrew! And even you may have good blood in your veins for all you know.

UNDERSHAFT. True. Probably I have. That is another argument in favor of a foundling.

LADY BRITOMART. Andrew: dont be aggravating. And dont be wicked. At present you are both.

UNDERSHAFT. This conversation is part of the Undershaft tradition, Biddy. Every Undershaft's wife has treated him to it ever since the house was founded. It is mere waste of breath. If the tradition be ever broken it will be for an abler man than Stephen.

LADY BRITOMART [*pouting*] Then go away.

UNDERSHAFT [*deprecatory*] Go away!

LADY BRITOMART. Yes: go away. If you will do nothing for Stephen, you are not wanted here. Go to your foundling, whoever he is; and look after h i m.

UNDERSHAFT. The fact is, Biddy—

LADY BRITOMART. Dont call me Biddy. I dont call you Andy.

UNDERSHAFT. I will not call my wife Britomart: it is not good sense. Seriously, my love, the Undershaft tradition has landed me in a difficulty. I am getting on in years; and my partner Lazarus has at last made a stand and insisted that the succession must be settled one way or the other; and of course he is quite right. You see, I havnt found a fit successor yet.

LADY BRITOMART [*obstinately*] There is Stephen.

UNDERSHAFT. Thats just it: all the foundlings I can find are exactly like Stephen.

411

LADY BRITOMART. Andrew!!

UNDERSHAFT. I want a man with no relations and no schooling: that is, a man who would be out of the running altogether if he were not a strong man. And I cant find him. Every blessed foundling nowadays is snapped up in his infancy by Barnardo homes, or School Board officers, or Boards of Guardians; and if he shews the least ability, he is fastened on by schoolmasters; trained to win scholarships like a race-horse; crammed with secondhand ideas; drilled and disciplined in docility and what they call good taste; and lamed for life so that he is fit for nothing but teaching. If you want to keep the foundry in the family, you had better find an eligible foundling and marry him to Barbara.

LADY BRITOMART. Ah! Barbara! Your pet! You would sacrifice Stephen to Barbara.

UNDERSHAFT. Cheerfully. And you, my dear, would boil Barbara to make soup for Stephen.

LADY BRITOMART. Andrew: this is not a question of our likings and dislikings: it is a question of duty. It is your duty to make Stephen your successor.

UNDERSHAFT. Just as much as it is your duty to submit to your husband. Come, Biddy! these tricks of the governing class are of no use with me. I am one of the governing class myself; and it is waste of time giving tracts to a missionary. I have the power in this matter; and I am not to be humbugged into using it for your purposes.

LADY BRITOMART. Andrew: you can talk my head off; but you cant change wrong into right. And your tie is all on one side. Put it straight.

UNDERSHAFT [disconcerted] It wont stay unless it's pinned— [He fumbles at it with childish grimaces].

Stephen comes in.

STEPHEN [at the door] I beg your pardon. [About to retire].

LADY BRITOMART. No: come in, Stephen. [Stephen comes forward to his mother's writing table].

412

UNDERSHAFT [*not very cordially*] Good afternoon.

STEPHEN [*coldly*] Good afternoon.

UNDERSHAFT [*to Lady Britomart*] He knows all about the tradition, I suppose?

LADY BRITOMART. Yes. [*To Stephen*]. It is what I told you last night, Stephen.

UNDERSHAFT [*sulkily*] I understand you want to come into the cannon business.

STEPHEN. *I* go into trade! Certainly not.

UNDERSHAFT [*opening his eyes, greatly eased in mind and manner*] Oh! in that case—

LADY BRITOMART. Cannons are not trade, Stephen. They are enterprise.

STEPHEN. I have no intention of becoming a man of business in any sense. I have no capacity for business and no taste for it. I intend to devote myself to politics.

UNDERSHAFT [*rising*] My dear boy: this is an immense relief to me. And I trust it may prove an equally good thing for the country. I was afraid you would consider yourself disparaged and slighted. [*He moves towards Stephen as if to shake hands with him*].

LADY BRITOMART [*rising and interposing*] Stephen: I cannot allow you to throw away an enormous property like this.

STEPHEN [*stiffly*] Mother: there must be an end of treating me as a child, if you please. [*Lady Britomart recoils, deeply wounded by his tone*]. Until last night I did not take your attitude seriously, because I did not think you meant it seriously. But I find now that you left me in the dark as to matters which you should have explained to me years ago. I am extremely hurt and offended. Any further discussion of my intentions had better take place with my father, as between one man and another.

LADY BRITOMART. Stephen! [*She sits down again, her eyes filling with tears*].

UNDERSHAFT [*with grave compassion*] You see, my

dear, it is only the big men who can be treated as children.

STEPHEN. I am sorry, mother, that you have forced me—

UNDERSHAFT [*stopping him*] Yes, yes, yes, yes: thats all right, Stephen. She wont interfere with you any more: your independence is achieved: you have won your latchkey. Dont rub it in; and above all, dont apologize. [*He resumes his seat*]. Now what about your future, as between one man and another—I beg your pardon, Biddy: as between two men and a woman.

LADY BRITOMART [*who has pulled herself together strongly*] I quite understand, Stephen. By all means go your own way if you feel strong enough. [*Stephen sits down magisterially in the chair at the writing table with an air of affirming his majority*].

UNDERSHAFT. It is settled that you do not ask for the succession to the cannon business.

STEPHEN. I hope it is settled that I repudiate the cannon business.

UNDERSHAFT. Come, come! dont be so devilishly sulky: it's boyish. Freedom should be generous. Besides, I owe you a fair start in life in exchange for disinheriting you. You cant become prime minister all at once. Havnt you a turn for something? What about literature, art and so forth?

STEPHEN. I have nothing of the artist about me, either in faculty or character, thank Heaven!

UNDERSHAFT. A philosopher, perhaps? Eh?

STEPHEN. I make no such ridiculous pretension.

UNDERSHAFT. Just so. Well, there is the army, the navy, the Church, the Bar. The Bar requires some ability. What about the Bar?

STEPHEN. I have not studied law. And I am afraid I have not the necessary push—I believe that is the name barristers give to their vulgarity—for success in pleading.

UNDERSHAFT. Rather a difficult case, Stephen. Hardly anything left but the stage, is there? [*Stephen makes an impatient movement*]. Well, come! is there a n y t h i n g

414

you know or care for?

STEPHEN [*rising and looking at him steadily*] I know the difference between right and wrong.

UNDERSHAFT [*hugely tickled*] You dont say so! What! no capacity for business, no knowledge of law, no sympathy with art, no pretension to philosophy; only a simple knowledge of the secret that has puzzled all the philosophers, baffled all the lawyers, muddled all the men of business, and ruined most of the artists: the secret of right and wrong. Why, man, youre a genius, a master of masters, a god! At twenty-four, too!

STEPHEN [*keeping his temper with difficulty*] You are pleased to be facetious. I pretend to nothing more than any honorable English gentleman claims as his birthright. [*He sits down angrily*].

UNDERSHAFT. Oh, thats everybody's birthright. Look at poor little Jenny Hill, the Salvation lassie! she would think you were laughing at her if you asked her to stand up in the street and teach grammar or geography or mathematics or even drawing room dancing; but it never occurs to her to doubt that she can teach morals and religion. You are all alike, you respectable people. You cant tell me the bursting strain of a ten-inch gun, which is a very simple matter; but you all think you can tell me the bursting strain of a man under temptation. You darent handle high explosives; but youre all ready to handle honesty and truth and justice and the whole duty of man, and kill one another at that game. What a country! What a world!

LADY BRITOMART [*uneasily*] What do you think he had better do, Andrew?

UNDERSHAFT. Oh, just what he wants to do. He knows nothing and he thinks he knows everything. That points clearly to a political career. Get him a private secretaryship to someone who can get him an Under Secretaryship; and then leave him alone. He will find his natural and proper place in the end on the Treasury Bench.

STEPHEN [*springing up again*] I am sorry, sir, that you

415

force me to forget the respect due to you as my father. I am an Englishman and I will not hear the Government of my country insulted. [*He thrusts his hands in his pockets, and walks angrily across to the window*].

UNDERSHAFT [*with a touch of brutality*] The government of your country! *I* am the government of your country: I, and Lazarus. Do you suppose that you and half a dozen amateurs like you, sitting in a row in that foolish gabble shop, can govern Undershaft and Lazarus? No, my friend: you will do what pays u s. You will make war when it suits us, and keep peace when it doesnt. You will find out that trade requires certain measures when we have decided on those measures. When I want anything to keep my dividends up, you will discover that my want is a national need. When other people want something to keep my dividends down, you will call out the police and military. And in return you shall have the support and applause of my newspapers, and the delight of imagining that you are a great statesman. Government of your country! Be off with you, my boy, and play with your caucuses and leading articles and historic parties and great leaders and burning questions and the rest of your toys. *I* am going back to my counting house to pay the piper and call the tune.

STEPHEN [*actually smiling, and putting his hand on his father's shoulder with indulgent patronage*] Really, my dear father, it is impossible to be angry with you. You don't know how absurd all this sounds to m e. You are very properly proud of having been industrious enough to make money; and it is greatly to your credit that you have made so much of it. But it has kept you in circles where you are valued for your money and deferred to for it, instead of in the doubtless very old-fashioned and behind-the-times public school and university where I formed my habits of mind. It is natural for you to think that money governs England; but you must allow me to think I know better.

UNDERSHAFT. And what d o e s govern England, pray?

STEPHEN. Character, father, character.

416

UNDERSHAFT. Whose character? Yours or mine?

STEPHEN. Neither yours nor mine, father, but the best elements in the English national character.

UNDERSHAFT. Stephen: Ive found your profession for you. Youre a born journalist. I'll start you with a high-toned weekly review. There!

Before Stephen can reply Sarah, Barbara, Lomax, and Cusins come in ready for walking. Barbara crosses the room to the window and looks out. Cusins drifts amiably to the armchair. Lomax remains near the door, whilst Sarah comes to her mother.

Stephen goes to the smaller writing table and busies himself with his letters.

SARAH. Go and get ready, mamma: the carriage is waiting. [LADY BRITOMART *leaves the room*].

UNDERSHAFT [*to Sarah*] Good day, my dear. Good afternoon, Mr Lomax.

LOMAX [*vaguely*] Ahdedoo.

UNDERSHAFT [*to Cusins*] Quite well after last night, Euripides, eh?

CUSINS. As well as can be expected.

UNDERSHAFT. Thats right. [*To Barbara*]. So you are coming to see my death and devastation factory, Barbara?

BARBARA [*at the window*] You came yesterday to see my salvation factory. I promised you a return visit.

LOMAX [*coming forward between Sarah and Undershaft*] Youll find it awfully interesting. Ive been through the Woolwich Arsenal; and it gives you a ripping feeling of security, you know, to think of the lot of beggars we could kill if it came to fighting. [*To Undershaft, with sudden solemnity*]. Still, it must be rather an awful reflection for you, from the religious point of view as it were. Youre getting on, you know, and all that.

SARAH. You dont mind Cholly's imbecility, papa, do you?

LOMAX [*much taken aback*] Oh I say!

UNDERSHAFT. Mr Lomax looks at the matter in a very proper spirit, my dear.

LOMAX. Just so. Thats all I meant, I assure you.

SARAH. Are you coming, Stephen?

STEPHEN. Well, I am rather busy—er— [*Magnanimously*] Oh well, yes: I'll come. That is, if there is room for me.

UNDERSHAFT. I can take two with me in a little motor I am experimenting with for field use. You wont mind its being rather unfashionable. It's not painted yet; but it's bullet proof.

LOMAX [*appalled at the prospect of confronting Wilton Crescent in an unpainted motor*] Oh I s a y!

SARAH. The carriage for me, thank you. Barbara doesnt mind what shes seen in.

LOMAX. I say, Dolly old chap: do you really mind the car being a guy? Because of course if you do I'll go in it. Still—

CUSINS. I prefer it.

LOMAX. Thanks awfully, old man. Come, my ownest. [*He hurries out to secure his seat in the carriage. Sarah follows him*].

CUSINS [*moodily walking across to Lady Britomart's writing table*] Why are we two coming to this Works Department of Hell? that is what I ask myself.

BARBARA. I have always thought of it as a sort of pit where lost creatures with blackened faces stirred up smoky fires and were driven and tormented by my father. Is it like that, dad?

UNDERSHAFT [*scandalized*] My dear! It is a spotlessly clean and beautiful hillside town.

CUSINS. With a Methodist chapel? Oh d o say theres a Methodist chapel.

UNDERSHAFT. There are two: a Primitive one and a sophisticated one. There is even an Ethical Society; but it is not much patronized, as my men are all strongly religious. In the High Explosives Sheds they object to the presence of Agnostics as unsafe.

CUSINS. And yet they dont object to you!

BARBARA. Do they obey all your orders?

UNDERSHAFT. I never give them any orders. When I speak to one of them it is "Well, Jones, is the baby doing well? and has Mrs Jones made a good recovery?" "Nicely, thank you, sir." And thats all.

CUSINS. But Jones has to be kept in order. How do you maintain discipline among your men?

UNDERSHAFT. I dont. They do. You see, the one thing Jones wont stand is any rebellion from the man under him, or any assertion of social equality between the wife of the man with 4 shillings a week less than himself, and Mrs Jones! Of course they all rebel against me, theoretically. Practically, every man of them keeps the man just below him in his place. I never meddle with them. I never bully them. I dont even bully Lazarus. I say that certain things are to be done; but I dont order anybody to do them. I dont say, mind you, that there is no ordering about and snubbing and even bullying. The men snub the boys and order them about; the carmen snub the sweepers; the artisans snub the unskilled laborers; the foremen drive and bully both the laborers and artisans; the assistant engineers find fault with the foremen; the chief engineers drop on the assistants; the departmental managers worry the chiefs; and the clerks have tall hats and hymnbooks and keep up the social tone by refusing to associate on equal terms with anybody. The result is a colossal profit, which comes to me.

CUSINS [*revolted*] You really are a—well, what I was saying yesterday.

BARBARA. What was he saying yesterday?

UNDERSHAFT. Never mind, my dear. He thinks I have made you unhappy. Have I?

BARBARA. Do you think I can be happy in this vulgar silly dress? I! who have worn the uniform. Do you understand what you have done to me? Yesterday I had a man's soul in my hand. I set him in the way of life with his face to salvation. But when we took your money he turned back to drunkenness and derision. [*With intense conviction*] I will never forgive you that. If I had a child, and you destroyed its body with your explosives—if you murdered Dolly with your horrible guns—I could forgive you if my forgiveness would open the gates of heaven to you. But to take a human soul from me, and turn it into the soul of a wolf! that is worse than any murder.

UNDERSHAFT. Does my daughter despair so easily? Can you strike a man to the heart and leave no mark on him?

BARBARA [*her face lighting up*] Oh, you are right: he can never be lost now: where was my faith?

CUSINS. Oh, clever clever devil!

BARBARA. You may be a devil; but God speaks through you sometimes. [*She takes her father's hands and kisses them*]. You have given me back my happiness: I feel it deep down now, though my spirit is troubled.

UNDERSHAFT. You have learnt something. That always feels at first as if you had lost something.

BARBARA. Well, take me to the factory of death; and let me learn something more. There must be some truth or other behind all this frightful irony. Come, Dolly. [*She goes out*].

CUSINS. My guardian angel! [*To Undershaft*] Avaunt! [*He follows Barbara*].

STEPHEN [*quietly, at the writing table*] You must not mind Cusins, father. He is a very amiable good fellow; but he is a Greek scholar and naturally a little eccentric.

UNDERSHAFT. Ah, quite so. Thank you, Stephen. Thank you. [*He goes out*].

Stephen smiles patronizingly; buttons his coat responsibly; and crosses the room to the door. Lady Britomart, dressed for out-of-doors, opens it before he reaches it. She looks round for the others; looks at Stephen; and turns to go without a word.

STEPHEN [*embarrassed*] Mother—

LADY BRITOMART. Dont be apologetic, Stephen. And dont forget that you have outgrown your mother. [*She goes out*].

Perivale St Andrews lies between two Middlesex hills, half climbing the northern one. It is an almost smokeless

420

*town of white walls, roofs of narrow green slates or red
tiles, tall trees, domes, campaniles, and slender chimney
shafts, beautifully situated and beautiful in itself. The best
view of it is obtained from the crest of a slope about half
a mile to the east, where the high explosives are dealt with.
The foundry lies hidden in the depths between, the tops of
its chimneys sprouting like huge skittles into the middle distance. Across the crest runs an emplacement of concrete,
with a firestep, and a parapet which suggests a fortification,
because there is a huge cannon of the obsolete Woolwich
Infant pattern peering across it at the town. The cannon is
mounted on an experimental gun carriage: possibly the
original model of the Undershaft disappearing rampart
gun alluded to by Stephen. The firestep, being a convenient
place to sit, is furnished here and there with straw disc
cushions; and at one place there is the additional luxury of
a fur rug.*

*Barbara is standing on the firestep, looking over the
parapet towards the town. On her right is the cannon; on
her left the end of a shed raised on piles, with a ladder of
three or four steps up to the door, which opens outwards and
has a little wooden landing at the threshold, with a fire
bucket in the corner of the landing. Several dummy soldiers more or less mutilated, with straw protruding from
their gashes, have been shoved out of the way under the
landing. A few others are nearly upright against the shed;
and one has fallen forward and lies, like a grotesque corpse,
on the emplacement. The parapet stops short of the shed,
leaving a gap which is the beginning of the path down the
hill through the foundry to the town. The rug is on the firestep near this gap. Down on the emplacement behind the
cannon is a trolley carrying a huge conical bombshell with
a red band painted on it. Further to the right is the door of
an office, which, like the sheds, is of the lightest possible
construction.*

Cusins arrives by the path from the town.

BARBARA. Well?

CUSINS. Not a ray of hope. Everything perfect! wonderful! real! It only needs a cathedral to be a heavenly city

instead of a hellish one.

BARBARA. Have you found out whether they have done anything for old Peter Shirley?

CUSINS. They have found him a job as gatekeeper and timekeeper. He's frightfully miserable. He calls the time-keeping brainwork, and says he isnt used to it; and his gate lodge is so splendid that hes ashamed to use the rooms, and skulks in the scullery.

BARBARA. Poor Peter!

Stephen arrives from the town. He carries a field-glass.

STEPHEN [*enthusiastically*] Have you two seen the place? Why did you leave us?

CUSINS. I wanted to see everything I was not intended to see; and Barbara wanted to make the men talk.

STEPHEN. Have you found anything discreditable?

CUSINS. No. They call him Dandy Andy and are proud of his being a cunning old rascal; but it's all horribly, frightfully, immorally, unanswerably perfect.

Sarah arrives.

SARAH. Heavens! what a place! [*She crosses to the trolley*]. Did you see the nursing home!? [*She sits down on the shell*].

STEPHEN. Did you see the libraries and schools!?

SARAH. Did you see the ball room and the banqueting chamber in the Town Hall!?

STEPHEN. Have you gone into the insurance fund, the pension fund, the building society, the various applications of co-operation!?

Undershaft comes from the office, with a sheaf of telegrams in his hand.

UNDERSHAFT. Well, have you seen everything? I'm sorry I was called away. [*Indicating the telegrams*] Good news from Manchuria.

STEPHEN. Another Japanese victory?

UNDERSHAFT. Oh, I dont know. Which side wins does not concern us here. No: the good news is that the aerial battleship is a tremendous success. At the first trial it has wiped out a fort with three hundred soldiers in it.

CUSINS [*from the platform*] Dummy soldiers?

MAJOR BARBARA

UNDERSHAFT [*striding across to Stephen and kicking the prostrate dummy brutally out of his way*] No: the real thing.

Cusins and Barbara exchange glances. Then Cusins sits on the step and buries his face in his hands. Barbara gravely lays her hand on his shoulder. He looks up at her in whimsical desperation.

UNDERSHAFT. Well, Stephen, what do you think of the place?

STEPHEN. Oh, magnificent. A perfect triumph of modern industry. Frankly, my dear father, I have been a fool: I had no idea of what it all meant: of the wonderful forethought, the power of organization, the administrative capacity, the financial genius, the colossal capital it represents. I have been repeating to myself as I came through your streets "Peace hath her victories no less renowned than War." I have only one misgiving about it all.

UNDERSHAFT. Out with it.

STEPHEN. Well, I cannot help thinking that all this provision for every want of your workmen may sap their independence and weaken their sense of responsibility. And greatly as we enjoyed our tea at that splendid restaurant —how they gave us all that luxury and cake and jam and cream for threepence I really cannot imagine!—still you must remember that restaurants break up home life. Look at the continent, for instance! Are you sure so much pampering is really good for the men's characters?

UNDERSHAFT. Well you see, my dear boy, when you are organizing civilization you have to make up your mind whether trouble and anxiety are good things or not. If you decide that they are, then, I take it, you simply dont organize civilization; and there you are, with trouble and anxiety enough to make us all angels! But if you decide the other way, you may as well go through with it. However, Stephen, our characters are safe here. A sufficient dose of anxiety is always provided by the fact that we may be blown to smithereens at any moment.

SARAH. By the way, papa, where do you make the explosives?

423

UNDERSHAFT. In separate little sheds, like that one. When one of them blows up, it costs very little; and only the people quite close to it are killed.

Stephen, who is quite close to it, looks at it rather scaredly, and moves away quickly to the cannon. At the same moment the door of the shed is thrown abruptly open; and a foreman in overalls and list slippers comes out on the little landing and holds the door for Lomax, who appears in the doorway.

LOMAX [*with studied coolness*] My good fellow: you neednt get into a state of nerves. Nothing's going to happen to you; and I suppose it wouldnt be the end of the world if anything did. A little bit of British pluck is what y o u want, old chap. [*He descends and strolls across to Sarah*].

UNDERSHAFT [*to the foreman*] Anything wrong, Bilton?

BILTON [*with ironic calm*] Gentleman walked into the high explosives shed and lit a cigaret, sir: thats all.

UNDERSHAFT. Ah, quite so. [*Going over to Lomax*] Do you happen to remember what you did with the match?

LOMAX. Oh come! I'm not a fool. I took jolly good care to blow it out before I chucked it away.

BILTON. The top of it was red hot inside, sir.

LOMAX. Well, suppose it was! I didnt chuck it into any of y o u r messes.

UNDERSHAFT. Think no more of it, Mr Lomax. By the way, would you mind lending me your matches?

LOMAX [*offering his box*] Certainly.

UNDERSHAFT. Thanks. [*He pockets the matches*].

LOMAX [*lecturing to the company generally*] You know, these high explosives dont go off like gunpowder, except when theyre in a gun. When theyre spread loose, you can put a match to them without the least risk: they just burn quietly like a bit of paper. [*Warming to the scientific interest of the subject*] Did you know that, Undershaft? Have you ever tried?

UNDERSHAFT. Not on a large scale, Mr Lomax. Bilton

424

will give you a sample of gun cotton when you are leaving if you ask him. You can experiment with it at home. [*Bilton looks puzzled*].

SARAH. Bilton will do nothing of the sort, papa. I suppose it's your business to blow up the Russians and Japs; but you might really stop short of blowing up poor Cholly. [*Bilton gives it up and retires into the shed*].

LOMAX. My ownest, there is no danger. [*He sits beside her on the shell*].

Lady Britomart arrives from the town with a bouquet.

LADY BRITOMART [*impetuously*] Andrew: you shouldnt have let me see this place.

UNDERSHAFT. Why, my dear?

LADY BRITOMART. Never mind why: you shouldnt have: thats all. To think of all that [*indicating the town*] being yours! and that you have kept it to yourself all these years!

UNDERSHAFT. It does not belong to me. I belong to it. It is the Undershaft inheritance.

LADY BRITOMART. It is not. Your ridiculous cannons and that noisy banging foundry may be the Undershaft inheritance; but all that plate and linen, all that furniture and those houses and orchards and gardens belong to us. They belong to m e: they are not a man's business. I wont give them up. You must be out of your senses to throw them all away; and if you persist in such folly, I will call in a doctor.

UNDERSHAFT [*stooping to smell the bouquet*] Where did you get the flowers, my dear?

LADY BRITOMART. Your men presented them to me in your William Morris Labor Church.

CUSINS. Oh! It needed only that. A Labor Church! [*He mounts the firestep distractedly, and leans with his elbows on the parapet, turning his back to them*].

LADY BRITOMART. Yes, with Morris's words in mosaic letters ten feet high round the dome. NO MAN IS GOOD ENOUGH TO BE ANOTHER MAN'S MASTER. The cynicism of it!

UNDERSHAFT. It shocked the men at first, I am afraid.

But now they take no more notice of it than of the ten commandments in church.

LADY BRITOMART. Andrew: you are trying to put me off the subject of the inheritance by profane jokes. Well, you shant. I dont ask it any longer for Stephen: he has inherited far too much of your perversity to be fit for it. But Barbara has rights as well as Stephen. Why should not Adolphus succeed to the inheritance? I could manage the town for him; and he can look after the cannons, if they are really necessary.

UNDERSHAFT. I should ask nothing better if Adolphus were a foundling. He is exactly the sort of new blood that is wanted in English business. But he's not a foundling; and theres an end of it. [*He makes for the office door*].

CUSINS [*turning to them*] Not quite. [*They all turn and stare at him*]. I think— Mind! I am not committing myself in any way as to my future course—but I t h i n k the foundling difficulty can be got over. [*He jumps down to the emplacement*].

UNDERSHAFT [*coming back to him*] What do you mean?

CUSINS. Well, I have something to say which is in the nature of a confession.

SARAH.
LADY BRITOMART. } Confession!
BARBARA.
STEPHEN.

LOMAX. Oh I say!

CUSINS. Yes, a confession. Listen, all. Until I met Barbara I thought myself in the main an honorable, truthful man, because I wanted the approval of my conscience more than I wanted anything else. But the moment I saw Barbara, I wanted her far more than the approval of my conscience.

LADY BRITOMART. Adolphus!

CUSINS. It is true. You accused me yourself, Lady Brit, of joining the Army to worship Barbara; and so I did. She bought my soul like a flower at a street corner; but she

426

bought it for herself.

UNDERSHAFT. What! Not for Dionysos or another?

CUSINS. Dionysos and all the others are in herself. I adored what was divine in her, and was therefore a true worshipper. But I was romantic about her too. I thought she was a woman of the people, and that a marriage with a professor of Greek would be far beyond the wildest social ambitions of her rank.

LADY BRITOMART. Adolphus!!

LOMAX. Oh I s a y!!!

CUSINS. When I learnt the horrible truth—

LADY BRITOMART. What do you mean by the horrible truth, pray?

CUSINS. That she was enormously rich; that her grandfather was an earl; that her father was the Prince of Darkness—

UNDERSHAFT. Chut!

CUSINS. —and that I was only an adventurer trying to catch a rich wife, then I stooped to deceive her about my birth.

BARBARA [rising] Dolly!

LADY BRITOMART. Your birth! Now Adolphus, dont dare to make up a wicked story for the sake of these wretched cannons. Remember: I have seen photographs of your parents; and the Agent General for South Western Australia knows them personally and has assured me that they are most respectable married people.

CUSINS. So they are in Australia; but here they are outcasts. Their marriage is legal in Australia, but not in England. My mother is my father's deceased wife's sister; and in this island I am consequently a foundling. [Sensation].

BARBARA. Silly! [She climbs to the cannon, and leans, listening, in the angle it makes with the parapet].

CUSINS. Is the subterfuge good enough, Machiavelli?

UNDERSHAFT [thoughtfully] Biddy: this may be a way out of the difficulty.

LADY BRITOMART. Stuff! A man cant make cannons any

the better for being his own cousin instead of his proper self. [*She sits down on the rug with a bounce that expresses her downright contempt for their casuistry*].

UNDERSHAFT [*to Cusins*] You are an educated man. That is against the tradition.

CUSINS. Once in ten thousand times it happens that the schoolboy is a born master of what they try to teach him. Greek has not destroyed my mind: it has nourished it. Besides, I did not learn it at an English public school.

UNDERSHAFT. Hm! Well, I cannot afford to be too particular: you have cornered the foundling market. Let it pass. You are eligible, Euripides: you are eligible.

BARBARA. Dolly: yesterday morning, when Stephen told us all about the tradition, you became very silent; and you have been strange and excited ever since. Were you thinking of your birth then?

CUSINS. When the finger of Destiny suddenly points at a man in the middle of his breakfast, it makes him thoughtful.

UNDERSHAFT. Aha! You have had your eye on the business, my young friend, have you?

CUSINS. Take care! There is an abyss of moral horror between me and your accursed aerial battleships.

UNDERSHAFT. Never mind the abyss for the present. Let us settle the practical details and leave your final decision open. You know that you will have to change your name. Do you object to that?

CUSINS. Would any man named Adolphus—any man called Dolly!—object to be called something else?

UNDERSHAFT. Good. Now, as to money! I propose to treat you handsomely from the beginning. You shall start at a thousand a year.

CUSINS [*with sudden heat, his spectacles twinkling with mischief*] A thousand! You dare offer a miserable thousand to the son-in-law of a millionaire! No, by Heavens, Machiavelli! you shall not cheat m e. You cannot do without me; and I can do without you. I must have two thousand five

428

hundred a year for two years. At the end of that time, if I am a failure, I go. But if I am a success, and stay on, you must give me the other five thousand.

UNDERSHAFT. What other five thousand?

CUSINS. To make the two years up to five thousand a year. The two thousand five hundred is only half pay in case I should turn out a failure. The third year I must have ten per cent on the profits.

UNDERSHAFT [*taken aback*] Ten per cent! Why, man, do you know what my profits are?

CUSINS. Enormous, I hope: otherwise I shall require twentyfive per cent.

UNDERSHAFT. But, Mr Cusins, this is a serious matter of business. You are not bringing any capital into the concern.

CUSINS. What! no capital! Is my mastery of Greek no capital? Is my access to the subtlest thought, the loftiest poetry yet attained by humanity, no capital? My character! my intellect! my life! my career! what Barbara calls my soul! are these no capital? Say another word; and I double my salary.

UNDERSHAFT. Be reasonable—

CUSINS [*peremptorily*] Mr Undershaft: you have my terms. Take them or leave them.

UNDERSHAFT [*recovering himself*] Very well. I note your terms; and I offer you half.

CUSINS [*disgusted*] Half!

UNDERSHAFT [*firmly*] Half.

CUSINS. You call yourself a gentleman; and you offer me half!!

UNDERSHAFT. I do not call myself a gentleman; but I offer you half.

CUSINS. This to your future partner! your successor! your son-in-law!

BARBARA. You are selling your own soul, Dolly, not mine. Leave me out of the bargain, please.

UNDERSHAFT. Come! I will go a step further for Barbara's sake. I will give you three fifths; but that is my last word.

CUSINS. Done!

LOMAX. Done in the eye! Why, *I* get only eight hundred, you know.

CUSINS. By the way, Mac, I am a classical scholar, not an arithmetical one. Is three fifths more than half or less?

UNDERSHAFT. More, of course.

CUSINS. I would have taken two hundred and fifty. How you can succeed in business when you are willing to pay all that money to a University don who is obviously not worth a junior clerk's wages!—well! What will Lazarus say?

UNDERSHAFT. Lazarus is a gentle romantic Jew who cares for nothing but string quartets and stalls at fashionable theatres. He will be blamed for your rapacity in money matters, poor fellow! as he has hitherto been blamed for mine. You are a shark of the first order, Euripides. So much the better for the firm!

BARBARA. Is the bargain closed, Dolly? Does your soul belong to him now?

CUSINS. No: the price is settled: that is all. The real tug of war is still to come. What about the moral question?

LADY BRITOMART. There is no moral question in the matter at all, Adolphus. You must simply sell cannons and weapons to people whose cause is right and just, and refuse them to foreigners and criminals.

UNDERSHAFT [*determinedly*] No: none of that. You must keep the true faith of an Armorer, or you dont come in here.

CUSINS. What on earth is the true faith of an Armorer?

UNDERSHAFT. To give arms to all men who offer an honest price for them, without respect of persons or principles: to aristocrat and republican, to Nihilist and Tsar, to Capitalist and Socialist, to Protestant and Catholic, to burglar and policeman, to black man, white man and yellow man, to all sorts and conditions, all nationalities, all faiths, all follies, all causes and all crimes. The first Undershaft wrote

430

up in his shop IF GOD GAVE THE HAND, LET NOT MAN WITH-HOLD THE SWORD. The second wrote up ALL HAVE THE RIGHT TO FIGHT: NONE HAVE THE RIGHT TO JUDGE. The third wrote up TO MAN THE WEAPON: TO HEAVEN THE VICTORY. The fourth had no literary turn; so he did not write up anything; but he sold cannons to Napoleon under the nose of George the Third. The fifth wrote up PEACE SHALL NOT PREVAIL SAVE WITH A SWORD IN HER HAND. The sixth, my master, was the best of all. He wrote up NOTHING IS EVER DONE IN THIS WORLD UNTIL MEN ARE PREPARED TO KILL ONE ANOTHER IF IT IS NOT DONE. After that, there was nothing left for the seventh to say. So he wrote up, simply, UNASHAMED.

CUSINS. My good Machiavelli, I shall certainly write something up on the wall; only, as I shall write it in Greek, you wont be able to read it. But as to your Armorer's faith, if I take my neck out of the noose of my own morality I am not going to put it into the noose of yours. I shall sell cannons to whom I please and refuse them to whom I please. So there!

UNDERSHAFT. From the moment when you become Andrew Undershaft, you will never do as you please again. Dont come here lusting for power, young man.

CUSINS. If power were my aim I should not come here for it. Y o u have no power.

UNDERSHAFT. None of my own, certainly.

CUSINS. I have more power than you, more will. You do not drive this place: it drives you. And what drives the place?

UNDERSHAFT [enigmatically] A will of which I am a part.

BARBARA [startled] Father! Do you know what you are saying; or are you laying a snare for my soul?

CUSINS. Dont listen to his metaphysics, Barbara. The place is driven by the most rascally part of society, the money hunters, the pleasure hunters, the military promotion hunters; and he is their slave.

431

UNDERSHAFT. Not necessarily. Remember the Armorer's Faith. I will take an order from a good man as cheerfully as from a bad one. If you good people prefer preaching and shirking to buying my weapons and fighting the rascals, dont blame me. I can make cannons: I cannot make courage and conviction. Bah! you th e me, Euripides, with your morality mongering. Ask Barbara: s h e understands. [*He suddenly reaches up and takes Barbara's hands, looking powerfully into her eyes*]. Tell him, my love, what power really means.

BARBARA [*hypnotized*] Before I joined the Salvation Army, I was in my own power; and the consequence was that I never knew what to do with myself. When I joined it, I had not time enough for all the things I had to do.

UNDERSHAFT [*approvingly*] Just so. And why was that, do you suppose?

BARBARA. Yesterday I should have said, because I was in the power of God. [*She resumes her self-possession, withdrawing her hands from his with a power equal to his own*]. But you came and shewed me that I was in the power of Bodger and Undershaft. Today I feel—oh! how can I put it into words? Sarah: do you remember the earthquake at Cannes, when we were little children?—how little the surprise of the first shock mattered compared to the dread and horror of waiting for the second? That is how I feel in this place today. I stood on the rock I thought eternal; and without a word of warning it reeled and crumbled under me. I was safe with an infinite wisdom watching me, an army marching to Salvation with me; and in a moment, at a stroke of your pen in a cheque book, I stood alone; and the heavens were empty. That was the first shock of the earthquake: I am waiting for the second.

UNDERSHAFT. Come, come, my daughter! dont make too much of your little tinpot tragedy. What do we do here when we spend years of work and thought and thousands of pounds of solid cash on a new gun or an aerial battleship that turns out just a hairsbreadth wrong after all? Scrap it.

432

Scrap it without wasting another hour or another pound on it. Well, you have made for yourself something that you call a morality or a religion or what not. It doesnt fit the facts. Well, scrap it. Scrap it and get one that does fit. That is what is wrong with the world at present. It scraps its obsolete steam engines and dynamos; but it wont scrap its old prejudices and its old moralities and its old religions and its old political constitutions. Whats the result? In machinery it does very well; but in morals and religion and politics it is working at a loss that brings it nearer bankruptcy every year. Dont persist in that folly. If your old religion broke down yesterday, get a newer and a better one for tomorrow.

BARBARA. Oh how gladly I would take a better one to my soul! But you offer me a worse one. [*Turning on him with sudden vehemence*] Justify yourself: shew me some light through the darkness of this dreadful place, with its beautifully clean workshops, and respectable workmen, and model homes.

UNDERSHAFT. Cleanliness and respectability do not need justification, Barbara: they justify themselves. I see no darkness here, no dreadfulness. In your Salvation shelter I saw poverty, misery, cold and hunger. You gave them bread and treacle and dreams of heaven. I give from thirty shillings a week to twelve thousand a year. They find their own dreams; but I look after the drainage.

BARBARA. And their souls?

UNDERSHAFT. I save their souls just as I saved yours.

BARBARA [*revolted*] Y o u saved my soul! What do you mean?

UNDERSHAFT. I fed you and clothed you and housed you. I took care that you should have money enough to live handsomely—more than enough; so that you could be wasteful, careless, generous. That saved your soul from the seven deadly sins.

BARBARA [*bewildered*] The seven deadly sins!

UNDERSHAFT. Yes, the deadly seven. [*Counting on his*

fingers] Food, clothing, firing, rent, taxes, respectability and children. Nothing can lift those seven millstones from Man's neck but money; and the spirit cannot soar until the millstones are lifted. I lifted them from your spirit. I enabled Barbara to become Major Barbara; and I saved her from the crime of poverty.

CUSINS. Do you call poverty a crime?

UNDERSHAFT. The worst of crimes. All the other crimes are virtues beside it: all the other dishonors are chivalry itself by comparison. Poverty blights whole cities; spreads horrible pestilences; strikes dead the very souls of all who come within sight, sound or smell of it. What y o u call crime is nothing: a murder here and a theft there, a blow now and a curse then: what do they matter? they are only the accidents and illnesses of life: there are not fifty genuine professional criminals in London. But there are millions of poor people, abject people, dirty people, ill fed, ill clothed people. They poison us morally and physically: they kill the happiness of society: they force us to do away with our own liberties and to organize unnatural cruelties for fear they should rise against us and drag us down into their abyss. Only fools fear crime: we all fear poverty. Pah! [*turning on Barbara*] you talk of your half-saved ruffian in West Ham: you accuse me of dragging his soul back to perdition. Well, bring him to me here; and I will drag his soul back again to salvation for you. Not by words and dreams; but by thirtyeight shillings a week, a sound house in a handsome street, and a permanent job. In three weeks he will have a fancy waistcoat; in three months a tall hat and a chapel sitting; before the end of the year he will shake hands with a duchess at a Primrose League meeting, and join the Conservative Party.

BARBARA. And will he be the better for that?

UNDERSHAFT. You know he will. Dont be a hypocrite, Barbara. He will be better fed, better housed, better clothed, better behaved; and his children will be pounds heavier and bigger. That will be better than an American cloth mattress in a shelter, chopping firewood, eating bread and treacle, and being forced to kneel down from time to time to thank heaven for it: knee drill, I think you call it. It is cheap work converting starving men with a Bible in one hand and a slice of bread in the other. I will undertake to convert West Ham to Mahometanism on the same terms. Try your hand on m y men: their souls are hungry because their bodies are full.

BARBARA. And leave the east end to starve?

UNDERSHAFT [*his energetic tone dropping into one of bitter and brooding remembrance*] I was an east ender. I moralized and starved until one day I swore that I would be a full-fed free man at all costs—that nothing should stop me except a bullet, neither reason nor morals nor the lives of other men. I said "Thou shalt starve ere I starve"; and with that word I became free and great. I was a dangerous man until I had my will: now I am a useful, beneficent, kindly person. That is the history of most self-made millionaires, I fancy. When it is the history of every Englishman we shall have an England worth living in.

LADY BRITOMART. Stop making speeches, Andrew. This is not the place for them.

UNDERSHAFT [*punctured*] My dear: I have no other means of conveying my ideas.

LADY BRITOMART. Your ideas are nonsense. You got on because you were selfish and unscrupulous.

UNDERSHAFT. Not at all. I had the strongest scruples about poverty and starvation. Your moralists are quite unscrupulous about both: they make virtues of them. I had rather be a thief than a pauper. I had rather be a murderer than a slave. I dont want to be either; but if you force the alternative on me, then, by Heaven, I'll choose the braver and more moral one. I hate poverty and slavery worse than any other crimes whatsoever. And let me tell you this. Poverty and slavery have stood up for centuries to your sermons

435

and leading articles: they will not stand up to my machine guns. Dont preach at them: dont reason with them. Kill them.

BARBARA. Killing. Is that your remedy for everything?

UNDERSHAFT. It is the final test of conviction, the only lever strong enough to overturn a social system, the only way of saying Must. Let six hundred and seventy fools loose in the street; and three policemen can scatter them. But huddle them together in a certain house in Westminster; and let them go through certain ceremonies and call themselves certain names until at last they get the courage to kill; and your six hundred and seventy fools become a government. Your pious mob fills up ballot papers and imagines it is governing its masters; but the ballot paper that really governs is the paper that has a bullet wrapped up in it.

CUSINS. That is perhaps why, like most intelligent people, I never vote.

UNDERSHAFT. Vote! Bah! When you vote, you only change the names of the cabinet. When you shoot, you pull down governments, inaugurate new epochs, abolish old orders and set up new. Is that historically true, Mr Learned Man, or is it not?

CUSINS. It is historically true. I loathe having to admit it. I repudiate your sentiments. I abhor your nature. I defy you in every possible way. Still, it is true. But it ought not to be true.

UNDERSHAFT. Ought! ought! ought! ought! ought! Are you going to spend your life saying ought, like the rest of our moralists? Turn your oughts into shalls, man. Come and make explosives with me. Whatever can blow men up can blow society up. The history of the world is the history of those who had courage enough to embrace this truth. Have you the courage to embrace it, Barbara?

LADY BRITOMART. Barbara, I positively forbid you to listen to your father's abominable wickedness. And you, Adolphus, ought to know better than to go about saying

436

that wrong things are true. What does it matter whether they are true if they are wrong?

UNDERSHAFT. What does it matter whether they are wrong if they are true?

LADY BRITOMART [*rising*] Children: come home instantly. Andrew: I am exceedingly sorry I allowed you to call on us. You are wickeder than ever. Come at once.

BARBARA [*shaking her head*] It's no use running away from wicked people, mamma.

LADY BRITOMART. It is every use. It shews your disapprobation of them.

BARBARA. It does not save them.

LADY BRITOMART. I can see that you are going to disobey me. Sarah: are you coming home or are you not?

SARAH. I daresay it's very wicked of papa to make cannons; but I dont think I shall cut him on that account.

LOMAX [*pouring oil on the troubled waters*] The fact is, you know, there is a certain amount of tosh about this notion of wickedness. It doesnt work. You must look at facts. Not that I would say a word in favor of anything wrong; but then, you see, all sorts of chaps are always doing all sorts of things; and we have to fit them in somehow, dont you know. What I mean is that you cant go cutting everybody; and thats about what it comes to. [*Their rapt attention to his eloquence makes him nervous*]. Perhaps I dont make myself clear.

LADY BRITOMART. You are lucidity itself, Charles. Because Andrew is successful and has plenty of money to give to Sarah, you will flatter him and encourage him in his wickedness.

LOMAX [*unruffled*] Well, where the carcase is, there will the eagles be gathered, dont you know. [*To Undershaft*] Eh? What?

UNDERSHAFT. Precisely. By the way, m a y I call you Charles?

LOMAX. Delighted. Cholly is the usual ticket.

UNDERSHAFT [*to Lady Britomart*] Bidd*y*—

437

LADY BRITOMART [*violently*] Dont dare call me Biddy. Charles Lomax: you are a fool. Adolphus Cusins: you are a Jesuit. Stephen: you are a prig. Barbara: you are a lunatic. Andrew: you are a vulgar tradesman. Now you all know my opinion; and m y conscience is clear, at all events. [*She sits down with a vehemence that the rug fortunately softens*].

UNDERSHAFT. My dear: you are the incarnation of morality. [*She snorts*]. Your conscience is clear and your duty done when you have called everybody names. Come, Euripides! it is getting late; and we all want to go home. Make up your mind.

CUSINS. Understand this, you old demon—

LADY BRITOMART. Adolphus!

UNDERSHAFT. Let him alone, Biddy. Proceed, Euripides.

CUSINS. You have me in a horrible dilemma. I want Barbara.

UNDERSHAFT. Like all young men, you greatly exaggerate the difference between one young woman and another.

BARBARA. Quite true, Dolly.

CUSINS. I also want to avoid being a rascal.

UNDERSHAFT [*with biting contempt*] You lust for personal righteousness, for self-approval, for what you call a good conscience, for what Barbara calls salvation, for what I call patronizing people who are not so lucky as yourself.

CUSINS. I do not: all the poet in me recoils from being a good man. But there are things in me that I must reckon with. Pity—

UNDERSHAFT. Pity! The scavenger of misery.

CUSINS. Well, love.

UNDERSHAFT. I know. You love the needy and the outcast: you love the oppressed races, the negro, the Indian ryot, the underdog everywhere. Do you love the Japanese? Do you love the French? Do you love the English?

CUSINS. No. Every true Englishman detests the English. We are the wickedest nation on earth; and our success is a moral horror.

UNDERSHAFT. That is what comes of your gospel of love, is it?

CUSINS. May I not love even my father-in-law?

UNDERSHAFT. Who wants your love, man? By what right do you take the liberty of offering it to me? I will have your due heed and respect, or I will kill you. But your love! Damn your impertinence!

CUSINS [*grinning*] I may not be able to control my affections, Mac.

UNDERSHAFT. You are fencing, Euripides. You are weakening: your grip is slipping. Come! try your last weapon. Pity and love have broken in your hand: forgiveness is still left.

CUSINS. No: forgiveness is a beggar's refuge. I am with you there: we must pay our debts.

UNDERSHAFT. Well said. Come! you will suit me. Remember the words of Plato.

CUSINS [*starting*] Plato! Y o u dare quote Plato to m e!

UNDERSHAFT. Plato says, my friend, that society cannot be saved until either the Professors of Greek take to making gunpowder, or else the makers of gunpowder become Professors of Greek.

CUSINS. Oh, tempter, cunning tempter!

UNDERSHAFT. Come! choose, man, choose.

CUSINS. But perhaps Barbara will not marry me if I make the wrong choice.

BARBARA. Perhaps not.

CUSINS [*desperately perplexed*] You hear!

BARBARA. Father: do you love nobody?

UNDERSHAFT. I love my best friend.

LADY BRITOMART. And who is that, pray?

UNDERSHAFT. My bravest enemy. That is the man who keeps me up to the mark.

CUSINS. You know, the creature is really a sort of poet in his way. Suppose he is a great man, after all!

UNDERSHAFT. Suppose you stop talking and make up

your mind, my young friend.

CUSINS. But you are driving me against my nature. I hate war.

UNDERSHAFT. Hatred is the coward's revenge for being intimidated. Dare you make war on war? Here are the means: my friend Mr Lomax is sitting on them.

LOMAX [*springing up*] Oh I say! You dont mean that this thing is loaded, do you? My ownest: come off it.

SARAH [*sitting placidly on the shell*] If I am to be blown up, the more thoroughly it is done the better. Dont fuss, Cholly.

LOMAX [*to Undershaft, strongly remonstrant*] Your own daughter, you know.

UNDERSHAFT. So I see. [*To Cusins*] Well, my friend, may we expect you here at six tomorrow morning?

CUSINS [*firmly*] Not on any account. I will see the whole establishment blown up with its own dynamite before I will get up at five. My hours are healthy, rational hours: eleven to five.

UNDERSHAFT. Come when you please: before a week you will come at six and stay until I turn you out for the sake of your health. [*Calling*] Bilton! [*He turns to Lady Britomart, who rises*]. My dear: let us leave these two young people to themselves for a moment. [*Bilton comes from the shed*]. I am going to take you through the gun cotton shed.

BILTON [*barring the way*] You cant take anything explosive in here, sir.

LADY BRITOMART. What do you mean? Are you alluding to me?

BILTON [*unmoved*] No, maam. Mr Undershaft has the other gentleman's matches in his pocket.

LADY BRITOMART [*abruptly*] Oh! I beg your pardon. [*She goes into the shed*].

UNDERSHAFT. Quite right, Bilton, quite right: here you are. [*He gives Bilton the box of matches*]. Come, Stephen. Come, Charles. Bring Sarah. [*He passes into the shed*].

Bilton opens the box and deliberately drops the matches into the fire-bucket.

LOMAX. Oh I say! [*Bilton stolidly hands him the empty box*]. Infernal nonsense! Pure scientific ignorance! [*He goes in*].

SARAH. Am I all right, Bilton?

BILTON. Youll have to put on list slippers, miss: thats all. Weve got em inside. [*She goes in*].

STEPHEN [*very seriously to Cusins*] Dolly, old fellow, think. Think before you decide. Do you feel that you are a sufficiently practical man? It is a huge undertaking, an enormous responsibility. All this mass of business will be Greek to you.

CUSINS. Oh, I think it will be much less difficult than Greek.

STEPHEN. Well, I just want to say this before I leave you to yourselves. Dont let anything I have said about right and wrong prejudice you against this great chance in life. I have satisfied myself that the business is one of the highest character and a credit to our company. [*Emotionally*] I am very proud of my father. I— [*Unable to proceed, he presses Cusins' hand and goes hastily into the shed, followed by Bilton*].

Barbara and Cusins, left alone together, look at one another silently.

CUSINS. Barbara: I am going to accept this offer.

BARBARA. I thought you would.

CUSINS. You understand, dont you, that I had to decide without consulting you. If I had thrown the burden of the choice on you, you would sooner or later have despised me for it.

BARBARA. Yes: I did not want you to sell your soul for me any more than for this inheritance.

CUSINS. It is not the sale of my soul that troubles me: I have sold it too often to care about that. I have sold it for a professorship. I have sold it for an income. I have sold it to escape being imprisoned for refusing to pay taxes for

441

hangmen's ropes and unjust wars and things that I abhor. What is all human conduct but the daily and hourly sale of our souls for trifles? What I am now selling it for is neither money nor position nor comfort, but for reality and for power.

BARBARA. You know that you will have no power, and that he has none.

CUSINS. I know. It is not for myself alone. I want to make power for the world.

BARBARA. I want to make power for the world too; but it must be spiritual power.

CUSINS. I think all power is spiritual: these cannons will not go off by themselves. I have tried to make spiritual power by teaching Greek. But the world can never be really touched by a dead language and a dead civilization. The people must have power; and the people cannot have Greek. Now the power that is made here can be wielded by all men.

BARBARA. Power to burn women's houses down and kill their sons and tear their husbands to pieces.

CUSINS. You cannot have power for good without having power for evil too. Even mother's milk nourishes murderers as well as heroes. This power which only tears men's bodies to pieces has never been so horribly abused as the intellectual power, the imaginative power, the poetic, religious power that can enslave men's souls. As a teacher of Greek I gave the intellectual man weapons against the common man. I now want to give the common man weapons against the intellectual man. I love the common people. I want to arm them against the lawyers, the doctors, the priests, the literary men, the professors, the artists, and the politicians, who, once in authority, are more disastrous and tyrannical than all the fools, rascals, and impostors. I want a power simple enough for common men to use, yet strong enough to force the intellectual oligarchy to use its genius for the general good.

BARBARA. Is there no higher power than that [*pointing*

442

to the shell].

CUSINS. Yes; but that power can destroy the higher powers just as a tiger can destroy a man: therefore Man must master that power first. I admitted this when the Turks and Greeks were last at war. My best pupil went out to fight for Hellas. My parting gift to him was not a copy of Plato's Republic, but a revolver and a hundred Undershaft cartridges. The blood of every Turk he shot—if he shot any—is on my head as well as on Undershaft's. That act committed me to this place for ever. Your father's challenge has beaten me. Dare I make war on war? I dare. I must. I will. And now, is it all over between us?

BARBARA [*touched by his evident dread of her answer*] Silly baby Dolly! How could it be!

CUSINS [*overjoyed*] Then you—you—you— Oh for my drum! [*He flourishes imaginary drumsticks*].

BARBARA [*angered by his levity*] Take care, Dolly, take care. Oh, if only I could get away from you and from father and from it all! if I could have the wings of a dove and fly away to heaven!

CUSINS. And leave m e!

BARBARA. Yes, you, and all the other naughty mischievous children of men. But I cant. I was happy in the Salvation Army for a moment. I escaped from the world into a paradise of enthusiasm and prayer and soul saving; but the moment our money ran short, it all came back to Bodger: it was he who saved our people: he, and the Prince of Darkness, my papa. Undershaft and Bodger: their hands stretch everywhere: when we feed a starving fellow creature, it is with their bread, because there is no other bread; when we tend the sick, it is in the hospitals they endow; if we turn from the churches they build, we must kneel on the stones of the streets they pave. As long as that lasts, there is no getting away from them. Turning our backs on Bodger and Undershaft is turning our backs on life.

CUSINS. I thought you were determined to turn your back on the wicked side of life.

BARBARA. There is no wicked side: life is all one. And I never wanted to shirk my share in whatever evil must be endured, whether it be sin or suffering. I wish I could cure you of middle-class ideas, Dolly.

CUSINS [*gasping*] Middle cl—! A snub! A social snub to m e! from the daughter of a foundling!

BARBARA. That is why I have no class, Dolly: I come straight out of the heart of the whole people. If I were middle-class I should turn my back on my father's business; and we should both live in an artistic drawing room, with you reading the reviews in one corner, and I in the other at the piano, playing Schumann: both very superior persons, and neither of us a bit of use. Sooner than that, I would sweep out the guncotton shed, or be one of Bodger's barmaids. Do you know what would have happened if you had refused papa's offer?

CUSINS. I wonder!

BARBARA. I should have given you up and married the man who accepted it. After all, my dear old mother has more sense than any of you. I felt like her when I saw this place—felt that I must have it—that never, never, never could I let it go; only she thought it was the houses and the kitchen ranges and the linen and china, when it was really all the human souls to be saved: not weak souls in starved bodies, sobbing with gratitude for a scrap of bread and treacle, but fullfed, quarrelsome, snobbish, uppish creatures, all standing on their little rights and dignities, and thinking that my father ought to be greatly obliged to them for making so much money for him—and so he ought. That is where salvation is really wanted. My father shall never throw it in my teeth again that my converts were bribed with bread. [*She is transfigured*]. I have got rid of the bribe of bread. I have got rid of the bribe of heaven. Let God's work be done for its own sake: the work he had to create us to do because it cannot be done except by living men and women. When I die, let him be in my debt, not I in his;

and let me forgive him as becomes a woman of my rank.

CUSINS. Then the way of life lies through the factory of death?

BARBARA. Yes, through the raising of hell to heaven and of man to God, through the unveiling of an eternal light in the Valley of The Shadow. [*Seizing him with both hands*] Oh, did you think my courage would never come back? did you believe that I was a deserter? that I, who have stood in the streets, and taken my people to my heart, and talked of the holiest and greatest things with them, could ever turn back and chatter foolishly to fashionable people about nothing in a drawing room? Never, never, never, never: Major Barbara will die with the colors. Oh! and I have my dear little Dolly boy still; and he has found me my place and my work. Glory Hallelujah! [*She kisses him*].

CUSINS. My dearest: consider my delicate health. I cannot stand as much happiness as you can.

BARBARA. Yes: it is not easy work being in love with me, is it? But it's good for you. [*She runs to the shed, and calls, childlike*] Mamma! Mamma! [*Bilton comes out of the shed, followed by Undershaft*]. I want Mamma.

UNDERSHAFT. She is taking off her list slippers, dear. [*He passes on to Cusins*]. Well? What does she say?

CUSINS. She has gone right up into the skies.

LADY BRITOMART [*coming from the shed and stopping on the steps, obstructing Sarah, who follows with Lomax. Barbara clutches like a baby at her mother's skirt*] Barbara: when will you learn to be independent and to act and think for yourself? I know as well as possible what that cry of "Mamma, Mamma," means. Always running to me!

SARAH [*touching Lady Britomart's ribs with her finger tips and imitating a bicycle horn*] Pip! pip!

LADY BRITOMART [*highly indignant*] How dare you say Pip! pip! to me, Sarah? You are both very naughty children. What do you want, Barbara?

445

BARBARA. I want a house in the village to live in with Dolly. [*Dragging at the skirt*] Come and tell me which one to take.

UNDERSHAFT [*to Cusins*] Six o'clock tomorrow morning, Euripides.

HEARTBREAK HOUSE

A FANTASIA IN THE RUSSIAN MANNER ON
ENGLISH THEMES

HEARTBREAK HOUSE AND HORSEBACK HALL

WHERE HEARTBREAK HOUSE STANDS

HEARTBREAK HOUSE is not merely the name of the play which follows this preface. It is cultured, leisured Europe before the war. When the play was begun not a shot had been fired; and only the professional diplomatists and the very few amateurs whose hobby is foreign policy even knew that the guns were loaded. A Russian playwright, Tchekov, had produced four fascinating dramatic studies of Heartbreak House, of which three, The Cherry Orchard, Uncle Vanya, and The Seagull, had been performed in England. Tolstoy, in his Fruits of Enlightenment, had shewn us through it in his most ferociously contemptuous manner. Tolstoy did not waste any sympathy on it: it was to him the house in which Europe was stifling its soul; and he knew that our utter enervation and futilization in that overheated drawing-room atmosphere was delivering the world over to the control of ignorant and soulless cunning and energy, with the frightful consequences which have now overtaken it. Tolstoy was no pessimist: he was not disposed to leave the house standing if he could bring it down about the ears of its pretty and amiable voluptuaries; and he wielded the pickaxe with a will. He treated the case of the inmates as one of opium poisoning, to be dealt with by seizing the patients roughly and exercising them violently until they were broad awake. Tchekov, more of a fatalist, had no faith in these charming people extricating themselves. They would, he thought, be sold up and sent adrift by the bailiffs; therefore he had no scruple in exploiting and even flattering their charm.

THE INHABITANTS

Tchekov's plays, being less lucrative than swings and roundabouts, got no further in England, where theatres are only ordinary commercial affairs, than a couple of performances by the Stage Society. We stared and said, "How Russian!" They did not strike me in that way. Just as Ibsen's intensely Norwegian plays exactly fitted every middle and

449

professional class suburb in Europe, these intensely Russian plays fitted all the country houses in Europe in which the pleasures of music, art, literature, and the theatre had supplanted hunting, shooting, fishing, flirting, eating, and drinking. The same nice people, the same utter futility. The nice people could read; some of them could write; and they were the only repositories of culture who had social opportunities of contact with our politicians, administrators, and newspaper proprietors, or any chance of sharing or influencing their activities. But they shrank from that contact. They hated politics. They did not wish to realize Utopia for the common people: they wished to realize their favorite fictions and poems in their own lives; and, when they could, they lived without scruple on incomes which they did nothing to earn. The women in their girlhood made themselves look like variety theatre stars, and settled down later into the types of beauty imagined by the previous generation of painters. They took the only part of our society in which there was leisure for high culture, and made it an economic, political, and, as far as practicable, a moral vacuum; and as Nature, abhorring the vacuum, immediately filled it up with sex and with all sorts of refined pleasures, it was a very delightful place at its best for moments of relaxation. In other moments it was disastrous. For prime ministers and their like, it was a veritable Capua.

HORSEBACK HALL

But where were our front benchers to nest if not here? The alternative to Heartbreak House was Horseback Hall, consisting of a prison for horses with an annex for the ladies and gentlemen who rode them, hunted them, talked about them, bought them and sold them, and gave nine-tenths of their lives to them, dividing the other tenth between charity, churchgoing (as a substitute for religion), and conservative electioneering (as a substitute for politics). It is true that the two establishments got mixed at the edges. Exiles from the library, the music room, and the picture gallery would be found languishing among the stables, miserably discontented; and hardy horsewomen who slept at the first chord of Schumann were born, horribly misplaced, into the garden of Klingsor; but sometimes one came upon horsebreakers and heartbreakers who could make the best of both worlds. As a rule, however, the two were apart and knew little of one another; so the prime minister folk had to choose between barbarism and Capua. And of the two atmospheres it is hard to say which was the more fatal to statesmanship.

REVOLUTION ON THE SHELF

Heartbreak House was quite familiar with revolutionary ideas on paper. It aimed at being advanced and free-thinking, and hardly ever went to church or kept the Sabbath except by a little extra fun at week-ends. When you spent a Friday to Tuesday in it you found on the shelf in your bedroom not only the books of poets and novelists, but of revolutionary biologists and even economists. Without at least a few plays by myself and Mr Granville Barker, and a few stories by Mr H. G. Wells, Mr Arnold Bennett, and Mr John Galsworthy, the house would have been out of the movement. You would find Blake among the poets, and beside him Bergson, Butler, Scott Haldane, the poems of Meredith and Thomas Hardy, and, generally speaking, all the literary implements for forming the mind of the perfect modern Socialist and Creative Evolutionist. It was a curious experience to spend Sunday in dipping into these books, and on Monday morning to read in the daily paper that the country had just been brought to the verge of anarchy because a new Home Secretary or chief of police, without an idea in his head that his great-grandmother might not have had to apologize for, had refused to "recognize" some powerful Trade Union, just as a gondola might refuse to recognize a 20,000-ton liner.

In short, power and culture were in separate compartments. The barbarians were not only literally in the saddle, but on the front bench in the House of Commons, with nobody to correct their incredible ignorance of modern thought and political science but upstarts from the counting-house, who had spent their lives furnishing their pockets instead of their minds. Both, however, were practised in dealing with money and with men, as far as acquiring the one and exploiting the other went; and although this is as undesirable an expertness as that of the medieval robber baron, it qualifies men to keep an estate or a business going in its old routine without necessarily understanding it, just as Bond Street tradesmen and domestic servants keep fashionable society going without any instruction in sociology.

THE CHERRY ORCHARD

The Heartbreak people neither could nor would do anything of the sort. With their heads as full of the Anticipations of Mr H. G. Wells as the heads of our actual rulers were empty even of the anticipations of Erasmus or Sir Thomas More, they refused the drudgery of politics, and would have made a very poor job of it if they had changed their minds. Not that they would have been allowed to meddle anyhow, as only through the accident of being a hereditary peer can anyone in these days of Votes for Everybody get into parliament if handicapped by a serious modern cultural equipment; but if they had, their habit of living in a vacuum would have left them helpless and ineffective in public affairs. Even in private life they were often helpless wasters of their inheritance, like the people in Tchekov's Cherry Orchard. Even those who lived within their incomes were really kept going by their solicitors and agents, being unable to manage an estate or run a business without continual prompting from those who have to learn how to do such things or starve.

From what is called Democracy no corrective to this state of things could be hoped. It is said that every people has the Government it deserves. It is more to the point that every Government has the electorate it deserves; for the orators of the front bench can edify or debauch an ignorant electorate at will. Thus our democracy moves in a vicious circle of reciprocal worthiness and unworthiness.

HEARTBREAK HOUSE
NATURE'S LONG CREDITS

Nature's way of dealing with unhealthy conditions is unfortunately not one that compels us to conduct a solvent hygiene on a cash basis. She demoralizes us with long credits and reckless overdrafts, and then pulls us up cruelly with catastrophic bankruptcies. Take, for example, common domestic sanitation. A whole city generation may neglect it utterly and scandalously, if not with absolute impunity, yet without any evil consequences that anyone thinks of tracing to it. In a hospital two generations of medical students may tolerate dirt and carelessness, and then go out into general practice to spread the doctrine that fresh air is a fad, and sanitation an imposture set up to make profits for plumbers. Then suddenly Nature takes her revenge. She strikes at the city with a pestilence and at the hospital with an epidemic of hospital gangrene, slaughtering right and left until the innocent young have paid for the guilty old, and the account is balanced. And then she goes to sleep again and gives another period of credit, with the same result.

This is what has just happened in our political hygiene. Political science has been as recklessly neglected by Governments and electorates during my lifetime as sanitary science was in the days of Charles the Second. In international relations diplomacy has been a boyishly lawless affair of family intrigues, commercial and territorial brigandage, torpors of pseudo-goodnature produced by laziness, and spasms of ferocious activity produced by terror. But in these islands we muddled through. Nature gave us a longer credit than she gave to France or Germany or Russia. To British centenarians who died in their beds in 1914, any dread of having to hide underground in London from the shells of an enemy seemed more remote and fantastic than a dread of the appearance of a colony of cobras and rattlesnakes in Kensington Gardens. In the prophetic works of Charles Dickens we were warned against many evils which have since come to pass; but of the evil of being slaughtered by a foreign foe on our own door-steps there was no shadow. Nature gave us a very long credit; and we abused it to the utmost. But when she struck at last she struck with a vengeance. For four years she smote our firstborn and heaped on us plagues of which Egypt never dreamed. They were all as preventible as the great Plague of London, and came solely because they had not been prevented. They were not undone by winning the war. The earth is still bursting with the dead bodies of the victors.

THE WICKED HALF CENTURY

It is difficult to say whether indifference and neglect are worse than false doctrine; but Heartbreak House and Horseback Hall unfortunately suffered from both. For half a century before the war civilization had been going to the devil very precipitately under the influence of a pseudo-science as disastrous as the blackest Calvinism. Calvinism taught that as we are predestinately saved or damned, nothing that we do can alter our destiny. Still, as Calvinism gave the individual no clue as to whether he had drawn a lucky number or an unlucky one, it left him a fairly strong interest in encouraging his hopes of salvation and allaying his fear of damnation by behaving as one of the elect might be expected to behave rather than as one of the reprobate. But in the middle of the XIX century naturalists and physicists assured the world, in the name of Science, that salvation and damnation are all nonsense, and that pre-destination is the central truth of religion, inasmuch as human beings are produced by their environment, their sins and good deeds being only a series of chemical and mechanical reactions over which they have no control. Such figments as mind, choice, purpose, conscience, will, and so forth, are, they taught, mere illusions, produced because they are useful in the continual struggle of the human machine to maintain its environment in a favorable condition, a process incidentally involving the ruthless destruction or subjection of its competitors for the supply (assumed to be

454

limited) of subsistence available. We taught Prussia this religion; and Prussia bettered our instruction so effectively that we presently found ourselves confronted with the necessity of destroying Prussia to prevent Prussia destroying us. And that has just ended in each destroying the other to an extent doubtfully reparable in our time.

It may be asked how so imbecile and dangerous a creed ever came to be accepted by intelligent beings. I will answer that question more fully in my next volume of plays, which will be entirely devoted to the subject. For the present I will only say that there were better reasons than the obvious one that such sham science as this opened a scientific career to very stupid men, and all the other careers to shameless rascals, provided they were industrious enough. It is true that this motive operated very powerfully; but when the new departure in scientific doctrine which is associated with the name of the great naturalist Charles Darwin began, it was not only a reaction against a barbarous pseudo-evangelical teleology intolerably obstructive to all scientific progress, but was accompanied, as it happened, by discoveries of extraordinary interest in physics, chemistry, and that lifeless method of evolution which its investigators called Natural Selection. Howbeit, there was only one result possible in the ethical sphere, and that was the banishment of conscience from human affairs, or, as Samuel Butler vehemently put it, "of mind from the universe."

HYPOCHONDRIA

Now Heartbreak House, with Butler and Bergson and Scott Haldane alongside Blake and the other major poets on its shelves (to say nothing of Wagner and the tone poets), was not so completely blinded by the doltish materialism of the laboratories as the uncultured world outside. But being an idle house it was a hypochondriacal house, always running after cures. It would stop eating meat, not on valid Shelleyan grounds, but in order to get rid of a bogey called Uric Acid; and it would actually let you pull all its teeth out to exorcise another demon named Pyorrhea. It was superstitious, and addicted to table-rapping, materialization séances, clairvoyance, palmistry, crystal-gazing and the like to such an extent that it may be doubted whether ever before in the history of the world did soothsayers, astrologers, and unregistered therapeutic specialists of all sorts flourish as they did during this half century of the drift to the abyss. The registered doctors and surgeons were hard put to it to compete with the unregistered. They were not clever enough to appeal to the imagination and sociability of the Heartbreakers by the arts of the actor, the orator, the poet, the winning conversationalist. They had to fall back coarsely on the terror of infection and death. They prescribed inoculations and operations. Whatever part of a human being could be cut out without necessarily killing him they cut out; and he often died (unnecessarily of course) in consequence. From such trifles as uvulas and tonsils they went on to ovaries and appendices until at last no one's inside was safe. They explained that the human intestine was too long, and that nothing could make a child of Adam healthy except short circuiting the pylorus by cutting a length out of the lower intestine and fastening it directly to the stomach. As their mechanist theory taught them that medicine was the business of the chemist's laboratory, and surgery of the carpenter's shop, and also that Science (by which they meant their practices) was so important that no consideration for the interests of any individual creature, whether frog or philosopher, much less the vulgar commonplaces of sentimental ethics, could weigh for a moment against the remotest off-chance of an addition to the body of scientific knowledge, they operated and vivisected and inoculated and lied on a stupendous scale, clamoring for and actually acquiring such legal powers over the bodies of their fellow-citizens as neither king, pope, nor parliament dare ever have claimed. The Inquisition itself was a Liberal institution compared to the General Medical Council.

456

HEARTBREAK HOUSE
THOSE WHO DO NOT KNOW HOW TO LIVE MUST MAKE A MERIT OF DYING

Heartbreak House was far too lazy and shallow to extricate itself from this palace of evil enchantment. It rhapsodized about love; but it believed in cruelty. It was afraid of the cruel people; and it saw that cruelty was at least effective. Cruelty did things that made money, whereas Love did nothing but prove the soundness of Larochefoucauld's saying that very few people would fall in love if they had never read about it. Heartbreak House, in short, did not know how to live, at which point all that was left to it was the boast that at least it knew how to die: a melancholy accomplishment which the outbreak of war presently gave it practically unlimited opportunities of displaying. Thus were the firstborn of Heartbreak House smitten; and the young, the innocent, the hopeful expiated the folly and worthlessness of their elders.

WAR DELIRIUM

Only those who have lived through a first-rate war, not in the field, but at home, and kept their heads, can possibly understand the bitterness of Shakespear and Swift, who both went through this experience. The horror of Peer Gynt in the madhouse, when the lunatics, exalted by illusions of splendid talent and visions of a dawning millennium, crowned him as their emperor, was tame in comparison. I do not know whether anyone really kept his head completely except those who had to keep it because they had to conduct the war at first hand. I should not have kept my own (as far as I did keep it) if I had not at once understood that as a scribe and speaker I too was under the most serious public obligation to keep my grip on realities; but this did not save me from a considerable degree of hyperaesthesia. There were of course some happy people to whom the war meant nothing: all political and general matters lying outside their little circle of interest. But the ordinary war-conscious civilian went mad, the main symptom being a conviction that the whole order of nature had been reversed. All foods, he felt, must now be adulterated. All schools must be closed. No advertisements must be sent to the newspapers, of which new editions must appear and be bought up every ten minutes. Travelling must be stopped, or, that being impossible, greatly hindered. All pretences about fine art and culture and the like must be flung off as an intolerable affectation; and the picture galleries and museums and schools at once occupied by war workers. The British Museum itself was saved only by a hairsbreadth. The sincerity of all this, and of much more which would not be believed if I chronicled it, may be established by one conclusive instance of the general craziness. Men were seized with the illusion that they could win the war by giving away money. And they not only subscribed millions to Funds of all sorts with no discoverable object, and to ridiculous voluntary organizations for doing what was plainly the business of the civil and military authorities, but actually handed out money to any thief in the street who had the presence of mind to pretend that he (or she) was "collecting" it for the annihilation of the enemy. Swindlers were emboldened to take offices; label themselves Anti-Enemy Leagues; and simply pocket the money that was heaped on them. Attractively dressed young women found that they had nothing to do but parade the streets, collecting box in hand, and live gloriously on the profits. Many months elapsed before, as a first sign of returning sanity, the police swept an Anti-Enemy secretary into prison *pour encourager les autres*, and the passionate penny collecting of the Flag Days was brought under some sort of regulation.

MADNESS IN COURT

The demoralization did not spare the Law Courts. Soldiers were acquitted, even on fully proved indictments for wilful murder, until at last the judges and magistrates had to announce that what was called the Unwritten Law, which meant simply that a soldier could do what he liked with impunity in civil life, was not the law of the land, and that

458

a Victoria Cross did not carry with it a perpetual plenary indulgence. Unfortunately the insanity of the juries and magistrates did not always manifest itself in indulgence. No person unlucky enough to be charged with any sort of conduct, however reasonable and salutary, that did not smack of war delirium had the slightest chance of acquittal. There were in the country, too, a certain number of people who had conscientious objections to war as criminal or unchristian. The Act of Parliament introducing Compulsory Military Service thoughtlessly exempted these persons, merely requiring them to prove the genuineness of their convictions. Those who did so were very ill-advised from the point of view of their own personal interest; for they were persecuted with savage logicality in spite of the law; whilst those who made no pretence of having any objection to war at all, and had not only had military training in Officers' Training Corps, but had proclaimed on public occasions that they were perfectly ready to engage in civil war on behalf of their political opinions, were allowed the benefit of the Act on the ground that they did not approve of this particular war. For the Christians there was no mercy. In cases where the evidence as to their being killed by ill treatment was so unequivocal that the verdict would certainly have been one of wilful murder had the prejudice of the coroner's jury been on the other side, their tormentors were gratuitously declared to be blameless. There was only one virtue, pugnacity: only one vice, pacifism. That is an essential condition of war; but the Government had not the courage to legislate accordingly; and its law was set aside for Lynch law.

The climax of legal lawlessness was reached in France. The greatest Socialist statesman in Europe, Jaurès, was shot and killed by a gentleman who resented his efforts to avert the war. M. Clemenceau was shot by another gentleman of less popular opinions, and happily came off no worse than having to spend a precautionary couple of days in bed. The slayer of Jaurès was recklessly acquitted: the would-be slayer of M. Clemenceau was carefully found guilty. There is no reason to doubt that the same thing would have happened in England if the war had begun with a successful attempt to assassinate Keir Hardie, and ended with an unsuccessful one to assassinate Mr Lloyd George.

THE LONG ARM OF WAR

The pestilence which is the usual accompaniment of war was called influenza. Whether it was really a war pestilence or not was made doubtful by the fact that it did its worst in places remote from the battle-fields, notably on the west coast of North America and in India. But the moral pestilence, which was unquestionably a war pestilence, reproduced this phenomenon. One would have supposed that the war fever would have raged most furiously in the countries actually under fire, and that the others would be more reasonable. Belgium and Flanders, where over large districts literally not one stone was left upon another as the opposed armies drove each other back and forward over it after terrific preliminary bombardments, might have been pardoned for relieving their feelings more emphatically than by shrugging their shoulders and saying "C'est la guerre." England, inviolate for so many centuries that the swoop of war on her homesteads had long ceased to be more credible than a return of the Flood, could hardly be expected to keep her temper sweet when she knew at last what it was to hide in cellars and underground railway stations, or lie quaking in bed, whilst bombs crashed, houses crumbled, and aircraft guns distributed shrapnel on friend and foe alike until certain shop windows in London, formerly full of fashionable hats, were filled with steel helmets. Slain and mutilated women and children, and burnt and wrecked dwellings, excuse a good deal of violent language, and produce a wrath on which many suns go down before it is appeased. Yet it was in the United States of America, where nobody slept the worse for the war, that the war fever went beyond all sense and reason. In European Courts

460

there was vindictive illegality: in American Courts there
was raving lunacy. It is not for me to chronicle the extrava-
gances of an Ally: let some candid American do that. I can
only say that to us sitting in our gardens in England, with
the guns in France making themselves felt by a throb in the
air as unmistakeable as an audible sound, or with tightening hearts studying the phases of the moon in London in
their bearing on the chances whether our houses would be
standing or ourselves alive next morning, the newspaper
accounts of the sentences American Courts were passing on
young girls and old men alike for the expression of opinions which were being uttered amid thundering applause
before huge audiences in England, and the more private
records of the methods by which the American War Loans
were raised, were so amazing that they put the guns and the
possibilities of a raid clean out of our heads for the moment.

THE RABID WATCHDOGS OF LIBERTY

Not content with these rancorous abuses of the existing
law, the war maniacs made a frantic rush to abolish all con-
stitutional guarantees of liberty and well-being. The ordinary law was superseded by Acts under which newspapers were seized and their printing machinery destroyed by
simple police raids *à la Russe*, and persons arrested and shot
without any pretence of trial by jury or publicity of procedure or evidence. Though it was urgently necessary that
production should be increased by the most scientific organization and economy of labor, and though no fact was
better established than that excessive duration and intensity
of toil reduces production heavily instead of increasing it,
the factory laws were suspended, and men and women
recklessly overworked until the loss of their efficiency became too glaring to be ignored. Remonstrances and warnings were met either with an accusation of pro-Germanism
or the formula, "Remember that we are at war now." I
have said that men assumed that war had reversed the order of nature, and that all was lost unless we did the exact
opposite of everything we had found necessary and bene-

461

ficial in peace. But the truth was worse than that. The war did not change men's minds in any such impossible way. What really happened was that the impact of physical death and destruction, the one reality that every fool can understand, tore off the masks of education, art, science, and religion from our ignorance and barbarism, and left us glorying grotesquely in the licence suddenly accorded to our vilest passions and most abject terrors. Ever since Thucydides wrote his history, it has been on record that when the angel of death sounds his trumpet the pretences of civilization are blown from men's heads into the mud like hats in a gust of wind. But when this scripture was fulfilled among us, the shock was not the less appalling because a few students of Greek history were not surprised by it. Indeed these students threw themselves into the orgy as shamelessly as the illiterate. The Christian priest joining in the war dance without even throwing off his cassock first, and the respectable school governor expelling the German professor with insult and bodily violence, and declaring that no English child should ever again be taught the language of Luther and Goethe, were kept in countenance by the most impudent repudiations of every decency of civilization and every lesson of political experience on the part of the very persons who, as university professors, historians, philosophers, and men of science, were the accredited custodians of culture. It was crudely natural, and perhaps necessary for recruiting purposes, that German militarism and German dynastic ambition should be painted by journalists and recruiters in black and red as European dangers (as in fact they are), leaving it to be inferred that our own militarism and our own political constitution are millennially democratic (which they certainly are not); but when it came to frantic denunciations of German chemistry, German biology, German poetry, German music, German literature, German philosophy, and even German engineering, as malignant abominations standing towards British and French chemistry and so forth in the relation of heaven to hell, it was clear that the utterers of such barbarous ravings had never really understood or cared for the arts and sciences they professed and were profaning, and were only the appallingly degenerate descendants of the men of the seventeenth and eighteenth centuries who, recognizing no national frontiers in the great realm of the human mind, kept the European comity of that realm loftily and even ostentatiously above the rancors of the battle-field. Tearing the Garter from the Kaiser's leg, striking the German dukes from the roll of our peerage, changing the King's illustrious and historically appropriate surname for that of a traditionless locality, was not a very dignified business; but the erasure of German names from the British rolls of science and learning was a confession that in England the little respect paid to science and learning is only an affectation which hides a savage contempt for both. One felt that the figure of St George and the Dragon on our coinage should be replaced by that of the soldier driving his spear through Archimedes. But by that time there was no coinage: only paper money in which ten shillings called itself a pound as confidently as the people who were disgracing their country called themselves patriots.

THE SUFFERINGS OF THE SANE

The mental distress of living amid the obscene din of all these carmagnoles and corobberies was not the only burden that lay on sane people during the war. There was also the emotional strain, complicated by the offended economic sense, produced by the casualty lists. The stupid, the selfish, the narrow-minded, the callous and unimaginative were spared a great deal. "Blood and destruction shall be so in use that mothers shall but smile when they behold their infants quartered by the hands of war," was a Shakespearean prophecy that very nearly came true; for when nearly every house had a slaughtered son to mourn, we should all have gone quite out of our senses if we had taken our own and our friends' bereavements at their peace value. It became necessary to give them a false value; to proclaim the young life worthily and gloriously sacrificed to redeem the liberty of mankind, instead of to expiate the heedlessness and folly of their fathers, and expiate it in vain. We had even to assume that the parents and not the children had made the sacrifice, until at last the comic papers were driven to satirize fat old men, sitting comfortably in club chairs, and boasting of the sons they had "given" to their country.

No one grudged these anodynes to acute personal grief; but they only embittered those who knew that the young men were having their teeth set on edge because their parents had eaten sour political grapes. Then think of the young men themselves! Many of them had no illusions about the policy that led to the war: they went clear-sighted to a horribly repugnant duty. Men essentially gentle and essentially wise, with really valuable work in hand, laid it down voluntarily and spent months forming fours in the barrack yard, and stabbing sacks of straw in the public eye, so that they might go out to kill and maim men as gentle as themselves. These men, who were perhaps, as a class, our most efficient soldiers (Frederick Keeling, for example), were not duped for a moment by the hypocritical melodrama that consoled and stimulated the others. They left their creative work to drudge at destruction, exactly as they would have left it to take their turn at the pumps in a sinking ship. They did not, like some of the conscientious objectors, hold back because the ship had been neglected by its officers and scuttled by its wreckers. The ship had to be saved, even if Newton had to leave his fluxions and Michael Angelo his marbles to save it; so they threw away the tools of their beneficent and ennobling trades, and took up the bloodstained bayonet and the murderous bomb, forcing themselves to pervert their divine instinct for perfect artistic execution to the effective handling of these diabolical things, and their economic faculty for organization to the contriving of ruin and slaughter. For it gave an ironic edge to their tragedy that the very talents they were forced to prostitute made the prostitution not only effective, but even

464

interesting; so that some of them were rapidly promoted, and found themselves actually becoming artists in war, with a growing relish for it, like Napoleon and all the other scourges of mankind, in spite of themselves. For many of them there was not even this consolation. They "stuck it," and hated it, to the end.

EVIL IN THE THRONE OF GOOD

This distress of the gentle was so acute that those who shared it in civil life, without having to shed blood with their own hands, or witness destruction with their own eyes, hardly care to obtrude their own woes. Nevertheless, even when sitting at home in safety, it was not easy for those who had to write and speak about the war to throw away their highest conscience, and deliberately work to a standard of inevitable evil instead of to the ideal of life more abundant. I can answer for at least one person who found the change from the wisdom of Jesus and St Francis to the morals of Richard III and the madness of Don Quixote extremely irksome. But that change had to be made; and we are all the worse for it, except those for whom it was not really a change at all, but only a relief from hypocrisy.

Think, too, of those who, though they had neither to write nor to fight, and had no children of their own to lose, yet knew the inestimable loss to the world of four years of the life of a generation wasted on destruction. Hardly one of the epoch-making works of the human mind might not have been aborted or destroyed by taking their authors away from their natural work for four critical years. Not only were Shakespears and Platos being killed outright; but many of the best harvests of the survivors had to be sown in the barren soil of the trenches. And this was no mere British consideration. To the truly civilized man, to the good European, the slaughter of the German youth was as disastrous as the slaughter of the English. Fools exulted in "German losses." They were our losses as well. Imagine exulting in the death of Beethoven because Bill Sikes dealt him his death blow!

HEARTBREAK HOUSE
STRAINING AT THE GNAT AND SWAL-
LOWING THE CAMEL

But most people could not comprehend these sorrows. There was a frivolous exultation in death for its own sake, which was at bottom an inability to realize that the deaths were real deaths and not stage ones. Again and again, when an air raider dropped a bomb which tore a child and its mother limb from limb, the people who saw it, though they had been reading with great cheerfulness of thousands of such happenings day after day in their newspapers, suddenly burst into furious imprecations on "the Huns" as murderers, and shrieked for savage and satisfying vengeance. At such moments it became clear that the deaths they had not seen meant no more to them than the mimic deaths of the cinema screen. Sometimes it was not necessary that death should be actually witnessed: it had only to take place under circumstances of sufficient novelty and proximity to bring it home almost as sensationally and effectively as if it had been actually visible.

For example, in the spring of 1915 there was an appalling slaughter of our young soldiers at Neuve Chapelle and at the Gallipoli landing. I will not go so far as to say that our civilians were delighted to have such exciting news to read at breakfast. But I cannot pretend that I noticed either in the papers, or in general intercourse, any feeling beyond the usual one that the cinema show at the front was going splendidly, and that our boys were the bravest of the brave. Suddenly there came the news that an Atlantic liner, the Lusitania, had been torpedoed, and that several well-known first class passengers, including a famous theatrical manager and the author of a popular farce, had been drowned, among others. The others included Sir Hugh Lane; but as he had only laid the country under great obligations in the sphere of the fine arts, no great stress was laid on that loss.

Immediately an amazing frenzy swept through the country. Men who up to that time had kept their heads

466

now lost them utterly. "Killing saloon passengers! What next?" was the essence of the whole agitation; but it is far too trivial a phrase to convey the faintest notion of the rage which possessed us. To me, with my mind full of the hideous cost of Neuve Chapelle, Ypres, and the Gallipoli landing, the fuss about the Lusitania seemed almost a heartless impertinence, though I was well acquainted personally with the three best-known victims, and understood, better perhaps than most people, the misfortune of the death of Lane. I even found a grim satisfaction, very intelligible to all soldiers, in the fact that the civilians who found the war such splendid British sport should get a sharp taste of what it was to the actual combatants. I expressed my impatience very freely, and found that my very straightforward and natural feeling in the matter was received as a monstrous and heartless paradox. When I asked those who gaped at me whether they had anything to say about the holocaust of Festubert, they gaped wider than before, having totally forgotten it, or rather, having never realized it. They were not heartless any more than I was; but the big catastrophe was too big for them to grasp, and the little one had been just the right size for them. I was not surprised. Have I not seen a public body for just the same reason pass a vote for £30,000 without a word, and then spend three special meetings, prolonged into the night, over an item of seven shillings for refreshments?

LITTLE MINDS AND BIG BATTLES

Nobody will be able to understand the vagaries of public feeling during the war unless they bear constantly in mind that the war in its entire magnitude did not exist for the average civilian. He could not conceive even a battle, much less a campaign. To the suburbs the war was nothing but a suburban squabble. To the miner and navvy it was only a series of bayonet fights between German champions and English ones. The enormity of it was quite beyond most of us. Its episodes had to be reduced to the dimensions of a railway accident or a shipwreck before it could produce any

467

effect on our minds at all. To us the ridiculous bombardments of Scarborough and Ramsgate were colossal tragedies, and the battle of Jutland a mere ballad. The words
"after thorough artillery preparation" in the news from the
front meant nothing to us; but when our seaside trippers
learned that an elderly gentleman at breakfast in a week-
end marine hotel had been interrupted by a bomb dropping into his egg-cup, their wrath and horror knew no
bounds. They declared that this would put a new spirit into
the army, and had no suspicion that the soldiers in the
trenches roared with laughter over it for days, and told
each other that it would do the blighters at home good to
have a taste of what the army was up against. Sometimes
the smallness of view was pathetic. A man would work at
home regardless of the call "to make the world safe for
democracy." His brother would be killed at the front. Immediately he would throw up his work and take up the war
as a family blood feud against the Germans. Sometimes it
was comic. A wounded man, entitled to his discharge, would
return to the trenches with a grim determination to find
the Hun who had wounded him and pay him out for it.

It is impossible to estimate what proportion of us, in
khaki or out of it, grasped the war and its political antecedents as a whole in the light of any philosophy of history or
knowledge of what war is. I doubt whether it was as high
as our proportion of higher mathematicians. But there can
be no doubt that it was prodigiously outnumbered by the
comparatively ignorant and childish. Remember that these
people had to be stimulated to make the sacrifices demanded
by the war, and that this could not be done by appeals to a
knowledge which they did not possess, and a comprehension
of which they were incapable. When the armistice at last
set me free to tell the truth about the war at the following
general election, a soldier said to a candidate whom I was
supporting "If I had known all that in 1914, they would
never have got me into khaki." And that, of course, was
precisely why it had been necessary to stuff him with a ro-

mance that any diplomatist would have laughed at. Thus
the natural confusion of ignorance was increased by a deliberately propagated confusion of nursery bogey stories
and melodramatic nonsense, which at last overreached itself and made it impossible to stop the war before we had
not only achieved the triumph of vanquishing the German
army and thereby overthrowing its militarist monarchy,
but made the very serious mistake of ruining the centre of
Europe, a thing that no sane European State could afford
to do.

THE DUMB CAPABLES AND THE NOISY INCAPABLES

Confronted with this picture of insensate delusion and
folly, the critical reader will immediately counterplead
that England all this time was conducting a war which involved the organization of several millions of fighting men
and of the workers who were supplying them with provisions, munitions, and transport, and that this could not
have been done by a mob of hysterical ranters. This is fortunately true. To pass from the newspaper offices and political platforms and club fenders and suburban drawing-
rooms to the Army and the munition factories was to pass
from Bedlam to the busiest and sanest of workaday worlds.
It was to rediscover England, and find solid ground for
the faith of those who still believed in her. But a necessary
condition of this efficiency was that those who were efficient
should give all their time to their business and leave the
rabble raving to its hearts' content. Indeed the raving was
useful to the efficient, because, as it was always wide of the
mark, it often distracted attention very conveniently from
operations that would have been defeated or hindered by
publicity. A precept which I endeavored vainly to popularize early in the war, "If you have anything to do go and
do it: if not, for heaven's sake get out of the way," was
only half carried out. Certainly the capable people went
and did it; but the incapables would by no means get out
of the way: they fussed and bawled and were only pre-

469

vented from getting very seriously into the way by the blessed fact that they never knew where the way was. Thus whilst all the efficiency of England was silent and invisible, all its imbecility was deafening the heavens with its clamor and blotting out the sun with its dust. It was also unfortunately intimidating the Government by its blusterings into using the irresistible powers of the State to intimidate the sensible people, thus enabling a despicable minority of would-be lynchers to set up a reign of terror which could at any time have been broken by a single stern word from a responsible minister. But our ministers had not that sort of courage: neither Heartbreak House nor Horseback Hall had bred it, much less the suburbs. When matters at last came to the looting of shops by criminals under patriotic pretexts, it was the police force and not the Government that put its foot down. There was even one deplorable moment, during the submarine scare, in which the Government yielded to a childish cry for the maltreatment of naval prisoners of war, and, to our great disgrace, was forced by the enemy to behave itself. And yet behind all this public blundering and misconduct and futile mischief, the effective England was carrying on with the most formidable capacity and activity. The ostensible England was making the empire sick with its incontinences, its ignorances, its ferocities, its panics, and its endless and intolerable blarings of Allied national anthems in season and out. The esoteric England was proceeding irresistibly to the conquest of Europe.

THE PRACTICAL BUSINESS MEN

From the beginning the useless people set up a shriek for "practical business men." By this they meant men who had become rich by placing their personal interests before those of the country, and measuring the success of every activity by the pecuniary profit it brought to them and to those on whom they depended for their supplies of capital. The pitiable failure of some conspicuous samples from the first batch we tried of these poor devils helped to give the whole public side of the war an air of monstrous and hope-

470

less farce. They proved not only that they were useless for public work, but that in a well-ordered nation they would never have been allowed to control private enterprise.

HOW THE FOOLS SHOUTED THE WISE MEN DOWN

Thus, like a fertile country flooded with mud, England shewed no sign of her greatness in the days when she was putting forth all her strength to save herself from the worst consequences of her littleness. Most of the men of action, occupied to the last hour of their time with urgent practical work, had to leave to idler people, or to professional rhetoricians, the presentation of the war to the reason and imagination of the country and the world in speeches, poems, manifestoes, picture posters, and newspaper articles. I have had the privilege of hearing some of our ablest commanders talking about their work; and I have shared the common lot of reading the accounts of that work given to the world by the newspapers. No two experiences could be more different. But in the end the talkers obtained a dangerous ascendancy over the rank and file of the men of action; for though the great men of action are always inveterate talkers and often very clever writers, and therefore cannot have their minds formed for them by others, the average man of action, like the average fighter with the bayonet, can give no account of himself in words even to himself, and is apt to pick up and accept what he reads about himself and other people in the papers, except when the writer is rash enough to commit himself on technical points. It was not uncommon during the war to hear a soldier, or a civilian engaged on war work, describing events within his own experience that reduced to utter absurdity the ravings and maunderings of his daily paper, and yet echo the opinions of that paper like a parrot. Thus, to escape from the prevailing confusion and folly, it was not enough to seek the company of the ordinary man of action: one had to get into contact with the master spirits. This was a privilege which only a handful of people could enjoy.

471

For the unprivileged citizen there was no escape. To him the whole country seemed mad, futile, silly, incompetent, with no hope of victory except the hope that the enemy might be just as mad. Only by very resolute reflection and reasoning could he reassure himself that if there was nothing more solid beneath these appalling appearances the war could not possibly have gone on for a single day without a total breakdown of its organization.

THE MAD ELECTION

Happy were the fools and the thoughtless men of action in those days. The worst of it was that the fools were very strongly represented in parliament, as fools not only elect fools, but can persuade men of action to elect them too. The election that immediately followed the armistice was perhaps the maddest that has ever taken place. Soldiers who had done voluntary and heroic service in the field were defeated by persons who had apparently never run a risk or spent a farthing that they could avoid, and who even had in the course of the election to apologize publicly for bawling Pacifist or Pro-German at their opponent. Party leaders seek such followers, who can always be depended on to walk tamely into the lobby at the party whip's orders, provided the leader will make their seats safe for them by the process which was called, in derisive reference to the war rationing system, "giving them the coupon." Other incidents were so grotesque that I cannot mention them without enabling the reader to identify the parties, which would not be fair, as they were no more to blame than thousands of others who must necessarily be nameless. The general result was patently absurd; and the electorate, disgusted at its own work, instantly recoiled to the opposite extreme, and cast out all the coupon candidates at the earliest bye-elections by equally silly majorities. But the mischief of the general election could not be undone; and the Government had not only to pretend to abuse its European victory as it had promised, but actually to do it by starving the enemies who had thrown down their arms. It

472

had, in short, won the election by pledging itself to be thriftlessly wicked, cruel, and vindictive; and it did not find it as easy to escape from this pledge as it had from nobler ones. The end, as I write, is not yet; but it is clear that this thoughtless savagery will recoil on the heads of the Allies so severely that we shall be forced by the sternest necessity to take up our share of healing the Europe we have wounded almost to death instead of attempting to complete her destruction.

YAHOO AND THE ANGRY APE

Contemplating this picture of a state of mankind so recent that no denial of its truth is possible, one understands Shakespear comparing Man to an angry ape, Swift describing him as a Yahoo rebuked by the superior virtue of the horse, and Wellington declaring that the British can behave themselves neither in victory nor defeat. Yet none of the three had seen war as we have seen it. Shakespear blamed great men, saying that "Could great men thunder as Jove himself does Jove would ne'er be quiet; for every pelting petty officer would use his heaven for thunder: nothing but thunder." What would Shakespear have said if he had seen something far more destructive than thunder in the hand of every village laborer, and found on the Messines Ridge the craters of the nineteen volcanoes that were let loose there at the touch of a finger that might have been a child's finger without the result being a whit less ruinous? Shakespear may have seen a Stratford cottage struck by one of Jove's thunderbolts, and have helped to extinguish the lighted thatch and clear away the bits of the broken chimney. What would he have said if he had seen Ypres as it is now, or returned to Stratford, as French peasants are returning to their homes today, to find the old familiar signpost inscribed "To Stratford, 1 mile," and at the end of the mile nothing but some holes in the ground and a fragment of a broken churn here and there? Would not the spectacle of the angry ape endowed with powers of destruction that Jove never pretended to, have beggared even his

473

command of words?

And yet, what is there to say except that war puts a strain on human nature that breaks down the better half of it, and makes the worse half a diabolical virtue? Better for us if it broke it down altogether; for then the warlike way out of our difficulties would be barred to us, and we should take greater care not to get into them. In truth, it is, as Byron said, "not difficult to die," and enormously difficult to live: that explains why, at bottom, peace is not only better than war, but infinitely more arduous. Did any hero of the war face the glorious risk of death more bravely than the traitor Bolo faced the ignominious certainty of it? Bolo taught us all how to die: can we say that he taught us all how to live? Hardly a week passes now without some soldier who braved death in the field so recklessly that he was decorated or specially commended for it, being haled before our magistrates for having failed to resist the paltriest temptations of peace, with no better excuse than the old one that "a man must live." Strange that one who, sooner than do honest work, will sell his honor for a bottle of wine, a visit to the theatre, and an hour with a strange woman, all obtained by passing a worthless cheque, could yet stake his life on the most desperate chances of the battle-field! Does it not seem as if, after all, the glory of death were cheaper than the glory of life? If it is not easier to attain, why do so many more men attain it? At all events it is clear that the kingdom of the Prince of Peace has not yet become the kingdom of this world. His attempts at invasion have been resisted far more fiercely than the Kaiser's. Successful as that resistance has been, it has piled up a sort of National Debt that is not the less oppressive because we have no figures for it and do not intend to pay it. A blockade that cuts off "the grace of our Lord" is in the long run less bearable than the blockades which merely cut off raw materials; and against that blockade our Armada is impotent. In the blockader's house, he has assured us, there are many

mansions; but I am afraid they do not include either Heartbreak House or Horseback Hall.

PLAGUE ON BOTH YOUR HOUSES!

Meanwhile the Bolshevist picks and petards are at work
on the foundations of both buildings; and though the Bol-
shevists may be buried in the ruins, their deaths will not
save the edifices. Unfortunately they can be built again.
Like Doubting Castle, they have been demolished many
times by successive Greathearts, and rebuilt by Simple,
Sloth, and Presumption, by Feeble Mind and Much Afraid,
and by all the jurymen of Vanity Fair. Another generation
of "secondary education" at our ancient public schools and
the cheaper institutions that ape them will be quite sufficient
to keep the two going until the next war.

For the instruction of that generation I leave these pages
as a record of what civilian life was during the war: a matter
on which history is usually silent. Fortunately it was a very
short war. It is true that the people who thought it could
not last more than six months were very signally refuted
by the event. As Sir Douglas Haig has pointed out, its
Waterloos lasted months instead of hours. But there would
have been nothing surprising in its lasting thirty years. If
it had not been for the fact that the blockade achieved the
amazing feat of starving out Europe, which it could not
possibly have done had Europe been properly organized
for war, or even for peace, the war would have lasted until
the belligerents were so tired of it that they could no longer
be compelled to compel themselves to go on with it. Considering its magnitude, the war of 1914–18 will certainly
be classed as the shortest in history. The end came so suddenly that the combatants literally stumbled over it; and
yet it came a full year later than it should have come if
the belligerents had not been far too afraid of one another
to face the situation sensibly. Germany, having failed to
provide for the war she began, failed again to surrender
before she was dangerously exhausted. Her opponents,

475

equally improvident, went as much too close to bankruptcy as Germany to starvation. It was a bluff at which both were bluffed. And, with the usual irony of war, it remains doubtful whether Germany and Russia, the defeated, will not be the gainers; for the victors are already busy fastening on themselves the chains they have struck from the limbs of the vanquished.

HOW THE THEATRE FARED

Let us now contract our view rather violently from the European theatre of war to the theatre in which the fights are sham fights, and the slain, rising the moment the curtain has fallen, go comfortably home to supper after washing off their rosepink wounds. It is nearly twenty years since I was last obliged to introduce a play in the form of a book for lack of an opportunity of presenting it in its proper mode by a performance in a theatre. The war has thrown me back on this expedient. Heartbreak House has not yet reached the stage. I have withheld it because the war has completely upset the economic conditions which formerly enabled serious drama to pay its way in London. The change is not in the theatres nor in the management of them, nor in the authors and actors, but in the audiences. For four years the London theatres were crowded every night with thousands of soldiers on leave from the front. These soldiers were not seasoned London playgoers. A childish experience of my own gave me a clue to their condition. When I was a small boy I was taken to the opera. I did not then know what an opera was, though I could whistle a good deal of opera music. I had seen in my mother's album photographs of all the great opera singers, mostly in evening dress. In the theatre I found myself before a gilded balcony filled with persons in evening dress whom I took to be the opera singers. I picked out one massive dark lady as Alboni, and wondered how soon she would stand up and sing. I was puzzled by the fact that I was made to sit with my back to the singers instead of facing them. When the curtain went up, my astonishment and delight were unbounded.

476

HEARTBREAK HOUSE
THE SOLDIER AT THE THEATRE FRONT

In 1915 I saw in the theatres men in khaki in just the same predicament. To everyone who had my clue to their state of mind it was evident that they had never been in a theatre before and did not know what it was. At one of our great variety theatres I sat beside a young officer, not at all a rough specimen, who, even when the curtain rose and enlightened him as to the place where he had to look for his entertainment, found the dramatic part of it utterly incomprehensible. He did not know how to play his part of the game. He could understand the people on the stage singing and dancing and performing gymnastic feats. He not only understood but intensely enjoyed an artist who imitated cocks crowing and pigs squeaking. But the people who pretended that they were somebody else, and that the painted picture behind them was real, bewildered him. In his presence I realized how very sophisticated the natural man has to become before the conventions of the theatre can be easily acceptable, or the purpose of the drama obvious to him.

Well, from the moment when the routine of leave for our soldiers was established, such novices, accompanied by damsels (called flappers) often as innocent as themselves, crowded the theatres to the doors. It was hardly possible at first to find stuff crude enough to nurse them on. The best music-hall comedians ransacked their memories for the oldest quips and the most childish antics to avoid carrying the military spectators out of their depth. I believe that this was a mistake as far as the novices were concerned. Shakespear, or the dramatized histories of George Barnwell, Maria Martin, or the Demon Barber of Fleet Street, would probably have been quite popular with them. But the novices were only a minority after all. The cultivated soldier, who in time of peace would look at nothing theatrical except the most advanced post-Ibsen plays in the most artistic settings, found himself, to his own astonishment, thirsting for silly jokes, dances, and brainlessly sensuous exhibitions

of pretty girls. The author of some of the most grimly serious plays of our time told me that after enduring the
trenches for months without a glimpse of the female of his
species, it gave him an entirely innocent but delightful
pleasure merely to see a flapper. The reaction from the
battle-field produced a condition of hyperaesthesia in which
all the theatrical values were altered. Trivial things gained
intensity and stale things novelty. The actor, instead of
having to coax his audiences out of the boredom which had
driven them to the theatre in an ill humor to seek some sort
of distraction, had only to exploit the bliss of smiling men
who were no longer under fire and under military discipline, but actually clean and comfortable and in a mood to
be pleased with anything and everything that a bevy of
pretty girls and a funny man, or even a bevy of girls pretending to be pretty and a man pretending to be funny,
could do for them.

Then could be seen every night in the theatres old-
fashioned farcical comedies, in which a bedroom, with four
doors on each side and a practicable window in the middle,
was understood to resemble exactly the bedroom in the
flats beneath and above, all three inhabited by couples con-
sumed with jealousy. When these people came home drunk
at night; mistook their neighbors' flats for their own; and
in due course got into the wrong beds, it was not only the
novices who found the resulting complications and scandals
exquisitely ingenious and amusing, nor their equally ver-
dant flappers who could not help squealing in a manner
that astonished the oldest performers when the gentleman
who had just come in drunk through the window pretended
to undress, and allowed glimpses of his naked person to
be descried from time to time. Men who had just read the
news that Charles Wyndham was dying, and were thereby
sadly reminded of Pink Dominos and the torrent of farcical
comedies that followed it in his heyday until every trick
of that trade had become so stale that the laughter they
provoked turned to loathing: these veterans also, when

478

they returned from the field, were as much pleased by what they knew to be stale and foolish as the novices by what they thought fresh and clever.

COMMERCE IN THE THEATRE

Wellington said that an army moves on its belly. So does a London theatre. Before a man acts he must eat. Before he performs plays he must pay rent. In London we have no theatres for the welfare of the people: they are all for the sole purpose of producing the utmost obtainable rent for the proprietor. If the twin flats and twin beds produce a guinea more than Shakespear, out goes Shakespear and in come the twin flats and the twin beds. If the brainless bevy of pretty girls and the funny man outbid Mozart, out goes Mozart.

UNSER SHAKESPEAR

Before the war an effort was made to remedy this by establishing a national theatre in celebration of the tercentenary of the death of Shakespear. A committee was formed; and all sorts of illustrious and influential persons lent their names to a grand appeal to our national culture. My play, The Dark Lady of The Sonnets, was one of the incidents of that appeal. After some years of effort the result was a single handsome subscription from a German gentleman. Like the celebrated swearer in the anecdote when the cart containing all his household goods lost its tailboard at the top of the hill and let its contents roll in ruin to the bottom, I can only say, "I cannot do justice to this situation," and let it pass without another word.

THE HIGHER DRAMA PUT OUT OF ACTION

The effect of the war on the London theatres may now be imagined. The beds and the bevies drove every higher form of art out of it. Rents went up to an unprecedented figure. At the same time prices doubled everywhere except at the theatre pay boxes, and raised the expenses of management to such a degree that unless the houses were quite full every night, profit was impossible. Even bare solvency

479

could not be attained without a very wide popularity. Now what had made serious drama possible to a limited extent before the war was that a play could pay its way even if the theatre were only half full until Saturday and three-quarters full then. A manager who was an enthusiast and a desperately hard worker, with an occasional grant-in-aid from an artistically disposed millionaire, and a due proportion of those rare and happy accidents by which plays of the higher sort turn out to be potboilers as well, could hold out for some years, by which time a relay might arrive in the person of another enthusiast. Thus and not otherwise occurred that remarkable revival of the British drama at the beginning of the century which made my own career as a playwright possible in England. In America I had already established myself, not as part of the ordinary theatre system, but in association with the exceptional genius of Richard Mansfield. In Germany and Austria I had no difficulty: the system of publicly aided theatres there, Court and Municipal, kept drama of the kind I dealt in alive; so that I was indebted to the Emperor of Austria for magnificent productions of my works at a time when the sole official attention paid me by the British Court was the announcement to the English-speaking world that certain plays of mine were unfit for public performance, a substantial set-off against this being that the British Court, in the course of its private playgoing, paid no regard to the bad character given me by the chief officer of its household.

Howbeit, the fact that my plays effected a lodgment on the London stage, and were presently followed by the plays of Granville Barker, Gilbert Murray, John Masefield, St John Hankin, Laurence Housman, Arnold Bennett, John Galsworthy, John Drinkwater, and others which would in the XIX century have stood rather less chance of production at a London theatre than the Dialogues of Plato, not to mention revivals of the ancient Athenian drama, and a restoration to the stage of Shakespear's plays as he wrote them, was made economically possible

480

solely by a supply of theatres which could hold nearly twice as much money as it cost to rent and maintain them. In such theatres work appealing to a relatively small class of cultivated persons, and therefore attracting only from half to three-quarters as many spectators as the more popular pastimes, could nevertheless keep going in the hands of young adventurers who were doing it for its own sake, and had not yet been forced by advancing age and responsibilities to consider the commercial value of their time and energy too closely. The war struck this foundation away in the manner I have just described. The expenses of running the cheapest west-end theatres rose to a sum which exceeded by twenty-five per cent the utmost that the higher drama can, as an ascertained matter of fact, be depended on to draw. Thus the higher drama, which has never really been a commercially sound speculation, now became an impossible one. Accordingly, attempts are being made to provide a refuge for it in suburban theatres in London and repertory theatres in the provinces. But at the moment when the army has at last disgorged the survivors of the gallant band of dramatic pioneers whom it swallowed, they find that the economic conditions which formerly made their work no worse than precarious now put it out of the question altogether, as far as the west end of London is concerned.

CHURCH AND THEATRE

I do not suppose many people care particularly. We are not brought up to care; and a sense of the national importance of the theatre is not born in mankind: the natural man, like so many of the soldiers at the beginning of the war, does not know what a theatre is. But please note that all these soldiers who did not know what a theatre was, knew what a church was. And they had been taught to respect churches. Nobody had ever warned them against a church as a place where frivolous women paraded in their best clothes; where stories of improper females like Potiphar's wife, and erotic poetry like the Song of Songs, were read aloud; where the sensuous and sentimental music of Schubert, Mendelssohn, Gounod, and Brahms was more popular than severe music by greater composers; where the prettiest sort of pretty pictures of pretty saints assailed the imagination and senses through stained-glass windows; and where sculpture and architecture came to the help of painting. Nobody ever reminded them that these things had sometimes produced such developments of erotic idolatry that men who were not only enthusiastic amateurs of literature, painting, and music, but famous practitioners of them, had actually exulted when mobs and even regular troops under express command had mutilated church statues, smashed church windows, wrecked church organs, and torn up the sheets from which the church music was read and sung. When they saw broken statues in churches, they were told that this was the work of wicked godless rioters, instead of, as it was, the work partly of zealots bent on driving the world, the flesh, and the devil out of the temple, and partly of insurgent men who had become intolerably poor because the temple had become a den of thieves. But all the sins and perversions that were so carefully hidden from them in the history of the Church were laid on the shoulders of the Theatre: that stuffy, uncomfortable place of penance in which we suffer so much inconvenience on the slenderest chance of gaining a scrap of food for our starving souls. When the Germans bombed the Cathedral of Rheims the world rang with the horror of the sacrilege. When they bombed the Little Theatre in the Adelphi, and narrowly missed bombing two writers of plays who lived within a few yards of it, the fact was not even mentioned in the papers. In point of appeal to the senses no theatre ever built could touch the fane at Rheims: no actress could rival its Virgin in beauty, nor any operatic tenor look otherwise than a fool beside its David. Its picture glass was glorious even to those who had seen the glass of Chartres. It was wonderful in its very grotesques: who would look at the Blondin Donkey after seeing its leviathans? In spite of the

Adam-Adelphian decoration on which Miss Kingston had lavished so much taste and care, the Little Theatre was in comparison with Rheims the gloomiest of little conventicles: indeed the cathedral must, from the Puritan point of view, have debauched a million voluptuaries for every one whom the Little Theatre had sent home thoughtful to a chaste bed after Mr Chesterton's Magic or Brieux's *Les Avariés*. Perhaps that is the real reason why the Church is lauded and the Theatre reviled. Whether or no, the fact remains that the lady to whose public spirit and sense of the national value of the theatre I owed the first regular public performance of a play of mine had to conceal her action as if it had been a crime, whereas if she had given the money to the Church she would have worn a halo for it. And I admit, as I have always done, that this state of things may have been a very sensible one. I have asked Londoners again and again why they pay half a guinea to go to a theatre when they can go to St Paul's or Westminster Abbey for nothing. Their only possible reply is that they want to see something new and possibly something wicked; but the theatres mostly disappoint both hopes. If ever a revolution makes me Dictator, I shall establish a heavy charge for admission to our churches. But everyone who pays at the church door shall receive a ticket entitling him or her to free admission to one performance at any theatre he or she prefers. Thus shall the sensuous charms of the church service be made to subsidize the sterner virtue of the drama.

THE NEXT PHASE

The present situation will not last. Although the newspaper I read at breakfast this morning before writing these words contains a calculation that no less than twenty-three wars are at present being waged to confirm the peace, England is no longer in khaki; and a violent reaction is setting in against the crude theatrical fare of the four terrible years. Soon the rents of theatres will once more be fixed on the assumption that they cannot always be full, nor even on the average half full week in and week out. Prices will change.

The higher drama will be at no greater disadvantage than it was before the war; and it may benefit, first, by the fact that many of us have been torn from the fools' paradise in which the theatre formerly traded, and thrust upon the sternest realities and necessities until we have lost both faith in and patience with the theatrical pretences that had no root either in reality or necessity; second, by the startling change made by the war in the distribution of income. It seems only the other day that a millionaire was a man with £50,000 a year. Today, when he has paid his income tax and super tax, and insured his life for the amount of his death duties, he is lucky if his net income is £10,000, though his nominal property remains the same. And this is the result of a Budget which is called "a respite for the rich." At the other end of the scale millions of persons have had regular incomes for the first time in their lives; and their men have been regularly clothed, fed, lodged, and taught to make up their minds that certain things have to be done, also for the first time in their lives. Hundreds of thousands of women have been taken out of their domestic cages and tasted both discipline and independence. The thoughtless and snobbish middle classes have been pulled up short by the very unpleasant experience of being ruined to an unprecedented extent. We have all had a tremendous jolt; and although the widespread notion that the shock of the war would automatically make a new heaven and a new earth, and that the dog would never go back to his vomit nor the sow to her wallowing in the mire, is already seen to be a delusion, yet we are far more conscious of our condition than we were, and far less disposed to submit to it. Revolution, lately only a sensational chapter in history or a demagogic claptrap, is now a possibility so imminent that hardly by trying to suppress it in other countries by arms and defamation, and calling the process anti-Bolshevism, can our Government stave it off at home.

Perhaps the most tragic figure of the day is the American President who was once a historian. In those days it became his task to tell us how, after that great war in America which was more clearly than any other war of our time a war for an idea, the conquerors, confronted with a heroic task of reconstruction, turned recreant, and spent fifteen years in abusing their victory under cover of pretending to accomplish the task they were doing what they could to make impossible. Alas! Hegel was right when he said that we learn from history that men never learn anything from history. With what anguish of mind the President sees that we, the new conquerors, forgetting everything we professed to fight for, are sitting down with watering mouths to a good square meal of ten years revenge upon and humiliation of our prostrate foe, can only be guessed by those who know, as he does, how hopeless is remonstrance, and how happy Lincoln was in perishing from the earth before his inspired messages became scraps of paper. He knows well that from the Peace Conference will come, in spite of his utmost, no edict on which he will be able, like Lincoln, to invoke "the considerate judgment of mankind, and the gracious favor of Almighty God." He led his people to destroy the militarism of Zabern; and the army they rescued is busy in Cologne imprisoning every German who does not salute a British officer; whilst the Government at home, asked whether it approves, replies that it does not propose even to discontinue this Zabernism when the Peace is concluded, but in effect looks forward to making Germans salute British officers until the end of the world. That is what war makes of men and women. It will wear off; and the worst it threatens is already proving impracticable; but before the humble and contrite heart ceases to be despised, the President and I, being of the same age, will be dotards. In the meantime there is, for him, another history to write; for me, another comedy to stage. Perhaps, after all, that is what wars are for, and what historians and playwrights are for. If men will not learn until their lessons are written in blood, why, blood they must have, their own for preference.

HEARTBREAK HOUSE
THE EPHEMERAL THRONES AND THE
ETERNAL THEATRE

To the theatre it will not matter. Whatever Bastilles fall, the theatre will stand. Apostolic Hapsburg has collapsed; All Highest Hohenzollern languishes in Holland, threatened with trial on a capital charge of fighting for his country against England; Imperial Romanoff, said to have perished miserably by a more summary method of murder, is perhaps alive or perhaps dead: nobody cares more than if he had been a peasant; the lord of Hellas is level with his lackeys in republican Switzerland; Prime Ministers and Commanders-in-Chief have passed from a brief glory as Solons and Caesars into failure and obscurity as closely on one another's heels as the descendants of Banquo; but Euripides and Aristophanes, Shakespear and Molière, Goethe and Ibsen remain fixed in their everlasting seats.

HOW WAR MUZZLES THE DRAMATIC
POET

As for myself, why, it may be asked, did I not write two plays about the war instead of two pamphlets on it? The answer is significant. You cannot make war on war and on your neighbor at the same time. War cannot bear the terrible castigation of comedy, the ruthless light of laughter that glares on the stage. When men are heroically dying for their country, it is not the time to shew their lovers and wives and fathers and mothers how they are being sacrificed to the blunders of boobies, the cupidity of capitalists, the ambition of conquerors, the electioneering of demagogues, the Pharisaism of patriots, the lusts and lies and rancors and bloodthirsts that love war because it opens their prison doors, and sets them in the thrones of power and popularity. For unless these things are mercilessly exposed they will hide under the mantle of the ideals on the stage just as they do in real life.

And though there may be better things to reveal, it may not, and indeed cannot, be militarily expedient to reveal them whilst the issue is still in the balance. Truth telling is not compatible with the defence of the realm. We are just now reading the revelations of our generals and admirals, unmuzzled at last by the armistice. During the war, General A, in his moving despatches from the field, told how General B had covered himself with deathless glory in such and such a battle. He now tells us that General B came within an ace of losing us the war by disobeying his orders on that occasion, and fighting instead of running away as he ought to have done. An excellent subject for comedy now that the war is over, no doubt; but if General A had let this out at the time, what would have been the effect on General B's soldiers? And had the stage made known what the Prime Minister and the Secretary of State for War who overruled General A thought of him, and what he thought of them, as now revealed in raging controversy, what would have been the effect on the nation? That is why comedy, though sorely tempted, had to be loyally silent; for the art of the dramatic poet knows no patriotism; recognizes no obligation but truth to natural history; cares not whether Germany or England perish; is ready to cry with Brynhild, "Lass' uns verderben, lachend zu grunde geh'n" sooner than deceive or be deceived; and thus becomes in time of war a greater military danger than poison, steel, or trinitrotoluene. That is why I had to withhold Heartbreak House from the footlights during the war; for the Germans might on any night have turned the last act from play into earnest, and even then might not have waited for their cues.

June 1919.

THE *hilly country in the middle of the north edge of Sussex, looking very pleasant on a fine evening at the end of September, is seen through the windows of a room which has been built so as to resemble the after part of an old-fashioned high-pooped ship with a stern gallery; for the windows are ship built with heavy timbering, and run right across the room as continuously as the stability of the wall allows. A row of lockers under the windows provides an unupholstered window-seat interrupted by twin glass doors, respectively halfway between the stern post and the sides. Another door strains the illusion a little by being apparently in the ship's port side, and yet leading, not to the open sea, but to the entrance hall of the house. Between this door and the stern gallery are bookshelves. There are electric light switches beside the door leading to the hall and the glass doors in the stern gallery. Against the starboard wall is a carpenter's bench. The vice has a board in its jaws; and the floor is littered with shavings, overflowing from a waste-paper basket. A couple of planes and a centrebit are on the bench. In the same wall, between the bench and the windows, is a narrow doorway with a half door, above which a glimpse of the room beyond shews that it is a shelved pantry with bottles and kitchen crockery.*

On the starboard side, but close to the middle, is a plain oak drawing-table with drawing-board, T-square, straightedges, set squares, mathematical instruments, saucers of water color, a tumbler of discolored water, Indian ink, pencils, and brushes on it. The drawing-board is set so that the draughtsman's chair has the window on its left hand. On the floor at the end of the table, on his right, is a ship's fire bucket. On the port side of the room, near the bookshelves, is a sofa with its back to the windows. It is a sturdy mahogany article, oddly upholstered in sailcloth, including the bolster, with a couple of blankets hanging over the back. Between the sofa and the drawing-table is a big wicker chair, with broad arms and a low sloping back, with its back

489

to the light. A small but stout table of teak, with a round top and gate legs, stands against the port wall between the door and the bookcase. It is the only article in the room that suggests (not at all convincingly) a woman's hand in the furnishing. The uncarpeted floor of narrow boards is caulked and holystoned like a deck.

The garden to which the glass doors lead dips to the south before the landscape rises again to the hills. Emerging from the hollow is the cupola of an observatory. Between the observatory and the house is a flagstaff on a little esplanade, with a hammock on the east side and a long garden seat on the west.

A young lady, gloved and hatted, with a dust coat on, is sitting in the window-seat with her body twisted to enable her to look out at the view. One hand props her chin: the other hangs down with a volume of the Temple Shakespear in it, and her finger stuck in the page she has been reading.

A clock strikes six.

The young lady turns and looks at her watch. She rises with an air of one who waits and is almost at the end of her patience. She is a pretty girl, slender, fair, and intelligent looking, nicely but not expensively dressed, evidently not a smart idler.

With a sigh of weary resignation she comes to the draughtsman's chair; sits down; and begins to read Shakespear. Presently the book sinks to her lap; her eyes close; and she dozes into a slumber.

An elderly womanservant comes in from the hall with three unopened bottles of rum on a tray. She passes through and disappears in the pantry without noticing the young lady. She places the bottles on the shelf and fills her tray with empty bottles. As she returns with these, the young lady lets her book drop, awakening herself, and startling the womanservant so that she all but lets the tray fall.

THE WOMANSERVANT. God bless us! [*The young lady picks up the book and places it on the table*]. Sorry to wake you, miss, I'm sure; but you are a stranger to me. What might you be waiting here for now?

THE YOUNG LADY. Waiting for somebody to shew some signs of knowing that I have been invited here.

THE WOMANSERVANT. Oh, youre invited, are you? And has nobody come? Dear! dear!

THE YOUNG LADY. A wild-looking old gentleman came and looked in at the window; and I heard him calling out "Nurse: there is a young and attractive female waiting in the poop. Go and see what she wants." Are you the nurse?

THE WOMANSERVANT. Yes, miss: I'm Nurse Guinness. That was old Captain Shotover, Mrs Hushabye's father. I heard him roaring; but I thought it was for something else. I suppose it was Mrs Hushabye that invited you, ducky?

THE YOUNG LADY. I understood her to do so. But really I think I'd better go.

NURSE GUINNESS. Oh, dont think of such a thing, miss. If Mrs Hushabye has forgotten all about it, it will be a pleasant surprise for her to see you, wont it?

THE YOUNG LADY. It has been a very unpleasant surprise to me to find that nobody expects me.

NURSE GUINNESS. Youll get used to it, miss: this house is full of surprises for them that dont know our ways.

CAPTAIN SHOTOVER [*looking in from the hall suddenly: an ancient but still hardy man with an immense white beard, in a reefer jacket with a whistle hanging from his neck*] Nurse: there is a hold-all and a handbag on the front steps for everybody to fall over. Also a tennis racquet. Who the devil left them there?

THE YOUNG LADY. They are mine, I'm afraid.

THE CAPTAIN [*advancing to the drawing-table*] Nurse: who is this misguided and unfortunate young lady?

NURSE GUINNESS. She says Miss Hessy invited her, sir.

THE CAPTAIN. And had she no friend, no parents, to warn her against my daughter's invitations? This is a pretty sort of house, by heavens! A young and attractive lady is invited here. Her luggage is left on the steps for hours; and

491

she herself is deposited in the poop and abandoned, tired and starving. This is our hospitality. These are our manners. No room ready. No hot water. No welcoming hostess. Our visitor is to sleep in the toolshed, and to wash in the duckpond.

NURSE GUINNESS. Now it's all right, Captain: I'll get the lady some tea; and her room shall be ready before she has finished it. [*To the young lady*] Take off your hat, ducky; and make yourself at home. [*She goes to the door leading to the hall*].

THE CAPTAIN [*as she passes him*] Ducky! Do you suppose, woman, that because this young lady has been insulted and neglected, you have the right to address her as you address my wretched children, whom you have brought up in ignorance of the commonest decencies of social intercourse?

NURSE GUINNESS. Never mind him, doty. [*Quite unconcerned, she goes out into the hall on her way to the kitchen*].

THE CAPTAIN. Madam: will you favor me with your name? [*He sits down in the big wicker chair*].

THE YOUNG LADY. My name is Ellie Dunn.

THE CAPTAIN. Dunn! I had a boatswain whose name was Dunn. He was originally a pirate in China. He set up as a ship's chandler with stores which I have every reason to believe he stole from me. No doubt he became rich. Are you his daughter?

ELLIE [*indignant*] No: certainly not. I am proud to be able to say that though my father has not been a successful man, nobody has ever had one word to say against him. I think my father is the best man I have ever known.

THE CAPTAIN. He must be greatly changed. Has he attained the seventh degree of concentration?

ELLIE. I dont understand.

THE CAPTAIN. But how could he, with a daughter? I, madam, have two daughters. One of them is Hesione Hushabye, who invited you here. I keep this house: she upsets it. I desire to attain the seventh degree of concentra-

492

tion: she invites visitors and leaves me to entertain them. [*Nurse Guinness returns with the tea-tray, which she places on the teak table*]. I have a second daughter who is, thank God, in a remote part of the Empire with her numskull of a husband. As a child she thought the figure-head of my ship, the Dauntless, the most beautiful thing on earth. He resembled it. He had the same expression: wooden yet enterprising. She married him, and will never set foot in this house again.

NURSE GUINNESS [*carrying the table, with the tea-things on it, to Ellie's side*] Indeed you never were more mistaken. She is in England this very moment. You have been told three times this week that she is coming home for a year for her health. And very glad you should be to see your own daughter again after all these years.

THE CAPTAIN. I am not glad. The natural term of the affection of the human animal for its offspring is six years. My daughter Ariadne was born when I was forty-six. I am now eighty-eight. If she comes, I am not at home. If she wants anything, let her take it. If she asks for me, let her be informed that I am extremely old, and have totally forgotten her.

NURSE GUINNESS. Thats no talk to offer to a young lady. Here, ducky, have some tea; and dont listen to him. [*She pours out a cup of tea*].

THE CAPTAIN [*rising wrathfully*] Now before high heaven they have given this innocent child Indian tea: the stuff they tan their own leather insides with. [*He seizes the cup and the tea-pot and empties both into the leathern bucket*].

ELLIE [*almost in tears*] Oh, please! I am so tired. I should have been glad of anything.

NURSE GUINNESS. Oh, what a thing to do! The poor lamb is ready to drop.

THE CAPTAIN. You shall have some of my tea. Do not touch that fly-blown cake: nobody eats it here except the dogs. [*He disappears into the pantry*].

493

HEARTBREAK HOUSE

NURSE GUINNESS. Theres a man for you! They say he sold himself to the devil in Zanzibar before he was a captain; and the older he grows the more I believe them.

A WOMAN'S VOICE [*in the hall*] Is anyone at home? Hesione! Nurse! Papa! Do come, somebody; and take in my luggage.

Thumping heard, as of an umbrella, on the wainscot.

NURSE GUINNESS. My gracious! It's Miss Addy, Lady Utterword, Mrs Hushabye's sister: the one I told the Captain about. [*Calling*] Coming, Miss, coming.

She carries the table back to its place by the door, and is hurrying out when she is intercepted by Lady Utterword, who bursts in much flustered. Lady Utterword, a blonde, is very handsome, very well dressed, and so precipitate in speech and action that the first impression (erroneous) is one of comic silliness.

LADY UTTERWORD. Oh, is that you, Nurse? How are you? You dont look a day older. Is nobody at home? Where is Hesione? Doesnt she expect me? Where are the servants? Whose luggage is that on the steps? Where's papa? Is everybody asleep? [*Seeing Ellie*] Oh! I beg your pardon. I suppose you are one of my nieces. [*Approaching her with outstretched arms*] Come and kiss your aunt, darling.

ELLIE. I'm only a visitor. It is my luggage on the steps.

NURSE GUINNESS. I'll go get you some fresh tea, ducky. [*She takes up the tray*].

ELLIE. But the old gentleman said he would make some himself.

NURSE GUINNESS. Bless you! he's forgotten what he went for already. His mind wanders from one thing to another.

LADY UTTERWORD. Papa, I suppose?

NURSE GUINNESS. Yes, Miss.

LADY UTTERWORD [*vehemently*] Dont be silly, Nurse. Dont call me Miss.

NURSE GUINNESS [*placidly*] No, lovey. [*She goes out

494

with the tea-tray].

LADY UTTERWORD [*sitting down with a flounce on the sofa*] I know what you must feel. Oh, this house, this house! I come back to it after twenty-three years; and it is just the same: the luggage lying on the steps, the servants spoilt and impossible, nobody at home to receive anybody, no regular meals, nobody ever hungry because they are always gnawing bread and butter or munching apples, and, what is worse, the same disorder in ideas, in talk, in feeling. When I was a child I was used to it: I had never known anything better, though I was unhappy, and longed all the time— oh, how I longed!—to be respectable, to be a lady, to live as others did, not to have to think of everything for myself. I married at nineteen to escape from it. My husband is Sir Hastings Utterword, who has been governor of all the crown colonies in succession. I have always been the mistress of Government House. I have been so happy: I had for-gotten that people could live like this. I wanted to see my father, my sister, my nephews and nieces (one ought to, you know), and I was looking forward to it. And now the state of the house! the way I'm received! the casual impudence of that woman Guinness, our old nurse! really Hesione might at least have been here: s o m e preparation might have been made for me. You must excuse my going on in this way; but I am really very much hurt and annoyed and dis-illusioned: and if I had realized it was to be like this, I wouldnt have come. I have a great mind to go away without another word. [*She is on the point of weeping*].

ELLIE [*also very miserable*] Nobody has been here to receive me either. I thought I ought to go away too. But how can I, Lady Utterword? My luggage is on the steps; and the station fly has gone.

The Captain emerges from the pantry with a tray of Chinese lacquer and a very fine tea-set on it. He rests it provisionally on the end of the table; snatches away the drawing-board, which he stands on the floor against the ta-ble legs; and puts the tray in the space thus cleared. Ellie pours out a cup greedily.

THE CAPTAIN. Your tea, young lady. What! another lady! I must fetch another cup. [*He makes for the pantry*].

LADY UTTERWORD [*rising from the sofa, suffused with emotion*] Papa! Dont you know me? I'm your daughter.

THE CAPTAIN. Nonsense! my daughter's upstairs asleep. [*He vanishes through the half door*].

Lady Utterword retires to the window to conceal her tears.

ELLIE [*going to her with the cup*] Dont be so distressed. Have this cup of tea. He is very old and very strange: he has been just like that to me. I know how dreadful it must be: my own father is all the world to me. Oh, I'm sure he didnt mean it.

The Captain returns with another cup.

THE CAPTAIN. Now we are complete. [*He places it on the tray*].

LADY UTTERWORD [*hysterically*] Papa: you cant have forgotten me. I am Ariadne. I'm little Paddy Patkins. Wont you kiss me? [*She goes to him and throws her arms round his neck*].

THE CAPTAIN [*woodenly enduring her embrace*] How can you be Ariadne? You are a middle-aged woman: well-preserved, madam, but no longer young.

LADY UTTERWORD. But think of all the years and years I have been away, papa. I have had to grow old, like other people.

THE CAPTAIN [*disengaging himself*] You should grow out of kissing strange men: they may be striving to attain the seventh degree of concentration.

LADY UTTERWORD. But I'm your daughter. You havnt seen me for years.

THE CAPTAIN. So much the worse! When our relatives are at home, we have to think of all their good points or it would be impossible to endure them. But when they are away, we console ourselves for their absence by dwelling on their vices. That is how I have come to think my absent

496

daughter Ariadne a perfect fiend; so do not try to ingratiate yourself here by impersonating her. [*He walks firmly away to the other side of the room*].

LADY UTTERWORD. Ingratiating myself indeed! [*With dignity*] Very well, papa. [*She sits down at the drawing-table and pours out tea for herself*].

THE CAPTAIN. I am neglecting my social duties. You remember Dunn? Billy Dunn?

LADY UTTERWORD. Do you mean that villainous sailor who robbed you?

THE CAPTAIN [*introducing Ellie*] His daughter. [*He sits down on the sofa*].

ELLIE [*protesting*] No—
Nurse Guinness returns with fresh tea.

THE CAPTAIN. Take that hogwash away. Do you hear?

NURSE. Youve actually remembered about the tea! [*To Ellie*] O, miss, he didnt forget you after all! You h a v e made an impression.

THE CAPTAIN [*gloomily*] Youth! beauty! novelty! They are badly wanted in this house. I am excessively old. Hesione is only moderately young. Her children are not youthful.

LADY UTTERWORD. How can children be expected to be youthful in this house? Almost before we could speak we were filled with notions that might have been all very well for pagan philosophers of fifty, but were certainly quite unfit for respectable people of any age.

NURSE. You were always for respectability, Miss Addy.

LADY UTTERWORD. Nurse: will you please remember that I am Lady Utterword, and not Miss Addy, nor lovey, nor darling, nor doty? Do you hear?

NURSE. Yes, ducky: all right. I'll tell them all they must call you my lady. [*She takes her tray out with undisturbed placidity*].

LADY UTTERWORD. What comfort? what sense is there in having servants with no manners?

ELLIE [*rising and coming to the table to put down her*

497

empty cup] Lady Utterword: do you think Mrs Hushabye really expects me?

LADY UTTERWORD. Oh, dont ask me. You can see for yourself that Ive just arrived; her only sister, after twenty-three years absence! and it seems that *I* am not expected.

THE CAPTAIN. What does it matter whether the young lady is expected or not? She is welcome. There are beds: there is food. I'll find a room for her myself. [*He makes for the door*].

ELLIE [*following him to stop him*] Oh please— [*He goes out*]. Lady Utterword: I dont know what to do. Your father persists in believing that my father is some sailor who robbed him.

LADY UTTERWORD. You had better pretend not to notice it. My father is a very clever man; but he always forgot things; and now that he is old, of course he is worse. And I must warn you that it is sometimes very hard to feel quite sure that he really forgets.

Mrs Hushabye bursts into the room tempestuously, and embraces Ellie. She is a couple of years older than Lady Utterword, and even better looking. She has magnificent black hair, eyes like the fishpools of Heshbon, and a nobly modelled neck, short at the back and low between her shoulders in front. Unlike her sister she is uncorseted and dressed anyhow in a rich robe of black pile that shews off her white skin and statuesque contour.

MRS HUSHABYE. Ellie, my darling, my pettikins [*kissing her*]: how long have you been here? Ive been at home all the time: I was putting flowers and things in your room; and when I just sat down for a moment to try how comfortable the armchair was I went off to sleep. Papa woke me and told me you were here. Fancy your finding no one, and being neglected and abandoned. [*Kissing her again*] My poor love! [*She deposits Ellie on the sofa. Meanwhile Ariadne has left the table and come over to claim her share of attention*]. Oh! youve brought someone with you. Introduce me.

498

LADY UTTERWORD. Hesione: is it possible that y o u dont know me?

MRS HUSHABYE [*conventionally*] Of course I remember your face quite well. Where have we met?

LADY UTTERWORD. Didnt papa tell you I was here? Oh! this is really too much. [*She throws herself sulkily into the big chair*].

MRS HUSHABYE. Papa!

LADY UTTERWORD. Yes: Papa. O u r papa, you unfeeling wretch. [*Rising angrily*] I'll go straight to a hotel.

MRS HUSHABYE [*seizing her by the shoulders*] My goodness gracious goodness, you dont mean to say that youre Addy!

LADY UTTERWORD. I certainly am Addy; and I dont think I can be so changed that you would not have recognized me if you had any real affection for me. And papa didnt think me even worth mentioning!

MRS HUSHABYE. What a lark! Sit down. [*She pushes her back into the chair instead of kissing her, and posts herself behind it*]. You d o look a swell. Youre much handsomer than you used to be. Youve made the acquaintance of Ellie, of course. She is going to marry a perfect hog of a millionaire for the sake of her father, who is as poor as a church mouse; and you must help me to stop her.

ELLIE. Oh p l e a s e, Hesione.

MRS HUSHABYE. My pettikins, the man's coming here today with your father to begin persecuting you; and everybody will see the state of the case in ten minutes; so whats the use of making a secret of it?

ELLIE. He is not a hog, Hesione. You dont know how wonderfully good he was to my father, and how deeply grateful I am to him.

MRS HUSHABYE [*to Lady Utterword*] Her father is a very remarkable man, Addy. His name is Mazzini Dunn. Mazzini was a celebrity of some kind who knew Ellie's grandparents. They were both poets, like the Brownings; and when her father came into the world Mazzini said

"Another soldier born for freedom!" So they christened him Mazzini; and he has been fighting for freedom in his quiet way ever since. Thats why he is so poor.

ELLIE. I am proud of his poverty.

MRS HUSHABYE. Of course you are, pettikins. Why not leave him in it, and marry someone you love?

LADY UTTERWORD [*rising suddenly and explosively*] Hesione: are you going to kiss me or are you not?

MRS HUSHABYE. What do you want to be kissed for?

LADY UTTERWORD. I d o n t want to be kissed; but I do want you to behave properly and decently. We are sisters. We have been separated for twenty-three years. You o u g h t to kiss me.

MRS HUSHABYE. Tomorrow morning, dear, before you make up. I hate the smell of powder.

LADY UTTERWORD. Oh! you unfeeling— [*She is interrupted by the return of the captain*].

THE CAPTAIN [*to Ellie*] Your room is ready. [*Ellie rises*]. The sheets were damp; but I have changed them. [*He makes for the garden door on the port side*].

LADY UTTERWORD. Oh! What about m y sheets?

THE CAPTAIN [*halting at the door*] Take my advice: air them; or take them off and sleep in blankets. You shall sleep in Ariadne's old room.

LADY UTTERWORD. Indeed I shall do nothing of the sort. That little hole! I am entitled to the best spare room.

THE CAPTAIN [*continuing unmoved*] She married a numskull. She told me she would marry anyone to get away from home.

LADY UTTERWORD. You are pretending not to know me on purpose. I will leave the house.

Mazzini Dunn enters from the hall. He is a little elderly man with bulging credulous eyes and earnest manners. He is dressed in a blue serge jacket suit with an unbuttoned mackintosh over it, and carries a soft black hat of clerical cut.

ELLIE. At last! Captain Shotover: here is my father.

HEARTBREAK HOUSE

THE CAPTAIN. This! Nonsense! not a bit like him. [*He goes away through the garden, shutting the door sharply behind him*].

LADY UTTERWORD. I will not be ignored and pretended to be somebody else. I will have it out with papa now, this instant. [*To Mazzini*] Excuse me. [*She follows the Captain out, making a hasty bow to Mazzini, who returns it*].

MRS HUSHABYE [*hospitably, shaking hands*] How good of you to come, Mr Dunn! You dont mind papa, do you? He is as mad as a hatter, you know, but quite harmless, and extremely clever. You will have some delightful talks with him.

MAZZINI. I hope so. [*To Ellie*] So here you are, Ellie, dear. [*He draws her arm affectionately through his*]. I must thank you, Mrs Hushabye, for your kindness to my daughter. I'm afraid she would have had no holiday if you had not invited her.

MRS HUSHABYE. Not at all. Very nice of her to come and attract young people to the house for us.

MAZZINI [*smiling*] I'm afraid Ellie is not interested in young men, Mrs Hushabye. Her taste is on the graver, solider side.

MRS HUSHABYE [*with a sudden rather hard brightness in her manner*] Wont you take off your overcoat, Mr Dunn? You will find a cupboard for coats and hats and things in the corner of the hall.

MAZZINI [*hastily releasing Ellie*] Yes—thank you—I had better— [*He goes out*].

MRS HUSHABYE [*emphatically*] The old brute!

ELLIE. Who?

MRS. HUSHABYE. Who! Him. He. It. [*Pointing after Mazzini*]. "Graver, solider tastes," indeed!

ELLIE [*aghast*] You dont mean that you were speaking like that of my father!

MRS HUSHABYE. I was. You know I was.

ELLIE [*with dignity*] I will leave your house at once.

501

[*She turns to the door*].

MRS HUSHABYE. If you attempt it, I'll tell your father why.

ELLIE [*turning again*] Oh! How can you treat a visitor like this, Mrs Hushabye?

MRS HUSHABYE. I thought you were going to call me Hesione.

ELLIE. Certainly not now?

MRS HUSHABYE. Very well: I'll tell your father.

ELLIE [*distressed*] Oh!

MRS HUSHABYE. If you turn a hair—if you take his part against me and against your own heart for a moment, I'll give that born soldier of freedom a piece of my mind that will stand him on his selfish old head for a week.

ELLIE. Hesione! My father selfish! How little you know—

She is interrupted by Mazzini, who returns, excited and perspiring.

MAZZINI. Ellie: Mangan has come: I thought youd like to know. Excuse me, Mrs Hushabye: the strange old gentleman—

MRS HUSHABYE. Papa. Quite so.

MAZZINI. Oh, I beg your pardon: of course: I was a little confused by his manner. He is making Mangan help him with something in the garden; and he wants me to—

A powerful whistle is heard.

THE CAPTAIN'S VOICE. Bosun ahoy! [*The whistle is repeated*].

MAZZINI [*flustered*] Oh dear! I believe he is whistling for me. [*He hurries out*].

MRS HUSHABYE. Now m y father is a wonderful man if you like.

ELLIE. Hesione: listen to me. You dont understand. My father and Mr Mangan were boys together. Mr Ma—

MRS HUSHABYE. I dont care what they were: we must sit down if you are going to begin as far back as that. [*She snatches at Ellie's waist, and makes her sit down on the sofa beside her*]. Now, pettikins: tell me all about Mr Mangan. They call him Boss Mangan, dont they? He is a Napoleon of industry and disgustingly rich, isnt he? Why isnt your father rich?

ELLIE. My poor father should never have been in business. His parents were poets; and they gave him the noblest ideas; but they could not afford to give him a profession.

MRS HUSHABYE. Fancy your grandparents, with their eyes in fine frenzy rolling! And so your poor father had to go into business. Hasnt he succeeded in it?

ELLIE. He always used to say he could succeed if he only had some capital. He fought his way along, to keep a roof over our heads and bring us up well; but it was always a struggle: always the same difficulty of not having capital enough. I dont know how to describe it to you.

MRS HUSHABYE. Poor Ellie! I know. Pulling the devil by the tail.

ELLIE [*hurt*] Oh no. Not like that. It was at least dignified.

MRS HUSHABYE. That made it all the harder, didnt it? *I* shouldn't have pulled the devil by the tail with dignity. I should have pulled hard—[*between her teeth*] h a r d. Well? Go on.

ELLIE. At last it seemed that all our troubles were at an end. Mr Mangan did an extraordinarily noble thing out of pure friendship for my father and respect for his character. He asked him how much capital he wanted, and gave it to him. I dont mean that he lent it to him, or that he invested it in his business. He just simply made him a present of it. Wasnt that splendid of him?

MRS HUSHABYE. On condition that you married him?

ELLIE. Oh no, no, no. This was when I was a child. He had never even seen me: he never came to our house. It was absolutely disinterested. Pure generosity.

MRS HUSHABYE. Oh! I beg the gentleman's pardon. Well, what became of the money?

ELLIE. We all got new clothes and moved into another

house. And I went to another school for two years.

MRS HUSHABYE. Only two years?

ELLIE. That was all; for at the end of two years my father was utterly ruined.

MRS HUSHABYE. How?

ELLIE. I dont know. I never could understand. But it was dreadful. When we were poor my father had never been in debt. But when he launched out into business on a large scale, he had to incur liabilities. When the business went into liquidation he owed more money than Mr Mangan had given him.

MRS HUSHABYE. Bit off more than he could chew, I suppose.

ELLIE. I think you are a little unfeeling about it.

MRS HUSHABYE. My pettikins: you mustnt mind my way of talking. I was quite as sensitive and particular as you once; but I have picked up so much slang from the children that I am really hardly presentable. I suppose your father had no head for business, and made a mess of it.

ELLIE. Oh, that just shews how entirely you are mistaken about him. The business turned out a great success. It now pays forty-four per cent after deducting the excess profits tax.

MRS HUSHABYE. Then why arnt you rolling in money?

ELLIE. I dont know. It seems very unfair to me. You see, my father was made bankrupt. It nearly broke his heart, because he had persuaded several of his friends to put money into the business. He was sure it would succeed; and events proved that he was quite right. But they all lost their money. It was dreadful. I dont know what we should have done but for Mr Mangan.

MRS HUSHABYE. What! Did the Boss come to the rescue again, after all his money being thrown away?

ELLIE. He did indeed, and never uttered a reproach to my father. He bought what was left of the business—the buildings and the machinery and things—from the official trustee for enough money to enable my father to pay six and

504

eightpence in the pound and get his discharge. Everyone pitied papa so much, and saw so plainly that he was an honorable man, that they let him off at six-and-eight pence instead of ten shillings. Then Mr Mangan started a company to take up the business, and made my father a manager in it to save us from starvation; for I wasnt earning anything then.

MRS HUSHABYE. Quite a romance. And when did the Boss develop the tender passion?

ELLIE. Oh, that was years after, quite lately. He took the chair one night at a sort of people's concert. I was singing there. As an amateur, you know: half a guinea for expenses and three songs with three encores. He was so pleased with my singing that he asked might he walk home with me. I never saw anyone so taken aback as he was when I took him home and introduced him to my father: his own manager. It was then that my father told me how nobly he had behaved. Of course it was considered a great chance for me, as he is so rich. And—and—we drifted into a sort of understanding—I suppose I should call it an engagement—[*She is distressed and cannot go on*].

MRS HUSHABYE [*rising and marching about*] You may have drifted into it; but you will bounce out of it, my pettikins, if I am to have anything to do with it.

ELLIE [*hopelessly*] No: it's no use. I am bound in honor and gratitude. I will go through with it.

MRS HUSHABYE [*behind the sofa, scolding down at her*] You know, of course, that it's not honorable or grateful to marry a man you dont love. Do you love this Mangan man?

ELLIE. Yes. At least—

MRS HUSHABYE. I dont want to know about "the least": I want to know the worst. Girls of your age fall in love with all sorts of impossible people, especially old people.

ELLIE. I like Mr Mangan very much; and I shall always be—

MRS HUSHABYE [*impatiently completing the sentence and prancing away intolerantly to starboard*] —grateful to

505

him for his kindness to dear father. I know. Anybody else?

ELLIE. What do you mean?

MRS HUSHABYE. Anybody else? Are you in love with anybody else?

ELLIE. Of course not.

MRS HUSHABYE. Humph! [*The book on the drawing-table catches her eye. She picks it up, and evidently finds the title very unexpected. She looks at Ellie, and asks, quaintly*]. Quite sure youre not in love with an actor?

ELLIE. No, no. Why? What put such a thing into your head?

MRS HUSHABYE. This is yours, isnt it? Why else should you be reading Othello?

ELLIE. My father taught me to love Shakespear.

MRS HUSHABYE [*flinging the book down on the table*] Really! your father does seem to be about the limit.

ELLIE [*naïvely*] Do you never read Shakespear, Hesione? That seems to me so extraordinary. I like Othello.

MRS HUSHABYE. Do you indeed? He was jealous, wasnt he?

ELLIE. Oh, not that. I think all the part about jealousy is horrible. But dont you think it must have been a wonderful experience for Desdemona, brought up so quietly at home, to meet a man who had been out in the world doing all sorts of brave things and having terrible adventures, and yet finding something in her that made him love to sit and talk with her and tell her about them?

MRS HUSHABYE. Thats your idea of romance, is it?

ELLIE. Not romance, exactly. It might really happen.

Ellie's eyes shew that she is not arguing, but in a day-dream. Mrs Hushabye, watching her inquisitively, goes deliberately back to the sofa and resumes her seat beside her.

MRS HUSHABYE. Ellie darling: have you noticed that some of those stories that Othello told Desdemona couldnt have happened?

ELLIE. Oh no. Shakespear thought they could have happened.

506

MRS HUSHABYE. Hm! Desdemona thought they could have happened. But they didnt.

ELLIE. Why do you look so enigmatic about it? You are such a sphinx: I never know what you mean.

MRS HUSHABYE. Desdemona would have found him out if she had lived, you know. I wonder was that why he strangled her!

ELLIE. Othello was not telling lies.

MRS HUSHABYE. How do you know?

ELLIE. Shakespear would have said if he was. Hesione: there are men who have done wonderful things: men like Othello, only, of course, white, and very handsome, and—

MRS HUSHABYE. Ah! Now we're coming to it. Tell me all about him. I knew there must be somebody, or youd never have been so miserable about Mangan: youd have thought it quite a lark to marry him.

ELLIE [*blushing vividly*] Hesione: you are dreadful. But I dont want to make a secret of it, though of course I dont tell everybody. Besides, I dont know him.

MRS HUSHABYE. Dont know him! What does that mean?

ELLIE. Well, of course I know him to speak to.

MRS HUSHABYE. But you want to know him ever so much more intimately, eh?

ELLIE. No no: I know him quite—almost intimately.

MRS HUSHABYE. You dont know him; and you know him almost intimately. How lucid!

ELLIE. I mean that he does not call on us. I—I got into conversation with him by chance at a concert.

MRS HUSHABYE. You seem to have rather a gay time at your concerts, Ellie.

ELLIE. Not at all: we talk to everyone in the green-room waiting for our turns. I thought he was one of the artists: he looked so splendid. But he was only one of the committee. I happened to tell him that I was copying a picture at the National Gallery. I make a little money that way. I cant paint much; but as it's always the same picture

I can do it pretty quickly and get two or three pounds for it. It happened that he came to the National Gallery one day.

MRS HUSHABYE. One student's day. Paid sixpence to stumble about through a crowd of easels, when he might have come in next day for nothing and found the floor clear! Quite by accident?

ELLIE [*triumphantly*] No. On purpose. He liked talking to me. He knows lots of the most splendid people. Fashionable women who are all in love with him. But he ran away from them to see me at the National Gallery and persuade me to come with him for a drive round Richmond Park in a taxi.

MRS HUSHABYE. My pettikins, you have been going it. It's wonderful what you good girls can do without anyone saying a word.

ELLIE. I am not in society, Hesione. If I didnt make acquaintances in that way I shouldnt have any at all.

MRS HUSHABYE. Well, no harm if you know how to take care of yourself. May I ask his name?

ELLIE [*slowly and musically*] Marcus Darnley.

MRS HUSHABYE [*echoing the music*] Marcus Darnley! What a splendid name!

ELLIE. Oh, I'm so glad you think so. I think so too; but I was afraid it was only a silly fancy of my own.

MRS HUSHABYE. Hm! Is he one of the Aberdeen Darnleys?

ELLIE. Nobody knows. Just fancy! He was found in an antique chest—

MRS HUSHABYE. A what?

ELLIE. An antique chest, one summer morning in a rose garden, after a night of the most terrible thunderstorm.

MRS HUSHABYE. What on earth was he doing in the chest? Did he get into it because he was afraid of the lightning?

ELLIE. Oh no, no: he was a baby. The name Marcus Darnley was embroidered on his babyclothes. And five hundred pounds in gold.

MRS HUSHABYE [*looking hard at her*] Ellie!

ELLIE. The garden of the Viscount—

MRS HUSHABYE. —de Rougemont?

ELLIE [*innocently*] No: de Larochejaquelin. A French family. A vicomte. His life has been one long romance. A tiger—

MRS HUSHABYE. Slain by his own hand?

ELLIE. Oh no: nothing vulgar like that. He saved the life of the tiger from a hunting party: one of King Edward's hunting parties in India. The King was furious: that was why he never had his military services properly recognized. But he doesnt care. He is a Socialist and despises rank, and has been in three revolutions fighting on the barricades.

MRS HUSHABYE. How can you sit there telling me such lies? You, Ellie, of all people! And I thought you were a perfectly simple, straightforward, good girl.

ELLIE [*rising, dignified but very angry*] Do you mean to say you dont believe me?

MRS HUSHABYE. Of course I dont believe you. Youre inventing every word of it. Do you take me for a fool?

Ellie stares at her. Her candor is so obvious that Mrs Hushabye is puzzled.

ELLIE. Goodbye, Hesione. I'm very sorry. I see now that it sounds very improbable as I tell it. But I cant stay if you think that way about me.

MRS HUSHABYE [*catching her dress*] You shant go. I couldnt be so mistaken: I know too well what liars are like. Somebody has really told you all this.

ELLIE [*flushing*] Hesione: dont say that you dont believe h i m. I couldnt bear that.

MRS HUSHABYE [*soothing her*] Of course I believe him, dearest. But you should have broken it to me by degrees. [*Drawing her back to her seat*] Now tell me all about him. Are you in love with him?

ELLIE. Oh no. I'm not so foolish. I dont fall in love with people. I'm not so silly as you think.

MRS HUSHABYE. I see. Only something to think about—

509

to give some interest and pleasure to life.

ELLIE. Just so. Thats all, really.

MRS HUSHABYE. It makes the hours go fast, doesnt it? No tedious waiting to go to sleep at nights and wondering whether you will have a bad night. How delightful it makes waking up in the morning! How much better than the happiest dream! All life transfigured! No more wishing one had an interesting book to read, because life is so much happier than any book! No desire but to be alone and not to have to talk to anyone: to be alone and just think about it.

ELLIE [embracing her] Hesione: you are a witch. How do you know? Oh, you are the most sympathetic woman in the world.

MRS HUSHABYE [caressing her] Pettikins, my pettikins: how I envy you! and how I pity you!

ELLIE. Pity me! Oh, why?

A very handsome man of fifty, with mousquetaire moustaches, wearing a rather dandified curly brimmed hat, and carrying an elaborate walking-stick, comes into the room from the hall, and stops short at sight of the women on the sofa.

ELLIE [seeing him and rising in glad surprise] Oh! Hesione: this is Mr Marcus Darnley.

MRS HUSHABYE [rising] What a lark! He is my husband.

ELLIE. But how— [She stops suddenly; then turns pale and sways].

MRS HUSHABYE [catching her and sitting down with her on the sofa] Steady, my pettikins.

THE MAN [with a mixture of confusion and effrontery, depositing his hat and stick on the teak table] My real name, Miss Dunn, is Hector Hushabye. I leave you to judge whether that is a name any sensitive man would care to confess to. I never use it when I can possibly help it. I have been away for nearly a month; and I had no idea you knew my wife, or that you were coming here. I am none the less delighted to find you in our little house.

510

ELLIE [*in great distress*] I dont know what to do. Please, may I speak to papa? Do leave me. I cant bear it.

MRS HUSHABYE. Be off, Hector.

HECTOR. I—

MRS HUSHABYE. Quick, quick. Get out.

HECTOR. If you think it better— [*He goes out, taking his hat with him but leaving the stick on the table*].

MRS HUSHABYE [*laying Ellie down at the end of the sofa*] Now, pettikins, he is gone. Theres nobody but me. You can let yourself go. Dont try to control yourself. Have a good cry.

ELLIE [*raising her head*] Damn!

MRS HUSHABYE. Splendid! Oh, what a relief! I thought you were going to be broken-hearted. Never mind me. Damn him again.

ELLIE. I am not damning him: I am damning myself for being such a fool. [*Rising*] How could I let myself be taken in so? [*She begins prowling to and fro, her bloom gone, looking curiously older and harder*].

MRS HUSHABYE [*cheerfully*] Why not, pettikins? Very few young women can resist Hector. I couldnt when I was your age. He is really rather splendid, you know.

ELLIE [*turning on her*] Splendid! Yes: splendid l o o k i n g, of course. But how can you love a liar?

MRS HUSHABYE. I dont know. But you can, fortunately. Otherwise there wouldnt be much love in the world.

ELLIE. But to lie like that! To be a boaster! a coward!

MRS HUSHABYE [*rising in alarm*] Pettikins: none of that, if you please. If you hint the slightest doubt of Hector's courage, he will go straight off and do the most horribly dangerous things to convince himself that he isnt a coward. He has a dreadful trick of getting out of one third-floor window and coming in at another, just to test his nerve. He has a whole drawerful of Albert Medals for saving people's lives.

ELLIE. He never told me that.

MRS HUSHABYE. He never boasts of anything he really

511

did: he cant bear it; and it makes him shy if anyone else does. All his stories are made-up stories.

ELLIE [*coming to her*] Do you mean that he is really brave, and really has adventures, and yet tells lies about things that he never did and that never happened?

MRS HUSHABYE. Yes, pettikins, I do. People dont have their virtues and vices in sets: they have them anyhow: all mixed.

ELLIE [*staring at her thoughtfully*] Theres something odd about this house, Hesione, and even about you. I dont know why I'm talking to you so calmly. I have a horrible fear that my heart is broken, but that heartbreak is not like what I thought it must be.

MRS HUSHABYE [*fondling her*] It's only life educating you, pettikins. How do you feel about Boss Mangan now?

ELLIE [*disengaging herself with an expression of distaste*] Oh, how can you remind me of him, Hesione?

MRS HUSHABYE. Sorry, dear. I think I hear Hector coming back. You dont mind now, do you, dear?

ELLIE. Not in the least. I'm quite cured.

Mazzini Dunn and Hector come in from the hall.

HECTOR [*as he opens the door and allows Mazzini to pass in*] One second more, and she would have been a dead woman!

MAZZINI. Dear! dear! what an escape! Ellie, my love: Mr Hushabye has just been telling me the most extraordinary—

ELLIE. Yes: Ive heard it. [*She crosses to the other side of the room*].

HECTOR [*following her*] Not this one: I'll tell it to you after dinner. I think youll like it. The truth is, I made it up for you, and was looking forward to the pleasure of telling it to you. But in a moment of impatience at being turned out of the room, I threw it away on your father.

ELLIE [*turning at bay with her back to the carpenter's bench, scornfully self-possessed*] It was not thrown away. He believes it. I should not have believed it.

512

MAZZINI [*benevolently*] Ellie is very naughty, Mr Hushabye. Of course she does not really think that. [*He goes to the bookshelves, and inspects the titles of the volumes*].

Boss Mangan comes in from the hall, followed by the Captain. Mangan, carefully frock-coated as for church or for a directors' meeting, is about fiftyfive, with a careworn, mistrustful expression, standing a little on an entirely imaginary dignity, with a dull complexion, straight, lustreless hair, and features so entirely commonplace that it is impossible to describe them.

CAPTAIN SHOTOVER [*to Mrs Hushabye, introducing the newcomer*] Says his name is Mangan. Not ablebodied.

MRS HUSHABYE [*graciously*] How do you do, Mr Mangan?

MANGAN [*shaking hands*] Very pleased.

CAPTAIN SHOTOVER. Dunn's lost his muscle, but recovered his nerve. Men seldom do after three attacks of delirium tremens. [*He goes into the pantry*].

MRS HUSHABYE. I congratulate you, Mr Dunn.

MAZZINI [*dazed*] I am a lifelong teetotaler.

MRS HUSHABYE. You will find it far less trouble to let papa have his own way than try to explain.

MAZZINI. But three attacks of delirium tremens, really!

MRS HUSHABYE [*to Mangan*] Do you know my husband, Mr. Mangan? [*She indicates Hector*].

MANGAN [*going to Hector, who meets him with outstretched hand*] Very pleased. [*Turning to Ellie*] I hope, Miss Ellie, you have not found the journey down too fatiguing. [*They shake hands*].

MRS HUSHABYE. Hector: shew Mr Dunn his room.

HECTOR. Certainly. Come along, Mr Dunn. [*He takes Mazzini out*].

ELLIE. You havnt shewn me my room yet, Hesione.

MRS HUSHABYE. How stupid of me! Come along. Make yourself quite at home, Mr Mangan. Papa will entertain you. [*She calls to the Captain in the pantry*] Papa: come

513

and explain the house to Mr Mangan.

She goes out with Ellie. The Captain comes from the pantry.

CAPTAIN SHOTOVER. Youre going to marry Dunn's daughter. Dont. Youre too old.

MANGAN [*staggered*] Well! Thats fairly blunt, Captain.

CAPTAIN SHOTOVER. It's true.

MANGAN. She doesnt think so.

CAPTAIN SHOTOVER. She does.

MANGAN. Older men than I have—

CAPTAIN SHOTOVER [*finishing the sentence for him*]—made fools of themselves. That, also, is true.

MANGAN [*asserting himself*] I dont see that this is any business of yours.

CAPTAIN SHOTOVER. It is everybody's business. The stars in their courses are shaken when such things happen.

MANGAN. I'm going to marry her all the same.

CAPTAIN SHOTOVER. How do you know?

MANGAN [*playing the strong man*] I intend to. I mean to. See? I never made up my mind to do a thing yet that I didnt bring it off. Thats the sort of man I am; and there will be a better understanding between us when you make up your mind to that, Captain.

CAPTAIN SHOTOVER. You frequent picture palaces.

MANGAN. Perhaps I do. Who told you?

CAPTAIN SHOTOVER. Talk like a man, not like a movy. You mean that you make a hundred thousand a year.

MANGAN. I dont boast. But when I meet a man that makes a hundred thousand a year, I take off my hat to that man, and stretch out my hand to him and call him brother.

CAPTAIN SHOTOVER. Then you also make a hundred thousand a year, hey?

MANGAN. No. I cant say that. Fifty thousand, perhaps.

CAPTAIN SHOTOVER. His half brother only. [*He turns away from Mangan with his usual abruptness, and collects the empty tea-cups on the Chinese tray*].

514

MANGAN [*irritated*] See here, Captain Shotover. I dont quite understand my position here. I came here on your daughter's invitation. Am I in her house or in yours?

CAPTAIN SHOTOVER. You are beneath the dome of heaven, in the house of God. What is true within these walls is true outside them. Go out on the seas; climb the mountains; wander through the valleys. She is still too young.

MANGAN [*weakening*] But I'm very little over fifty.

CAPTAIN SHOTOVER. You are still less under sixty. Boss Mangan: you will not marry the pirate's child. [*He carries the tray away into the pantry*].

MANGAN [*following him to the half door*] What pirate's child? What are you talking about?

CAPTAIN SHOTOVER [*in the pantry*] Ellie Dunn. You will not marry her.

MANGAN. Who will stop me?

CAPTAIN SHOTOVER [*emerging*] My daughter. [*He makes for the door leading to the hall*].

MANGAN [*following him*] Mrs Hushabye! Do you mean to say she brought me down here to break it off?

CAPTAIN SHOTOVER [*stopping and turning on him*] I know nothing more than I have seen in her eye. She w i l l break it off. Take my advice: marry a West Indian negress: they make excellent wives. I was married to one myself for two years.

MANGAN. Well, I a m damned!

CAPTAIN SHOTOVER. I thought so. I was, too, for many years. The negress redeemed me.

MANGAN [*feebly*] This is queer. I ought to walk out of this house.

CAPTAIN SHOTOVER. Why?

MANGAN. Well, many men would be offended by your style of talking.

CAPTAIN SHOTOVER. Nonsense! It's the other sort of talking that makes quarrels. Nobody ever quarrels with me.

A gentleman, whose firstrate tailoring and frictionless

515

manners proclaim the wellbred West Ender, comes in from the hall. He has an engaging air of being young and unmarried, but on close inspection is found to be at least over forty.

THE GENTLEMAN. Excuse my intruding in this fashion; but there is no knocker on the door; and the bell does not seem to ring.

CAPTAIN SHOTOVER. Why should there be a knocker? Why should the bell ring? The door is open.

THE GENTLEMAN. Precisely. So I ventured to come in.

CAPTAIN SHOTOVER. Quite right. I will see about a room for you. [*He makes for the door*].

THE GENTLEMAN [*stopping him*] But I'm afraid you dont know who I am.

CAPTAIN SHOTOVER. Do you suppose that at my age I make distinctions between one fellowcreature and another? [*He goes out. Mangan and the newcomer stare at one another*].

MANGAN. Strange character, Captain Shotover, sir.

THE GENTLEMAN. Very.

CAPTAIN SHOTOVER [*shouting outside*] Hesione: another person has arrived and wants a room. Man about town, well dressed, fifty.

THE GENTLEMAN. Fancy Hesione's feelings! May I ask are you a member of the family?

MANGAN. No.

THE GENTLEMAN. I am. At least a connexion.

Mrs Hushabye comes back.

MRS HUSHABYE. How do you do? How good of you to come!

THE GENTLEMAN. I am very glad indeed to make your acquaintance, Hesione. [*Instead of taking her hand he kisses her. At the same moment the Captain appears in the doorway*]. You will excuse my kissing your daughter, Captain, when I tell you that—

CAPTAIN SHOTOVER. Stuff! Everyone kisses my daughter. Kiss her as much as you like. [*He makes for the pantry*].

516

THE GENTLEMAN. Thank you. One moment, Captain. [*The Captain halts and turns. The gentleman goes to him affably*]. Do you happen to remember—but probably you dont, as it occurred many years ago—that your younger daughter married a numskull?

CAPTAIN SHOTOVER. Yes. She said she'd marry anybody to get away from this house. I should not have recognized you: your head is no longer like a walnut. Your aspect is softened. You have been boiled in bread and milk for years and years, like other married men. Poor devil! [*He disappears into the pantry*].

MRS HUSHABYE [*going past Mangan to the gentleman and scrutinizing him*]. I dont believe you are Hastings Utterword.

THE GENTLEMAN. I am not.

MRS HUSHABYE. Then what business had you to kiss me?

THE GENTLEMAN. I thought I would like to. The fact is, I am Randall Utterword, the unworthy younger brother of Hastings. I was abroad diplomatizing when he was married.

LADY UTTERWORD [*dashing in*] Hesione: where is the key of the wardrobe in my room? My diamonds are in my dressing-bag: I must lock it up— [*Recognizing the stranger with a shock*] Randall: how dare you? [*She marches at him past Mrs Hushabye, who retreats and joins Mangan near the sofa*].

RANDALL. How dare I what? I am not doing anything.

LADY UTTERWORD. Who told you I was here?

RANDALL. Hastings. You had just left when I called on you at Claridge's; so I followed you down here. You are looking extremely well.

LADY UTTERWORD. Dont presume to tell me so.

MRS HUSHABYE. What is wrong with Mr Randall, Addy?

LADY UTTERWORD [*recollecting herself*] Oh, nothing. But he has no right to come bothering you and papa without being invited. [*She goes to the window-seat and sits down, turning away from them ill-humoredly and looking into the garden, where Hector and Ellie are now seen strolling together*].

MRS HUSHABYE. I think you have not met Mr Mangan, Addy.

LADY UTTERWORD [*turning her head and nodding coldly to Mangan*] I beg your pardon. Randall: you have flustered me so: I made a perfect fool of myself.

MRS HUSHABYE. Lady Utterword. My sister. My y o u n g e r sister.

MANGAN [*bowing*] Pleased to meet you, Lady Utterword.

LADY UTTERWORD [*with marked interest*] Who is that gentleman walking in the garden with Miss Dunn?

MRS HUSHABYE. I dont know. She quarrelled mortally with my husband only ten minutes ago; and I didnt know anyone else had come. It must be a visitor. [*She goes to the window to look*]. Oh, it i s Hector. Theyve made it up.

LADY UTTERWORD. Your husband! That handsome man?

MRS HUSHABYE. Well, why shouldnt my husband be a handsome man?

RANDALL [*joining them at the window*] One's husband never is, Ariadne. [*He sits by Lady Utterword, on her right*].

MRS HUSHABYE. One's sister's husband always is, Mr Randall.

LADY UTTERWORD. Dont be vulgar, Randall. And you, Hesione, are just as bad.

Ellie and Hector come in from the garden by the starboard door. Randall rises. Ellie retires into the corner near the pantry. Hector comes forward; and Lady Utterword rises looking her very best.

MRS HUSHABYE. Hector: this is Addy.

HECTOR [*apparently surprised*] Not this lady.

LADY UTTERWORD [*smiling*] Why not?

HEARTBREAK HOUSE

HECTOR [*looking at her with a piercing glance of deep but respectful admiration, his moustache bristling*] I thought— [*Pulling himself together*] I beg your pardon, Lady Utterword. I am extremely glad to welcome you at last under our roof. [*He offers his hand with grave courtesy*].

MRS HUSHABYE. She wants to be kissed, Hector.

LADY UTTERWORD. Hesione! [*But she still smiles*].

MRS HUSHABYE. Call her Addy; and kiss her like a good brother-in-law; and have done with it. [*She leaves them to themselves*].

HECTOR. Behave yourself, Hesione. Lady Utterword is entitled not only to hospitality but to civilization.

LADY UTTERWORD [*gratefully*] Thank you, Hector. [*They shake hands cordially*].

Mazzini Dunn is seen crossing the garden from starboard to port.

CAPTAIN SHOTOVER [*coming from the pantry and addressing Ellie*] Your father has washed himself.

ELLIE [*quite self-possessed*] He often does, Captain Shotover.

CAPTAIN SHOTOVER. A strange conversion! I saw him through the pantry window.

Mazzini Dunn enters through the port window door, newly washed and brushed, and stops, smiling benevolently, between Mangan and Mrs Hushabye.

MRS HUSHABYE [*introducing*] Mr Mazzini Dunn, Lady Ut—oh, I forgot: youve met. [*Indicating Ellie*] Miss Dunn.

MAZZINI [*walking across the room to take Ellie's hand, and beaming at his own naughty irony*] I have met Miss Dunn also. She is my daughter. [*He draws her arm through his caressingly*].

MRS HUSHABYE. Of course: how stupid! Mr Utterword, my sister's-er—

RANDALL [*shaking hands agreeably*] Her brother-in-law, Mr Dunn. How do you do?

MRS HUSHABYE. This is my husband.

HECTOR. We have met, dear. Dont introduce us any more. [*He moves away to the big chair, and adds*] Wont you sit down, Lady Utterword? [*She does so very graciously*].

MRS HUSHABYE. Sorry. I hate it: it's like making people shew their tickets.

MAZZINI [*sententiously*] How little it tells us, after all! The great question is, not who we are, but what we are.

CAPTAIN SHOTOVER. Ha! What are you?

MAZZINI [*taken aback*] What am I?

CAPTAIN SHOTOVER. A thief, a pirate, and a murderer.

MAZZINI. I assure you you are mistaken.

CAPTAIN SHOTOVER. An adventurous life; but what does it end in? Respectability. A ladylike daughter. The language and appearance of a city missionary. Let it be a warning to all of you. [*He goes out through the garden*].

DUNN. I hope nobody here believes that I am a thief, a pirate, or a murderer. Mrs Hushabye: will you excuse me a moment? I must really go and explain. [*He follows the Captain*].

MRS HUSHABYE [*as he goes*] It's no use. Youd really better— [*But Dunn has vanished*]. We had better all go out and look for some tea. We never have regular tea; but you can always get some when you want: the servants keep it stewing all day. The kitchen veranda is the best place to ask. May I shew you? [*She goes to the starboard door*].

RANDALL [*going with her*] Thank you, I dont think I'll take any tea this afternoon. But if you will shew me the garden—?

MRS HUSHABYE. Theres nothing to see in the garden except papa's observatory, and a gravel pit with a cave where he keeps dynamite and things of that sort. However, it's pleasanter out of doors; so come along.

RANDALL. Dynamite! Isnt that rather risky?

MRS HUSHABYE. Well, we dont sit in the gravel pit when theres a thunderstorm.

LADY UTTERWORD. Thats something new. What is the dynamite for?

HECTOR. To blow up the human race if it goes too far. He is trying to discover a psychic ray that will explode all the explosives at the will of a Mahatma.

ELLIE. The Captain's tea is delicious, Mr Utterword.

MRS HUSHABYE [*stopping in the doorway*] Do you mean to say that youve had some of my father's tea? that you got round him before you were ten minutes in the house?

ELLIE. I did.

MRS HUSHABYE. You little devil! [*She goes out with Randall*].

MANGAN. Wont you come, Miss Ellie?

ELLIE. I'm too tired. I'll take a book up to my room and rest a little. [*She goes to the bookshelf*].

MANGAN. Right. You cant do better. But I'm disappointed. [*He follows Randall and Mrs Hushabye*].

Ellie, Hector, and Lady Utterword are left. Hector is close to Lady Utterword. They look at Ellie, waiting for her to go.

ELLIE [*looking at the title of a book*] Do you like stories of adventure, Lady Utterword?

LADY UTTERWORD [*patronizingly*] Of course, dear.

ELLIE. Then I'll leave you to Mr Hushabye. [*She goes out through the hall*].

HECTOR. That girl is mad about tales of adventure. The lies I have to tell her!

LADY UTTERWORD [*not interested in Ellie*] When you saw me what did you mean by saying that you thought, and then stopping short? What did you think?

HECTOR [*folding his arms and looking down at her magnetically*] May I tell you?

LADY UTTERWORD. Of course.

HECTOR. It will not sound very civil. I was on the point of saying "I thought you were a plain woman."

LADY UTTERWORD. Oh for shame, Hector! What right

had you to notice whether I am plain or not?

HECTOR. Listen to me, Ariadne. Until today I have seen only photographs of you; and no photograph can give the strange fascination of the daughters of that supernatural old man. There is some damnable quality in them that destroys men's moral sense, and carries them beyond honor and dishonor. You know that, dont you?

LADY UTTERWORD. Perhaps I do, Hector. But let me warn you once for all that I am a rigidly conventional woman. You may think because I'm a Shotover that I'm a Bohemian, because we are all so horribly Bohemian. But I'm not. I hate and loathe Bohemianism. No child brought up in a strict Puritan household ever suffered from Puritanism as I suffered from our Bohemianism.

HECTOR. Our children are like that. They spend their holidays in the houses of their respectable schoolfellows.

LADY UTTERWORD. I shall invite them for Christmas.

HECTOR. Their absence leaves us both without our natural chaperons.

LADY UTTERWORD. Children are certainly very inconvenient sometimes. But intelligent people can always manage, unless they are Bohemians.

HECTOR. You are no Bohemian; but you are no Puritan either: your attraction is alive and powerful. What sort of woman do you count yourself?

LADY UTTERWORD. I am a woman of the world, Hector; and I can assure you that if you will only take the trouble always to do the perfectly correct thing, and to say the perfectly correct thing, you can do just what you like. An ill-conducted, careless woman gets simply no chance. An ill-conducted, careless man is never allowed within arms length of any woman worth knowing.

HECTOR. I see. You are neither a Bohemian woman nor a Puritan woman. You are a dangerous woman.

LADY UTTERWORD. On the contrary, I am a safe woman.

HECTOR. You are a most accursedly attractive woman. Mind: I am not making love to you. I do not like being

522

attracted. But you had better know how I feel if you are going to stay here.

LADY UTTERWORD. You are an exceedingly clever lady-killer, Hector. And terribly handsome. I am quite a good player, myself, at that game. Is it quite understood that we are only playing?

HECTOR. Quite. I am deliberately playing the fool, out of sheer worthlessness.

LADY UTTERWORD [*rising brightly*] Well, you are my brother-in-law. Hesione asked you to kiss me. [*He seizes her in his arms, and kisses her strenuously*]. Oh! that was a little more than play, brother-in-law. [*She pushes him suddenly away*]. You shall not do that again.

HECTOR. In effect, you got your claws deeper into me than I intended.

MRS HUSHABYE [*coming in from the garden*] Dont let me disturb you: I only want a cap to put on daddiest. The sun is setting; and he'll catch cold. [*She makes for the door leading to the hall*].

LADY UTTERWORD. Your husband is quite charming, darling. He has actually condescended to kiss me at last. I shall go into the garden: it's cooler now. [*She goes out by the port door*].

MRS HUSHABYE. Take care, dear child. I dont believe any man can kiss Addy without falling in love with her. [*She goes into the hall*].

HECTOR [*striking himself on the chest*] Fool! Goat!

Mrs Hushabye comes back with the Captain's cap.

HECTOR. Your sister is an extremely enterprising old girl. Wheres Miss Dunn!

MRS HUSHABYE. Mangan says she has gone up to her room for a nap. Addy wont let you talk to Ellie: she has marked you for her own.

HECTOR. She has the diabolical family fascination. I began making love to her automatically. What am I to do? I cant fall in love; and I cant hurt a woman's feelings by telling her so when she falls in love with me. And as

523

women are always falling in love with my moustache I get landed in all sorts of tedious and terrifying flirtations in which I'm not a bit in earnest.

MRS HUSHABYE. Oh, neither is Addy. She has never been in love in her life, though she has always been trying to fall in head over ears. She is worse than you, because you had one real go at least, with me.

HECTOR. That was a confounded madness. I cant believe that such an amazing experience is common. It has left its mark on me. I believe that is why I have never been able to repeat it.

MRS HUSHABYE [laughing and caressing his arm] We were frightfully in love with one another, Hector. It was such an enchanting dream that I have never been able to grudge it to you or anyone else since. I have invited all sorts of pretty women to the house on the chance of giving you another turn. But it has never come off.

HECTOR. I dont know that I want it to come off. It was damned dangerous. You fascinated me; but I loved you; so it was heaven. This sister of yours fascinates me; but I hate her; so it is hell. I shall kill her if she persists.

MRS HUSHABYE. Nothing will kill Addy: she is as strong as a horse. [Releasing him] Now I am going off to fascinate somebody.

HECTOR. The Foreign Office toff? Randall?

MRS HUSHABYE. Goodness gracious, no! Why should I fascinate him?

HECTOR. I presume you dont mean the bloated capitalist, Mangan?

MRS HUSHABYE. Hm! I think he had better be fascinated by me than by Ellie. [She is going into the garden when the Captain comes in from it with some sticks in his hand]. What have you got there, daddiest?

CAPTAIN SHOTOVER. Dynamite.

MRS HUSHABYE. Youve been to the gravel pit. Dont drop it about the house: theres a dear. [She goes into the garden, where the evening light is now very red].

524

HECTOR. Listen, O sage. How long dare you concentrate on a feeling without risking having it fixed in your consciousness all the rest of your life?

CAPTAIN SHOTOVER. Ninety minutes. An hour and a half. [*He goes into the pantry*].

Hector, left alone, contracts his brows, and falls into a daydream. He does not move for some time. Then he folds his arms. Then, throwing his hands behind him, and gripping one with the other, he strides tragically once to and fro. Suddenly he snatches his walking-stick from the teak table, and draws it; for it is a sword-stick. He fights a desperate duel with an imaginary antagonist, and after many vicissitudes runs him through the body up to the hilt. He sheathes his sword and throws it on the sofa, falling into another reverie as he does so. He looks straight into the eyes of an imaginary woman; seizes her by the arms; and says in a deep and thrilling tone "Do you love me!" The Captain comes out of the pantry at this moment; and Hector, caught with his arms stretched out and his fists clenched, has to account for his attitude by going through a series of gymnastic exercises.

CAPTAIN SHOTOVER. That sort of strength is no good. You will never be as strong as a gorilla.

HECTOR. What is the dynamite for?

CAPTAIN SHOTOVER. To kill fellows like Mangan.

HECTOR. No use. They will always be able to buy more dynamite than you.

CAPTAIN SHOTOVER. I will make a dynamite that he cannot explode.

HECTOR. And that you can, eh?

CAPTAIN SHOTOVER. Yes: when I have attained the seventh degree of concentration.

HECTOR. Whats the use of that? You never do attain it.

CAPTAIN SHOTOVER. What then is to be done? Are we to be kept for ever in the mud by these hogs to whom the universe is nothing but a machine for greasing their bristles and filling their snouts?

525

HECTOR. Are Mangan's bristles worse than Randall's lovelocks?

CAPTAIN SHOTOVER. We must win powers of life and death over them both. I refuse to die until I have invented the means.

HECTOR. Who are we that we should judge them?

CAPTAIN SHOTOVER. What are they that they should judge us? Yet they do, unhesitatingly. There is enmity between our seed and their seed. They know it and act on it, strangling our souls. They believe in themselves. When we believe in ourselves, we shall kill them.

HECTOR. It is the same seed. You forget that your pirate has a very nice daughter. Mangan's son may be a Plato: Randall's a Shelley. What was my father?

CAPTAIN SHOTOVER. The damndest scoundrel I ever met. [*He replaces the drawing-board; sits down at the table; and begins to mix a wash of color*].

HECTOR. Precisely. Well, dare you kill his innocent grandchildren?

CAPTAIN SHOTOVER. They are mine also.

HECTOR. Just so. We are members one of another. [*He throws himself carelessly on the sofa*]. I tell you I have often thought of this killing of human vermin. Many men have thought of it. Decent men are like Daniel in the lion's den: their survival is a miracle; and they do not always survive. We live among the Mangans and Randalls and Billie Dunns as they, poor devils, live among the disease germs and the doctors and the lawyers and the parsons and the restaurant chefs and the tradesmen and the servants and all the rest of the parasites and blackmailers. What are our terrors to theirs? Give me the power to kill them; and I'll spare them in sheer—

CAPTAIN SHOTOVER [*cutting in sharply*] Fellow feeling?

HECTOR. No. I should kill myself if I believed that. I must believe that my spark, small as it is, is divine, and that the red light over their door is hell fire. I should spare them in simple magnanimous pity.

CAPTAIN SHOTOVER. You cant spare them until you have the power to kill them. At present they have the power to kill you. There are millions of blacks over the water for them to train and let loose on us. Theyre going to do it. Theyre doing it already.

HECTOR. They are too stupid to use their power.

CAPTAIN SHOTOVER [*throwing down his brush and coming to the end of the sofa*] Do not deceive yourself: they do use it. We kill the better half of ourselves every day to propitiate them. The knowledge that these people are there to render all our aspirations barren prevents us having the aspirations. And when we are tempted to seek their destruction they bring forth demons to delude us, disguised as pretty daughters, and singers and poets and the like, for whose sake we spare them.

HECTOR [*sitting up and leaning towards him*] May not Hesione be such a demon, brought forth by you lest I should slay you?

CAPTAIN SHOTOVER. That is possible. She has used you up, and left you nothing but dreams, as some women do.

HECTOR. Vampire women, demon women.

CAPTAIN SHOTOVER. Men think the world well lost for them, and lose it accordingly. Who are the men that do things? The husbands of the shrew and of the drunkard, the men with the thorn in the flesh. [*Walking distractedly away towards the pantry*] I must think these things out. [*Turning suddenly*] But I go on with the dynamite none the less. I will discover a ray mightier than any X-ray: a mind ray that will explode the ammunition in the belt of my adversary before he can point his gun at me. And I must hurry. I am old: I have no time to waste in talk. [*He is about to go into the pantry, and Hector is making for the hall, when Hesione comes back*].

MRS HUSHABYE. Daddiest: you and Hector must come and help me to entertain all these people. What on earth were you shouting about?

527

HECTOR [*stopping in the act of turning the door handle*] He is madder than usual.

MRS HUSHABYE. We all are.

HECTOR. I must change. [*He resumes his door opening*].

MRS HUSHABYE. Stop, stop. Come back, both of you. Come back. [*They return, reluctantly*]. Money is running short.

HECTOR. Money! Where are my April dividends?

MRS HUSHABYE. Where is the snow that fell last year?

CAPTAIN SHOTOVER. Where is all the money you had for that patent lifeboat I invented?

MRS HUSHABYE. Five hundred pounds; and I have made it last since Easter!

CAPTAIN SHOTOVER. Since Easter! Barely four months! Monstrous extravagance! I could live for seven years on £500.

MRS HUSHABYE. Not keeping open house as we do here, daddiest.

CAPTAIN SHOTOVER. Only £500 for that lifeboat! I got twelve thousand for the invention before that.

MRS HUSHABYE. Yes, dear; but that was for the ship with the magnetic keel that sucked up submarines. Living at the rate we do, you cannot afford life-saving inventions. Cant you think of something that will murder half Europe at one bang?

CAPTAIN SHOTOVER. No. I am ageing fast. My mind does not dwell on slaughter as it did when I was a boy. Why doesnt your husband invent something? He does nothing but tell lies to women.

HECTOR. Well, that is a form of invention, is it not? However, you are right: I ought to support my wife.

MRS HUSHABYE. Indeed you shall do nothing of the sort: I should never see you from breakfast to dinner. I want my husband.

HECTOR [*bitterly*] I might as well be your lapdog.

MRS HUSHABYE. Do you want to be my breadwinner,

like the other poor husbands?

HECTOR. No, by thunder! What a damned creature a husband is anyhow!

MRS HUSHABYE [*to the Captain*] What about that harpoon cannon?

CAPTAIN SHOTOVER. No use. It kills whales, not men.

MRS HUSHABYE. Why not? You fire the harpoon out of a cannon. It sticks in the enemy's general; you wind him in; and there you are.

HECTOR. You are your father's daughter, Hesione.

CAPTAIN SHOTOVER. There is something in it. Not to wind in generals: they are not dangerous. But one could fire a grapnel and wind in a machine gun or even a tank. I will think it out.

MRS HUSHABYE [*squeezing the Captain's arm affectionately*] Saved! You a r e a darling, daddiest. Now we must go back to these dreadful people and entertain them.

CAPTAIN SHOTOVER. They have had no dinner. Dont forget that.

HECTOR. Neither have I. And it is dark: it must be all hours.

MRS HUSHABYE. Oh, Guinness will produce some sort of dinner for them. The servants always take jolly good care that there is food in the house.

CAPTAIN SHOTOVER [*raising a strange wail in the darkness*] What a house! What a daughter!

MRS HUSHABYE [*raving*] What a father!

HECTOR [*following suit*] What a husband!

CAPTAIN SHOTOVER. Is there no thunder in heaven?

HECTOR. Is there no beauty, no bravery, on earth?

MRS HUSHABYE. What do men want? They have their food, their firesides, their clothes mended, and our love at the end of the day. Why are they not satisfied? Why do they envy us the pain with which we bring them into the world, and make strange dangers and torments for themselves to be even with us?

CAPTAIN SHOTOVER [*weirdly chanting*]

529

I built a house for my daughters, and opened the doors thereof,

That men might come for their choosing, and their betters spring from their love;

But one of them married a numskull;

HECTOR [*taking up the rhythm*]

The other a liar wed;

MRS HUSHABYE [*completing the stanza*]

And now must she lie beside him, even as she made her bed.

LADY UTTERWORD [*calling from the garden*] Hesione! Hesione! Where are you?

HECTOR. The cat is on the tiles.

MRS HUSHABYE. Coming, darling, coming. [*She goes quickly into the garden*].

The Captain goes back to his place at the table.

HECTOR [*going into the hall*] Shall I turn up the lights for you?

CAPTAIN SHOTOVER. No. Give me deeper darkness. Money is not made in the light.

END OF ACT I

ACT II

THE *same room, with the lights turned up and the curtains drawn. Ellie comes in, followed by Mangan. Both are dressed for dinner. She strolls to the drawing-table. He comes between the table and the wicker chair.*

MANGAN. What a dinner! I dont call it a dinner: I call it a meal.

ELLIE. I am accustomed to meals, Mr Mangan, and very lucky to get them. Besides, the captain cooked some macaroni for me.

MANGAN [*shuddering liverishly*] Too rich: I cant eat such things. I suppose it's because I have to work so much with my brain. Thats the worst of being a man of business: you are always thinking, thinking, thinking. By the way, now that we are alone, may I take the opportunity to come to a little understanding with you?

ELLIE [*settling into the draughtsman's seat*] Certainly. I should like to.

MANGAN [*taken aback*] Should you? That surprises me; for I thought I noticed this afternoon that you avoided me all you could. Not for the first time either.

ELLIE. I was very tired and upset. I wasn't used to the ways of this extraordinary house. Please forgive me.

MANGAN. Oh, thats all right: I dont mind. But Captain Shotover has been talking to me about you. You and me, you know.

ELLIE [*interested*] The Captain! What did he say?

MANGAN. Well, he noticed the difference between our ages.

ELLIE. He notices everything.

MANGAN. You dont mind, then?

ELLIE. Of course I know quite well that our engagement—

MANGAN. Oh! you call it an engagement.

ELLIE. Well, isnt it?

MANGAN. Oh, yes, yes: no doubt it is if you hold to it.

531

This is the first time youve used the word; and I didnt quite know where we stood: thats all. [*He sits down in the wicker chair; and resigns himself to allow her to lead the conversation*]. You were saying——?

ELLIE. Was I? I forget. Tell me. Do you like this part of the country? I heard you ask Mr Hushabye at dinner whether there are any nice houses to let down here.

MANGAN. I like the place. The air suits me. I shouldnt be surprised if I settled down here.

ELLIE. Nothing would please me better. The air suits me too. And I want to be near Hesione.

MANGAN [*with growing uneasiness*] The air may suit us; but the question is, should we suit one another? Have you thought about that?

ELLIE. Mr. Mangan: we must be sensible, mustnt we? It's no use pretending that we are Romeo and Juliet. But we can get on very well together if we choose to make the best of it. Your kindness of heart will make it easy for me.

MANGAN [*leaning forward, with the beginning of something like deliberate unpleasantness in his voice*] Kindness of heart, eh? I ruined your father, didnt I?

ELLIE. Oh, not intentionally.

MANGAN. Yes I did. Ruined him on purpose.

ELLIE. On purpose!

MANGAN. Not out of ill-nature, you know. And youll admit that I kept a job for him when I had finished with him. But business is business; and I ruined him as a matter of business.

ELLIE. I dont understand how that can be. Are you trying to make me feel that I need not be grateful to you, so that I may choose freely?

MANGAN [*rising aggressively*] No. I mean what I say.

ELLIE. But how could it possibly do you any good to ruin my father? The money he lost was yours.

MANGAN [*with a sour laugh*] W a s mine! It i s mine, Miss Ellie, and all the money the other fellows lost too. [*He shoves his hands into his pockets and shews his teeth*].

I just smoked them out like a hive of bees. What do you say to that? A bit of a shock, eh?

ELLIE. It would have been, this morning. N o w! you cant think how little it matters. But it's quite interesting. Only, you must explain it to me. I dont understand it. [*Propping her elbows on the drawing-board and her chin on her hands, she composes herself to listen with a combination of conscious curiosity with unconscious contempt which provokes him to more and more unpleasantness, and an attempt at patronage of her ignorance*].

MANGAN. Of course you dont understand: what do you know about business? You just listen and learn. Your father's business was a new business; and I dont start new businesses: I let other fellows start them. They put all their money and their friends' money into starting them. They wear out their souls and bodies trying to make a success of them. Theyre what you call enthusiasts. But the first dead lift of the thing is too much for them; and they havnt enough financial experience. In a year or so they have either to let the whole show go bust, or sell out to a new lot of fellows for a few deferred ordinary shares: that is, if theyre lucky enough to get anything at all. As likely as not the very same thing happens to the new lot. They put in more money and a couple of years more work; and then perhaps t h e y have to sell out to a third lot. If it's really a big thing the third lot will have to sell out too, and leave t h e i r work and t h e i r money behind them. And thats where the real business man comes in: where I come in. But I'm cleverer than some: I dont mind dropping a little money to start the process. I took your father's measure. I saw that he had a sound idea, and that he would work himself silly for it if he got the chance. I saw that he was a child in business, and was dead certain to outrun his expenses and be in too great a hurry to wait for his market. I knew that the surest way to ruin a man who doesnt know how to handle money is to give him some. I explained my idea to some friends in the city, and they found the money;

533

for I take no risks in ideas, even when theyre my own. Your father and the friends that ventured their money with him were no more to me than a heap of squeezed lemons. Youve been wasting your gratitude: my kind heart is all rot. I'm sick of it. When I see your father beaming at me with his moist, grateful eyes, regularly wallowing in gratitude, I sometimes feel I must tell him the truth or burst. What stops me is that I know he wouldnt believe me. He'd think it was my modesty, as you did just now. He'd think anything rather than the truth, which is that he's a blamed fool, and I am a man that knows how to take care of himself. [*He throws himself back into the big chair with large self-approval*]. Now what do you think of me, Miss Ellie?

ELLIE [*dropping her hands*] How strange! that my mother, who knew nothing at all about business, should have been quite right about you! She always said—not before papa, of course, but to us children—that you were just that sort of man.

MANGAN [*sitting up, much hurt*] Oh! did she? And yet she'd have let you marry me.

ELLIE. Well, you see, Mr Mangan, my mother married a very good man—for whatever you may think of my father as a man of business, he is the soul of goodness—and she is not at all keen on my doing the same.

MANGAN. Anyhow, you dont want to marry me now, do you?

ELLIE [*very calmly*] Oh, I think so. Why not?

MANGAN [*rising aghast*] Why not!

ELLIE. I dont see why we shouldnt get on very well together.

MANGAN. Well, but look here, you know— [*He stops, quite at a loss*].

ELLIE [*patiently*] Well?

MANGAN. Well, I thought you were rather particular about people's characters.

ELLIE. If we women were particular about men's char-

534

acters, we should never get married at all, Mr Mangan.

MANGAN. A child like you talking of "we women"! What next! Youre not in earnest?

ELLIE. Yes I am. Arnt you?

MANGAN. You mean to hold me to it?

ELLIE. Do you wish to back out of it?

MANGAN. Oh no. Not exactly back out of it.

ELLIE. Well?

He has nothing to say. With a long whispered whistle, he drops into the wicker chair and stares before him like a beggared gambler. But a cunning look soon comes into his face. He leans over towards her on his right elbow, and speaks in a low steady voice.

MANGAN. Suppose I told you I was in love with another woman!

ELLIE [*echoing him*] Suppose I told you I was in love with another man!

MANGAN [*bouncing angrily out of his chair*] I'm not joking.

ELLIE. Who told you *I* was?

MANGAN. I tell you I'm serious. Youre too young to be serious; but youll have to believe me. I want to be near your friend Mrs Hushabye. I'm in love with her. Now the murder's out.

ELLIE. I want to be near your friend Mr Hushabye. I'm in love with him. [*She rises and adds with a frank air*] Now we are in one another's confidence, we shall be real friends. Thank you for telling me.

MANGAN [*almost beside himself*] Do you think I'll be made a convenience of like this?

ELLIE. Come, Mr Mangan! you made a business convenience of my father. Well, a woman's business is marriage. Why shouldnt I make a domestic convenience of you?

MANGAN. Because I dont choose, see? Because I'm not a silly gull like your father. Thats why.

ELLIE [*with serene contempt*] You are not good enough to clean my father's boots, Mr Mangan; and I am paying

535

you a great compliment in condescending to make a convenience of you, as you call it. Of course you are free to throw over our engagement if you like; but, if you do, youll never enter Hesione's house again: I will take care of that.

MANGAN [*gasping*] You little devil, youve done me. [*On the point of collapsing into the big chair again he recovers himself*] Wait a bit, though: youre not so cute as you think. You cant beat Boss Mangan as easy as that. Suppose I go straight to Mrs Hushabye and tell her that youre in love with her husband.

ELLIE. She knows it.

MANGAN. You told her!!!

ELLIE. She told me.

MANGAN [*clutching at his bursting temples*] Oh, this is a crazy house. Or else I'm going clean off my chump. Is she making a swop with you—she to have your husband and you to have hers?

ELLIE. Well, you dont want us both, do you?

MANGAN [*throwing himself into the chair distractedly*] My brain wont stand it. My head's going to split. Help! Help me to hold it. Quick: hold it: squeeze it. Save me. [*Ellie comes behind his chair; clasps his head hard for a moment; then begins to draw her hands from his forehead back to his ears*]. Thank you. [*Drowsily*] Thats very refreshing. [*Waking a little*] Don't you hypnotize me, though. Ive seen men made fools of by hypnotism.

ELLIE [*steadily*] Be quiet. Ive seen men made fools of without hypnotism.

MANGAN [*humbly*] You dont dislike touching me, I hope. You never touched me before, I noticed.

ELLIE. Not since you fell in love naturally with a grown-up nice woman, who will never expect you to make love to her. And I will never expect him to make love to me.

MANGAN. He may, though.

ELLIE [*making her passes rhythmically*] Hush. Go to

536

sleep. Do you hear? You are to go to sleep, go to sleep, go to sleep; be quiet, deeply deeply quiet; sleep, sleep, sleep, sleep, sleep.

He falls asleep. Ellie steals away; turns the light out; and goes into the garden.

Nurse Guinness opens the door and is seen in the light which comes in from the hall.

GUINNESS [*speaking to someone outside*] Mr Mangan's not here, ducky: theres no one here. It's all dark.

MRS HUSHABYE [*without*] Try the garden. Mr Dunn and I will be in my boudoir. Shew him the way.

GUINNESS. Yes, ducky. [*She makes for the garden door in the dark; stumbles over the sleeping Mangan; and screams*]. Ahoo! Oh Lord, sir! I beg your pardon, I'm sure: I didnt see you in the dark. Who is it? [*She goes back to the door and turns on the light*]. Oh, Mr Mangan, sir, I hope I havnt hurt you plumping into your lap like that. [*Coming to him*] I was looking for you, sir. Mrs Husha-bye says will you please— [*Noticing that he remains quite insensible*] Oh, my good Lord, I hope I havnt killed him. Sir! Mr Mangan! Sir! [*She shakes him; and he is rolling inertly off the chair on the floor when she holds him up and props him against the cushion*]. Miss Hessy! Miss Hessy! Quick, doty darling. Miss Hessy! [*Mrs Hushabye comes in from the hall, followed by Mazzini Dunn*]. Oh, Miss Hessy, Ive been and killed him.

Mazzini runs round the back of the chair to Mangan's right hand, and sees that the nurse's words are apparently only too true.

MAZZINI. What tempted you to commit such a crime, woman?

MRS HUSHABYE [*trying not to laugh*] Do you mean you did it on purpose?

GUINNESS. Now is it likely I'd kill any man on purpose? I fell over him in the dark; and I'm a pretty tidy weight. He never spoke nor moved until I shook him; and then he would have dropped dead on the floor. Isnt it tiresome?

537

MRS HUSHABYE [*going past the nurse to Mangan's side, and inspecting him less credulously than Mazzini*] Nonsense! he is not dead: he is only asleep. I can see him breathing.

GUINNESS. But why wont he wake?

MAZZINI [*speaking very politely into Mangan's ear*] Mangan! My dear Mangan! [*He blows into Mangan's ear*].

MRS HUSHABYE. Thats no good. [*She shakes him vigorously*]. Mr Mangan: wake up. Do you hear? [*He begins to roll over*]. Oh! Nurse, nurse: he's falling: help me.

Nurse Guinness rushes to the rescue. With Mazzini's assistance, Mangan is propped safely up again.

GUINNESS [*behind the chair; bending over to test the case with her nose*] Would he be drunk, do you think, pet?

MRS HUSHABYE. Had he any of papa's rum?

MAZZINI. It cant be that: he is most abstemious. I am afraid he drank too much formerly, and has to drink too little now. You know, Mrs Hushabye, I really think he has been hypnotized.

GUINNESS. Hip no what, sir?

MAZZINI. One evening at home, after we had seen a hypnotizing performance, the children began playing at it; and Ellie stroked my head. I assure you I went off dead asleep; and they had to send for a professional to wake me up after I had slept eighteen hours. They had to carry me upstairs; and as the poor children were not very strong, they let me slip; and I rolled right down the whole flight and never woke up. [*Mrs Hushabye splutters*]. Oh, you may laugh, Mrs Hushabye; but I might have been killed.

MRS HUSHABYE. I couldnt have helped laughing even if you had been, Mr Dunn. So Ellie has hypnotized him. What fun!

MAZZINI. Oh no, no, no. It was such a terrible lesson to her: nothing would induce her to try such a thing again.

MRS HUSHABYE. Then who did it? *I* didnt.

MAZZINI. I thought perhaps the Captain might have

538

done it unintentionally. He is so fearfully magnetic: I feel vibrations whenever he comes close to me.

GUINNESS. The Captain will get him out of it anyhow, sir: I'll back him for that. I'll go fetch him. [*She makes for the pantry*].

MRS HUSHABYE. Wait a bit. [*To Mazzini*] You say he is all right for eighteen hours?

MAZZINI. Well, *I* was asleep for eighteen hours.

MRS HUSHABYE. Were you any the worse for it?

MAZZINI. I dont quite remember. They had poured brandy down my throat, you see; and—

MRS HUSHABYE. Quite. Anyhow, you survived. Nurse, darling: go and ask Miss Dunn to come to us here. Say I want to speak to her particularly. You will find her with Mr Hushabye probably.

GUINNESS. I think not, ducky: Miss Addy is with him. But I'll find her and send her to you. [*She goes out into the garden*].

MRS HUSHABYE [*calling Mazzini's attention to the figure on the chair*] Now, Mr Dunn, look. Just look. Look hard. Do you still intend to sacrifice your daughter to that thing?

MAZZINI [*troubled*] You have completely upset me, Mrs Hushabye, by all you have said to me. That anyone could imagine that I—*I*, a consecrated soldier of freedom, if I may say so—could sacrifice Ellie to anybody or anyone, or that I should ever have dreamed of forcing her inclinations in any way, is a most painful blow to my—well, I suppose you would say to my good opinion of myself.

MRS HUSHABYE [*rather stolidly*] Sorry.

MAZZINI [*looking forlornly at the body*] What is your objection to poor Mangan, Mrs Hushabye? He looks all right to me. But then I am so accustomed to him.

MRS HUSHABYE. Have you no heart? Have you no sense? Look at the brute! Think of poor weak innocent Ellie in the clutches of this slavedriver, who spends his life making thousands of rough violent workmen bend to his

539

will and sweat for him: a man accustomed to have great masses of iron beaten into shape for him by steam-hammers! to fight with women and girls over a halfpenny an hour ruthlessly! a captain of industry, I think you call him, dont you? Are you going to fling your delicate, sweet, helpless child into such a beast's claws just because he will keep her in an expensive house and make her wear diamonds to shew how rich he is?

MAZZINI [*staring at her in wide-eyed amazement*] Bless you, dear Mrs Hushabye, what romantic ideas of business you have! Poor dear Mangan isnt a bit like that.

MRS HUSHABYE [*scornfully*] Poor dear Mangan indeed!

MAZZINI. But he doesnt know anything about machinery. He never goes near the men: he couldnt manage them: he is afraid of them. I never can get him to take the least interest in the works: he hardly knows more about them than you do. People are cruelly unjust to Mangan: they think he is all rugged strength just because his manners are bad.

MRS HUSHABYE. Do you mean to tell me he isnt strong enough to crush poor little Ellie?

MAZZINI. Of course it's very hard to say how any marriage will turn out; but speaking for myself, I should say that he wont have a dog's chance against Ellie. You know, Ellie has remarkable strength of character. I think it is because I taught her to like Shakespear when she was very young.

MRS HUSHABYE [*contemptuously*] Shakespear! The next thing you will tell me is that you could have made a great deal more money than Mangan. [*She retires to the sofa, and sits down at the port end of it in the worst of humors*].

MAZZINI [*following her and taking the other end*] No: I'm no good at making money. I dont care enough for it, somehow. I'm not ambitious! that must be it. Mangan is wonderful about money: he thinks of nothing else. He is so dreadfully afraid of being poor. I am always thinking of other things: even at the works I think of the things we are doing and not of what they cost. And the worst of it is, poor Mangan doesnt know what to do with his money when he gets it. He is such a baby that he doesnt know even what to eat and drink: he has ruined his liver eating and drinking the wrong things; and now he can hardly eat at all. Ellie will diet him splendidly. You will be surprised when you come to know him better: he is really the most helpless of mortals. You get quite a protective feeling towards him.

MRS HUSHABYE. Then who manages his business, pray?

MAZZINI. I do. And of course other people like me.

MRS HUSHABYE. Footling people, you mean.

MAZZINI. I suppose youd think us so.

MRS HUSHABYE. And pray why dont you do without him if youre all so much cleverer?

MAZZINI. Oh, we couldnt: we should ruin the business in a year. I've tried; and I know. We should spend too much on everything. We should improve the quality of the goods and make them too dear. We should be sentimental about the hard cases among the workpeople. But Mangan keeps us in order. He is down on us about every extra halfpenny. We could never do without him. You see, he will sit up all night thinking of how to save sixpence. Wont Ellie make him jump, though, when she takes his house in hand!

MRS HUSHABYE. Then the creature is a fraud even as a captain of industry!

MAZZINI. I am afraid all the captains of industry are what y o u call frauds, Mrs Hushabye. Of course there are some manufacturers who really do understand their own works; but they dont make as high a rate of profit as Mangan does. I assure you Mangan is quite a good fellow in his way. He means well.

MRS HUSHABYE. He doesnt look well. He is not in his first youth, is he?

MAZZINI. After all, no husband is in his first youth for

very long, Mrs Hushabye. And men cant afford to marry in their first youth nowadays.

MRS HUSHABYE. Now if *I* said that, it would sound witty. Why cant y o u say it wittily? What on earth is the matter with you? Why dont you inspire everybody with confidence? with respect?

MAZZINI [*humbly*] I think that what is the matter with me is that I am poor. You dont know what that means at home. Mind: I dont say they have ever complained. Theyve all been wonderful: theyve been proud of my poverty. Theyve even joked about it quite often. But my wife has had a very poor time of it. She has been quite resigned—

MRS HUSHABYE [*shuddering involuntarily*]!!

MAZZINI. There! You see, Mrs Hushabye. I dont want Ellie to live on resignation.

MRS HUSHABYE. Do you want her to have to resign herself to living with a man she doesnt love?

MAZZINI [*wistfully*] Are you sure that would be worse than living with a man she did love, if he was a footling person?

MRS HUSHABYE [*relaxing her contemptuous attitude, quite interested in Mazzini now*] You know, I really think you must love Ellie very much; for you become quite clever when you talk about her.

MAZZINI. I didnt know I was so very stupid on other subjects.

MRS HUSHABYE. You are, sometimes.

MAZZINI [*turning his head away; for his eyes are wet*] I have learnt a good deal about myself from you, Mrs Hushabye; and I'm afraid I shall not be the happier for your plain speaking. But if you thought I needed it to make me think of Ellie's happiness you were very much mistaken.

MRS HUSHABYE [*leaning towards him kindly*] Have I been a beast?

MAZZINI [*pulling himself together*] It doesnt matter about me, Mrs Hushabye. I think you like Ellie; and that is enough for me.

542

MRS HUSHABYE. I'm beginning to like you a little. I perfectly loathed you at first. I thought you the most odious, self-satisfied, boresome elderly prig I ever met.

MAZZINI [*resigned, and now quite cheerful*] I daresay I am all that. I never have been a favorite with gorgeous women like you. They always frighten me.

MRS HUSHABYE [*pleased*] Am I a gorgeous woman, Mazzini? I shall fall in love with you presently.

MAZZINI [*with placid gallantry*] No you wont, Hesione. But you would be quite safe. Would you believe it that quite a lot of women have flirted with me because I am quite safe? But they get tired of me for the same reason.

MRS HUSHABYE [*mischievously*]. Take care. You may not be so safe as you think.

MAZZINI. Oh yes, quite safe. You see, I have been in love really: the sort of love that only happens once. [*Softly*] Thats why Ellie is such a lovely girl.

MRS HUSHABYE. Well, really, you a r e coming out. Are you quite sure you wont let me tempt you into a second grand passion?

MAZZINI. Quite. It wouldnt be natural. The fact is, you dont strike on my box, Mrs Hushabye; and I certainly dont strike on yours.

MRS HUSHABYE. I see. Your marriage was a safety match.

MAZZINI. What a very witty application of the expression I used! I should never have thought of it.

Ellie comes in from the garden, looking anything but happy.

MRS HUSHABYE [*rising*] Oh! here is Ellie at last. [*She goes behind the sofa*].

ELLIE [*on the threshold of the starboard door*] Guinness said you wanted me: you and papa.

MRS HUSHABYE. You have kept us waiting so long that it almost came to—well, never mind. Your father is a very wonderful man [*she ruffles his hair affectionately*]: the only one I ever met who could resist me when I made myself really agreeable. [*She comes to the big chair, on Mangan's left*]. Come here. I have something to shew you. [*Ellie strolls listlessly to the other side of the chair*]. Look.

ELLIE [*contemplating Mangan without interest*] I know. He is only asleep. We had a talk after dinner; and he fell asleep in the middle of it.

MRS HUSHABYE. You did it, Ellie. You put him asleep.

MAZZINI [*rising quickly and coming to the back of the chair*] Oh, I hope not. Did you, Ellie?

ELLIE [*wearily*] He asked me to.

MAZZINI. But it's dangerous. You know what happened to me.

ELLIE [*utterly indifferent*] Oh, I daresay I can wake him. If not, somebody else can.

MRS HUSHABYE. It doesnt matter, anyhow, because I have at last persuaded your father that you dont want to marry him.

ELLIE [*suddenly coming out of her listlessness, much vexed*] But why did you do that, Hesione? I do want to marry him. I fully intend to marry him.

MAZZINI. Are you quite sure, Ellie? Mrs Hushabye has made me feel that I may have been thoughtless and selfish about it.

ELLIE [*very clearly and steadily*] Papa. When Mrs Hushabye takes it on herself to explain to you what I think or dont think, shut your ears tight; and shut your eyes too. Hesione knows nothing about me: she hasnt the least notion of the sort of person I am, and never will. I promise you I wont do anything I dont want to do and mean to do for my own sake.

MAZZINI. You are quite, quite sure?

ELLIE. Quite, quite sure. Now you must go away and leave me to talk to Mrs Hushabye.

MAZZINI. But I should like to hear. Shall I be in the way?

ELLIE [*inexorable*] I had rather talk to her alone.

MAZZINI [*affectionately*] Oh, well, I know what a nuisance parents are, dear. I will be good and go. [*He goes to the garden door*]. By the way, do you remember the address of that professional who woke me up? Dont you think I had better telegraph to him?

MRS HUSHABYE [*moving towards the sofa*] It's too late to telegraph tonight.

MAZZINI. I suppose so. I do hope he'll wake up in the course of the night. [*He goes out into the garden*].

ELLIE [*turning vigorously on Hesione the moment her father is out of the room*] Hesione: what the devil do you mean by making mischief with my father about Mangan?

MRS HUSHABYE [*promptly losing her temper*] Dont you dare speak to me like that, you little minx. Remember that you are in my house.

ELLIE. Stuff! Why dont you mind your own business? What is it to you whether I choose to marry Mangan or not?

MRS HUSHABYE. Do you suppose you can bully me, you miserable little matrimonial adventurer?

ELLIE. Every woman who hasnt any money is a matrimonial adventurer. It's easy for you to talk: you have never known what it is to want money; and you can pick up men as if they were daisies. I am poor and respectable—

MRS HUSHABYE [*interrupting*] Ho! respectable! How did you pick up Mangan? How did you pick up my husband? You have the audacity to tell me that I am a—a—a—

ELLIE. A siren. So you are. You were born to lead men by the nose: if you werent, Marcus would have waited for me, perhaps.

MRS HUSHABYE [*suddenly melting and half laughing*] Oh, my poor Ellie, my pettikins, my unhappy darling! I am so sorry about Hector. But what can I do? It's not my fault: I'd give him to you if I could.

ELLIE. I dont blame you for that.

MRS HUSHABYE. What a brute I was to quarrel with you and call you names! Do kiss me and say youre not

545

angry with me.

ELLIE [*fiercely*] Oh, dont slop and gush and be sentimental. Dont you see that unless I can be hard—as hard as nails—I shall go mad? I dont care a damn about your calling me names: do you think a woman in my situation can feel a few hard words?

MRS HUSHABYE. Poor little woman! Poor little situation!

ELLIE. I suppose you think youre being sympathetic. You are just foolish and stupid and selfish. You see me getting a smasher right in the face that kills a whole part of my life: the best part that can never come again; and you think you can help me over it by a little coaxing and kissing. When I want all the strength I can get to lean on: something iron, something stony, I dont care how cruel it is, you go all mushy and want to slobber over me. I'm not angry; I'm not unfriendly; but for God's sake do pull yourself together; and dont think that because youre on velvet and always have been, women who are in hell can take it as easily as you.

MRS HUSHABYE [*shrugging her shoulders*] Very well. [*She sits down on the sofa in her old place*]. But I warn you that when I am neither coaxing and kissing nor laughing, I am just wondering how much longer I can stand living in this cruel, damnable world. You object to the siren: well, I drop the siren. You want to rest your wounded bosom against a grindstone. Well [*folding her arms*], here is the grindstone.

ELLIE [*sitting down beside her, appeased*] Thats better: you really have the trick of falling in with everyone's mood; but you dont understand, because you are not the sort of woman for whom there is only one man and only one chance.

MRS HUSHABYE. I certainly dont understand how your marrying that object [*indicating Mangan*] will console you for not being able to marry Hector.

ELLIE. Perhaps you dont understand why I was quite

a nice girl this morning, and am now neither a girl nor particularly nice.

MRS HUSHABYE. Oh yes, I do. It's because you have made up your mind to do something despicable and wicked.

ELLIE. I dont think so, Hesione. I must make the best of my ruined house.

MRS HUSHABYE. Pooh! Youll get over it. Your house isnt ruined.

ELLIE. Of course I shall get over it. You dont suppose I'm going to sit down and die of a broken heart, I hope, or be an old maid living on a pittance from the Sick and Indigent Room-keepers' Association. But my heart i s broken, all the same. What I mean by that is that I know that what has happened to me with Marcus will not happen to me ever again. In the world for me there is Marcus and a lot of other men of whom one is just the same as another. Well, if I cant have love, thats no reason why I should have poverty. If Mangan has nothing else, he has money.

MRS HUSHABYE. And are there no y o u n g men with money?

ELLIE. Not within my reach. Besides, a young man would have the right to expect love from me, and would perhaps leave me when he found I could not give it to him. Rich young men can get rid of their wives, you know, pretty cheaply. But this object, as you call him, can expect nothing more from me than I am prepared to give him.

MRS HUSHABYE. He will be your owner, remember. If he buys you, he will make the bargain pay him and not you. Ask your father.

ELLIE [*rising and strolling to the chair to contemplate their subject*] You need not trouble on that score, Hesione. I have more to give Boss Mangan than he has to give me: it is I who am buying him, and at a pretty good price too, I think. Women are better at that sort of bargain than men. I have taken the Boss's measure; and ten Boss Mangans shall not prevent me doing far more as I please as his wife than I have ever been able to do as a poor girl. [*Stooping to the recumbent figure*] Shall they, Boss? I think not. [*She passes on to the drawing-table, and leans against the end of it, facing the windows*]. I shall not have to spend most of my time wondering how long my gloves will last, anyhow.

MRS HUSHABYE [*rising superbly*] Ellie: you are a wicked sordid little beast. And to think that I actually condescended to fascinate that creature there to save you from him! Well, let me tell you this: if you make this disgusting match, you will never see Hector again if I can help it.

ELLIE [*unmoved*] I nailed Mangan by telling him that if he did not marry me he should never see you again. [*She lifts herself on her wrists and seats herself on the end of the table*].

MRS HUSHABYE [*recoiling*] Oh!

ELLIE. So you see I am not unprepared for your playing that trump against me. Well, you just try it: thats all. I should have made a man of Marcus, not a household pet.

MRS HUSHABYE [*flaming*] You dare!

ELLIE [*looking almost dangerous*] Set him thinking about me if y o u dare.

MRS HUSHABYE. Well, of all the impudent little fiends I ever met! Hector says there is a certain point at which the only answer you can give to a man who breaks all the rules is to knock him down. What would you say if I were to box your ears?

ELLIE [*calmly*] I should pull your hair.

MRS HUSHABYE [*mischievously*] That wouldnt hurt me. Perhaps it comes off at night.

ELLIE [*so taken aback that she drops off the table and runs to her*] Oh, you dont mean to say, Hesione, that your beautiful black hair is false?

MRS HUSHABYE [*patting it*] Dont tell Hector. He believes in it.

ELLIE [*groaning*] Oh! Even the hair that ensnared him false! Everything false!

MRS HUSHABYE. Pull it and try. Other women can

snare men in their hair; but I can swing a baby on mine. Aha! you cant do that, Goldylocks.

ELLIE [*heartbroken*] No. You have stolen m y babies.

MRS HUSHABYE. Pettikins: dont make me cry. You know, what you said about my making a household pet of him is a little true. Perhaps he ought to have waited for you. Would any other woman on earth forgive you?

ELLIE. Oh, what right had you to take him all for yourself! [*Pulling herself together*] There! You couldnt help it: neither of us could help it. He couldnt help it. No: dont say anything more: I cant bear it. Let us wake the object. [*She begins stroking Mangan's head, reversing the movement with which she put him to sleep*]. Wake up, do you hear? You are to wake up at once. Wake up, wake up, wake—

MANGAN [*bouncing out of the chair in a fury and turning on them*] Wake up! So you think Ive been asleep, do you? [*He kicks the chair violently back out of his way, and gets between them*]. You throw me into a trance so that I cant move hand or foot—I might have been buried alive! it's a mercy I wasnt—and then you think I was only asleep. If youd let me drop the two times you rolled me about, my nose would have been flattened for life against the floor. But Ive found you all out, anyhow. I know the sort of people I'm among now. Ive heard every word youve said, you and your precious father, and [*to Mrs Hushabye*] you too. So I'm an object, am I? I'm a thing, am I? I'm a fool that hasnt sense enough to feed myself properly, am I? I'm afraid of the men that would starve if it werent for the wages I give them, am I? I'm nothing but a disgusting old skinflint to be made a convenience of by designing women and fool managers of my works, am I? I'm—

MRS HUSHABYE [*with the most elegant aplomb*] Sh-sh-sh-sh-sh! Mr Mangan: you are bound in honor to obliterate from your mind all you heard while you were pretending to be asleep. It was not meant for you to hear.

MANGAN. Pretending to be asleep! Do you think if I

was only pretending that I'd have sprawled there helpless, and listened to such unfairness, such lies, such injustice and plotting and backbiting and slandering of me, if I could have up and told you what I thought of you! I wonder I didnt burst.

MRS HUSHABYE [*sweetly*] You dreamt it all, Mr Mangan. We were only saying how beautifully peaceful you looked in your sleep. That was all, wasnt it, Ellie? Believe me, Mr Mangan, all those unpleasant things came into your mind in the last half second before you woke. Ellie rubbed your hair the wrong way; and the disagreeable sensation suggested a disagreeable dream.

MANGAN [*doggedly*] I believe in dreams.

MRS HUSHABYE. So do I. But they go by contraries, dont they?

MANGAN [*depths of emotion suddenly welling up in him*] I shant forget, to my dying day, that when you gave me the glad eye that time in the garden, you were making a fool of me. That was a dirty low mean thing to do. You had no right to let me come near you if I disgusted you. It isnt my fault if I'm old and havnt a moustache like a bronze candlestick as your husband has. There are things no decent woman would do to a man—like a man hitting a woman in the breast.

Hesione, utterly shamed, sits down on the sofa and covers her face with her hands. Mangan sits down also on his chair and begins to cry like a child. Ellie stares at them. Mrs Hushabye, at the distressing sound he makes, takes down her hands and looks at him. She rises and runs to him.

MRS HUSHABYE. Dont cry: I cant bear it. Have I broken your heart? I didnt know you had one. How could I?

MANGAN. I'm a man aint I?

MRS HUSHABYE [*half coaxing, half rallying, altogether tenderly*] Oh no: not what I call a man. Only a Boss: just that and nothing else. What business has a Boss with a heart?

MANGAN. Then youre not a bit sorry for what you did,

550

nor ashamed?

MRS HUSHABYE. I was ashamed for the first time in my life when you said that about hitting a woman in the breast, and I found out what I'd done. My very bones blushed red. Youve had your revenge, Boss. Arnt you satisfied?

MANGAN. Serve you right! Do you hear? Serve you right! Youre just cruel. Cruel.

MRS HUSHABYE. Yes: cruelty would be delicious if one could only find some sort of cruelty that didnt really hurt. By the way [*sitting down beside him on the arm of the chair*], whats your name? It's not really Boss, is it?

MANGAN [*shortly*] If you want to know, my name's Alfred.

MRS HUSHABYE [*springing up*] Alfred! Ellie: he was christened after Tennyson!!!

MANGAN [*rising*] I was christened after my uncle, and never had a penny from him, damn him! What of it?

MRS HUSHABYE. It comes to me suddenly that you are a real person: that you had a mother, like anyone else. [*Putting her hands on his shoulders and surveying him*] Little Alf!

MANGAN. Well, you have a nerve.

MRS HUSHABYE. And you have a heart, Alfy, a whimpering little heart, but a real one. [*Releasing him suddenly*] Now run and make it up with Ellie. She has had time to think what to say to you, which is more than I had. [*She goes out quickly into the garden by the port door*].

MANGAN. That woman has a pair of hands that go right through you.

ELLIE. Still in love with her, in spite of all we said about you?

MANGAN. Are all women like you two? Do they never think of anything about a man except what they can get out of him? Y o u werent even thinking that about me. You were only thinking whether your gloves would last.

ELLIE. I shall not have to think about that when we are married.

MANGAN. And you think I am going to marry you after what I heard there!

ELLIE. You heard nothing from me that I did not tell you before.

MANGAN. Perhaps you think I cant do without you.

ELLIE. I think you would feel lonely without us all now, after coming to know us so well.

MANGAN [*with something like a yell of despair*] Am I never to have the last word?

CAPTAIN SHOTOVER [*appearing at the starboard garden door*] There is a soul in torment here. What is the matter?

MANGAN. This girl doesnt want to spend her life wondering how long her gloves will last.

CAPTAIN SHOTOVER [*passing through*] Dont wear any. I never do. [*He goes into the pantry*].

LADY UTTERWORD [*appearing at the port garden door, in a handsome dinner dress*] Is anything the matter?

ELLIE. This gentleman wants to know is he never to have the last word?

LADY UTTERWORD [*coming forward to the sofa*] I should let him have it, my dear. The important thing is not to have the last word, but to have your own way.

MANGAN. She wants both.

LADY UTTERWORD. She wont get them, Mr Mangan. Providence always has the last word.

MANGAN [*desperately*] Now y o u are going to come religion over me. In this house a man's mind might as well be a football. I'm going. [*He makes for the hall, but is stopped by a hail from the Captain, who has just emerged from his pantry*].

CAPTAIN SHOTOVER. Whither away, Boss Mangan?

MANGAN. To hell out of this house: let that be enough for you and all here.

CAPTAIN SHOTOVER. You were welcome to come: you are free to go. The wide earth, the high seas, the spacious skies are waiting for you outside.

LADY UTTERWORD. But your things, Mr Mangan. Your

bags, your comb and brushes, your pyjamas—

HECTOR [*who has just appeared in the port doorway in a handsome Arab costume*] Why should the escaping slave take his chains with him?

MANGAN. Thats right, Hushabye. Keep the pyjamas, my lady; and much good may they do you.

HECTOR [*advancing to Lady Utterword's left hand*] Let us all go out into the night and leave everything behind us.

MANGAN. You stay where you are, the lot of you. I want no company, especially female company.

ELLIE. Let him go. He is unhappy here. He is angry with us.

CAPTAIN SHOTOVER. Go, Boss Mangan; and when you have found the land where there is happiness and where there are no women, send me its latitude and longitude; and I will join you there.

LADY UTTERWORD. You will certainly not be comfortable without your luggage, Mr Mangan.

ELLIE [*impatient*] Go, go: why dont you go? It is a heavenly night: you can sleep on the heath. Take my waterproof to lie on: it is hanging up in the hall.

HECTOR. Breakfast at nine, unless you prefer to breakfast with the Captain at six.

ELLIE. Good night, Alfred.

HECTOR. Alfred! [*He runs back to the door and calls into the garden*] Randall: Mangan's Christian name is Alfred.

RANDALL [*appearing in the starboard doorway in evening dress*] Then Hesione wins her bet.

Mrs Hushabye appears in the port doorway. She throws her left arm round Hector's neck; draws him with her to the back of the sofa; and throws her right arm round Lady Utterword's neck.

MRS HUSHABYE. They wouldnt believe me, Alf.

They contemplate him.

MANGAN. Is there any more of you coming in to look at

me, as if I was the latest thing in a menagerie?

MRS HUSHABYE. You a r e the latest thing in this menagerie.

Before Mangan can retort, a fall of furniture is heard from upstairs; then a pistol shot, and a yell of pain. The staring group breaks up in consternation.

MAZZINI'S VOICE [*from above*] Help! A burglar! Help!

HECTOR [*his eyes blazing*] A burglar!!!

MRS HUSHABYE. No, Hector: youll be shot. [*But it is too late: he has dashed out past Mangan, who hastily moves towards the bookshelves out of his way*].

CAPTAIN SHOTOVER [*blowing his whistle*] All hands aloft! [*He strides out after Hector*].

LADY UTTERWORD. My diamonds! [*She follows the Captain*].

RANDALL [*rushing after her*] No, Ariadne. Let me.

ELLIE. Oh, is papa shot? [*She runs out*].

MRS HUSHABYE. Are you frightened, Alf?

MANGAN. No. It aint my house, thank God.

MRS HUSHABYE. If they catch a burglar, shall we have to go into court as witnesses, and be asked all sorts of questions about our private lives?

MANGAN. You wont be believed if you tell the truth.

Mazzini, terribly upset, with a duelling pistol in his hand, comes from the hall, and makes his way to the drawing-table.

MAZZINI. Oh, my dear Mrs Hushabye, I might have killed him. [*He throws the pistol on the table and staggers round to the chair*]. I hope you wont believe I really intended to.

Hector comes in, marching an old and villainous looking man before him by the collar. He plants him in the middle of the room and releases him.

Ellie follows, and immediately runs across to the back of her father's chair and pats his shoulders.

RANDALL [*entering with a poker*] Keep your eye on this

554

door, Mangan. I'll look after the other. [*He goes to the starboard door and stands on guard there*].

Lady Utterword comes in after Randall, and goes between Mrs Hushabye and Mangan.

Nurse Guinness brings up the rear, and waits near the door, on Mangan's left.

MRS HUSHABYE. What has happened?

MAZZINI. Your housekeeper told me there was somebody upstairs, and gave me a pistol that Mr Hushabye had been practising with. I thought it would frighten him; but it went off at a touch.

THE BURGLAR. Yes, and took the skin off my ear. Precious near took the top off my head. Why dont you have a proper revolver instead of a thing like that, that goes off if you as much as blow on it?

HECTOR. One of my duelling pistols. Sorry.

MAZZINI. He put his hands up and said it was a fair cop.

THE BURGLAR. So it was. Send for the police.

HECTOR. No, by thunder! It was not a fair cop. We were four to one.

MRS HUSHABYE. What will they do to him?

THE BURGLAR. Ten years. Beginning with solitary. Ten years off my life. I shant serve it all: I'm too old. It will see me out.

LADY UTTERWORD. You should have thought of that before you stole my diamonds.

THE BURGLAR. Well, youve got them back, lady: havnt you? Can you give me back the years of my life you are going to take from me?

MRS HUSHABYE. Oh, we cant bury a man alive for ten years for a few diamonds.

THE BURGLAR. Ten little shining diamonds! Ten long black years!

LADY UTTERWORD. Think of what it is for us to be dragged through the horrors of a criminal court, and have all our family affairs in the papers! If you were a native, and Hastings could order you a good beating and send you

555

away, I shouldnt mind; but here in England there is no real protection for any respectable person.

THE BURGLAR. I'm too old to be giv a hiding, lady. Send for the police and have done with it. It's only just and right you should.

RANDALL [*who has relaxed his vigilance on seeing the burglar so pacifically disposed, and comes forward swinging the poker between his fingers like a well-folded umbrella*] It is neither just nor right that we should be put to a lot of inconvenience to gratify your moral enthusiasm, my friend. You had better get out, while you have the chance.

THE BURGLAR [*inexorably*] No. I must work my sin off my conscience. This has come as a sort of call to me. Let me spend the rest of my life repenting in a cell. I shall have my reward above.

MANGAN [*exasperated*] The very burglars cant behave naturally in this house.

HECTOR. My good sir: you must work out your salvation at somebody else's expense. Nobody here is going to charge you.

THE BURGLAR. Oh, you wont charge me, wont you?

HECTOR. No. I'm sorry to be inhospitable; but will you kindly leave the house?

THE BURGLAR. Right. I'll go to the police station and give myself up. [*He turns resolutely to the door; but Hector stops him*].

HECTOR.	Oh no. You mustnt do that.
RANDALL.	No, no. Clear out, man, cant you; and dont be a fool.
MRS HUSHABYE.	Dont be so silly. Cant you repent at home?

LADY UTTERWORD. You will have to do as you are told.

THE BURGLAR. It's compounding a felony, you know.

MRS HUSHABYE. This is utterly ridiculous. Are we to be forced to prosecute this man when we dont want to?

THE BURGLAR. Am I to be robbed of my salvation to save you the trouble of spending a day at the sessions? Is that justice? Is it right? Is it fair to me?

MAZZINI [*rising and leaning across the table persuasively as if it were a pulpit desk or a shop counter*] Come, come! let me shew you how you can turn your very crimes to account. Why not set up as a locksmith? You must know more about locks than most honest men?

THE BURGLAR. Thats true, sir. But I couldnt set up as a locksmith under twenty pounds.

RANDALL. Well, you can easily steal twenty pounds. You will find it in the nearest bank.

THE BURGLAR [*horrified*] Oh what a thing for a gentleman to put into the head of a poor criminal scrambling out of the bottomless pit as it were! Oh, shame on you, sir! Oh, God forgive you! [*He throws himself into the big chair and covers his face as if in prayer*].

LADY UTTERWORD. Really, Randall!

HECTOR. It seems to me that we shall have to take up a collection for this inopportunely contrite sinner.

LADY UTTERWORD. But twenty pounds is ridiculous.

THE BURGLAR [*looking up quickly*] I shall have to buy a lot of tools, lady.

LADY UTTERWORD. Nonsense: you have your burgling kit.

THE BURGLAR. Whats a jimmy and a centrebit and an acetylene welding plant and a bunch of skeleton keys? I shall want a forge, and a smithy, and a shop, and fittings. I cant hardly do it for twenty.

HECTOR. My worthy friend, we havnt got twenty pounds.

THE BURGLAR [*now master of the situation*] You can raise it among you, cant you?

MRS HUSHABYE. Give him a sovereign, Hector, and get rid of him.

HECTOR [*giving him a pound*] There! Off with you.

THE BURGLAR [*rising and taking the money very ungratefully*] I wont promise nothing. You have more on you than a quid: all the lot of you, I mean.

LADY UTTERWORD [*vigorously*] Oh, let us prosecute him and have done with it. I have a conscience too, I hope; and I do not feel at all sure that we have any right to let him go, especially if he is going to be greedy and impertinent.

THE BURGLAR [*quickly*] All right, lady, all right. Ive no wish to be anything but agreeable. Good evening, ladies and gentlemen; and thank you kindly.

He is hurrying out when he is confronted in the doorway by Captain Shotover.

CAPTAIN SHOTOVER [*fixing the burglar with a piercing regard*] Whats this? Are there two of you?

THE BURGLAR [*falling on his knees before the Captain in abject terror*] Oh my good Lord, what have I done? Dont tell me its y o u r house Ive broken into, Captain Shotover.

The Captain seizes him by the collar; drags him to his feet; and leads him to the middle of the group, Hector falling back beside his wife to make way for them.

CAPTAIN SHOTOVER [*turning him towards Ellie*] Is that your daughter? [*He releases him*].

THE BURGLAR. Well, how do I know, Captain? You know the sort of life you and me has led. Any young lady of that age might be my daughter anywhere in the wide world, as you might say.

CAPTAIN SHOTOVER [*to Mazzini*] You are not Billy Dunn. This is Billy Dunn. Why have you imposed on me?

THE BURGLAR [*indignantly to Mazzini*] Have you been giving yourself out to be me? You, that nigh blew my head off! Shooting y o u r s e l f, in a manner of speaking!

MAZZINI. My dear Captain Shotover, ever since I came into this house I have done hardly anything else but assure you that I am not Mr William Dunn, but Mazzini Dunn, a very different person.

THE BURGLAR. He dont belong to my branch, Captain. Theres two sets in the family: the thinking Dunns and the drinking Dunns, each going their own ways. I'm a drinking

558

Dunn: he's a thinking Dunn. But that didnt give him any right to shoot me.

CAPTAIN SHOTOVER. So youve turned burglar, have you?

THE BURGLAR. No, Captain: I wouldnt disgrace our old sea calling by such a thing. I am no burglar.

LADY UTTERWORD. What were you doing with my diamonds?

GUINNESS. What did you break into the house for if youre no burglar?

RANDALL. Mistook the house for your own and came in by the wrong window, eh?

THE BURGLAR. Well, it's no use my telling you a lie: I can take in most captains, but not Captain Shotover, because he sold himself to the devil in Zanzibar, and can divine water, spot gold, explode a cartridge in your pocket with a glance of his eye, and see the truth hidden in the heart of man. But I'm no burglar.

CAPTAIN SHOTOVER. Are you an honest man?

THE BURGLAR. I dont set up to be better than my fellow-creatures, and never did, as you well know, Captain. But what I do is innocent and pious. I enquire about for houses where the right sort of people live. I work it on them same as I worked it here. I break into the house; put a few spoons or diamonds in my pocket; make a noise; get caught; and take up a collection. And you wouldnt believe how hard it is to get caught when youre actually trying to. I have knocked over all the chairs in a room without a soul paying any attention to me. In the end I have had to walk out and leave the job.

RANDALL. When that happens, do you put back the spoons and diamonds?

THE BURGLAR. Well, I dont fly in the face of Providence, if thats what you want to know.

CAPTAIN SHOTOVER. Guinness: you remember this man?

GUINNESS. I should think I do, seeing I was married to him, the blackguard!

HESIONE } [*exclaiming* { Married to him!
LADY UTTERWORD } *together*] { Guinness!!

THE BURGLAR. It wasnt legal. Ive been married to no end of women. No use coming that over me.

CAPTAIN SHOTOVER. Take him to the forecastle. [*He flings him to the door with a strength beyond his years*].

GUINNESS. I suppose you mean the kitchen. They wont have him there. Do you expect servants to keep company with thieves and all sorts?

CAPTAIN SHOTOVER. Land-thieves and water-thieves are the same flesh and blood. I'll have no boatswain on my quarter-deck. Off with you both.

THE BURGLAR. Yes, Captain. [*He goes out humbly*].

MAZZINI. Will it be safe to have him in the house like that?

GUINNESS. Why didnt you shoot him, sir? If I'd known who he was, I'd have shot him myself. [*She goes out*].

MRS HUSHABYE. Do sit down, everybody. [*She sits down on the sofa*].

They all move except Ellie. Mazzini resumes his seat. Randall sits down in the window seat near the starboard door, again making a pendulum of his poker, and studying it as Galileo might have done. Hector sits on his left, in the middle. Mangan, forgotten, sits in the port corner. Lady Utterword takes the big chair. Captain Shotover goes into the pantry in deep abstraction. They all look after him; and Lady Utterword coughs consciously.

MRS HUSHABYE. So Billy Dunn was poor nurse's little romance. I knew there had been somebody.

RANDALL. They will fight their battles over again and enjoy themselves immensely.

LADY UTTERWORD [*irritably*] You are not married; and you know nothing about it, Randall. Hold your tongue.

RANDALL. Tyrant!

MRS HUSHABYE. Well, we have had a very exciting evening. Everything will be an anticlimax after it. We'd better all go to bed.

RANDALL. Another burglar may turn up.

MAZZINI. Oh, impossible! I hope not.

RANDALL. Why not? There is more than one burglar in England.

MRS HUSHABYE. What do you say, Alf?

MANGAN [*huffily*] Oh, I dont matter. I'm forgotten. The burglar has put my nose out of joint. Shove me into a corner and have done with me.

MRS HUSHABYE [*jumping up mischievously, and going to him*] Would you like a walk on the heath, Alfred? With me?

ELLIE. Go, Mr Mangan. It will do you good. Hesione will soothe you.

MRS HUSHABYE [*slipping her arm under his and pulling him upright*] Come, Alfred. There is a moon: it's like the night in Tristan and Isolde. [*She caresses his arm and draws him to the port garden door*].

MANGAN [*writhing but yielding*] How you can have the face—the heart— [*He breaks down and is heard sobbing as she takes him out*].

LADY UTTERWORD. What an extraordinary way to behave! What is the matter with the man?

ELLIE [*in a strangely calm voice, staring into an imaginary distance*] His heart is breaking: that is all. [*The Captain appears at the pantry door, listening*]. It is a curious sensation: the sort of pain that goes mercifully beyond our powers of feeling. When your heart is broken, your boats are burned: nothing matters any more. It is the end of happiness and the beginning of peace.

LADY UTTERWORD [*suddenly rising in a rage, to the astonishment of the rest*] How dare you?

HECTOR. Good heavens! Whats the matter?

RANDALL [*in a warning whisper*] Tch—tch—tch! Steady.

ELLIE [*surprised and haughty*] I was not addressing you particularly, Lady Utterword. And I am not accustomed to be asked how dare I.

561

LADY UTTERWORD. Of course not. Anyone can see how badly you have been brought up.

MAZZINI. Oh, I hope not, Lady Utterword. Really!

LADY UTTERWORD. I know very well what you meant. The impudence!

ELLIE. What on earth do you mean?

CAPTAIN SHOTOVER [*advancing to the table*] She means that her heart will not break. She has been longing all her life for someone to break it. At last she has become afraid she has none to break.

LADY UTTERWORD [*flinging herself on her knees and throwing her arms round him*] Papa: dont say you think Ive no heart.

CAPTAIN SHOTOVER [*raising her with grim tenderness*] If you had no heart how could you want to have it broken, child?

HECTOR [*rising with a bound*] Lady Utterword: you are not to be trusted. You have made a scene. [*He runs out into the garden through the starboard door*].

LADY UTTERWORD. Oh! Hector, Hector! [*She runs out after him*].

RANDALL. Only nerves, I assure you. [*He rises and follows her, waving the poker in his agitation*]. Ariadne! Ariadne! For God's sake be careful. You will— [*He is gone*].

MAZZINI [*rising*] How distressing! Can I do anything, I wonder?

CAPTAIN SHOTOVER [*promptly taking his chair and setting to work at the drawing-board*] No. Go to bed. Goodnight.

MAZZINI [*bewildered*] Oh! Perhaps you are right.

ELLIE. Goodnight, dearest. [*She kisses him*].

MAZZINI. Goodnight, love. [*He makes for the door, but turns aside to the bookshelves*]. I'll just take a book. [*He takes one*]. Goodnight. [*He goes out, leaving Ellie alone with the Captain*].

The Captain is intent on his drawing. Ellie, standing

sentry over his chair, contemplates him for a moment.

ELLIE. Does nothing ever disturb you, Captain Shotover?

CAPTAIN SHOTOVER. Ive stood on the bridge for eighteen hours in a typhoon. Life here is stormier; but I can stand it.

ELLIE. Do you think I ought to marry Mr Mangan?

CAPTAIN SHOTOVER [*never looking up*] One rock is as good as another to be wrecked on.

ELLIE. I am not in love with him.

CAPTAIN SHOTOVER. Who said you were?

ELLIE. You are not surprised?

CAPTAIN SHOTOVER. Surprised! At m y age!

ELLIE. It seems to me quite fair. He wants me for one thing: I want him for another.

CAPTAIN SHOTOVER. Money?

ELLIE. Yes.

CAPTAIN SHOTOVER. Well, one turns the cheek: the other kisses it. One provides the cash: the other spends it.

ELLIE. Who will have the best of the bargain, I wonder?

CAPTAIN SHOTOVER. You. These fellows live in an office all day. You will have to put up with him from dinner to breakfast; but you will both be asleep most of that time. All day you will be quit of him; and you will be shopping with his money. If that is too much for you, marry a seafaring man: you will be bothered with him only three weeks in the year, perhaps.

ELLIE. That would be best of all, I suppose.

CAPTAIN SHOTOVER. It's a dangerous thing to be married right up to the hilt, like my daughter's husband. The man is at home all day, like a damned soul in hell.

ELLIE. I never thought of that before.

CAPTAIN SHOTOVER. If youre marrying for business, you cant be too businesslike.

ELLIE. Why do women always want other women's husbands?

CAPTAIN SHOTOVER. Why do horse-thieves prefer a

563

horse that is broken-in to one that is wild?

ELLIE [*with a short laugh*] I suppose so. What a vile world it is!

CAPTAIN SHOTOVER. It doesnt concern me. I'm nearly out of it.

ELLIE. And I'm only just beginning.

CAPTAIN SHOTOVER. Yes; so look ahead.

ELLIE. Well, I think I am being very prudent.

CAPTAIN SHOTOVER. I didnt say prudent. I said look ahead.

ELLIE. Whats the difference?

CAPTAIN SHOTOVER. It's prudent to gain the whole world and lose your own soul. But dont forget that your soul sticks to you if you stick to it; but the world has a way of slipping through your fingers.

ELLIE [*wearily, leaving him and beginning to wander restlessly about the room*] I'm sorry, Captain Shotover; but it's no use talking like that to me. Old-fashioned people are no use to me. Old-fashioned people think you can have a soul without money. They think the less money you have, the more soul you have. Young people nowadays know better. A soul is a very expensive thing to keep: much more so than a motor car.

CAPTAIN SHOTOVER. Is it? How much does your soul eat?

ELLIE. Oh, a lot. It eats music and pictures and books and mountains and lakes and beautiful things to wear and nice people to be with. In this country you cant have them without lots of money: that is why our souls are so horribly starved.

CAPTAIN SHOTOVER. Mangan's soul lives on pigs' food.

ELLIE. Yes: money is thrown away on him. I suppose his soul was starved when he was young. But it will not be thrown away on me. It is just because I want to save my soul that I am marrying for money. All the women who are not fools do.

CAPTAIN SHOTOVER. There are other ways of getting

money. Why dont you steal it?

ELLIE. Because I dont want to go to prison.

CAPTAIN SHOTOVER. Is that the only reason? Are you quite sure honesty has nothing to do with it?

ELLIE. Oh, you are very old-fashioned, Captain. Does any modern girl believe that the legal and illegal ways of getting money are the honest and dishonest ways? Mangan robbed my father and my father's friends. I should rob all the money back from Mangan if the police would let me. As they wont, I must get it back by marrying him.

CAPTAIN SHOTOVER. I cant argue: I'm too old: my mind is made up and finished. All I can tell you is that, old-fashioned or new-fashioned, if you sell yourself, you deal your soul a blow that all the books and pictures and concerts and scenery in the world wont heal. [*He gets up suddenly and makes for the pantry*].

ELLIE [*running after him and seizing him by the sleeve*] Then why did you sell yourself to the devil in Zanzibar?

CAPTAIN SHOTOVER [*stopping, startled*] What?

ELLIE. You shall not run away before you answer. I have found out that trick of yours. If you sold yourself, why shouldnt I?

CAPTAIN SHOTOVER. I had to deal with men so degraded that they wouldnt obey me unless I swore at them and kicked them and beat them with my fists. Foolish people took young thieves off the streets; flung them into a training ship where they were taught to fear the cane instead of fearing God; and thought theyd made men and sailors of them by private subscription. I tricked these thieves into believing I'd sold myself to the devil. It saved my soul from the kicking and swearing that was damning me by inches.

ELLIE [*releasing him*] I shall pretend to sell myself to Boss Mangan to save my soul from the poverty that is damning m e by inches.

CAPTAIN SHOTOVER. Riches will damn you ten times deeper. Riches wont save even your body.

ELLIE. Old-fashioned again. We know now that the

565

soul is the body, and the body the soul. They tell us they are different because they want to persuade us that we can keep our souls if we let them make slaves of our bodies. I am afraid you are no use to me, Captain.

CAPTAIN SHOTOVER. What did you expect? A Savior, eh? Are you old-fashioned enough to believe in that?

ELLIE. No. But I thought you were very wise, and might help me. Now I have found you out. You pretend to be busy, and think of fine things to say, and run in and out to surprise people by saying them, and get away before they can answer you.

CAPTAIN SHOTOVER. It confuses me to be answered. It discourages me. I cannot bear men and women. I h a v e to run away. I must run away now. [*He tries to*].

ELLIE [*again seizing his arm*] You shall not run away from me. I can hypnotize you. You are the only person in the house I can say what I like to. I know you are fond of me. Sit down. [*She draws him to the sofa*].

CAPTAIN SHOTOVER [*yielding*] Take care: I am in my dotage. Old men are dangerous: it doesnt matter to them what is going to happen to the world.

They sit side by side on the sofa. She leans affectionately against him with her head on his shoulder and her eyes half closed.

ELLIE [*dreamily*] I should have thought nothing else mattered to old men. They cant be very interested in what is going to happen to themselves.

CAPTAIN SHOTOVER. A man's interest in the world is only the overflow from his interest in himself. When you are a child your vessel is not yet full; so you care for nothing but your own affairs. When you grow up, your vessel overflows; and you are a politician, a philosopher, or an explorer and adventurer. In old age the vessel dries up: there is no overflow: you are a child again. I can give you the memories of my ancient wisdom: mere scraps and leavings; but I no longer really care for anything but my own little wants and hobbies. I sit here working out my old ideas

566

as a means of destroying my fellow-creatures. I see my
daughters and their men living foolish lives of romance and
sentiment and snobbery. I see you, the younger generation,
turning from their romance and sentiment and snobbery to
money and comfort and hard common sense. I was ten times
happier on the bridge in the typhoon, or frozen into Arctic
ice for months in darkness, than you or they have ever been.
You are looking for a rich husband. At your age I looked
for hardship, danger, horror, and death, that I might feel
the life in me more intensely. I did not let the fear of death
govern my life; and my reward was, I had my life. You are
going to let the fear of poverty govern your life; and your
reward will be that you will eat, but you will not live.

ELLIE [*sitting up impatiently*] But what can I do? I am
not a sea captain: I cant stand on bridges in typhoons, or go
slaughtering seals and whales in Greenland's icy mountains.
They wont let women be captains. Do you want me to be a
stewardess?

CAPTAIN SHOTOVER. There are worse lives. The stew-
ardesses could come ashore if they liked; but they sail and
sail and sail.

ELLIE. What could they do ashore but marry for
money? I dont want to be a stewardess: I am too bad a
sailor. Think of something else for me.

CAPTAIN SHOTOVER. I cant think so long and continuously. I am too old. I must go in and out. [*He tries to rise*].

ELLIE [*pulling him back*] You shall not. You are happy
here, arnt you?

CAPTAIN SHOTOVER. I tell you it's dangerous to keep
me. I cant keep awake and alert.

ELLIE. What do you run away for? To sleep?

CAPTAIN SHOTOVER. No. To get a glass of rum.

ELLIE [*frightfully disillusioned*] Is t h a t it? How disgusting! Do you like being drunk?

CAPTAIN SHOTOVER. No: I dread being drunk more than
anything in the world. To be drunk means to have dreams;
to go soft; to be easily pleased and deceived; to fall into the

567

clutches of women. Drink does that for you when you are young. But when you are old: very very old, like me, the dreams come by themselves. You dont know how terrible that is: you are young: you sleep at night only, and sleep soundly. But later on you will sleep in the afternoon. Later still you will sleep even in the morning; and you will awake tired, tired of life. You will never be free from dozing and dreams: the dreams will steal upon your work every ten minutes unless you can awaken yourself with rum. I drink now to keep sober; but the dreams are conquering: rum is not what it was: I have had ten glasses since you came; and it might be so much water. Go get me another: Guinness knows where it is. You had better see for yourself the horror of an old man drinking.

ELLIE. You shall not drink. Dream. I like you to dream. You must never be in the real world when we talk together.

CAPTAIN SHOTOVER. I am too weary to resist or too weak. I am in my second childhood. I do not see you as you really are. I cant remember what I really am. I feel nothing but the accursed happiness I have dreaded all my life long: the happiness that comes as life goes, the happiness of yielding and dreaming instead of resisting and doing, the sweetness of the fruit that is going rotten.

ELLIE. You dread it almost as much as I used to dread losing my dreams and having to fight and do things. But that is all over for me: m y dreams are dashed to pieces. I should like to marry a very old, very rich man. I should like to marry you. I had much rather marry you than marry Mangan. Are you very rich?

CAPTAIN SHOTOVER. No. Living from hand to mouth. And I have a wife somewhere in Jamaica: a black one. My first wife. Unless she's dead.

ELLIE. What a pity! I feel so happy with you. [*She takes his hand, almost unconsciously, and pats it*]. I thought I should never feel happy again.

CAPTAIN SHOTOVER. Why?

ELLIE. Dont you know?

568

CAPTAIN SHOTOVER. No.

ELLIE. Heartbreak. I fell in love with Hector, and didnt know he was married.

CAPTAIN SHOTOVER. Heartbreak? Are you one of those who are so sufficient to themselves that they are only happy when they are stripped of everything, even of hope?

ELLIE [*gripping the hand*] It seems so; for I feel now as if there was nothing I could not do, because I want nothing.

CAPTAIN SHOTOVER. Thats the only real strength. Thats genius. Thats better than rum.

ELLIE [*throwing away his hand*] Rum! Why did you spoil it?

Hector and Randall come in from the garden through the starboard door.

HECTOR. I beg your pardon. We did not know there was anyone here.

ELLIE [*rising*] That means that you want to tell Mr Randall the story about the tiger. Come, Captain: I want to talk to my father; and you had better come with me.

CAPTAIN SHOTOVER [*rising*] Nonsense! the man is in bed.

ELLIE. Aha! Ive caught you. My real father has gone to bed; but the father you gave me is in the kitchen. You knew quite well all along. Come. [*She draws him out into the garden with her through the port door*].

HECTOR. Thats an extraordinary girl. She has the Ancient Mariner on a string like a Pekinese dog.

RANDALL. Now that they have gone, shall we have a friendly chat?

HECTOR. You are in what is supposed to be my house. I am at your disposal.

Hector sits down in the draughtsman's chair, turning it to face Randall, who remains standing, leaning at his ease against the carpenter's bench.

RANDALL. I take it that we may be quite frank. I mean about Lady Utterword.

HECTOR. Y o u may. I have nothing to be frank about. I never met her until this afternoon.

RANDALL [*straightening up*] What! But you are her sister's husband.

HECTOR. Well, if you come to that, you are her husband's brother.

RANDALL. But you seem to be on intimate terms with her.

HECTOR. So do you.

RANDALL. Yes; but I a m on intimate terms with her. I have known her for years.

HECTOR. It took her years to get to the same point with you that she got to with me in five minutes, it seems.

RANDALL [*vexed*] Really, Ariadne is the limit. [*He moves away huffishly towards the windows*].

HECTOR [*coolly*] She is, as I remarked to Hesione, a very enterprising woman.

RANDALL [*returning, much troubled*] You see, Hushabye, you are what women consider a good-looking man.

HECTOR. I cultivated that appearance in the days of my vanity; and Hesione insists on my keeping it up. She makes me wear these ridiculous things [*indicating his Arab costume*] because she thinks me absurd in evening dress.

RANDALL. Still, you d o keep it up, old chap. Now, I assure you I have not an atom of jealousy in my disposition—

HECTOR. The question would seem to be rather whether your brother has any touch of that sort.

RANDALL. What! Hastings! Oh, dont trouble about Hastings. He has the gift of being able to work sixteen hours a day at the dullest detail, and actually likes it. That gets him to the top wherever he goes. As long as Ariadne takes care that he is fed regularly, he is only too thankful to anyone who will keep her in good humor for him.

HECTOR. And as she has all the Shotover fascination, there is plenty of competition for the job, eh?

RANDALL [*angrily*] She encourages them. Her conduct is perfectly scandalous. I assure you, my dear fellow, I

570

havnt an atom of jealousy in my composition; but she makes herself the talk of every place she goes to by her thoughtlessness. It's nothing more: she doesnt really care for the men she keeps hanging about her; but how is the world to know that? It's not fair to Hastings. It's not fair to me.

HECTOR. Her theory is that her conduct is so correct—

RANDALL. Correct! She does nothing but make scenes from morning till night. You be careful, old chap. She will get you into trouble: that is, she would if she really cared for you.

HECTOR. Doesnt she?

RANDALL. Not a scrap. She may want your scalp to add to her collection; but her true affection has been engaged years ago. You had really better be careful.

HECTOR. Do you suffer much from this jealousy?

RANDALL. Jealousy! I jealous! My dear fellow, havnt I told you that there is not an atom of—

HECTOR. Yes. And Lady Utterword told me she never made scenes. Well, dont waste your jealousy on my moustache. Never waste jealousy on a real man: it is the imaginary hero that supplants us all in the long run. Besides, jealousy does not belong to your easy man-of-the-world pose, which you carry so well in other respects.

RANDALL. Really, Hushabye, I think a man may be allowed to be a gentleman without being accused of posing.

HECTOR. It is a pose like any other. In this house we know all the poses: our game is to find out the man under the pose. The man under your pose is apparently Ellie's favorite, Othello.

RANDALL. Some of your games in this house are damned annoying, let me tell you.

HECTOR. Yes: I have been their victim for many years. I used to writhe under them at first; but I became accustomed to them. At last I learned to play them.

RANDALL. If it's all the same to you, I had rather you didnt play them on me. You evidently dont quite understand my character, or my notions of good form.

HECTOR. Is it your notion of good form to give away Lady Utterword?

RANDALL [*a childishly plaintive note breaking into his huff*] I have not said a word against Lady Utterword. This is just the conspiracy over again.

HECTOR. What conspiracy?

RANDALL. You know very well, sir. A conspiracy to make me out to be pettish and jealous and childish and everything I am not. Everyone knows I am just the opposite.

HECTOR [*rising*] Something in the air of the house has upset you. It often does have that effect. [*He goes to the garden door and calls Lady Utterword with commanding emphasis*] Ariadne!

LADY UTTERWORD [*at some distance*] Yes.

RANDALL. What are you calling her for? I want to speak—

LADY UTTERWORD [*arriving breathless*] Yes. You really are a terribly commanding person. Whats the matter?

HECTOR. I do not know how to manage your friend Randall. No doubt you do.

LADY UTTERWORD. Randall: have you been making yourself ridiculous, as usual? I can see it in your face. Really, you are the most pettish creature.

RANDALL. You know quite well, Ariadne, that I have not an ounce of pettishness in my disposition. I have made myself perfectly pleasant here. I have remained absolutely cool and imperturbable in the face of a burglar. Imperturbability is almost too strong a point of mine. But [*putting his foot down with a stamp, and walking angrily up and down the room*] I i n s i s t on being treated with a certain consideration. I will not allow Hushabye to take liberties with me. I will not stand your encouraging people as you do.

HECTOR. The man has a rooted delusion that he is your husband.

LADY UTTERWORD. I know. He is jealous. As if he had any right to be! He compromises me everywhere. He makes scenes all over the place. Randall: I will not allow it.

I simply will not allow it. You had no right to discuss me with Hector. I will not be discussed by men.

HECTOR. Be reasonable, Ariadne. Your fatal gift of beauty forces men to discuss you.

LADY UTTERWORD. Oh indeed! what about y o u r fatal gift of beauty?

HECTOR. How can I help it?

LADY UTTERWORD. You could cut off your moustache: I cant cut off my nose. I get my whole life messed up with people falling in love with me. And then Randall says I run after men.

RANDALL. I—

LADY UTTERWORD. Yes you do: you said it just now. Why cant you think of something else than women? Napoleon was quite right when he said that women are the occupation of the idle man. Well, if ever there was an idle man on earth, his name is Randall Utterword.

RANDALL. Ariad—

LADY UTTERWORD [overwhelming him with a torrent of words] Oh yes you are: it's no use denying it. What have you ever done? What good are you? You are as much trouble in the house as a child of three. You couldnt live without your valet.

RANDALL. This is—

LADY UTTERWORD. Laziness! You are laziness incarnate. You are selfishness itself. You are the most uninteresting man on earth. You cant even gossip about anything but yourself and your grievances and your ailments and the people who have offended you. [Turning to Hector] Do you know what they call him, Hector?

HECTOR ⎱ [speaking ⎰ Please dont tell me.
RANDALL ⎰ together] ⎱ I'll not stand it—

LADY UTTERWORD. Randall the Rotter: that is his name in good society.

RANDALL [shouting] I'll not bear it, I tell you. Will you listen to me, you infernal— [He chokes].

LADY UTTERWORD. Well: go on. What were you going

573

to call me? An infernal what? Which unpleasant animal is it to be this time?

RANDALL [*foaming*] There is no animal in the world so hateful as a woman can be. You are a maddening devil. Hushabye: you will not believe me when I tell you that I have loved this demon all my life; but God knows I have paid for it. [*He sits down in the draughtsman's chair, weeping*].

LADY UTTERWORD [*standing over him with triumphant contempt*] Cry-baby!

HECTOR [*gravely, coming to him*] My friend: the Shotover sisters have two strange powers over men. They can make them love; and they can make them cry. Thank your stars that you are not married to one of them.

LADY UTTERWORD [*haughtily*] And pray, Hector—

HECTOR [*suddenly catching her round the shoulders; swinging her right round him and away from Randall; and gripping her throat with the other hand*] Ariadne: if you attempt to start on me, I'll choke you: do you hear? The cat-and-mouse game with the other sex is a good game; but I can play your head off at it. [*He throws her, not at all gently, into the big chair, and proceeds, less fiercely but firmly*]. It is true that Napoleon said that woman is the occupation of the idle man. But he added that she is the relaxation of the warrior. Well, *I* am the warrior. So take care.

LADY UTTERWORD [*not in the least put out, and rather pleased by his violence*] My dear Hector: I have only done what you asked me to do.

HECTOR. How do you make that out, pray?

LADY UTTERWORD. You called me in to manage Randall, didnt you? You said you couldnt manage him yourself.

HECTOR. Well, what if I did? I did not ask you to drive the man mad.

LADY UTTERWORD. He isnt mad. Thats the way to manage him. If you were a mother, youd understand.

574

HECTOR. Mother! What are you up to now?

LADY UTTERWORD. It's quite simple. When the children got nerves and were naughty, I smacked them just enough to give them a good cry and a healthy nervous shock. They went to sleep and were quite good afterwards. Well, I cant smack Randall: he is too big; so when he gets nerves and is naughty, I just rag him till he cries. He will be all right now. Look: he is half asleep already. [*Which is quite true*].

RANDALL [*waking up indignantly*] I'm not. You are most cruel, Ariadne. [*Sentimentally*] But I suppose I must forgive you, as usual. [*He checks himself in the act of yawning*].

LADY UTTERWORD [*to Hector*] Is the explanation satisfactory, dread warrior?

HECTOR. Some day I shall kill you, if you go too far. I thought you were a fool.

LADY UTTERWORD [*laughing*] Everybody does, at first. But I am not such a fool as I look. [*She rises complacently*]. Now, Randall: go to bed. You will be a good boy in the morning.

RANDALL [*only very faintly rebellious*] I'll go to bed when I like. It isnt ten yet.

LADY UTTERWORD. It is long past ten. See that he goes to bed at once, Hector. [*She goes into the garden*].

HECTOR. Is there any slavery on earth viler than this slavery of men to women?

RANDALL [*rising resolutely*] I'll not speak to her tomorrow. I'll not speak to her for another week. I'll give her s u c h a lesson. I'll go straight to bed without bidding her goodnight. [*He makes for the door leading to the hall*].

HECTOR. You are under a spell, man. Old Shotover sold himself to the devil in Zanzibar. The devil gave him a black witch for a wife; and these two demon daughters are their mystical progeny. I am tied to Hesione's apron-string; but I'm her husband; and if I did go stark staring mad about her, at least we became man and wife. But why should

575

y o u let yourself be dragged about and beaten by Ariadne as a toy donkey is dragged about and beaten by a child? What do you get by it? Are you her lover?

RANDALL. You must not misunderstand me. In a higher sense—in a Platonic sense—

HECTOR. Psha! Platonic sense! She makes you her servant; and when pay-day comes round, she bilks you: that is what you mean.

RANDALL [*feebly*] Well, if I dont mind, I dont see what business it is of yours. Besides, I tell you I am going to punish her. You shall see: *I* know how to deal with women. I'm really very sleepy. Say goodnight to Mrs Hushabye for me, will you, like a good chap. Goodnight. [*He hurries out*].

HECTOR. Poor wretch! Oh women! women! women! [*He lifts his fists in invocation to heaven*]. Fall. Fall and crush. [*He goes out into the garden*].

END OF ACT II

576

ACT III

IN the garden, Hector, as he comes out through the glass door of the poop, finds Lady Utterword lying voluptuously in the hammock on the east side of the flagstaff, in the circle of light cast by the electric arc, which is like a moon in its opal globe. Beneath the head of the hammock, a campstool. On the other side of the flagstaff, on the long garden seat, Captain Shotover is asleep, with Ellie beside him, leaning affectionately against him on his right hand. On his left is a deck chair. Behind them in the gloom, Hesione is strolling about with Mangan. It is a fine still night, moonless.

LADY UTTERWORD. What a lovely night! It seems made for us.

HECTOR. The night takes no interest in us. What are we to the night? [He sits down moodily in the deck chair].

ELLIE [dreamily, nestling against the Captain] Its beauty soaks into my nerves. In the night there is peace for the old and hope for the young.

HECTOR. Is that remark your own?

ELLIE. No. Only the last thing the Captain said before he went to sleep.

CAPTAIN SHOTOVER. I'm not asleep.

HECTOR. Randall is. Also Mr Mazzini Dunn. Mangan too, probably.

MANGAN. No.

HECTOR. Oh, you are there. I thought Hesione would have sent you to bed by this time.

MRS HUSHABYE [coming to the back of the garden seat, into the light, with Mangan] I think I shall. He keeps telling me he has a presentiment that he is going to die. I never met a man so greedy for sympathy.

MANGAN [plaintively] But I have a presentiment. I really have. And you wouldnt listen.

MRS HUSHABYE. I was listening for something else. There was a sort of splendid drumming in the sky. Did none of you hear it? It came from a distance and then died away.

577

MANGAN. I tell you it was a train.

MRS HUSHABYE. And *I* tell you, Alf, there is no train at this hour. The last is nine fortyfive.

MANGAN. But a goods train.

MRS HUSHABYE. Not on our little line. They tack a truck on to the passenger train. What can it have been, Hector?

HECTOR. Heaven's threatening growl of disgust at us useless futile creatures. [*Fiercely*] I tell you, one of two things must happen. Either out of that darkness some new creation will come to supplant us as we have supplanted the animals, or the heavens will fall in thunder and destroy us.

LADY UTTERWORD [*in a cool instructive manner, wallowing comfortably in her hammock*] We have not supplanted the animals, Hector. Why do you ask heaven to destroy this house, which could be made quite comfortable if Hesione had any notion of how to live? Dont you know what is wrong with it?

HECTOR. We are wrong with it. There is no sense in us. We are useless, dangerous, and ought to be abolished.

LADY UTTERWORD. Nonsense! Hastings told me the very first day he came here, nearly twentyfour years ago, what is wrong with the house.

CAPTAIN SHOTOVER. What! The numskull said there was something wrong with my house!

LADY UTTERWORD. I said Hastings said it; and he is not in the least a numskull.

CAPTAIN SHOTOVER. Whats wrong with my house?

LADY UTTERWORD. Just what is wrong with a ship, papa. Wasnt it clever of Hastings to see that?

CAPTAIN SHOTOVER. The man's a fool. Theres nothing wrong with a ship.

LADY UTTERWORD. Yes there is.

MRS HUSHABYE. But what is it? Dont be aggravating, Addy.

LADY UTTERWORD. Guess.

HECTOR. Demons. Daughters of the witch of Zanzibar. Demons.

LADY UTTERWORD. Not a bit. I assure you, all this house needs to make it a sensible, healthy, pleasant house, with good appetites and sound sleep in it, is horses.

MRS HUSHABYE. Horses! What rubbish!

LADY UTTERWORD. Yes: horses. Why have we never been able to let this house? Because there are no proper stables. Go anywhere in England where there are natural, wholesome, contented, and really nice English people; and what do you always find? That the stables are the real centre of the household; and that if any visitor wants to play the piano the whole room has to be upset before it can be opened, there are so many things piled on it. I never lived until I learned to ride; and I shall never ride really well because I didnt begin as a child. There are only two classes in good society in England: the equestrian classes and the neurotic classes. It isnt mere convention: everybody can see that the people who hunt are the right people and the people who dont are the wrong ones.

CAPTAIN SHOTOVER. There is some truth in this. My ship made a man of me; and a ship is the horse of the sea.

LADY UTTERWORD. Exactly how Hastings explained your being a gentleman.

CAPTAIN SHOTOVER. Not bad for a numskull. Bring the man here with you next time: I must talk to him.

LADY UTTERWORD. Why is Randall such an obvious rotter? He is well bred; he has been at a public school and a university; he has been in the Foreign Office; he knows the best people and has lived all his life among them. Why is he so unsatisfactory, so contemptible? Why cant he get a valet to stay with him longer than a few months? Just because he is too lazy and pleasure-loving to hunt and shoot. He strums the piano, and sketches, and runs after married women, and reads literary books and poems. He actually plays the flute: but I never let him bring it into my house.

If he would only— [*She is interrupted by the melancholy strains of a flute coming from an open window above. She raises herself indignantly in the hammock*]. Randall: you have not gone to bed. Have you been listening? [*The flute replies pertly*]:

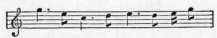

How vulgar! Go to bed instantly, Randall: how dare you? [*The window is slammed down. She subsides*]. How can anyone care for such a creature!

MRS HUSHABYE. Addy: do you think Ellie ought to marry poor Alfred merely for his money?

MANGAN [*much alarmed*] Whats that? Mrs. Hushabye: are my affairs to be discussed like this before everybody?

LADY UTTERWORD. I dont think Randall is listening now.

MANGAN. Everybody is listening. It isnt right.

MRS HUSHABYE. But in the dark, what does it matter? Ellie doesnt mind. Do you, Ellie?

ELLIE. Not in the least. What is your opinion, Lady Utterword? You have so much good sense.

MANGAN. But it isnt right. It— [*Mrs Hushabye puts her hand on his mouth*]. Oh, very well.

LADY UTTERWORD. How much money have you, Mr Mangan?

MANGAN. Really— No: I cant stand this.

LADY UTTERWORD. Nonsense, Mr Mangan! It all turns on your income, doesnt it?

MANGAN. Well, if you come to that, how much money has she?

ELLIE. None.

LADY UTTERWORD. You are answered, Mr Mangan. And now, as you have made Miss Dunn throw her cards on the table, you cannot refuse to shew your own.

MRS HUSHABYE. Come, Alf! out with it! How much?

MANGAN [*baited out of all prudence*] Well, if you want

to know, I have no money and never had any.

MRS HUSHABYE. Alfred: you mustnt tell naughty stories.

MANGAN. I'm not telling you stories. I'm telling you the raw truth.

LADY UTTERWORD. Then what do you live on, Mr Mangan?

MANGAN. Travelling expenses. And a trifle of commission.

CAPTAIN SHOTOVER. What more have any of us but travelling expenses for our life's journey?

MRS HUSHABYE. But you have factories and capital and things?

MANGAN. People think I have. People think I'm an industrial Napoleon. Thats why Miss Ellie wants to marry me. But I tell you I have nothing.

ELLIE. Do you mean that the factories are like Marcus's tigers? That they dont exist?

MANGAN. They exist all right enough. But theyre not mine. They belong to syndicates and shareholders and all sorts of lazy good-for-nothing capitalists. I get money from such people to start the factories. I find people like Miss Dunn's father to work them, and keep a tight hand so as to make them pay. Of course I make them keep me going pretty well; but it's a dog's life; and I dont own anything.

MRS HUSHABYE. Alfred, Alfred: you are making a poor mouth of it to get out of marrying Ellie.

MANGAN. I'm telling the truth about my money for the first time in my life; and it's the first time my word has ever been doubted.

LADY UTTERWORD. How sad! Why dont you go in for politics, Mr Mangan?

MANGAN. Go in for politics! Where have you been living? I a m in politics.

LADY UTTERWORD. I'm sure I beg your pardon. I never heard of you.

MANGAN. Let me tell you, Lady Utterword, that the

Prime Minister of this country asked me to join the Government without even going through the nonsense of an election, as the dictator of a great public department.

LADY UTTERWORD. As a Conservative or a Liberal?

MANGAN. No such nonsense. As a practical business man. [*They all burst out laughing*]. What are you all laughing at?

MRS HUSHABYE. Oh, Alfred, Alfred!

ELLIE. You! who have to get my father to do everything for you!

MRS HUSHABYE. You! who are afraid of your own workmen!

HECTOR. You! with whom three women have been playing cat and mouse all the evening!

LADY UTTERWORD. You must have given an immense sum to the party funds, Mr Mangan.

MANGAN. Not a penny out of my own pocket. The syndicate found the money: they knew how useful I should be to them in the Government.

LADY UTTERWORD. This is most interesting and unexpected, Mr Mangan. And what have your administrative achievements been, so far?

MANGAN. Achievements? Well, I dont know what you call achievements; but Ive jolly well put a stop to the games of the other fellows in the other departments. Every man of them thought he was going to save the country all by himself, and do me out of the credit and out of my chance of a title. I took good care that if they wouldnt let me do it they shouldnt do it themselves either. I may not know anything about my own machinery; but I know how to stick a ramrod into the other fellow's. And now they all look the biggest fools going.

HECTOR. And in heaven's name, what do you look like?

MANGAN. I look like the fellow that was too clever for all the others, dont I? If that isnt a triumph of practical business, what is?

HECTOR. Is this England, or is it a madhouse?

LADY UTTERWORD. Do you expect to save the country, Mr Mangan?

MANGAN. Well, who else will? Will your Mr Randall save it?

LADY UTTERWORD. Randall the rotter! Certainly not.

MANGAN. Will your brother-in-law save it with his moustache and his fine talk?

HECTOR. Yes, if they will let me.

MANGAN [*sneering*] Ah! W i l l they let you?

HECTOR. No. They prefer you.

MANGAN. Very well then, as youre in a world where I'm appreciated and youre not, youd best be civil to me, hadnt you? Who else is there but me?

LADY UTTERWORD. There is Hastings. Get rid of your ridiculous sham democracy; and give Hastings the necessary powers, and a good supply of bamboo to bring the British native to his senses: he will save the country with the greatest ease.

CAPTAIN SHOTOVER. It had better be lost. Any fool can govern with a stick in his hand. *I* could govern that way. It is not God's way. The man is a numskull.

LADY UTTERWORD. The man is worth all of you rolled into one. What do y o u say, Miss Dunn?

ELLIE. I think my father would do very well if people did not put upon him and cheat him and despise him because he is so good.

MANGAN [*contemptuously*] I think I see Mazzini Dunn getting into parliament or pushing his way into the Government. Weve not come to that yet, thank God! What do you say, Mrs Hushabye?

MRS HUSHABYE. Oh, *I* say it matters very little which of you governs the country so long as we govern you.

HECTOR. We? Who is we, pray?

MRS HUSHABYE. The devil's granddaughters, dear. The lovely women.

HECTOR [*raising his hands as before*] Fall, I say; and deliver us from the lures of Satan!

ELLIE. There seems to be nothing real in the world except my father and Shakespear. Marcus's tigers are false; Mr Mangan's millions are false; there is nothing really strong and true about Hesione but her beautiful black hair; and Lady Utterword's is too pretty to be real. The one thing that was left to me was the Captain's seventh degree of concentration; and that turns out to be—

CAPTAIN SHOTOVER. Rum.

LADY UTTERWORD [*placidly*] A good deal of my hair is quite genuine. The Duchess of Dithering offered me fifty guineas for this [*touching her forehead*] under the impression that it was a transformation; but it is all natural except the color.

MANGAN [*wildly*] Look here: I'm going to take off all my clothes. [*He begins tearing off his coat*].

LADY UTTERWORD.		Mr Mangan!
CAPTAIN SHOTOVER.	[*in consternation*]	Whats that?
HECTOR.		Ha! ha! Do. Do.
ELLIE.		Please dont.

MRS HUSHABYE [*catching his arm and stopping him*] Alfred: for shame! Are you mad?

MANGAN. Shame! What shame is there in this house? Let's all strip stark naked. We may as well do the thing thoroughly when we're about it. Weve stripped ourselves morally naked: well, let us strip ourselves physically naked as well, and see how we like it. I tell you I cant bear this. I was brought up to be respectable. I dont mind the women dyeing their hair and the men drinking: it's human nature. But it's not human nature to tell everybody about it. Every time one of you opens your mouth I go like this [*he cowers as if to avoid a missile*] afraid of what will come next. How are we to have any self-respect if we dont keep it up that we're better than we really are?

LADY UTTERWORD. I quite sympathize with you, Mr

Mangan. I have been through it all; and I know by experience that men and women are delicate plants and must be cultivated under glass. Our family habit of throwing stones in all directions and letting the air in is not only unbearably rude, but positively dangerous. Still, there is no use catching physical colds as well as moral ones; so please keep your clothes on.

MANGAN. I'll do as I like: not what you tell me. Am I a child or a grown man? I wont stand this mothering tyranny. I'll go back to the city, where I'm respected and made much of.

MRS HUSHABYE. Goodbye, Alf. Think of us sometimes in the city. Think of Ellie's youth!

ELLIE. Think of Hesione's eyes and hair!

CAPTAIN SHOTOVER. Think of this garden in which you are not a dog barking to keep the truth out!

HECTOR. Think of Lady Utterword's beauty! her good sense! her style!

LADY UTTERWORD. Flatterer. Think, Mr Mangan, whether you can really do any better for yourself elsewhere: that is the essential point, isnt it?

MANGAN [*surrendering*] All right: all right. I'm done. Have it your own way. Only let me alone. I dont know whether I'm on my head or my heels when you all start on me like this. I'll stay. I'll marry her. I'll do anything for a quiet life. Are you satisfied now?

ELLIE. No. I never really intended to make you marry me, Mr Mangan. Never in the depths of my soul. I only wanted to feel my strength: to know that you could not escape if I chose to take you.

MANGAN [*indignantly*] What! Do you mean to say you are going to throw me over after my acting so handsome?

LADY UTTERWORD. I should not be too hasty, Miss Dunn. You can throw Mr Mangan over at any time up to the last moment. Very few men in his position go bankrupt.

You can live very comfortably on his reputation for immense wealth.

ELLIE. I cannot commit bigamy, Lady Utterword.

MRS HUSHABYE.	*[exclaiming all together]*	Bigamy! Whatever on earth are you talking about, Ellie?
LADY UTTERWORD.		Bigamy! What do you mean, Miss Dunn?
MANGAN.		Bigamy! Do you mean to say youre married already?
HECTOR.		Bigamy! This is some enigma.

ELLIE. Only half an hour ago I became Captain Shotover's white wife.

MRS HUSHABYE. Ellie! What nonsense! Where?

ELLIE. In heaven, where all true marriages are made.

LADY UTTERWORD. Really, Miss Dunn! Really, papa!

MANGAN. He told me *I* was too old! And him a mummy!

HECTOR [*quoting Shelley*]

"Their altar the grassy earth outspread,
And their priest the muttering wind."

ELLIE. Yes: I, Ellie Dunn, give my broken heart and my strong sound soul to its natural captain, my spiritual husband and second father.

She draws the Captain's arm through hers, and pats his hand. The Captain remains fast asleep.

MRS HUSHABYE. Oh, thats very clever of you, pettikins. V e r y clever. Alfred: you could never have lived up to Ellie. You must be content with a little share of me.

MANGAN [*sniffing and wiping his eyes*] It isnt kind— [*His emotion chokes him*].

LADY UTTERWORD. You are well out of it, Mr Mangan. Miss Dunn is the most conceited young woman I have met since I came back to England.

MRS HUSHABYE. Oh, Ellie isnt conceited. Are you, pettikins?

ELLIE. I know my strength now, Hesione.

MANGAN. Brazen, I call you. Brazen.

MRS HUSHABYE. Tut tut, Alfred: dont be rude. Dont you feel how lovely this marriage night is, made in heaven? Arnt you happy, you and Hector? Open your eyes: Addy and Ellie look beautiful enough to please the most fastidious man: we live and love and have not a care in the world. We women have managed all that for you. Why in the name of common sense do you go on as if you were two miserable wretches?

CAPTAIN SHOTOVER. I tell you happiness is no good. You can be happy when you are only half alive. I am happier now I am half dead than ever I was in my prime. But there is no blessing on my happiness.

ELLIE [*her face lighting up*] Life with a blessing! that is what I want. Now I know the real reason why I couldnt marry Mr Mangan: there would be no blessing on our marriage. There is a blessing on my broken heart. There is a blessing on your beauty, Hesione. There is a blessing on your father's spirit. Even on the lies of Marcus there is a blessing; but on Mr Mangan's money there is none.

MANGAN. I dont understand a word of that.

ELLIE. Neither do I. But I know it means something.

MANGAN. Dont say there was any difficulty about the blessing. I was ready to get a bishop to marry us.

MRS HUSHABYE. Isnt he a fool, pettikins?

HECTOR [*fiercely*] Do not scorn the man. We are all fools.

Mazzini, in pyjamas and a richly colored silk dressing-gown, comes from the house, on Lady Utterword's side.

MRS HUSHABYE. Oh! here comes the only man who ever resisted me. Whats the matter, Mr Dunn? Is the house on fire?

MAZZINI. Oh no: nothing's the matter: but really it's

587

impossible to go to sleep with such an interesting conversation going on under one's window, and on such a beautiful night too. I just had to come down and join you all. What has it all been about?

MRS HUSHABYE. Oh, wonderful things, soldier of freedom.

HECTOR. For example, Mangan, as a practical business man, has tried to undress himself and has failed ignominiously; whilst you, as an idealist, have succeeded brilliantly.

MAZZINI. I hope you dont mind my being like this, Mrs Hushabye. [*He sits down on the campstool*].

MRS HUSHABYE. On the contrary, I could wish you always like that.

LADY UTTERWORD. Your daughter's match is off, Mr Dunn. It seems that Mr Mangan, whom we all supposed to be a man of property, owns absolutely nothing.

MAZZINI. Well of course I knew that, Lady Utterword. But if people believe in him and are always giving him money, whereas they dont believe in me and never give me any, how can I ask poor Ellie to depend on what I can do for her?

MANGAN. Dont you run away with this idea that I have nothing. I——

HECTOR. Oh, dont explain. We understand. You have a couple of thousand pounds in exchequer bills, 50,000 shares worth tenpence a dozen, and half a dozen tabloids of cyanide of potassium to poison yourself with when you are found out. Thats the reality of your millions.

MAZZINI. Oh no, no, no. He is quite honest: the businesses are genuine and perfectly legal.

HECTOR [*disgusted*] Yah! Not even a great swindler!

MANGAN. So you think. But Ive been too many for some honest men, for all that.

LADY UTTERWORD. There is no pleasing you, Mr Mangan. You are determined to be neither rich nor poor, honest

HEARTBREAK HOUSE

nor dishonest.

MANGAN. There you go again. Ever since I came into this silly house I have been made to look like a fool, though I'm as good a man in this house as in the city.

ELLIE [*musically*] Yes: this silly house, this strangely happy house, this agonizing house, this house without foundations. I shall call it Heartbreak House.

MRS HUSHABYE. Stop, Ellie; or I shall howl like an animal.

MANGAN [*breaks into a low snivelling*] !!!

MRS HUSHABYE. There! you have set Alfred off.

ELLIE. I like him best when he is howling.

CAPTAIN SHOTOVER. Silence! [*Mangan subsides into silence*]. I say, let the heart break in silence.

HECTOR. Do you accept that name for your house?

CAPTAIN SHOTOVER. It is not my house: it is only my kennel.

HECTOR. We have been too long here. We do not live in this house: we haunt it.

LADY UTTERWORD [*heart torn*] It is dreadful to think how you have been here all these years while I have gone round the world. I escaped young; but it has drawn me back. It wants to break my heart too. But it shant. I have left you and it behind. It was silly of me to come back. I felt sentimental about papa and Hesione and the old place. I felt them calling to me.

MAZZINI. But what a very natural and kindly and charming human feeling, Lady Utterword!

LADY UTTERWORD. So I thought, Mr Dunn. But I know now that it was only the last of my influenza. I found that I was not remembered and not wanted.

CAPTAIN SHOTOVER. You left because you did not want us. Was there no heartbreak in that for your father? You tore yourself up by the roots; and the ground healed up and brought forth fresh plants and forgot you. What right had you to come back and probe old wounds?

MRS HUSHABYE. You were a complete stranger to me at first, Addy; but now I feel as if you had never been away.

LADY UTTERWORD. Thank you, Hesione; but the influenza is quite cured. The place may be Heartbreak House to you, Miss Dunn, and to this gentleman from the city who seems to have so little self-control; but to me it is only a very ill-regulated and rather untidy villa without any stables.

HECTOR. Inhabited by—?

ELLIE. A crazy old sea captain and a young singer who adores him.

MRS HUSHABYE. A sluttish female, trying to stave off a double chin and an elderly spread, vainly wooing a born soldier of freedom.

MAZZINI. Oh, really, Mrs Hushabye—

MANGAN. A member of His Majesty's Government that everybody sets down as a nincompoop: dont forget him, Lady Utterword.

LADY UTTERWORD. And a very fascinating gentleman whose chief occupation is to be married to my sister.

HECTOR. All heartbroken imbeciles.

MAZZINI. Oh no. Surely, if I may say so, rather a favorable specimen of what is best in our English culture. You are very charming people, most advanced, unprejudiced, frank, humane, unconventional, democratic, free-thinking, and everything that is delightful to thoughtful people.

MRS HUSHABYE. You do us proud, Mazzini.

MAZZINI. I am not flattering, really. Where else could I feel perfectly at ease in my pyjamas? I sometimes dream that I am in very distinguished society, and suddenly I have nothing on but my pyjamas! Sometimes I havnt even pyjamas. And I always feel overwhelmed with confusion. But here, I dont mind in the least: it seems quite natural.

LADY UTTERWORD. An infallible sign that you are not now in really distinguished society, Mr Dunn. If you were in my house, you w o u l d feel embarrassed.

590

MAZZINI. I shall take particular care to keep out of your house, Lady Utterword.

LADY UTTERWORD. You will be quite wrong, Mr Dunn. I should make you very comfortable; and you would not have the trouble and anxiety of wondering whether you should wear your purple and gold or your green and crimson dressing-gown at dinner. You complicate life instead of simplifying it by doing these ridiculous things.

ELLIE. Y o u r house is not Heartbreak House: is it, Lady Utterword?

HECTOR. Yet she breaks hearts, easy as her house is. That poor devil upstairs with his flute howls when she twists his heart, just as Mangan howls when my wife twists his.

LADY UTTERWORD. That is because Randall has nothing to do but have his heart broken. It is a change from having his head shampooed. Catch anyone breaking Hastings' heart!

CAPTAIN SHOTOVER. The numskull wins, after all.

LADY UTTERWORD. I shall go back to my numskull with the greatest satisfaction when I am tired of you all, clever as you are.

MANGAN [huffily] I never set up to be clever.

LADY UTTERWORD. I forgot you, Mr Mangan.

MANGAN. Well, I dont see that quite, either.

LADY UTTERWORD. You may not be clever, Mr Mangan; but you are successful.

MANGAN. But I dont want to be regarded merely as a successful man. I have an imagination like anyone else. I have a presentiment—

MRS HUSHABYE. Oh, you are impossible, Alfred. Here I am devoting myself to you; and you think of nothing but your ridiculous presentiment. You bore me. Come and talk poetry to me under the stars. [She drags him away into the darkness].

MANGAN [tearfully, as he disappears] Yes: it's all very well to make fun of me; but if you only knew—

591

HECTOR [*impatiently*] How is all this going to end?

MAZZINI. It wont end, Mr Hushabye. Life doesnt end: it goes on.

ELLIE. Oh, it cant go on for ever. I'm always expecting something. I dont know what it is; but life must come to a point sometime.

LADY UTTERWORD. The point for a young woman of your age is a baby.

HECTOR. Yes, but, damn it, I have the same feeling; and *I* cant have a baby.

LADY UTTERWORD. By deputy, Hector.

HECTOR. But I h a v e children. All that is over and done with for me: and yet I too feel that this cant last. We sit here talking, and leave everything to Mangan and to chance and to the devil. Think of the powers of destruction that Mangan and his mutual admiration gang wield! It's madness: it's like giving a torpedo to a badly brought up child to play at earthquakes with.

MAZZINI. I know. I used often to think about that when I was young.

HECTOR. Think! Whats the good of thinking about it? Why didnt you do something?

MAZZINI. But I did. I joined societies and made speeches and wrote pamphlets. That was all I could do. But, you know, though the people in the societies thought they knew more than Mangan, most of them wouldnt have joined if they had known as much. You see they had never had any money to handle or any men to manage. Every year I expected a revolution, or some frightful smash-up: it seemed impossible that we could blunder and muddle on any longer. But nothing happened, except, of course, the usual poverty and crime and drink that we are used to. Nothing ever does happen. It's amazing how well we get along, all things considered.

LADY UTTERWORD. Perhaps somebody cleverer than you and Mr Mangan was at work all the time.

MAZZINI. Perhaps so. Though I was brought up not to

believe in anything, I often feel that there is a great deal to be said for the theory of an overruling Providence, after all.

LADY UTTERWORD. Providence! I meant Hastings.

MAZZINI. Oh, I beg your pardon, Lady Utterword.

CAPTAIN SHOTOVER. Every drunken skipper trusts to Providence. But one of the ways of Providence with drunken skippers is to run them on the rocks.

MAZZINI. Very true, no doubt, at sea. But in politics, I assure you, they only run into jellyfish. Nothing happens.

CAPTAIN SHOTOVER. At sea nothing happens to the sea. Nothing happens to the sky. The sun comes up from the east and goes down to the west. The moon grows from a sickle to an arc lamp, and comes later and later until she is lost in the light as other things are lost in the darkness. After the typhoon, the flying-fish glitter in the sunshine like birds. It's amazing how t h e y get along, all things considered. Nothing happens, except something not worth mentioning.

ELLIE. What is that, O Captain, my captain?

CAPTAIN SHOTOVER [*savagely*] Nothing but the smash of the drunken skipper's ship on the rocks, the splintering of her rotten timbers, the tearing of her rusty plates, the drowning of the crew like rats in a trap.

ELLIE. Moral: dont take rum.

CAPTAIN SHOTOVER [*vehemently*] That is a lie, child. Let a man drink ten barrels of rum a day, he is not a drunken skipper until he is a drifting skipper. Whilst he can lay his course and stand on his bridge and steer it, he is no drunkard. It is the man who lies drinking in his bunk and trusts to Providence that I call the drunken skipper, though he drank nothing but the waters of the River Jordan.

ELLIE. Splendid! And you havnt had a drop for an hour. You see you dont need it: your own spirit is not dead.

CAPTAIN SHOTOVER. Echoes: nothing but echoes. The last shot was fired years ago.

HECTOR. And this ship that we are all in? This soul's prison we call England?

CAPTAIN SHOTOVER. The captain is in his bunk, drinking bottled ditch-water; and the crew is gambling in the forecastle. She will strike and sink and split. Do you think the laws of God will be suspended in favor of England because you were born in it?

HECTOR. Well, I dont mean to be drowned like a rat in a trap. I still have the will to live. What am I to do?

CAPTAIN SHOTOVER. Do? Nothing simpler. Learn your business as an Englishman.

HECTOR. And what may my business as an Englishman be, pray?

CAPTAIN SHOTOVER. Navigation. Learn it and live; or leave it and be damned.

ELLIE. Quiet, quiet: youll tire yourself.

MAZZINI. I thought all that once, Captain; but I assure you nothing will happen.

A dull distant explosion is heard.

HECTOR [*starting up*] What was that?

CAPTAIN SHOTOVER. Something happening. [*He blows his whistle*]. Breakers ahead!

The light goes out.

HECTOR [*furiously*] Who put that light out? Who dared put that light out?

NURSE GUINNESS [*running in from the house to the middle of the esplanade*] I did, sir. The police have telephoned to say we'll be summoned if we dont put that light out: it can be seen for miles.

HECTOR. It shall be seen for a hundred miles. [*He dashes into the house*].

NURSE GUINNESS. The rectory is nothing but a heap of bricks, they say. Unless we can give the rector a bed he has nowhere to lay his head this night.

CAPTAIN SHOTOVER. The Church is on the rocks, breaking up. I told him it would unless it headed for God's open sea.

594

NURSE GUINNESS. And you are all to go down to the cellars.

CAPTAIN SHOTOVER. Go there yourself, you and all the crew. Batten down the hatches.

NURSE GUINNESS. And hide beside the coward I married! I'll go on the roof first. [*The lamp lights up again*]. There! Mr Hushabye's turned it on again.

THE BURGLAR [*hurrying in and appealing to Nurse Guinness*] Here: wheres the way to that gravel pit? The boot-boy says theres a cave in the gravel pit. Them cellars is no use. Wheres the gravel pit, Captain?

NURSE GUINNESS. Go straight on past the flagstaff until you fall into it and break your dirty neck. [*She pushes him contemptuously towards the flagstaff, and herself goes to the foot of the hammock and waits there, as it were by Ariadne's cradle*].

Another and louder explosion is heard. The burglar stops and stands trembling.

ELLIE [*rising*] That was nearer.

CAPTAIN SHOTOVER. The next one will get us. [*He rises*]. Stand by, all hands, for judgment.

THE BURGLAR. Oh my Lordy God! [*He rushes away frantically past the flagstaff into the gloom*].

MRS HUSHABYE [*emerging panting from the darkness*] Who was that running away? [*She comes to Ellie*]. Did you hear the explosions? And the sound in the sky: it's splendid: it's like an orchestra: it's like Beethoven.

ELLIE. By thunder, Hesione: it i s Beethoven.

She and Hesione throw themselves into one another's arms in wild excitement. The light increases.

MAZZINI [*anxiously*] The light is getting brighter.

NURSE GUINNESS [*looking up at the house*] It's Mr Hushabye turning on all the lights in the house and tearing down the curtains.

RANDALL [*rushing in in his pyjamas, distractedly waving a flute*] Ariadne: my soul, my precious, go down to the cellars: I beg and implore you, go down to the cellars!

595

LADY UTTERWORD [*quite composed in her hammock*] The governor's wife in the cellars with the servants! Really, Randall!

RANDALL. But what shall I do if you are killed?

LADY UTTERWORD. You will probably be killed, too, Randall. Now play your flute to shew that you are not afraid; and be good. Play us Keep the home fires burning.

NURSE GUINNESS [*grimly*] T h e y l l keep the home fires burning for us: them up there.

RANDALL [*having tried to play*] My lips are trembling. I cant get a sound.

MAZZINI. I hope poor Mangan is safe.

MRS HUSHABYE. He is hiding in the cave in the gravel pit.

CAPTAIN SHOTOVER. My dynamite drew him there. It is the hand of God.

HECTOR [*returning from the house and striding across to his former place*] There is not half light enough. We should be blazing to the skies.

ELLIE [*tense with excitement*] Set fire to the house, Marcus.

MRS HUSHABYE. My house! No.

HECTOR. I thought of that; but it would not be ready in time.

CAPTAIN SHOTOVER. The judgment has come. Courage will not save you; but it will shew that your souls are still alive.

MRS HUSHABYE. Sh-sh! Listen: do you hear it now? It's magnificent.

They all turn away from the house and look up, listening.

HECTOR [*gravely*] Miss Dunn: you can do no good here. We of this house are only moths flying into the candle. You had better go down to the cellar.

ELLIE [*scornfully*] I d o n t think.

MAZZINI. Ellie, dear, there is no disgrace in going to

596

the cellar. An officer would order his soldiers to take cover. Mr Hushabye is behaving like an amateur. Mangan and the burglar are acting very sensibly; and it is they who will survive.

ELLIE. Let them. I shall behave like an amateur. But why should you run any risk?

MAZZINI. Think of the risk those poor fellows up there are running!

NURSE GUINNESS. Think of t h e m, indeed, the murdering blackguards! What next?

A terrific explosion shakes the earth. They reel back into their seats, or clutch the nearest support. They hear the falling of the shattered glass from the windows.

MAZZINI. Is anyone hurt?

HECTOR. Where did it fall?

NURSE GUINNESS [*in hideous triumph*] Right in the gravel pit: I seen it. Serve un right! I seen it. [*She runs away towards the gravel pit, laughing harshly*].

HECTOR. One husband gone.

CAPTAIN SHOTOVER. Thirty pounds of good dynamite wasted.

MAZZINI. Oh, poor Mangan!

HECTOR. Are you immortal that you need pity him? Our turn next.

They wait in silence and intense expectation. Hesione and Ellie hold each other's hand tight.

A distant explosion is heard.

MRS HUSHABYE [*relaxing her grip*] Oh! they have passed us.

LADY UTTERWORD. The danger is over, Randall. Go to bed.

CAPTAIN SHOTOVER. Turn in, all hands. The ship is safe. [*He sits down and goes asleep*].

ELLIE [*disappointedly*] Safe!

HECTOR [*disgustedly*] Yes, safe. And how damnably dull the world has become again suddenly! [*He sits down*].

MAZZINI [*sitting down*] I was quite wrong, after all. It

597

HEARTBREAK HOUSE

is we who have survived; and Mangan and the burglar —

HECTOR. —the two burglars—

LADY UTTERWORD. —the two practical men of business—

MAZZINI. —both gone. And the poor clergyman will have to get a new house.

MRS HUSHABYE. But what a glorious experience! I hope theyll come again tomorrow night.

ELLIE [*radiant at the prospect*] Oh, I hope so.

Randall at last succeeds in keeping the home fires burning on his flute.

CURTAIN

CAPTAIN BRASSBOUND'S CONVERSION

AN ADVENTURE

1899

CAPTAIN BRASSBOUND'S CONVERSION

ACT I

ON the heights overlooking the harbor of Mogador, a seaport on the west coast of Morocco, the missionary, in the coolness of the late afternoon, is following the precept of Voltaire by cultivating his garden. He is an elderly Scotchman, spiritually a little weatherbeaten, as having to navigate his creed in strange waters crowded with other craft, but still a convinced son of the Free Church and the North African Mission, with a faithful brown eye, and a peaceful soul. Physically a wiry small-knit man, well tanned, clean shaven, with delicate resolute features and a twinkle of mild humor. He wears the sun helmet and pagri, the neutral-tinted spectacles, and the white canvas Spanish sand shoes of the modern Scotch missionary; but instead of a cheap tourist's suit from Glasgow, a grey flannel shirt with white collar, a green sailor knot tie with a cheap pin in it, he wears a suit of clean white linen, acceptable in color, if not in cut, to the Moorish mind.

The view from the garden includes much Atlantic Ocean and a long stretch of sandy coast to the south, swept by the north east trade wind, and scantily nourishing a few stunted pepper trees, mangy palms, and tamarisks. The prospect ends, as far as the land is concerned, in little hills that come nearly to the sea: rudiments, these, of the Atlas Mountains. The missionary, having had daily opportunities of looking at this seascape for thirty years or so, pays no heed to it, being absorbed in trimming a huge red geranium bush, to English eyes unnaturally big, which, with a dusty smilax or two, is the sole product of his pet flower-bed. He is sitting to his work on a Moorish stool. In the middle of the garden there is a pleasant seat in the shade of a tamarisk tree. The house is in the south west corner of the garden, and the geranium bush in the north east corner.

At the garden-door of the house there appears presently a man who is clearly no barbarian, being in fact a less agreeable product peculiar to modern commercial civilization.

CAPTAIN BRASSBOUND'S CONVERSION

His frame and flesh are those of an ill-nourished lad of seventeen; but his age is inscrutable: only the absence of any sign of grey in his mud colored hair suggests that he is at all events probably under forty, without prejudice to the possibility of his being under twenty. A Londoner would recognize him at once as an extreme but hardy specimen of the abortion produced by nurture in a city slum. His utterance, affectedly pumped and hearty, and naturally vulgar and nasal, is ready and fluent: nature, a Board School education, and some kerbstone practice having made him a bit of an orator. His dialect, apart from its base nasal delivery, is not unlike that of smart London society in its tendency to replace diphthongs by vowels (sometimes rather prettily) and to shuffle all the traditional vowel pronunciations. He pronounces ow as ah, and i as aw, using the ordinary ow for o, i for ā, ă for ŭ, and ĕ for ă, with this reservation, that when any vowel is followed by an r, he signifies its presence, not by pronouncing the r, which he never does under these circumstances, but by prolonging and modifying the vowel, sometimes even to the extreme degree of pronouncing it properly. As to his yol for l (a compendious delivery of the provincial eh-al), and other metropolitan refinements, amazing to all but cockneys, they cannot be indicated, save in the above imperfect manner, without the aid of a phonetic alphabet. He is dressed in somebody else's very second best as a coast guardsman, and gives himself the airs of a stage tar with sufficient success to pass as a possible fish porter of bad character in casual employment during busy times at Billingsgate. His manner shews an earnest disposition to ingratiate himself with the missionary, probably for some dishonest purpose.

THE MAN. Awtenoon, Mr Renkin. [*The missionary sits up quickly, and turns, resigning himself dutifully to the interruption*]. Yr honor's eolth.

RANKIN [*reservedly*] Good afternoon, Mr Drinkwotter.

DRINKWATER. Youre not best pleased to be hinterrapted

602

CAPTAIN BRASSBOUND'S CONVERSION

in yr bit o gawdnin baw the lawk o me, gavner.

RANKIN. A missionary knows nothing of leks of that soart, or of disleks either, Mr Drinkwotter. What can I do for ye?

DRINKWATER [*heartily*] Nathink, gavner. Awve bror noos fer yer.

RANKIN. Well, sit ye doon.

DRINKWATER. Aw thenk yr honor. [*He sits down on the seat under the tree and composes himself for conversation*]. Hever ear o Jadge Ellam?

RANKIN. Sir Howrrd Hallam?

DRINKWATER. Thets im—enginest jadge in Hingland! —awlus gives the ket wen its robbry with voylence, bless is awt. Aw sy nathink agin im: awm all fer lor mawseolf, aw em.

RANKIN. Well?

DRINKWATER. Hever ear of is sist-in-lor: Lidy Sisly Winefleet?

RANKIN. Do ye mean the celebrated leddy—the traveller?

DRINKWATER. Yuss: should think aw doo. Walked acrost Harfricar with nathink but a little dawg, and wrowt abaht it in the Dily Mile (*the Daily Mail, a popular London newspaper*), she did.

RANKIN. Is she Sir Howrrd Hallam's sister-in-law?

DRINKWATER. Deceased wawfe's sister: yuss: thets wot s h e is.

RANKIN. Well, what about them?

DRINKWATER. Wot abaht them! Waw, theyre e a h. Lannid aht of a steam yacht in Mogador awber not twenty minnits agow. Gorn to the British cornsl's. E'll send em orn to you: e ynt got naowheres to put em. Sor em awr (*hire*) a Harab an two Krooboys to kerry their laggige. Thort awd cam an teoll yer.

RANKIN. Thank you. Its verra kind of you, Mr Drinkwotter.

DRINKWATER. Downt mention it, gavner. Lor bless yer,

603

wawnt it you as converted me? Wot was aw wen aw cam eah but a pore lorst sinner? Downt aw ow y'a turn fer thet? Besawds, gavner, this Lidy Sisly Winefleet mawt wornt to tike a walk crost Morocker—a rawd inter the mahntns or sech lawk. Weoll, as you knaow, gavner, thet cawnt be done eah withaht a hescort.

RANKIN. It's impoassible: th' would oall b' murrdered. Morocco is not lek the rest of Africa.

DRINKWATER. No, gavner: these eah Moors ez their religion; an it mikes em dinegerous. Hever convert a Moor, gavner?

RANKIN [with a rueful smile] No.

DRINKWATER [solemnly] Nor hever will, gavner.

RANKIN. I have been at work here for twenty-five years, Mr Drinkwotter; and you are my first and only convert.

DRINKWATER. Downt seem naow good, do it, gavner?

RANKIN. I dont say that. I hope I have done some good. They come to me for medicine when they are ill; and they call me the Christian who is not a thief. T h a t is something.

DRINKWATER. Their mawnds kennot rawse to Christiennity lawk hahrs ken, gavner: thets ah it is. Weoll, ez haw was syin, if a hescort is wornted, theres maw friend and commawnder Kepn Brarsbahnd of the schooner Thenksgivin, an is crew, incloodin mawseolf, will see the lidy an Jadge Ellam through henny little excursion in reason. Yr honor mawt mention it.

RANKIN. I will certainly not propose anything so dangerous as an excursion.

DRINKWATER [virtuously] Naow, gavner, nor would I awst you to. [Shaking his head] Naow, naow: it i s dinegerous. But hall the more call for a hescort if they should ev it hin their mawnds to gow.

RANKIN. I hope they wont.

DRINKWATER. An sow aw do too, gavner.

RANKIN [pondering] Tis strange that they should come to Mogador, of all places; and to my house! I once met

604

Sir Howrrd Hallam, years ago.

DRINKWATER [*amazed*] Naow! didger? Think o thet, gavner! Waw, sow aw did too. But it were a misunnerstendin, thet wors. Lef the court withaht a stine on maw kerrickter, aw did.

RANKIN [*with some indignation*] I hope you dont think I met Sir Howrrd in that way.

DRINKWATER. Mawt yeppn to the honestest, best meanin pusson, aw do assure yer, gavner.

RANKIN. I would have you to know that I met him privately, Mr Drinkwotter. His brother was a dear friend of mine. Years ago. He went out to the West Indies.

DRINKWATER. The Wust Hindies! Jist acrost there, tather sawd thet howcean [*pointing seaward*]! Dear me! We cams hin with vennity, an we deepawts in dawkness. Downt we, gavner?

RANKIN [*pricking up his ears*] Eh? Have you been reading that little book I gave you?

DRINKWATER. Aw hev, et odd tawms. Very camfitn, gavner. [*He rises, apprehensive lest further catechism should find him unprepared*]. Awll sy good awtenoon, gavner: youre busy hexpectin o Sr Ahrd an Lidy Sisly, ynt yer? [*About to go*].

RANKIN [*stopping him*] No, stop: we're oalways ready for travellers here. I have something else to say—a question to ask you.

DRINKWATER [*with misgiving, which he masks by exaggerating his hearty sailor manner*] An weollcome, yr honor.

RANKIN. Who is this Captain Brassbound?

DRINKWATER [*guiltily*] Kepn Brarsbahnd! E's—weoll, e's maw Kepn, gavner.

RANKIN. Yes. Well?

DRINKWATER [*feebly*] Kepn of the schooner Thenksgivin, gavner.

RANKIN [*searchingly*] Have ye ever haird of a bad character in these seas called Black Paquito?

DRINKWATER [*with a sudden radiance of complete en-*

lightenment] Aoh, nar aw tikes yer wiv me, yr honor. Nah sammun es bin a teolln you thet Kepn Brarsbahnd an Bleck Pakeetow is hawdentically the sime pussn. Ynt thet sow?

RANKIN. That is so. [*Drinkwater slaps his knee triumphantly. The missionary proceeds determinedly*]. And the someone was a verra honest, straightforward man, as far as I could judge.

DRINKWATER [*embracing the implication*] Course e wors, gavner. Ev aw said a word agin him? Ev aw nah?

RANKIN. But is Captain Brassbound Black Paquito then?

DRINKWATER. Waw, its the nime is blessed mather give im at er knee, bless is little awt! Ther ynt naow awm in it. She were a Wust Hinjin—howver there agin, yer see [*pointing seaward*]—leastwaws, naow she wornt: she were a Brazilian, aw think; an Pakeetow's Brazilian for a bloomin little perrit—awskin yr pawdn for the word. [*Sentimentally*] Lawk as a Hinglish lidy mawt call er little boy Birdie.

RANKIN [*not quite convinced*] But why B l a c k Paquito?

DRINKWATER [*artlessly*] Waw, the bird in its netral stite bein green, an e evin bleck air, y' knaow—

RANKIN [*cutting him short*] I see. And now I will put ye another question. W h a t is Captain Brassbound, or Paquito, or whatever he calls himself.

DRINKWATER [*officiously*] Brarsbahnd, gavner. Awlus calls isseolf Brarsbahnd.

RANKIN. Well, Brassbound then. What is he?

DRINKWATER [*fervently*] You awks me wot e is, gavner?

RANKIN [*firmly*] I do.

DRINKWATER [*with rising enthusiasm*] An shll aw teoll yer wot e is, yr honor?

RANKIN [*not at all impressed*] If ye will be so good, Mr Drinkwotter.

DRINKWATER [*with overwhelming conviction*] Then

606

awll teoll you, gavner, wot he is. Ee's a Paffick Genlmn: thets wot e is.

RANKIN [*gravely*] Mr Drinkwotter: pairfection is an attribute, not of West Coast captains, but of thr Maaker. And there are gentlemen and gentlemen in the world, espaecially in these latitudes. Which sort of gentleman is he?

DRINKWATER. Hinglish genlmn, gavner. Hinglish speakin; Hinglish fawther; West Hinjin plawnter; Hinglish true blue breed. [*Reflectively*] Tech o brahn from the mather, preps, she bein Brazilian.

RANKIN. Now on your faith as a Christian, Felix Drinkwotter, is Captain Brassbound a slaver or not?

DRINKWATER [*surprised into his natural cockney pertness*] Naow e ynt.

RANKIN. Are ye s u r e?

DRINKWATER. Waw, a sliver is abaht the wanne thing in the wy of a genlmn o fortn thet e y n t.

RANKIN. Ive haird that expression "gentleman of fortune" before, Mr Drinkwotter. It means pirate. Do ye know that?

DRINKWATER. Bless yr awt, y' cawnt be a pawrit naradys. Waw, the aw seas is wuss pleest nor Piccadilly Suckus. If aw was to do orn thet there Hetlentic Howcean the things aw did as a bwoy in the Worterleoo Rowd, awd ev maw air cat afore aw could turn maw ed. Pawrit be blaowed!— awskink yr pawdn, gavner. Nah, jest to shaow you ah little thet there striteforard man y' mide mention on knaowed wot e was atorkin abaht: oo would you spowse was the marster to which Kepn Brarsbahnd served apprentice, as yr mawt sy?

RANKIN. I dont know.

DRINKWATER. Gawdn, gavner, Gawdn. Gawdn o Kawtoom—stetcher stends in Trifawlgr Square to this dy. Trined Bleck Pakeetow in smawshin hap the slive riders, e did. Promist Gawdn e wouldnt never smaggle slives nor

607

gin, an [*with suppressed aggravation*] w o w n t, gavner, not if we gows dahn on ahr bloomin bended knees to im **to** do it.

RANKIN [*drily*] And d o ye go down on your bended knees to him to do it?

DRINKWATER [*somewhat abashed*] Some of huz is hanconverted men, gavner; an they sy: You smaggles wanne thing, Kepn; waw not hanather?

RANKIN. Weve come to it at last. I thought so. Captain Brassbound is a smuggler.

DRINKWATER. Weoll, waw not? Waw not, gavner? Ahrs is a Free Tride nition. It gows agin us as Hinglishmen to see these bloomin furriners settin ap their Castoms Ahses and spheres o hinfluence and sich lawk hall owver Arfricar. Daownt Harfricar belong as much to huz as to them? thets wot we sy. Ennywys, there ynt naow awm in ahr business. All we daz is hescort, tourist h o r commercial. Cook's hexcursions to the Hatlas Mahntns: thets hall it is. Waw, its spreadin civlawzytion, it is. Ynt it nah?

RANKIN. You think Captain Brassbound's crew sufficiently equipped for that, do you?

DRINKWATER. Hee-quipped! Haw should think sow. Lawtnin rawfles, twelve shots in the meggezine! Oo's to storp us?

RANKIN. The most dangerous chieftain in these parts, the Sheikh Sidi el Assif, has a new American machine pistol which fires ten bullets without loadin; and his rifle has sixteen shots in the magazine.

DRINKWATER [*indignantly*] Yuss; an the people that sells sich things into the ends o' them eathen bleck niggers calls theirseolves Christians! Its a crool shime, sow it is.

RANKIN. If a man has the heart to pull the trigger, it matters little what color his hand is, Mr Drinkwotter. Have ye anything else to say to me this afternoon?

DRINKWATER [*rising*] Nathink, gavner, cept to wishyer the bust o yolth, and a many cornverts. Awtenoon, gavner.

As Drinkwater turns to go, a Moorish porter comes

CAPTAIN BRASSBOUND'S CONVERSION

from the house with two Krooboys.

THE PORTER [*at the door, addressing Rankin*] Bikouros (*Moroccan for Epicurus, a general Moorish name for the missionaries, who are supposed by the Moors to have chosen their calling through a love of luxurious idleness*): I have brought to your house a Christian dog and his woman.

DRINKWATER. Theres eathen menners fer yer! Calls Sr Ahrd Ellam an Lidy Winefleet a Christian dorg and is woman! If ee ed you in the dorck et the Centl Crimnal, youd fawnd aht oo was the dorg and oo was is marster, pretty quick, y o u would.

RANKIN. Have you broat their boxes?

THE PORTER. By Allah, two camel loads!

RANKIN. Have you been paid?

THE PORTER. Only one miserable dollar, Bikouros. I have brought them to your house. They will pay you. Give me something for bringing gold to your door.

DRINKWATER. Yah! You oughter bin bawn a Christian, you ought. You knaow too mach.

RANKIN. You have broat onnly trouble and expense to my door, Hassan; and you know it. Have I ever charged your wife and children for my medicines?

HASSAN [*philosophically*] It is always permitted by the Prophet to ask, Bikouros. [*He goes cheerfully into the house with the Krooboys*].

DRINKWATER. Jist thort eed trah it orn, e did. Hooman nitre is the sime everywheres. Them eathens is jast lawk you an' me, gavner.

A lady and gentleman, both English, come into the garden. The gentleman, more than elderly, is facing old age on compulsion, not resignedly. He is clean shaven, and has a brainy rectangular forehead, a resolute nose with strongly governed nostrils, and a tightly fastened down mouth which has evidently shut in much temper and anger in its time. He has a habit of deliberately assumed authority and dignity, but is trying to take life more genially and easily in his character of tourist, which is further borne out

609

CAPTAIN BRASSBOUND'S CONVERSION

by his white hat and summery racecourse attire.

The lady is between thirty and forty, tall, very good-looking, sympathetic, intelligent, tender and humorous, dressed with cunning simplicity not as a businesslike, tailor made, gaitered tourist, but as if she lived at the next cottage and had dropped in for tea in blouse and flowered straw hat. A woman of great vitality and humanity, who begins a casual acquaintance at the point usually attained by English people after thirty years' acquaintance when they are capable of reaching it at all. She pounces genially on Drinkwater, who is smirking at her, hat in hand, with an air of hearty welcome. The gentleman, on the other hand, comes down the side of the garden next the house, instinctively maintaining a distance between himself and the others.

THE LADY [*to Drinkwater*] Howdyedo? Are you the missionary?

DRINKWATER [*modestly*] Naow, lidy, aw will not deceive you, thow the mistike his but netral. Awm wanne of the missionary's good works, lidy—is first cornvert, a umble British seaman—countrymen o yours, lidy, and of is lawdship's. This eah is Mr Renkin, the bust worker in the wust cowst vawnyard. [*Introducing the judge*] Mr Renkin: is lawdship Sr Ahrd Ellam. [*He withdraws discreetly into the house*].

SIR HOWARD [*to Rankin*] I am sorry to intrude on you, Mr Rankin; but in the absence of a hotel there seems to be no alternative.

LADY CICELY [*beaming on him*] Besides, we would so much r a t h e r stay with you, if you will have us, Mr Rankin.

SIR HOWARD [*introducing her*] My sister-in-law, Lady Cicely Waynflete, Mr Rankin.

RANKIN. I am glad to be of service to your leddyship. You will be wishing to have some tea after your journey, I'm thinking.

LADY CICELY. Thoughtful man that you are, Mr Ran-
610

kin. But weve had some already on board the yacht. And Ive arranged everything with your servants; so you must go on gardening just as if we were not here.

SIR HOWARD. I am sorry to have to warn you, Mr Rankin, that Lady Cicely, from travelling in Africa, has acquired a habit of walking into people's houses and behaving as if she were in her own.

LADY CICELY. But, my dear Howard, I assure you the natives like it.

RANKIN [*gallantly*] So do I.

LADY CICELY [*delighted*] Oh, that is so nice of you, Mr Rankin. This is a delicious country! And the people seem so good! They have such nice faces! We had such a handsome Moor to carry our luggage up! And two perfect pets of Krooboys! Did you notice their faces, Howard?

SIR HOWARD. I did; and I can confidently say, after a long experience of faces of the worst type looking at me from the dock, that I have never seen so entirely villainous a trio as that Moor and the two Krooboys, to whom you gave five dollars when they would have been perfectly satisfied with one.

RANKIN [*throwing up his hands*] Five dollars! Tis easy to see you are not Scotch, my leddy.

LADY CICELY. O, poor things, they must want it more than we do; and you know, Howard, that Mahometans never spend money in drink.

RANKIN. Excuse me a moment, my leddy. I have a word in season to say to that same Moor. [*He goes into the house*].

LADY CICELY [*walking about the garden, looking at the view and at the flowers*] I think this is a perfectly heavenly place.

Drinkwater returns from the house with a chair.

DRINKWATER [*placing the chair for Sir Howard*] Awskink yr pawdn for the libbety, Sr Ahrd.

SIR HOWARD [*looking at him*] I have seen you before somewhere.

DRINKWATER. You ev, Sr Ahrd. But aw do assure yer it were hall a mistike.

SIR HOWARD. As usual. [*He sits down*]. Wrongfully convicted, of course.

DRINKWATER [*with sly delight*] Naow, gavner. [*Half whispering, with an ineffable grin*]. Wrongfully hacquittid!

SIR HOWARD. Indeed! Thats the first case of the kind I have ever met.

DRINKWATER. Lawd, Sr Ahrd, wot jagginses them jurymen was! You an me knaowed it too, didnt we?

SIR HOWARD. I daresay we did. I am sorry to say I forget the exact nature of the difficulty you were in. Can you refresh my memory?

DRINKWATER. Owny the aw sperrits o youth, y' lawdship. Worterleoo Rowd kice. Wot they calls Ooliganism.

SIR HOWARD. Oh! You were a Hooligan, were you?

LADY CICELY [*puzzled*] A Hooligan!

DRINKWATER [*deprecatingly*] Nime giv huz pore thortless leds baw a gent on the Dily Chrornicle, lidy. [*Rankin returns. Drinkwater immediately withdraws, stopping the missionary for a moment near the threshold to say, touching his forelock*]. Awll eng abaht within ile, gavner, hin kice aw should be wornted. [*He goes into the house with soft steps*].

Lady Cicely sits down on the bench under the tamarisk. Rankin takes his stool from the flowerbed and sits down on her left, Sir Howard being on her right.

LADY CICELY. What a pleasant face your sailor friend has, Mr Rankin! He has been so frank and truthful with us. You know I dont think anybody can pay me a greater compliment than to be quite sincere with me at first sight. Its the perfection of natural good manners.

SIR HOWARD. You must not suppose, Mr Rankin, that my sister-in-law talks nonsense on purpose. She will continue to believe in your friend until he steals her watch; and even then she will find excuses for him.

CAPTAIN BRASSBOUND'S CONVERSION

RANKIN [*drily changing the subject*] And how have ye been, Sir Howrrd, since our last meeting that morning nigh forty year ago down at the docks in London?

SIR HOWARD [*greatly surprised, pulling himself together*] Our last meeting! Mr Rankin: have I been unfortunate enough to forget an old acquaintance?

RANKIN. Well, perhaps hardly an acquaintance, Sir Howrrd. But I was a close friend of your brother Miles; and when he sailed for Brazil I was one of the little party that saw him off. You were one of the party also, if I'm not mistaken. I took particular notice of you because you were Miles's brother and I had never seen ye before. But ye had no call to take notice of me.

SIR HOWARD [*reflecting*] Yes: there was a young friend of my brother's who might well be you. But the name, as I recollect it, was Leslie.

RANKIN. That was me, sir. My name is Leslie Rankin; and your brother and I were always Miles and Leslie to one another.

SIR HOWARD [*pluming himself a little*] Ah! that explains it. I can trust my memory still, Mr Rankin; though some people do complain that I am growing old.

RANKIN. And where may Miles be now, Sir Howard?

SIR HOWARD [*abruptly*] Dont you know that he is dead?

RANKIN [*much shocked*] Never haird of it. Dear, dear: I shall never see him again; and I can scarcely bring his face to mind after all these years. [*With moistening eyes, which at once touch Lady Cicely's sympathy*]. I'm right sorry—right sorry.

SIR HOWARD [*decorously subduing his voice*] Yes: he did not live long: indeed, he never came back to England. It must be nearly thirty years ago now that he died in the West Indies on his property there.

RANKIN [*surprised*] His proaperty! Miles with a proaperty!

SIR HOWARD. Yes: he became a planter, and did well out there, Mr Rankin. The history of that property is a very curious and interesting one—at least it is so to a lawyer like myself.

RANKIN. I should be glad to hear it for Miles's sake, though I am no lawyer, Sir Howrrd.

LADY CICELY. I never knew you had a brother, Howard?

SIR HOWARD [*not pleased by this remark*] Perhaps because you never asked me. [*Turning more blandly to Rankin*]. I will tell you the story, Mr Rankin. When Miles died, he left an estate in one of the West Indian islands. It was in charge of an agent who was a sharpish fellow, with all his wits about him. Now, sir, that man did a thing which probably could hardly be done with impunity even here in Morocco, under the most barbarous of surviving civilizations. He quite simply took the estate for himself and kept it.

RANKIN. But how about the law?

SIR HOWARD. The law, sir, in that island, consisted practically of the Attorney General and the Solicitor General; and these gentlemen were both retained by the agent. Consequently there was no solicitor in the island to take up the case against him.

RANKIN. Is such a thing possible today in the British Empire?

SIR HOWARD [*calmly*] Oh, quite. Quite.

LADY CICELY. But could not a firstrate solicitor have been sent out from London?

SIR HOWARD. No doubt, by paying him enough to compensate him for giving up his London practice: that is, rather more than there was any reasonable likelihood of the estate proving worth.

RANKIN. Then the estate was lost?

SIR HOWARD. Not permanently. It is in my hands at present.

RANKIN. Then how did ye get it back?

SIR HOWARD [*with crafty enjoyment of his own cunning*] By hoisting the rogue with his own petard. I had to leave matters as they were for many years; for I had my own position in the world to make. But at last I made it. In the course of a holiday trip to the West Indies, I found that this dishonest agent had left the island, and placed the estate in the hands of an agent of his own, whom he was foolish enough to pay very badly. I put the case before that agent; and he decided to treat the estate as my property. The robber now found himself in exactly the same position he had formerly forced me into. Nobody in the island would act against me, least of all the Attorney and Solicitor General, who appreciated my influence at the Colonial Office. And so I got the estate back. "The mills of the gods grind slowly," Mr Rankin; "but they grind exceeding small."

LADY CICELY. Now I suppose if I'd done such a clever thing in England, youd have sent me to prison.

SIR HOWARD. Probably, unless you had taken care to keep outside the law against conspiracy. Whenever you wish to do anything against the law, Cicely, always consult a good solicitor first.

LADY CICELY. So I do. But suppose your agent takes it into his head to give the estate back to his wicked old employer!

SIR HOWARD. I heartily wish he would.

RANKIN [*openeyed*] You wish he w o u l d!!

SIR HOWARD. Yes. A few years ago the collapse of the West Indian sugar industry converted the income of the estate into an annual loss of about £150 a year. If I cant sell it soon, I shall simply abandon it—unless you, Mr Rankin, would like to take it as a present.

RANKIN [*laughing*] I thank your lordship: we have estates enough of that sort in Scotland. Youre setting with your back to the sun, Leddy Ceecily, and losing something worth looking at. See there. [*He rises and points seaward, where the rapid twilight of the latitude has begun*].

LADY CICELY [*getting up to look and uttering a cry of admiration*] Oh, how lovely!

615

SIR HOWARD [*also rising*] What are those hills over there to the southeast?

RANKIN. They are the outposts, so to speak, of the Atlas Mountains.

LADY CICELY. The Atlas Mountains! Where Shelley's witch lived! We'll make an excursion to them tomorrow, Howard.

RANKIN. Thats impossible, my leddy. The natives are verra dangerous.

LADY CICELY. Why? Has any explorer been shooting them?

RANKIN. No. But every man of them believes he will go to Heaven if he kills an unbeliever.

LADY CICELY. Bless you, dear Mr Rankin, the people in England believe that they will go to heaven if they give all their property to the poor. But they dont do it. I'm not a bit afraid of that.

RANKIN. But they are not accustomed to see women going about unveiled.

LADY CICELY. I always get on best with people when they can see my face.

SIR HOWARD. Cicely: you are talking great nonsense; and you know it. These people have no laws to restrain them, which means, in plain English, that they are habitual thieves and murderers.

RANKIN. Nay, nay: not exactly that, Sir Howarrd.

LADY CICELY [*indignantly*] Of course not. You always think, Howard, that nothing prevents people killing each other but the fear of your hanging them for it. But what nonsense that is! And how wicked! If these people werent here for some good purpose, they wouldnt have been made, would they, Mr Rankin?

RANKIN. That is a point, certainly, Leddy Ceecily.

SIR HOWARD. Oh, if you are going to talk theology—

LADY CICELY. Well, why not? theology is as respectable as law, I should think. Besides, I'm only talking common-

616

sense. Why do people get killed by savages? Because instead of being polite to them, and saying Howdyedo? like me, people aim pistols at them. Ive been among savages—cannibals and all sorts. Everybody said theyd kill me. But when I met them, I said Howdyedo? and they were quite nice. The kings always wanted to marry me.

SIR HOWARD. That does not seem to me to make you any safer here, Cicely. You shall certainly not stir a step beyond the protection of the consul, if I can help it, without a strong escort.

LADY CICELY. I dont want an escort.

SIR HOWARD. I do. And I suppose you will expect me to accompany you.

RANKIN. Tis not safe, Leddy Ceecily. Really and truly, tis not safe. The tribes are verra fierce; and there are cities here that no Christian has ever set foot in. If you go without being well protected, the first chief you meet will seize you and send you back again to prevent his followers murdering you.

LADY CICELY. Oh, how nice of him, Mr Rankin!

RANKIN. He would not do it for your sake, Leddy Ceecily, but for his own. The Sultan would get into trouble with England if you were killed; and the Sultan would kill the chief to pacify the English government.

LADY CICELY. But I always go everywhere. I k n o w the people here wont touch me. They have such nice faces and such pretty scenery.

SIR HOWARD [to Rankin, sitting down again resignedly] You can imagine how much use there is in talking to a woman who admires the faces of the ruffians who infest these ports, Mr Rankin. Can anything be done in the way of an escort?

RANKIN. There is a certain Captain Brassbound here who trades along the coast, and occasionally escorts parties of merchants on journeys into the interior. I understand that he served under Gordon in the Soudan.

617

SIR HOWARD. That sounds promising. But I should like to know a little more about him before I trust myself in his hands.

RANKIN. I quite agree with you, Sir Howrrd. I'll send Felix Drinkwotter for him. [*He claps his hands. An Arab boy appears at the house door*]. Muley: is sailor man here? [*Muley nods*]. Tell sailor man bring captain. [*Muley nods and goes*].

SIR HOWARD. Who is Drinkwater?

RANKIN. His agent, or mate: I dont rightly know which.

LADY CICELY. Oh, if he has a mate named Felix Drinkwater, it must be quite a respectable crew. It is such a nice name.

RANKIN. You saw him here just now. He is a convert of mine.

LADY CICELY [*delighted*] That nice truthful sailor!

SIR HOWARD [*horrified*] What! The Hooligan!

RANKIN [*puzzled*] Hooligan? No, my lord: he is an Englishman.

SIR HOWARD. My dear Mr Rankin, this man was tried before me on a charge of street ruffianism.

RANKIN. So he told me. He was badly broat up, I am afraid. But he is now a converted man.

LADY CICELY. Of course he is. His telling you so frankly proves it. You know, really, Howard, all those poor people whom you try are more sinned against than sinning. If you would only talk to them in a friendly way instead of passing cruel sentences on them, you would find them quite nice to you. [*Indignantly*] I wont have this poor man trampled on merely because his mother brought him up as a Hooligan. I am sure nobody could be nicer than he was when he spoke to us.

SIR HOWARD. In short, we are to have an escort of Hooligans commanded by a filibuster. Very well, very well. You will most likely admire all their faces; and I have no doubt at all that they will admire yours.

Drinkwater comes from the house with an Italian

618

dressed in a much worn suit of blue serge, a dilapidated Alpine hat, and boots laced with scraps of twine. He remains near the door, whilst Drinkwater comes forward between Sir Howard and Lady Cicely.

DRINKWATER. Yr honor's servant. [*To the Italian*] Mawtzow: is lawdship Sr Ahrd Ellam. [*Marzo touches his hat*]. Er Lidyship Lidy Winefleet. [*Marzo touches his hat*]. Hawtellian shipmite, lidy. Hahr chef.

LADY CICELY [*nodding affably to Marzo*] Howdyedo? I love Italy. What part of it were you born in?

DRINKWATER. Wornt bawn in Hitly at all, lidy. Bawn in Ettn Gawdn (*Hatton Garden*). Hawce barrer an street pianner Hawtellian, lidy: thets wot e is. Kepn Brarsbahnd's respects to yr honors; an e awites yr commawnds.

RANKIN. Shall we go indoors to see him?

SIR HOWARD. I think we had better have a look at him by daylight.

RANKIN. Then we must lose no time: the dark is soon down in this latitude. [*To Drinkwater*] Will ye ask him to step out here to us, Mr Drinkwotter?

DRINKWATER. Rawt you aw, gavner. [*He goes officiously into the house*].

Lady Cicely and Rankin sit down as before to receive the Captain. The light is by this time waning rapidly, the darkness creeping west into the orange crimson.

LADY CICELY [*whispering*] Dont you feel rather creepy, Mr Rankin? I wonder what he'll be like.

RANKIN. I misdoubt me he will not answer, your leddyship.

There is a scuffling noise in the house; and Drinkwater shoots out through the doorway across the garden with every appearance of having been violently kicked. Marzo immediately hurries down the garden on Sir Howard's right out of the neighborhood of the doorway.

DRINKWATER [*trying to put a cheerful air on much mortification and bodily anguish*] Narsty step to thet ere door—tripped me hap, it did. [*Raising his voice and nar-*

619

rowly escaping a squeak of pain]. Kepn Brarsbahnd. [*He gets as far from the house as possible, on Rankin's left. Rankin rises to receive his guest*].

An olive complexioned man with dark southern eyes and hair comes from the house. Age about 36. Handsome features, but joyless; dark eyebrows drawn towards one another; mouth set grimly; nostrils large and strained: a face set to one tragic purpose. A man of few words, fewer gestures, and much significance. On the whole, interesting, and even attractive, but not friendly. He stands for a moment, saturnine in the ruddy light, to see who is present, looking in a singular and rather deadly way at Sir Howard; then with some surprise and uneasiness at Lady Cicely. Finally he comes down into the middle of the garden, and confronts Rankin, who has been staring at him in consternation from the moment of his entrance, and continues to do so in so marked a way that the glow in Brassbound's eyes deepens as he begins to take offence.

BRASSBOUND. Well, sir, have you stared your fill at me?

RANKIN [*recovering himself with a start*] I ask your pardon for my bad manners, Captain Brassbound. Ye are extraordinair lek an auld college friend of mine, whose face I said not ten minutes gone that I could no longer bring to mind. It was as if he had come from the grave to remind me of it.

BRASSBOUND. Why have you sent for me?

RANKIN. We have a matter of business with ye, Captain.

BRASSBOUND. Who are "we"?

RANKIN. This is Sir Howarrd Hallam, who will be well known to ye as one of Her Majesty's judges.

BRASSBOUND [*turning the singular look again on Sir Howard*] The friend of the widow! the protector of the fatherless!

SIR HOWARD [*startled*] I did not know I was so favorably spoken of in these parts, Captain Brassbound. We want an escort for a trip into the mountains.

BRASSBOUND [*ignoring this announcement*] Who is the lady?

RANKIN. Lady Ceecily Waynflete, his lordship's sister-in-law.

LADY CICELY. Howdyedo, Captain Brassbound? [*He bows gravely*].

SIR HOWARD [*a little impatient of these questions, which strike him as somewhat impertinent*] Let us come to business, if you please. We are thinking of making a short excursion to see the country about here. Can you provide us with an escort of respectable, trustworthy men?

BRASSBOUND. No.

DRINKWATER [*in strong remonstrance*] Nah, nah, nah! Nah look eah, Kepn, y' knaow—

BRASSBOUND [*between his teeth*] Hold your tongue.

DRINKWATER [*abjectly*] Yuss, Kepn.

RANKIN. I understood it was your business to provide escorts, Captain Brassbound.

BRASSBOUND. You were rightly informed. That i s my business.

LADY CICELY. Then why wont you do it for us?

BRASSBOUND. You are not content with an escort. You want respectable, trustworthy men. You should have brought a division of London policemen with you. M y men are neither respectable nor trustworthy.

DRINKWATER [*unable to contain himself*] Nah, nah, look eah, Kepn. If you want to be moddist, be moddist on your aown accahnt, nort on mawn.

BRASSBOUND. You see what my men are like. That rascal [*Indicating Marzo*] would cut a throat for a dollar if he had courage enough.

MARZO. I not understand. I no spik Englis.

BRASSBOUND. This thing [*pointing to Drinkwater*] is the greatest liar, thief, drunkard, and rapscallion on the west coast.

DRINKWATER [*affecting an ironic indifference*] Gow

orn, gow orn. Sr Ahrd ez erd witnesses to maw kerrickter afoah. *E* knaows ah mech to blieve of em.

LADY CICELY. Captain Brassbound: I have heard all that before about the blacks; and I found them very nice people when they were properly treated.

DRINKWATER [*chuckling: the Italian is also grinning*] Nah, Kepn, nah! Owp yr prahd o y'seolf nah.

BRASSBOUND. I quite understand the proper treatment for him, madam. If he opens his mouth again without my leave, I will break every bone in his skin.

LADY CICELY [*in her most sunnily matter-of-fact way*] Does Captain Brassbound always treat you like this, Mr Drinkwater?

Drinkwater hesitates, and looks apprehensively at the Captain.

BRASSBOUND. Answer, you dog, when the lady orders you. [*To Lady Cicely*] Do not address him as Mr Drinkwater, madam: he is accustomed to be called Brandyfaced Jack.

DRINKWATER [*indignantly*] Eah, aw sy! nah look eah, Kepn: maw nime is Drinkworter. You awsk em et Sin Jorn's in the Worterleoo Rowd. Orn maw grenfawther's tombstown, it is.

BRASSBOUND. It will be on your own tombstone, presently, if you cannot hold your tongue. [*Turning to the others*] Let us understand one another, if you please. An escort here, or anywhere where there are no regular disciplined forces, is what its captain makes it. If I undertake this business, *I* shall be your escort. I may require a dozen men, just as I may require a dozen horses. Some of the horses will be vicious; so will all the men. If either horse or man tries any of his viciousness on me, so much the worse for him; but it will make no difference to you. I will order my men to behave themselves before the lady; and they shall obey their orders. But the lady will please understand that I take my own way with them and suffer no interference.

LADY CICELY. Captain Brassbound: I dont want an escort at all. It will simply get us all into danger; and I shall have the trouble of getting it out again. Thats what escorts always do. But since Sir Howard prefers an escort, I think you had better stay at home and let me take charge of it. I know your men will get on perfectly well if theyre properly treated.

DRINKWATER [*with enthusiasm*] Feed aht o yr and, lidy, we would.

BRASSBOUND [*with sardonic assent*] Good. I agree. [*To Drinkwater*] You shall go without me.

DRINKWATER [*terrified*] Eah! Wot are you a syin orn? We cawnt gow withaht yer. [*To Lady Cicely*] Naow, lidy: it wouldnt be for yr hown good. Yer cawnt hexpect a lot o poor honeddikited men lawk huz to ran ahrseolvs into dineger withaht naow Kepn to teoll us wot to do. Naow, lidy: hoonawted we stend: deevawdid we fall.

LADY CICELY. Oh, if you prefer your captain, have him by all means. Do you l i k e to be treated as he treats you?

DRINKWATER [*with a smile of vanity*] Weoll, lidy: y' cawnt deenaw that e's a Paffick Genlmn. Bit hawbitrairy, preps; but hin a genlmn you looks for sich. It tikes a hawbitrairy wanne to knock aht them eathen Shikes, aw teoll yer.

BRASSBOUND. Thats enough. Go.

DRINKWATER. Weoll, aw was hownly a teolln the lidy thet— [*A threatening movement from Brassbound cuts him short. He flies for his life into the house, followed by the Italian*].

BRASSBOUND. Your ladyship sees. These men serve me by their own free choice. If they are dissatisfied, they go. If *I* am dissatisfied, they go. They take care that I am not dissatisfied.

SIR HOWARD [*who has listened with approval and growing confidence*] Captain Brassbound: you are the man I want. If your terms are at all reasonable, I will accept your services if we decide to make an excursion. You do not object, Cicely, I hope.

LADY CICELY. Oh no. After all, those men must really

like you, Captain Brassbound. I feel sure you have a kind heart. You have such nice eyes.

SIR HOWARD [*scandalized*] My d e a r Cicely: you really must restrain your expressions of confidence in people's eyes and faces. [*To Brassbound*] Now, about terms, Captain?

BRASSBOUND. Where do you propose to go?

SIR HOWARD. I hardly know. Where c a n we go, Mr Rankin?

RANKIN. Take my advice, Sir Howrrd. Dont go far.

BRASSBOUND. I can take you to Meskala, from which you can see the Atlas Mountains. From Meskala I can take you to an ancient castle in the hills, where you can put up as long as you please. The customary charge is half a dollar a man per day and his food. *I* charge double.

SIR HOWARD. I suppose you answer for your men being sturdy fellows, who will stand to their guns if necessary.

BRASSBOUND. I can answer for their being more afraid of me than of the Moors.

LADY CICELY. That doesnt matter in the least, Howard. The important thing, Captain Brassbound, is: first, that we should have as few men as possible, because men give such a lot of trouble travelling. And then, they must have good lungs and not be always catching cold. Above all, their clothes must be of good wearing material. Otherwise I shall be nursing and stitching and mending all the way; and it will be trouble enough, I assure you, to keep them washed and fed without that.

BRASSBOUND [*haughtily*] My men, madam, are not children in the nursery.

LADY CICELY [*with unanswerable conviction*] Captain Brassbound: a l l men are children in the nursery. I see that you dont notice things. That poor Italian had only one proper bootlace: the other was a bit of string. And I am sure from Mr Drinkwater's complexion that he ought to have some medicine.

BRASSBOUND [*outwardly determined not to be trifled*

624

with: inwardly puzzled and rather daunted] Madam: if you want an escort, I can provide you with an escort. If you want a Sunday School treat, I can n o t provide it

LADY CICELY [*with sweet melancholy*] Ah, dont you wish you could, Captain? Oh, if I could only shew you my children from Waynflete Sunday School! The darlings would love this place, with all the camels and black men. I'm sure you would enjoy having them here, Captain Brassbound; and it would be such an education for your men! [*Brassbound stares at her with drying lips*].

SIR HOWARD. Cicely: when you have quite done talking nonsense to Captain Brassbound, we can proceed to make some definite arrangements with him.

LADY CICELY. But it's arranged already. We'll start at eight o'clock tomorrow morning, if you please, Captain. Never mind about the Italian: I have a big box of clothes with me for my brother in Rome; and there are some boot-laces in it. Now go home to bed and dont fuss yourself. All you have to do is to bring your men round; and I'll see to the rest. Men are always so nervous about moving. Goodnight. [*She offers him her hand. Surprised he pulls off his cap for the first time. Some scruple prevents him from taking her hand at once. He hesitates; then turns to Sir Howard and addresses him with warning earnestness*].

BRASSBOUND. Sir Howard Hallam: I advise you not to attempt this expedition.

SIR HOWARD. Indeed! Why?

BRASSBOUND. You are safe here. I warn you, in those hills there is a justice that is not the justice of your courts in England. If you have wronged a man, you may meet that man there. If you have wronged a woman, you may meet her son there. The justice of those hills is the justice of vengeance.

SIR HOWARD [*faintly amused*]. You are superstitious, Captain. Most sailors are, I notice. However, I have complete confidence in your escort.

BRASSBOUND [*almost threateningly*] Take care. The

CAPTAIN BRASSBOUND'S CONVERSION

avenger may be one of the escort.

SIR HOWARD. I have already met the only member of your escort who might have borne a grudge against me, Captain; and he was acquitted.

BRASSBOUND. You are fated to come, then?

SIR HOWARD [*smiling*] It seems so.

BRASSBOUND. On your head be it! [*To Lady Cicely, accepting her hand at last*] Goodnight.

He goes. It is by this time starry night.

END OF ACT I

626

ACT II

MIDDAY. A room in a Moorish castle. A divan seat runs round the dilapidated adobe walls, which are partly painted, partly faced with white tiles patterned in green and yellow. The ceiling is made up of little squares, painted in bright colors, with gilded edges, and ornamented with gilt knobs. On the cement floor are mattings, sheepskins, and leathern cushions with geometrical patterns on them. There is a tiny Moorish table in the middle; and at it a huge saddle, with saddle cloths of various colors, shewing that the room is used by foreigners accustomed to chairs. Anyone sitting at the table in this seat would have the chief entrance, a large horseshoe arch, on his left, and another saddle seat between him and the arch; whilst, if susceptible to draughts, he would probably catch cold from a little Moorish door in the wall behind him to his right.

Two or three of Brassbound's men, overcome by the midday heat, sprawl supine on the floor, with their reefer coats under their heads, their knees uplifted, and their calves laid comfortably on the divan. Those who wear shirts have them open at the throat for greater coolness. Some have jerseys. All wear boots and belts, and have guns ready to their hands. One of them, lying with his head against the second saddle seat, wears what was once a fashionable white English yachting suit. He is evidently a pleasantly worthless young English gentleman gone to the bad, but retaining sufficient self-respect to shave carefully and brush his hair, which is wearing thin, and does not seem to have been luxuriant even in its best days.

The silence is broken only by the snores of the young gentleman, whose mouth has fallen open, until a few distant shots half waken him. He shuts his mouth convulsively, and opens his eyes sleepily. A door is violently kicked outside; and the voice of Drinkwater is heard raising urgent alarm.

DRINKWATER. Wot ow! Wike ap there, will yr. Wike

627

ap. [*He rushes in through the horseshoe arch, hot and excited, and runs round, kicking the sleepers*]. Nah then. Git ap. Git ap, will yr, Kiddy Redbrook. [*He gives the young gentleman a rude shove*].

REDBROOK [*sitting up*] Stow that, will you. Whats amiss?

DRINKWATER [*disgusted*] Wots amiss! Didnt eah naow fawrin, I spowse.

REDBROOK. No.

DRINKWATER [*sneering*] Naow. Thort it sifer nort, didnt yr?

REDBROOK [*with crisp intelligence*] What! Youre running away, are you? [*He springs up, crying*] Look alive, Johnnies: theres danger. Brandyfaced Jack's on the run. [*They spring up hastily, grasping their guns*].

DRINKWATER. Dineger! Yuss: should think there wors dineger. It's howver, thow, as it mowstly his baw the tawm y o u r e awike. [*They relapse into lassitude*]. Waw wasnt you on the look-aht to give us a end? Bin hattecked baw the Benny Seeras (*Beni Siras*), we ev, an ed to rawd for it pretty strite, too, aw teoll yr. Mawtzow is it: the bullet glawnst all rahnd is bloomin brisket. Brarsbahnd e dropt the Shike's oss at six unnern fifty yawds. [*Bustling them about*] Nah then: git the plice ready for the British herristorcracy, Lawd Ellam and Lidy Wineflete.

REDBROOK. Lady faint, eh?

DRINKWATER. Fynt! Not lawkly. Wornted to gow an talk to the Benny Seeras: blaow me if she didnt! Harskʳ huz wot we was frahtnd of. Tyin ap Mawtzow's wound, she is, like a bloomin orspittle nass. [*Sir Howard, with a copious pagri on his white hat, enters through the horseshoe arch, followed by a couple of men supporting the wounded Marzo, who, weeping and terrorstricken by the prospect of death and of subsequent torments for which he is conscious of having eminently qualified himself, has his coat off and a bandage round his chest. One of his supporters is a black-bearded, thickset, slow, middle-aged man with an air of*]

*damaged respectability named—as it afterwards appears—
Johnson. Lady Cicely walks beside Marzo. Redbrook, a
little shamefaced, crosses the room to the opposite wall as
far away as possible from the visitors. Drinkwater turns and
receives them with jocular ceremony.*] Weolcome to Brarsbahnd Cawstl, Sr Ahrd an lidy. This eah is the corfee and
commercial room.

*Sir Howard goes to the table and sits on the saddle,
rather exhausted. Lady Cicely comes to Drinkwater.*

LADY CICELY. Where is Marzo's bed?

DRINKWATER. Is bed, lidy? Weoll: e ynt petickler, lidy.
E ez is chawce of henny flegstown agin thet wall.

*They deposit Marzo on the flags against the wall close
to the little door. He groans. Johnson phlegmatically leaves
him and joines Redbrook.*

LADY CICELY. But you cant leave him there in that state.

DRINKWATER. Ow: e's hall rawt. [*Strolling up callously
to Marzo*] Youre hall rawt, ynt yer, Mawtzow? [*Marzo
whimpers*]. Corse y'aw.

LADY CICELY [*to Sir Howard*] Did you ever see such a
helpless lot of poor creatures? [*She makes for the little
door*].

DRINKWATER. Eah! [*He runs to the door and places
himself before it*]. Where mawt yr lidyship be gowin?

LADY CICELY. I'm going through every room in this
castle to find a proper place to put that man. And now I'll
tell you where y o u r e going. Youre going to get some
water for Marzo, who is very thirsty. And then, when Ive
chosen a room for him, youre going to make a bed for him
there.

DRINKWATER [*sarcastically*] Ow! Henny ather little
suvvice? Mike yrseolf at owm, y' knaow, lidy.

LADY CICELY [*considerately*] Dont go if youd rather
not, Mr Drinkwater. Perhaps youre too tired. [*Turning to
the archway*] I'll ask Captain Brassbound: he wont mind.

DRINKWATER [*terrified, running after her and getting
between her and the arch*] Naow, naow! Naow, lidy: downt

629

you gow disturbin the kepn. Awll see to it.

LADY CICELY [*gravely*] I was sure you would, Mr Drinkwater. You have such a kind face. [*She turns back and goes out through the small door*].

DRINKWATER [*looking after her*] Garn!

SIR HOWARD [*to Drinkwater*] Will you ask one of your friends to shew me to my room whilst you are getting the water?

DRINKWATER [*insolently*] Yr room! Ow: this ynt good enaf fr yr, ynt it? [*Ferociously*] Oo a you orderin abaht, ih?

SIR HOWARD [*rising quietly, and taking refuge between Redbrook and Johnson, whom he addresses*] Can you find me a more private room than this?

JOHNSON [*shaking his head*] Ive no orders. You must wait til the capn comes, sir.

DRINKWATER [*following Sir Howard*] Yuss; an whawl youre witin, yll tike your horders from me: see?

JOHNSON [*with slow severity, to Drinkwater*] Look here: do you see three genlmen talkin to one another here, civil and private, eh?

DRINKWATER [*chapfallen*] No offence, Miste Jornsn—

JOHNSON [*ominously*] Ay; but there is offence. Wheres your manners, you guttersnipe? [*Turning to Sir Howard*] Thats the curse o this kind o life, sir: you got to associate with all sorts. My father, sir, was Capn Johnson o Hull—owned his own schooner, sir. We're mostly genlemen here, sir, as youll find, except the poor ignorant foreigner and that there scum of the submerged tenth. [*Contemptuously talking at Drinkwater*]. He aint nobody's son: he's only a offspring o coster folk or such.

DRINKWATER [*bursting into tears*] Clawss feelin! thets wot it is; clawss feelin! Wot are yer, arter all, bat a bloomin gang o wust cowst cazhls (*casual ward paupers*)? [*Johnson is scandalized; and there is a general thrill of indignation*]. Better ev naow fembly, an rawse aht of it, lawk me, than ev a specble one and disgrice it, lawk you.

JOHNSON. Brandyfaced Jack: I name you for conduct

CAPTAIN BRASSBOUND'S CONVERSION

and language unbecoming to a gentleman. Those who agree will signify the same in the usual manner.

ALL [*vehemently*] Aye.

DRINKWATER [*wildly*] Naow.

JOHNSON. Felix Drinkwater: are you goin out, or are you goin to wait til youre chucked out? You can cry in the passage. If you give any trouble, youll have something to cry for.

They make a threatening movement towards Drinkwater.

DRINKWATER [*whimpering*] You lee me alown: awm gowin. Theres n'maw true demmecrettick feelin eah than there is in the owl bloomin M division of Noontn Corzwy coppers [*Newington Causeway policemen*].

As he slinks away in tears towards the arch, Brassbound enters. Drinkwater promptly shelters himself on the captain's left hand, the others retreating to the opposite side as Brassbound advances to the middle of the room. Sir Howard retires behind them and seats himself on the divan, much fatigued.

BRASSBOUND [*to Drinkwater*] What are you snivelling at?

DRINKWATER. You awsk the wust cowst herristorcracy. They fawnds maw corNduck hanbecammin to a genlmn.

Brassbound is about to ask Johnson for an explanation, when Lady Cicely returns through the little door, and comes between Brassbound and Drinkwater.

LADY CICELY [*to Drinkwater*] Have you fetched the water?

DRINKWATER. Yuss: nah y o u begin orn me. [*He weeps afresh*].

LADY CICELY [*surprised*] Oh! This wont do, Mr Drinkwater. If you cry, I cant let you nurse your friend.

DRINKWATER [*frantic*] Thetll brike maw awt, wownt it nah? [*With a lamentable sob, he throws himself down on the divan, raging like an angry child*].

LADY CICELY [*after contemplating him in astonishment

631

for a moment] Captain Brassbound: are there any char-women in the Atlas Mountains?

BRASSBOUND. There are people here who work if you pay them, as there are elsewhere.

LADY CICELY. This castle is very romantic, Captain; but it hasnt had a spring cleaning since the Prophet lived in it. Theres only one room I can put the wounded man into. Its the only one that has a bed in it: the second room on the right out of that passage.

BRASSBOUND [*haughtily*] That is my room, madam.

LADY CICELY [*relieved*] Oh, thats all right. It would have been so awkward if I had had to ask one of your men to turn out. You wont mind, I know. [*All the men stare at her. Even Drinkwater forgets his sorrows in his stupefaction*].

BRASSBOUND. Pray, madam, have you made any arrangements for my accommodation?

LADY CICELY [*reassuringly*] Yes: you can have my room instead, wherever it may be: I'm sure you chose me a nice one. I must be near my patient; and I dont mind roughing it. Now I must have Marzo moved very carefully. Where is that truly gentlemanly Mr Johnson?—oh, there you are, Mr Johnson. [*She runs to Johnson, past Brassbound, who has to step back hastily out of her way with every expression frozen out of his face except one of extreme and indignant dumbfoundedness*]. Will you ask your strong friend to help you with Marzo: strong people are always so gentle.

JOHNSON. Let me introdooce Mr Redbrook. Your ladyship may know his father, the very Rev. Dean Redbrook. [*He goes to Marzo*].

REDBROOK. Happy to oblige you, Lady Cicely.

LADY CICELY [*shaking hands*] Howdyedo? Of course I knew your father—Dunham wasnt it? Were you ever called—

REDBROOK. The kid? Yes.

LADY CICELY. But why—

632

REDBROOK [*anticipating the rest of the question*] Cards and drink, Lady Sis. [*He follows Johnson to the patient. Lady Cicely goes too*]. Now, Count Marzo. [*Marzo groans as Johnson and Redbrook raise him*].

LADY CICELY. Now theyre n o t hurting you, Marzo. They couldn't be more gentle.

MARZO. Drink.

LADY CICELY. I'll get you some water myself. Your friend Mr Drinkwater was too overcome—take care of the corner—thats it—the second door on the right. [*She goes out with Marzo and his bearers through the little door*].

BRASSBOUND [*still staring*] Well, I a m damned!

DRINKWATER [*getting up*] Weoll, blimey!

BRASSBOUND [*turning irritably on him*] What did you say?

DRINKWATER. Weoll, wot did yer sy yrseolf, kepn? Fust tawm aw yever see y' afride of ennybody. [*The others laugh*].

BRASSBOUND. Afraid!

DRINKWATER [*maliciously*] She's took y' bed from hander yr for a bloomin penny hawcemen. If y' ynt afride, let eah yer speak ap to er wen she cams bawck agin.

BRASSBOUND [*to Sir Howard*] I wish you to understand, Sir Howard, that in this castle, it is *I* who give orders, and no one else. Will you be good enough to let Lady Cicely Waynflete know that.

SIR HOWARD [*sitting up on the divan and pulling himself together*] You will have ample opportunity for speaking to Lady Cicely yourself when she returns. [*Drinkwater chuckles; and the rest grin*].

BRASSBOUND. My manners are rough, Sir Howard. I have no wish to frighten the lady.

SIR HOWARD. Captain Brassbound: if you can frighten Lady Cicely, you will confer a great obligation on her family. If she had any sense of danger, perhaps she would keep out of it.

BRASSBOUND. Well, sir, if she were ten Lady Cicelys,

she must consult me while she is here.

DRINKWATER. Thets rawt, kepn. Lets eah you steblish yr hawthority. [*Brassbound turns impatiently on him: he retreats remonstrating*] Nah, nah, nah!

SIR HOWARD. If you feel at all nervous, Captain Brassbound, I will mention the matter with pleasure.

BRASSBOUND. Nervous, sir! no. Nervousness is not in my line. You will find me perfectly capable of saying what I want to say—with considerable emphasis, if necessary. [*Sir Howard assents with a polite but incredulous nod*].

DRINKWATER. Eah, eah!

Lady Cicely returns with Johnson and Redbrook. She carries a jar.

LADY CICELY [*stopping between the door and the arch*] Now for the water. Where is it?

REDBROOK. Theres a well in the courtyard. I'll come and work the bucket.

LADY CICELY. So good of you, Mr Kidbrook. [*She makes for the horseshoe arch, followed by Redbrook*].

DRINKWATER. Nah, Kepn Brarsbahnd: you got sathink to sy to the lidy, ynt yr?

LADY CICELY [*stopping*] I'll come back to hear it presently, Captain. And oh, while I remember it, [*coming forward between Brassbound and Drinkwater*] do please tell me, Captain, if I interfere with your arrangements in any way. If I disturb you the least bit in the world, stop me at once. You have all the responsibility; and your comfort and your authority must be the first thing. Youll tell me, wont you?

BRASSBOUND [*awkwardly, quite beaten*] Pray do as you please, madam.

LADY CICELY. Thank you. Thats so like you, Captain. Thank you. Now, Mr Redbrook! Show me the way to the well. [*She follows Redbrook out through the arch*].

DRINKWATER. Yah! Yah! Shime! Beat baw a woman!

JOHNSON [*coming forward on Brassbound's right*] Whats wrong, now?

634

DRINKWATER [*with an air of disappointment and disillusionment*] Downt awsk me, Miste Jornsn. The kepn's naow clawss arter all.

BRASSBOUND [*a little shamefacedly*] What has she been fixing up in there, Johnson?

JOHNSON. Well: Marzo's in your bed. Lady wants to make a kitchen of the Sheikh's audience chamber, and to put me and the Kid handy in his bedroom in case Marzo gets erysipelas and breaks out violent. From what I can make out, she means to make herself matron of this institution. I spose its all right, isn't it?

DRINKWATER. Yuss, an horder huz abaht as if we was keb tahts! An the kepn afride to talk bawck at er!

Lady Cicely returns with Redbrook. She carries the jar full of water.

LADY CICELY [*putting down the jar, and coming between Brassbound and Drinkwater as before*] And now, Captain, before I go to poor Marzo, what have you to say to me?

BRASSBOUND. I! Nothing.

DRINKWATER. Downt fank it, gavner. Be a men!

LADY CICELY [*looking at Drinkwater, puzzled*] Mr Drinkwater said you had.

BRASSBOUND [*recovering himself*] It was only this. That fellow there [*pointing to Drinkwater*] is subject to fits of insolence. If he is impertinent to your ladyship, or disobedient, you have my authority to order him as many kicks as you think good for him; and I will see that he gets them.

DRINKWATER [*lifting up his voice in protest*] Nah, nah—

LADY CICELY. Oh, I couldnt think of such a thing, Captain Brassbound. I am sure it would hurt Mr Drinkwater.

DRINKWATER [*lachrymosely*] Lidy's hinkyp'ble o sich bawbrous usage.

LADY CICELY. But theres one thing I s h o u l d like, if Mr Drinkwater wont mind my mentioning it. It's so important if he's to attend on Marzo.

BRASSBOUND. What is that?

LADY CICELY. Well—you w o n t mind, Mr Drinkwater, will you?

DRINKWATER [*suspiciously*] Wot is it?

LADY CICELY. There would be so much less danger of erysipelas if you would be so good as to take a bath.

DRINKWATER [*aghast*] A bawth!

BRASSBOUND [*in tones of command*] Stand by, all hands. [*They stand by*]. Take that man and wash him. [*With a roar of laughter they seize him*].

DRINKWATER [*in an agony of protest*] Naow, naow. Look eah—

BRASSBOUND [*ruthlessly*] In c o l d water.

DRINKWATER [*shrieking*] Na-a-a-a-ow. Aw cawnt aw teol yer. Naow. Aw sy, look eah. Naow, naow, naow, naow, naow, NAOW!!!

He is dragged away through the arch in a whirlwind of laughter, protests and tears.

LADY CICELY. I'm afraid he isnt used to it, poor fellow; but r e a l l y it will do him good, Captain Brassbound. Now I must be off to my patient. [*She takes up her jar and goes out by the little door, leaving Brassbound and Sir Howard alone together*].

SIR HOWARD [*rising*] And now, Captain Brass—

BRASSBOUND [*cutting him short with a fierce contempt that astonishes him*] I will attend to you presently. [*Calling*]. Johnson. Send me Johnson there. And Osman. [*He pulls off his coat and throws it on the table, standing at his ease in his blue jersey*].

SIR HOWARD [*after a momentary flush of anger, with a controlled force that compels Brassbound's attention in spite of himself*] You seem to be in a strong position with reference to these men of yours.

BRASSBOUND. I am in a strong position with reference to everyone in this castle.

SIR HOWARD [*politely but threateningly*] I have just

636

been noticing that you think so. I do not agree with you. Her Majesty's Government, Captain Brassbound, has a strong arm and a long arm. If anything disagreeable happens to me or to my sister-in-law, that arm will be stretched out. If that happens you will not be in a strong position. Excuse my reminding you of it.

BRASSBOUND [*grimly*] Much good may it do you! [*Johnson comes in through the arch*]. Where is Osman, the Sheikh's messenger? I want him too.

JOHNSON. Coming, Captain. He had a prayer to finish.

Osman, a tall, skinny, whiteclad, elderly Moor, appears in the archway.

BRASSBOUND. Osman Ali [*Osman comes forward between Brassbound and Johnson*]: you have seen this unbeliever [*indicating Sir Howard*] come in with us?

OSMAN. Yea, and the shameless one with the naked face, who flattered my countenance and offered me her hand.

JOHNSON. Yes; and you took it too, Johnny, didnt you?

BRASSBOUND. Take horse, then; and ride fast to your master the Sheikh Sidi el Assif—

OSMAN [*proudly*] Kinsman to the Prophet.

BRASSBOUND. Tell him what you have seen here. That is all. Johnson: give him a dollar; and note the hour of his going, that his master may know how fast he rides.

OSMAN. The believer's word shall prevail with Allah and his servant Sidi el Assif.

BRASSBOUND. Off with you.

OSMAN. Make good thy master's word ere I go out from his presence, O Johnson el Hull.

JOHNSON. He wants the dollar.

Brassbound gives Osman a coin.

OSMAN [*bowing*] Allah will make hell easy for the friend of Sidi el Assif and his servant. [*He goes out through the arch*].

BRASSBOUND [*to Johnson*] Keep the men out of this

until the Sheikh comes. I have business to talk over. When he does come, we must keep together all: Sidi el Assif's natural instinct will be to cut every Christian throat here.

JOHNSON. We look to you, Captain, to square him, since you invited him over.

BRASSBOUND. You can depend on me; and you know it, I think.

JOHNSON [*phlegmatically*] Yes: we know it. [*He is going out when Sir Howard speaks*].

SIR HOWARD. You know also, Mr Johnson, I hope, that you can depend on m e.

JOHNSON [*turning*] On y o u, sir?

SIR HOWARD. Yes: on me. If my throat is cut, the Sultan of Morocco may send Sidi's head with a hundred thousand dollars blood-money to the Colonial Office; but it will not be enough to save his kingdom—any more than it would save your life, if your Captain here did the same thing.

JOHNSON [*struck*] Is that so, Captain?

BRASSBOUND. I know the gentleman's value—better perhaps than he knows it himself. I shall not lose sight of it.

Johnson nods gravely, and is going out when Lady Cicely returns softly by the little door and calls to him in a whisper. She has taken off her travelling things and put on an apron. At her chatelaine is a case of sewing materials.

LADY CICELY. Mr Johnson. [*He turns*]. Ive got Marzo to sleep. Would you mind asking the gentlemen not to make a noise under his window in the courtyard.

JOHNSON. Right, maam. [*He goes out*].

Lady Cicely sits down at the tiny table, and begins stitching at a sling bandage for Marzo's arm. Brassbound walks up and down on her right, muttering to himself so ominously that Sir Howard quietly gets out of his way by crossing to the other side and sitting down on the second saddle seat.

SIR HOWARD. Are you yet able to attend to me for a

638

moment, Captain Brassbound.

BRASSBOUND [*still walking about*] What do you want?

SIR HOWARD. Well, I am afraid I want a little privacy, and, if you will allow me to say so, a little civility. I am greatly obliged to you for bringing us safely off today when we were attacked. So far, you have carried out your contract. But since we have been your guests here, your tone and that of the worst of your men has changed—intentionally changed, I think.

BRASSBOUND [*stopping abruptly and flinging the announcement at him*] You are not my guest: you are my prisoner.

SIR HOWARD. Prisoner!

Lady Cicely, after a single glance up, continues stitching, apparently quite unconcerned.

BRASSBOUND. I warned you. You should have taken my warning.

SIR HOWARD [*immediately taking the tone of cold disgust for moral delinquency*] Am I to understand, then, that you are a brigand? Is this a matter of ransom?

BRASSBOUND [*with unaccountable intensity*] All the wealth of England shall not ransom you.

SIR HOWARD. Then what do you expect to gain by this?

BRASSBOUND. Justice on a thief and a murderer.

Lady Cicely lays down her work and looks up anxiously.

SIR HOWARD [*deeply outraged, rising with venerable dignity*] Sir: do you apply those terms to me?

BRASSBOUND. I do. [*He turns to Lady Cicely, and adds, pointing contemptuously to Sir Howard*]. Look at him. You would not take this virtuously indignant gentleman for the uncle of a brigand, would you?

Sir Howard starts. The shock is too much for him: he sits down again, looking very old; and his hands tremble; but his eyes and mouth are intrepid, resolute, and angry.

LADY CICELY. Uncle! What do you mean?

BRASSBOUND. Has he never told you about my mother?

639

this fellow who puts on ermine and scarlet and calls himself Justice.

SIR HOWARD [*almost voiceless*] You are the son of that woman!

BRASSBOUND [*fiercely*] "That woman!" [*He makes a movement as if to rush at Sir Howard*].

LADY CICELY [*rising quickly and putting her hand on his arm*] Take care. You mustnt strike an old man.

BRASSBOUND [*raging*] He did not spare my mother—"that woman," he calls her—because of her sex. I will not spare him because of his age. [*Lowering his tone to one of sullen vindictiveness*]. But I am not going to strike him. [*Lady Cicely releases him, and sits down, much perplexed. Brassbound continues, with an evil glance at Sir Howard*]. I shall do no more than justice.

SIR HOWARD [*recovering his voice and vigor*] Justice! I think you mean vengeance, disguised as justice by your passions.

BRASSBOUND. To many and many a poor wretch in the dock y o u have brought vengeance in that disguise—the vengeance of society, disguised as justice by i t s passions. Now the justice you have outraged meets you disguised as vengeance. How do you like it?

. SIR HOWARD. I shall meet it, I trust, as becomes an innocent man and an upright judge. What do you charge against me?

BRASSBOUND. I charge you with the death of my mother and the theft of my inheritance.

SIR HOWARD. As to your inheritance, sir, it was yours whenever you came forward to claim it. Three minutes ago I did not know of your existence. I affirm that most solemnly. I never knew—never dreamt—that my brother Miles left a son. As to your mother, her case was a hard one—perhaps the hardest that has come within even my experience. I mentioned it, as such, to Mr Rankin, the missionary, the evening we met you. As to her death, you know—you m u s t know—that she died in her native
640

country, years after our last meeting. Perhaps you were too young to know that she could hardly have expected to live long.

BRASSBOUND. You mean that she drank.

SIR HOWARD. *I* did not say so. I do not think she was always accountable for what she did.

BRASSBOUND. Yes: she was mad too; and whether drink drove her to madness or madness drove her to drink matters little. The question is, who drove her to both?

SIR HOWARD. I presume the dishonest agent who seized her estate did. I repeat, it was a hard case—a frightful injustice. But it could not be remedied.

BRASSBOUND. You told her so. When she would not take that false answer you drove her from your doors. When she exposed you in the street and threatened to take with her own hands the redress the law denied her, you had her imprisoned, and forced her to write you an apology and leave the country to regain her liberty and save herself from a lunatic asylum. And when she was gone, and dead, and forgotten, you found for yourself the remedy you could not find for her. You recovered the estate easily enough then, robber and rascal that you are. Did he tell the missionary that, Lady Cicely, eh?

LADY CICELY [*sympathetically*] Poor woman! [*To Sir Howard*] Couldnt you have helped her, Howard?

SIR HOWARD. No. This man may be ignorant enough to suppose that when I was a struggling barrister I could do everything I did when I was Attorney General. You know better. There is some excuse for his mother. She was an uneducated Brazilian, knowing nothing of English society, and driven mad by injustice.

BRASSBOUND. Your defence—

SIR HOWARD [*interrupting him determinedly*] I do not defend myself. I call on you to obey the law.

BRASSBOUND. I intend to do so. The law of the Atlas Mountains is administered by the Sheikh Sidi el Assif. He will be here within an hour. He is a judge, like yourself.

You can talk law to him. He will give you both the law and the prophets.

SIR HOWARD. Does he know what the power of England is?

BRASSBOUND. He knows that the Mahdi killed my master Gordon, and that the Mahdi died in his bed and went to paradise.

SIR HOWARD. Then he knows also that England's vengeance was on the Mahdi's track.

BRASSBOUND. Ay, on the track of the railway from the Cape to Cairo? Who are you, that a nation should go to war for you? If you are missing, what will your news-papers say? A foolhardy tourist! What will your learned friends at the bar say? That it was time for you to make room for younger and better men. Y o u a national hero! You had better find a goldfield in the Atlas Mountains. Then all the governments of Europe will rush to your rescue. Until then, take care of yourself; for you are going to see at last the hypocrisy in the sanctimonious speech of the judge who is sentencing you, instead of the despair in the white face of the wretch you are recommending to the mercy of your God.

SIR HOWARD [*deeply and personally offended by this slight to his profession, and for the first time throwing away his assumed dignity and rising to approach Brassbound with his fists clenched; so that Lady Cicely lifts one eye from her work to assure herself that the table is between them*] I have no more to say to you, sir. I am not afraid of you, nor of any bandit with whom you may be in league. As to your property, it is ready for you as soon as you come to your senses and claim it as your father's heir. Commit a crime, and you will become an outlaw, and not only lose the property, but shut the doors of civilization against yourself for ever.

BRASSBOUND. I will not sell my mother's revenge for ten properties.

LADY CICELY [*placidly*] Besides, really, Howard, as the

property now costs £150 a year to keep up instead of bringing in anything, I am afraid it would not be of much use to him. [*Brassbound stands amazed at this revelation*].

SIR HOWARD [*taken aback*] I must say, Cicely, I think you might have chosen a more suitable moment to men-- tion that fact.

BRASSBOUND [*with disgust*] Agh! Trickster! Lawyer! Even the price you offer for your life is to be paid in false coin. [*Calling*] Hallo there! Johnson! Redbrook! Some of you there! [*To Sir Howard*] You ask for a little pri- vacy: you shall have it. I will not endure the company of such a fellow.

SIR HOWARD [*very angry, and full of the crustiest pluck*] You insult me, sir. You are a rascal. You are a ras- cal.

Johnson, Redbrook, and a few others come in through the arch.

BRASSBOUND. Take this man away.

JOHNSON. Where are we to put him?

BRASSBOUND. Put him where you please so long as you can find him when he is wanted.

SIR HOWARD. You will be laid by the heels yet, my friend.

REDBROOK [*with cheerful tact*] Tut tut, Sir Howard: whats the use of talking back? Come along: we'll make you comfortable.

Sir Howard goes out through the arch between John- son and Redbrook, muttering wrathfully. The rest, ex- cept Brassbound and Lady Cicely, follow.

Brassbound walks up and down the room, nursing his indignation. In doing so he unconsciously enters upon an unequal contest with Lady Cicely, who sits quietly stitch- ing. It soon becomes clear that a tranquil woman can go on sewing longer than an angry man can go on fuming. Further, it begins to dawn on Brassbound's wrath-blurred perception that Lady Cicely has at some unnoticed stage in the proceedings finished Marzo's bandage, and is now

643

stitching a coat. He stops; glances at his shirt-sleeves; finally realizes the situation.

BRASSBOUND. What are you doing there, madam?

LADY CICELY. Mending your coat, Captain Brassbound.

BRASSBOUND. I have no recollection of asking you to take that trouble.

LADY CICELY. No: I dont suppose you even knew it was torn. Some men are b o r n untidy. You cannot very well receive Sidi el—whats his name?—with your sleeve half out.

BRASSBOUND [*disconcerted*] I—I dont know how it got torn.

LADY CICELY. You should not get virtuously indignant with people. It bursts clothes more than anything else, Mr Hallam.

BRASSBOUND [*flushing quickly*] I beg you will not call me Mr Hallam. I hate the name.

LADY CICELY. Black Paquito is your pet name, isnt it?

BRASSBOUND [*huffily*] I am not usually called so to my face.

LADY CICELY [*turning the coat a little*] I'm so sorry. [*She takes another piece of thread and puts it into her needle, looking placidly and reflectively upward meanwhile*]. Do you know, you are wonderfully like your uncle.

BRASSBOUND. Damnation!

LADY CICELY. Eh?

BRASSBOUND. If I thought my veins contained a drop of his black blood, I would drain them empty with my knife. I have no relations. I had a mother: that was all.

LADY CICELY [*unconvinced*] I daresay you have your mother's complexion. But didnt you notice Sir Howard's temper, his doggedness, his high spirit: above all, his belief in ruling people by force, as you rule your men; and in revenge and punishment, just as you want to revenge your mother? Didnt you recognize yourself in that?

644

BRASSBOUND [*startled*] Myself!—in that!

LADY CICELY [*returning to the tailoring question as if her last remark were of no consequence whatever*] Did this sleeve catch you at all under the arm? Perhaps I had better make it a little easier for you.

BRASSBOUND [*irritably*] Let my coat alone. It will do very well as it is. Put it down.

LADY CICELY. Oh, dont ask me to sit doing nothing. It bores me so.

BRASSBOUND. In Heaven's name then, do what you like! Only dont worry me with it.

LADY CICELY. I'm so sorry. All the Hallams are irritable.

BRASSBOUND [*penning up his fury with difficulty*] As I have already said, that remark has no application to me.

LADY CICELY [*resuming her stitching*] Thats so funny! They all hate to be told that they are like one another.

BRASSBOUND [*with the beginnings of despair in his voice*] Why did you come here? My trap was laid for him, not for you. Do you know the danger you are in?

LADY CICELY. Theres always a danger of something or other. Do you think it's worth bothering about?

BRASSBOUND [*scolding her*] Do I t h i n k! Do you think my coat's worth mending?

LADY CICELY [*prosaically*] Oh yes: it's not so far gone as that.

BRASSBOUND. Have you any feeling? Or are you a fool?

LADY CICELY. I'm afraid I'm a dreadful fool. But I cant help it. I was made so, I suppose.

BRASSBOUND. Perhaps you dont realize that your friend my good uncle will be pretty fortunate if he is allowed to live out his life as a slave with a set of chains on him?

LADY CICELY. Oh, I dont know about that, Mr H—I mean Captain Brassbound. Men are always thinking that they are going to do something grandly wicked to their enemies; but when it comes to the point, really bad men

645

are just as rare as really good ones.

BRASSBOUND. You forget that I am like my uncle, according to you. Have you any doubt as to the reality of h i s badness?

LADY CICELY. Bless me! your uncle Howard is one of the most harmless of men—much nicer than most professional people. Of course he does dreadful things as a judge; but then if you take a man and pay him £5,000 a year to be wicked, and praise him for it, and have policemen and courts and laws and juries to drive him into it so that he cant help doing it, what can you expect? Sir Howard's all right when he's left to himself. We caught a burglar one night at Waynflete when he was staying with us; and I insisted on his locking the poor man up, until the police came, in a room with a window opening on the lawn. The man came back next day and said he must return to a life of crime unless I gave him a job in the garden; and I did. It was much more sensible than giving him ten years penal servitude: Howard admitted it. So you see he's not a bit bad really.

BRASSBOUND. He had a fellow feeling for the thief, knowing he was a thief himself. Do you forget that he sent my mother to prison.

LADY CICELY [softly] Were you very fond of your poor mother, and always very good to her?

BRASSBOUND [rather taken aback] I was not worse than other sons, I suppose.

LADY CICELY [opening her eyes very widely] Oh! Was t h a t all?

BRASSBOUND [exculpating himself, full of gloomy remembrances] You dont understand. It was not always possible to be very tender with my mother. She had unfortunately a very violent temper; and she—she—

LADY CICELY. Yes: so you told Howard. [With genuine pity for him]. You must have had a very unhappy childhood.

BRASSBOUND [grimly] Hell. That was what my child-

646

hood was. Hell.

LADY CICELY. Do you think she would really have killed Howard, as she threatened, if he hadnt sent her to prison?

BRASSBOUND [*breaking out again, with a growing sense of being morally trapped*] What if she did? Why did he rob her? Why did he not help her to get the estate, as he got it for himself afterwards?

LADY CICELY. He says he couldnt, you know. But perhaps the real reason was that he didnt like her. You know, dont you, that if you dont like people you think of all the reasons for not helping them, and if you like them you think of all the opposite reasons.

BRASSBOUND. But his duty as a brother!

LADY CICELY. Are you going to do your duty as a nephew!

BRASSBOUND. Dont quibble with me. I am going to do my duty as a son; and you know it.

LADY CICELY. But I should have thought that the time for that was in your mother's lifetime, when you could have been kind and forbearing with her. Hurting your uncle wont do her any good, you know.

BRASSBOUND. It will teach other scoundrels to respect widows and orphans. Do you forget that there is such a thing as justice?

LADY CICELY [*gaily shaking out the finished coat*] Oh, if you are going to dress yourself in ermine and call yourself Justice, I give you up. You are just your uncle over again; only he gets £5,000 a year for it, and you do it for nothing. [*She holds the coat up to see whether any further repairs are needed*].

BRASSBOUND [*sulkily*] You twist my words very cleverly. But no man or woman has ever changed me.

LADY CICELY. Dear me! That must be very nice for the people you deal with, because they can always depend on you; but isnt it rather inconvenient for yourself when you change your mind?

647

BRASSBOUND. I never change my mind.

LADY CICELY [*rising with the coat in her hands*] Oh! Oh!! Nothing will ever persuade me that you are as pigheaded as that.

BRASSBOUND [*offended*] Pigheaded!

LADY CICELY [*with quick, caressing apology*] No, no, no. I didnt mean that. Firm! Unalterable! Resolute! Iron-willed! Stonewall Jackson! Thats the idea, isnt it?

BRASSBOUND [*hopelessly*] You are laughing at me.

LADY CICELY. No: trembling, I assure you. Now will you try this on for me: I'm so afraid I have made it too tight under the arm. [*She holds it behind him*].

BRASSBOUND [*obeying mechanically*] You take me for a fool, I think. [*He misses the sleeve*].

LADY CICELY. No: all men look foolish when they are feeling for their sleeves—

BRASSBOUND. Agh! [*He turns and snatches the coat from her; then puts it on himself and buttons the lowest button*].

LADY CICELY [*horrified*] Stop. No. You must n e v e r pull a coat at the skirts, Captain Brassbound: it spoils the sit of it. Allow me. [*She pulls the lapels of his coat vigorously forward*]. Put back your shoulders. [*He frowns, but obeys*]. Thats better. [*She buttons the top button*]. Now button the rest from the top down. D o e s it catch you at all under the arm?

BRASSBOUND [*miserably—all resistance beaten out of him*] No.

LADY CICELY. Thats right. Now before I go back to poor Marzo, say thank you to me for mending your jacket, like a nice polite sailor.

BRASSBOUND [*sitting down at the table in great agitation*] Damn you! you have belittled my whole life to me. [*He bows his head on his hands, convulsed*].

LADY CICELY [*quite understanding, and putting her hand kindly on his shoulder*] Oh no. I am sure you have done lots of kind things and brave things, if you could

648

only recollect them. With Gordon for instance? Nobody can belittle that.

He looks up at her for a moment; then kisses her hand. She presses his and turns away with her eyes so wet that she sees Drinkwater, coming in through the arch just then, with a prismatic halo round him. Even when she sees him clearly, she hardly recognizes him; for he is ludicrously clean and smoothly brushed; and his hair, formerly mud color, is now a lively red.

DRINKWATER. Look eah, kepn. [*Brassbound springs up and recovers himself quickly*]. Eahs the bloomin Shike jest appeahd on the orawzn wiv abaht fifty men. Thyll be eah insawd o ten minnits, they will.

LADY CICELY. The Sheikh!

BRASSBOUND. Sidi el Assif and fifty men! [*To Lady Cicely*] You were too late: I gave you up my vengeance when it was no longer in my hand. [*To Drinkwater*] Call all hands to stand by and shut the gates. Then all here to me for orders; and bring the prisoner.

DRINKWATER. Rawt, kepn. [*He runs out*].

LADY CICELY. Is there really any danger for Howard?

BRASSBOUND. Yes. Danger for all of us unless I keep to my bargain with this fanatic.

LADY CICELY. What bargain?

BRASSBOUND. I pay him so much a head for every party I escort through to the interior. In return he protects me and lets my caravans alone. But I have sworn an oath to him to take only Jews and true believers—no Christians, you understand.

LADY CICELY. Then why did you take us?

BRASSBOUND. I took my uncle on purpose—and sent word to Sidi that he was here.

LADY CICELY. Well, thats a pretty kettle of fish, isnt it?

BRASSBOUND. I will do what I can to save him—and you. But I fear my repentance has come too late, as repentance usually does.

649

LADY CICELY [*cheerfully*] Well, I must go and look after Marzo, at all events. [*She goes out through the little door. Johnson, Redbrook, and the rest come in through the arch, with Sir Howard, still very crusty and determined. He keeps close to Johnson, who comes to Brassbound's right, Redbrook taking the other side*].

BRASSBOUND. Wheres Drinkwater?

JOHNSON. On the lookout. Look here, Capn; we dont half like this job. The gentleman has been talking to us a bit; and we think that he is a gentleman, and talks straight sense.

REDBROOK. Righto, Brother Johnson. [*To Brassbound*] Wont do, governor. Not good enough.

BRASSBOUND [*fiercely*] Mutiny, eh?

REDBROOK. Not at all, governor. Dont talk Tommy rot with Brother Sidi only five minutes gallop off. Cant hand over an Englishman to a nigger to have his throat cut.

BRASSBOUND [*unexpectedly acquiescing*] Very good. You know, I suppose, that if you break my bargain with Sidi, youll have to defend this place and fight for your lives in five minutes. That cant be done without discipline: you know that too. I'll take my part with the rest under whatever leader you are willing to obey. So choose your captain and look sharp about it. [*Murmurs of surprise and discontent*].

VOICES. No, no. Brassbound must command.

BRASSBOUND. Youre wasting your five minutes. Try Johnson.

JOHNSON. No. I havnt the head for it.

BRASSBOUND. Well, Redbrook.

REDBROOK. Not this Johnny, thank you. Havnt character enough.

BRASSBOUND. Well, theres Sir Howard Hallam for you! H e has character enough.

A VOICE. He's too old.

ALL. No, no. Brassbound, Brassbound.

JOHNSON. Theres nobody but you, Captain.

REDBROOK. The mutiny's over, governor. You win, hands down.

BRASSBOUND [*turning on them*] Now listen, you, all of you. If I am to command here, I am going to do what I like, not what you like. I'll give this gentleman here to Sidi or to the devil if I choose. I'll not be intimidated or talked back to. Is that understood?

REDBROOK [*diplomatically*] He's offered a present of five hundred quid if he gets safe back to Mogador, governor. Excuse my mentioning it.

SIR HOWARD. Myself a n d Lady Cicely.

BRASSBOUND. What! A judge compound a felony! You greenhorns, he is more likely to send you all to penal servitude if you are fools enough to give him the chance.

VOICES. So he would. Whew! [*Murmurs of conviction*].

REDBROOK. Righto, governor. Thats the ace of trumps.

BRASSBOUND [*to Sir Howard*] Now, have you any other card to play? Any other bribe? Any other threat? Quick. Time presses.

SIR HOWARD. My life is in the hands of Providence. Do your worst.

BRASSBOUND. Or my best. I still have that choice.

DRINKWATER [*running in*] Look eah, kepn. Eahs anather lot cammin from the sahth heast. Hunnerds of em, this tawm. The owl dezzit is lawk a bloomin Awd Pawk demonstration. Aw blieve its the Kidy from Kintorfy. [*General alarm. All look to Brassbound*].

BRASSBOUND [*eagerly*] The Cadi! How far off?

DRINKWATER. Matter o two mawl.

BRASSBOUND. We're saved. Open the gates to the Sheikh. [*They stare at him*]. Look alive there.

DRINKWATER [*appalled, almost in tears*] Naow, naow. Lissen, kepn [*pointing to Sir Howard*]: e'll give huz fawv unnerd red uns. [*To the others*] Ynt yer spowk to im, Miste Jornson—Miste Redbrook—

BRASSBOUND [*cutting him short*] Now then, do you understand plain English? Johnson and Redbrook: take what men you want and open the gates to the Sheikh. Let him come straight to me. Look alive, will you.

JOHNSON. Ay ay, sir.

REDBROOK. Righto, governor.

They hurry out, with a few others. Drinkwater stares after them, dumbfounded by their obedience.

BRASSBOUND [*taking out a pistol*] You wanted to sell me to my prisoner, did you, you dog.

DRINKWATER [*falling on his knees with a yell*] Naow! [*Brassbound turns on him as if to kick him. He scrambles away and takes refuge behind Sir Howard*].

BRASSBOUND. Sir Howard Hallam: you have one chance left. The Cadi of Kintafi stands superior to the Sheikh as the responsible governor of the whole province. It is the Cadi who will be sacrificed by the Sultan if England demands satisfaction for any injury to you. If we can hold the Sheikh in parley until the Cadi arrives, you may frighten the Cadi into forcing the Sheikh to release you. The Cadi's coming is a lucky chance for y o u.

SIR HOWARD. If it were a real chance, you would not tell me of it. Dont try to play cat and mouse with me, man.

DRINKWATER [*aside to Sir Howard, as Brassbound turns contemptuously away to the other side of the room*] It ynt mach of a chawnst, Sir Ahrd. But if there was a ganbowt in Mogador Awbr, awd put a bit on it, aw would.

Johnson, Redbrook, and the others return, rather mistrustfully ushering in Sidi el Assif, attended by Osman and a troop of Arabs. Brassbound's men keep together on the archway side, backing their captain. Sidi's followers cross the room behind the table and assemble near Sir Howard, who stands his ground. Drinkwater runs across to Brassbound and stands at his elbow as he turns to face Sidi.

Sidi el Assif, clad in spotless white, is a nobly handsome Arab, hardly thirty, with fine eyes, bronzed com-

CAPTAIN BRASSBOUND'S CONVERSION

plexion, and instinctively dignified carriage. He places himself between the two groups, with Osman in attendance at his right hand.

OSMAN [*pointing out Sir Howard*] This is the infidel, Cadi. [*Sir Howard bows to Sidi, but, being an infidel, receives only the haughtiest stare in acknowledgement*]. This [*pointing to Brassbound*] is Brassbound the Franguestani captain, the servant of Sidi.

DRINKWATER [*not to be outdone, points out the Sheikh and Osman to Brassbound*] This eah is the Commawnder of the Fythful an is Vizzeer Hosman.

SIDI. Where is the woman?

OSMAN. The shameless one is not here.

BRASSBOUND. Sidi el Assif, kinsman of the Prophet: you are welcome.

REDBROOK [*with much aplomb*] There is no majesty and no might save in Allah, the Glorious, the Great!

DRINKWATER. Eah, eah!

OSMAN [*to Sidi*] The servant of the captain makes his profession of faith as a true believer.

SIDI. It is well.

BRASSBOUND [*aside to Redbrook*] Where did you pick that up?

REDBROOK [*aside to Brassbound*] Captain Burton's Arabian Nights—copy in the library of the National Liberal Club.

LADY CICELY [*calling without*] Mr Drinkwater. Come and help me with Marzo. [*The Sheikh pricks up his ears. His nostrils and eyes expand*].

OSMAN. The shameless one!

BRASSBOUND [*to Drinkwater, seizing him by the collar and slinging him towards the door*] Off with you.

Drinkwater goes out through the little door.

OSMAN. Shall we hide her face before she enters?

SIDI. No.

Lady Cicely, who has resumed her travelling equipment, and has her hat slung across her arm, comes through

653

the little door supporting Marzo, who is very white, but able to get about. Drinkwater has his other arm. Redbrook hastens to relieve Lady Cicely of Marzo, taking him into the group behind Brassbound. Lady Cicely comes forward between Brassbound and the Sheikh, to whom she turns affably.

LADY CICELY [*proffering her hand*] Sidi el Assif, isnt it? Howdyedo? [*He recoils, blushing somewhat*].

OSMAN [*scandalized*] Woman touch not the kinsman of the Prophet.

LADY CICELY. Oh, I see. I'm being presented at court. Very good. [*She makes a presentation curtsey*].

REDBROOK. Sidi el Assif: this is one of the mighty women Sheikhs of Franguestan. She goes unveiled among Kings; and only princes may touch her hand.

LADY CICELY. Allah upon thee, Sidi el Assif! Be a good little Sheikh, and shake hands.

SIDI [*timidly touching her hand*] Now this is a wonderful thing, and worthy to be chronicled with the story of Solomon and the Queen of Sheba. Is it not so, Osman Ali?

OSMAN. Allah upon thee, master! it is so.

SIDI. Brassbound Ali: the oath of a just man fulfils itself without many words. The infidel Cadi, thy captive, falls to my share.

BRASSBOUND [*firmly*] It cannot be, Sidi el Assif. [*Sidi's brows contract gravely*]. The price of his blood will be required of our lord the Sultan. I will take him to Morocco and deliver him up there.

SIDI [*impressively*] Brassbound: I am in mine own house and amid mine own people. *I* am the Sultan here. Consider what you say; for when my word goes forth for life or death, it may not be recalled.

BRASSBOUND. Sidi el Assif: I will buy the man from you at what price you choose to name; and if I do not pay faithfully, you shall take my head for his.

SIDI. It is well. You shall keep the man, and give me

654

the woman in payment.

SIR HOWARD AND BRASSBOUND [*with the same impulse*] No, no.

LADY CICELY [*eagerly*] Yes, yes. Certainly, Mr Sidi. Certainly.

Sidi smiles gravely.

SIR HOWARD. Impossible.

BRASSBOUND. You dont know what youre doing.

LADY CICELY. Oh, dont I? Ive not crossed Africa and stayed with six cannibal chiefs for nothing. [*To the Sheikh*] It's all right, Mr Sidi: I shall be delighted.

SIR HOWARD. You are mad. Do you suppose this man will treat you as a European gentleman would?

LADY CICELY. No: he'll treat me like one of Nature's gentlemen: look at his perfectly splendid face! [*Addressing Osman as if he was her oldest and most attached retainer*]. Osman: be sure you choose me a good horse; and get a nice strong camel for my luggage.

Osman, after a moment of stupefaction, hurries out. Lady Cicely puts on her hat and pins it to her hair, the Sheikh gazing at her during the process with timid admiration.

DRINKWATER [*chuckling*] She'll mawch em all to church next Sunder lawk a bloomin lot o cherry kids: you see if she downt.

LADY CICELY [*busily*] Goodbye, Howard: dont be anxious about me; and above all, dont bring a parcel of men with guns to rescue me. I shall be all right now that I am getting away from the escort. Captain Brassbound: I rely on you to see that Sir Howard gets safe to Mogador. [*Whispering*] Take your hand off that pistol. [*He takes his hand out of his pocket, reluctantly*]. Goodbye.

A tumult without. They all turn apprehensively to the arch. Osman rushes in.

OSMAN. The Cadi, the Cadi. He is in anger. His men are upon us. Defend—

CAPTAIN BRASSBOUND'S CONVERSION

The Cadi, a vigorous, fatfeatured, choleric, whitehaired and bearded elder, rushes in, cudgel in hand, with an overwhelming retinue, and silences Osman with a sounding thwack. In a moment the back of the room is crowded with his followers. The Sheikh retreats a little towards his men; and the Cadi comes impetuously forward between him and Lady Cicely.

THE CADI. Now woe upon thee, Sidi el Assif, thou child of mischief!

SIDI [*sternly*] Am I a dog, Muley Othman, that thou speakest thus to me?

THE CADI. Wilt thou destroy thy country, and give us all into the hands of them that set the sea on fire but yesterday with their ships of war? Where are the Franguestani captives?

LADY CICELY. Here we are, Cadi. How d'ye do?

THE CADI. Allah upon thee, thou moon at the full! Where is thy kinsman, the Cadi of Franguestan? I am his friend, his servant. I come on behalf of my master the Sultan to do him honor, and to cast down his enemies.

SIR HOWARD. You are very good, I am sure.

SIDI [*graver than ever*] Muley Othman—

THE CADI [*fumbling in his breast*] Peace, peace, thou inconsiderate one. [*He takes out a letter*].

BRASSBOUND. Cadi—

THE CADI. Oh thou dog, thou, thou accursed Brassbound, son of a wanton: it is thou hast led Sidi el Assif into this wrongdoing. Read this writing that thou hast brought upon me from the commander of the warship.

BRASSBOUND. Warship! [*He takes the letter and opens it, his men whispering to one another very low-spiritedly meanwhile*].

REDBROOK. Warship! Whew!

JOHNSON. Gunboat, praps.

DRINKWATER. Lawk bloomin Worterleoo buses, they are, on this cowst.

656

Brassbound folds up the letter, looking glum.

SIR HOWARD [*sharply*] Well, sir, are we not to have the benefit of that letter? Your men are waiting to hear it, I think.

BRASSBOUND. It is not a British ship. [*Sir Howard's face falls*].

LADY CICELY. What is it, then?

BRASSBOUND. An American cruiser. The Santiago.

THE CADI [*tearing his beard*] Woe! alas! it is where they set the sea on fire.

SIDI. Peace, Muley Othman: Allah is still above us.

JOHNSON. Would you mind readin it to us, capn?

BRASSBOUND [*grimly*] Oh, I'll read it to you. "Mogador Harbor. 26 Sept 1899. Captain Hamlin Kearney, of the cruiser Santiago, presents the compliments of the United States to the Cadi Muley Othman el Kintafi, and announces that he is coming to look for the two British travellers Sir Howard Hallam and Lady Cicely Waynflete, in the Cadi's jurisdiction. As the search will be conducted with machine guns, the prompt return of the travellers to Mogador Harbor will save much trouble to all parties."

THE CADI. As I live, O Cadi, and thou, moon of loveliness, ye shall be led back to Mogador with honor. And thou, accursed Brassbound, shalt go thither a prisoner in chains, thou and thy people. [*Brassbound and his men make a movement to defend themselves*]. Seize them.

LADY CICELY. Oh, please dont fight. [*Brassbound, seeing that his men are hopelessly outnumbered, makes no resistance. They are made prisoners by the Cadi's followers*].

SIDI [*attempting to draw his scimitar*] The woman is mine: I will not forego her. [*He is seized and overpowered after a Homeric struggle*].

SIR HOWARD [*drily*] I told you you were not in a strong position, Captain Brassbound. [*Looking implacably at him*]

You are laid by the heels, my friend, as I said you would be.

LADY CICELY. But I assure you —

BRASSBOUND [*interrupting her*] What have you to assure him of? You persuaded me to spare him. Look at his face. Will you be able to persuade him to spare me?

END OF ACT II

ACT III

TORRID *forenoon filtered through small Moorish windows high up in the adobe walls of the largest room in Leslie Rankin's house. A clean cool room, with the table (a Christian article) set in the middle, a presidentially elbowed chair behind it, and an inkstand and paper ready for the sitter. A couple of cheap American chairs right and left of the table, facing the same way as the presidential chair, give a judicial aspect to the arrangement. Rankin is placing a little tray with a jug and some glasses near the inkstand when Lady Cicely's voice is heard at the door, which is behind him in the corner to his right.*

LADY CICELY. Good morning. May I come in?

RANKIN. Certainly. [*She comes in to the nearest end of the table. She has discarded all travelling equipment, and is dressed exactly as she might be in Surrey on a very hot day*]. Sit ye doon, Leddy Ceecily.

LADY CICELY [*sitting down*] How nice youve made the room for the inquiry!

RANKIN [*doubtfully*] I could wish there were more chairs. Yon American captain will preside in this; and that leaves but one for Sir Howrrd and one for your leddyship. I could almost be tempted to call it a maircy that your friend that owns the yacht has sprained his ankle and cannot come. I misdoubt me it will not look judeecial to have Captain Kearney's officers squatting on the floor.

LADY CICELY. Oh, they wont mind. What about the prisoners?

RANKIN. They are to be broat here from the town gaol presently.

LADY CICELY. And where is that silly old Cadi, and my handsome Sheikh Sidi? I must see them before the inquiry, or theyll give Captain Kearney quite a false impression of what happened.

RANKIN. But ye cannot see them. They decamped last night, back to their castles in the Atlas.

659

LADY CICELY [*delighted*] No!

RANKIN. Indeed and they did. The poor Cadi is so tarrified by all he has haird of the destruction of the Spanish fleet, that he darent trust himself in the captain's hands. [*Looking reproachfully at her*] On your journey back here, ye seem to have frightened the poor man yourself, Leddy Ceecily, by talking to him about the fanatical Chreestianity of the Americans. Ye have largely yourself to thank if he's gone.

LADY CICELY. Allah be praised! W h a t a weight off our minds, Mr Rankin!

RANKIN [*puzzled*] And why? Do ye not understand how necessary their evidence is?

LADY CICELY. T h e i r evidence! It would spoil everything. They would perjure themselves out of pure spite against poor Captain Brassbound.

RANKIN [*amazed*] Do ye call him p o o r Captain Brassbound! Does not your leddyship know that this Brassbound is—Heaven forgive me for judging him!—a precious scoundrel? Did ye not hear what Sir Howrrd told me on the yacht last night?

LADY CICELY. All a mistake, Mr Rankin: all a mistake, I assure you. You said just now, Heaven forgive you for judging him! Well, thats just what the whole quarrel is about. Captain Brassbound is just like you: he thinks we have no right to judge one another; and as Sir Howard gets £5,000 a year for doing nothing else but judging people, he thinks poor Captain Brassbound a regular Anarchist. They quarrelled dreadfully at the castle. You mustnt mind what Sir Howard says about him: you really mustnt.

RANKIN. But his conduct—

LADY CICELY. Perfectly saintly, Mr Rankin. Worthy of yourself in your best moments. He forgave Sir Howard, and did all he could to save him.

RANKIN. Ye astoanish me, Leddy Ceecily.

LADY CICELY. And think of the temptation to behave badly when he had us all there helpless!

660

CAPTAIN BRASSBOUND'S CONVERSION

RANKIN. The temptation! ay: thats true. Yere ower bonny to be cast away among a parcel o lone, lawless men, my leddy.

LADY CICELY [*naïvely*] Bless me, thats quite true; and I never thought of it! Oh, after that you really must do all you can to help Captain Brassbound.

RANKIN [*reservedly*] No: I cannot say that, Leddy Ceecily. I doubt he has imposed on your good nature and sweet disposeetion. I had a crack with the Cadi as well as with Sir Howrrd; and there is little question in my mind but that Captain Brassbound is no better than a breegand.

LADY CICELY [*apparently deeply impressed*] I wonder whether he can be, Mr Rankin. If you think so, thats heavily against him in my opinion, because you have more knowledge of men than anyone else here. Perhaps I'm mistaken. I only thought you might like to help him as the son of your old friend.

RANKIN [*startled*] The son of my old friend! What d'ye mean?

LADY CICELY. Oh! Didnt Sir Howard tell you that? Why, Captain Brassbound turns out to be Sir Howard's nephew, the son of the brother you knew.

RANKIN [*overwhelmed*] I saw the likeness the night he came here! It's true: it's true. Uncle and nephew!

LADY CICELY. Yes: thats why they quarrelled so.

RANKIN [*with a momentary sense of ill usage*] I think Sir Howrrd might have told me that.

LADY CICELY. Of course he o u g h t to have told you. You see he only tells one side of the story. That comes from his training as a barrister. You mustnt think he's naturally deceitful: if he'd been brought up as a clergyman, he'd have told you the whole truth as a matter of course.

RANKIN [*too much perturbed to dwell on his grievance*] Leddy Ceecily: I must go to the prison and see the lad. He may have been a bit wild; but I cant leave poor Miles's son unbefriended in a foreign gaol.

LADY CICELY [*rising, radiant*] Oh, how good of you!

661

You have a real kind heart of gold, Mr Rankin. Now, before you go, shall we just put our heads together, and consider how to give Miles's son every chance—I mean of course every chance that he ought to have.

RANKIN [*rather addled*] I am so confused by this astoanishing news—

LADY CICELY. Yes, yes: of course you are. But dont you think he would make a better impression on the American captain if he were a little more respectably dressed?

RANKIN. Mebbe. But how can that be remedied here in Mogador?

LADY CICELY. Oh, Ive thought of that. You know I'm going back to England by way of Rome, Mr Rankin; and I'm bringing a portmanteau full of clothes for my brother there: he's ambassador, you know, and has to be v e r y particular as to what he wears. I had the portmanteau brought here this morning. Now would you mind taking it to the prison, and smartening up Captain Brassbound a little. Tell him he ought to do it to shew his respect for me; and he will. It will be quite easy: there are two Krooboys waiting to carry the portmanteau. You will: I know you will. [*She edges him to the door*]. And do you think there is time to get him shaved?

RANKIN [*succumbing, half bewildered*] I'll do my best.

LADY CICELY. I know you will. [*As he is going out*] Oh! one word, Mr Rankin. [*He comes back*]. The Cadi didnt know that Captain Brassbound was Sir Howard's nephew, did he?

RANKIN. No.

LADY CICELY. Then he must have misunderstood everything quite dreadfully. I'm afraid, Mr Rankin—though you know best, of course—that we are bound not to repeat anything at the inquiry that the Cadi said. He didnt know, you see.

RANKIN [*cannily*] I take your point, Leddy Ceecily. It alters the case. I shall certainly make no allusion to it.

LADY CICELY [*magnanimously*] Well, then, I wont

either. There!

They shake hands on it. Sir Howard comes in.

SIR HOWARD. Good morning, Mr Rankin. I hope you got home safely from the yacht last night.

RANKIN. Quite safe, thank ye, Sir Howrrd.

LADY CICELY. Howard: he's in a hurry. Dont make him stop to talk.

SIR HOWARD. Very good, very good. [*He comes to the table and takes Lady Cicely's chair*].

RANKIN. Oo revoir, Leddy Ceecily.

LADY CICELY. Bless you, Mr Rankin. [*Rankin goes out. She comes to the other end of the table, looking at Sir Howard with a troubled, sorrowfully sympathetic air, but unconsciously making her right hand stalk about the table on the tips of its fingers in a tentative stealthy way which would put Sir Howard on his guard if he were in a suspicious frame of mind, which, as it happens, he is not*]. I'm s o sorry for you, Howard, about this unfortunate inquiry.

SIR HOWARD [*swinging round on his chair, astonished*] Sorry for m e! Why?

LADY CICELY. It will look so dreadful. Your own nephew, you know.

SIR HOWARD. Cicely: an English judge has no nephews, no sons even, when he has to carry out the law.

LADY CICELY. But then he oughtnt to have any property either. People will never understand about the West Indian Estate. Theyll think youre the wicked uncle out of the Babes in the Wood. [*With a fresh gush of compassion*]. I'm so s o sorry for you.

SIR HOWARD [*rather stiffly*] I really do not see how I need your commiseration, Cicely. The woman was an impossible person, half mad, half drunk. Do you understand what such a creature is when she has a grievance, and imagines some innocent person to be the author of it?

LADY CICELY [*with a touch of impatience*] Oh, quite. T h a t l l be made clear enough. I can see it all in the papers already: our half mad, half drunk sister-in-law, mak-

663

ing scenes with you in the street, with the police called in, and prison and all the rest of it. The family will be furious. [*Sir Howard quails. She instantly follows up her advantage with*] Think of papa!

SIR HOWARD. I shall expect Lord Waynflete to look at the matter as a reasonable man.

LADY CICELY. Do you think he's so greatly changed as that, Howard?

SIR HOWARD [*falling back on the fatalism of the depersonalized public man*] My dear Cicely: there is no use discussing the matter. It cannot be helped, however disagreeable it may be.

LADY CICELY. Of course not. Thats whats so dreadful. Do you think people will understand?

SIR HOWARD. I really cannot say. Whether they do or not, *I* cannot help it.

LADY CICELY. If you were anybody but a judge, it wouldn't matter so much. But a judge mustnt even be misunderstood. [*Despairingly*] Oh, it's dreadful, Howard: it's terrible! What would poor Mary say if she were alive now?

SIR HOWARD [*with emotion*] I dont think, Cicely, that my dear wife would misunderstand me.

LADY CICELY. No: s h e ' d know you mean well. And when you came home and said, "Mary: Ive just told all the world that your sister-in-law was a police court criminal, and that I sent her to prison; and your nephew is a brigand, and I'm sending him to prison," she'd have thought it must be all right because you did it. But you dont think she would have l i k e d it, any more than papa and the rest of us, do you?

SIR HOWARD [*appalled*] But what am I to do? Do you ask me to compound a felony?

LADY CICELY [*sternly*] Certainly not. I would not allow such a thing, even if you were wicked enough to attempt it. No. What I say is, that you ought not to tell the story yourself.

SIR HOWARD. Why?

LADY CICELY. Because everybody would say you are such a clever lawyer you could make a poor simple sailor like Captain Kearney believe anything. The proper thing for you to do, Howard, is to let m e tell the exact truth. Then you can simply say that you are bound to confirm me. Nobody can blame you for that.

SIR HOWARD [*looking suspiciously at her*] Cicely: you are up to some devilment.

LADY CICELY [*promptly washing her hands of his interests*] Oh, very well. Tell the story yourself, in your own clever way. I only proposed to tell the exact truth. You call that devilment. So it is, I daresay, from a lawyer's point of view.

SIR HOWARD. I hope youre not offended.

LADY CICELY [*With the utmost goodhumor*] My dear Howard, not a bit. Of course youre right: you know how these things ought to be done. I'll do e x a c t l y what you tell me, and confirm everything you say.

SIR HOWARD [*alarmed by the completeness of his victory*] Oh, my dear, you mustnt act in my interest. You must give your evidence with absolute impartiality. [*She nods, as if thoroughly impressed and reproved, and gazes at him with the steadfast candor peculiar to liars who read novels. His eyes turn to the ground; and his brow clouds perplexedly. He rises; rubs his chin nervously with his forefinger; and adds*] I think, perhaps, on reflection, that there is something to be said for your proposal to relieve me of the very painful duty of telling what has occurred.

LADY CICELY [*holding off*] But youd do it so very much better.

SIR HOWARD. For that very reason, perhaps, it had better come from you.

LADY CICELY [*reluctantly*] Well, if youd rather.

SIR HOWARD. But mind, Cicely, the exact truth.

LADY CICELY [*with conviction*] The exact truth. [*They shake hands on it*].

665

CAPTAIN BRASSBOUND'S CONVERSION

SIR HOWARD [*holding her hand*] Fiat justitia: ruat cœlum!

LADY CICELY. Let Justice be done, though the ceiling fall!

An American bluejacket appears at the door.

BLUEJACKET. Captain Kearney's cawmpliments to Lady Waynflete; and may he come in?

LADY CICELY. Yes. By all means. Where are the prisoners?

BLUEJACKET. Party gawn to the jail to fetch em, marm.

LADY CICELY. Thank you. I should like to be told when they are coming, if I might.

BLUEJACKET. You shall so, marm. [*He stands aside, saluting, to admit his captain, and goes out*].

Captain Hamlin Kearney is a robustly built western American, with the keen, squeezed, wind beaten eyes and obstinately enduring mouth of his profession. A curious ethnological specimen, with all the nations of the old world at war in his veins, he is developing artificially in the direction of sleekness and culture under the restraints of an overwhelming dread of European criticism, and climatically in the direction of the indigenous North American, who is already in possession of his hair, his cheek-bones, and the manlier instincts in him which the sea has rescued from civilization. The world, pondering on the great part of its own future which is in his hands, contemplates him with wonder as to what the devil he will evolve into in another century or two. Meanwhile he presents himself to Lady Cicely as a blunt sailor who has something to say to her concerning her conduct which he wishes to put politely, as becomes an officer addressing a lady, but also with an emphatically implied rebuke, as an American addressing an English person who has taken a liberty.

LADY CICELY [*as he enters*] So glad youve come, Captain Kearney.

KEARNEY [*coming between Sir Howard and Lady Cicely*] When we parted yesterday ahfternoon, Lady
666

Waynflete, I was unaware that in the course of your visit to my ship you had entirely altered the sleeping arrangements of my stokers. I thahnk you. As captain of the ship, I am customairily cawnsulted before the orders of English visitors are carried out; but as your alterations appear to cawndooce to the comfort of the men, I have not interfered with them.

LADY CICELY. How clever of you to find out! I believe you know every bolt in that ship.

Kearney softens perceptibly.

SIR HOWARD. I am really very sorry that my sister-in-law has taken so serious a liberty, Captain Kearney. It is a mania of hers—simply a mania. Why did your men pay any attention to her?

KEARNEY [*with gravely dissembled humor*] Well, I ahsked that question too. I said, Why did you obey that lady's orders instead of waiting for mine? They said they didnt see exactly how they could refuse. I ahsked whether they cawnsidered that discipline. They said, Well, sir, will you talk to the lady yourself next time?

LADY CICELY. I'm s o sorry. But you know, Captain, the one thing that one misses on board a man-of-war is a woman.

KEARNEY. We often feel that deprivation verry keenly, Lady Waynflete.

LADY CICELY. My uncle is first Lord of the Admiralty; and I am always telling him what a scandal it is that an English captain should be forbidden to take his wife on board to look after the ship.

KEARNEY. Stranger still, Lady Waynflete, he is not forbidden to take any other lady. Yours is an extraordinairy country—to an American.

LADY CICELY. But it's most serious, Captain. The poor men go melancholy mad, and ram each other's ships and do all sorts of things.

SIR HOWARD. Cicely: I beg you will not talk nonsense to Captain Kearney. Your ideas on some subjects are really hardly decorous.

LADY CICELY [*to Kearney*] Thats what English people are like, Captain Kearney. They wont hear of anything concerning your poor sailors except Nelson and Trafalgar. Y o u understand me, dont you?

KEARNEY [*gallantly*] I cawnsider that you have more sense in your wedding ring finger than the British Ahdmiralty has in its whole cawnstitootion, Lady Waynflete.

LADY CICELY. Of course I have. Sailors always understand things.

The bluejacket reappears.

BLUEJACKET [*to Lady Cicely*] Prisoners coming up the hill, marm.

KEARNEY [*turning sharply on him*] Who sent you in to say that?

BLUEJACKET [*calmly*] British lady's orders, sir. [*He goes out, unruffled, leaving Kearney dumbfounded*].

SIR HOWARD [*contemplating Kearney's expression with dismay*] I am really very sorry, Captain Kearney. I am quite aware that Lady Cicely has no right whatever to give orders to your men.

LADY CICELY. I didnt give orders: I just asked him. He has such a nice face! Dont you think so, Captain Kearney? [*He gasps, speechless*]. And now will you excuse me a moment. I want to speak to somebody before the inquiry begins. [*She hurries out*].

KEARNEY. There is sertnly a wonderful chahm about the British aristocracy, Sir Howard Hallam. Are they all like that? [*He takes the presidential chair*].

SIR HOWARD [*resuming his seat on Kearney's right*] Fortunately not, Captain Kearney. Half a dozen such women would make an end of law in England in six months.

The bluejacket comes to the door again.

BLUEJACKET. All ready, sir.

KEARNEY. Verry good. *I*'m waiting.

The bluejacket turns and intimates this to those without. The officers of the Santiago enter.

668

CAPTAIN BRASSBOUND'S CONVERSION

SIR HOWARD [*rising and bobbing to them in a judicial manner*] Good morning, gentlemen.

They acknowledge the greeting rather shyly, bowing or touching their caps, and stand in a group behind Kearney.

KEARNEY [*to Sir Howard*] You will be glahd to hear that I have a verry good account of one of our prisoners from our chahplain, who visited them in the gaol. He has expressed a wish to be cawnverted to Episcopalianism.

SIR HOWARD [*drily*] Yes, I think I know him.

KEARNEY. Bring in the prisoners.

BLUEJACKET [*at the door*] They are engaged with the British lady, sir. Shall I ask her—

KEARNEY [*jumping up and exploding in storm piercing tones*] Bring in the prisoners. Tell the lady those are my orders. Do you hear? Tell her so. [*The bluejacket goes out dubiously. The officers look at one another in mute comment on the unaccountable pepperiness of their commander*].

SIR HOWARD [*suavely*] Mr Rankin will be present, I presume.

KEARNEY [*angrily*] Rahnkin! Who is Rahnkin?

SIR HOWARD. Our host the missionary.

KEARNEY [*subsiding unwillingly*] Oh! Rahnkin, is he? He'd better look sharp or he'll be late. [*Again exploding*] What are they doing with those prisoners?

Rankin hurries in, and takes his place near Sir Howard.

SIR HOWARD. This is Mr Rankin, Captain Kearney.

RANKIN. Excuse my delay, Captain Kearney. The leddy sent me on an errand. [*Kearney grunts*]. I thoaght I should be late. But the first thing I heard when I arrived was your officer giving your compliments to Leddy Ceecily, and would she kindly allow the prisoners to come in, as you were anxious to see her again. Then I knew I was in time.

KEARNEY. Oh, that was it, was it? May I ask, sir, did you notice any sign on Lady Waynflete's part of cawmplying with that verry moderate request?

669

CAPTAIN BRASSBOUND'S CONVERSION

LADY CICELY [*outside*] Coming, coming.

The prisoners are brought in by a guard of armed blue-jackets. Drinkwater first, again elaborately clean, and conveying by a virtuous and steadfast smirk a cheerful confidence in his innocence. Johnson solid and inexpressive, Redbrook unconcerned and debonair, Marzo uneasy. These four form a little group together on the captain's left. The rest wait unintelligently on Providence in a row against the wall on the same side, shepherded by the bluejackets. The first bluejacket, a petty officer, posts himself on the Captain's right, behind Rankin and Sir Howard. Finally Brassbound appears with Lady Cicely on his arm. He is in fashionable frock coat and trousers, spotless collar and cuffs, and elegant boots. He carries a glossy tall hat in his hand. To an unsophisticated eye, the change is monstrous and appalling; and its effect on himself is so unmanning that he is quite out of countenance—a shaven Samson. Lady Cicely, however, is greatly pleased with it; and the rest regard it as an unquestionable improvement. The officers fall back gallantly to allow her to pass. Kearney rises to receive her, and stares with some surprise at Brassbound as she stops at the table on his left. Sir Howard rises punctiliously when Kearney rises and sits when he sits.

KEARNEY. Is this another gentleman of your party, Lady Waynflete? I presume I met you lahst night, sir, on board the yacht.

BRASSBOUND. No. I am your prisoner. My name is Brassbound.

DRINKWATER [*officiously*] Kepn Brarsbahnd, of the schooner Thenksgiv—

REDBROOK [*hastily*] Shut up, you fool. [*He elbows Drinkwater into the background*].

KEARNEY [*surprised and rather suspicious*] Well, I hardly understahnd this. However, if you are Captain Brassbound, you can take your place with the rest. [*Brassbound joins Redbrook and Johnson. Kearney sits down again, after inviting Lady Cicely, with a solemn gesture,*

670

to take the vacant chair]. Now let me see. You are a man of experience in these matters, Sir Howard Hallam. If you had to conduct this business, how would you start?

LADY CICELY. He'd call on the counsel for the prosecution, wouldnt you, Howard?

SIR HOWARD. But there is no counsel for the prosecution, Cicely.

LADY CICELY. Oh yes there is. I'm counsel for the prosecution. You mustnt let Sir Howard make a speech, Captain Kearney: his doctors have positively forbidden anything of that sort. Will you begin with me?

KEARNEY. By your leave, Lady Waynflete, I think I will just begin with myself. Sailor fashion will do as well here as lawyer fashion.

LADY CICELY. Ever so much better, d e a r Captain Kearney. [*Silence. Kearney composes himself to speak. She breaks out again*]. You look so nice as a judge!

A general smile. Drinkwater splutters into a half suppressed laugh.

REDBROOK [*in a fierce whisper*] Shut up, you fool, will you? [*Again he pushes him back with a furtive kick*].

SIR HOWARD [*remonstrating*] Cicely!

KEARNEY [*grimly keeping his countenance*] Your ladyship's cawmpliments will be in order at a later stage. Captain Brassbound: the position is this. My ship, the United States cruiser Santiago, was spoken off Mogador lahst Thursday by the yacht Redgauntlet. The owner of the aforesaid yacht, who is not present through having sprained his ahnkle, gave me sertn information. In cawnsequence of that information the Santiago made the twenty knots to Mogador Harbor inside of fifty-seven minutes. Before noon next day a messenger of mine gave the Cadi of the district sertn information. In cawnsequence of that information the Cadi stimulated himself to some ten knots an hour, and lodged you and your men in Mogador gaol at my disposal. The Cadi then went back to his mountain fahstnesses; so we shall not have the pleasure of his company here today. Do

671

you follow me so far?

BRASSBOUND. Yes. I know what you did and what the Cadi did. The point is, why did you do it?

KEARNEY. With doo patience we shall come to that presently. Mr Rahnkin: will you kindly take up the parable?

RANKIN. On the very day that Sir Howrrd and Lady Cicely started on their excursion I was applied to for medicine by a follower of the Sheikh Sidi el Assif. He told me I should never see Sir Howrrd again, because his master knew he was a Christian and would take him out of the hands of Captain Brassbound. I hurried on board the yacht and told the owner to scour the coast for a gunboat or cruiser to come into the harbor and put persuasion on the authorities. [*Sir Howard turns and looks at Rankin with a sudden doubt of his integrity as a witness*].

KEARNEY. But I understood from our chahplain that you reported Captain Brassbound as in league with the Sheikh to deliver Sir Howard up to him.

RANKIN. That was my first hasty conclusion, Captain Kearney. But it appears that the compact between them was that Captain Brassbound should escort travellers under the Sheikh's protection at a certain payment per head, provided none of them were Christians. As I understand it, he tried to smuggle Sir Howrrd through under this compact, and the Sheikh found him out.

DRINKWATER. Rawt, gavner. Thets jest ah it wors. The Kepn—

REDBROOK [*again suppressing him*] Shut up, you fool, I tell you.

SIR HOWARD [*to Rankin*] May I ask have you had any conversation with Lady Cicely on this subject?

RANKIN [*naïvely*] Yes. [*Sir Howard grunts emphatically, as who should say "I thought so." Rankin continues, addressing the court*]. May I say how sorry I am that there are so few chairs, Captain and gentlemen.

KEARNEY [*with genial American courtesy*] Oh, t h a t s all right, Mr Rahnkin. Well, I see no harm so far: its hu-

672

man fawlly, but not human crime. Now the counsel for the prosecution can proceed to prosecute. The floor is yours, Lady Waynflete.

LADY CICELY [*rising*] I can only tell you the exact truth—

DRINKWATER [*involuntarily*] Naow, downt do thet, lidy—

REDBROOK [*as before*] S h u t up, you fool, will you.

LADY CICELY. We had a most delightful trip in the hills; and Captain Brassbound's men could not have been nicer—I must say that for them—until we saw a tribe of Arabs—such nice looking men!—and then the poor things were frightened.

KEARNEY. The Arabs?

LADY CICELY. No: Arabs are never frightened. The escort, of course: escorts are always frightened. I wanted to speak to the Arab chief; but Captain Brassbound cruelly shot his horse; and the chief shot the Count; and then—

KEARNEY. The Count! What Count?

LADY CICELY. Marzo. Thats Marzo [*pointing to Marzo, who grins and touches his forehead*].

KEARNEY [*slightly overwhelmed by the unexpected profusion of incident and character in her story*] Well, what happened then?

LADY CICELY. Then the escort ran away—all escorts do—and dragged me into the castle, which you really ought to make them clean and whitewash thoroughly, Captain Kearney. Then Captain Brassbound and Sir Howard turned out to be related to one another [*sensation*]; and then of course there was a quarrel. The Hallams always quarrel.

SIR HOWARD [*rising to protest*] Cicely! Captain Kearney: this man told me—

LADY CICELY [*swiftly interrupting him*] You mustnt say what people told you: it's not evidence. [*Sir Howard chokes with indignation*].

KEARNEY [*calmly*] Allow the lady to pro-ceed, Sir Howard Hallam.

SIR HOWARD [*recovering his self-control with a gulp, and resuming his seat*] I beg your pardon, Captain Kearney.

LADY CICELY. Then Sidi came.

KEARNEY. Sidney! Who was Sidney?

LADY CICELY. No, Sidi. The Sheikh. Sidi el Assif. A noble creature, with such a fine face! He fell in love with me at first sight—

SIR HOWARD [*remonstrating*] Cicely!

LADY CICELY. He did: you know he did. You told me to tell the exact truth.

KEARNEY. I can readily believe it, madam. Proceed.

LADY CICELY. Well, that put the poor fellow into a most cruel dilemma. You see, he could claim to carry off Sir Howard, because Sir Howard is a Christian. But as I am only a woman, he had no claim to me.

KEARNEY [*somewhat sternly, suspecting Lady Cicely of aristocratic atheism*] But you are a Christian woman.

LADY CICELY. No: the Arabs dont count women. They dont believe we have any souls.

RANKIN. That is true, Captain: the poor benighted creatures!

LADY CICELY. Well, what was he to do? He wasnt in love with Sir Howard; and he w a s in love with me. So he naturally offered to swop Sir Howard for me. Dont you think that was nice of him, Captain Kearney?

KEARNEY. I should have done the same myself, Lady Waynflete. Proceed.

LADY CICELY. Captain Brassbound, I must say, was nobleness itself, in spite of the quarrel between himself and Sir Howard. He refused to give up either of us, and was on the point of fighting for us when in came the Cadi with your most amusing and delightful letter, captain, and bundled us all back to Mogador after calling my poor Sidi the most dreadful names, and putting all the blame on Captain Brassbound. So here we are. Now, Howard, isnt that the exact truth, every word of it?

SIR HOWARD. It is the truth, Cicely, and nothing but the

674

truth. But the English law requires a witness to tell the w h o l e truth.

LADY CICELY. What nonsense! As if anybody ever knew the whole truth about anything! [*Sitting down, much hurt and discouraged*] I'm sorry you wish Captain Kearney to understand that I am an untruthful witness.

SIR HOWARD. No: but—

LADY CICELY. Very well, then: please dont say things that convey that impression.

KEARNEY. But Sir Howard told me yesterday that Captain Brassbound threatened to sell him into slavery.

LADY CICELY [*springing up again*] Did Sir Howard tell you the things he said about Captain Brassbound's mother? [*Renewed sensation*]. I told you they quarrelled, Captain Kearney. I said so, didnt I?

REDBROOK [*crisply*] Distinctly. [*Drinkwater opens his mouth to corroborate*]. Shut up, you fool.

LADY CICELY. Of course I did. Now, Captain Kearney, do y o u want me—does Sir Howard want me—does a n y - b o d y want me to go into the details of that shocking family quarrel? Am I to stand here in the absence of any individual of my own sex and repeat the language of two angry men?

KEARNEY [*rising impressively*] The United States navy will have no hahnd in offering any violence to the pure instincts of womanhood. Lady Waynflete: I thahnk you for the delicacy with which you have given your evidence. [*Lady Cicely beams on him gratefully and sits down triumphant*]. Captain Brassbound: I shall not hold you respawnsible for what you may have said when the English bench addressed you in the language of the English forecastle— [*Sir Howard is about to protest*]. No, Sir Howard Hallam; excuse m e. In moments of pahssion I have called a man that myself. We are all glahd to find real flesh and blood beneath the ermine of the judge. We will now drop a subject that should never have been broached in a lady's presence. [*He resumes his seat, and adds, in a businesslike tone*] Is there anything further before we release these men?

BLUEJACKET. There are some dawcuments handed over by the Cadi, sir. He reckoned they were sort of magic spells. The chahplain ordered them to be reported to you and burnt, with your leave, sir.

KEARNEY. What are they?

BLUEJACKET [*reading from a list*] Four books, torn and dirty, made up of separate numbers, value each wawn penny, and entitled Sweeny Todd, the Demon Barber of London; The Skeleton Horseman—

DRINKWATER [*rushing forward in painful alarm and anxiety*] It's maw lawbrary, gavner. Downt burn em.

KEARNEY. Youll be better without that sort of reading, my man.

DRINKWATER [*in intense distress, appealing to Lady Cicely*] Downt let em burn em, lidy. They dassent if you horder em not to. [*With desperate eloquence*] Yer dunno wot them books is to me. They took me aht of the sawdid reeyellities of the Worterleoo Rowd. They formed maw mawnd: they shaowed me sathink awgher than the squalor of a corster's lawf—

REDBROOK [*collaring him*] Oh shut up, you fool. Get out. Hold your ton—

DRINKWATER [*frantically breaking from him*] Lidy, lidy: sy a word for me. Ev a feelin awt. [*His tears choke him: he clasps his hands in dumb entreaty*].

LADY CICELY [*touched*] Dont burn his books, Captain. Let me give them back to him.

KEARNEY. The books will be handed over to the lady.

DRINKWATER [*in a small voice*] Thenkyer, lidy. [*He retires among his comrades, snivelling subduedly*].

REDBROOK [*aside to him as he passes*] You silly ass, you. [*Drinkwater sniffs and does not reply*].

KEARNEY. I suppose you and your men accept this lady's account of what passed, Captain Brassbound.

BRASSBOUND [*gloomily*] Yes. It is true—as far as it goes.

KEARNEY [*impatiently*] Do you wawnt it to go any further?

MARZO. She leave out something. Arab shoot me. She nurse me. She cure me.

KEARNEY. And who are you, pray?

MARZO [*seized with a sanctimonious desire to demonstrate his higher nature*] Only dam thief. Dam liar. Dam rascal. She no lady.

JOHNSON [*revolted by the seeming insult to the English peerage from a low Italian*] What? Whats that you say?

MARZO. No lady nurse dam rascal. Only saint. She saint. She get me to heaven—get us all to heaven. We do what we like now.

LADY CICELY. Indeed you will do nothing of the sort, Marzo, unless you like to behave yourself very nicely indeed. What hour did you say we were to lunch at, Captain Kearney?

KEARNEY. You recall me to my dooty, Lady Waynflete. My barge will be ready to take off you and Sir Howard to the Santiago at one o'clawk. [*He rises*]. Captain Brassbound: this innquery has elicited no reason why I should detain you or your men. I advise you to ahct as escort in future to heathens exclusively. Mr Rahnkin: I thahnk you in the name of the United States for the hospitahlity you have extended to us today; and I invite you to accompany me bahck to my ship with a view to lunch at half-past-one. Gentlemen: we will wait on the governor of the gaol on our way to the harbor. [*He goes out, following his officers, and followed by the bluejackets and the petty officer*].

SIR HOWARD [*to Lady Cicely*] Cicely: in the course of my professional career I have met with unscrupulous witnesses, and, I am sorry to say, unscrupulous counsel also. But the combination of unscrupulous witness and unscrupulous counsel I have met today has taken away my breath.

677

You have made me your accomplice in defeating justice.

LADY CICELY. Yes: arent you glad it's been defeated for once? [*She takes his arm to go out with him*] Captain Brassbound: I will come back to say goodbye before I go. [*He nods gloomily. She goes out with Sir Howard, following the Captain and his staff*].

RANKIN [*running to Brassbound and taking both his hands*] I'm right glad yere cleared. I'll come back and have a crack with ye when yon lunch is over. God bless ye. [*He goes out quickly*].

Brassbound and his men, left by themselves in the room, free and unobserved, go straight out of their senses. They laugh; they dance; they embrace one another; they set to partners and waltz clumsily; they shake hands repeatedly and maudlinly. Three only retain some sort of self-possession. Marzo, proud of having successfully thrust himself into a leading part in the recent proceedings and made a dramatic speech, inflates his chest, curls his scanty moustache, and throws himself into a swaggering pose, chin up and right foot forward, despising the emotional English barbarians around him. Brassbound's eyes and the working of his mouth shew that he is infected with the general excitement; but he bridles himself savagely. Redbrook, trained to affect indifference, grins cynically; winks at Brassbound; and finally relieves himself by assuming the character of a circus ring-master, flourishing an imaginary whip and egging on the rest to wilder exertions. A climax is reached when Drinkwater, let loose without a stain on his character for the second time, is rapt by belief in his star into an ecstasy in which, scorning all partnership, he becomes as it were a whirling dervish, and executes so miraculous a clog dance that the others gradually cease their slower antics to stare at him.

BRASSBOUND [*tearing off his hat and striding forward as Drinkwater collapses, exhausted, and is picked up by Redbrook*] Now to get rid of this respectable clobber and feel like a man again. Stand by, all hands, to jump on the
678

captain's tall hat. [*He puts the hat down and prepares to jump on it. The effect is startling, and takes him completely aback. His followers, far from appreciating his iconoclasm, are shocked into scandalized sobriety, except Redbrook, who is intensely tickled by their prudery*].

DRINKWATER. Naow, look eah, kepn: that ynt rawt. Dror a lawn somewhere.

JOHNSON. I say nothin agen a bit of fun, Capn; but lets be gentlemen.

REDBROOK. I suggest to you, Brassbound, that the clobber belongs to Lady Sis. Aint you going to give it back to her?

BRASSBOUND [*picking up the hat and brushing the dust off it anxiously*] Thats true. I'm a fool. All the same, she shall not see me again like this. [*He pulls off the coat and waistcoat together*]. Does any man here know how to fold up this sort of thing properly?

REDBROOK. Allow me, governor. [*He takes the coat and waistcoat to the table, and folds them up*].

BRASSBOUND [*loosening his collar and the front of his shirt*] Brandyfaced Jack: youre looking at these studs. I know whats in your mind.

DRINKWATER [*indignantly*] Naow yer downt: nort a bit on it. Wots in maw mawnd is secrifawce, seolf-secrifawce.

BRASSBOUND. If one brass pin of that lady's property is missing, I'll hang you with my own hands at the gaff of the Thanksgiving—and would, if she were lying under the guns of all the fleets in Europe. [*He pulls off the shirt and stands in his blue jersey, with his hair ruffled. He passes his hand through it and exclaims*] Now I am half a man, at any rate.

REDBROOK. A horrible combination, governor: churchwarden from the waist down, and the rest pirate. Lady Sis wont speak to you in it.

BRASSBOUND. I'll change altogether. [*He leaves the room to get his own trousers*].

REDBROOK [*softly*] Look here, Johnson, and gents gen-

679

erally. [*They gather about him*]. Spose she takes him back to England!

MARZO [*trying to repeat his success*] Im! Im only dam pirate. She saint, I tell you—no take any man nowhere.

JOHNSON [*severely*] Dont you be a ignorant and immoral foreigner. [*The rebuke is well received; and Marzo is hustled into the background and extinguished*]. She wont take him for harm; but she might take him for good. And then where should we be?

DRINKWATER. Brarsbahnd ynt the ownly kepn in the world. Wot mikes a kepn is brines an knollidge o lawf. It ynt thet thers naow sitch pusson: its thet you dunno where to look fr im. [*The implication that he is such a person is so intolerable that they receive it with a prolonged burst of booing*].

BRASSBOUND [*returning in his own clothes, getting into his jacket as he comes*] Stand by, all. [*They start asunder guiltily, and wait for orders*]. Redbrook: you pack that clobber in the lady's portmanteau, and put it aboard the yacht for her. Johnson: you take all hands aboard the Thanksgiving; look through the stores; weigh anchor; and make all ready for sea. Then send Jack to wait for me at the slip with a boat; and give me a gunfire for a signal. Lose no time.

JOHNSON. Ay, ay, sir. All aboard, mates.

ALL. Ay, ay. [*They rush out tumultously*].

When they are gone, Brassbound sits down at the end of the table, with his elbows on it and his head on his fists, gloomily thinking. Then he takes from the breast pocket of his jacket a leather case, from which he extracts a scrappy packet of dirty letters and newspaper cuttings. These he throws on the table. Next comes a photograph in a cheap frame. He throws it down untenderly beside the papers; then folds his arms, and is looking at it with grim distaste when Lady Cicely enters. His back is towards her; and he does not hear her. Perceiving this, she shuts the door loudly enough to attract attention. He starts up.

680

CAPTAIN BRASSBOUND'S CONVERSION

LADY CICELY [*coming to the opposite end of the table*] So youve taken off all my beautiful clothes!

BRASSBOUND. Your brother's, you mean. A man should wear his own clothes; and a man should tell his own lies. I'm sorry you had to tell mine for me today.

LADY CICELY. Oh, women spend half their lives telling little lies for men, and sometimes big ones. We're used to it. But mind! I dont admit that I told any today.

BRASSBOUND. How did you square my uncle?

LADY CICELY. I dont understand the expression.

BRASSBOUND. I mean—

LADY CICELY. I'm afraid we havnt time to go into what you mean before lunch. I want to speak to you about your future. May I?

BRASSBOUND [*darkening a little, but politely*] Sit down. [*She sits down. So does he*].

LADY CICELY. What are your plans?

BRASSBOUND. I have no plans. You will hear a gun fired in the harbor presently. That will mean that the Thanksgiving's anchor's weighed and that she is waiting for her captain to put out to sea. And her captain doesnt know now whether to turn her head north or south.

LADY CICELY. Why not north for England?

BRASSBOUND. Why not south for the Pole?

LADY CICELY. But you must do something with yourself?

BRASSBOUND [*settling himself with his fists and elbows weightily on the table and looking straight and powerfully at her*] Look you: when you and I first met, I was a man with a purpose. I stood alone: I saddled no friend, woman or man, with that purpose, because it was against law, against religion, against my own credit and safety. But I believed in it; and I stood alone for it, as a man should stand for his belief, against law and religion as much as against wickedness and selfishness. Whatever I may be, I am none of your fairweather sailors thatll do nothing for their creed but go to Heaven for it. I was ready to go to hell for mine.

681

Perhaps you dont understand that.

LADY CICELY. Oh bless you, yes. Its so very like a certain sort of man.

BRASSBOUND. I daresay; but Ive not met many of that sort. Anyhow, that was what I was like. I dont say I was happy in it; but I wasnt unhappy, because I wasnt drifting. I was steering a course and had work in hand. Give a man health and a course to steer; and he'll never stop to trouble about whether he's happy or not.

LADY CICELY. Sometimes he wont even stop to trouble about whether other people are happy or not.

BRASSBOUND. I dont deny that: nothing makes a man so selfish as work. But I was not self-seeking: it seemed to me that I had put justice above self. I tell you life meant something to me then. Do you see that dirty little bundle of scraps of paper?

LADY CICELY. What are they?

BRASSBOUND. Accounts cut out of newspapers. Speeches made by my uncle at charitable dinners, or sentencing men to death—pious, highminded speeches by a man who was to me a thief and a murderer! To my mind they were more weighty, more momentous, better revelations of the wickedness of law and respectability than the book of the prophet Amos. What are they now? [*He quietly tears the newspaper cuttings into little fragments and throws them away, looking fixedly at her meanwhile*].

LADY CICELY. Well, thats a comfort, at all events.

BRASSBOUND. Yes; but its a part of my life gone: y o u r doing, remember. What have I left? See here! [*he takes up the letters*] the letters my uncle wrote to my mother, with her comments on their cold drawn insolence, their treachery and cruelty. And the piteous letters she wrote to him later on, returned unopened. Must they go too?

LADY CICELY [*uneasily*] I cant ask you to destroy your mother's letters.

BRASSBOUND. Why not, now that you have taken the

meaning out of them? [*He tears them*]. Is that a comfort too?

LADY CICELY. It's a little sad; but perhaps it is best so.

BRASSBOUND. That leaves one relic: her portrait. [*He plucks the photograph out of its cheap case*].

LADY CICELY [*with vivid curiosity*] Oh, let me see. [*He hands it to her. Before she can control herself, her expression changes to one of unmistakable disappointment and repulsion*].

BRASSBOUND [*with a single sardonic cachinnation*] Ha! You expected something better than that. Well, youre right. Her face does not look well opposite yours.

LADY CICELY [*distressed*] I said nothing.

BRASSBOUND. What could you say? [*He takes back the portrait: she relinquishes it without a word. He looks at it; shakes his head; and takes it quietly between his finger and thumb to tear it*].

LADY CICELY [*staying his hand*] Oh, not your mother's picture!

BRASSBOUND. If that were your picture, would you like your son to keep it for younger and better women to see?

LADY CICELY [*releasing his hand*]. Oh, you are dreadful! Tear it, tear it. [*She covers her eyes for a moment to shut out the sight*].

BRASSBOUND [*tearing it quietly*] You killed her for me that day in the castle; and I am better without her. [*He throws away the fragments*]. Now everything is gone. You have taken the old meaning out of my life; but you have put no new meaning into it. I can see that you have some clue to the world that makes all its difficulties easy for you; but I'm not clever enough to seize it. Youve lamed me by shewing me that I take life the wrong way when I'm left to myself.

LADY CICELY. Oh no. Why do you say that?

BRASSBOUND. What else can I say? See what Ive done! My uncle is no worse a man than myself—better, most

683

likely; for he has a better head and a higher place. Well, I took him for a villain out of a storybook. My mother would have opened anybody else's eyes: she shut mine. I'm a stupider man than Brandyfaced Jack even; for he got his romantic nonsense out of his penny numbers and such like trash; but I got just the same nonsense out of life and experience. [*Shaking his head*] It was vulgar—v u l g a r. I see that now; for youve opened my eyes to the past; but what good is that for the future? What am I to do? Where am I to go?

LADY CICELY. It's quite simple. Do whatever you like. Thats what I always do.

BRASSBOUND. That answer is no good to me. What I like is to have something to do; and I have nothing. You might as well talk like the missionary and tell me to do my duty.

LADY CICELY [*quickly*] Oh no thank you. Ive had quite enough of your duty, and Howard's duty. Where would you both be now if I'd let you do it?

BRASSBOUND. We'd have been somewhere, at all events. It seems to me that now I am nowhere.

LADY CICELY. But arnt you coming back to England with us?

BRASSBOUND. What for?

LADY CICELY. Why, to make the most of your opportunities.

BRASSBOUND. What opportunities?

LADY CICELY. Dont you understand that when you are the nephew of a great bigwig, and have influential connexions, and good friends among them, lots of things can be done for you that are never done for ordinary ship captains?

BRASSBOUND. Ah; but I'm not an aristocrat, you see. And like most poor men, I'm proud. I don't like being patronized.

LADY CICELY. What is the use of saying that? In my world, which is now your world—o u r world—getting patronage is the whole art of life. A man cant have a career without it.

BRASSBOUND. In my world a man can navigate a ship and get his living by it.

LADY CICELY. Oh, I see youre one of the Idealists—the Impossibilists! We have them, too, occasionally, in our world. There's only one thing to be done with them.

BRASSBOUND. Whats that?

LADY CICELY. Marry them straight off to some girl with enough money for them, and plenty of sentiment. Thats t h e i r fate.

BRASSBOUND. Youve spoiled even that chance for me. Do you think I could look at any ordinary woman after you? You seem to be able to make me do pretty well what you like; but you cant make me marry anybody but yourself.

LADY CICELY. Do you know, Captain Paquito, that Ive married no less than seventeen men [*Brassbound stares*] to other women. And they all opened the subject by saying that they would never marry anybody but me.

BRASSBOUND. Then I shall be the first man you ever found to stand to his word.

LADY CICELY [*part pleased, part amused, part sympathetic*] Do you really want a wife?

BRASSBOUND. I want a commander. Dont undervalue me: I am a good man when I have a good leader. I have courage: I have determination: I'm not a drinker: I can command a schooner and a shore party if I cant command a ship or an army. When work is put upon me, I turn neither to save my life nor to fill my pocket. Gordon trusted me; and he never regretted it. If you trust me, you shant regret it. All the same, theres something wanting in me: I suppose I'm stupid.

LADY CICELY. Oh, youre not stupid.

BRASSBOUND. Yes I am. Since you saw me for the first time in that garden, youve heard me say nothing clever. And Ive heard you say nothing that didnt make me laugh, or make me feel friendly, as well as telling me what to think

685

and what to do. Thats what I mean by real cleverness. Well, I havnt got it. I can give an order when I know what order to give. I can make men obey it, willing or unwilling. But I'm stupid, I tell you: stupid. When theres no Gordon to command me, I cant think of what to do. Left to myself, Ive become half a brigand. I can kick that little gutter-scrub Drinkwater; but I find myself doing what he puts into my head because I cant think of anything else. When you came, I took your orders as naturally as I took Gordon's, though I little thought my next commander would be a woman. I want to take service under you. And theres no way in which that can be done except marrying you. Will you let me do it?

LADY CICELY. I'm afraid you dont quite know how odd a match it would be for me according to the ideas of English society.

BRASSBOUND. I care nothing about English society: let it mind its own business.

LADY CICELY [*rising, a little alarmed*] Captain Paquito: I am not in love with you.

BRASSBOUND [*also rising, with his gaze still steadfastly on her*] I didnt suppose you were: the commander is not usually in love with his subordinate.

LADY CICELY. Nor the subordinate with the commander.

BRASSBOUND [*assenting firmly*] Nor the subordinate with the commander.

LADY CICELY [*learning for the first time in her life what terror is, as she finds that he is unconsciously mesmerizing her*] Oh, you are dangerous!

BRASSBOUND. Come: are you in love with anybody else? Thats the question.

LADY CICELY [*shaking her head*] I have never been in love with any real person; and I never shall. How could I manage people if I had that mad little bit of self left in me? Thats my secret.

BRASSBOUND. Then throw away the last bit of self. Marry me.

686

LADY CICELY [*vainly struggling to recall her wandering will*] Must I?

BRASSBOUND. There is no must. You c a n. I ask you to. My fate depends on it.

LADY CICELY. It's frightful; for I dont mean to—dont wish to.

BRASSBOUND. But you will.

LADY CICELY [*quite lost, slowly stretches out her hand to give it to him*] I— [*gunfire from the Thanksgiving. His eyes dilate. It wakes her from her trance*]. What is that?

BRASSBOUND. It is farewell. Rescue for you—safety, freedom! You were made to be something better than the wife of Black Paquito. [*He kneels and takes her hands*]. You can do no more for me now: I have blundered somehow on the secret of command at last [*he kisses her hands*]: thanks for that, and for a man's power and purpose restored and righted. And farewell, farewell, farewell.

LADY CICELY [*in a strange ecstasy, holding his hands as he rises*] Oh, farewell. With my heart's deepest feeling, farewell, farewell.

BRASSBOUND. With my heart's noblest honor and triumph, farewell. [*He turns and flies*].

LADY CICELY. How glorious! how glorious! And what an escape!

CURTAIN

NOTES TO CAPTAIN BRASSBOUND'S CONVERSION

SOURCES OF THE PLAY

I CLAIM as a notable merit in the authorship of this play that I have been intelligent enough to steal its scenery, its surroundings, its atmosphere, its geography, its knowledge of the east, its fascinating Cadis and Krooboys and Sheikhs and mud castles from an excellent book of philosophic travel and vivid adventure entitled Mogreb-el-Acksa (Morocco the Most Holy) by Cunninghame Graham. My own first hand knowledge of Morocco is based on a morning's walk through Tangier, and a cursory observation of the coast through a binocular from the deck of an Orient steamer, both later in date than the writing of the play.

Cunninghame Graham is the hero of his own book; but I have not made him the hero of my play, because so incredible a personage must have destroyed its likelihood—such as it is. There are moments when I do not myself believe in his existence. And yet he must be real; for I have seen him with these eyes; and I am one of the few men living who can decipher the curious alphabet in which he writes his private letters. The man is on public record too. The battle of Trafalgar Square, in which he personally and bodily assailed civilization as represented by the concentrated military and constabular forces of the capital of the world, can scarcely be forgotten by the more discreet spectators, of whom I was one. On that occasion civilization, qualitatively his inferior, was quantitatively so hugely in excess of him that it put him in prison, but had not sense enough to keep him there. Yet his getting out of prison was as nothing compared to his getting into the House of Commons. How he did it I know not; but the thing certainly happened, somehow. That he made pregnant utterances as a legislator may be taken as proved by the keen philosophy of the travels and tales he has since tossed to us; but the House, strong in stupidity, did not understand him until in an inspired moment he voiced a universal impulse by bluntly damning its hypocrisy. Of all the eloquence of that silly parliament, there remains only one single damn. It has survived the front bench speeches of the eighties as the word of Cervantes survives the oraculations of the Dons and Deys who put him, too, in prison. The shocked house demanded that he should withdraw his cruel word. "I never withdraw," said he; and I promptly stole the potent phrase for the sake of its perfect style, and used it as a cockade for the Bulgarian hero of Arms and the Man. The theft prospered; and I naturally take the first opportunity of repeating it. In what other Lepantos besides Trafalgar Square Cunninghame Graham has fought, I cannot tell. He is a fascinating mystery to a sedentary person like myself. The horse, a dangerous animal whom, when I cannot avoid, I propitiate with apples and sugar, he bestrides and dominates fearlessly, yet with a true republican sense of the rights of the four-legged fellow-creature whose martyrdom, and man's shame therein, he has told most powerfully in his Cavalry, a tale with an edge that will cut the soft cruel hearts and strike fire from the hard kind ones. He handles the other lethal weapons as familiarly as the pen: medieval sword and modern Mauser are to him as umbrellas and kodaks are to me. His tales of adventure have the true Cervantes touch of the man who has been there—so refreshingly different from the scenes imagined by bloody-minded clerks who escape from their servitude into literature to tell us how men and cities are conceived in the counting house and the volunteer corps. He is, I understand, a Spanish hidalgo: hence the superbity of his portrait by Lavery (Velasquez being no longer available). He is, I know, a Scotch laird. How he contrives to be authentically the two things at the same time is no more intelligible to me than the fact that everything that has even happened to him seems to have happened in Paraguay or Texas instead of in Spain or Scotland. He is, I regret to add, an impenitent and unashamed dandy: such boots, such a hat, would have dazzled D'Orsay himself.

With that hat he once saluted me in Regent St. when I was walking with my mother. Her interest was instantly kindled; and the following conversation ensued. "Who is that?" "Cunninghame Graham." "Nonsense! Cunninghame Graham is one of your Socialists: that man is a gentleman." This is the punishment of vanity, a fault I have myself always avoided, as I find conceit less troublesome and much less expensive. Later on somebody told him of Tarudant, a city in Morocco in which no Christian had ever set foot. Concluding at once that it must be an exceptionally desirable place to live in, he took ship and horse; changed the hat for a turban; and made straight for the sacred city, via Mogador. How he fared, and how he fell into the hands of the Cadi of Kintafi, who rightly held that there was more danger to Islam in one Cunninghame Graham than in a thousand Christians, may be learnt from his account of it in Mogreb-el-Acksa, without which Captain Brassbound's Conversion would never have been written.

I am equally guiltless of any exercise of invention concerning the story of the West Indian estate which so very nearly serves as a peg to hang Captain Brassbound. To Mr Frederick Jackson of Hindhead, who, against all his principles, encourages and abets me in my career as a dramatist, I owe my knowledge of those main facts of the case which became public through an attempt to make the House of Commons act on them. This being so, I must add that the character of Captain Brassbound's mother, like the recovery of the estate by the next heir, is an interpolation of my own. It is not, however, an invention. One of the evils of the pretence that our institutions represent abstract principles of justice instead of being mere social scaffolding is that persons of a certain temperament take the pretence seriously, and, when the law is on the side of injustice, will not accept the situation, and are driven mad by their vain struggle against it. Dickens has drawn the type in his Man from Shropshire in Bleak House. Most public men and all lawyers have been appealed to by victims of this sense of injustice—the most unhelpable of afflictions in a society like ours.

ENGLISH AND AMERICAN DIALECTS

The fact that English is spelt conventionally and not phonetically makes the art of recording speech almost impossible. What is more, it places the modern dramatist, who writes for America as well as England, in a most trying position. Take for example my American captain and my English lady. I have spelt the word conduce, as uttered by the American captain, as cawndooce, to suggest (very roughly) the American pronunciation to English readers. Then why not spell the same word, when uttered by Lady Cicely, as kerndewce, to suggest the English pronunciation to American readers? To this I have absolutely no defence: I can only plead that an author who lives in England necessarily loses his consciousness of the peculiarities of English speech, and sharpens his consciousness of the points in which American speech differs from it; so that it is more convenient to leave English peculiarities to be recorded by American authors. I must, however, most vehemently disclaim any intention of suggesting that English pronunciation is authoritative and correct. My own tongue is neither American English nor English English, but Irish English; so I am as nearly impartial in the matter as it is in human nature to be. Besides, there is no standard English pronunciation any more than there is an American one: in England every county has its catchwords, just as no doubt every State in the Union has. I cannot believe that the pioneer American, for example, can spare time to learn that last refinement of modern speech, the exquisite diphthong, a farfetched combination of the French eu and the English e, with which a New Yorker pronounces such words as world, bird, &c. I have spent months without success in trying to achieve glibness with it.

To Felix Drinkwater also I owe some apology for implying that all his vowel pronunciations are unfashionable.

They are very far from being so. As far as my social experience goes (and I have kept very mixed company) there is no class in English society in which a good deal of Drinkwater pronunciation does not pass unchallenged save by the expert phonetician. This is no mere rash and ignorant jibe of my own at the expense of my English neighbors. Academic authority in the matter of English speech is represented at present by Mr Henry Sweet, of the University of Oxford, whose *Elementarbuch des gesprochenen Englisch,* translated into his native language for the use of British islanders as a Primer of Spoken English, is the most accessible standard work on the subject. In such words as plum, come, humbug, up, gun, etc., Mr Sweet's evidence is conclusive. Ladies and gentlemen in Southern England pronounce them as plam, kam, hambag, ap, gan, etc., exactly as Felix Drinkwater does. I could not claim Mr Sweet's authority if I dared to whisper that such coster English as the rather pretty dahn tahn for down town, or the decidedly ugly cowcow for cocoa is current in very polite circles. The entire nation, costers and all, would undoubtedly repudiate any such pronunciation as vulgar. All the same, if I were to attempt to represent current "smart" cockney speech as I have attempted to represent Drinkwater's, without the niceties of Mr Sweet's Romic alphabets, I am afraid I should often have to write dahn tahn and cowcow as being at least nearer to the actual sound than down town and cocoa. And this would give such offence that I should have to leave the country; for nothing annoys a native speaker of English more than a faithful setting down in phonetic spelling of the sounds he utters. He imagines that a departure from conventional spelling indicates a departure from the correct standard English of good society. Alas! this correct standard English of good society is unknown to phoneticians. It is only one of the many figments that bewilder our poor snobbish brains. No such thing exists; but what does that matter to people trained from infancy to make a point of honor of belief in abstractions and incredibilities? And so I

692

am compelled to hide Lady Cicely's speech under the veil of conventional orthography.

I need not shield Drinkwater, because he will never read my book. So I have taken the liberty of making a special example of him, as far as that can be done without a phonetic alphabet, for the benefit of the mass of readers outside London who still form their notions of cockney dialect on Sam Weller. When I came to London in 1876, the Sam Weller dialect had passed away so completely that I should have given it up as a literary fiction if I had not discovered it surviving in a Middlesex village, and heard of it from an Essex one. Some time in the eighties the late Andrew Tuer called attention in the Pall Mall Gazette to several peculiarities of modern cockney, and to the obsolescence of the Dickens dialect that was still being copied from book to book by authors who never dreamt of using their ears, much less of training them to listen. Then came Mr Anstey's cockney dialogues in Punch, a great advance, and Mr Chevalier's coster songs and patter. The Tompkins verses contributed by Mr. Barry Pain to the London Daily Chronicle also did something to bring the literary convention for cockney English up to date. But Tompkins sometimes perpetuated horrible solecisms. He would pronounce face as fice, accurately enough; but he would rhyme it quite impossibly to nice, which Tompkins would have pronounced as nawce: for example Mawl Enn Rowd for Mile End Road. This aw for i, which I have made Drinkwater use, is the latest stage of the old diphthongal oi, which Mr Chevalier still uses. Irish, Scotch, and north country readers must remember that Drinkwater's rs are absolutely unpronounced when they follow a vowel, though they modify the vowel very considerably. Thus, though luggage is pronounced by him as laggige, turn is not pronounced as tarn, but as teun with the eu sounded as in French. The London r seems thoroughly understood in America, with the result, however, that the use of the r by Artemus Ward and other American dialect writers causes Irish people to misread them grotesquely. I once saw the pronunciation of *malheureux* represented in a cockney handbook by mal-err-err: not at all a bad makeshift to instruct a Londoner, but out of the question elsewhere in the British Isles. In America, representations of English speech dwell too derisively on the dropped or interpolated h. American writers have apparently not noticed the fact that the south English h is not the same as the never-dropped Irish and American h, and that to ridicule an Englishman for dropping it is as absurd as to ridicule the whole French and Italian nation for doing the same. The American h, helped out by a general agreement to pronounce wh as hw, is tempestuously audible, and cannot be dropped without being immediately missed. The London h is so comparatively quiet at all times, and so completely inaudible in wh, that it probably fell out of use simply by escaping the ears of children learning to speak. However that may be, it is kept alive only by the literate classes who are reminded constantly of its existence by seeing it on paper. Roughly speaking, I should say that in England he who bothers about his hs is a fool, and he who ridicules a dropped h a snob. As to the interpolated h, my experience as a London vestryman has convinced me that it is often effective as a means of emphasis, and that the London language would be poorer without it. The objection to it is no more respectable than the objection of a street boy to a black man or to a lady in knickerbockers.

I have made only the most perfunctory attempt to represent the dialect of the missionary. There is no literary notation for the grave music of good Scotch.

BLACKDOWN,
August 1900.

THE MAN OF DESTINY

1896

THE MAN OF DESTINY

THE *twelfth of May, 1796, in north Italy, at Tavazzano, on the road from Lodi to Milan. The afternoon sun is blazing serenely over the plains of Lombardy, treating the Alps with respect and the anthills with indulgence, neither disgusted by the basking of the swine in the villages nor hurt by its cool reception in the churches, but ruthlessly disdainful of two hordes of mischievous insects which are the French and Austrian armies. Two days before, at Lodi, the Austrians tried to prevent the French from crossing the river by the narrow bridge there; but the French, commanded by a general aged 27, Napoleon Bonaparte, who does not respect the rules of war, rushed the fireswept bridge, supported by a tremendous cannonade in which the young general assisted with his own hands. Cannonading is his technical speciality: he has been trained in the artillery under the old régime, and made perfect in the military arts of shirking his duties, swindling the paymaster over travelling expenses, and dignifying war with the noise and smoke of cannon, as depicted in all military portraits. He is, however, an original observer, and has perceived, for the first time since the invention of gunpowder, that a cannon ball, if it strikes a man, will kill him. To a thorough grasp of this remarkable discovery he adds a highly evolved faculty for physical geography and for the calculation of times and distances. He has prodigious powers of work, and a clear realistic knowledge of human nature in public affairs, having seen it exhaustively tested in that department during the French Revolution. He is imaginative without illusions, and creative without religion, loyalty, patriotism or any of the common ideals. Not that he is incapable of these ideals: on the contrary, he has swallowed them all in his boyhood, and now, having a keen dramatic faculty, is extremely clever at playing upon them by the arts of the actor and stage manager. Withal, he is no spoiled child. Poverty, ill-luck, the shifts of impecunious shabbygentility, repeated failure as a would-be author, humiliation*

697

as a rebuffed time server, reproof and punishment as an incompetent and dishonest officer, an escape from dismissal from the service so narrow that if the emigration of the nobles had not raised the value of even the most rascally lieutenant to the famine price of a general he would have been swept contemptuously from the army: these trials have ground his conceit out of him, and forced him to be self-sufficient and to understand that to such men as he is the world will give nothing that he cannot take from it by force. In this the world is not free from cowardice and folly; for Napoleon, as a merciless cannonader of political rubbish, is making himself useful: indeed, it is even now impossible to live in England without sometimes feeling how much that country lost in not being conquered by him as well as by Julius Cæsar.

However, on this May afternoon in 1796, it is early days with him. He has but recently been promoted general, partly by using his wife to seduce the Directory (then governing France); partly by the scarcity of officers caused by the emigration as aforesaid; partly by his faculty of knowing a country, with all its roads, rivers, hills and valleys, as he knows the palm of his hand; and largely by that new faith of his in the efficacy of firing cannons at people. His army is, as to discipline, in a state which has so greatly shocked some modern writers before whom the following story has been enacted, that they, impressed with the later glory of "L'Empereur," have altogether refused to credit it. But Napoleon is not L'Empereur yet: his men call him Le Petit Caporal, as he is still in the stage of gaining influence over them by displays of pluck. He is not in a position to force his will on them in orthodox military fashion by the cat o' nine tails. The French Revolution, which has escaped suppression solely through the monarchy's habit of being at least four years in arrear with its soldiers in the matter of pay, has substituted for that habit, as far as possible, the habit of not paying at all, except in promises and patriotic flatteries which are not compatible with martial

698

law of the Prussian type. Napoleon has therefore approached the Alps in command of men without money, in rags, and consequently indisposed to stand much discipline, especially from upstart generals. This circumstance, which would have embarrassed an idealist soldier, has been worth a thousand cannon to Napoleon. He has said to his army "You have patriotism and courage; but you have no money, no clothes, and hardly anything to eat. In Italy there are all these things, and glory as well, to be gained by a devoted army led by a general who regards loot as the natural right of the soldier. I am such a general. En avant, mes enfants!" The result has entirely justified him. The army conquers Italy as the locusts conquered Cyprus. They fight all day and march all night, covering impossible distances and appearing in incredible places, not because every soldier carries a field marshal's baton in his knapsack, but because he hopes to carry at least half a dozen silver forks there next day.

It must be understood, by the way, that the French army does not make war on the Italians. It is there to rescue them from the tyranny of their Austrian conquerors, and confer republican institutions on them; so that in incidentally looting them it merely makes free with the property of its friends, who ought to be grateful to it, and perhaps would be if ingratitude were not the proverbial failing of their country. The Austrians, whom it fights, are a thoroughly respectable regular army, well disciplined, commanded by gentlemen versed in orthodox campaigning: at the head of them Beaulieu, practising the classic art of war under orders from Vienna, and getting horribly beaten by Napoleon, who acts on his own responsibility in defiance of professional precedents or orders from Paris. Even when the Austrians win a battle, all that is necessary is to wait until their routine obliges them to return to their quarters for afternoon tea, so to speak, and win it back again from them: a course pursued later on with brilliant success at Marengo. On the whole, with his foe handicapped by Austrian states-

*manship, classic generalship, and the exigencies of the aris-
tocratic social structure of Viennese society, Napoleon finds
it possible to be irresistible without working heroic miracles.
The world, however, likes miracles and heroes, and is quite
incapable of conceiving the action of such forces as academic
militarism or Viennese drawing-roomism. Hence it has
already begun to manufacture "L'Empereur," and thus to
make it difficult for the romanticists of a hundred years
later to credit the hitherto unrecorded little scene now in
question at Tavazzano.*

*The best quarters in Tavazzano are at a little inn, the
first house reached by travellers passing through the place
from Milan to Lodi. It stands in a vineyard; and its principal room, a pleasant refuge from the summer heat, is open
so widely at the back to this vineyard that it is almost a large
veranda. The bolder children, much excited by the alarums
and excursions of the past few days, and by an irruption of
French troops at six o'clock, know that the French commander has quartered himself in this room, and are divided
between a craving to peep in at the front windows, and a
mortal dread of the sentinel, a young gentleman-soldier
who, having no natural moustache, has had a most ferocious
one painted on his face with boot blacking by his sergeant. As
his heavy uniform, like all the uniforms of that day, is de-
signed for parade without the least reference to his health
or comfort, he perspires profusely in the sun; and his
painted moustache has run in little streaks down his chin
and round his neck, except where it has dried in stiff
japanned flakes and had its sweeping outline chipped off in
grotesque little bays and headlands, making him unspeakably ridiculous in the eye of History a hundred years later,
but monstrous and horrible to the contemporary north
Italian infant, to whom nothing would seem more natural
than that he should relieve the monotony of his guard by
pitchforking a stray child up on his bayonet, and eating it
uncooked. Nevertheless one girl of bad character, in whom
an instinct of privilege with soldiers is already stirring, does*

THE MAN OF DESTINY

*peep in at the safest window for a moment before a glance
and a clink from the sentinel sends her flying. Most of what
she sees she has seen before: the vineyard at the back, with
the old winepress and a cart among the vines; the door
close on her right leading to the street entry; the landlord's best sideboard, now in full action for dinner, further
back on the same side; the fireplace on the other side with a
couch near it; another door, leading to the inner rooms,
between it and the vineyard; and the table in the middle set
out with a repast of Milanese risotto, cheese, grapes, bread,
olives, and a big wickered flask of red wine.*

*The landlord, Giuseppe Grandi, she knows well. He
is a swarthy vivacious shrewdly cheerful black-curled bullet
headed grinning little innkeeper of forty. Naturally an excellent host, he is in the highest spirits this evening at his
good fortune in having as his guest the French commander
to protect him against the license of the troops. He actually
sports a pair of gold earrings which would otherwise have
been hidden carefully under the winepress with his little
equipment of silver plate.*

*Napoleon, sitting facing her on the further side of the
table, she sees for the first time. He is working hard, partly
at his meal, which he has discovered how to dispatch in
ten minutes by attacking all the courses simultaneously
(this practice is the beginning of his downfall), and partly
at a military map on which he from time to time marks the
position of the forces by taking a grapeskin from his mouth
and planting it on the map with his thumb like a wafer.
There is no revolutionary untidiness about his dress or
person; but his elbow has displaced most of the dishes and
glasses; and his long hair trails into the risotto when he
forgets it and leans more intently over the map.*

GIUSEPPE. Will your excellency—

NAPOLEON [*intent on his map, but cramming himself
mechanically with his left hand*] Dont talk. I'm busy.

GIUSEPPE [*with perfect good humor*] Excellency: I
obey.

THE MAN OF DESTINY

NAPOLEON. Some red ink.

GIUSEPPE. Alas! excellency, there is none.

NAPOLEON [*with Corsican facetiousness*] Kill something and bring me its blood.

GIUSEPPE [*grinning*] There is nothing but your excellency's horse, the sentinel, the lady upstairs, and my wife.

NAPOLEON. Kill your wife.

GIUSEPPE. Willingly, your excellency; but unhappily I am not strong enough. She would kill me.

NAPOLEON. That will do equally well.

GIUSEPPE. Your excellency does me too much honor. [*Stretching his hand towards the flask*] Perhaps some wine will answer your excellency's purpose.

NAPOLEON [*hastily protecting the flask, and becoming quite serious*] Wine! No: that would be waste. You are all the same: waste! waste! waste! [*He marks the map with gravy, using his fork as a pen*]. Clear away. [*He finishes his wine; pushes back his chair; and uses his napkin, stretching his legs and leaning back, but still frowning and thinking*].

GIUSEPPE [*clearing the table and removing the things to a tray on the sideboard*] Every man to his trade, excellency. We innkeepers have plenty of cheap wine: we think nothing of spilling it. You great generals have plenty of cheap blood: you think nothing of spilling it. Is it not so, excellency?

NAPOLEON. Blood costs nothing: wine costs money. [*He rises and goes to the fireplace*].

GIUSEPPE. They say you are careful of everything except human life, excellency.

NAPOLEON. Human life, my friend, is the only thing that takes care of itself. [*He throws himself at his ease on the couch*].

GIUSEPPE [*admiring him*] Ah, excellency, what fools we all are beside you! If I could only find out the secret of your success!

NAPOLEON. You would make yourself Emperor of

702

Italy, eh?

GIUSEPPE. Too troublesome, excellency: I leave all that to you. Besides, what would become of my inn if I were Emperor? See how you enjoy looking on at me whilst I keep the inn for you and wait on you! Well, I shall enjoy looking on at you whilst you become Emperor of Europe, and govern the country for me. [*As he chatters, he takes the cloth off deftly without removing the map, and finally takes the corners in his hands and the middle in his mouth, to fold it up*].

NAPOLEON. Emperor of Europe, eh? Why only Europe?

GIUSEPPE. Why, indeed? Emperor of the world, excellency! Why not? [*He folds and rolls up the cloth, emphasizing his phrase by the steps of the process*]. One man is like another [*fold*]: one country is like another [*fold*]: one battle is like another. [*At the last fold, he slaps the cloth on the table and deftly rolls it up, adding, by way of peroration*] Conquer one: conquer all. [*He takes the cloth to the sideboard, and puts it in a drawer*].

NAPOLEON. And govern for all; fight for all; be everybody's servant under cover of being everybody's master. Giuseppe.

GIUSEPPE [*at the sideboard*] Excellency?

NAPOLEON. I forbid you to talk to me about myself.

GIUSEPPE [*coming to the foot of the couch*] Pardon. Your excellency is so unlike other great men. It is the subject they like best.

NAPOLEON. Well, talk to me about the subject they like next best, whatever that may be.

GIUSEPPE [*unabashed*] Willingly, your excellency. Has your excellency by any chance caught a glimpse of the lady upstairs?

NAPOLEON [*sitting up promptly*]. How old is she?

GIUSEPPE. The right age, excellency.

NAPOLEON. Do you mean seventeen or thirty?

GIUSEPPE. Thirty, excellency.

NAPOLEON. Goodlooking?

GIUSEPPE. I cannot see with your excellency's eyes: every man must judge that for himself. In my opinion, excellency, a fine figure of a lady. [*Slyly*] Shall I lay the table for her collation here?

NAPOLEON [*brusquely, rising*] No: lay nothing here until the officer for whom I am waiting comes back. [*He looks at his watch, and takes to walking to and fro between the fireplace and the vineyard*].

GIUSEPPE [*with conviction*] Excellency: believe me, he has been captured by the accursed Austrians. He dare not keep you waiting if he were at liberty.

NAPOLEON [*turning at the edge of the shadow of the veranda*] Giuseppe: if that turns out to be true, it will put me into such a temper that nothing short of hanging you and your whole household, including the lady upstairs, will satisfy me.

GIUSEPPE. We are all cheerfully at your excellency's disposal, except the lady. I cannot answer for her; but no lady could resist you, General.

NAPOLEON [*sourly, resuming his march*] Hm! Y o u will never be hanged. There is no satisfaction in hanging a man who does not object to it.

GIUSEPPE [*sympathetically*] Not the least in the world, excellency: is there? [*Napoleon again looks at his watch, evidently growing anxious*]. Ah, one can see that you are a great man, General: you know how to wait. If it were a corporal now, or a sub-lieutenant, at the end of three minutes he would be swearing, fuming, threatening, pulling the house about our ears.

NAPOLEON. Giuseppe: your flatteries are insufferable. Go and talk outside. [*He sits down again at the table, with his jaws in his hands, and his elbows propped on the map, poring over it with a troubled expression*].

GIUSEPPE. Willingly, your excellency. You shall not be disturbed. [*He takes up the tray and prepares to withdraw*].

THE MAN OF DESTINY

NAPOLEON. The moment he comes back, send him to me.

GIUSEPPE. Instantaneously, your excellency.

A LADY'S VOICE [*calling from some distant part of the inn*] Giusep-pe! [*The voice is very musical, and the two final notes make an ascending interval*].

NAPOLEON [*startled*] Who's that?

GIUSEPPE. The lady, excellency.

NAPOLEON. The lady upstairs?

GIUSEPPE. Yes, excellency. The strange lady.

NAPOLEON. Strange? Where does she come from?

GIUSEPPE [*with a shrug*] Who knows? She arrived here just before your excellency in a hired carriage belonging to the Golden Eagle at Borghetto. By herself, excellency. No servants. A dressing bag and a trunk: that is all. The postillion says she left a horse at the Golden Eagle. A charger, with military trappings.

NAPOLEON. A woman with a charger! French or Austrian?

GIUSEPPE. French, excellency.

NAPOLEON. Her husband's charger, no doubt. Killed at Lodi, poor fellow.

THE LADY'S VOICE [*the two final notes now making a peremptory descending interval*] Giuseppe!

NAPOLEON [*rising to listen*] Thats not the voice of a woman whose husband was killed yesterday.

GIUSEPPE. Husbands are not always regretted, excellency. [*Calling*] Coming, lady, coming. [*He makes for the inner door*].

NAPOLEON [*arresting him with a strong hand on his shoulder*] Stop. Let h e r come.

VOICE. Giuseppe!! [*Impatiently*].

GIUSEPPE. Let me go, excellency. It is my point of honor as an innkeeper to come when I am called. I appeal to you as a soldier.

A MAN'S VOICE [*outside, at the inn door, shouting*] Here, someone. Hollo! Landlord! Where are you?

705

[*Somebody raps vigorously with a whip handle on a bench in the passage*].

NAPOLEON [*suddenly becoming the commanding officer again and throwing Giuseppe off*] My man at last. [*Pointing to the inner door*] Go. Attend to your business: the lady is calling you. [*He goes to the fireplace and stands with his back to it with a determined military air*].

GIUSEPPE [*with bated breath, snatching up his tray*] Certainly, excellency. [*He hurries out by the inner door*].

THE MAN'S VOICE [*impatiently*] Are you all asleep here?

The other door is kicked rudely open. A dusty sublieutenant bursts into the room. He is a tall chuckle-headed young man of twenty-four, with the complexion and style of a man of rank, and a self-assurance on that ground which the French Revolution has failed to shake in the smallest degree. He has a thick silly lip, an eager credulous eye, an obstinate nose, and a loud confident voice. A young man without fear, without reverence, without imagination, without sense, hopelessly insusceptible to the Napoleonic or any other idea, stupendously egotistical, eminently qualified to rush in where angels fear to tread, yet of a vigorous babbling vitality which bustles him into the thick of things. He is just now boiling with vexation, attributable by a superficial observer to his impatience at not being promptly attended to by the staff of the inn, but in which a more discerning eye can perceive a certain moral depth, indicating a more permanent and momentous grievance. On seeing Napoleon, he is sufficiently taken aback to check himself and salute; but he does not betray by his manner any of that prophetic consciousness of Marengo and Austerlitz, Waterloo and St Helena, or the Napoleonic pictures of Delaroche and Meissonier, which later ages expect from him.

NAPOLEON [*watch in hand*] Well, sir, you have come at last. Your instructions were that I should arrive here at six, and find you waiting for me with my mail from Paris and with despatches. It is now twenty minutes to eight. You were sent on this service as a hard rider with the fastest horse in the camp. You arrived a hundred minutes late, on foot. Where is your horse?

THE LIEUTENANT [*moodily pulling off his gloves and dashing them with his cap and whip on the table*] Ah! where indeed? Thats just what I should like to know, General. [*With emotion*] You dont know how fond I was of that horse.

NAPOLEON [*angrily sarcastic*] Indeed! [*With sudden misgiving*] Where are the letters and despatches?

THE LIEUTENANT [*importantly, rather pleased than otherwise at having some remarkable news*] I dont know.

NAPOLEON [*unable to believe his ears*] You dont know!

LIEUTENANT. No more than you do, General. Now I suppose I shall be court-martialled. Well, I dont mind being court-martialled; but [*with solemn determination*] I tell you, General, if ever I catch that innocent looking youth, I'll spoil his beauty, the slimy little liar! I'll make a picture of him. I'll—

NAPOLEON [*advancing from the hearth to the table*] What innocent looking youth? Pull yourself together, sir, will you; and give an account of yourself.

LIEUTENANT [*facing him at the opposite side of the table, leaning on it with his fists*] Oh, I'm all right, General: I'm perfectly ready to give an account of myself. I shall make the court-martial thoroughly understand that the fault was not mine. Advantage has been taken of the better side of my nature; and I'm not ashamed of it. But with all respect to you as my commanding officer, General, I say again that if ever I set eyes on that son of Satan, I'll—

NAPOLEON [*angrily*] So you said before.

LIEUTENANT [*drawing himself upright*] I say it again. Just wait until I catch him. Just wait: thats all. [*He folds his arms resolutely, and breathes hard, with compressed lips*].

NAPOLEON. I a m waiting, sir. For your explanation.

LIEUTENANT [*confidently*] Youll change your tone,

707

General, when you hear what has happened to me.

NAPOLEON. Nothing has happened to you, sir: you are alive and not disabled. Where are the papers entrusted to you?

LIEUTENANT. Nothing happened to me! Nothing!! He swore eternal brotherhood with me. Was that nothing? He said my eyes reminded him of his sister's eyes. Was that nothing? He cried—actually cried—over the story of my separation from Angelica. Was that nothing? He paid for both bottles of wine, though he only ate bread and grapes himself. Perhaps you call that nothing. He gave me his pistols and his horse and his despatches—most important despatches—and let me go away with them. [*Triumphantly, seeing that he has reduced Napoleon to blank stupefaction*] Was t h a t nothing?

NAPOLEON [*enfeebled by astonishment*] What did he do that for?

LIEUTENANT [*as if the reason were obvious*] To shew his confidence in me, of course. [*Napoleon's jaw does not exactly drop; but its hinges become nerveless*]. And I was worthy of his confidence: I brought them all back honorably. But would you believe it? when I trusted him with m y pistols, and m y horse, and m y despatches—

NAPOLEON. What the devil did you do that for?

LIEUTENANT. I'm telling you: to shew my confidence in him. And he betrayed it! abused it! never came back again! The thief! the swindler! the heartless treacherous little blackguard! You call that nothing, I suppose. But look here, General: [*again resorting to the table with his fist for greater emphasis*] y o u may put up with this outrage from the Austrians if you like; but speaking for myself personally, I tell you that if ever I catch—

NAPOLEON [*turning on his heel in disgust and irritably resuming his march to and fro*] Yes: you have said that more than once already.

LIEUTENANT [*excitedly*] More than once! I'll say it fifty times; and whats more, I'll do it. Youll see, General.

I'll shew my confidence in him, so I will. I'll—

NAPOLEON. Yes, yes, sir: no doubt you will. What kind of man was he?

LIEUTENANT. Well, I should think you ought to be able to tell from his conduct the kind of man he was.

NAPOLEON. Psha! What was he like?

LIEUTENANT. Like! He was like—well, you ought to have just seen the fellow: that will give you a notion of what he was like. He wont be like it five minutes after I catch him; for I tell you that if ever—

NAPOLEON [*shouting furiously for the innkeeper*] Giuseppe! [*To the lieutenant, out of all patience*] Hold your tongue, sir, if you can.

LIEUTENANT [*plaintively*] I warn you it's no use trying to put the blame on me. How was I to know the sort of fellow he was? [*He takes a chair from between the sideboard and the outer door; places it near the table; and sits down*]. If you only knew how hungry and tired I am, youd have more consideration.

GIUSEPPE [*returning*] What is it, excellency?

NAPOLEON [*struggling with his temper*] Take this—this officer. Feed him; and put him to bed, if necessary. When he is in his right mind again, find out what has happened to him and bring me word. [*To the lieutenant*] Consider yourself under arrest, sir.

LIEUTENANT [*with sulky stiffness*] I was prepared for that. It takes a gentleman to understand a gentleman. [*He throws his sword on the table*].

GIUSEPPE [*with sympathetic concern*] Have you been attacked by the Austrians, lieutenant? Dear! dear! dear!

LIEUTENANT [*contemptuously*] Attacked! I could have broken his back between my finger and thumb. I wish I had, now. No: it was by appealing to the better side of my nature: thats what I cant get over. He said he'd never met a man he liked so much as me. He put his handkerchief round my neck because a gnat bit me, and my stock was chafing it. Look! [*He pulls a handkerchief from his stock. Giuseppe takes it and examines it].*

GIUSEPPE [*to Napoleon*] A lady's handkerchief, excellency. [*He smells it*]. Perfumed.

NAPOLEON. Eh? [*He takes it and looks at it attentively*]. Hm! [*He smells it*]. Ha! [*He walks thoughtfully across the room, looking at the handkerchief, which he finally sticks in the breast of his coat*].

LIEUTENANT. Good enough for him, anyhow. I noticed that he had a woman's hands when he touched my neck, with his coaxing fawning ways, the mean effeminate little hound. [*Lowering his voice with thrilling intensity*]. But mark my words, General. If ever—

THE LADY'S VOICE [*outside, as before*] Giuseppe!

LIEUTENANT [*petrified*] What was that?

GIUSEPPE. Only a lady upstairs, lieutenant, calling me.

LIEUTENANT. Lady!

VOICE. Giuseppe, Giuseppe: where a r e you?

LIEUTENANT [*murderously*] Give me that sword. [*He snatches up the sword and draws it*].

GIUSEPPE [*rushing forward and seizing his right arm*] What are you thinking of, lieutenant? It's a lady: dont you hear? It's a woman's voice.

LIEUTENANT. It's h i s voice, I tell you. Let me go. [*He breaks away, and rushes to the edge of the veranda, where he posts himself, sword in hand, watching the door like a cat watching a mousehole*].

It opens; and the Strange Lady steps in. She is tall and extraordinarily graceful, with a delicately intelligent, apprehensive, questioning face: perception in the brow, sensitiveness in the nostrils, character in the chin: all keen, refined, and original. She is very feminine, but by no means weak: the lithe tender figure is hung on a strong frame: the hands and feet, neck and shoulders, are useful vigorous members, of full size in proportion to her stature, which perceptibly exceeds that of Napoleon and the innkeeper, and leaves her at no disadvantage with the lieutenant. Only, her elegance and radiant charm keep the secret of her size and strength. She is not, judging by her dress, an admirer of the latest fashions of the Directory; or perhaps she uses up her old dresses for travelling. At all events she wears no jacket with extravagant lappels, no Greco-Tallien sham chiton, nothing, indeed, that the Princess de Lamballe might not have worn. Her dress of flowered silk is long waisted, with a Watteau pleat behind, but with the paniers reduced to mere rudiments, as she is too tall for them. It is cut low in the neck, where it is eked out by a creamy fichu. She is fair, with golden brown hair and grey eyes.

She enters with the self-possession of a woman accustomed to the privileges of rank and beauty. The innkeeper, who has excellent natural manners, is highly appreciative of her. Napoleon is smitten self-conscious. His color deepens: he becomes stiffer and less at ease than before. She is advancing in an infinitely well bred manner to pay her respects to him when the lieutenant pounces on her and seizes her right wrist. As she recognizes him, she becomes deadly pale. There is no mistaking her expression: a revelation of some fatal error, utterly unexpected, has suddenly appalled her in the midst of tranquillity, security, and victory. The next moment a wave of angry color rushes up from beneath the creamy fichu and drowns her whole face. One can see that she is blushing all over her body. Even the lieutenant, ordinarily incapable of observation, can see a thing when it is painted red for him. Interpreting the blush as the involuntary confession of black deceit confronted with its victim, he addresses her in a loud crow of retributive triumph.

LIEUTENANT. So Ive got you, my lad. So youve disguised yourself, have you? [*In a voice of thunder, releasing her wrist*]. Take off that skirt.

GIUSEPPE [*remonstrating*] Oh, lieutenant!

LADY [*affrighted, but highly indignant at his having dared to touch her*] Gentlemen: I appeal to you. [*To Napoleon*] You, sir, are an officer: a general. You will protect me, will you not?

LIEUTENANT. Never you mind him, General. Leave me to deal with him.

NAPOLEON. With him! With whom, sir? Why do you treat this lady in such a fashion?

LIEUTENANT. Lady! He's a man! the man I shewed my confidence in. [*Raising his sword*]. Here, you—

LADY [*running behind Napoleon and in her agitation clasping to her breast the arm which he extends before her as a fortification*] Oh, thank you, General. Keep him away.

NAPOLEON. Nonsense, sir. This is certainly a lady [*she suddenly drops his arm and blushes again*]; and you are under arrest. Put down your sword, sir, instantly.

LIEUTENANT. General: I tell you he's an Austrian spy. He passed himself off on me as one of General Masséna's staff this afternoon; and now he's passing himself off on you as a woman. Am I to believe my own eyes or not?

LADY. General: it must be my brother. He is on General Masséna's staff. He is very like me.

LIEUTENANT [*his mind giving way*] Do you mean to say that youre not your brother, but your sister? the sister who was so like me? who had my beautiful blue eyes? It's a lie: your eyes are not like mine: theyre exactly like your own.

NAPOLEON [*with contained exasperation*] Lieutenant: will you obey my orders and leave the room, since you are convinced at last that this is no gentleman?

LIEUTENANT. Gentleman! I should think not. No gentleman would have abused my confid—

NAPOLEON [*out of all patience*] That will do, sir: do you hear? Will you leave the room? I order you to leave the room.

LADY. Oh pray let me go instead.

NAPOLEON [*drily*] Excuse me, madam. With all possible respect for your brother, I do not yet understand what an officer on General Masséna's staff wants with my letters. I have some questions to put to you.

THE MAN OF DESTINY

GIUSEPPE [*discreetly*] Come, lieutenant. [*He opens the door*].

LIEUTENANT. I'm off. General: take warning by me: be on your guard against the better side of your nature. [*To the lady*] Madam: my apologies. I thought you were the same person, only of the opposite sex; and that naturally misled me.

LADY [*recovering her good humor*] It was not your fault, was it? I'm so glad youre not angry with me any longer, lieutenant. [*She offers her hand*].

LIEUTENANT [*bending gallantly to kiss it*] Oh, madam, not the lea— [*Checking himself and looking at it*]. You have your brother's hand. And the same sort of ring!

LADY [*sweetly*] We are twins.

LIEUTENANT. That accounts for it. [*He kisses her hand*]. A thousand pardons. I didnt mind about the despatches at all: thats more the General's affair than mine: it was the abuse of my confidence through the better side of my nature. [*Taking his cap, gloves and whip from the table and going*] Youll excuse my leaving you, General, I hope. Very sorry, I'm sure. [*He talks himself out of the room. Giuseppe follows him and shuts the door*].

NAPOLEON [*looking after them with concentrated irritation*] Idiot!

The Strange Lady smiles sympathetically. He comes frowning down the room between the table and the fireplace, all his awkwardness gone now that he is alone with her.

LADY. How can I thank you, General, for your protection?

NAPOLEON [*turning on her suddenly*] My despatches: come! [*He puts out his hand for them*].

LADY. General! [*She involuntarily puts her hands on her fichu as if to protect something there*].

NAPOLEON. You tricked that blockhead out of them. You disguised yourself as a man. I want my despatches.

713

They are there in the bosom of your dress, under your hands.

LADY [*quickly removing her hands*] Oh how unkindly you are speaking to me! [*She takes her handkerchief from her fichu*]. You frighten me. [*She touches her eyes as if to wipe away a tear*].

NAPOLEON. I see you dont know me, madam, or you would save yourself the trouble of pretending to cry.

LADY [*producing an effect of smiling through her tears*] Yes, I do know you. You are the famous General Buonaparte. [*She gives the name a marked Italian pronunciation: Bwawna-parr-te*].

NAPOLEON [*angrily, with the French pronunciation*] Bonaparte, Madam, Bonaparte. The papers, if you please.

LADY. But I assure you— [*He snatches the handkerchief rudely*]. General! [*Indignantly*].

NAPOLEON [*taking the other handkerchief from his breast*] You lent one of your handkerchiefs to my lieutenant when you robbed him. [*He looks at the two handkerchiefs*]. They match one another. [*He smells them*]. The same scent. [*He flings them down on the table*]. I am waiting for my despatches. I shall take them, if necessary, with as little ceremony as I took the handkerchief.

LADY [*in dignified reproof*] General: do you threaten women?

NAPOLEON [*bluntly*] Yes.

LADY [*disconcerted, trying to gain time*] But I dont understand. I—

NAPOLEON. You understand perfectly. You came here because your Austrian employers calculated that I was six leagues away. I am always to be found where my enemies dont expect me. You have walked into the lion's den. Come! you are a brave woman. Be a sensible one: I have no time to waste. The papers. [*He advances a step ominously*].

LADY [*breaking down in the childish rage of impotence, and throwing herself in tears on the chair left beside the table by the lieutenant*] I brave! How little you know! I

714

have spent the day in an agony of fear. I have a pain here from the tightening of my heart at every suspicious look, every threatening movement. Do you think everyone is as brave as you? Oh, why will not you brave people do the brave things? Why do you leave them to us, who have no courage at all? I'm not brave: I shrink from violence: danger makes me miserable.

NAPOLEON [*interested*] Then why have you thrust yourself into danger?

LADY. Because there is no other way: I can trust nobody else. And now it is all useless: all because of you, who have no fear because you have no heart, no feeling, no— [*She breaks off, and throws herself on her knees*]. Ah, General, let me go: let me go without asking any questions. You shall have your despatches and letters: I swear it.

NAPOLEON [*holding out his hand*] Yes: I am waiting for them.

She gasps, daunted by his ruthless promptitude into despair of moving him by cajolery. She looks up perplexedly at him, racking her brains for some device to outwit him. He meets her regard inflexibly.

LADY [*rising at last with a quiet little sigh*] I will get them for you. They are in my room. [*She turns to the door*].

NAPOLEON. I shall accompany you, madam.

LADY [*drawing herself up with a noble air of offended delicacy*] I cannot permit you, General, to enter my chamber.

NAPOLEON. Then you shall stay here, madam, whilst I have your chamber searched for my papers.

LADY [*spitefully, openly giving up her plan*] You may save yourself the trouble. They are not there.

NAPOLEON. No: I have already told you where they are. [*Pointing to her breast*].

LADY [*with pretty piteousness*] General: I only want to keep one little private letter. Only one. Let me have it.

NAPOLEON [*cold and stern*] Is that a reasonable demand, madam?

LADY [*encouraged by his not refusing point-blank*] No; but that is why you must grant it. Are your own demands reasonable? thousands of lives for the sake of your victories, your ambitions, your destiny! And what I ask is such a little thing. And I am only a weak woman, and you a brave man. [*She looks at him with her eyes full of tender pleading, and is about to kneel to him again*].

NAPOLEON [*brusquely*] Get up, get up. [*He turns moodily away and takes a turn across the room, pausing for a moment to say, over his shoulder*] Youre talking nonsense; and you know it. [*She sits down submissively on the couch. When he turns and sees her despair, he feels that his victory is complete, and that he may now indulge in a little play with his victim. He comes back and sits beside her. She looks alarmed and moves a little away from him; but a ray of rallying hope beams from her eye. He begins like a man enjoying some secret joke*]. How do you know I am a brave man?

LADY [*amazed*] You! General Buonaparte. [*Italian pronunciation*].

NAPOLEON. Yes, I, General Bonaparte. [*Emphasizing the French pronunciation*].

LADY. Oh, how can you ask such a question? you! who stood only two days ago at the bridge at Lodi, with the air full of death, fighting a duel with cannons across the river! [*Shuddering*] Oh, you d o brave things.

NAPOLEON. So do you.

LADY. I! [*With a sudden odd thought*] Oh! Are you a coward?

NAPOLEON [*laughing grimly and slapping his knees*] That is the one question you must never ask a soldier. The sergeant asks after the recruit's height, his age, his wind, his limb, but never after his courage.

LADY [*as if she had found it no laughing matter*] Ah, you can laugh at fear. Then you dont know what fear is.

NAPOLEON. Tell me this. Suppose you could have got

that letter by coming to me over the bridge at Lodi the day before yesterday! Suppose there had been no other way, and that this was a sure way—if only you escaped the cannon! [*She shudders and covers her eyes for a moment with her hands*]. Would you have been afraid?

LADY. Oh, horribly afraid, agonizingly afraid. [*She presses her hands on her heart*]. It hurts only to imagine it.

NAPOLEON [*inflexibly*] Would you have come for the despatches?

LADY [*overcome by the imagined horror*] Dont ask me. I m u s t have come.

NAPOLEON. Why?

LADY. Because I must. Because there would have been no other way.

NAPOLEON [*with conviction*] Because you would have wanted my letter enough to bear your fear. [*He rises suddenly, and deliberately poses for an oration*]. There is only one universal passion: fear. Of all the thousand qualities a man may have, the only one you will find as certainly in the youngest drummer boy in my army as in me, is fear. It is fear that makes men fight: it is indifference that makes them run away: fear is the mainspring of war. Fear! I know fear well, better than you, better than any woman. I once saw a regiment of good Swiss soldiers massacred by a mob in Paris because I was afraid to interfere: I felt myself a coward to the tips of my toes as I looked on at it. Seven months ago I revenged my shame by pounding that mob to death with cannon balls. Well, what of that? Has fear ever held a man back from anything he really wanted—or a woman either? Never. Come with me; and I will shew you twenty thousand cowards who will risk death every day for the price of a glass of brandy. And do you think there are no women in the army, braver than the men, though their lives are worth more? Psha! I think nothing of your fear or your bravery. If you had had to come across to me at Lodi, you would not have been afraid: once on the bridge, every other feeling would have gone down before the necessity—the n e c e s s i t y—for making your way to my side and getting what you wanted.

And now, suppose you had done all this! suppose you had come safely out with that letter in your hand, knowing that when the hour came, your fear had tightened, not your heart, but your grip of your own purpose! that it had ceased to be fear, and had become strength, penetration, vigilance, iron resolution! how would you answer then if you were asked whether you were a coward?

LADY [*rising*] Ah, you are a hero, a real hero.

NAPOLEON. Pooh! theres no such thing as a real hero. [*He strolls about the room, making light of her enthusiasm, but by no means displeased with himself for having evoked it*].

LADY. Ah yes, there is. There is a difference between what you call my bravery and yours. You wanted to win the battle of Lodi for yourself and not for anyone else, didnt you?

NAPOLEON. Of course. [*Suddenly recollecting himself*] Stop: no. [*He pulls himself piously together, and says, like a man conducting a religious service*] I am only the servant of the French republic, following humbly in the footsteps of the heroes of classical antiquity. I win battles for humanity: for my country, not for myself.

LADY [*disappointed*] Oh, then you are only a womanish hero after all. [*She sits down again, all her enthusiasm gone*].

NAPOLEON [*greatly astonished*] Womanish!

LADY [*listlessly*] Yes, like me. [*With deep melancholy*] Do you think that if I wanted those despatches only for myself, I dare venture into a battle for them? No: if that were all, I should not have the courage to ask to see you at your hotel, even. My courage is mere slavishness: it is of no use to me for my own purposes. It is only through love, through pity, through the instinct to save and protect someone else, that I can do the things that terrify me.

NAPOLEON [*contemptuously*] Pshaw! [*He turns slight-*

ingly away from her].

LADY. Aha! now you see that I'm not really brave. [*Relapsing into petulant listlessness*] But what right have you to despise me if you only win your battles for others? for your country! through patriotism! That is what I call womanish: it is so like a Frenchman!

NAPOLEON [*furiously*] I am no Frenchman.

LADY [*innocently*] I thought you said you won the battle of Lodi for your country, General Bu— shall I pronounce it in Italian or French?

NAPOLEON. You are presuming on my patience, madam. I was born a French subject, but not in France.

LADY [*affecting a marked access of interest in him*] You were not born a subject at all, I think.

NAPOLEON [*greatly pleased*] Eh? Eh? You think not.

LADY. I am sure of it.

NAPOLEON. Well, well, perhaps not. [*The self-complacency of his assent catches his own ear. He stops short, reddening. Then, composing himself into a solemn attitude, modelled on the heroes of classical antiquity, he takes a high moral tone*]. But we must not live for ourselves alone, little one. Never forget that we should always think of others, and work for others, and lead and govern them for their own good. Self-sacrifice is the foundation of all true nobility of character.

LADY [*again relaxing her attitude with a sigh*] Ah, it is easy to see that you have never tried it, General.

NAPOLEON [*indignantly, forgetting all about Brutus and Scipio*] What do you mean by that speech, madam?

LADY. Havent you noticed that people always exaggerate the value of the things they havent got? The poor think they need nothing but riches to be quite happy and good. Everybody worships truth, purity, unselfishness, for the same reason: because they have no experience of them. Oh, if they only knew!

NAPOLEON [*with angry derision*] If they only knew! Pray do y o u know?

LADY. Yes. I had the misfortune to be born good. [*Glancing up at him for a moment*] And it i s a misfortune, I can tell you, General. I really am truthful and unselfish and all the rest of it; and it's nothing but cowardice; want of character; want of being really, strongly, positively one-self.

NAPOLEON. Ha? [*Turning to her quickily with a flash of strong interest*].

LADY [*earnestly, with rising enthusiasm*] What is the secret of your power? Only that you believe in yourself. You can fight and conquer for yourself and for nobody else. You are not afraid of your own destiny. You teach us what we all might be if we had the will and courage; and that [*suddenly sinking on her knees before him*] is why we all begin to worship you. [*She kisses his hands*].

NAPOLEON [*embarrassed*] Tut tut! Pray rise, madam.

LADY. Do not refuse my homage: it is your right. You will be Emperor of France—

NAPOLEON [*hurriedly*] Take care. Treason!

LADY [*insisting*] Yes, Emperor of France; then of Europe; perhaps of the world. I am only the first subject to swear allegiance. [*Again kissing his hand*] My Emperor!

NAPOLEON [*overcome, raising her*] Pray! pray! No, no: this is folly. Come: be calm, be calm. [*Petting her*] There! there! my girl.

LADY [*struggling with happy tears*] Yes, I know it is an impertinence in me to tell you what you must know far better than I do. But you are not angry with me, are you?

NAPOLEON. Angry! No, no: not a bit, not a bit. Come: you are a very clever and sensible and interesting woman. [*He pats her on the cheek*]. Shall we be friends?

LADY [*enraptured*] Your friend! You will let me be your friend! Oh! [*She offers him both her hands with a radiant smile*]. You see: I shew my confidence in you.

This incautious echo of the lieutenant undoes her. Napoleon starts: his eyes flash: he utters a yell of rage.

NAPOLEON. What!!!

THE MAN OF DESTINY

LADY. Whats the matter?

NAPOLEON. Shew your confidence in me! So that I may shew my confidence in you in return by letting you give me the slip with the despatches, eh? Ah, Dalila, Dalila, you have been trying your tricks on me; and I have been as gross a gull as my jackass of a lieutenant. [*Menacingly*] Come: the despatches. Quick: I am not to be trifled with now.

LADY [*flying round the couch*] General—

NAPOLEON. Quick, I tell you. [*He passes swiftly up the middle of the room and intercepts her as she makes for the vineyard*].

LADY [*at bay, confronting him and giving way to her temper*] You dare address me in that tone.

NAPOLEON. Dare!

LADY. Yes, dare. Who are you that you should presume to speak to me in that coarse way? Oh, the vile, vulgar Corsican adventurer comes out in you very easily.

NAPOLEON [*beside himself*] You she devil! [*Savagely*] Once more, and only once, will you give me those papers or shall I tear them from you?—by force!

LADY. Tear them from me: by force!

As he glares at her like a tiger about to spring, she crosses her arms on her breast in the attitude of a martyr. The gesture and pose instantly awaken his theatrical instinct: he forgets his rage in the desire to shew her that in acting, too, she has met her match. He keeps her a moment in suspense; then suddenly clears up his countenance; puts his hands behind him with provoking coolness; looks at her up and down a couple of times; takes a pinch of snuff; wipes his fingers carefully and puts up his handkerchief, her heroic pose becoming more and more ridiculous all the time.

NAPOLEON [*at last*] Well?

LADY [*disconcerted, but with her arms still crossed devotedly*] Well: what are you going to do?

NAPOLEON. Spoil your attitude.

LADY. You brute! [*Abandoning the attitude, she comes*

721

THE MAN OF DESTINY

to the end of the couch, where she turns with her back to it, leaning against it and facing him with her hands behind her].

NAPOLEON. Ah, thats better. Now listen to me. I like you. Whats more, I value your respect.

LADY. You value what you have not got, then.

NAPOLEON. I shall have it presently. Now attend to me. Suppose I were to allow myself to be abashed by the respect due to your sex, your beauty, your heroism and all the rest of it! Suppose I, with nothing but such sentimental stuff to stand between these muscles of mine and those papers which you have about you, and which I want and mean to have! suppose I, with the prize within my grasp, were to falter and sneak away with my hands empty; or, what would be worse, cover up my weakness by playing the magnanimous hero, and sparing you the violence I dared not use! would you not despise me from the depths of your woman's soul? Would any woman be such a fool? Well, Bonaparte can rise to the situation and act like a woman when it is necessary. Do you understand?

The lady, without speaking, stands upright, and takes a packet of papers from her bosom. For a moment she has an intense impulse to dash them in his face. But her good breeding cuts her off from any vulgar method of relief. She hands them to him politely, only averting her head. The moment he takes them, she hurries across to the other side of the room; sits down; and covers her face with her hands.

NAPOLEON [*gloating over the papers*] Aha! Thats right. Thats right. [*Before he opens them, he looks at her and says*] Excuse me. [*He sees that she is hiding her face*]. Very angry with me, eh? [*He unties the packet, the seal of which is already broken, and puts it on the table to examine its contents*].

LADY [*quietly, taking down her hands and shewing that she is not crying, but only thinking*] No. You were right. But I am sorry for you.

722

NAPOLEON [*pausing in the act of taking the uppermost paper from the packet*] Sorry for me! Why?

LADY. I am going to see you lose your honor.

NAPOLEON. Hm! Nothing worse than that? [*He takes up the paper*].

LADY. And your happiness.

NAPOLEON. Happiness! Happiness is the most tedious thing in the world to me. Should I be what I am if I cared for happiness? Anything else?

LADY. Nothing.

NAPOLEON. Good.

LADY. Except that you will cut a very foolish figure in the eyes of France.

NAPOLEON [*quickly*] What? [*The hand unfolding the paper involuntarily stops. The lady looks at him enigmatically, in tranquil silence. He throws the letter down and breaks out into a torrent of scolding*]. What do you mean? Eh? Are you at your tricks again? Do you think I dont know what these papers contain? I'll tell you. First, my information as to Beaulieu's retreat. There are only two things he can do—leather-brained idiot that he is!—shut himself up in Mantua or violate the neutrality of Venice by taking Peschiera. You are one of old Leatherbrain's spies: he has discovered that he has been betrayed, and has sent you to intercept the information at all hazards. As if that could save him from m e, the old fool! The other papers are only my private letters from Paris, of which you know nothing.

LADY [*prompt and businesslike*] General: let us make a fair division. Take the information your spies have sent you about the Austrian army; and give me the Paris correspondence. That will content me.

NAPOLEON [*his breath taken away by the coolness of the proposal*] A fair di— [*He gasps*]. It seems to me, madam, that you have come to regard my letters as your own property, of which I am trying to rob you.

LADY [*earnestly*] No: on my honor I ask for no letter

723

of yours: not a word that has been written by you or to you. That packet contains a stolen letter: a letter written by a woman to a man: a man not her husband: a letter that means disgrace, infamy—

NAPOLEON. A love letter?

LADY [*bitter-sweetly*] What else but a love letter could stir up so much hate?

NAPOLEON. Why is it sent to me? To put the husband in my power, eh?

LADY. No, no: it can be of no use to you: I swear that it will cost you nothing to give it to me. It has been sent to you out of sheer malice: solely to injure the woman who wrote it.

NAPOLEON. Then why not send it to her husband instead of to me?

LADY [*completely taken aback*] Oh! [*Sinking back into the chair*] I—I dont know. [*She breaks down*].

NAPOLEON. Aha! I thought so: a little romance to get the papers back. Per Bacco, I cant help admiring you. I wish I could lie like that. It would save me a great deal of trouble.

LADY [*wringing her hands*] Oh, how *I* wish I really had told you some lie! You would have believed me then. The truth is the one thing that nobody will believe.

NAPOLEON [*with coarse familiarity, treating her as if she were a vivandière*] Capital! Capital! [*He puts his hands behind him on the table, and lifts himself on to it, sitting with his arms akimbo and his legs wide apart*]. Come: I am a true Corsican in my love for stories. But I could tell them better than you if I set my mind to it. Next time you are asked why a letter compromising a wife should not be sent to her husband, answer simply that the husband wouldnt read it. Do you suppose, you goose, that a man wants to be compelled by public opinion to make a scene, to fight a duel, to break up his household, to injure his career by a scandal, when he can avoid it all by taking care not to know?

724

THE MAN OF DESTINY

LADY [*revolted*] Suppose that packet contained a letter about your own wife?

NAPOLEON [*offended, coming off the table*] You are impertinent, madam.

LADY [*humbly*] I beg your pardon. Cæsar's wife is above suspicion.

NAPOLEON [*with a deliberate assumption of superiority*] You have committed an indiscretion. I pardon you. In future, do not permit yourself to introduce real persons in your romances.

LADY [*politely ignoring a speech which is to her only a breach of good manners*] General: there really is a woman's letter there. [*Pointing to the packet*] Give it to me.

NAPOLEON [*with brute conciseness*] Why?

LADY. She is an old friend: we were at school together. She has written to me imploring me to prevent the letter falling into your hands.

NAPOLEON. Why has it been sent to me?

LADY. Because it compromises the director Barras.

NAPOLEON [*frowning, evidently startled*] Barras! [*Haughtily*] Take care, madam. The director Barras is my attached personal friend.

LADY [*nodding placidly*] Yes. You became friends through your wife.

NAPOLEON. Again! Have I not forbidden you to speak of my wife? [*She keeps looking curiously at him, taking no account of the rebuke. More and more irritated, he drops his haughty manner, of which he is himself somewhat impatient, and says suspiciously, lowering his voice*] Who is this woman with whom you sympathize so deeply?

LADY. Oh, General! How could I tell you that?

NAPOLEON [*ill humoredly, beginning to walk about again in angry perplexity*] Ay, ay: stand by one another. You are all the same, you women.

LADY [*indignantly*] We are not all the same, any more than you are. Do you think that if *I* loved another man, I should pretend to go on loving my husband, or be afraid

725

to tell him or all the world? But this woman is not made that way. She governs men by cheating them; and they like it, and let her govern them. [*She turns her back to him in disdain*].

NAPOLEON [*not attending to her*] Barras? Barras? [*Very threateningly, his face darkening*] Take care. Take care: do you hear? You may go too far.

LADY [*innocently turning her face to him*] Whats the matter?

NAPOLEON. What are you hinting at? Who is this woman?

LADY [*meeting his angry searching gaze with tranquil indifference as she sits looking up at him*] A vain, silly, extravagant creature, with a very able and ambitious husband who knows her through and through: knows that she has lied to him about her age, her income, her social position, about everything that silly women lie about: knows that she is incapable of fidelity to any principle or any person; and yet can not help loving her—can not help his man's instinct to make use of her for his own advancement with Barras.

NAPOLEON [*in a stealthy coldly furious whisper*] This is your revenge, you she cat, for having had to give me the letters.

LADY. Nonsense! Or do you mean that y o u are that sort of man?

NAPOLEON [*exasperated, clasps his hands behind him, his fingers twitching, and says, as he walks irritably away from her to the fireplace*] This woman will drive me out of my senses. [*To her*] Begone.

LADY [*seated immovably*] Not without that letter.

NAPOLEON. Begone, I tell you. [*Walking from the fireplace to the vineyard and back to the table*] You shall have no letter. I dont like you. Youre a detestable woman, and as ugly as Satan. I dont choose to be pestered by strange women. Be off. [*He turns his back on her. In quiet amusement, she leans her cheek on her hand and laughs at him.*

726

He turns again, angrily mocking her] Ha! ha! ha! What are you laughing at?

LADY. At you, General. I have often seen persons of your sex getting into a pet and behaving like children; but I never saw a really great man do it before.

NAPOLEON [*brutally, flinging the words in her face*] Psha! Flattery! Flattery! Coarse, impudent flattery!

LADY [*springing up with a bright flush in her cheeks*] Oh, you are too bad. Keep your letters. Read the story of your own dishonor in them; and much good may they do you. Goodbye. [*She goes indignantly towards the inner door*].

NAPOLEON. My own——! Stop. Come back. Come back, I order you. [*She proudly disregards his savagely peremptory tone and continues on her way to the door. He rushes at her; seizes her by the arm; and drags her back*]. Now, what do you mean? Explain. Explain. I tell you, or—— [*Threatening her. She looks at him with unflinching defiance*]. Rrrr! you obstinate devil, you. [*Throwing her arm away*] Why cant you answer a civil question?

LADY [*deeply offended by his violence*] Why do you ask me? You have the explanation.

NAPOLEON. Where?

LADY [*pointing to the letters on the table*] There. You have only to read it.

He snatches the packet up; hesitates; looks at her suspiciously; and throws it down again.

NAPOLEON. You seem to have forgotten your solicitude for the honor of your old friend.

LADY. I do not think she runs any risk now. She does not quite understand her husband.

NAPOLEON. I am to read the letter, then? [*He stretches out his hand as if to take up the packet again, with his eye on her*].

LADY. I do not see how you can very well avoid doing so now. [*He instantly withdraws his hand*] Oh, dont be afraid. You will find many interesting things in it.

THE MAN OF DESTINY

NAPOLEON. For instance?

LADY. For instance, a duel with Barras, a domestic scene, a broken household, a public scandal, a checked career, all sorts of things.

NAPOLEON. Hm! [*He looks at her; takes up the packet and looks at it, pursing his lips and balancing it in his hand; looks at her again; passes the packet into his left hand and puts it behind his back, raising his right to scratch the back of his head as he turns and goes up to the edge of the vineyard, where he stands for a moment looking out into the vines, deep in thought. The Lady watches him in silence, somewhat slightingly. Suddenly he turns and comes back again, full of force and decision*]. I grant your request, madam. Your courage and resolution deserve to succeed. Take the letters for which you have fought so well; and remember henceforth that you found the vile vulgar Corsican adventurer as generous to the vanquished after the battle as he was resolute in the face of the enemy before it. [*He offers her the packet*].

LADY [*without taking it, looking hard at him*] What are you at now, I wonder? [*He dashes the packet furiously to the floor*]. Aha! Ive spoilt t h a t attitude, I think. [*She makes him a pretty mocking curtsey*].

NAPOLEON [*snatching it up again*] Will you take the letters and begone? [*Advancing and thrusting them upon her*].

LADY [*escaping round the table*] No: I dont want your letters.

NAPOLEON. Ten minutes ago, nothing else would satisfy you.

LADY [*keeping the table carefully between them*] Ten minutes ago you had not insulted me beyond all bearing.

NAPOLEON. I— [*swallowing his spleen*] I apologize.

LADY [*coolly*] Thanks. [*With forced politeness he offers her the packet across the table. She retreats a step out of its reach and says*] But dont you want to know whether the Austrians are at Mantua or Peschiera?

728

NAPOLEON. I have already told you that I can conquer my enemies without the aid of spies, madam.

LADY. And the letter? dont you want to read that?

NAPOLEON. You have said that it is not addressed to me. I am not in the habit of reading other people's letters. [*He again offers the packet*].

LADY. In that case there can be no objection to your keeping it. All I wanted was to prevent your reading it. [*Cheerfully*] G o o d afternoon, General. [*She turns coolly towards the inner door*].

NAPOLEON [*angrily flinging the packet on the couch*] Heaven grant me patience! [*He goes determinedly to the door, and places himself before it*]. Have you any sense of personal danger? Or are you one of those women who like to be beaten black and blue?

LADY. Thank you, General: I have no doubt the sensation is very voluptuous; but I had rather not. I simply want to go home: thats all. I was wicked enough to steal your despatches; but you have got them back; and you have forgiven me, because [*delicately reproducing his rhetorical cadence*] you are as generous to the vanquished after the battle as you are resolute in the face of the enemy before it. Wont you say goodbye to me? [*She offers her hand sweetly*].

NAPOLEON [*repulsing the advance with a gesture of concentrated rage, and opening the door to call fiercely*] Giuseppe! [*Louder*] Giuseppe! [*He bangs the door to, and comes to the middle of the room. The Lady goes a little way into the vineyard to avoid him*].

GIUSEPPE [*appearing at the door*] Excellency?

NAPOLEON. Where is that fool?

GIUSEPPE. He has had a good dinner, according to your instructions, excellency, and is now doing me the honor to gamble with me to pass the time.

NAPOLEON. Send him here. B r i n g him here. Come with him. [*Giuseppe, with unruffled readiness, hurries off. Napoleon turns curtly to the lady, saying*] I must trouble

729

THE MAN OF DESTINY

you to remain some moments longer, madam. [*He comes to the couch*].

She comes from the vineyard along the opposite side of the room to the sideboard, and posts herself there, leaning against it, watching him. He takes the packet from the couch and deliberately buttons it carefully into his breast pocket, looking at her meanwhile with an expression which suggests that she will soon find out the meaning of his proceedings, and will not like it. Nothing more is said until the lieutenant arrives followed by Giuseppe, who stands modestly in attendance at the table. The lieutenant, without cap, sword or gloves, and much improved in temper and spirits by his meal, chooses the lady's side of the room, and waits, much at his ease, for Napoleon to begin.

NAPOLEON. Lieutenant.

LIEUTENANT [*encouragingly*] General.

NAPOLEON. I cannot persuade this lady to give me much information; but there can be no doubt that the man who tricked you out of your charge was, as she admitted to you, her brother.

LIEUTENANT [*triumphantly*] What did I tell you, General! What did I tell you!

NAPOLEON. You must find that man. Your honor is at stake; and the fate of the campaign, the destiny of France, of Europe, of humanity, perhaps, may depend on the information those despatches contain.

LIEUTENANT. Yes, I suppose they really are rather serious. [*As if this had hardly occurred to him before*].

NAPOLEON [*energetically*] They are so serious, sir, that if you do not recover them, you will be degraded in the presence of your regiment.

LIEUTENANT. Whew! The regiment wont like that, I can tell you.

NAPOLEON. Personally I am sorry for you. I would willingly hush up the affair if it were possible. But I shall be called to account for not acting on the despatches. I shall have to prove to all the world that I never received them.

730

THE MAN OF DESTINY

no matter what the consequences may be to you. I am sorry; but you see that I cannot help myself.

LIEUTENANT [*goodnaturedly*] Oh, dont take it to heart, General: it's really very good of you. Never mind what happens to me: I shall scrape through somehow; and we'll beat the Austrians for you, despatches or no despatches. I hope you wont insist on my starting off on a wild goose chase after the fellow now. I havnt a notion where to look for him.

GIUSEPPE [*deferentially*] You forget, Lieutenant: he has your horse.

LIEUTENANT [*starting*] I forgot that. [*Resolutely*] I'll go after him, General: I'll find that horse if it's alive anywhere in Italy. And I shant forget the despatches: never fear. Giuseppe: go and saddle one of those mangy old post-horses of yours while I get my cap and sword and things. Quick march. Off with you. [*Bustling him*].

GIUSEPPE. Instantly, Lieutenant, instantly. [*He disappears in the vineyard, where the light is now reddening with the sunset*].

LIEUTENANT [*looking about him on his way to the inner door*] By the way, General, did I give you my sword or did I not? Oh, I remember now. [*Fretfully*] It's all that nonsense about putting a man under arrest: one never knows where to find— [*He talks himself out of the room*].

LADY [*still at the sideboard*] What does all this mean, General?

NAPOLEON. He will not find your brother.

LADY. Of course not. Theres no such person.

NAPOLEON. The despatches will be irrecoverably lost.

LADY. Nonsense! They are inside your coat.

NAPOLEON. You will find it hard, I think, to prove that wild statement. [*The lady starts. He adds, with clinching emphasis*] Those papers are lost.

LADY [*anxiously, advancing to the corner of the table*] And that unfortunate young man's career will be sacrificed?

NAPOLEON. H i s career! The fellow is not worth the

731

gunpowder it would cost to have him shot. [*He turns contemptuously and goes to the hearth, where he stands with his back to her*].

LADY [*wistfully*] You are very hard. Men and women are nothing to you but things to be used, even if they are broken in the use.

NAPOLEON [*turning on her*] Which of us has broken this fellow? I or you? Who tricked him out of the despatches? Did you think of his career then?

LADY [*conscience-stricken*] Oh, I never thought of that. It was wicked of me; but I couldnt help it, could I? How else could I have got the papers? [*Supplicating*] General: you will save him from disgrace.

NAPOLEON [*laughing sourly*] Save him yourself, since you are so clever: it was you who ruined him. [*With savage intensity*] I h a t e a bad soldier.

He goes out determinedly through the vineyard. She follows him a few steps with an appealing gesture, but is interrupted by the return of the lieutenant, gloved and capped, with his sword on, ready for the road. He is crossing to the outer door when she intercepts him.

LADY. Lieutenant.

LIEUTENANT [*importantly*] You mustnt delay me, you know. Duty, madam, duty.

LADY [*imploringly*] Oh, sir, what are you going to do to my poor brother?

LIEUTENANT. Are you very fond of him?

LADY. I should die if anything happened to him. You must spare him. [*The lieutenant shakes his head gloomily*]. Yes, yes: you must: you shall: he is not fit to die. Listen to me. If I tell you where to find him—if I undertake to place him in your hands a prisoner, to be delivered up by you to General Bonaparte—will you promise me on your honor as an officer and a gentleman not to fight with him or treat him unkindly in any way?

LIEUTENANT. But suppose he attacks me. He has my pistols.

732

LADY. He is too great a coward.

LIEUTENANT. I dont feel so sure about that. He's capable of anything.

LADY. If he attacks you, or resists you in any way, I release you from your promise.

LIEUTENANT. My promise! I didnt mean to promise. Look here: youre as bad as he is: youve taken an advantage of me through the better side of my nature. What about my horse?

LADY. It is part of the bargain that you are to have your horse and pistols back.

LIEUTENANT. Honor bright?

LADY. Honor bright. [*She offers her hand*].

LIEUTENANT [*taking it and holding it*] All right: I'll be as gentle as a lamb with him. His sister's a very pretty woman. [*He attempts to kiss her*].

LADY [*slipping away from her*] Oh, Lieutenant! You forget: your career is at stake—the destiny of Europe—of humanity.

LIEUTENANT. Oh, bother the destiny of humanity! [*Making for her*] Only a kiss.

LADY [*retreating round the table*] Not until you have regained your honor as an officer. Remember: you have not captured my brother yet.

LIEUTENANT [*seductively*] Youll tell me where he is, wont you?

LADY. I have only to send him a certain signal; and he will be here in quarter of an hour.

LIEUTENANT. He's not far off, then.

LADY. No: quite close. Wait here for him: when he gets my message he will come here at once and surrender himself to you. You understand?

LIEUTENANT [*intellectually overtaxed*] Well, it's a little complicated; but I daresay it will be all right.

LADY. And now, whilst youre waiting, dont you think you had better make terms with the General?

LIEUTENANT. Oh, look here: this is getting frightfully

complicated. What terms?

LADY. Make him promise that if you catch my brother he will consider that you have cleared your character as a soldier. He will promise anything you ask on that condition.

LIEUTENANT. Thats not a bad idea. Thank you: I think I'll try it.

LADY. Do. And mind, above all things, dont let him see how clever you are.

LIEUTENANT. I understand. He'd be jealous.

LADY. Dont tell him anything except that you are resolved to capture my brother or perish in the attempt. He wont believe you. Then you will produce my brother—

LIEUTENANT [*interrupting as he masters the plot*] And have the laugh at him! I say: what a jolly clever woman you are! [*Shouting*] Giuseppe!

LADY. Sh! Not a word to Giuseppe about me. [*She puts her finger on her lips. He does the same. They look at one another warningly. Then, with a ravishing smile, she changes the gesture into wafting him a kiss, and runs out through the inner door. Electrified, he bursts into a volley of chuckles*].

Giuseppe comes back by the outer door.

GIUSEPPE. The horse is ready, Lieutenant.

LIEUTENANT. I'm not going just yet. Go and find the General and tell him I want to speak to him.

GIUSEPPE [*shaking his head*] That will never do, Lieutenant.

LIEUTENANT. Why not?

GIUSEPPE. In this wicked world a general may send for a lieutenant; but a lieutenant must not send for a general.

LIEUTENANT. Oh, you think he wouldnt like it. Well, perhaps youre right: one has to be awfully particular about that sort of thing now we're a republic.

Napoleon reappears, advancing from the vineyard, buttoning the breast of his coat, pale and full of gnawing thoughts.

734

THE MAN OF DESTINY

GIUSEPPE [*unconscious of Napoleon's approach*] Quite true, Lieutenant, quite true. You are all like innkeepers now in France: you have to be polite to everybody.

NAPOLEON [*putting his hand on Giuseppe's shoulder*] And that destroys the whole value of politeness, eh?

LIEUTENANT. The very man I wanted! See here, General: suppose I catch that fellow for you!

NAPOLEON [*with ironical gravity*] You will not catch him, my friend.

LIEUTENANT. Aha! you think so; but youll see. Just wait. Only, if I do catch him and hand him over to you, will you cry quits? Will you drop all this about degrading me in the presence of my regiment? Not that *I* mind, you know; but still no regiment likes to have all the other regiments laughing at it.

NAPOLEON [*a cold ray of humor striking pallidly across his gloom*] What shall we do with this officer, Giuseppe? Everything he says is wrong.

GIUSEPPE [*promptly*] Make him a general, excellency; and then everything he says will be right.

LIEUTENANT [*crowing*] Haw-aw! [*He throws himself ecstatically on the couch to enjoy the joke*].

NAPOLEON [*laughing and pinching Giuseppe's ear*] You are thrown away in this inn, Giuseppe. [*He sits down and places Giuseppe before him like a schoolmaster with a pupil*]. Shall I take you away with me and make a man of you?

GIUSEPPE [*shaking his head rapidly and repeatedly*] No no no no no no no. All my life long people have wanted to make a man of me. When I was a boy, our good priest wanted to make a man of me by teaching me to read and write. Then the organist at Melegnano wanted to make a man of me by teaching me to read music. The recruiting sergeant would have made a man of me if I had been a few inches taller. But it always meant making me work; and I am too lazy for that, thank Heaven! So I taught myself to cook and became an innkeeper; and now I keep servants to

THE MAN OF DESTINY

do the work, and have nothing to do myself except talk, which suits me perfectly.

NAPOLEON [*looking at him thoughtfully*] You are satisfied?

GIUSEPPE [*with cheerful conviction*] Quite, excellency.

NAPOLEON. And you have no devouring devil inside you who must be fed with action and victory: gorged with them night and day: who makes you pay, with the sweat of your brain and body, weeks of Herculean toil for ten minutes of enjoyment: who is at once your slave and your tyrant, your genius and your doom: who brings you a crown in one hand and the oar of a galley slave in the other: who shews you all the kingdoms of the earth and offers to make you their master on condition that you become their servant! have you nothing of that in you?

GIUSEPPE. Nothing of it! Oh, I assure you, excellency, m y devouring devil is far worse than that. He offers me no crowns and kingdoms: he expects to get everything for nothing: sausages! omelettes! grapes! cheese! polenta! wine! three times a day, excellency: nothing less will content him.

LIEUTENANT. Come: drop it. Giuseppe: youre making me feel hungry again.

Giuseppe, with an apologetic shrug, retires from the conversation.

NAPOLEON [*turning to the lieutenant with sardonic politeness*] I hope *I* have not been making you feel ambitious.

LIEUTENANT. Not at all: I dont fly so high. Besides, I'm better as I am: men like me are wanted in the army just now. The fact is, the Revolution was all very well for civilians; but it wont work in the army. You know what soldiers are, General: they w i l l have men of family for their officers. A subaltern must be a gentleman, because he's so much in contact with the men. But a general, or even a colonel, may be any sort of riff-raff if he understands his job well enough. A lieutenant is a gentleman: all the rest

736

is chance. Why, who do you suppose won the battle of Lodi?
I'll tell you. My horse did.

NAPOLEON. [*rising*] Your folly is carrying you too far,
sir. Take care.

LIEUTENANT. Not a bit of it. You remember all that red-
hot cannonade across the river: the Austrians blazing away
at you to keep you from crossing, and you blazing away at
them to keep them from setting the bridge on fire? Did you
notice where I was then?

NAPOLEON. I am sorry. I am afraid I was rather occupied at the moment.

GIUSEPPE [*with eager admiration*] They say you
jumped off your horse and worked the big guns with your
own hands, General.

LIEUTENANT. That was a mistake: an officer should
never let himself down to the level of his men. [*Napoleon
looks at him dangerously, and begins to walk tigerishly to
and fro*]. But you might have been firing away at the Austrians still if we cavalry fellows hadnt found the ford and
got across and turned old Beaulieu's flank for you. You
know you didnt dare give the order to charge the bridge
until you saw us on the other side. Consequently, I say that
whoever found that ford won the battle of Lodi. Well, who
found it? I was the first man to cross; and I know. It was
my horse that found it. [*With conviction, as he rises from
the couch*] That horse is the true conqueror of the Austrians.

NAPOLEON [*passionately*] You idiot: I'll have you shot
for losing those despatches: I'll have you blown from the
mouth of a cannon: nothing less could make any impression
on you. [*Baying at him*] Do you hear? Do you understand?

*A French officer enters unobserved, carrying his
sheathed sabre in his hand.*

LIEUTENANT [*unabashed*] If I dont capture him, General. Remember the if.

NAPOLEON. If!! Ass: there is no such man.

THE OFFICER [*suddenly stepping between them and*

THE MAN OF DESTINY

speaking in the unmistakable voice of the Strange Lady]
Lieutenant: I am your prisoner. [*She offers him her sabre*].

Napoleon gazes at her for a moment thunderstruck; then seizes her by the wrist and drags her roughly to him, looking closely and fiercely at her to satisfy himself as to her identity; for it now begins to darken rapidly into night, the red glow over the vineyard giving way to clear starlight].

NAPOLEON. Pah! [*He flings her hand away with an exclamation of disgust, and turns his back on her with his hand in his breast, his brow lowering and his toes twitching*].

LIEUTENANT [*triumphantly, taking the sabre*] No such man! eh, General? [*To the Lady*] I say: wheres my horse?

LADY. Safe at Borghetto, waiting for you, Lieutenant.

NAPOLEON [*turning on them*] Where are the despatches?

LADY. You would never guess. They are in the most unlikely place in the world. Did you meet my sister here, any of you?

LIEUTENANT. Yes. Very nice woman. She's wonderfully like you; but of course she's better-looking.

LADY [*mysteriously*] Well, do you know that she is a witch?

GIUSEPPE [*in terror, crossing himself*] Oh, no, no, no. It is not safe to jest about such things. I cannot have it in my house, excellency.

LIEUTENANT. Yes, drop it. Youre my prisoner, you know. Of course I dont believe in any such rubbish; but still it's not a proper subject for joking.

LADY. But this is very serious. My sister has bewitched the General. [*Giuseppe and the lieutenant recoil from Napoleon*]. General: open your coat: you will find the despatches in the breast of it. [*She puts her hand quickly on his breast*]. Yes: there they are: I can feel them. Eh? [*She looks up into his face half coaxingly, half mockingly*]. Will you allow me, General? [*She takes a button as if to unbutton his coat, and pauses for permission*].

738

NAPOLEON [*inscrutably*] If you dare.

LADY. Thank you. [*She opens his coat and takes out the despatches*]. There! [*To Giuseppe, shewing him the despatches*] See!

GIUSEPPE [*flying to the outer door*] No, in heaven's name! Theyre bewitched.

LADY [*turning to the lieutenant*] Here, Lieutenant: you are not afraid of them.

LIEUTENANT [*retreating*] Keep off. [*Seizing the hilt of the sabre*] Keep off, I tell you.

LADY [*to Napoleon*] They belong to you, General. Take them.

GIUSEPPE. Dont touch them, excellency. Have nothing to do with them.

LIEUTENANT. Be careful, General: be careful.

GIUSEPPE. Burn them. And burn the witch too.

LADY [*to Napoleon*] Shall I burn them?

NAPOLEON [*thoughtfully*] Yes, burn them. Giuseppe: go and fetch a light.

GIUSEPPE [*trembling and stammering*] Do you mean go alone? in the dark? with a witch in the house?

NAPOLEON. Psha! Youre a poltroon. [*To the lieutenant*] Oblige me by going, Lieutenant.

LIEUTENANT [*remonstrating*] Oh, I say, General! No, look here, you know: nobody can say I'm a coward after Lodi. But to ask me to go into the dark by myself without a candle after such an awful conversation is a little too much. How would you like to do it yourself?

NAPOLEON [*irritably*] You refuse to obey my order?

LIEUTENANT [*resolutely*] Yes I do. It's not reasonable. But I'll tell you what I'll do. If Giuseppe goes, I'll go with him and protect him.

NAPOLEON [*to Giuseppe*] There! will that satisfy you? Be off, both of you.

GIUSEPPE [*humbly, his lips trembling*] W-willingly, your excellency. [*He goes reluctantly towards the inner door*]. Heaven protect me! [*To the lieutenant*] After you,

Lieutenant.

LIEUTENANT. Youd better go first: I dont know the way.

GIUSEPPE. You cant miss it. Besides [*imploringly, laying his hand on his sleeve*] I am only a poor innkeeper: you are a man of family.

LIEUTENANT. Theres something in that. Here: you neednt be in such a fright. Take my arm. [*Giuseppe does so*]. Thats the way. [*They go out, arm in arm*].

It is now starry night. The lady throws the packet on the table and seats herself at her ease on the couch, enjoying the sensation of freedom from petticoats].

LADY. Well, General: Ive beaten you.

NAPOLEON [*walking about*] You are guilty of indelicacy: of unwomanliness. Is that costume proper?

LADY. It seems to me much the same as yours.

NAPOLEON. Psha! I blush for you.

LADY [*naïvely*] Yes: soldiers blush so easily. [*He growls and turns away. She looks mischievously at him, balancing the despatches in her hand*]. Wouldnt you like to read these before theyre burnt, General? You must be dying with curiosity. Take a peep. [*She throws the packet on the table, and turns her face away from it*]. I wont look.

NAPOLEON. I have no curiosity whatever, madam. But since you are evidently burning to read them, I give you leave to do so.

LADY. Oh, Ive read them already.

NAPOLEON [*starting*] What!

LADY. I read them the first thing after I rode away on that poor lieutenant's horse. So you see I know whats in them; and you dont.

NAPOLEON. Excuse me. I read them when I was out there in the vineyard ten minutes ago.

LADY Oh! [*jumping up*] Oh, General: Ive not beaten you after all. I do admire you so. [*He laughs and pats her cheek*]. This time, really and truly without shamming, I do you homage. [*Kissing his hand*].

NAPOLEON [*quickly withdrawing it*] Brr! Dont do that. No more witchcraft.

LADY. I want to say something to you; only you would misunderstand it.

NAPOLEON. Need that stop you?

LADY. Well, it is this. I adore a man who is not afraid to be mean and selfish.

NAPOLEON [*indignantly*] I am neither mean nor selfish.

LADY. Oh, you dont appreciate yourself. Besides, I dont really mean meanness and selfishness.

NAPOLEON. Thank you. I thought perhaps you did.

LADY. Well, of course I d o. But what I mean is a certain strong simplicity about you.

NAPOLEON. Thats better.

LADY. You didnt want to read the letters; but you were curious about what was in them. So you went into the garden and read them when no one was looking, and then came back and pretended you hadnt. Thats the meanest thing I ever knew any man do; but it exactly fulfilled your purpose; and so you werent a bit afraid or ashamed to do it.

NAPOLEON [*abruptly*] Where did you pick up all these vulgar scruples? this [*with contemptuous emphasis*] conscience of yours? I took you for a lady: an aristocrat. Was your grandfather a shopkeeper, pray?

LADY. No: he was an Englishman.

NAPOLEON. That accounts for it. The English are a nation of shopkeepers. Now I understand why youve beaten me.

LADY. Oh, I havnt beaten you. And I'm not English.

NAPOLEON. Yes you are: English to the backbone. Listen to me: I will explain the English to you.

LADY [*eagerly*] Do. [*With a lively air of anticipating an intellectual treat, she sits down on the couch and composes herself to listen to him. Secure of his audience, he at once nerves himself for a performance. He considers a little before he begins; so as to fix her attention by a moment of suspense. His style is at first modelled on Talma's in Cor-*

neille's Cinna; but it is somewhat lost in the darkness, and Talma presently gives way to Napoleon, the voice coming through the gloom with startling intensity].

NAPOLEON. There are three sorts of people in the world: the low people, the middle people, and the high people. The low people and the high people are alike in one thing: they have no scruples, no morality. The low are beneath morality, the high above it. I am not afraid of either of them; for the low are unscrupulous without knowledge, so that they make an idol of me; whilst the high are unscrupulous without purpose, so that they go down before my will. Look you: I shall go over all the mobs and all the courts of Europe as a plough goes over a field. It is the middle people who are dangerous: they have both knowledge and purpose. But they, too, have their weak point. They are full of scruples: chained hand and foot by their morality and respectability.

LADY. Then you will beat the English; for all shopkeepers are middle people.

NAPOLEON. No, because the English are a race apart. No Englishman is too low to have scruples: no Englishman is high enough to be free from their tyranny. But every Englishman is born with a certain miraculous power that makes him master of the world. When he wants a thing, he never tells himself that he wants it. He waits patiently until there comes into his mind, no one knows how, a burning conviction that it is his moral and religious duty to conquer those who possess the thing he wants. Then he becomes irresistible. Like the aristocrat, he does what pleases him and grabs what he covets: like the shopkeeper, he pursues his purpose with the industry and steadfastness that come from strong religious conviction and deep sense of moral responsibility. He is never at a loss for an effective moral attitude. As the great champion of freedom and national independence, he conquers and annexes half the world, and calls it Colonization. When he wants a new market for his adulterated Manchester goods, he sends a

742

missionary to teach the natives the Gospel of Peace. The natives kill the missionary: he flies to arms in defence of Christianity; fights for it; conquers for it; and takes the market as a reward from heaven. In defence of his island shores, he puts a chaplain on board his ship; nails a flag with a cross on it to his top-gallant mast; and sails to the ends of the earth, sinking, burning, and destroying all who dispute the empire of the seas with him. He boasts that a slave is free the moment his foot touches British soil; and he sells the children of his poor at six years of age to work under the lash in his factories for sixteen hours a day. He makes two revolutions, and then declares war on our one in the name of law and order. There is nothing so bad or so good that you will not find Englishmen doing it; but you will never find an Englishman in the wrong. He does everything on principle. He fights you on patriotic principles; he robs you on business principles; he enslaves you on imperial principles; he bullies you on manly principles; he supports his king on loyal principles and cuts off his king's head on republican principles. His watchword is always Duty; and he never forgets that the nation which lets its duty get on the opposite side to its interest is lost. He—

LADY. W-w-w-w-w-wh! Do stop a moment. I want to know how you make me out to be English at this rate.

NAPOLEON [*dropping his rhetorical style*] It's plain enough. You wanted some letters that belonged to me. You have spent the morning in stealing them: yes, stealing them, by highway robbery. And you have spent the afternoon in putting me in the wrong about them: in assuming that it was *I* who wanted to steal y o u r letters: in explaining that it all came about through my meanness and selfishness, and your goodness, your devotion, your self-sacrifice. Thats English.

LADY. Nonsense! I am sure I am not a bit English. The English are a very stupid people.

NAPOLEON. Yes, too stupid sometimes to know when theyre beaten. But I grant that your brains are not English. You see, though your grandfather was an Englishman, your grandmother was—what? A Frenchwoman?

LADY. Oh no. An Irishwoman.

NAPOLEON [*quickly*] Irish! [*Thoughtfully*] Yes: I forgot the Irish. An English army led by an Irish general: that might be a match for a French army led by an Italian general. [*He pauses, and adds, half jestingly, half moodily*] At all events, y o u have beaten me; and what beats a man first will beat him last. [*He goes meditatively into the moonlit vineyard and looks up*].

She steals out after him. She ventures to rest her hand on his shoulder, overcome by the beauty of the night and emboldened by its obscurity].

LADY [*softly*] What are you looking at?

NAPOLEON [*pointing up*] My star.

LADY. You believe in that?

NAPOLEON. I do.

They look at it for a moment, she leaning a little on his shoulder.

LADY. Do you know that the English say that a man's star is not complete without a woman's garter?

NAPOLEON [*scandalized: abruptly shaking her off and coming back into the room*] Pah! the hypocrites! If the French said that, how they would hold up their hands in pious horror! [*He goes to the inner door and holds it open, shouting*] Hallo! Giuseppe! Wheres that light, man? [*He comes between the table and the sideboard, and moves the second chair to the table, beside his own*]. We have still to burn the letter. [*He takes up the packet*].

Giuseppe comes back, pale and still trembling, carrying in one hand a branched candlestick with a couple of candles alight, and a broad snuffers tray in the other.

GIUSEPPE [*piteously, as he places the light on the table*] Excellency: what were you looking up at just now? Out there! [*He points across his shoulder to the vineyard, but is afraid to look round*].

NAPOLEON [*unfolding the packet*] What is that to you?

THE MAN OF DESTINY

GIUSEPPE. Because the witch is gone: vanished; and no one saw her go out.

LADY [*coming behind him from the vineyard*] We were watching her riding up to the moon on your broomstick, Giuseppe. You will never see her again.

GIUSEPPE. Gesu Maria! [*He crosses himself and hurries out*].

NAPOLEON [*throwing down the letters in a heap on the table*] Now! [*He sits down at the table in the chair which he has just placed*].

LADY. Yes; but you know you have THE letter in your pocket. [*He smiles; takes a letter from his pocket; and tosses it on top of the heap. She holds it up and looks at him, saying*] About Cæsar's wife.

NAPOLEON. Cæsar's wife is above suspicion. Burn it.

LADY [*taking up the snuffers and holding the letter to the candle flame with it*] I wonder would Cæsar's wife be above suspicion if she saw us here together!

NAPOLEON [*echoing her, with his elbows on the table and his cheeks on his hands, looking at the letter*] I wonder!

The Strange Lady puts the letter down alight on the snuffers tray, and sits down beside Napoleon, in the same attitude, elbows on table, cheeks on hands, watching it burn. When it is burnt, they simultaneously turn their eyes and look at one another. The curtain steals down and hides them.

ANDROCLES AND THE LION

A FABLE PLAY

PREFACE ON THE PROSPECTS OF
CHRISTIANITY
WHY NOT GIVE CHRISTIANITY A TRIAL?

THE question seems a hopeless one after 2000 years of resolute adherence to the old cry of "Not this man, but Barabbas." Yet it is beginning to look as if Barabbas was a failure, in spite of his strong right hand, his victories, his empires, his millions of money, and his moralities and churches and political constitutions. "This man" has not been a failure yet; for nobody has ever been sane enough to try his way. But he has had one quaint triumph. Barabbas has stolen his name and taken his cross as a standard. There is a sort of compliment in that. There is even a sort of loyalty in it, like that of the brigand who breaks every law and yet claims to be a patriotic subject of the king who makes them. We have always had a curious feeling that though we crucified Christ on a stick, he somehow managed to get hold of the right end of it, and that if we were better men we might try his plan. There have been one or two grotesque attempts at it by inadequate people, such as the Kingdom of God in Munster, which was ended by a crucifixion so much more atrocious than the one on Calvary that the bishop who took the part of Annas went home and died of horror. But responsible people have never made such attempts. The moneyed, respectable, capable world has been steadily anti-Christian and Barabbasque since the crucifixion; and the specific doctrine of Jesus has not in all that time been put into political or general social practice. I am no more a Christian than Pilate was, or you, gentle reader; and yet, like Pilate, I greatly prefer Jesus to Annas and Caiaphas; and I am ready to admit that after contemplating the world and human nature for nearly sixty years, I see no way out of the world's misery but the way which would have been found by Christ's will if he had undertaken the work of a modern practical statesman.

Pray do not at this early point lose patience with me and shut the book. I assure you I am as sceptical and scientific

ANDROCLES AND THE LION

and modern a thinker as you will find anywhere. I grant you I know a great deal more about economics and politics than Jesus did, and can do things he could not do. I am by all Barabbasque standards a person of much better character and standing, and greater practical sense. I have no sympathy with vagabonds and talkers who try to reform society by taking men away from their regular productive work and making vagabonds and talkers of them too; and if I had been Pilate I should have recognized as plainly as he the necessity for suppressing attacks on the existing social order, however corrupt that order might be, by people with no knowledge of government and no power to construct political machinery to carry out their views, acting on the very dangerous delusion that the end of the world was at hand. I make no defence of such Christians as Savonarola and John of Leyden: they were scuttling the ship before they had learned how to build a raft; and it became necessary to throw them overboard to save the crew. I say this to set myself right with respectable society; but I must still insist that if Jesus could have worked out the practical problems of a Communist constitution, an admitted obligation to deal with crime without revenge or punishment, and a full assumption by humanity of divine responsibilities, he would have conferred an incalculable benefit on mankind, because these distinctive demands of his are now turning out to be good sense and sound economics.

I say distinctive, because his common humanity and his subjection to time and space (that is, to the Syrian life of his period) involved his belief in many things, true and false, that in no way distinguish him from other Syrians of that time. But such common beliefs do not constitute specific Christianity any more than wearing a beard, working in a carpenter's shop, or believing that the earth is flat and that the stars could drop on it from heaven like hailstones. Christianity interests practical statesmen now because of the doctrines that distinguished Christ from the Jews and the Barabbasques generally, including ourselves.

750

WHY JESUS MORE THAN ANOTHER?

I do not imply, however, that these doctrines were peculiar to Christ. A doctrine peculiar to one man would be only a craze, unless its comprehension depended on a development of human faculty so rare that only one exceptionally gifted man possessed it. But even in this case it would be useless, because incapable of spreading. Christianity is a step in moral evolution which is independent of any individual preacher. If Jesus had never existed (and that he ever existed in any other sense than that in which Shakespear's Hamlet existed has been vigorously questioned) Tolstoy would have thought and taught and quarrelled with the Greek Church all the same. Their creed has been fragmentarily practised to a considerable extent in spite of the fact that the laws of all countries treat it, in effect, as criminal. Many of its advocates have been militant atheists. But for some reason the imagination of white mankind has picked out Jesus of Nazareth as *the* Christ, and attributed all the Christian doctrines to him; and as it is the doctrine and not the man that matters, and, as, besides, one symbol is as good as another provided everyone attaches the same meaning to it, I raise, for the moment, no question as to how far the gospels are original, and how far they consist of Greek and Chinese interpolations. The record that Jesus said certain things is not invalidated by a demonstration that Confucius said them before him. Those who claim a literal divine paternity for him cannot be silenced by the discovery that the same claim was made for Alexander and Augustus. And I am not just now concerned with the credibility of the gospels as records of fact; for I am not acting as a detective, but turning our modern lights on to certain ideas and doctrines in them which disentangle themselves from the rest because they are flatly contrary to common practice, common sense, and common belief, and yet have, in the teeth of dogged incredulity and recalcitrance, produced an irresistible impression that Christ, though rejected by his posterity as an unpractical dreamer, and executed by his contemporaries as a dangerous anarchist and blasphemous madman, was greater than his judges.

WAS JESUS A COWARD?

I know quite well that this impression of superiority is not produced on everyone, even of those who profess extreme susceptibility to it. Setting aside the huge mass of inculcated Christ-worship which has no real significance because it has no intelligence, there is, among people who are really free to think for themselves on the subject, a great deal of hearty dislike of Jesus and of contempt for his failure to save himself and overcome his enemies by personal bravery and cunning as Mahomet did. I have heard this feeling expressed far more impatiently by persons brought up in England as Christians than by Mahometans, who are, like their prophet, very civil to Jesus, and allow him a place in their esteem and veneration at least as high as we accord to John the Baptist. But this British bulldog contempt is founded on a complete misconception of his reasons for submitting voluntarily to an ordeal of torment and death. The modern Secularist is often so determined to regard Jesus as a man like himself and nothing more, that he slips unconsciously into the error of assuming that Jesus shared that view. But it is quite clear from the New Testament writers (the chief authorities for believing that Jesus ever existed) that Jesus at the time of his death believed himself to be the Christ, a divine personage. It is therefore absurd to criticize his conduct before Pilate as if he were Colonel Roosevelt or Admiral von Tirpitz or even Mahomet. Whether you accept his belief in his divinity as fully as Simon Peter did, or reject it as a delusion which led him to submit to torture and sacrifice his life without resistance in the conviction that he would presently rise again in glory, you are equally bound to admit that, far from behaving like a coward or a sheep, he shewed considerable physical fortitude in going through a cruel ordeal against which he could have defended himself as effectually as he cleared the money-changers out of the temple. "Gentle Jesus, meek and mild"

PREFACE

is a snivelling modern invention, with no warrant in the gospels. St Matthew would as soon have thought of applying such adjectives to Judas Maccabeus as to Jesus; and even St Luke, who makes Jesus polite and gracious, does not make him meek. The picture of him as an English curate of the farcical comedy type, too meek to fight a policeman, and everybody's butt, may be useful in the nursery to soften children; but that such a figure could ever have become a centre of the world's attention is too absurd for discussion: grown men and women may speak kindly of a harmless creature who utters amiable sentiments and is a helpless nincompoop when he is called on to defend them; but they will not follow him, nor do what he tells them, because they do not wish to share his defeat and disgrace.

WAS JESUS A MARTYR?

It is important therefore that we should clear our minds of the notion that Jesus died, as some of us are in the habit of declaring, for his social and political opinions. There have been many martyrs to those opinions; but he was not one of them, nor, as his words shew, did he see any more sense in martyrdom than Galileo did. He was executed by the Jews for the blasphemy of claiming to be a God; and Pilate, to whom this was a mere piece of superstitious nonsense, let them execute him as the cheapest way of keeping them quiet, on the formal plea that he had committed treason against Rome by saying that he was the King of the Jews. He was not falsely accused, nor denied full opportunities of defending himself. The proceedings were quite straightforward and regular; and Pilate, to whom the appeal lay, favored him and despised his judges, and was evidently willing enough to be conciliated. But instead of denying the charge, Jesus repeated the offence. He knew what he was doing: he had alienated numbers of his own disciples and been stoned in the streets for doing it before. He was not lying: he believed literally what he said. The horror of the High Priest was perfectly natural: he was a Primate confronted with a heterodox street preacher uttering what

753

seemed to him an appalling and impudent blasphemy. The fact that the blasphemy was to Jesus a simple statement of fact, and that it has since been accepted as such by all western nations, does not invalidate the proceedings, nor give us the right to regard Annas and Caiaphas as worse men than the Archbishop of Canterbury and the Head Master of Eton. If Jesus had been indicted in a modern court, he would have been examined by two doctors; found to be obsessed by a delusion; declared incapable of pleading; and sent to an asylum: that is the whole difference. But please note that when a man is charged before a modern tribunal (to take a case that happened the other day) of having asserted and maintained that he was an officer returned from the front to receive the Victoria Cross at the hands of the King, although he was in fact a mechanic, nobody thinks of treating him as afflicted with a delusion. He is punished for false pretences, because his assertion is credible and therefore misleading. Just so, the claim to divinity made by Jesus was to the High Priest, who looked forward to the coming of a Messiah, one that might conceivably have been true, and might therefore have misled the people in a very dangerous way. That was why he treated Jesus as an impostor and a blasphemer where we should have treated him as a madman.

THE GOSPELS WITHOUT PREJUDICE

All this will become clear if we read the gospels without prejudice. When I was young it was impossible to read them without fantastic confusion of thought. The confusion was so utterly confounded that it was called the proper spirit to read the Bible in. Jesus was a baby; and he was older than creation. He was a man who could be persecuted, stoned, scourged, and killed; and he was a god, immortal and all-powerful, able to raise the dead and call millions of angels to his aid. It was a sin to doubt either view of him: that is, it was a sin to reason about him; and the end was that you did not reason about him, and read about him only when you were compelled. When you heard the gospel

754

stories read in church, or learnt them from painters and poets, you came out with an impression of their contents that would have astonished a Chinaman who had read the story without prepossession. Even sceptics who were specially on their guard, put the Bible in the dock, and read the gospels with the object of detecting discrepancies in the four narratives to shew that the writers were as subject to error as the writers of yesterday's newspaper.

All this has changed greatly within two generations. Today the Bible is so little read that the language of the Authorized Version is rapidly becoming obsolete; so that even in the United States, where the old tradition of the verbal infallibility of "the book of books" lingers more strongly than anywhere else except perhaps in Ulster, re-translations into modern English have been introduced perforce to save its bare intelligibility. It is quite easy today to find cultivated persons who have never read the New Testament, and on whom therefore it is possible to try the experiment of asking them to read the gospels and state what they have gathered as to the history and views and character of Christ.

THE GOSPELS NOW UNINTELLIGIBLE TO NOVICES

But it will not do to read the gospels with a mind furnished only for the reception of, say, a biography of Goethe. You will not make sense of them, nor even be able without impatient weariness to persevere in the task of going steadily through them, unless you know something of the history of the human imagination as applied to religion. Not long ago I asked a writer of distinguished intellectual competence whether he had made a study of the gospels since his childhood. His reply was that he had lately tried, but "found it all such nonsense that I could not stick it." As I do not want to send anyone to the gospels with this result, I had better here give a brief exposition of how much of the history of religion is needed to make the gospels and the conduct and ultimate fate of Jesus intelligible and interesting.

WORLDLINESS OF THE MAJORITY

The first common mistake to get rid of is that mankind consists of a great mass of religious people and a few eccentric atheists. It consists of a huge mass of worldly people, and a small percentage of persons deeply interested in religion and concerned about their own souls and other people's; and this section consists mostly of those who are passionately affirming the established religion and those who are passionately attacking it, the genuine philosophers being very few. Thus you never have a nation of millions of Wesleys and one Tom Paine. You have a million Mr Worldly Wisemans, one Wesley, with his small congregation, and one Tom Paine, with *his* smaller congregation. The passionately religious are a people apart; and if they were not hopelessly outnumbered by the worldly, they would turn the world upside down, as St Paul was reproached, quite justly, for wanting to do. Few people can number among their personal acquaintances a single atheist or a single Plymouth Brother. Unless a religious turn in ourselves has led us to seek the little Societies to which these rare birds belong, we pass our lives among people who, whatever creeds they may repeat, and in whatever temples they may avouch their respectability and wear their Sunday clothes, have robust consciences, and hunger and thirst, not for righteousness, but for rich feeding and comfort and social position and attractive mates and ease and pleasure and respect and consideration: in short, for love and money. To these people one morality is as good as another provided they are used to it and can put up with its restrictions without unhappiness; and in the maintenance of this morality they will fight and punish and coerce without scruple. They may not be the salt of the earth, these Philistines; but they are the substance of civilization; and they save society from ruin by criminals and conquerors as well as by Savonarolas and Knipperdollings. And as they know, very sensibly, that a little religion is good for children and serves morality, keeping the poor in goodhumor or in awe by promising rewards in heaven or threatening torments in hell, they encourage the religious people up to a certain point: for instance, if Savonarola only tells the ladies of Florence that they ought to tear off their jewels and finery and sacrifice them to God, they offer him a cardinal's hat, and praise him as a saint; but if he induces them to actually do it, they burn him as a public nuisance.

RELIGION OF THE MINORITY. SALVATIONISM

The religion of the tolerated religious minority has always been essentially the same religion: that is why its changes of name and form have made so little difference. That is why, also, a nation so civilized as the English can convert negroes to their faith with great ease, but cannot convert Mahometans or Jews. The negro finds in civilized Salvationism an unspeakably more comforting version of his crude creed; but neither Saracen nor Jew sees any advantage in it over his own version. The Crusader was surprised to find the Saracen quite as religious and moral as himself, and rather more than less civilized. The Latin Christian has nothing to offer the Greek Christian that Greek Christianity has not already provided. They are all, at root, Salvationists.

Let us trace this religion of Salvation from its beginnings. So many things that man does not himself contrive or desire are always happening: death, plagues, tempests, blights, floods, sunrise and sunset, growths and harvests and decay, and Kant's two wonders of the starry heavens above us and the moral law within us, that we conclude that somebody must be doing it all, or that somebody is doing the good and somebody else doing the evil, or that armies of invisible persons, beneficent and malevolent, are doing it; hence you postulate gods and devils, angels and demons. You propitiate these powers with presents, called sacrifices, and flatteries, called praises. Then the Kantian moral law within you makes you conceive your god as a judge; and straightway you try to corrupt him, also with presents and

757

flatteries. This seems shocking to us; but our objection to it is quite a recent development: no longer ago than Shakespear's time it was thought quite natural that litigants should give presents to human judges; and the buying off of divine wrath by actual money payments to priests, or, in the reformed churches which discountenance this, by subscriptions to charities and church building and the like, is still in full swing. Its practical disadvantage is that though it makes matters very easy for the rich, it cuts off the poor from all hope of divine favor. And this quickens the moral criticism of the poor to such an extent, that they soon find the moral law within them revolting against the idea of buying off the deity with gold and gifts, though they are still quite ready to buy him off with the paper money of praise and professions of repentance. Accordingly, you will find that though a religion may last unchanged for many centuries in primitive communities where the conditions of life leave no room for poverty and riches, and the process of propitiating the supernatural powers is as well within the means of the least of the members as within those of the headman, yet when commercial civilization arrives, and capitalism divides the people into a few rich and a great many so poor that they can barely live, a movement for religious reform will arise among the poor, and will be essentially a movement for cheap or entirely gratuitous salvation.

To understand what the poor mean by propitiation, we must examine for a moment what they mean by justice.

THE DIFFERENCE BEWEEN ATONEMENT AND PUNISHMENT

The primitive idea of justice is partly legalized revenge and partly expiation by sacrifice. It works out from both sides in the notion that two blacks make a white, and that when a wrong has been done, it should be paid for by an equivalent suffering. It seems to the Philistine majority a matter of course that this compensating suffering should be inflicted on the wrongdoer for the sake of its deterrent effect on other would-be wrongdoers; but a moment's re-

758

flection will shew that this utilitarian application corrupts the whole transaction. For example, the shedding of innocent blood cannot be balanced by the shedding of guilty blood. Sacrificing a criminal to propitiate God for the murder of one of his righteous servants is like sacrificing a mangy sheep or an ox with the rinderpest: it calls down divine wrath instead of appeasing it. In doing it we offer God as a sacrifice the gratification of our own revenge and the protection of our own lives without cost to ourselves; and cost to ourselves is the essence of sacrifice and expiation. However much the Philistines have succeeded in confusing these things in practice, they are to the Salvationist sense distinct and even contrary. The Baronet's cousin in Dickens's novel, who, perplexed by the failure of the police to discover the murderer of the baronet's solicitor, said "Far better hang wrong fellow than no fellow," was not only expressing a very common sentiment, but trembling on the brink of the rarer Salvationist opinion that it is much better to hang the wrong fellow: that, in fact, the wrong fellow is the right fellow to hang.

The point is a cardinal one, because until we grasp it not only does historical Christianity remain unintelligible to us, but those who do not care a rap about historical Christianity may be led into the mistake of supposing that if we discard revenge, and treat murderers exactly as God treated Cain: that is, exempt them from punishment by putting a brand on them as unworthy to be sacrificed, and let them face the world as best they can with that brand on them, we should get rid both of punishment and sacrifice. It would not at all follow: on the contrary, the feeling that there must be an expiation of the murder might quite possibly lead to our putting some innocent person—the more innocent the better—to a cruel death to balance the account with divine justice.

SALVATION AT FIRST A CLASS PRIVILEGE; AND THE REMEDY

Thus, even when the poor decide that the method of

purchasing salvation by offering rams and goats or bringing gold to the altar must be wrong because they cannot afford it, we still do not feel "saved" without a sacrifice and a victim. In vain do we try to substitute mystical rites that cost nothing, such as circumcision, or, as a substitute for that, baptism. Our sense of justice still demands an expiation, a sacrifice, a sufferer for our sins. And this leaves the poor man still in his old difficulty; for if it was impossible for him to procure rams and goats and shekels, how much more impossible is it for him to find a neighbor who will voluntarily suffer for his sins: one who will say cheerfully "You have committed a murder. Well, never mind: I am willing to be hanged for it in your stead"?

Our imagination must come to our rescue. Why not, instead of driving ourselves to despair by insisting on a separate atonement by a separate redeemer for every sin, have one great atonement and one great redeemer to compound for the sins of the world once for all? Nothing easier, nothing cheaper. The yoke is easy, the burden light. All you have to do when the redeemer is once found (or invented by the imagination) is to believe in the efficacy of the transaction, and you are saved. The rams and goats cease to bleed; the altars which ask for expensive gifts and continually renewed sacrifices are torn down; and the Church of the single redeemer and the single atonement rises on the ruins of the old temples, and becomes a single Church of the Christ.

RETROSPECTIVE ATONEMENT; AND THE EXPECTATION OF THE REDEEMER

But this does not happen at once. Between the old costly religion of the rich and the new gratuitous religion of the poor there comes an interregnum in which the redeemer, though conceived by the human imagination, is not yet found. He is awaited and expected under the names of the Christ, the Messiah, Baldur the Beautiful, or what not; but he has not yet come. Yet the sinners are not therefore in despair. It is true that they cannot say, as we say, "The

Christ has come, and has redeemed us"; but they can say "The Christ will come, and will redeem us," which, as the atonement is conceived as retrospective, is equally consoling. There are periods when nations are seething with this expectation and crying aloud with prophecy of the Redeemer through their poets. To feel that atmosphere we have only to take up the Bible and read Isaiah at one end of such a period and Luke and John at the other.

COMPLETION OF THE SCHEME BY LUTHER AND CALVIN

We now see our religion as a quaint but quite intelligible evolution from crude attempts to propitiate the destructive forces of Nature among savages to a subtle theology with a costly ritual of sacrifice possible only to the rich as a luxury, and finally to the religion of Luther and Calvin. And it must be said for the earlier forms that they involved very real sacrifices. The sacrifice was not always vicarious, and is not yet universally so. In India men pay with their own skins, torturing themselves hideously to attain holiness. In the west, saints amazed the world with their austerities and self-scourgings and confessions and vigils. But Luther delivered us from all that. His reformation was a triumph of imagination and a triumph of cheapness. It brought you complete salvation and asked you for nothing but faith. Luther did not know what he was doing in the scientific sociological way in which we know it; but his instinct served him better than knowledge could have done; for it was instinct rather than theological casuistry that made him hold so resolutely to Justification by Faith as the trump card by which he should beat the Pope, or, as he would have put it, the sign in which he should conquer. He may be said to have abolished the charge for admission to heaven. Paul had advocated this; but Luther and Calvin did it.

JOHN BARLEYCORN

There is yet another page in the history of religion which must be conned and digested before the career of Jesus can be fully understood. People who can read long books will find it in Frazer's Golden Bough. Simpler folk will find it in the peasant's song of John Barleycorn, now made accessible to our drawing room amateurs in the admirable collections of Somersetshire Folk Songs by Mr Cecil Sharp. From Frazer's *magnum opus* you will learn how the same primitive logic which makes the Englishman believe today that by eating a beefsteak he can acquire the strength and courage of the bull, and to hold that belief in the face of the most ignominious defeats by vegetarian wrestlers and racers and bicyclists, led the first men who conceived God as capable of incarnation to believe that they could acquire a spark of his divinity by eating his flesh and drinking his blood. And from the song of John Barleycorn you may learn how the miracle of the seed, the growth, and the harvest, still the most wonderful of all the miracles and as inexplicable as ever, taught the primitive husbandman, and, as we must now affirm, taught him quite rightly, that God is in the seed, and that God is immortal. And thus it became the test of Godhead that nothing that you could do to it could kill it, and that when you buried it, it would rise again in renewed life and beauty and give mankind eternal life on condition that it was eaten and drunk, and again slain and buried, to rise again for ever and ever. You may, and indeed must, use John Barleycorn "right barbarouslee," cutting him "off at knee" with your scythes, scourging him with your flails, burying him in the earth; and he will not resist you nor reproach you, but will rise again in golden beauty amidst a great burst of sunshine and bird music, and save you and renew your life. And from the interweaving of these two traditions with the craving for the Redeemer, you at last get the conviction that when the Redeemer comes he will be immortal; he will give us his body to eat and his blood to drink; and he will prove his divinity by suffering a barbarous death without resistance or reproach, and rise from the dead and return to the earth in glory as the giver of life eternal.

LOOKING FOR THE END OF THE WORLD

Yet another persistent belief has beset the imagination

of the religious ever since religion spread among the poor, or, rather, ever since commercial civilization produced a hopelessly poor class cut off from enjoyment in this world. That belief is that the end of this world is at hand, and that it will presently pass away and be replaced by a kingdom of happiness, justice, and bliss in which the rich and the oppressors and the unjust shall have no share. We are all familiar with this expectation: many of us cherish some pious relative who sees in every great calamity a sign of the approaching end. Warning pamphlets are in constant circulation: advertisements are put in the papers and paid for by those who are convinced, and who are horrified at the indifference of the irreligious to the approaching doom. And revivalist preachers, now as in the days of John the Baptist, seldom fail to warn their flocks to watch and pray, as the great day will steal upon them like a thief in the night, and cannot be long deferred in a world so wicked. This belief also associates itself with Barleycorn's second coming; so that the two events become identified at last.

There is the other and more artificial side of this belief, on which it is an inculcated dread. The ruler who appeals to the prospect of heaven to console the poor and keep them from insurrection also curbs the vicious by threatening them with hell. In the Koran we find Mahomet driven more and more to this expedient of government; and experience confirms his evident belief that it is impossible to govern without it in certain phases of civilization. We shall see later on that it gives a powerful attraction to the belief in a Redeemer, since it adds to remorse of conscience, which hardened men bear very lightly, a definite dread of hideous and eternal torture.

THE HONOR OF DIVINE PARENTAGE

One more tradition must be noted. The consummation of praise for a king is to declare that he is the son of no earthly father, but of a god. His mother goes into the temple of Apollo, and Apollo comes to her in the shape of a serpent, or the like. The Roman emperors, following the example of

763

Augustus, claimed the title of God. Illogically, such divine kings insist a good deal on their royal human ancestors. Alexander, claiming to be the son of Apollo, is equally determined to be the son of Philip. As the gospels stand, St Matthew and St Luke give genealogies (the two are different) establishing the descent of Jesus through Joseph from the royal house of David, and yet declare that not Joseph but the Holy Ghost was the father of Jesus. It is therefore now held that the story of the Holy Ghost is a later interpolation borrowed from the Greek and Roman imperial tradition. But experience shews that simultaneous faith in the descent from David and the conception by the Holy Ghost is possible. Such double beliefs are entertained by the human mind without uneasiness or consciousness of the contradiction involved. Many instances might be given: a familiar one to my generation being that of the Tichborne claimant, whose attempt to pass himself off as a baronet was supported by an association of laborers on the ground that the Tichborne family, in resisting it, were trying to do a laborer out of his rights. It is quite possible that Matthew and Luke may have been unconscious of the contradiction: indeed the interpolation theory does not remove the difficulty, as the interpolators themselves must have been unconscious of it. A better ground for suspecting interpolation is that St Paul knew nothing of the divine birth, and taught that Jesus came into the world at his birth as the son of Joseph, but rose from the dead after three days as the son of God. Here again, few notice the discrepancy: the three views are accepted simultaneously without intellectual discomfort. We can provisionally entertain half a dozen contradictory versions of an event if we feel either that it does not greatly matter, or that there is a category attainable in which the contradictions are reconciled.

But that is not the present point. All that need be noted here is that the legend of divine birth was sure to be attached sooner or later to very eminent persons in Roman imperial times, and that modern theologians, far from discrediting it, have very logically affirmed the miraculous conception not only of Jesus but of his mother.

With no more scholarly equipment than a knowledge of these habits of the human imagination, anyone may now read the four gospels without bewilderment, and without the contemptuous incredulity which spoils the temper of many modern atheists, or the senseless credulity which sometimes makes pious people force us to shove them aside in emergencies as impracticable lunatics when they ask us to meet violence and injustice with dumb submission in the belief that the strange demeanor of Jesus before Pilate was meant as an example of normal human conduct. Let us admit that without the proper clues the gospels are, to a modern educated person, nonsensical and incredible, whilst the apostles are unreadable. But with the clues, they are fairly plain sailing. Jesus becomes an intelligible and consistent person. His reasons for going "like a lamb to the slaughter" instead of saving himself as Mahomet did, become quite clear. The narrative becomes as credible as any other historical narrative of its period.

MATTHEW

THE ANNUNCIATION:
THE MASSACRE: THE FLIGHT

Let us begin with the gospel of Matthew, bearing in mind that it does not profess to be the evidence of an eyewitness. It is a chronicle, founded, like other chronicles, on such evidence and records as the chronicler could get hold of. The only one of the evangelists who professes to give first-hand evidence as an eyewitness naturally takes care to say so; and the fact that Matthew makes no such pretension, and writes throughout as a chronicler, makes it clear that he is telling the story of Jesus as Holinshed told the story of Macbeth, except that, for a reason to be given later on, he must have collected his material and completed his book within the lifetime of persons contemporary with Jesus. Allowance must also be made for the fact that the gospel is

written in the Greek language, whilst the first-hand traditions and the actual utterances of Jesus must have been in
Aramic, the dialect of Palestine. These distinctions are important, as you will find if you read Holinshed or Froissart
and then read Benvenuto Cellini. You do not blame Holinshed or Froissart for believing and repeating the things they
had read or been told, though you cannot always believe
these things yourself. But when Cellini tells you that he saw
this or did that, and you find it impossible to believe him,
you lose patience with him, and are disposed to doubt everything in his autobiography. Do not forget, then, that Matthew is Holinshed and not Benvenuto. The very first pages
of his narrative will put your attitude to the test.

Matthew tells us that the mother of Jesus was betrothed
to a man of royal pedigree named Joseph, who was rich
enough to live in a house in Bethlehem to which kings could
bring gifts of gold without provoking any comment. An
angel announces to Joseph that Jesus is the son of the Holy
Ghost, and that he must not accuse her of infidelity because
of her bearing a son of which he is not the father; but this
episode disappears from the subsequent narrative: there is
no record of its having been told to Jesus, nor any indication
of his having any knowledge of it. The narrative, in fact,
proceeds in all respects as if the annunciation formed no
part of it.

Herod the Tetrarch, believing that a child has been born
who will destroy him, orders all the male children to be
slaughtered; and Jesus escapes by the flight of his parents
into Egypt, whence they return to Nazareth when the danger is over. Here it is necessary to anticipate a little by saying
that none of the other evangelists accepts this story, as none
of them except John, who throws over Matthew altogether,
shares his craze for treating history and biography as mere
records of the fulfilment of ancient Jewish prophecies. This
craze no doubt led him to seek for some legend bearing out
Hosea's "Out of Egypt have I called my son," and Jere-
miah's Rachel weeping for her children: in fact, he says so.

PREFACE

Nothing that interests us nowadays turns on the credibility of the massacre of the innocents and the flight into Egypt. We may forget them, and proceed to the important part of the narrative, which skips at once to the manhood of Jesus.

JOHN THE BAPTIST

At this moment, a Salvationist prophet named John is stirring the people very strongly. John has declared that the rite of circumcision is insufficient as a dedication of the individual to God, and has substituted the rite of baptism. To us, who are accustomed to baptism as a matter of course, and to whom circumcision is a rather ridiculous foreign practice of no consequence, the sensational effect of such a heresy as this on the Jews is not apparent: it seems to us as natural that John should have baptized people as that the rector of our village should do so. But, as St Paul found to his cost later on, the discarding of circumcision for baptism was to the Jews as startling a heresy as the discarding of transubstantiation in the Mass was to the Catholics of the XVI century.

JESUS JOINS THE BAPTISTS

Jesus entered as a man of thirty (Luke says) into the religious life of his time by going to John the Baptist and demanding baptism from him, much as certain well-to-do young gentlemen forty years ago "joined the Socialists." As far as established Jewry was concerned, he burnt his boats by this action, and cut himself off from the routine of wealth, respectability, and orthodoxy. He then began preaching John's gospel, which, apart from the heresy of baptism, the value of which lay in its bringing the Gentiles (that is, the uncircumcized) within the pale of salvation, was a call to the people to repent of their sins, as the kingdom of heaven was at hand. Luke adds that he also preached the communism of charity; told the surveyors of taxes not to over-assess the taxpayers; and advised soldiers to be content with their wages and not to be violent or lay false accusations. There is no record of John going beyond this.

THE SAVAGE JOHN AND THE CIVILIZED JESUS

Jesus went beyond it very rapidly, according to Matthew. Though, like John, he became an itinerant preacher, he departed widely from John's manner of life. John went into the wilderness, not into the synagogues; and his baptismal font was the river Jordan. He was an ascetic, clothed in skins and living on locusts and wild honey, practising a savage austerity. He courted martyrdom, and met it at the hands of Herod. Jesus saw no merit either in asceticism or martyrdom. In contrast to John he was essentially a highly-civilized, cultivated person. According to Luke, he pointed out the contrast himself, chaffing the Jews for complaining that John must be possessed by the devil because he was a teetotaller and vegetarian, whilst, because Jesus was neither one nor the other, they reviled him as a gluttonous man and a winebibber, the friend of the officials and their mistresses. He told straitlaced disciples that they would have trouble enough from other people without making any for themselves, and that they should avoid martyrdom and enjoy themselves whilst they had the chance. "When they persecute you in this city," he says, "flee into the next." He preaches in the synagogues and in the open air indifferently, just as they come. He repeatedly says, "I desire mercy and not sacrifice," meaning evidently to clear himself of the inveterate superstition that suffering is gratifying to God. "Be not, as the Pharisees, of a sad countenance," he says. He is convivial, feasting with Roman officials and sinners. He is careless of his person, and is remonstrated with for not washing his hands before sitting down to table. The followers of John the Baptist, who fast, and who expect to find the Christians greater ascetics than themselves, are disappointed at finding that Jesus and his twelve friends do not fast; and Jesus tells them that they should rejoice in him instead of being melancholy. He is jocular, and tells them they will all have as much fasting as they want soon enough, whether they like it or not. He is not afraid of disease, and dines with

768

a leper. A woman, apparently to protect him against infection, pours a costly unguent on his head, and is rebuked because what it cost might have been given to the poor. He poohpoohs that lowspirited view, and says, as he said when he was reproached for not fasting, that the poor are always there to be helped, but that he is not there to be anointed always, implying that you should never lose a chance of being happy when there is so much misery in the world. He breaks the Sabbath; is impatient of conventionality when it is uncomfortable or obstructive; and outrages the feelings of the Jews by breaches of it. He is apt to accuse people who feel that way of hypocrisy. Like the late Samuel Butler, he regards disease as a department of sin, and on curing a lame man, says "Thy sins are forgiven" instead of "Arise and walk," subsequently maintaining, when the Scribes reproach him for assuming power to forgive sin as well as to cure disease, that the two come to the same thing. He has no modest affectations, and claims to be greater than Solomon or Jonah. When reproached, as Bunyan was, for resorting to the art of fiction when teaching in parables, he justifies himself on the ground that art is the only way in which the people can be taught. He is, in short, what we should call an artist and a Bohemian in his manner of life.

JESUS NOT A PROSELYTIST

A point of considerable practical importance today is that he expressly repudiates the idea that forms of religion, once rooted, can be weeded out and replanted with the flowers of a foreign faith. "If you try to root up the tares you will root up the wheat as well." Our proselytizing missionary enterprises are thus flatly contrary to his advice; and their results appear to bear him out in his view that if you convert a man brought up in another creed, you inevitably demoralize him. He acts on this view himself, and does not convert his disciples from Judaism to Christianity. To this day a Christian would be in religion a Jew initiated by baptism instead of circumcision, and accepting Jesus as the Messiah, and his teachings as of higher authority than those of Moses, but for the action of the Jewish priests, who, to save Jewry from being submerged in the rising flood of Christianity after the capture of Jerusalem and the destruction of the Temple, set up what was practically a new religious order, with new Scriptures and elaborate new observances, and to their list of the accursed added one Jeschu, a bastard magician, whose comic rogueries brought him to a bad end like Punch or Til Eulenspiegel: an invention which cost them dear when the Christians got the upper hand of them politically. The Jew as Jesus, himself a Jew, knew him, never dreamt of such things, and could follow Jesus without ceasing to be a Jew.

THE TEACHINGS OF JESUS

So much for his personal life and temperament. His public career as a popular preacher carries him equally far beyond John the Baptist. He lays no stress on baptism or vows, and preaches conduct incessantly. He advocates communism, the widening of the private family with its cramping ties into the great family of mankind under the fatherhood of God, the abandonment of revenge and punishment, the counteracting of evil by good instead of by a hostile evil, and an organic conception of society in which you are not an independent individual but a member of society, your neighbor being another member, and each of you members one of another, as two fingers on a hand, the obvious conclusion being that unless you love your neighbor as yourself and he reciprocates you will both be the worse for it. He conveys all this with extraordinary charm, and entertains his hearers with fables (parables) to illustrate them. He has no synagogue or regular congregation, but travels from place to place with twelve men whom he has called from their work as he passed, and who have abandoned it to follow him.

THE MIRACLES

He has certain abnormal powers by which he can perform miracles. He is ashamed of these powers, but, being extremely compassionate, cannot refuse to exercise them when afflicted people beg him to cure them, when multi-

tudes of people are hungry, and when his disciples are terrified by storms on the lakes. He asks for no reward, but begs
the people not to mention these powers of his. There are two
obvious reasons for his dislike of being known as a worker
of miracles. One is the natural objection of all men who
possess such powers, but have far more important business
in the world than to exhibit them, to be regarded primarily
as charlatans, besides being pestered to give exhibitions to
satisfy curiosity. The other is that his view of the effect of
miracles upon his mission is exactly that taken later on by
Rousseau. He perceives that they will discredit him and
divert attention from his doctrine by raising an entirely
irrelevant issue between his disciples and his opponents.

Possibly my readers may not have studied Rousseau's
Letters Written From The Mountain, which may be regarded as the classic work on miracles as credentials of divine
mission. Rousseau shews, as Jesus foresaw, that the miracles
are the main obstacle to the acceptance of Christianity, because their incredibility (if they were not incredible they
would not be miracles) makes people sceptical as to the
whole narrative, credible enough in the main, in which they
occur, and suspicious of the doctrine with which they are
thus associated. "Get rid of the miracles," said Rousseau,
"and the whole world will fall at the feet of Jesus Christ."
He points out that miracles offered as evidence of divinity,
and failing to convince, make divinity ridiculous. He says,
in effect, there is nothing in making a lame man walk: thousands of lame men have been cured and have walked without any miracle. Bring me a man with only one leg and make
another grow instantaneously on him before my eyes, and I
will be really impressed; but mere cures of ailments that
have often been cured before are quite useless as evidence of
anything else than desire to help and power to cure.

Jesus, according to Matthew, agreed so entirely with
Rousseau, and felt the danger so strongly, that when people
who were not ill or in trouble came to him and asked him to
exercise his powers as a sign of his mission, he was irritated

beyond measure, and refused with an indignation which they, not seeing Rousseau's point, must have thought very unreasonable. To be called "an evil and adulterous generation" merely for asking a miracle worker to give an exhibition of his powers, is rather a startling experience. Mahomet, by the way, also lost his temper when people asked him to perform miracles. But Mahomet expressly disclaimed any unusual powers; whereas it is clear from Matthew's story that Jesus (unfortunately for himself, as he thought) had some powers of healing. It is also obvious that the exercise of such powers would give rise to wild tales of magical feats which would expose their hero to condemnation as an impostor among people whose good opinion was of great consequence to the movement started by his mission.

But the deepest annoyance arising from the miracles would be the irrelevance of the issue raised by them. Jesus's teaching has nothing to do with miracles. If his mission had been simply to demonstrate a new method of restoring lost eyesight, the miracle of curing the blind would have been entirely relevant. But to say "You should love your enemies; and to convince you of this I will now proceed to cure this gentleman of cataract" would have been, to a man of Jesus's intelligence, the proposition of an idiot. If it could be proved today that not one of the miracles of Jesus actually occurred, that proof would not invalidate a single one of his didactic utterances; and conversely, if it could be proved that not only did the miracles actually occur, but that he had wrought a thousand other miracles a thousand times more wonderful, not a jot of weight would be added to his doctrine. And yet the intellectual energy of sceptics and divines has been wasted for generations in arguing about the miracles on the assumption that Christianity is at stake in the controversy as to whether the stories of Matthew are false or true. According to Matthew himself, Jesus must have known this only too well; for wherever he went he was assailed with a clamor for miracles, though his doctrine created bewilderment.

772

So much for the miracles! Matthew tells us further, that Jesus declared that his doctrines would be attacked by Church and State, and that the common multitude were the salt of the earth and the light of the world. His disciples, in their relations with the political and ecclesiastical organizations, would be as sheep among wolves.

MATTHEW IMPUTES BIGOTRY TO JESUS

Matthew, like most biographers, strives to identify the opinions and prejudices of his hero with his own. Although he describes Jesus as tolerant even to carelessness, he draws the line at the Gentile, and represents Jesus as a bigoted Jew who regards his mission as addressed exclusively to "the lost sheep of the house of Israel." When a woman of Canaan begged Jesus to cure her daughter, he first refused to speak to her, and then told her brutally that "It is not meet to take the children's bread and cast it to the dogs." But when the woman said, "Truth, Lord; yet the dogs eat of the crumbs which fall from their master's table," she melted the Jew out of him and made Christ a Christian. To the woman whom he had just called a dog he said, "O woman, great is thy faith: be it unto thee even as thou wilt." This is somehow one of the most touching stories in the gospel; perhaps because the woman rebukes the prophet by a touch of his own finest quality. It is certainly out of character; but as the sins of good men are always out of character, it is not safe to reject the story as invented in the interest of Matthew's determination that Jesus shall have nothing to do with the Gentiles. At all events, there the story is; and it is by no means the only instance in which Matthew reports Jesus, in spite of the charm of his preaching, as extremely uncivil in private intercourse.

THE GREAT CHANGE

So far the history is that of a man sane and interesting apart from his special gifts as orator, healer, and prophet. But a startling change occurs. One day, after the disciples have discouraged him for a long time by their misunderstandings of his mission, and their speculations as to whether

773

he is one of the old prophets come again, and if so, which, his disciple Peter suddenly solves the problem by exclaiming, "Thou art the Christ, the son of the living God." At this Jesus is extraordinarily pleased and excited. He declares that Peter has had a revelation straight from God. He makes a pun on Peter's name, and declares him the founder of his Church. And he accepts his destiny as a god by announcing that he will be killed when he goes to Jerusalem; for if he is really the Christ, it is a necessary part of his legendary destiny that he shall be slain. Peter, not understanding this, rebukes him for what seems mere craven melancholy; and Jesus turns fiercely on him and cries, "Get thee behind me, Satan."

Jesus now becomes obsessed with a conviction of his divinity, and talks about it continually to his disciples, though he forbids them to mention it to others. They begin to dispute among themselves as to the position they shall occupy in heaven when his kingdom is established. He rebukes them strenuously for this, and repeats his teaching that greatness means service and not domination; but he himself, always instinctively somewhat haughty, now becomes arrogant, dictatorial, and even abusive, never replying to his critics without an insulting epithet, and even cursing a fig-tree which disappoints him when he goes to it for fruit. He assumes all the traditions of the folk-lore gods, and announces that, like John Barleycorn, he will be barbarously slain and buried, but will rise from the earth and return to life. He attaches to himself the immemorial tribal ceremony of eating the god, by blessing bread and wine and handing them to his disciples with the words "This is my body: this is my blood." He forgets his own teaching and threatens eternal fire and eternal punishment. He announces, in addition to his Barleycorn resurrection, that he will come to the world a second time in glory and establish his kingdom on earth. He fears that this may lead to the appearance of impostors claiming to be himself, and declares explicitly and repeatedly that no matter what wonders these impostors

774

may perform, his own coming will be unmistakable, as the stars will fall from heaven, and trumpets be blown by angels. Further he declares that this will take place during the lifetime of persons then present.

JERUSALEM AND THE MYSTICAL SACRIFICE

In this new frame of mind he at last enters Jerusalem amid great popular curiosity; drives the moneychangers and sacrifice sellers out of the temple in a riot; refuses to interest himself in the beauties and wonders of the temple building on the ground that presently not a stone of it shall be left on another; reviles the high priests and elders in intolerable terms; and is arrested by night in a garden to avoid a popular disturbance. He makes no resistance, being persuaded that it is part of his destiny as a god to be murdered and to rise again. One of his followers shews fight, and cuts off the ear of one of his captors. Jesus rebukes him, but does not attempt to heal the wound, though he declares that if he wished to resist he could easily summon twelve million angels to his aid. He is taken before the high priest and by him handed over to the Roman governor, who is puzzled by his silent refusal to defend himself in any way, or to contradict his accusers or their witnesses, Pilate having naturally no idea that the prisoner conceives himself as going through an inevitable process of torment, death, and burial as a prelude to resurrection. Before the high priest he has also been silent except that when the priest asks him is he the Christ, the Son of God, he replies that they shall all see the Son of Man sitting at the right hand of power, and coming on the clouds of heaven. He maintains this attitude with frightful fortitude whilst they scourge him, mock him, torment him, and finally crucify him between two thieves. His prolonged agony of thirst and pain on the cross at last breaks his spirit, and he dies with a cry of "My God: why hast Thou forsaken me?"

NOT THIS MAN BUT BARABBAS

Meanwhile he has been definitely rejected by the people as well as by the priests. Pilate, pitying him, and unable to make out exactly what he has done (the blasphemy that has horrified the high priest does not move the Roman), tries to get him off by reminding the people that they have, by custom, the right to have a prisoner released at that time, and suggests that he should release Jesus. But they insist on his releasing a prisoner named Barabbas instead, and on having Jesus crucified. Matthew gives no clue to the popularity of Barabbas, describing him simply as "a notable prisoner." The later gospels make it clear, very significantly, that his offence was sedition and insurrection; that he was an advocate of physical force; and that he had killed his man. The choice of Barabbas thus appears as a popular choice of the militant advocate of physical force as against the unresisting advocate of mercy.

THE RESURRECTION

Matthew then tells how after three days an angel opened the family vault of one Joseph, a rich man of Arimathea, who had buried Jesus in it, whereupon Jesus rose and returned from Jerusalem to Galilee and resumed his preaching with his disciples, assuring them that he would now be with them to the end of the world.

At that point the narrative abruptly stops. The story has no ending.

DATE OF MATTHEW'S NARRATIVE

One effect of the promise of Jesus to come again in glory during the lifetime of some of his hearers is to date the gospel without the aid of any scholarship. It must have been written during the lifetime of Jesus's contemporaries: that is, whilst it was still possible for the promise of his Second Coming to be fulfilled. The death of the last person who had been alive when Jesus said "There be some of them that stand here that shall in no wise taste death til they see the Son of Man coming in his kingdom" destroyed the last possibility of the promised Second Coming, and bore out the incredulity of Pilate and the Jews. And as Matthew writes as one believing in that Second Coming, and in fact left his story unfinished to be ended by it, he must have produced his gospel within a lifetime of the crucifixion. Also, he must have believed that reading books would be one of the pleasures of the kingdom of heaven on earth.

CLASS TYPE OF MATTHEW'S JESUS

One more circumstance must be noted as gathered from Matthew. Though he begins his story in such a way as to suggest that Jesus belonged to the privileged classes, he mentions later on that when Jesus attempted to preach in his own country, and had no success there, the people said, "Is not this the carpenter's son?" But Jesus's manner throughout is that of an aristocrat, or at the very least the son of a rich bourgeois, and by no means a lowly-minded one at that. We must be careful therefore to conceive Joseph, not as a modern proletarian carpenter working for weekly wages, but as a master craftsman of royal descent. John the Baptist may have been a Keir Hardie; but the Jesus of Matthew is of the Ruskin-Morris class.

This haughty characterization is so marked that if we had no other documents concerning Jesus than the gospel of Matthew, we should not feel as we do about him. We should have been much less loth to say, "There is a man here who was sane until Peter hailed him as the Christ, and who then became a monomaniac." We should have pointed out that his delusion is a very common delusion among the insane, and that such insanity is quite consistent with the retention of the argumentative cunning and penetration which Jesus displayed in Jerusalem after his delusion had taken complete hold of him. We should feel horrified at the scourging and mocking and crucifixion just as we should if Ruskin had been treated in that way when he also went mad, instead of being cared for as an invalid. And we should have had no clear perception of any special significance in his way of calling the Son of God the Son of Man. We should have noticed that he was a Communist; that he regarded much of what we call law and order as machinery for robbing the poor under legal forms; that he thought domestic ties a snare for the soul; that he agreed with the proverb "The

777

nearer the Church, the farther from God"; that he saw very plainly that the masters of the community should be its servants and not its oppressors and parasites; and that though he did not tell us not to fight our enemies, he did tell us to love them, and warned us that they who draw the sword shall perish by the sword. All this shews a great power of seeing through vulgar illusions, and a capacity for a higher morality than has yet been established in any civilized community; but it does not place Jesus above Confucius or Plato, not to mention more modern philosophers and moralists.

MARK

THE WOMEN DISCIPLES AND THE
ASCENSION

Let us see whether we can get anything more out of Mark, whose gospel, by the way, is supposed to be older than Matthew's. Mark is brief; and it does not take long to discover that he adds nothing to Matthew except the ending of the story by Christ's ascension into heaven, and the news that many women had come with Jesus to Jerusalem, including Mary Magdalene, out of whom he had cast seven devils. On the other hand Mark says nothing about the birth of Jesus, and does not touch his career until his adult baptism by John. He apparently regards Jesus as a native of Nazareth, as John does, and not of Bethlehem, as Matthew and Luke do, Bethlehem being the city of David, from whom Jesus is said by Matthew and Luke to be descended. He describes John's doctrine as "Baptism of repentance unto remission of sins": that is, a form of Salvationism. He tells us that Jesus went into the synagogues and taught, not as the Scribes but as one having authority: that is, we infer, he preaches his own doctrine as an original moralist instead of repeating what the books say. He describes the miracle of Jesus reaching the boat by walking across the sea, but says nothing about Peter trying to do the same. Mark sees what he relates more vividly than Matthew, and gives touches of detail that bring the event more clearly before the reader. He says, for instance, that when Jesus walked on the waves

778

to the boat, he was passing it by when the disciples called out to him. He seems to feel that Jesus's treatment of the woman of Canaan requires some apology, and therefore says that she was a Greek of Syrophenician race, which probably excused any incivility to her in Mark's eyes. He represents the father of the boy whom Jesus cured of epilepsy after the transfiguration as a sceptic who says "Lord, I believe: help thou mine unbelief." He tells the story of the widow's mite, omitted by Matthew. He explains that Barabbas was "lying bound with them that made insurrection, men who in the insurrection had committed murder." Joseph of Arimathea, who buried Jesus in his own tomb, and who is described by Matthew as a disciple, is described by Mark as "one who also himself was looking for the kingdom of God," which suggests that he was an independent seeker. Mark earns our gratitude by making no mention of the old prophecies, and thereby not only saves time, but avoids the absurd implication that Christ was merely going through a predetermined ritual, like the works of a clock, instead of living. Finally Mark reports Christ as saying, after his resurrection, that those who believe in him will be saved and those who do not, damned; but it is impossible to discover whether he means anything by a state of damnation beyond a state of error. The paleographers regard this passage as tacked on by a later scribe.

On the whole Mark leaves the modern reader where Matthew left him.

LUKE

LUKE THE LITERARY ARTIST

When we come to Luke, we come to a later story-teller, and one with a stronger natural gift for his art. Before you have read twenty lines of Luke's gospel you are aware that you have passed from the chronicler writing for the sake of recording important facts, to the artist, telling the story for the sake of telling it. At the very outset he achieves the most charming idyll in the Bible: the story of Mary crowded out of the inn into the stable and laying her newly-born son in the

779

manger, and of the shepherds abiding in the field keeping watch over their flocks by night, and how the angel of the Lord came upon them, and the glory of the Lord shone around them, and suddenly there was with the angel a multitude of the heavenly host. These shepherds go to the stable and take the place of the kings in Matthew's chronicle. So completely has this story conquered and fascinated our imagination that most of us suppose all the gospels to contain it; but it is Luke's story and his alone: none of the others have the smallest hint of it.

THE CHARM OF LUKE'S NARRATIVE

Luke gives the charm of sentimental romance to every incident. The Annunciation, as described by Matthew, is made to Joseph, and is simply a warning to him not to divorce his wife for misconduct. In Luke's gospel it is made to Mary herself, at much greater length, with a sense of the ecstasy of the bride of the Holy Ghost. Jesus is refined and softened almost out of recognition: the stern peremptory disciple of John the Baptist, who never addresses a Pharisee or a Scribe without an insulting epithet, becomes a considerate, gentle, sociable, almost urbane person; and the Chauvinist Jew becomes a pro-Gentile who is thrown out of the synagogue in his own town for reminding the congregation that the prophets had sometimes preferred Gentiles to Jews. In fact they try to throw him down from a sort of Tarpeian rock which they use for executions; but he makes his way through them and escapes: the only suggestion of a feat of arms on his part in the gospels. There is not a word of the Syrophenician woman. At the end he is calmly superior to his sufferings; delivers an address on his way to execution with unruffled composure; does not despair on the cross; and dies with perfect dignity, commending his spirit to God, after praying for the forgiveness of his persecutors on the ground that "They know not what they do." According to Matthew, it is part of the bitterness of his death that even the thieves who are crucified with him revile him. According to Luke, only one of them does this; and he is rebuked by the other, who begs Jesus to remember him when he comes into his kingdom. To which Jesus replies, "This day shalt thou be with me in Paradise," implying that he will spend the three days of his death there. In short, every device is used to get rid of the ruthless horror of the Matthew chronicle, and to relieve the strain of the Passion by touching episodes, and by representing Christ as superior to human suffering. It is Luke's Jesus who has won our hearts.

THE TOUCH OF PARISIAN ROMANCE

Luke's romantic shrinking from unpleasantness, and his sentimentality, are illustrated by his version of the woman with the ointment. Matthew and Mark describe it as taking place in the house of Simon the Leper, where it is objected to as a waste of money. In Luke's version the leper becomes a rich Pharisee; the woman becomes a Dame aux Camellias; and nothing is said about money and the poor. The woman washes the feet of Jesus with her tears and dries them with her hair; and he is reproached for suffering a sinful woman to touch him. It is almost an adaptation of the unromantic Matthew to the Parisian stage. There is a distinct attempt to increase the feminine interest all through. The slight lead given by Mark is taken up and developed. More is said about Jesus's mother and her feelings. Christ's following of women, just mentioned by Mark to account for their presence at his tomb, is introduced earlier; and some of the women are named; so that we are introduced to Joanna the wife of Chuza, Herod's steward, and Susanna. There is the quaint little domestic episode between Mary and Martha. There is the parable of the Prodigal Son, appealing to the indulgence romance has always shewn to Charles Surface and Des Grieux. Women follow Jesus to the cross; and he makes them a speech beginning "Daughters of Jerusalem." Slight as these changes may seem, they make a great change in the atmosphere. The Christ of Matthew could never have become what is vulgarly called a woman's hero (though the truth is that the popular demand for sentiment, as far as it is not simply human, is more manly than womanly); but the Christ of Luke has made possible those pictures which now hang in many ladies' chambers, in which Jesus is represented exactly as he is represented in the Lourdes cinematograph, by a handsome actor. The only touch of realism which Luke does not instinctively suppress for the sake of producing this kind of amenity is the reproach addressed to Jesus for sitting down to table without washing his hands; and that is retained because an interesting discourse hangs on it.

WAITING FOR THE MESSIAH

Another new feature in Luke's story is that it begins in a world in which everyone is expecting the advent of the Christ. In Matthew and Mark, Jesus comes into a normal Philistine world like our own of today. Not until the Baptist foretells that one greater than himself shall come after him does the old Jewish hope of a Messiah begin to stir again; and as Jesus begins as a disciple of John, and is baptized by him, nobody connects him with that hope until Peter has the sudden inspiration which produces so startling an effect on Jesus. But in Luke's gospel men's minds, and especially women's minds, are full of eager expectation of a Christ not only before the birth of Jesus, but before the birth of John the Baptist, the event with which Luke begins his story. Whilst Jesus and John are still in their mothers' wombs, John leaps at the approach of Jesus when the two mothers visit one another. At the circumcision of Jesus pious men and women hail the infant as the Christ.

The Baptist himself is not convinced; for at quite a late period in his former disciple's career he sends two young men to ask Jesus is he really the Christ. This is noteworthy because Jesus immediately gives them a deliberate exhibition of miracles, and bids them tell John what they have seen, and ask him what he thinks *now*. This is in complete contradiction to what I have called the Rousseau view of miracles as inferred from Matthew. Luke shews all a romancer's thoughtlessness about miracles: he regards them as "signs": that is, as proofs of the divinity of the person performing them, and not merely of thaumaturgic powers. He revels in miracles just as he revels in parables: they make such capital stories. He cannot allow the calling of Peter, James, and John from their boats to pass without a comic miraculous overdraft of fishes, with the net sinking the boats and provoking Peter to exclaim, "Depart from me; for I am a sinful man, O Lord," which should probably be translated, "I want no more of your miracles: natural fishing is good enough for my boats."

There are some other novelties in Luke's version. Pilate sends Jesus to Herod, who happens to be in Jerusalem just then, because Herod had expressed some curiosity about him; but nothing comes of it: the prisoner will not speak to him. When Jesus is ill received in a Samaritan village James and John propose to call down fire from heaven and destroy it; and Jesus replies that he is come not to destroy lives but to save them. The bias of Jesus against lawyers is emphasized, and also his resolution not to admit that he is more bound to his relatives than to strangers. He snubs a woman who blesses his mother. As this is contrary to the traditions of sentimental romance, Luke would presumably have avoided it had he not become persuaded that the brotherhood of Man and the Fatherhood of God are superior even to sentimental considerations. The story of the lawyer asking what are the two chief commandments is changed by making Jesus put the question to the lawyer instead of answering it.

As to doctrine, Luke is only clear when his feelings are touched. His logic is weak; for some of the sayings of Jesus are pieced together wrongly, as anyone who has read them in the right order and context in Matthew will discover at once. He does not make anything new out of Christ's mission, and, like the other evangelists, thinks that the whole point of it is that Jesus was the long expected Christ, and that he will presently come back to earth and establish his kingdom, having duly died and risen again after three days. Yet Luke not only records the teaching as to communism and the discarding of hate, which have, of course, nothing to do with the Second Coming, but quotes one very remarkable saying which is not compatible with it, which is, that people must not go about asking where the kingdom of heaven is, and saying "Lo, here!" and "Lo, there!" because the kingdom of heaven is within them. But Luke has no sense that this belongs to a quite different order of thought to his Christianity, and retains undisturbed his view of the kingdom as a locality as definite as Jerusalem or Madagascar.

JOHN

A NEW STORY AND A NEW CHARACTER

The gospel of John is a surprise after the others. Matthew, Mark and Luke describe the same events in the same order (the variations in Luke are negligible), and their gospels are therefore called the synoptic gospels. They tell substantially the same story of a wandering preacher who at the end of his life came to Jerusalem. John describes a preacher who spent practically his whole adult life in the capital, with occasional visits to the provinces. His circumstantial account of the calling of Peter and the sons of Zebedee is quite different from the others; and he says nothing about their being fishermen. He says expressly that Jesus, though baptized by John, did not himself practise baptism, and that his disciples did. Christ's agonized appeal against his doom in the garden of Gethsemane becomes a cold-blooded suggestion made in the temple at a much earlier period. Jesus argues much more; complains a good deal of the unreasonableness and dislike with which he is met; is by no means silent before Caiaphas and Pilate; lays much greater stress on his resurrection and on the eating of his body (losing all his disciples except the twelve in consequence); says many apparently contradictory and nonsensical things to which no ordinary reader can now find any clue; and gives the impression of an educated, not to say sophisticated mystic, different both in character and schooling from the simple and downright preacher of Matthew and Mark, and the urbane easy-minded charmer of Luke. Indeed, the Jews say of him

784

"How knoweth this man letters, having never learnt?"

JOHN THE IMMORTAL EYE-WITNESS

John, moreover, claims to be not only a chronicler but a witness. He declares that he is "the disciple whom Jesus loved," and that he actually leaned on the bosom of Jesus at the last supper and asked in a whisper which of them it was that should betray him. Jesus whispered that he would give a sop to the traitor, and thereupon handed one to Judas, who ate it and immediately became possessed by the devil. This is more natural than the other accounts, in which Jesus openly indicates Judas without eliciting any protest or exciting any comment. It also implies that Jesus deliberately bewitched Judas in order to bring about his own betrayal. Later on John claims that Jesus said to Peter "If I will that John tarry til I come, what is that to thee?" and John, with a rather obvious mock modesty, adds that he must not claim to be immortal, as the disciples concluded; for Christ did not use that expression, but merely remarked "If I will that he tarry til I come." No other evangelist claims personal intimacy with Christ, or even pretends to be his contemporary (there is no ground for identifying Matthew the publican with Matthew the Evangelist); and John is the only evangelist whose account of Christ's career and character is hopelessly irreconcilable with Matthew's. He is almost as bad as Matthew, by the way, in his repeated explanations of Christ's actions as having no other purpose than to fulfill the old prophecies. The impression is more unpleasant, because, as John, unlike Matthew, is educated, subtle, and obsessed with artificial intellectual mystifications, the discovery that he is stupid or superficial in so simple a matter strikes one with distrust and dislike, in spite of his great literary charm, a good example of which is his transfiguration of the harsh episode of the Syrophenician woman into the pleasant story of the woman of Samaria. This perhaps is why his claim to be John the disciple, or to be a contemporary of Christ or even of any survivor of Christ's generation, has been disputed, and finally, it seems, disallowed. But I repeat, I take no note here of the disputes of experts as to the date of the gospels, not because I am not acquainted with them, but because, as the earliest codices are Greek manuscripts of the fourth century A. D., and the Syrian ones are translations from the Greek, the paleographic expert has no difficulty in arriving at whatever conclusion happens to suit his beliefs or disbeliefs; and he never succeeds in convincing the other experts except when they believe or disbelieve exactly as he does. Hence I conclude that the dates of the original narratives cannot be ascertained, and that we must make the best of the evangelists' own accounts of themselves. There is, as we have seen, a very marked difference between them, leaving no doubt that we are dealing with four authors of well-marked diversity; but they all end in an attitude of expectancy of the Second Coming which they agree in declaring Jesus to have positively and unequivocally promised within the lifetime of his contemporaries. Any believer compiling a gospel after the last of these contemporaries had passed away, would either reject and omit the tradition of that promise on the ground that since it was not fulfilled, and could never now be fulfilled, it could not have been made, or else have had to confess to the Jews, who were the keenest critics of the Christians, that Jesus was either an impostor or the victim of a delusion. Now all the evangelists except Matthew expressly declare themselves to be believers; and Matthew's narrative is obviously not that of a sceptic. I therefore assume as a matter of common sense that, interpolations apart, the gospels are derived from narratives written in the first century A. D. I include John, because though it may be claimed that he hedged his position by claiming that Christ, who specially loved him, endowed him with a miraculous life until the Second Coming, the conclusion being that John is alive at this moment, I cannot believe that a literary forger could hope to save the situation by so outrageous a pretension. Also, John's narrative is in many passages nearer to the realities of public life than the simple chronicle of Matthew or the sentimental romance of Luke. This may be because

John was obviously more a man of the world than the others, and knew, as mere chroniclers and romancers never know, what actually happens away from books and desks. But it may also be because he saw and heard what happened instead of collecting traditions about it. The paleographers and daters of first quotations may say what they please: John's claim to give evidence as an eyewitness whilst the others are only compiling history is supported by a certain verisimilitude which appeals to me as one who has preached a new doctrine and argued about it, as well as written stories. This verisimilitude may be dramatic art backed by knowledge of public life; but even at that we must not forget that the best dramatic art is the operation of a divinatory instinct for truth. Be that as it may, John was certainly not the man to believe in the Second Coming and yet give a date for it after that date had passed. There is really no escape from the conclusion that the originals of all the gospels date from the period within which there was still a possibility of the Second Coming occurring at the promised time.

THE PECULIAR THEOLOGY OF JESUS

In spite of the suspicions roused by John's idiosyncrasies, his narrative is of enormous importance to those who go to the gospels for a credible modern religion. For it is John who adds to the other records such sayings as that "I and my father are one"; that "God is a spirit"; that the aim of Jesus is not only that the people should have life, but that they should have it "more abundantly" (a distinction much needed by people who think a man is either alive or dead, and never consider the important question how much alive he is); and that men should bear in mind what they were told in the 82nd Psalm: that they are gods, and are responsible for the doing of the mercy and justice of God. The Jews stoned him for saying these things, and, when he remonstrated with them for stupidly stoning one who had done nothing to them but good works, replied "For a good work we stone thee not; but for blasphemy, because that thou, being a man, makest thyself God." He insists (refer-

ring to the 82nd Psalm) that if it is part of their own religion
that they are gods on the assurance of God himself, it cannot
be blasphemy for him, whom the Father sanctified and sent
into the world, to say "I am the son of God." But they will
not have this at any price; and he has to escape from their
fury. Here the point is obscured by the distinction made by
Jesus between himself and other men. He says, in effect, "If
you are gods, then, *à fortiori*, I am a god." John makes him
say this, just as he makes him say "I am the light of the
world." But Matthew makes him say to the people "Ye are
the light of the world." John has no grip of the significance
of these scraps which he has picked up: he is far more interested in a notion of his own that men can escape death
and do even more extraordinary things than Christ himself:
in fact, he actually represents Jesus as promising this explicitly, and is finally led into the audacious hint that he,
John, is himself immortal in the flesh. Still, he does not miss
the significant sayings altogether. However inconsistent
they may be with the doctrine he is consciously driving at,
they appeal to some sub-intellectual instinct in him that
makes him stick them in, like a child sticking tinsel stars
on the robe of a toy angel.

John does not mention the ascension; and the end of his
narrative leaves Christ restored to life, and appearing from
time to time among his disciples. It is on one of these occasions that John describes the miraculous draught of fishes
which Luke places at the other end of Christ's career, at the
call of the sons of Zebedee.

JOHN AGREED AS TO THE TRIAL AND CRUCIFIXION

Although John, following his practice of shewing Jesus's
skill as a debater, makes him play a less passive part at his
trial, he still gives substantially the same account of it as all
the rest. And the question that would occur to any modern
reader never occurs to him, any more than it occurred to
Matthew, Mark, or Luke. That question is, Why on earth
did not Jesus defend himself, and make the people rescue

him from the High Priest? He was so popular that they were unable to prevent him driving the moneychangers out of the temple, or to arrest him for it. When they did arrest him afterwards, they had to do it at night in a garden. He could have argued with them as he had often done in the temple, and justified himself both to the Jewish law and to Caesar. And he had physical force at his command to back up his arguments: all that was needed was a speech to rally his followers; and he was not gagged. The reply of the evangelists would have been that all these inquiries are idle, because if Jesus had wished to escape, he could have saved himself all that trouble by doing what John describes him as doing: that is, casting his captors to the earth by an exertion of his miraculous power. If you asked John why he let them get up again and torment and execute him, John would have replied that it was part of the destiny of God to be slain and buried and to rise again, and that to have avoided this destiny would have been to repudiate his Godhead. And that is the only apparent explanation. Whether you believe with the evangelists that Christ could have rescued himself by a miracle, or, as a modern Secularist, point out that he could have defended himself effectually, the fact remains that according to all the narratives he did not do so. He had to die like a god, not to save himself "like one of the princes."[1] The consensus on this point is important, because it proves the absolute sincerity of Jesus's declaration that he was a god. No impostor would have accepted such dreadful consequences without an effort to save himself. No impostor would have been nerved to endure them by the conviction that he would rise from the grave and live again after three

[1] Jesus himself had referred to that psalm (LXXXII) in which men who have judged unjustly and accepted the persons of the wicked (including by anticipation practically all the white inhabitants of the British Isles and the North American continent, to mention no other places) are condemned in the words, "I have said, ye are gods; and all of ye are children of the Most High; but ye shall die like men, and fall like one of the princes."

days. If we accept the story at all, we must believe this, and believe also that his promise to return in glory and establish his kingdom on earth within the lifetime of men then living, was one which he believed that he could, and indeed must fulfil. Two evangelists declare that in his last agony he despaired, and reproached God for forsaking him. The other two represent him as dying in unshaken conviction and charity with the simple remark that the ordeal was finished. But all four testify that his faith was not deceived, and that he actually rose again after three days. And I think it unreasonable to doubt that all four wrote their narratives in full faith that the other promise would be fulfilled too, and that they themselves might live to witness the Second Coming.

CREDIBILITY OF THE GOSPELS

It will be noted by the older among my readers, who are sure to be obsessed more or less by elderly wrangles as to whether the gospels are credible as matter-of-fact narratives, that I have hardly raised this question, and have accepted the credible and incredible with equal complacency. I have done this because credibility is a subjective condition, as the evolution of religious belief clearly shews. Belief is not dependent on evidence and reason. There is as much evidence that the miracles occurred as that the battle of Waterloo occurred, or that a large body of Russian troops passed through England in 1914 to take part in the war on the western front. The reasons for believing in the murder of Pompey are the same as the reasons for believing in the raising of Lazarus. Both have been believed and doubted by men of equal intelligence. Miracles, in the sense of phenomena we cannot explain, surround us on every hand: life itself is the miracle of miracles. Miracles in the sense of events that violate the normal course of our experience are vouched for every day: the flourishing Church of Christ Scientist is founded on a multitude of such miracles. Nobody believes all the miracles: everybody believes some of them. I cannot tell why men who will not believe that Jesus ever existed yet believe firmly that Shakespear was Bacon. I cannot tell why people who believe that angels appeared and fought on our side at the battle of Mons, and who believe that miracles occur quite frequently at Lourdes, nevertheless boggle at the miracle of the liquefaction of the blood of St Januarius, and reject it as a trick of priestcraft. I cannot tell why people who will not believe Matthew's story of three kings bringing costly gifts to the cradle of Jesus, believe Luke's story of the shepherds and the stable. I cannot tell why people, brought up to believe the Bible in the old literal way as an infallible record and revelation, and rejecting that view later on, begin by rejecting the Old Testament, and give up the belief in a brimstone hell before they give up (if they ever do) the belief in a heaven of harps, crowns, and thrones. I cannot tell why people who will not believe in baptism on any terms believe in vaccination with the cruel fanaticism of inquisitors. I am convinced that if a dozen sceptics were to draw up in parallel columns a list of the events narrated in the gospels which they consider credible and incredible respectively, their lists would be different in several particulars. Belief is literally a matter of taste.

FASHIONS IN BELIEF

Now matters of taste are mostly also matters of fashion. We are conscious of a difference between medieval fashions in belief and modern fashions. For instance, though we are more credulous than men were in the Middle Ages, and entertain such crowds of fortune-tellers, magicians, miracle workers, agents of communication with the dead, discoverers of the elixir of life, transmuters of metals, and healers of all sorts, as the Middle Ages never dreamed of as possible, yet we will not take our miracles in the form that convinced the Middle Ages. Arithmetical numbers appealed to the Middle Ages just as they do to us, because they are difficult to deal with, and because the greatest masters of numbers, the Newtons and Leibnitzes, rank among the greatest men. But there are fashions in numbers too. The Middle Ages took a fancy to some familiar number like seven; and because it was an odd number, and the world was made in seven days, and there are seven stars in Charles's Wain, and for a dozen other reasons, they were ready to believe anything that had a seven or a seven times seven in it. Seven deadly sins, seven swords of sorrow in the heart of the Virgin, seven champions of Christendom, seemed obvious and reasonable things to believe in simply because they were seven. To us, on the contrary, the number seven is the stamp of superstition. We will believe in nothing less than millions. A medieval doctor gained his patient's confidence by telling him that his vitals were being devoured by seven worms. Such a diagnosis would ruin a modern physician. The modern physician tells his patient that he is ill because every drop of his blood is swarming with a million microbes; and the patient believes him abjectly and instantly. Had a bishop told William the Conqueror that the sun was seventy-seven miles distant from the earth, William would have believed him not only out of respect for the Church, but because he would have felt that seventy-seven miles was the proper distance. The Kaiser, knowing just as little about it as the Conqueror, would send that bishop to an asylum. Yet he (I presume) unhesitatingly accepts the estimate of ninety-two and nine-tenths millions of miles, or whatever the latest big figure may be.

CREDIBILITY AND TRUTH

And here I must remind you that our credulity is not to be measured by the truth of the things we believe. When men believed that the earth was flat, they were not credulous: they were using their common sense, and, if asked to prove that the earth was flat, would have said simply, "Look at it." Those who refuse to believe that it is round are exercising a wholesome scepticism. The modern man who believes that the earth is round is grossly credulous. Flat Earth men drive him to fury by confuting him with the greatest ease when he tries to argue about it. Confront him with a theory that the earth is cylindrical, or annular, or hour-glass shaped, and he is lost. The thing he believes may be true, but that is not why he believes it: he believes it because in some mysterious way it appeals to his imagination. If you ask him why he believes that the sun is ninety-odd million miles off, either he will have to confess that he doesnt know, or he will say that Newton proved it. But he has not read the treatise in which Newton proved it, and does not even know that it was written in Latin. If you press an Ulster Protestant as to why he regards Newton as an infallible authority, and St Thomas Aquinas or the Pope as superstitious liars whom, after his death, he will have the pleasure of watching from his place in heaven whilst they roast in eternal flame, or if you ask me why I take into serious consideration Colonel Sir Almroth Wright's estimates of the number of streptococci contained in a given volume of serum whilst I can only laugh at the earlier estimates of the number of angels that can be accommodated on the point of a needle, no reasonable reply is possible except that somehow sevens and angels are out of fashion, and billions and streptococci are all the rage. I simply cannot tell you why Bacon, Montaigne, and Cervantes had a quite different fashion of credulity and incredulity from the Venerable Bede and Piers Plowman and the divine doctors of the Aquinas-Aristotle school, who were certainly no stupider, and had the same facts before them. Still less can I explain why, if we assume that these leaders of thought had all reasoned out their beliefs, their authority seemed conclusive to one generation and blasphemous to another, neither generation having followed the reasoning or gone into the facts of the matter for itself at all.

It is therefore idle to begin disputing with the reader as to what he should believe in the gospels and what he should disbelieve. He will believe what he can, and disbelieve what he must. If he draws any lines at all, they will be quite arbitrary ones. St John tells us that when Jesus explicitly claimed divine honors by the sacrament of his body and blood, so many of his disciples left him that their number was reduced to twelve. Many modern readers will not hold out so long: they will give in at the first miracle. Others will discriminate. They will accept the healing miracles, and reject the feeding of the multitude. To some the walking on

793

the water will be a legendary exaggeration of a swim, ending in an ordinary rescue of Peter; and the raising of Lazarus will be only a similar glorification of a commonplace feat of artificial respiration, whilst others will scoff at it as a planned imposture in which Lazarus acted as a confederate. Between the rejection of the stories as wholly fabulous and the acceptance of them as the evangelists themselves mean them to be accepted, there will be many shades of belief and disbelief, of sympathy and derision. It is not a question of being a Christian or not. A Mahometan Arab will accept literally and without question parts of the narrative which an English Archbishop has to reject or explain away; and many Theosophists and lovers of the wisdom of India, who never enter a Christian Church except as sightseers, will revel in parts of John's gospel which mean nothing to a pious matter-of-fact Bradford manufacturer. Every reader takes from the Bible what he can get. In submitting a précis of the gospel narratives I have not implied any estimate either of their credibility or of their truth. I have simply informed him or reminded him, as the case may be, of what those narratives tell us about their hero.

CHRISTIAN ICONOLATRY AND THE PERIL OF THE ICONOCLAST

I must now abandon this attitude, and make a serious draft on the reader's attention by facing the question whether, if and when the medieval and Methodist will-to-believe the Salvationist and miraculous side of the gospel narratives fails us, as it plainly has failed the leaders of modern thought, there will be anything left of the mission of Jesus: whether, in short, we may not throw the gospels into the waste-paper basket, or put them away on the fiction shelf of our libraries. I venture to reply that we shall be, on the contrary, in the position of the man in Bunyan's riddle who found that "the more he threw away, the more he had." We get rid, to begin with, of the idolatrous or iconographic worship of Christ. By this I mean literally that worship which is given to pictures and statues of him, and to finished and unalterable stories about him. The test of the prevalence of this is that if you speak or write of Jesus as a real live person, or even as a still active God, such wor-shippers are more horrified than Don Juan was when the statue stepped from its pedestal and came to supper with him. You may deny the divinity of Jesus; you may doubt whether he ever existed; you may reject Christianity for Judaism, Mahometanism, Shintoism, or Fire Worship; and the iconolaters, placidly contemptuous, will only classify you as a freethinker or a heathen. But if you venture to wonder how Christ would have looked if he had shaved and had his hair cut, or what size in shoes he took, or whether he swore when he stood on a nail in the carpenter's shop, or could not button his robe when he was in a hurry, or whether he laughed over the repartees by which he baffled the priests when they tried to trap him into sedition and blasphemy, or even if you tell any part of his story in the vivid terms of modern colloquial slang, you will produce an extraordinary dismay and horror among the iconolaters. You will have made the picture come out of its frame, the statue descend from its pedestal, the story become real, with all the incalculable consequences that may flow from this terrifying miracle. It is at such moments that you realize that the iconolaters have never for a moment conceived Christ as a real person who meant what he said, as a fact, as a force like electricity, only needing the invention of suitable political machinery to be applied to the affairs of mankind with revolutionary effect.

Thus it is not disbelief that is dangerous in our society: it is belief. The moment it strikes you (as it may any day) that Christ is not the lifeless harmless image he has hitherto been to you, but a rallying centre for revolutionary influences which all established States and Churches fight, you must look to yourselves; for you have brought the image to life; and the mob may not be able to bear that horror.

THE ALTERNATIVE TO BARABBAS

But mobs must be faced if civilization is to be saved. It

did not need the present war to shew that neither the iconographic Christ nor the Christ of St Paul has succeeded in
effecting the salvation of human society. Whilst I write, the
Turks are said to be massacring the Armenian Christians
on an unprecedented scale; but Europe is not in a position
to remonstrate; for her Christians are slaying one another
by every device which civilization has put within their
reach as busily as they are slaying the Turks. Barabbas is
triumphant everywhere; and the final use he makes of his
triumph is to lead us all to suicide with heroic gestures and
resounding lies. Now those who, like myself, see the Barabbasque social organization as a failure, and are convinced
that the Life Force (or whatever you choose to call it) cannot be finally beaten by any failure, and will even supersede
humanity by evolving a higher species if we cannot master
the problems raised by the multiplication of our own numbers, have always known that Jesus had a real message, and
have felt the fascination of his character and doctrine. Not
that we should nowadays dream of claiming any supernatural authority for him, much less the technical authority
which attaches to an educated modern philosopher and
jurist. But when, having entirely got rid of Salvationist
Christianity, and even contracted a prejudice against Jesus
on the score of his involuntary connection with it, we engage
on a purely scientific study of economics, criminology, and
biology, and find that our practical conclusions are virtually
those of Jesus, we are distinctly pleased and encouraged to
find that we were doing him an injustice, and that the nim-
bus that surrounds his head in the pictures may be inter-
preted some day as a light of science rather than a declaration of sentiment or a label of idolatry.

The doctrines in which Jesus is thus confirmed are,
roughly, the following:

1. The kingdom of heaven is within you. You are the
son of God; and God is the son of man. God is a spirit, to
be worshipped in spirit and in truth, and not an elderly
gentleman to be bribed and begged from. We are members

one of another; so that you cannot injure or help your neighbor without injuring or helping yourself. God is your father: you are here to do God's work; and you and your father are one.

2. Get rid of property by throwing it into the common stock. Dissociate your work entirely from money payments. If you let a child starve you are letting God starve. Get rid of all anxiety about tomorrow's dinner and clothes, because you cannot serve two masters: God and Mammon.

3. Get rid of judges and punishment and revenge. Love your neighbor as yourself, he being a part of yourself. And love your enemies: they are your neighbors.

4. Get rid of your family entanglements. Every mother you meet is as much your mother as the woman who bore you. Every man you meet is as much your brother as the man she bore after you. Dont waste your time at family funerals grieving for your relatives: attend to life, not to death: there are as good fish in the sea as ever came out of it, and better. In the kingdom of heaven, which, as aforesaid, is within you, there is no marriage nor giving in marriage, because you cannot devote your life to two divinities: God and the person you are married to.

Now these are very interesting propositions; and they become more interesting every day, as experience and science drive us more and more to consider them favorably. In considering them, we shall waste our time unless we give them a reasonable construction. We must assume that the man who saw his way through such a mass of popular passion and illusion as stands between us and a sense of the value of such teaching was quite aware of all the objections that occur to an average stockbroker in the first five minutes. It is true that the world is governed to a considerable extent by the considerations that occur to stockbrokers in the first five minutes; but as the result is that the world is so badly governed that those who know the truth can hardly bear to live in it, an objection from an average stockbroker constitutes in itself a *prima facie* case for any social reform.

All the same, we must reduce the ethical counsels and
proposals of Jesus to modern practice if they are to be of any
use to us. If we ask our stockbroker to act simply as Jesus
advised his disciples to act, he will reply, very justly, "You
are advising me to become a tramp." If we urge a rich man
to sell all that he has and give it to the poor, he will inform
us that such an operation is impossible. If he sells his shares
and his lands, their purchaser will continue all those activities which oppress the poor. If all the rich men take the
advice simultaneously the shares will fall to zero and the
lands be unsaleable. If one man sells out and throws the
money into the slums, the only result will be to add himself
and his dependents to the list of the poor, and to do no good
to the poor beyond giving a chance few of them a drunken
spree. We must therefore bear in mind that whereas, in the
time of Jesus, and in the ages which grew darker and darker
after his death until the darkness, after a brief false dawn in
the Reformation and the Renascence, culminated in the
commercial night of the nineteenth century, it was believed
that you could not make men good by Act of Parliament,
we now know that you cannot make them good in any other
way, and that a man who is better than his fellows is a
nuisance. The rich man must sell up not only himself but
his whole class; and that can be done only through the
Chancellor of the Exchequer. The disciple cannot have his
bread without money until there is bread for everybody
without money; and that requires an elaborate municipal
organization of the food supply, rate supported. Being members one of another means One Man One Vote, and One
Woman One Vote, and universal suffrage and equal incomes and all sorts of modern political measures. Even in
Syria in the time of Jesus his teachings could not possibly
have been realized by a series of independent explosions of
personal righteousness on the part of the separate units of
the population. Jerusalem could not have done what even a

village community cannot do, and what Robinson Crusoe himself could not have done if his conscience, and the stern compulsion of Nature, had not imposed a common rule on the half dozen Robinson Crusoes who struggled within him for not wholly compatible satisfactions. And what cannot be done in Jerusalem or Juan Fernandez cannot be done in London, New York, Paris, and Berlin.

In short, Christianity, good or bad, right or wrong, must perforce be left out of the question in human affairs until it is made practically applicable to them by complicated political devices; and to pretend that a field preacher under the governorship of Pontius Pilate, or even Pontius Pilate himself in council with all the wisdom of Rome, could have worked out applications of Christianity or any other system of morals for the twentieth century, is to shelve the subject much more effectually than Nero and all its other persecutors ever succeeded in doing. Personal righteousness, and the view that you cannot make people moral by Act of Parliament, is, in fact, the favorite defensive resort of the people who, consciously or subconsciously, are quite determined not to have their property meddled with by Jesus or any other reformer.

MODERN COMMUNISM

Now let us see what modern experience and sociology have to say to the suggestion of Jesus that you should get rid of your property by throwing it into the common stock. One can hear the Pharisees of Jerusalem and Chorazin and Bethsaida saying, "My good fellow, if you were to divide up the wealth of Judea equally today, before the end of the year you would have rich and poor, poverty and affluence, just as you have today; for there will always be the idle and the industrious, the thrifty and the wasteful, the drunken and the sober; and, as you yourself have very justly observed, the poor we shall have always with us." And we can hear the reply, "Woe unto you, liars and hypocrites; for ye have this very day divided up the wealth of the country yourselves, as must be done every day (for man liveth not otherwise than

799

from hand to mouth, nor can fish and eggs endure for ever); and ye have divided it unjustly; also ye have said that my reproach to you for having the poor always with you was a law unto you that this evil should persist and stink in the nostrils of God to all eternity; wherefore I think that Lazarus will yet see you beside Dives in hell." Modern Capitalism has made short work of the primitive pleas for inequality. The Pharisees themselves have organized communism in capital. Joint stock is the order of the day. An attempt to return to individual properties as the basis of our production would smash civilization more completely than ten revolutions. You cannot get the fields tilled today until the farmer becomes a co-operator. Take the shareholder to his railway, and ask him to point out to you the particular length of rail, the particular seat in the railway carriage, the particular lever in the engine that is his very own and nobody elses; and he will shun you as a madman, very wisely. And if, like Ananias and Sapphira, you try to hold back your little shop or what not from the common stock, represented by the Trust, or Combine, or Kartel, the Trust will presently freeze you out and rope you in and finally strike you dead industrially as thoroughly as St Peter himself. There is no longer any practical question open as to Communism in production: the struggle today is over the distribution of the product: that is, over the daily dividing-up which is the first necessity of organized society.

REDISTRIBUTION

Now it needs no Christ to convince anybody today that our system of distribution is wildly and monstrously wrong. We have million-dollar babies side by side with paupers worn out by a long life of unremitted drudgery. One person in every five dies in a workhouse, a public hospital, or a madhouse. In cities like London the proportion is very nearly one in two. Naturally so outrageous a distribution has to be effected by violence pure and simple. If you demur, you are sold up. If you resist the selling up you are

bludgeoned and imprisoned, the process being euphemistic-
ally called the maintenance of law and order. Iniquity can
go no further. By this time nobody who knows the figures
of the distribution defends them. The most bigoted British
Conservative hesitates to say that his king should be much
poorer than Mr Rockefeller, or to proclaim the moral superiority of prostitution to needlework on the ground that it
pays better. The need for a drastic redistribution of income
in all civilized countries is now as obvious and as generally
admitted as the need for sanitation.

SHALL HE WHO MAKES, OWN?

It is when we come to the question of the proportions in
which we are to redistribute that controversy begins. We
are bewildered by an absurdly unpractical notion that in
some way a man's income should be given to him, not to
enable him to live, but as a sort of Sunday School Prize
for good behavior. And this folly is complicated by a less
ridiculous but quite as unpractical belief that it is possible
to assign to each person the exact portion of the national income that he or she has produced. To a child it seems that
the blacksmith has made a horse-shoe, and that therefore
the horse-shoe is his. But the blacksmith knows that the
horse-shoe does not belong solely to him, but to his landlord, to the rate collector and taxgatherer, to the men from
whom he bought the iron and anvil and the coals, leaving
only a scrap of its value for himself; and this scrap he has to
exchange with the butcher and baker and the clothier for
the things that he really appropriates as living tissue or its
wrappings, paying for all of them more than their cost; for
these fellow traders of his have also their landlords and
moneylenders to satisfy. If, then, such simple and direct
village examples of apparent individual production turn out
on a moment's examination to be the products of an elaborate social organization, what is to be said of such products
as dreadnoughts, factory-made pins and needles, and steel
pens? If God takes the dreadnought in one hand and a steel
pen in the other, and asks Job who made them, and to whom

they should belong by maker's right, Job must scratch his puzzled head with a potsherd and be dumb, unless indeed it strikes him that God is the ultimate maker, and that all we have a right to do with the product is to feed his lambs.

LABOR TIME

So maker's right as an alternative to taking the advice of Jesus would not work. In practice nothing was possible in that direction but to pay a worker by labor time: so much an hour or day or week or year. But how much? When that question came up, the only answer was "as little as he can be starved into accepting," with the ridiculous results already mentioned, and the additional anomaly that the largest share went to the people who did not work at all, and the least to those who worked hardest. In England nine-tenths of the wealth goes into the pockets of one-tenth of the population.

THE DREAM OF DISTRIBUTION
ACCORDING TO MERIT

Against this comes the protest of the Sunday School theorists "Why not distribute according to merit?" Here one imagines Jesus, whose smile has been broadening down the ages as attempt after attempt to escape from his teaching has led to deeper and deeper disaster, laughing outright. Was ever so idiotic a project mooted as the estimation of virtue in money? The London School of Economics is, we must suppose, to set examination papers with such questions as, "Taking the money value of the virtues of Jesus as 100, and of Judas Iscariot as zero, give the correct figures for, respectively, Pontius Pilate, the proprietor of the Gadarene swine, the widow who put her mite in the poor-box, Mr Horatio Bottomley, Shakespear, Mr Jack Johnson, Sir Isaac Newton, Palestrina, Offenbach, Sir Thomas Lipton, Mr Paul Cinquevalli, your family doctor, Florence Nightingale, Mrs Siddons, your charwoman, the Archbishop of Canterbury, and the common hangman." Or "The late Mr Barney Barnato received as his lawful income three thousand times as much money as an English agricultural laborer of good general character. Name the principal virtues in which Mr

PREFACE

Barnato exceeded the laborer three thousandfold; and give in figures the loss sustained by civilization when Mr Barnato was driven to despair and suicide by the reduction of his multiple to one thousand." The Sunday School idea, with its principle "to each the income he deserves," is really too silly for discussion. Hamlet disposed of it three hundred years ago. "Use every man after his deserts, and who shall scape whipping?" Jesus remains unshaken as the practical man; and we stand exposed as the fools, the blunderers, the unpractical visionaries. The moment you try to reduce the Sunday School idea to figures you find that it brings you back to the hopeless plan of paying for a man's time; and your examination paper will read "The time of Jesus was worth nothing (he complained that the foxes had holes and the birds of the air nests whilst he had not a place to lay his head). Dr Crippen's time was worth, say, three hundred and fifty pounds a year. Criticize this arrangement; and, if you dispute its justice, state in pounds, dollars, francs and marks, what their relative time wages ought to have been." Your answer may be that the question is in extremely bad taste and that you decline to answer it. But you cannot object to being asked how many minutes of a bookmaker's time are worth two hours of an astronomer's?

VITAL DISTRIBUTION

In the end you are forced to ask the question you should have asked at the beginning. What do you give a man an income for? Obviously to keep him alive. Since it is evident that the first condition on which he can be kept alive without enslaving somebody else is that he shall produce an equivalent for what it costs to keep him alive, we may quite rationally compel him to abstain from idling by whatever means we employ to compel him to abstain from murder, arson, forgery, or any other crime. The one supremely foolish thing to do with him is to do nothing: that is, to be as idle, lazy, and heartless in dealing with him as he is in dealing with us. Even if we provided work for him instead of basing, as we do, our whole industrial system on successive com-

803

petitive waves of overwork with their ensuing troughs of unemployment, we should still sternly deny him the alternative of not doing it; for the result must be that he will become poor and make his children poor if he has any; and poor people are cancers in the commonwealth, costing far more than if they were handsomely pensioned off as incurables. Jesus had more sense than to propose anything of the sort. He said to his disciples, in effect, "Do your work for love; and let the other people lodge and feed and clothe you for love." Or, as we should put it nowadays, "for nothing." All human experience and all natural uncommercialized human aspiration point to this as the right path. The Greeks said, "First secure an independent income; and then practise virtue." We all strive towards an independent income. We all know as well as Jesus did that if we have to take thought for the morrow as to whether there shall be anything to eat or drink it will be impossible for us to think of nobler things, or live a higher life than that of a mole, whose life is from beginning to end a frenzied pursuit of food. Until the community is organized in such a way that the fear of bodily want is forgotten as completely as the fear of wolves already is in civilized capitals, we shall never have a decent social life. Indeed the whole attraction of our present arrangement lies in the fact that it does relieve a handful of us from this fear; but as the relief is effected stupidly and wickedly by making the favored handful parasitic on the rest, they are smitten with the degeneracy which seems to be the inevitable biological penalty of complete parasitism. They corrupt culture and statecraft instead of contributing to them, their excessive leisure being as mischievous as the excessive toil of the laborers. Anyhow, the moral is clear. The two main problems of organized society: how to produce subsistence enough for all its members, and how to prevent the theft of that subsistence by idlers, should be carefully dissociated; for the triumphant solution of the first by our inventors and chemists has been offset by the disastrous failure of our rulers to solve the other. Optimism on this point is only wilful blindness: we all have the hard fact of the failure before us. The only people who cling to the lazy delusion that it is possible to find a just distribution that will work automatically are those who postulate some revolutionary change like land nationalization, which by itself would obviously only force into greater urgency the problem of how to distribute the product of the land among all the individuals in the community.

EQUAL DISTRIBUTION

When that problem is at last faced, the question of the proportion in which the national income shall be distributed can have only one answer. All our shares must be equal. It has always been so: it always will be so. It is true that the incomes of robbers vary considerably from individual to individual; and the variation is reflected in the incomes of their parasites. The commercialization of certain exceptional talents has also produced exceptional incomes, direct and derivative. Persons who live on rent of land and capital are economically, though not legally, in the category of robbers, and have grotesquely different incomes. But in the huge mass of mankind variation of income from individual to individual is unknown, because it is ridiculously impracticable. As a device for persuading a carpenter that a judge is a creature of superior nature to himself, to be deferred and submitted to even to the death, we may give a carpenter a hundred pounds a year and a judge five thousand; but the wage for one carpenter is the wage for all the carpenters: the salary for one judge is the salary for all the judges.

THE CAPTAIN AND THE CABIN BOY

Nothing, therefore, is really in question, or ever has been, but the differences between class incomes. Already there is economic equality between captains, and economic equality between cabin boys. What is at issue still is whether there shall be economic equality between captains and cabin boys. What would Jesus have said? Presumably he would have said that if your only object is to produce a captain and

805

a cabin boy for the purpose of transferring you from Liverpool to New York, or to manœuvre a fleet and carry powder from the magazine to the gun, then you need give no more than a shilling to the cabin boy for every pound you give to the more expensively trained captain. But if in addition to this you desire to allow the two human souls which are inseparable from the captain and the cabin boy, and which alone differentiate them from the donkey-engine, to develop all their possibilities, then you may find the cabin boy costing rather more than the captain, because cabin boy's work does not do so much for the soul as captain's work. Consequently you will have to give him at least as much as the captain unless you definitely wish him to be a lower creature, in which case the sooner you are hanged as an abortionist the better. That is the fundamental argument.

THE POLITICAL AND BIOLOGICAL OBJECTIONS TO INEQUALITY

But there are other reasons for objecting to class stratification of income which have heaped themselves up since the time of Jesus. In politics it defeats every form of government except that of a necessarily corrupt oligarchy. Democracy in the most democratic modern republics: France and the United States for example, is an imposture and a delusion. It reduces justice and law to a farce: law becomes merely an instrument for keeping the poor in subjection; and accused workmen are tried, not by a jury of their peers, but by conspiracies of their exploiters. The press is the press of the rich and the curse of the poor: it becomes dangerous to teach men to read. The priest becomes the mere complement of the policeman in the machinery by which the countryhouse oppresses the village. Worst of all, marriage becomes a class affair: the infinite variety of choice which nature offers to the young in search of a mate is narrowed to a handful of persons of similar income; and beauty and health become the dreams of artists and the advertisements of quacks instead of the normal conditions of life. Society is not only divided but actually destroyed in all directions by inequality of income between classes: such stability as it has is due to the huge blocks of people between whom there is equality of income.

JESUS AS ECONOMIST

It seems therefore that we must begin by holding the right to an income as sacred and equal, just as we now begin by holding the right to life as sacred and equal. Indeed the one right is only a restatement of the other. To hang me for cutting a dock laborer's throat after making much of me for leaving him to starve when I do not happen to have a ship for him to unload is idiotic; for as he does far less mischief with his throat cut than when he is starving, a rational society would esteem the cutthroat more highly than the capitalist. The thing has become so obvious, and the evil so unendurable, that if our attempt at civilization is not to perish like all the previous ones, we shall have to organize our society in such a way as to be able to say to every person in the land, "Take no thought, saying What shall we eat? or What shall we drink? or Wherewithal shall we be clothed?" We shall then no longer have a race of men whose hearts are in their pockets and safes and at their bankers. As Jesus said, where your treasure is, there will your heart be also. That was why he recommended that money should cease to be a treasure, and that we should take steps to make ourselves utterly reckless of it, setting our minds free for higher uses. In other words, that we should all be gentlemen and take care of our country because our country takes care of us, instead of the commercialized cads we are, doing everything and anything for money, and selling our souls and bodies by the pound and the inch after wasting half the day haggling over the price. Decidedly, whether you think Jesus was God or not, you must admit that he was a first-rate political economist.

JESUS AS BIOLOGIST

He was also, as we now see, a first-rate biologist. It took a century and a half of evolutionary preachers, from Buffon and Goethe to Butler and Bergson, to convince us that we and our father are one; that as the kingdom of heaven is within us we need not go about looking for it and crying Lo here! and Lo there!; that God is not a picture of a pompous person in white robes in the family Bible, but a spirit; that it is through this spirit that we evolve towards greater abundance of life; that we are the lamps in which the light of the world burns: that, in short, we are gods though we die like men. All that is today sound biology and psychology; and the efforts of Natural Selectionists like Weismann to reduce evolution to mere automatism have not touched the doctrine of Jesus, though they have made short work of the theologians who conceived God as a magnate keeping men and angels as Lord Rothschild keeps buffaloes and emus at Tring.

MONEY THE MIDWIFE OF SCIENTIFIC COMMUNISM

It may be asked here by some simple-minded reader why we should not resort to crude Communism as the disciples were told to do. This would be quite practicable in a village where production was limited to the supply of the primitive wants which nature imposes on all human beings alike. We know that people need bread and boots without waiting for them to come and ask for these things and offer to pay for them. But when civilization advances to the point at which articles are produced that no man absolutely needs and that only some men fancy or can use, it is necessary that individuals should be able to have things made to their order and at their own cost. It is safe to provide bread for everybody because everybody wants and eats bread; but it would be absurd to provide microscopes and trombones, pet snakes and polo mallets, alembics and test tubes for everybody, as nine-tenths of them would be wasted; and the nine-tenths of the population who do not use such things would object to their being provided at all. We have in the invaluable instrument called money a means of enabling every individual to order and pay for the particular things he desires over and above the things he must consume in order to remain alive, plus the things the State insists on his having and using whether he wants to or not: for example, clothes, sanitary arrangements, armies and navies. In large communities, where even the most eccentric demands for manufactured articles average themselves out until they can be foreseen within a negligible margin of error, direct communism (Take what you want without payment, as the people do in Morris's News From Nowhere) will, after a little experience, be found not only practicable but highly economical to an extent that now seems impossible. The sportsmen, the musicians, the physicists, the biologists will get their apparatus for the asking as easily as their bread, or, as at present, their paving, street lighting, and bridges; and the deaf man will not object to contribute to communal flutes when the musician has to contribute to communal ear trumpets. There are cases (for example, radium) in which the demand may be limited to the merest handful of laboratory workers, and in which nevertheless the whole community must pay because the price is beyond the means of any individual worker. But even when the utmost allowance is made for extensions of communism that now seem fabulous, there will still remain for a long time to come regions of supply and demand in which men will need and use money or individual credit, and for which, therefore, they must have individual incomes. Foreign travel is an obvious instance. We are so far from even national communism still, that we shall probably have considerable developments of local communism before it becomes possible for a Manchester man to go up to London for a day without taking any money with him. The modern practical form of the communism of Jesus is therefore, for the present, equal distribution of the surplus of the national income that is not absorbed by simple communism.

JUDGE NOT

In dealing with crime and the family, modern thought and experience have thrown no fresh light on the views of Jesus. When Swift had occasion to illustrate the corruption of our civilization by making a catalogue of the types of scoundrels it produces, he always gave judges a conspicuous place alongside of them they judged. And he seems to have done this not as a restatement of the doctrine of Jesus, but as the outcome of his own observation and judgment. One of Mr Gilbert Chesterton's stories has for its hero a judge who, whilst trying a criminal case, is so overwhelmed by the absurdity of his position and the wickedness of the things it forces him to do, that he throws off the ermine there and then, and goes out into the world to live the life of an honest man instead of that of a cruel idol. There has also been a propaganda of a soulless stupidity called Determinism, representing man as a dead object driven hither and thither by his environment, antecedents, circumstances, and so forth, which nevertheless does remind us that there are limits to the number of cubits an individual can add to his stature morally or physically, and that it is silly as well as cruel to torment a man five feet high for not being able to pluck fruit that is within the reach of men of average height. I have known a case of an unfortunate child being beaten for not being able to tell the time after receiving an elaborate explanation of the figures on a clock dial, the fact being that she was short-sighted and could not see them. This is a typical illustration of the absurdities and cruelties into which we are led by the counter-stupidity to Determinism: the doctrine of Free Will. The notion that people can be good if they like, and that you should give them a powerful additional motive for goodness by tormenting them when they do evil, would soon reduce itself to absurdity if its application were not kept within the limits which nature sets to the self-control of most of us. Nobody supposes that a man with no ear for music or no mathematical faculty could be compelled on pain of death, however cruelly inflicted, to hum all the themes of Beethoven's symphonies or to complete Newton's work on fluxions.

LIMITS TO FREE WILL

Consequently such of our laws as are not merely the

intimidations by which tyrannies are maintained under pretext of law, can be obeyed through the exercise of a quite
common degree of reasoning power and self-control. Most
men and women can endure the ordinary annoyances and
disappointments of life without committing murderous assaults. They conclude therefore that any person can refrain
from such assaults if he or she chooses to, and proceed to
reinforce self-control by threats of severe punishment. But
in this they are mistaken. There are people, some of them
possessing considerable powers of mind and body, who can
no more restrain the fury into which a trifling mishap throws
them than a dog can restrain himself from snapping if he is
suddenly and painfully pinched. People fling knives and
lighted paraffin lamps at one another in a dispute over a
dinner-table. Men who have suffered several long sentences
of penal servitude for murderous assaults will, the very day
after they are released, seize their wives and cast them under
drays at an irritating word. We have not only people who
cannot resist an opportunity of stealing for the sake of satisfying their wants, but even people who have a specific mania
for stealing, and do it when they are in no need of the things
they steal. Burglary fascinates some men as sailoring fascinates some boys. Among respectable people how many are
there who can be restrained by the warnings of their doctors
and the lessons of experience from eating and drinking
more than is good for them? It is true that between self-
controlled people and ungovernable people there is a narrow
margin of moral malingerers who can be made to behave
themselves by the fear of consequences; but it is not worth
while maintaining an abominable system of malicious, deliberate, costly and degrading ill-treatment of criminals
for the sake of these marginal cases. For practical dealing
with crime, Determinism or Predestination is quite a good
working rule. People without self-control enough for social
purposes may be killed, or may be kept in asylums with a
view to studying their condition and ascertaining whether
it is curable. To torture them and give ourselves virtuous

airs at their expense is ridiculous and barbarous; and the desire to do it is vindictive and cruel. And though vindictiveness and cruelty are at least human qualities when they are frankly proclaimed and indulged, they are loathsome when they assume the robes of Justice. Which, I take it, is why Shakespear's Isabella gave such a dressing-down to Judge Angelo, and why Swift reserved the hottest corner of his hell for judges. Also, of course, why Jesus said "Judge not that ye be not judged" and "If any man hear my words and believe not, I judge him not" because "he hath one that judgeth him": namely, the Father who is one with him.

When we are robbed we generally appeal to the criminal law, not considering that if the criminal law were effective we should not have been robbed. That convicts us of vengeance.

I need not elaborate the argument further. I have dealt with it sufficiently elsewhere. I have only to point out that we have been judging and punishing ever since Jesus told us not to; and I defy anyone to make out a convincing case for believing that the world has been any better than it would have been if there had never been a judge, a prison, or a gallows in it all that time. We have simply added the misery of punishment to the misery of crime, and the cruelty of the judge to the cruelty of the criminal. We have taken the bad man, and made him worse by torture and degradation, incidentally making ourselves worse in the process. It does not seem very sensible, does it? It would have been far easier to kill him as kindly as possible, or to label him and leave him to his conscience, or to treat him as an invalid or a lunatic is now treated (it is only of late years, by the way, that madmen have been delivered from the whip, the chain, and the cage); and this, I presume, is the form in which the teaching of Jesus could have been put into practice.

JESUS ON MARRIAGE AND THE FAMILY

When we come to marriage and the family, we find Jesus making the same objection to that individual appropriation of human beings which is the essence of matrimony as to

812

the individual appropriation of wealth. A married man, he said, will try to please his wife, and a married woman to please her husband, instead of doing the work of God. This is another version of "Where your treasure is, there will your heart be also." Eighteen hundred years later we find a very different person from Jesus, Talleyrand to wit, saying the same thing. A married man with a family, said Talleyrand, will do anything for money. Now this, though not a scientifically precise statement, is true enough to be a moral objection to marriage. As long as a man has a right to risk his life or his livelihood for his ideas he needs only courage and conviction to make his integrity unassailable. But he forfeits that right when he marries. It took a revolution to rescue Wagner from his Court appointment at Dresden; and his wife never forgave him for being glad and feeling free when he lost it and threw her back into poverty. Millet might have gone on painting potboiling nudes to the end of his life if his wife had not been of a heroic turn herself. Women, for the sake of their children and parents, submit to slaveries and prostitutions that no unattached woman would endure.

This was the beginning and the end of the objection of Jesus to marriage and family ties, and the explanation of his conception of heaven as a place where there should be neither marrying nor giving in marriage. Now there is no reason to suppose that when he said this he did not mean it. He did not, as St Paul did afterwards in his name, propose celibacy as a rule of life; for he was not a fool, nor, when he denounced marriage, had he yet come to believe, as St Paul did, that the end of the world was at hand and there was therefore no more need to replenish the earth. He must have meant that the race should be continued without dividing with women and men the allegiance the individual owes to God within him. This raises the practical problem of how we are to secure the spiritual freedom and integrity of the priest and the nun without their barrenness and uncompleted experience. Luther the priest did not solve the problem by marrying a nun: he only testified in the most convincing and practical way to the fact that celibacy was a worse failure than marriage.

WHY JESUS DID NOT MARRY

To all appearance the problem oppresses only a few exceptional people. Thoroughly conventional women married to thoroughly conventional men should not be conscious of any restriction: the chain not only leaves them free to do whatever they want to do, but greatly facilitates their doing it. To them an attack on marriage is not a blow struck in defence of their freedom but at their rights and privileges. One would expect that they would not only demur vehemently to the teachings of Jesus in this matter, but object strongly to his not having been a married man himself. Even those who regard him as a god descended from his throne in heaven to take on humanity for a time might reasonably declare that the assumption of humanity must have been incomplete at its most vital point if he were a celibate. But the facts are flatly contrary. The mere thought of Jesus as a married man is felt to be blasphemous by the most conventional believers; and even those of us to whom Jesus is no supernatural personage, but a prophet only as Mahomet was a prophet, feel that there was something more dignified in the bachelordom of Jesus than in the spectacle of Mahomet lying distracted on the floor of his harem whilst his wives stormed and squabbled and henpecked round him. We are not surprised that when Jesus called the sons of Zebedee to follow him, he did not call their father, and that the disciples, like Jesus himself, were all men without family entanglements. It is evident from his impatience when people excused themselves from following him because of their family funerals, or when they assumed that his first duty was to his mother, that he had found family ties and domestic affections in his way at every turn, and had become persuaded at last that no man could follow his inner light until he was free from their compulsion. The absence of any protest against this tempts us to

814

declare that on this question of marriage there are no conventional people; and that everyone of us is at heart a good Christian sexually.

INCONSISTENCY OF THE SEX INSTINCT

But the question is not so simple as that. Sex is an exceedingly subtle and complicated instinct; and the mass of mankind neither know nor care much about freedom of conscience, which is what Jesus was thinking about, and are concerned almost to obsession with sex, as to which Jesus said nothing. In our sexual natures we are torn by an irresistible attraction and an overwhelming repugnance and disgust. We have two tyrannous physical passions: concupiscence and chastity. We become mad in pursuit of sex: we become equally mad in the persecution of that pursuit. Unless we gratify our desire the race is lost: unless we restrain it we destroy ourselves. We are thus led to devise marriage institutions which will at the same time secure opportunities for the gratification of sex and raise up innumerable obstacles to it; which will sanctify it and brand it as infamous; which will identify it with virtue and with sin simultaneously. Obviously it is useless to look for any consistency in such institutions; and it is only by continual reform and readjustment, and by a considerable elasticity in their enforcement, that a tolerable result can be arrived at. I need not repeat here the long and elaborate examination of them that I prefixed to my play entitled Getting Married. Here I am concerned only with the views of Jesus on the question; and it is necessary, in order to understand the attitude of the world towards them, that we should not attribute the general approval of the decision of Jesus to remain unmarried as an endorsement of his views. We are simply in a state of confusion on the subject; but it is part of the confusion that we should conclude that Jesus was a celibate, and shrink even from the idea that his birth was a natural one, yet cling with ferocity to the sacredness of the institution which provides a refuge from celibacy.

815

FOR BETTER FOR WORSE

Jesus, however, did not express a complicated view of marriage. His objection to it was quite simple, as we have seen. He perceived that nobody could live the higher life unless money and sexual love were obtainable without sacrificing it; and he saw that the effect of marriage as it existed among the Jews (and as it still exists among ourselves) was to make the couples sacrifice every higher consideration until they had fed and pleased one another. The worst of it is that this dangerous preposterousness in marriage, instead of improving as the general conduct of married couples improves, becomes much worse. The selfish man to whom his wife is nothing but a slave, the selfish woman to whom her husband is nothing but a scapegoat and a breadwinner, are not held back from spiritual or any other adventures by fear of their effect on the welfare of their mates. Their wives do not make recreants and cowards of them: their husbands do not chain them to the cradle and the cooking range when their feet should be beautiful on the mountains. It is precisely as people become more kindly, more conscientious, more ready to shoulder the heavier part of the burden (which means that the strong shall give way to the weak and the slow hold back the swift), that marriage becomes an intolerable obstacle to individual evolution. And that is why the revolt against marriage of which Jesus was an exponent always recurs when civilization raises the standard of marital duty and affection, and at the same time produces a greater need for individual freedom in pursuit of a higher evolution.

THE REMEDY

This, fortunately, is only one side of marriage; and the question arises, can it not be eliminated? The reply is reassuring: of course it can. There is no mortal reason in the nature of things why a married couple should be economically dependent on one another. The Communism advocated by Jesus, which we have seen to be entirely practicable, and indeed inevitable if our civilization is to be saved from collapse, gets rid of that difficulty completely. And with the

816

economic dependence will go the force of the outrageous claims that derive their real sanction from the economic pressure behind them. When a man allows his wife to turn him from the best work he is capable of doing, and to sell his soul at the highest commercial prices obtainable; when he allows her to entangle him in a social routine that is wearisome and debilitating to him, or tie him to her apron strings when he needs that occasional solitude which is one of the most sacred of human rights, he does so because he has no right to impose eccentric standards of expenditure and unsocial habits on her, and because these conditions have produced by their pressure so general a custom of chaining wedded couples to one another that married people are coarsely derided when their partners break the chain. And when a woman is condemned by her parents to wait in genteel idleness and uselessness for a husband when all her healthy social instincts call her to acquire a profession and work, it is again her economic dependence on them that makes their tyranny effective.

THE CASE FOR MARRIAGE

Thus, though it would be too much to say that everything that is obnoxious in marriage and family life will be cured by Communism, yet it can be said that it will cure what Jesus objected to in these institutions. He made no comprehensive study of them: he only expressed his own grievance with an overwhelming sense that it is a grievance so deep that all the considerations on the other side are as dust in the balance. Obviously there are such considerations, and very weighty ones too. When Talleyrand said that a married man with a family is capable of anything, he meant anything evil; but an optimist may declare, with equal half truth, that a married man is capable of anything good; that marriage turns vagabonds into steady citizens; and that men and women will, for love of their mates and children, practise virtues that unattached individuals are incapable of. It is true that too much of this domestic virtue is self-denial, which is not a virtue at all; but then the following of the inner light at all costs is largely self-indulgence, which is just as suicidal, just as weak, just as cowardly as self-denial. Ibsen, who takes us into the matter far more resolutely than Jesus, is unable to find any golden rule: both Brand and Peer Gynt come to a bad end; and though Brand does not do as much mischief as Peer, the mischief he does do is of extraordinary intensity.

CELIBACY NO REMEDY

We must, I think, regard the protest of Jesus against marriage and family ties as the claim of a particular kind of individual to be free from them because they hamper his own work intolerably. When he said that if we are to follow him in the sense of taking up his work we must give up our family ties, he was simply stating a fact; and to this day the Roman Catholic priest, the Buddhist lama, and the fakirs of all the eastern denominations accept the saying. It is also accepted by the physically enterprising, the explorers, the restlessly energetic of all kinds: in short, by the adventurous. The greatest sacrifice in marriage is the sacrifice of the adventurous attitude towards life: the being settled. Those who are born tired may crave for settlement; but to fresher and stronger spirits it is a form of suicide.

Now to say of any institution that it is incompatible with both the contemplative and adventurous life is to disgrace it so vitally that all the moralizings of all the Deans and Chapters cannot reconcile our souls to its slavery. The unmarried Jesus and the unmarried Beethoven, the unmarried Joan of Arc, Clare, Teresa, Florence Nightingale seem as they should be; and the saying that there is always something ridiculous about a married philosopher becomes inevitable. And yet the celibate is still more ridiculous than the married man: the priest, in accepting the alternative of celibacy, disables himself; and the best priests are those who have been men of this world before they became men of the world to come. But as the taking of vows does not annul an existing marriage, and a married man cannot become a priest, we are again confronted with the absurdity that the best priest is a reformed rake. Thus does marriage, itself intolerable, thrust us upon intolerable alternatives. The practical solution is to make the individual economically independent of marriage and the family, and to make marriage as easily dissoluble as any other partnership: in other words, to accept the conclusions to which experience is slowly driving both our sociologists and our legislators. This will not instantly cure all the evils of marriage, nor root up at one stroke its detestable tradition of property in human bodies. But it will leave Nature free to effect a cure; and in free soil the root may wither and perish.

This disposes of all the opinions and teachings of Jesus which are still matters of controversy. They are all in line with the best modern thought. He told us what we have to do; and we have had to find the way to do it. Most of us are still, as most were in his own time, extremely recalcitrant, and are being forced along that way by painful pressure of circumstances, protesting at every step that nothing will induce us to go; that it is a ridiculous way, a disgraceful way, a socialistic way, an atheistic way, an immoral way, and that the vanguard ought to be ashamed of themselves and must be made to turn back at once. But they find that they have to follow the vanguard all the same if their lives are to be worth living.

AFTER THE CRUCIFIXION

Let us now return to the New Testament narrative; for what happened after the disappearance of Jesus is instructive. Unfortunately, the crucifixion was a complete political success. I remember that when I described it in these terms once before, I greatly shocked a most respectable newspaper in my native town, the Dublin Daily Express, because my journalistic phrase shewed that I was treating it as an ordinary event like Home Rule or the Insurance Act: that is (though this did not occur to the editor), as a real event which had really happened, instead of a portion of the Church service. I can only repeat, assuming as I am that it *was* a real event and did actually happen, that it was as complete a success as any in history. Christianity as a specific doctrine was slain with Jesus, suddenly and utterly. He was hardly cold in his grave, or high in his heaven (as you please), before the apostles dragged the tradition of him down to the level of the thing it has remained ever since. And that thing the intelligent heathen may study, if they would be instructed in it by modern books, in Samuel Butler's novel, The Way of All Flesh.

THE VINDICTIVE MIRACLES AND THE STONING OF STEPHEN

Take, for example, the miracles. Of Jesus alone of all the Christian miracle workers there is no record, except in certain gospels that all men reject, of a malicious or destructive miracle. A barren fig-tree was the only victim of his anger. Every one of his miracles on sentient subjects was an act of kindness. John declares that he healed the wound of the man whose ear was cut off (by Peter, John says) at the arrest in the garden. One of the first things the apostles did with their miraculous power was to strike dead a wretched man and his wife who had defrauded them by holding back some money from the common stock. They struck people blind or dead without remorse, judging because they had been judged. They healed the sick and raised the dead apparently in a spirit of pure display and advertisement. Their doctrine did not contain a ray of that light which reveals Jesus as one of the redeemers of men from folly and error. They cancelled him, and went back straight to John the Baptist and his formula of securing remission of sins by repentance and the rite of baptism (being born again of water and the spirit). Peter's first harangue softens us by the human touch of its exordium, which was a quaint assurance to his hearers that they must believe him to be sober because it was too early in the day to get drunk; but of Jesus he had nothing to say except that he was the Christ foretold by the prophets as coming from the seed of David, and that they must believe this and be baptized. To this the other apostles added incessant denunciations of the Jews for having crucified him,

820

and threats of the destruction that would overtake them if they did not repent: that is, if they did not join the sect which the apostles were now forming. A quite intolerable young speaker named Stephen delivered an oration to the council, in which he first inflicted on them a tedious sketch of the history of Israel, with which they were presumably as well acquainted as he, and then reviled them in the most insulting terms as "stiffnecked and uncircumcized." Finally, after boring and annoying them to the utmost bearable extremity, he looked up and declared that he saw the heavens open, and Christ standing on the right hand of God. This was too much: they threw him out of the city and stoned him to death. It was a severe way of suppressing a tactless and conceited bore; but it was pardonable and human in comparison to the slaughter of poor Ananias and Sapphira.

PAUL

Suddenly a man of genius, Paul, violently anti-Christian, enters on the scene, holding the clothes of the men who are stoning Stephen. He persecutes the Christians with great vigor, a sport which he combines with the business of a tentmaker. This temperamental hatred of Jesus, whom he has never seen, is a pathological symptom of that particular sort of conscience and nervous constitution which brings its victims under the tyranny of two delirious terrors: the terror of sin and the terror of death, which may be called also the terror of sex and the terror of life. Now Jesus, with his healthy conscience on his higher plane, was free from these terrors. He consorted freely with sinners, and was never concerned for a moment, as far as we know, about whether his conduct was sinful or not; so that he has forced us to accept him as the man without sin. Even if we reckon his last days as the days of his delusion, he none the less gave a fairly convincing exhibition of superiority to the fear of death. This must have both fascinated and horrified Paul, or Saul, as he was first called. The horror accounts for his fierce persecution of the Christians. The fascination accounts for the strangest of his fancies: the fancy for attach-

ing the name of Jesus Christ to the great idea which flashed
upon him on the road to Damascus, the idea that he could
not only make a religion of his two terrors, but that the
movement started by Jesus offered him the nucleus for his
new Church. It was a monstrous idea; and the shock of it,
as he afterwards declared, struck him blind for days. He
heard Jesus calling to him from the clouds, "Why persecute me?" His natural hatred of the teacher for whom Sin
and Death had no terrors turned into a wild personal worship of him which has the ghastliness of a beautiful thing
seen in a false light.

The chronicler of the Acts of the Apostles sees nothing
of the significance of this. The great danger of conversion
in all ages has been that when the religion of the high mind
is offered to the lower mind, the lower mind, feeling its
fascination without understanding it, and being incapable
of rising to it, drags it down to its level by degrading it.
Years ago I said that the conversion of a savage to Christianity is the conversion of Christianity to savagery. The
conversion of Paul was no conversion at all: it was Paul who
converted the religion that had raised one man above sin
and death into a religion that delivered millions of men so
completely into their dominion that their own common
nature became a horror to them, and the religious life became a denial of life. Paul had no intention of surrendering
either his Judaism or his Roman citizenship to the new
moral world (as Robert Owen called it) of Communism and
Jesuism. Just as in our own time Karl Marx, not content
to take political economy as he found it, insisted on re-
building it from the bottom upwards in his own way, and
thereby gave a new lease of life to the errors it was just out-
growing, so Paul reconstructed the old Salvationism from
which Jesus had vainly tried to redeem him, and produced
a fantastic theology which is still the most amazing thing of
the kind known to us. Being intellectually an inveterate
Roman Rationalist, always discarding the irrational real
thing for the unreal but ratiocinable postulate, he began by

822

discarding Man as he is, and substituted a postulate which he called Adam. And when he was asked, as he surely must have been in a world not wholly mad, what had become of the natural man, he replied "Adam *is* the natural man." This was confusing to simpletons, because according to tradition Adam was certainly the name of the natural man as created in the garden of Eden. It was as if a preacher of our own time had described as typically British Frankenstein's monster, and called him Smith, and somebody, on demanding what about the man in the street, had been told "Smith *is* the man in the street." The thing happens often enough; for indeed the world is full of these Adams and Smiths and men in the street and average sensual men and economic men and womanly women and what not, all of them imaginary Atlases carrying imaginary worlds on their unsubstantial shoulders.

The Eden story provided Adam with a sin: the "original sin" for which we are all damned. Baldly stated, this seems ridiculous; nevertheless it corresponds to something actually existent not only in Paul's consciousness but in our own. The original sin was not the eating of the forbidden fruit, but the consciousness of sin which the fruit produced. The moment Adam and Eve tasted the apple they found themselves ashamed of their sexual relation, which until then had seemed quite innocent to them; and there is no getting over the hard fact that this shame, or state of sin, has persisted to this day, and is one of the strongest of our instincts. Thus Paul's postulate of Adam as the natural man was pragmatically true: it worked. But the weakness of Pragmatism is that most theories will work if you put your back into making them work, provided they have some point of contact with human nature. Hedonism will pass the pragmatic test as well as Stoicism. Up to a certain point every social principle that is not absolutely idiotic works: Autocracy works in Russia and Democracy in America; Atheism works in France, Polytheism in India, Monotheism throughout Islam, and Pragmatism, or No-ism, in England. Paul's fantastic conception of the damned Adam, represented by Bunyan as a pilgrim with a great burden of sins on his back, corresponded to the fundamental condition of evolution, which is, that life, including human life, is continually evolving, and must therefore be continually ashamed of itself and its present and past. Bunyan's pilgrim wants to get rid of his bundle of sins; but he also wants to reach "yonder shining light"; and when at last his bundle falls off him into the sepulchre of Christ, his pilgrimage is still unfinished and his hardest trials still ahead of him. His conscience remains uneasy; "original sin" still torments him; and his adventure with Giant Despair, who throws him into the dungeon of Doubting Castle, from which he escapes by the use of a skeleton key, is more terrible than any he met whilst the bundle was still on his back. Thus Bunyan's allegory of human nature breaks through the Pauline theology at a hundred points. His theological allegory, The Holy War, with its troops of Election Doubters, and its cavalry of "those that rode Reformadoes," is, as a whole, absurd, impossible, and, except in passages where the artistic old Adam momentarily got the better of the Salvationist theologian, hardly readable.

Paul's theory of original sin was to some extent idiosyncratic. He tells us definitely that he finds himself quite well able to avoid the sinfulness of sex by practising celibacy; but he recognizes, rather contemptuously, that in this respect he is not as other men are, and says that they had better marry than burn, thus admitting that though marriage may lead to placing the desire to please wife or husband before the desire to please God, yet preoccupation with unsatisfied desire may be even more ungodly than preoccupation with domestic affection. This view of the case inevitably led him to insist that a wife should be rather a slave than a partner, her real function being, not to engage a man's love and loyalty, but on the contrary to release them for God by relieving the man of all preoccupation with sex just as in her capacity of housekeeper and cook she relieves his preoccupation with hunger by the simple expedient of satisfying his appetite. This slavery also justifies itself pragmatically by working effectively; but it has made Paul the eternal enemy of Woman. Incidentally it has led to many foolish surmises about Paul's personal character and circumstances, by people so enslaved by sex that a celibate appears to them a sort of monster. They forget that not only whole priesthoods, official and unofficial, from Paul to Carlyle and Ruskin, have defied the tyranny of sex, but immense numbers of ordinary citizens of both sexes have, either voluntarily or under pressure of circumstances easily surmountable, saved their energies for less primitive activities.

Howbeit, Paul succeeded in stealing the image of Christ crucified for the figure-head of his Salvationist vessel, with its Adam posing as the natural man, its doctrine of original sin, and its damnation avoidable only by faith in the sacrifice of the cross. In fact, no sooner had Jesus knocked over the dragon of superstition than Paul boldly set it on its legs again in the name of Jesus.

THE CONFUSION OF CHRISTENDOM

Now it is evident that two religions having such contrary effects on mankind should not be confused as they are under a common name. There is not one word of Pauline Christianity in the characteristic utterances of Jesus. When Saul watched the clothes of the men who stoned Stephen, he was not acting upon beliefs which Paul renounced. There is no record of Christ's having ever said to any man: "Go and sin as much as you like: you can put it all on me." He said "Sin no more," and insisted that he was putting up the standard of conduct, not debasing it, and that the righteousness of the Christian must exceed that of the Scribe and Pharisee. The notion that he was shedding his blood in order that every petty cheat and adulterator and libertine might wallow in it and come out whiter than snow, cannot be imputed to him on his own authority. "I come as an infallible patent medicine for bad consciences" is not one of the sayings in the gospels. If Jesus could have been consulted on Bunyan's

allegory as to that business of the burden of sin dropping
from the pilgrim's back when he caught sight of the cross,
we must infer from his teaching that he would have told
Bunyan in forcible terms that he had never made a greater
mistake in his life, and that the business of a Christ was to
make self-satisfied sinners feel the burden of their sins and
stop committing them instead of assuring them that they
could not help it, as it was all Adam's fault, but that it did
not matter as long as they were credulous and friendly about
himself. Even when he believed himself to be a god, he did
not regard himself as a scapegoat. He was to take away the
sins of the world by good government, by justice and mercy,
by setting the welfare of little children above the pride of
princes, by casting all the quackeries and idolatries which
now usurp and malversate the power of God into what our
local authorities quaintly call the dust destructor, and by
riding on the clouds of heaven in glory instead of in a thou-
sand-guinea motor car. That was delirious, if you like; but
it was the delirium of a free soul, not of a shamebound one
like Paul's. There has really never been a more monstrous
imposition perpetrated than the imposition of the limitations of Paul's soul upon the soul of Jesus.

THE SECRET OF PAUL'S SUCCESS

Paul must soon have found that his followers had gained
peace of mind and victory over death and sin at the cost of
all moral responsibility; for he did his best to reintroduce it
by making good conduct the test of sincere belief, and insisting that sincere belief was necessary to salvation. But as
his system was rooted in the plain fact that as what he called
sin includes sex and is therefore an ineradicable part of
human nature (why else should Christ have had to atone for
the sin of all future generations?) it was impossible for him
to declare that sin, even in its wickedest extremity, could
forfeit the sinner's salvation if he repented and believed.
And to this day Pauline Christianity is, and owes its enormous vogue to being, a premium on sin. Its consequences
have had to be held in check by the worldlywise majority

through a violently anti-Christian system of criminal law and stern morality. But of course the main restraint is human nature, which has good impulses as well as bad ones, and refrains from theft and murder and cruelty, even when it is taught that it can commit them all at the expense of Christ and go happily to heaven afterwards, simply because it does not always want to murder or rob or torture.

It is now easy to understand why the Christianity of Jesus failed completely to establish itself politically and socially, and was easily suppressed by the police and the Church, whilst Paulinism overran the whole western civilized world, which was at that time the Roman Empire, and was adopted by it as its official faith, the old avenging gods falling helplessly before the new Redeemer. It still retains, as we may see in Africa, its power of bringing to simple people a message of hope and consolation that no other religion offers. But this enchantment is produced by its spurious association with the personal charm of Jesus, and exists only for untrained minds. In the hands of a logical Frenchman like Calvin, pushing it to its utmost conclusions, and devising "institutes" for hardheaded adult Scots and literal Swiss, it becomes the most infernal of fatalisms; and the lives of civilized children are blighted by its logic whilst negro piccaninnies are rejoicing in its legends.

PAUL'S QUALITIES

Paul, however, did not get his great reputation by mere imposition and reaction. It is only in comparison with Jesus (to whom many prefer him) that he appears common and conceited. Though in The Acts he is only a vulgar revivalist, he comes out in his own epistles as a genuine poet, though by flashes only. He is no more a Christian than Jesus was a Baptist: he is a disciple of Jesus only as Jesus was a disciple of John. He does nothing that Jesus would have done, and says nothing that Jesus would have said, though much, like the famous ode to charity, that he would have admired. He is more Jewish than the Jews, more Roman than the Romans, proud both ways, full of startling confessions and self-reve-

827

lations that would not surprise us if they were slipped into the pages of Nietzsche, tormented by an intellectual conscience that demanded an argued case even at the cost of sophistry, with all sorts of fine qualities and occasional illuminations, but always hopelessly in the toils of Sin, Death, and Logic, which had no power over Jesus. As we have seen, it was by introducing this bondage and terror of his into the Christian doctrine that he adapted it to the Church and State systems which Jesus transcended, and made it practicable by destroying the specifically Jesuist side of it. He would have been quite in his place in any modern Protestant State; and he, not Jesus, is the true head and founder of our Reformed Church, as Peter is of the Roman Church. The followers of Paul and Peter made Christendom, whilst the Nazarenes were wiped out.

THE ACTS OF THE APOSTLES

Here we may return to the narrative called The Acts of the Apostles, which we left at the point where the stoning of Stephen was followed by the introduction of Paul. The author of The Acts, though a good story-teller, like Luke, was (herein also like Luke) much weaker in power of thought than in imaginative literary art. Hence we find Luke credited with the authorship of The Acts by people who like stories and have no aptitude for theology, whilst the book itself is denounced as spurious by Pauline theologians because Paul, and indeed all the apostles, are represented in it as very commonplace revivalists, interesting us by their adventures more than by any qualities of mind or character. Indeed, but for the epistles, we should have a very poor opinion of the apostles. Paul in particular is described as setting a fashion which has remained in continual use to this day. Whenever he addresses an audience, he dwells with great zest on his misdeeds before his pseudo conversion, with the effect of throwing into stronger relief his present state of blessedness; and he tells the story of that conversion over and over again, ending with exhortations to the hearers to come and be saved, and threats of the wrath that will overtake them if they refuse. At any revival meeting today the same thing may be heard, followed by the same conversions. This is natural enough; but it is totally unlike the preaching of Jesus, who never talked about his personal history, and never "worked up" an audience to hysteria. It aims at a purely nervous effect; it brings no enlightenment; the most ignorant man has only to become intoxicated with his own vanity, and mistake his self-satisfaction for the Holy Ghost, to become qualified as an apostle; and it has absolutely nothing to do with the characteristic doctrines of Jesus. The Holy Ghost may be at work all round producing wonders of art and science, and strengthening men to endure all sorts of martyrdoms for the enlargement of knowledge, and the enrichment and intensification of life ("that ye may have life more abundantly"); but the apostles, as described in The Acts, take no part in the struggle except as persecutors and revilers. To this day, when their successors get the upper hand, as in Geneva (Knox's "perfect city of Christ") and in Scotland and Ulster, every spiritual activity but moneymaking and churchgoing is stamped out; heretics are ruthlessly persecuted; and such pleasures as money can purchase are suppressed so that its possessors are compelled to go on making money because there is nothing else to do. And the compensation for all this privation is partly an insane conceit of being the elect of God, with a reserved seat in heaven, and partly, since even the most infatuated idiot cannot spend his life admiring himself, the less innocent excitement of punishing other people for not admiring him, and the nosing out of the sins of the people who, being intelligent enough to be incapable of mere dull self-righteousness, and highly susceptible to the beauty and interest of the real workings of the Holy Ghost, try to live more rational and abundant lives. The abominable amusement of terrifying children with threats of hell is another of these diversions, and perhaps the vilest and most mischievous of them. The net result is that the imitators of the apostles, whether they are called Holy Willies or Stigginses in derision, or, in admiration, Puritans or saints, are, outside their own congregations, and to a considerable extent inside them, heartily detested. Now nobody detests Jesus, though many who have been tormented in their childhood in his name include him in their general loathing of everything connected with the word religion; whilst others, who know him only by misrepresentation as a sentimental pacifist and an ascetic, include him in their general dislike of that type of character. In the same way a student who has had to "get up" Shakespear as a college subject may hate Shakespear; and people who dislike the theatre may include Molière in that dislike without ever having read a line of his or witnessed one of his plays; but nobody with any knowledge of Shakespear or Molière could possibly detest them, or read without pity and horror a description of their being insulted, tortured, and killed. And the same is true of Jesus. But it requires the most strenuous effort of conscience to refrain from crying "Serve him right" when we read of the stoning of Stephen; and nobody has ever cared twopence about the martyrdom of Peter: many better men have died worse deaths: for example, honest Hugh Latimer, who was burned by us, was worth fifty Stephens and a dozen Peters. One feels at last that when Jesus called Peter from his boat, he spoiled an honest fisherman, and made nothing better out of the wreck than a salvation monger.

THE CONTROVERSIES ON BAPTISM AND TRANSUBSTANTIATION

Meanwhile the inevitable effect of dropping the peculiar doctrines of Jesus and going back to John the Baptist, was to make it much easier to convert Gentiles than Jews; and it was by following the line of least resistance that Paul became the apostle to the Gentiles. The Jews had their own rite of initiation: the rite of circumcision; and they were fiercely jealous for it, because it marked them as the chosen people of God, and set them apart from the Gentiles, who were simply the uncircumcized. When Paul, finding that baptism made way faster among the Gentiles than among the Jews, as it enabled them to plead that they too were sanctified by a rite of later and higher authority than the Mosaic rite, he was compelled to admit that circumcision did not matter; and this, to the Jews, was an intolerable blasphemy. To Gentiles like ourselves, a good deal of the Epistle to the Romans is now tedious to unreadableness because it consists of a hopeless attempt by Paul to evade the conclusion that if a man were baptized it did not matter a rap whether he was circumcized or not. Paul claims circumcision as an excellent thing in its way for a Jew; but if it has no efficacy towards salvation, and if salvation is the one thing needful—and Paul was committed to both propositions—his pleas in mitigation only made the Jews more determined to stone him.

Thus from the very beginning of apostolic Christianity, it was hampered by a dispute as to whether salvation was to be attained by a surgical operation or by a sprinkling of water: mere rites on which Jesus would not have wasted twenty words. Later on, when the new sect conquered the Gentile west, where the dispute had no practical application, the other ceremony—that of eating the god—produced a still more disastrous dispute, in which a difference of belief, not as to the obligation to perform the ceremony, but as to whether it was a symbolic or a real ingestion of divine substance, produced persecution, slaughter, hatred, and everything that Jesus loathed, on a monstrous scale.

But long before that, the superstitions which had fastened on the new faith made trouble. The parthenogenetic birth of Christ, simple enough at first as a popular miracle, was not left so simple by the theologians. They began to ask of what substance Christ was made in the womb of the virgin. When the Trinity was added to the faith the question arose, was the virgin the mother of God or only the mother of Jesus? Arian schisms and Nestorian schisms arose on these questions; and the leaders of the resultant agitations rancorously deposed one another and excommunicated one another according to their luck in enlisting the

emperors on their side. In the IV century they began to burn
one another for differences of opinion in such matters. In
the VIII century Charlemagne made Christianity compulsory by killing those who refused to embrace it; and though
this made an end of the voluntary character of conversion,
Charlemagne may claim to be the first Christian who put
men to death for any point of doctrine that really mattered.
From his time onward the history of Christian controversy
reeks with blood and fire, torture and warfare. The Crusades,
the persecutions in Albi and elsewhere, the Inquisition, the
"wars of religion" which followed the Reformation, all presented themselves as Christian phenomena; but who can
doubt that they would have been repudiated with horror by
Jesus? Our own notion that the massacre of St Bartholo-
mew's was an outrage on Christianity, whilst the campaigns
of Gustavus Adolphus, and even of Frederick the Great,
were a defence of it, is as absurd as the opposite notion that
Frederick was Antichrist and Torquemada and Ignatius
Loyola men after the very heart of Jesus. Neither they nor
their exploits had anything to do with him. It is probable
that Archbishop Laud and John Wesley died equally persuaded that he in whose name they had made themselves
famous on earth would receive them in Heaven with open
arms. George Fox the Quaker would have had ten times their
chance; and yet Fox made rather a miserable business of life.

Nevertheless all these perversions of the doctrine of
Jesus derived their moral force from his credit, and so had
to keep his gospel alive. When the Protestants translated
the Bible into the vernacular and let it loose among the
people, they did an extremely dangerous thing, as the mischief which followed proves; but they incidentally let loose
the sayings of Jesus in open competition with the sayings of
Paul and Koheleth and David and Solomon and the authors
of Job and the Pentateuch; and, as we have seen, Jesus seems
to be the winning name. The glaring contradiction between
his teaching and the practice of all the States and all the
Churches is no longer hidden. And it may be that though

PREFACE

nineteen centuries have passed since Jesus was born (the date of his birth is now quaintly given as 7 B.C., though some contend for 100 B.C.), and though his Church has not yet been founded nor his political system tried, the bankruptcy of all the other systems when audited by our vital statistics, which give us a final test for all political systems, is driving us hard into accepting him, not as a scapegoat, but as one who was much less of a fool in practical matters than we have hitherto all thought him.

THE ALTERNATIVE CHRISTS

Let us now clear up the situation a little. The New Testament tells two stories for two different sorts of readers. One is the old story of the achievement of our salvation by the sacrifice and atonement of a divine personage who was barbarously slain and rose again on the third day: the story as it was accepted by the apostles. And in this story the political, economic, and moral views of the Christ have no importance: the atonement is everything; and we are saved by our faith in it, and not by works or opinions (other than that particular opinion) bearing on practical affairs.

The other is the story of a prophet who, after expressing several very interesting opinions as to practical conduct, both personal and political, which are now of pressing importance, and instructing his disciples to carry them out in their daily life, lost his head; believed himself to be a crude legendary form of god; and under that delusion courted and suffered a cruel execution in the belief that he would rise from the dead and come in glory to reign over a regenerated world. In this form, the political, economic, and moral opinions of Jesus, as guides to conduct, are interesting and important: the rest is mere psychopathy and superstition. The accounts of the resurrection, the parthenogenetic birth, and the more incredible miracles are rejected as inventions; and such episodes as the conversation with the devil are classed with similar conversations recorded of St Dunstan, Luther, Bunyan, Swedenborg, and Blake.

833

CREDULITY NO CRITERION

This arbitrary acceptance and rejection of parts of the gospel is not peculiar to the Secularist view. We have seen Luke and John reject Matthew's story of the massacre of the innocents and the flight into Egypt without ceremony. The notion that Matthew's manuscript is a literal and infallible record of facts, not subject to the errors that beset all earthly chroniclers, would have made John stare, being as it is a comparatively modern fancy of intellectually untrained people who keep the Bible on the same shelf with Napoleon's Book of Fate, Old Moore's Almanack, and handbooks of therapeutic herbalism. You may be a fanatical Salvationist and reject more miracle stories than Huxley did; and you may utterly repudiate Jesus as the Savior and yet cite him as a historical witness to the possession by men of the most marvellous thaumaturgical powers. "Christ Scientist" and Jesus the Mahatma are preached by people whom Peter would have struck dead as worse infidels than Simon Magus; and the Atonement is preached by Baptist and Congregationalist ministers whose views of the miracles are those of Ingersoll and Bradlaugh. Luther, who made a clean sweep of all the saints with their million miracles, and reduced the Blessed Virgin herself to the status of an idol, concentrated Salvationism to a point at which the most execrable murderer who believes in it when the rope is round his neck, flies straight to the arms of Jesus, whilst Tom Paine and Shelley fall into the bottomless pit to burn there to all eternity. And sceptical physicists like Sir William Crookes demonstrate by laboratory experiments that "mediums" like Dunglas Home can make the pointer of a springbalance go round without touching the weight suspended from it.

BELIEF IN PERSONAL IMMORTALITY NO CRITERION

Nor is belief in individual immortality any criterion. Theosophists, rejecting vicarious atonement so sternly that they insist that the smallest of our sins brings its Karma, also

834

insist on individual immortality and metempsychosis in
order to provide an unlimited field for Karma to be worked
out by the unredeemed sinner. The belief in the prolonga-
tion of individual life beyond the grave is far more real and
vivid among table-rapping Spiritualists than among conventional Christians. The notion that those who reject the
Christian (or any other) scheme of salvation by atonement
must reject also belief in personal immortality and in miracles is as baseless as the notion that if a man is an atheist
he will steal your watch.

I could multiply these instances to weariness. The main
difference that set Gladstone and Huxley by the ears is not
one between belief in supernatural persons or miraculous
events and the sternest view of such belief as a breach of intellectual integrity: it is the difference between belief in the
efficacy of the crucifixion as an infallible cure for guilt, and
a congenital incapacity for believing this, or (the same thing)
desiring to believe it.

THE SECULAR VIEW NATURAL, NOT RATIONAL, THEREFORE INEVITABLE

It must therefore be taken as a flat fundamental modern
fact, whether we like it or not, that whilst many of us cannot
believe that Jesus got his curious grip of our souls by mere
sentimentality, neither can we believe that he was John Barleycorn. The more our reason and study lead us to believe
that Jesus was talking the most penetrating good sense when
he preached Communism; when he declared that the reality
behind the popular belief in God was a creative spirit in ourselves called by him the Heavenly Father and by us Evolution, Élan Vital, Life Force and other names; when he pro-
tested against the claims of marriage and the family to appropriate that high part of our energy that was meant for the
service of his Father, the more impossible it becomes for us
to believe that he was talking equally good sense when he so
suddenly announced that he was himself a visible concrete
God; that his flesh and blood were miraculous food for us;
that he must be tortured and slain in the traditional manner

835

and would rise from the dead after three days; and that at his Second Coming the stars would fall from heaven and he become king of an earthly paradise. But it is easy and reasonable to believe that an overwrought preacher at last went mad as Swift and Ruskin and Nietzsche went mad. Every asylum has in it a patient suffering from the delusion that he is a god, yet otherwise sane enough. These patients do not nowadays declare that they will be barbarously slain and will rise from the dead, because they have lost that tradition of the destiny of godhead; but they claim everything appertaining to divinity that is within their knowledge.

Thus the gospels as memoirs and suggestive statements of sociological and biological doctrine, highly relevant to modern civilization, though ending in the history of a psychopathic delusion, are quite credible, intelligible, and interesting to modern thinkers. In any other light they are neither credible, intelligible, nor interesting except to people upon whom the delusion imposes.

"THE HIGHER CRITICISM"

Historical research and paleographic criticism will no doubt continue their demonstrations that the New Testament, like the Old, seldom tells a single story or expounds a single doctrine, and gives us often an accretion and conglomeration of widely discrete and even unrelated traditions and doctrines. But these disintegrations, though technically interesting to scholars, and gratifying or exasperating, as the case may be, to people who are merely defending or attacking the paper fortifications of the infallibility of the Bible, have hardly anything to do with the purpose of these pages. I have mentioned the fact that most of the authorities are now agreed (for the moment) that the date of the birth of Jesus may be placed at about 7 B.C.; but they do not therefore date their letters 1923, nor, I presume, do they expect me to do so. What I am engaged in is a criticism (in the Kantian sense) of an established body of belief which has become an actual part of the mental fabric of my readers; and I should be the most exasperating of triflers and pedants if

836

PREFACE

I were to digress into a criticism of some other belief or no-belief which my readers might conceivably profess if they were erudite Scriptural paleographers and historians, in which case, by the way, they would have to change their views so frequently that the gospel they received in their childhood would dominate them after all by its superior persistency. The chaos of mere facts in which the Sermon on the Mount and the Ode to Charity suggest nothing but disputes as to whether they are interpolations or not, in which Jesus becomes nothing but a name suspected of belonging to ten different prophets or executed persons, in which Paul is only the man who could not possibly have written the epistles attributed to him, in which Chinese sages, Greek philosophers, Latin authors, and writers of ancient anonymous inscriptions are thrown at our heads as the sources of this or that scrap of the Bible, is neither a religion nor a criticism of religion: one does not offer the fact that a good deal of the medieval building in Peterborough Cathedral was found to be flagrant jerry-building as a criticism of the Dean's sermons. For good or evil, we have made a synthesis out of the literature we call the Bible; and though the discovery that there is a good deal of jerry-building in the Bible is interesting in its way, because everything about the Bible is interesting, it does not alter the synthesis very materially even for the paleographers, and does not alter it at all for those who know no more about modern paleography than Archbishop Ussher did. I have therefore indicated little more of the discoveries than Archbishop Ussher might have guessed for himself if he had read the Bible without prepossessions.

For the rest, I have taken the synthesis as it really lives and works in men. After all, a synthesis is what you want: it is the case you have to judge brought to an apprehensible issue for you. Even if you have little more respect for synthetic biography than for synthetic rubber, synthetic milk, and the still unachieved synthetic protoplasm which is to enable us to make different sorts of men as a pastrycook

837

makes different sorts of tarts, the practical issue still lies as plainly before you as before the most credulous votaries of what pontificates as the Higher Criticism.

THE PERILS OF SALVATIONISM

The secular view of Jesus is powerfully reinforced by the increase in our day of the number of people who have had the means of educating and training themselves to the point at which they are not afraid to look facts in the face, even such terrifying facts as sin and death. The result is greater sternness in modern thought. The conviction is spreading that to encourage a man to believe that though his sins be as scarlet he can be made whiter than snow by an easy exercise of self-conceit, is to encourage him to be a rascal. It did not work so badly when you could also conscientiously assure him that if he let himself be caught napping in the matter of faith by death, a red-hot hell would roast him alive to all eternity. In those days a sudden death —the most enviable of all deaths—was regarded as the most frightful calamity. It was classed with plague, pestilence, and famine, battle and murder, in our prayers. But belief in that hell is fast vanishing. All the leaders of thought have lost it; and even for the rank and file it has fled to those parts of Ireland and Scotland which are still in the seventeenth century. Even there, it is tacitly reserved for the other fellow.

THE IMPORTANCE OF HELL IN THE SALVATION SCHEME

The seriousness of throwing over hell whilst still clinging to the Atonement is obvious. If there is no punishment for sin there can be no self-forgiveness for it. If Christ paid our score, and if there is no hell and therefore no chance of our getting into trouble by forgetting the obligation, then we can be as wicked as we like with impunity inside the secular law, even from self-reproach, which becomes mere ingratitude to the Savior. On the other hand, if Christ did not pay our score, it still stands against us; and such debts make us extremely uncomfortable. The drive of evolution,

838

which we call conscience and honor, seizes on such slips, and shames us to the dust for being so low in the scale as to be capable of them. The "saved" thief experiences an ecstatic happiness which can never come to the honest atheist: he is tempted to steal again to repeat the glorious sensation. But if the atheist steals he has no such happiness. He is a thief and knows that he is a thief. Nothing can rub that off him. He may try to soothe his shame by some sort of restitution or equivalent act of benevolence; but that does not alter the fact that he did steal; and his conscience will not be easy until he has conquered his will to steal and changed himself into an honest man by developing that divine spark within him which Jesus insisted on as the everyday reality of what the atheist denies.

Now though the state of the believers in the Atonement may thus be the happier, it is most certainly not more desirable from the point of view of the community. The fact that a believer is happier than a sceptic is no more to the point than the fact that a drunken man is happier than a sober one. The happiness of credulity is a cheap and dangerous quality of happiness, and by no means a necessity of life. Whether Socrates got as much happiness out of life as Wesley is an unanswerable question; but a nation of Socrateses would be much safer and happier than a nation of Wesleys; and its individuals would be higher in the evolutionary scale. At all events it is in the Socratic man and not in the Wesleyan that our hope lies now.

THE RIGHT TO REFUSE ATONEMENT

Consequently, even if it were mentally possible for all of us to believe in the Atonement, we should have to cry off it, as we evidently have a right to do. Every man to whom salvation is offered has an inalienable natural right to say "No, thank you: I prefer to retain my full moral responsibility: it is not good for me to be able to load a scapegoat with my sins: I should be less careful how I committed them if I knew they would cost me nothing." Then, too, there is the attitude of Ibsen: that iron moralist to whom the whole scheme of salvation was only an ignoble attempt to cheat God; to get into heaven without paying the price. To be let off, to beg for and accept eternal life as a present instead of earning it, would be mean enough even if we accepted the contempt of the Power on whose pity we were trading; but to bargain for a crown of glory as well! that was too much for Ibsen: it provoked him to exclaim, "Your God is an old man whom you cheat," and to lash the deadened conscience of the nineteenth century back to life with a whip of scorpions.

THE TEACHING OF CHRISTIANITY

And there I must leave the matter to such choice as your nature allows you. The honest teacher who has to make known to a novice the facts about Christianity cannot in any essential regard, I think, put the facts otherwise than as I have put them. If children are to be delivered from the proselytizing atheist on the one hand, and the proselytizing nun in the convent school on the other, with all the other proselytizers that lie between them, they must not be burdened with idle controversies as to whether there was ever such a person as Jesus or not. When Hume said that Joshua's campaigns were impossible, Whately did not wrangle about it: he proved, on the same lines, that the campaigns of Napoleon were impossible. Only fictitious characters will stand Hume's sort of examination: nothing will ever make Edward the Confessor and St Louis as real to us as Don Quixote and Mr Pickwick. We must cut the controversy short by declaring that there is the same evidence for the existence of Jesus as for that of any other person of his time; and the fact that you may not believe everything Matthew tells you no more disproves the existence of Jesus than the fact that you do not believe everything Macaulay tells you disproves the existence of William III. The gospel narratives in the main give you a biography which is quite credible and accountable on purely secular grounds when you have trimmed off everything that Hume or Grimm or Rousseau or Huxley or any modern bishop could reject as fanciful. Without going further than this, you can become a follower of Jesus just as you can become a follower of Confucius or Lao Tse, and may therefore call yourself a Jesuist, or even a Christian, if you hold, as the strictest Secularist quite legitimately may, that all prophets are inspired, and all men with a mission, Christs.

The teacher of Christianity has then to make known to the child, first the song of John Barleycorn, with the fields and seasons as witness to its eternal truth. Then, as the child's mind matures, it can learn, as historical and psychological phenomena, the tradition of the scapegoat, the Redeemer, the Atonement, the Resurrection, the Second Coming, and how, in a world saturated with this tradition, Jesus has been largely accepted as the long expected and often prophesied Redeemer, the Messiah, *the* Christ. It is open to the child also to accept him. If the child is built like Gladstone, he will accept Jesus as his Savior, and Peter and John the Baptist as the Savior's revealer and forerunner respectively. If he is built like Huxley, he will take the secular view, in spite of all that a pious family can do to prevent him. The important thing now is that the Gladstones and Huxleys should no longer waste their time irrelevantly and ridiculously wrangling about the Gadarene swine, and that they should make up their minds as to the soundness of the secular doctrines of Jesus; for it is about these that they may come to blows in our own time.

CHRISTIANITY AND THE EMPIRE

Finally, let us ask why it is that the old superstitions have so suddenly lost countenance that although, to the utter disgrace of the nation's leaders and rulers, the laws by which persecutors can destroy or gag all freedom of thought and speech in these matters are still unrepealed and ready to the hand of our bigots and fanatics (quite recently a respectable shopkeeper was convicted of "blasphemy" for saying that if a modern girl accounted for an illicit pregnancy by saying she had conceived of the Holy Ghost, we should know what to think: a remark which would never have

841

occurred to him had he been properly taught how the story was grafted on the gospel), yet somehow they are used only against poor men, and that only in a half-hearted way. When we consider that from the time when the first scholar ventured to whisper as a professional secret that the Pentateuch could not possibly have been written by Moses to the time within my own recollection when Bishop Colenso, for saying the same thing openly, was inhibited from preaching and actually excommunicated, eight centuries elapsed (the point at issue, though technically interesting to paleographers and historians, having no more bearing on human welfare than the controversy as to whether uncial or cursive is the older form of writing); yet now, within fifty years of Colenso's heresy, there is not a Churchman of any authority living, or an educated layman, who could without ridicule declare that Moses wrote the Pentateuch as Pascal wrote his Thoughts or D'Aubigny his History of the Reformation, or that St Jerome wrote the passage about the three witnesses in the Vulgate, or that there are less than three different accounts of the creation jumbled together in the book of Genesis. Now the maddest Progressive will hardly contend that our growth in wisdom and liberality has been greater in the last half century than in the sixteen half centuries preceding: indeed it would be easier to sustain the thesis that the last fifty years have witnessed a distinct reaction from Victorian Liberalism to Collectivism which has perceptibly strengthened the State Churches. Yet the fact remains that whereas Byron's Cain, published a century ago, is a leading case on the point that there is no copyright in a blasphemous book, the Salvation Army might now include it among its publications without shocking anyone.

I suggest that the causes which have produced this sudden clearing of the air include the transformation of many modern States, notably the old self-contained French Republic and the tight little Island of Britain, into empires which overflow the frontiers of all the Churches. In India, for example, there are less than four million Christians out of a population of three hundred and sixteen and a half millions. The King of England is the defender of the faith; but what faith is now *the* faith? The inhabitants of this island would, within the memory of persons still living, have claimed that their faith is surely *the* faith of God, and that all others are heathen. But we islanders are only forty-five millions; and if we count ourselves all as Christians, there are still seventy-seven and a quarter million Mahometans in the Empire. Add to these the Hindoos and Buddhists, Sikhs and Jains, whom I was taught in my childhood, by way of religious instruction, to regard as gross idolaters consigned to eternal perdition, but whose faith I can now be punished for disparaging by a provocative word, and you have a total of over three hundred and forty-two and a quarter million heretics to swamp our forty-five million Britons, of whom, by the way, only six thousand call themselves distinctively "disciples of Christ," the rest being members of the Church of England and other denominations whose discipleship is less emphatically affirmed. In short, the Englishman of today, instead of being, like the forefathers whose ideas he clings to, a subject of a State practically wholly Christian, is now crowded, and indeed considerably overcrowded, into a corner of an Empire in which the Christians are a mere eleven per cent of the population; so that the Nonconformist who allows his umbrella stand to be sold up rather than pay rates towards the support of a Church of England school, finds himself paying taxes not only to endow the Church of Rome in Malta, but to send Christians to prison for the blasphemy of offering Bibles for sale in the streets of Khartoum.

Turn to France, a country ten times more insular in its preoccupation with its own language, its own history, its own character, than we, who have always been explorers and colonizers and grumblers. This once self-centred nation is forty millions strong. The total population of the French Republic is about one hundred and fourteen millions. The French are not in our hopeless Christian minority of eleven

843

per cent; but they are in a minority of thirty-five per cent, which is fairly conclusive. And, being a more logical people than we, they have officially abandoned Christianity and declared that the French State has no specific religion.

Neither has the British State, though it does not say so. No doubt there are many innocent people in England who take Charlemagne's view, and would, as a matter of course, offer our eighty-nine per cent of "pagans, I regret to say" the alternative of death or Christianity but for a vague impression that these lost ones are all being converted gradually by the missionaries. But no statesman can entertain such ludicrously parochial delusions. No English king or French president can possibly govern on the assumption that the theology of Peter and Paul, Luther and Calvin, has any objective validity, or that the Christ is more than the Buddha or Jehovah more than Krishna, or Jesus more or less human than Mahomet or Zoroaster or Confucius. He is actually compelled, in so far as he makes laws against blasphemy at all, to treat all the religions, including Christianity, as blasphemous when paraded before people who are not accustomed to them and do not want them. And even that is a concession to a mischievous intolerance which an empire should use its control of education to eradicate.

On the other hand, Governments cannot really divest themselves of religion, or even of dogma. When Jesus said that people should not only live but live more abundantly, he was dogmatizing; and many Pessimist sages, including Shakespear, whose hero begged his friend to refrain from suicide in the words "Absent thee from felicity awhile," would say dogmatizing very perniciously. Indeed many preachers and saints declare, some of them in the name of Jesus himself, that this world is a vale of tears, and that our lives had better be passed in sorrow and even in torment, as a preparation for a better life to come. Make these sad people comfortable; and they baffle you by putting on hair shirts.

None the less, Governments must proceed on dogmatic assumptions, whether they call them dogmas or not; and they must clearly be assumptions common enough to stamp those who reject them as eccentrics or lunatics. And the greater and more heterogeneous the population the commoner the assumptions must be. A Trappist monastery can be conducted on assumptions which would in twenty-four hours provoke the village at its gates to insurrection. That is because the monastery selects its people; and if a Trappist does not like it he can leave it. But a subject of the British Empire or the French Republic is not selected; and if he does not like it he must lump it; for emigration is practicable only within narrow limits, and seldom provides an effective remedy, all civilizations being now much alike.

To anyone capable of comprehending government at all it must be evident without argument that the set of fundamental assumptions drawn up in the thirty-nine articles or in the Westminster Confession are wildly impossible as political constitutions for modern empires. A personal profession of them by any person disposed to take such professions seriously would practically disqualify him for high imperial office. A Calvinist Viceroy of India and a Particular Baptist Secretary of State for Foreign Affairs would wreck the empire. The Stuarts wrecked even the tight little island which was the nucleus of the empire by their Scottish logic and theological dogma; and it may be sustained very plausibly that the alleged aptitude of the English for self-government, which is contradicted by every chapter of their history, is really only an incurable inaptitude for theology, and indeed for co-ordinated thought in any direction, which makes them equally impatient of systematic despotism and systematic good government: their history being that of a badly governed and accidentally free people (comparatively). Thus our success in colonizing, as far as it has not been produced by exterminating the natives, has been due to our indifference to the salvation of our subjects. Ireland is the exception which proves the rule; for Ireland, the standing instance of the inability of the English to colonize without extermination of natives, is also the one country under British rule in which the conquerors and colonizers proceeded on the assumption that their business was to establish Protestantism as well as to make money and thereby secure at least the lives of the unfortunate inhabitants out of whose labor it could be made. At this moment Ulster is refusing to accept fellow-citizenship with the other Irish provinces because the south believes in St Peter and Bossuet, and the north in St Paul and Calvin. Imagine the effect of trying to govern India or Egypt from Belfast or from the Vatican!

The position is perhaps graver for France than for England, because the sixty-five per cent of French subjects who are neither French nor Christian nor Modernist includes some thirty millions of negroes who are susceptible, and indeed highly susceptible, of conversion to those salvationist forms of pseudo-Christianity which have produced all the persecutions and religious wars of the last fifteen hundred years. When the late explorer Sir Henry Stanley told me of the emotional grip which Christianity had over the Baganda tribes, and read me their letters, which were exactly like medieval letters in their literal faith and ever-present piety, I said "Can these men handle a rifle?" To which Stanley replied with some scorn "Of course they can, as well as any white man." Now at this moment (1915) a vast European war is being waged, in which the French are using Senegalese soldiers. I ask the French Government, which, like our own Government, is deliberately leaving the religious instruction of these negroes in the hands of missions of Petrine Catholics and Pauline Calvinists, whether they have considered the possibility of a new series of crusades, by ardent African Salvationists, to rescue Paris from the grip of the modern scientific "infidel," and to raise the cry of "Back to the Apostles: back to Charlemagne!"

We are more fortunate in that an overwhelming majority of our subjects are Hindoos, Mahometans, and Buddhists: that is, they have, as a prophylactic against salvationist Christianity, highly civilized religions of their own. Mahometanism, which Napoleon at the end of his career classed as perhaps the best popular religion for modern political use, might in some respects have arisen as a reformed Christianity if Mahomet had had to deal with a population of seventeenth-century Christians instead of Arabs who worshipped stones. As it is, men do not reject Mahomet for Calvin; and to offer a Hindoo so crude a theology as ours in exchange for his own, or our Jewish canonical literature as an improvement on Hindoo scripture, is to offer old lamps for older ones in a market where the oldest lamps, like old furniture in England, are the most highly valued.

Yet, I repeat, government is impossible without a religion: that is, without a body of common assumptions. The open mind never acts: when we have done our utmost to arrive at a reasonable conclusion, we still, when we can reason and investigate no more, must close our minds for the moment with a snap, and act dogmatically on our conclusions. The man who waits to make an entirely reasonable will dies intestate. A man so reasonable as to have an open mind about theft and murder, or about the need for food and reproduction, might just as well be a fool and a scoundrel for any use he could be as a legislator or a State official. The modern pseudo-democratic statesman, who says that he is only in power to carry out the will of the people, and moves only as the cat jumps, is clearly a political and intellectual brigand. The rule of the negative man who has no convictions means in practice the rule of the positive mob. Freedom of conscience as Cromwell used the phrase is an excellent thing; nevertheless if any man had proposed to give effect to freedom of conscience as to cannibalism in England, Cromwell would have laid him by the heels almost as promptly as he would have laid a Roman Catholic, though in Fiji at the same moment he would have supported heartily the freedom of conscience of a vegetarian who disparaged the sacred diet of Long Pig.

Here then comes in the importance of the repudiation by Jesus of proselytism. His rule "Dont pull up the tares: sow

847

the wheat: if you try to pull up the tares you will pull up
the wheat with it" is the only possible rule for a statesman
governing a modern empire, or a voter supporting such a
statesman. There is nothing in the teaching of Jesus that
cannot be assented to by a Brahman, a Mahometan, a Buddhist or a Jew, without any question of their conversion to
Christianity. In some ways it is easier to reconcile a Mahometan to Jesus than a British parson, because the idea of a
professional priest is unfamiliar and even monstrous to a
Mahometan (the tourist who persists in asking who is the
dean of St Sophia puzzles beyond words the sacristan who
lends him a huge pair of slippers); and Jesus never suggested that his disciples should separate themselves from
the laity: he picked them up by the wayside, where any man
or woman might follow him. For priests he had not a civil
word; and they shewed their sense of his hostility by getting
him killed as soon as possible. He was, in short, a thoroughgoing anti-Clerical. And though, as we have seen, it is only
by political means that his doctrine can be put into practice,
he not only never suggested a sectarian theocracy as a form
of government, and would certainly have prophesied the
downfall of the late President Kruger if he had survived to
his time, but, when challenged, he refused to teach his disciples not to pay tribute to Caesar, admitting that Caesar,
who presumably had the kingdom of heaven within him as
much as any disciple, had his place in the scheme of things.
Indeed the apostles made this an excuse for carrying sub-
servience to the State to a pitch of idolatry that ended in the
theory of the divine right of kings, and provoked men to cut
kings' heads off to restore some sense of proportion in the
matter. Jesus certainly did not consider the overthrow of the
Roman empire or the substitution of a new ecclesiastical
organization for the Jewish Church or for the priesthood of
the Roman gods as part of his program. He said that God
was better than Mammon; but he never said that Tweedledum was better than Tweedledee; and that is why it is now
possible for British citizens and statesmen to follow Jesus,

though they cannot possibly follow either Tweedledum or Tweedledee without bringing the empire down with a crash on their heads. And at that I must leave it.

LONDON, *December* 1915.

ANDROCLES AND THE LION
PROLOGUE

OVERTURE: *forest sounds, roaring of lions, Christian hymn faintly.*

A jungle path. A lion's roar, a melancholy suffering roar, comes from the jungle. It is repeated nearer. The lion limps from the jungle on three legs, holding up his right forepaw, in which a huge thorn sticks. He sits down and contemplates it. He licks it. He shakes it. He tries to extract it by scraping it along the ground, and hurts himself worse. He roars piteously. He licks it again. Tears drop from his eyes. He limps painfully off the path and lies down under the trees, exhausted with pain. Heaving a long sigh, like wind in a trombone, he goes to sleep.

Androcles and his wife Megaera come along the path. He is a small, thin, ridiculous little man who might be any age from thirty to fifty-five. He has sandy hair, watery compassionate blue eyes, sensitive nostrils, and a very presentable forehead; but his good points go no further: his arms and legs and back, though wiry of their kind, look shrivelled and starved. He carries a big bundle, is very poorly clad, and seems tired and hungry.

His wife is a rather handsome pampered slattern, well fed and in the prime of life. She has nothing to carry, and has a stout stick to help her along.

MEGAERA [*suddenly throwing down her stick*] I wont go another step.

ANDROCLES [*pleading wearily*] Oh, not again, dear. Whats the good of stopping every two miles and saying you wont go another step? We must get on to the next village before night. There are wild beasts in this wood: lions, they say.

MEGAERA. I dont believe a word of it. You are always threatening me with wild beasts to make me walk the very soul out of my body when I can hardly drag one foot before another. We havnt seen a single lion yet.

ANDROCLES. Well, dear, do you want to see one?

MEGAERA [*tearing the bundle from his back*] You cruel brute, you dont care how tired I am, or what becomes of me [*she throws the bundle on the ground*]: always thinking of your-

851

self. Self! self! self! always yourself! [*She sits down on the bundle*].

ANDROCLES [*sitting down sadly on the ground with his elbows on his knees and his head in his hands*] We all have to think of ourselves occasionally, dear.

MEGAERA. A man ought to think of his wife sometimes.

ANDROCLES. He cant always help it, dear. You make me think of you a good deal. Not that I blame you.

MEGAERA. Blame me! I should think not indeed. Is it my fault that I'm married to you?

ANDROCLES. No, dear: that is my fault.

MEGAERA. Thats a nice thing to say to me. Arnt you happy with me?

ANDROCLES. I dont complain, my love.

MEGAERA. You ought to be ashamed of yourself.

ANDROCLES. I am, my dear.

MEGAERA. Youre not: you glory in it.

ANDROCLES. In what, darling?

MEGAERA. In everything. In making me a slave, and making yourself a laughing-stock. It's not fair. You get me the name of being a shrew with your meek ways, always talking as if butter wouldnt melt in your mouth. And just because I look a big strong woman, and because I'm goodhearted and a bit hasty, and because youre always driving me to do things I'm sorry for afterwards, people say "Poor man: what a life his wife leads him!" Oh, if they only knew! And you think I dont know. But I do, I do, [*screaming*] I do.

ANDROCLES. Yes, my dear: I know you do.

MEGAERA. Then why dont you treat me properly and be a good husband to me?

ANDROCLES. What can I do, my dear?

MEGAERA. What can you do! You can return to your duty, and come back to your home and your friends, and sacrifice to the gods as all respectable people do, instead of having us hunted out of house and home for being dirty disreputable blaspheming atheists.

ANDROCLES. I'm not an atheist, dear: I am a Christian.

ANDROCLES AND THE LION

MEGAERA. Well, isnt that the same thing, only ten times worse? Everybody knows that the Christians are the very lowest of the low.

ANDROCLES. Just like us, dear.

MEGAERA. Speak for yourself. Dont you dare to compare me to common people. My father owned his own public-house; and sorrowful was the day for me when you first came drinking in our bar.

ANDROCLES. I confess I was addicted to it, dear. But I gave it up when I became a Christian.

MEGAERA. Youd much better have remained a drunkard. I can forgive a man being addicted to drink: it's only natural; and I dont deny I like a drop myself sometimes. What I cant stand is your being addicted to Christianity. And whats worse again, your being addicted to animals. How is any woman to keep her house clean when you bring in every stray cat and lost cur and lame duck in the whole country-side? You took the bread out of my mouth to feed them: you know you did: dont attempt to deny it.

ANDROCLES. Only when they were hungry and you were getting too stout, dearie.

MEGAERA. Yes: insult me, do. [Rising] Oh! I wont bear it another moment. You used to sit and talk to those dumb brute beasts for hours, when you hadnt a word for me.

ANDROCLES. They never answered back, darling. [He rises and again shoulders the bundle].

MEGAERA. Well, if youre fonder of animals than of your own wife, you can live with them here in the jungle. Ive had enough of them and enough of you. I'm going back. I'm going home.

ANDROCLES [barring the way back] No, dearie: dont take on like that. We cant go back. Weve sold everything: we should starve; and I should be sent to Rome and thrown to the lions—

MEGAERA. Serve you right! I wish the lions joy of you. [Screaming] Are you going to get out of my way and let me go home?

853

ANDROCLES. No, dear—

MEGAERA. Then I'll make my way through the forest; and when I'm eaten by the wild beasts youll know what a wife youve lost. [*She dashes into the jungle and nearly falls over the sleeping lion*]. Oh! Oh! Andy! Andy! [*She totters back and collapses into the arms of Androcles, who, crushed by her weight, falls on his bundle*].

ANDROCLES [*extracting himself from beneath her and slapping her hands in great anxiety*] What is it, my precious, my pet? Whats the matter? [*He raises her head. Speechless with terror, she points in the direction of the sleeping lion. He steals cautiously towards the spot indicated by Megaera. She rises with an effort and totters after him*].

MEGAERA. No, Andy: youll be killed. Come back.

The lion utters a long snoring sigh. Androcles sees the lion, and recoils fainting into the arms of Megaera, who falls back on the bundle. They roll apart and lie staring in terror at one another. The lion is heard groaning heavily in the jungle.

ANDROCLES [*whispering*] Did you see? A lion.

MEGAERA [*despairing*] The gods have sent him to punish us because youre a Christian. Take me away, Andy. Save me.

ANDROCLES [*rising*] Meggy: theres one chance for you. Itll take him pretty nigh twenty minutes to eat me (I'm rather stringy and tough) and you can escape in less time than that.

MEGAERA. Oh, dont talk about eating. [*The lion rises with a great groan and limps towards them*]. Oh! [*She faints*].

ANDROCLES [*quaking, but keeping between the lion and Megaera*] Dont you come near my wife, do you hear? [*The lion groans. Androcles can hardly stand for trembling*]. Meggy: run. Run for your life. If I take my eye off him, it's all up. [*The lion holds up his wounded paw and flaps it piteously before Androcles*]. Oh, he's lame, poor old chap! He's got a thorn in his paw. A frightfully big thorn. [*Full of sympathy*] Oh, poor old man! Did um get an awful thorn into um's toot-sums wootsums? Has it made um too sick to eat a nice little Christian man for um's breakfast? Oh, a nice little Christian

854

man will get um's thorn out for um; and then um shall eat the nice Christian man and the nice Christian man's nice big tender wifey pifey. [*The lion responds by moans of self-pity*]. Yes, yes, yes, yes, yes. Now, now [*taking the paw in his hand*], um is not to bite and not to scratch, not even if it hurts a very very little. Now make velvet paws. Thats right. [*He pulls gingerly at the thorn. The lion, with an angry yell of pain, jerks back his paw so abruptly that Androcles is thrown on his back*]. Steadeee! Oh, did the nasty cruel little Christian man hurt the sore paw? [*The lion moans assentingly but apologetically*]. Well, one more little pull and it will be all over. Just one little, little, leetle pull; and then um will live happily ever after. [*He gives the thorn another pull. The lion roars and snaps his jaws with a terrifying clash*]. Oh, mustnt frighten um's good kind doctor, um's affectionate nursey. That didnt hurt at all: not a bit. Just one more. Just to shew how the brave big lion can bear pain, not like the little crybaby Christian man. Oopsh! [*The thorn comes out. The lion yells with pain, and shakes his paw wildly*]. Thats it! [*Holding up the thorn*]. Now it's out. Now lick um's paw to take away the nasty inflammation. See? [*He licks his own hand. The lion nods intelligently and licks his paw industriously*]. Clever little liony-piony! Understands um's dear old friend Andy Wandy. [*The lion licks his face*]. Yes, kissums Andy Wandy. [*The lion, wagging his tail violently, rises on his hind legs, and embraces Androcles, who makes a wry face and cries*] Velvet paws! Velvet paws! [*The lion draws in his claws*]. Thats right. [*He embraces the lion, who finally takes the end of his tail in one paw, places that tight round Androcles' waist, resting it on his hip. Androcles takes the other paw in his hand, stretches out his arm, and the two waltz rapturously round and round and finally away through the jungle*].

MEGAERA [*who has revived during the waltz*] Oh, you coward, you havnt danced with me for years; and now you go off dancing with a great brute beast that you havnt known for ten minutes and that wants to eat your own wife. Coward! Coward! Coward! [*She rushes off after them into the jungle*].

ACT I

EVENING. *The end of three converging roads to Rome. Three triumphal arches span them where they debouch on a square at the gate of the city. Looking north through the arches one can see the campagna threaded by the three long dusty tracks. On the east and west sides of the square are long stone benches. An old beggar sits on the east side, his bowl at his feet.*

Through the eastern arch a squad of Roman soldiers tramps along escorting a batch of Christian prisoners of both sexes and all ages, among them one Lavinia, a good-looking resolute young woman, apparently of higher social standing than her fellow-prisoners. A centurion, carrying his vinewood cudgel, trudges alongside the squad, on its right, in command of it. All are tired and dusty; but the soldiers are dogged and indifferent, the Christians lighthearted and determined to treat their hardships as a joke and encourage one another.

A bugle is heard far behind on the road, where the rest of the cohort is following.

CENTURION [*stopping*] Halt! Orders from the Captain. [*They halt and wait*]. Now then, you Christians, none of your larks. The Captain's coming. Mind you behave yourselves. No singing. Look respectful. Look serious, if youre capable of it. See that big building over there! Thats the Coliseum. Thats where youll be thrown to the lions or set to fight the gladiators presently. Think of that; and itll help you to behave properly before the Captain. [*The Captain arrives*]. Attention! Salute! [*The soldiers salute*].

A CHRISTIAN [*cheerfully*] God bless you, Captain!

THE CENTURION [*scandalized*] Silence!

The Captain, a patrician, handsome, about thirty-five, very cold and distinguished, very superior and authoritative, steps up on a stone seat at the west side of the square, behind the centurion, so as to dominate the others more effectually.

THE CAPTAIN. Centurion.

THE CENTURION [*standing at attention and saluting*] Sir?

THE CAPTAIN [*speaking stiffly and officially*] You will re-

856

ANDROCLES AND THE LION

mind your men, Centurion, that we are now entering Rome. You will instruct them that once inside the gates of Rome they are in the presence of the Emperor. You will make them understand that the lax discipline of the march cannot be permitted here. You will instruct them to shave every day, not every week. You will impress on them particularly that there must be an end to the profanity and blasphemy of singing Christian hymns on the march. I have to reprimand you, Centurion, for not only allowing this, but actually doing it yourself.

THE CENTURION [*apologetic*] The men march better, Captain.

THE CAPTAIN. No doubt. For that reason an exception is made in the case of the march called Onward Christian Soldiers. This may be sung, except when marching through the forum or within hearing of the Emperor's palace; but the words must be altered to "Throw them to the Lions."

The Christians burst into shrieks of uncontrollable laughter, to the great scandal of the Centurion.

CENTURION. Silence! Silen-n-n-n-nce! Wheres your behavior? Is that the way to listen to an officer? [*To the Captain*] Thats what we have to put up with from these Christians every day, sir. Theyre always laughing and joking something scandalous. Theyve no religion: thats how it is.

LAVINIA. But I think the Captain meant us to laugh, Centurion. It was so funny.

CENTURION. Youll find out how funny it is when youre thrown to the lions tomorrow. [*To the Captain, who looks displeased*] Beg pardon, Sir. [*To the Christians*] Silennnnce!

THE CAPTAIN. You are to instruct your men that all intimacy with Christian prisoners must now cease. The men have fallen into habits of dependence upon the prisoners, especially the female prisoners, for cooking, repairs to uniforms, writing letters, and advice in their private affairs. In a Roman soldier such dependence is inadmissible. Let me see no more of it whilst we are in the city. Further, your orders are that in addressing Christian prisoners, the man-

857

ners and tone of your men must express abhorrence and contempt. Any shortcoming in this respect will be regarded as a breach of discipline. [*He turns to the prisoners*] Prisoners.

CENTURION [*fiercely*] Prisonerrrrrs! Tention! Silence!

THE CAPTAIN. I call your attention, prisoners, to the fact that you may be called on to appear in the Imperial Circus at any time from tomorrow onwards according to the requirements of the managers. I may inform you that as there is a shortage of Christians just now, you may expect to be called on very soon.

LAVINIA. What will they do to us, Captain?

CENTURION. Silence!

THE CAPTAIN. The women will be conducted into the arena with the wild beasts of the Imperial Menagerie, and will suffer the consequences. The men, if of an age to bear arms, will be given weapons to defend themselves, if they choose, against the Imperial Gladiators.

LAVINIA. Captain: is there no hope that this cruel persecution—

CENTURION [*shocked*] Silence! Hold your tongue, there. Persecution, indeed!

THE CAPTAIN [*unmoved and somewhat sardonic*] Persecution is not a term applicable to the acts of the Emperor. The Emperor is the Defender of the Faith. In throwing you to the lions he will be upholding the interests of religion in Rome. If you were to throw him to the lions, that would no doubt be persecution.

The Christians again laugh heartily.

CENTURION [*horrified*] Silence, I tell you! Keep silence there. Did anyone ever hear the like of this?

LAVINIA. Captain: there will be nobody to appreciate your jokes when we are gone.

THE CAPTAIN [*unshaken in his official delivery*] I call the attention of the female prisoner Lavinia to the fact that as the Emperor is a divine personage, her imputation of cruelty is not only treason, but sacrilege. I point out to her further that there is no foundation for the charge, as the Emperor does not desire that any prisoner should suffer; nor can any Christian be harmed save through his or her own obstinacy. All that is necessary is to sacrifice to the gods: a simple and convenient ceremony effected by dropping a pinch of incense on the altar, after which the prisoner is at once set free. Under such circumstances you have only your own perverse folly to blame if you suffer. I suggest to you that if you cannot burn a morsel of incense as a matter of conviction, you might at least do so as a matter of good taste, to avoid shocking the religious convictions of your fellow citizens. I am aware that these considerations do not weigh with Christians; but it is my duty to call your attention to them in order that you may have no ground for complaining of your treatment, or of accusing the Emperor of cruelty when he is shewing you the most signal clemency. Looked at from this point of view, every Christian who has perished in the arena has really committed suicide.

LAVINIA. Captain: your jokes are too grim. Do not think it is easy for us to die. Our faith makes life far stronger and more wonderful in us than when we walked in darkness and had nothing to live for. Death is harder for us than for you: the martyr's agony is as bitter as his triumph is glorious.

THE CAPTAIN [*rather troubled, addressing her personally and gravely*] A martyr, Lavinia, is a fool. Your death will prove nothing.

LAVINIA. Then why kill me?

THE CAPTAIN. I mean that truth, if there be any truth, needs no martyrs.

LAVINIA. No; but my faith, like your sword, needs testing. Can you test your sword except by staking your life on it?

THE CAPTAIN [*suddenly resuming his official tone*] I call the attention of the female prisoner to the fact that Christians are not allowed to draw the Emperor's officers into arguments and put questions to them for which the military regulations provide no answer. [*The Christians titter*].

LAVINIA. Captain: how c a n you?

THE CAPTAIN. I call the female prisoner's attention speci-

ally to the fact that four comfortable homes have been offered
her by officers of this regiment, of which she can have her
choice the moment she chooses to sacrifice as all wellbred
Roman ladies do. I have no more to say to the prisoners.

CENTURION. Dismiss! But stay where you are.

THE CAPTAIN. Centurion: you will remain here with your
men in charge of the prisoners until the arrival of three
Christian prisoners in the custody of a cohort of the tenth
legion. Among these prisoners you will particularly identify
an armorer named Ferrovius, of dangerous character and
great personal strength, and a Greek tailor reputed to be a
sorcerer, by name Androcles. You will add the three to your
charge here and march them all to the Coliseum, where you
will deliver them into the custody of the master of the gladiators and take his receipt, countersigned by the keeper of
the beasts and the acting manager. You understand your
instructions?

CENTURION. Yes, sir.

THE CAPTAIN. Dismiss. [*He throws off his air of parade,
and descends from his perch. The Centurion seats himself on it
and prepares for a nap, whilst his men stand at ease. The Christians sit down on the west side of the square, glad to rest. Lavinia
alone remains standing to speak to the Captain*].

LAVINIA. Captain: is this man who is to join us the famous
Ferrovius, who has made such wonderful conversions in the
northern cities?

THE CAPTAIN. Yes. We are warned that he has the
strength of an elephant and the temper of a mad bull. Also
that he is stark mad. Not a model Christian, it would seem.

LAVINIA. You need not fear him if he is a Christian,
Captain.

THE CAPTAIN [*coldly*] I shall not fear him in any case,
Lavinia.

LAVINIA [*her eyes dancing*] How brave of you, Captain!

THE CAPTAIN. You are right: it was a silly thing to say.
[*In a lower tone, humane and urgent*] Lavinia: do Christians
know how to love?

860

LAVINIA [*composedly*] Yes, Captain: they love even their enemies.

THE CAPTAIN. Is that easy?

LAVINIA. Very easy, Captain, when their enemies are as handsome as you.

THE CAPTAIN. Lavinia: you are laughing at me.

LAVINIA. At you, Captain! Impossible.

THE CAPTAIN. Then you are flirting with me, which is worse. Dont be foolish.

LAVINIA. But such a very handsome captain.

THE CAPTAIN. Incorrigible! [*Urgently*] Listen to me. The men in that audience tomorrow will be the vilest of voluptuaries: men in whom the only passion excited by a beautiful woman is a lust to see her tortured and torn shrieking limb from limb. It is a crime to gratify that passion. It is offering yourself for violation by the whole rabble of the streets and the riff-raff of the court at the same time. Why will you not choose rather a kindly love and an honorable alliance?

LAVINIA. They cannot violate my soul. I alone can do that by sacrificing to false gods.

THE CAPTAIN. Sacrifice then to the true God. What does his name matter? We call him Jupiter. The Greeks call him Zeus. Call him what you will as you drop the incense on the altar flame: He will understand.

LAVINIA. No. I couldnt. That is the strange thing, Captain, that a little pinch of incense should make all that difference. Religion is such a great thing that when I meet really religious people we are friends at once, no matter what name we give to the divine will that made us and moves us. Oh, do you think that I, a woman, would quarrel with you for sacrificing to a woman god like Diana, if Diana meant to you what Christ means to me? No: we should kneel side by side before her altar like two children. But when men who believe neither in my god nor in their own—men who do not know the meaning of the word religion—when these men drag me to the foot of an iron statue that has become the symbol of the terror and darkness through which they walk, of their cruelty and greed, of their hatred of God and their oppression of man—when they ask me to pledge my soul before the people that this hideous idol is God, and that all this wickedness and falsehood is divine truth, I cannot do it, not if they could put a thousand cruel deaths on me. I tell you, it is physically impossible. Listen, Captain: did you ever try to catch a mouse in your hand? Once there was a dear little mouse that used to come out and play on my table as I was reading. I wanted to take him in my hand and caress him; and sometimes he got among my books so that he could not escape me when I stretched out my hand. And I did stretch out my hand; but it always came back in spite of me. I was not afraid of him in my heart; but my hand refused: it is not in the nature of my hand to touch a mouse. Well, Captain, if I took a pinch of incense in my hand and stretched it out over the altar fire, my hand would come back. My body would be true to my faith even if you could corrupt my mind. And all the time I should believe more in Diana than my persecutors have ever believed in anything. Can you understand that?

THE CAPTAIN [*simply*] Yes: I understand that. But my hand would not come back. The hand that holds the sword has been trained not to come back from anything but victory.

LAVINIA. Not even from death?

THE CAPTAIN. Least of all from death.

LAVINIA. Then I must not come back from death either. A woman has to be braver than a soldier.

THE CAPTAIN. Prouder, you mean.

LAVINIA [*startled*] Prouder! You call our courage pride!

THE CAPTAIN. There is no such thing as courage: there is only pride. You Christians are the proudest devils on earth.

LAVINIA [*hurt*] Pray God then my pride may never become a false pride. [*She turns away as if she did not wish to continue the conversation, but softens and says to him with a smile*] Thank you for trying to save me.

THE CAPTAIN. I knew it was no use; but one tries in spite of one's knowledge.

862

ANDROCLES AND THE LION

LAVINIA. Something stirs, even in the iron breast of a Roman soldier?

THE CAPTAIN. It will soon be iron again. I have seen many women die, and forgotten them in a week.

LAVINIA. Remember me for a fortnight, handsome Captain. I shall be watching you, perhaps.

THE CAPTAIN. From the skies? Do not deceive yourself, Lavinia. There is no future for you beyond the grave.

LAVINIA. What does that matter? Do you think I am only running away from the terrors of life into the comfort of heaven? If there were no future, or if the future were one of torment, I should have to go just the same. The hand of God is upon me.

THE CAPTAIN. Yes: when all is said, we are both patricians, Lavinia, and must die for our beliefs. Farewell. [*He offers her his hand. She takes it and presses it. He walks away, trim and calm. She looks after him for a moment, and cries a little as he disappears through the eastern arch. A trumpet-call is heard from the road through the western arch*].

CENTURION [*waking up and rising*] Cohort of the tenth with prisoners. Two file out with me to receive them. [*He goes out through the western arch, followed by four soldiers in two files*].

Lentulus and Metellus come into the square from the west side with a little retinue of servants. Both are young courtiers, dressed in the extremity of fashion. Lentulus is slender, fair-haired, epicene. Metellus is manly, compactly built, olive skinned, not a talker.

LENTULUS. Christians, by Jove! Lets chaff them.

METELLUS. Awful brutes. If you knew as much about them as I do you wouldnt want to chaff them. Leave them to the lions.

LENTULUS [*indicating Lavinia, who is still looking towards the arches after the Captain*] That woman's got a figure. [*He walks past her, staring at her invitingly; but she is preoccupied and is not conscious of him*]. Do you turn the other cheek when they kiss you?

863

LAVINIA [*starting*] What?

LENTULUS. Do you turn the other cheek when they kiss you, fascinating Christian?

LAVINIA. Dont be foolish. [*To Metellus, who has remained on her right, so that she is between them*] Please dont let your friend behave like a cad before the soldiers. How are they to respect and obey patricians if they see them behaving like street boys? [*Sharply to Lentulus*] Pull yourself together, man. Hold your head up. Keep the corners of your mouth firm; and treat me respectfully. What do you take me for?

LENTULUS [*irresolutely*] Look here, you know: I—you—I—

LAVINIA. Stuff! Go about your business. [*She turns decisively away and sits down with her comrades, leaving him disconcerted*].

METELLUS. You didnt get much out of that. I told you they were brutes.

LENTULUS. Plucky little filly! I suppose she thinks I care. [*With an air of indifference he strolls with Metellus to the east side of the square, where they stand watching the return of the Centurion through the western arch with his men, escorting three prisoners: Ferrovius, Androcles, and Spintho. Ferrovius is a powerful, choleric man in the prime of life, with large nostrils, staring eyes, and a thick neck: a man whose sensibilities are keen and violent to the verge of madness. Spintho is a debauchee, the wreck of a good-looking man gone hopelessly to the bad. Androcles is overwhelmed with grief, and is restraining his tears with great difficulty*].

THE CENTURION [*to Lavinia*] Here are some pals for you. This little bit is Ferrovius that you talk so much about. [*Ferrovius turns on him threateningly. The Centurion holds up his left forefinger in admonition*]. Now remember that youre a Christian, and that youve got to return good for evil. [*Ferrovius controls himself convulsively; moves away from temptation to the east side near Lentulus; clasps his hands in silent prayer; and throws himself on his knees*]. Thats the way to manage them, eh! This fine fellow [*indicating Androcles, who*
864

comes to his left, and makes Lavinia a heart-broken salutation]
is a sorcerer. A Greek tailor, he is. A real sorcerer, too: no
mistake about it. The tenth marches with a leopard at the
head of the column. He made a pet of the leopard; and now
he's crying at being parted from it. *[Androcles sniffs lament-
ably].* Aint you, old chap? Well, cheer up, we march with a
Billy goat *[Androcles brightens up]* thats killed two leopards
and ate a turkey-cock. You can have him for a pet if you like.
*[Androcles, quite consoled, goes past the Centurion to Lavinia,
and sits down contentedly on the ground on her left].* This dirty
dog *[collaring Spintho]* is a real Christian. He mobs the
temples, he does *[at each accusation he gives the neck of
Spintho's tunic a twist]*; he goes smashing things mad drunk,
he does; he steals the gold vessels, he does; he assaults the
priestesses, he does—yah! *[He flings Spintho into the middle
of the group of prisoners].* Youre the sort that makes duty a
pleasure, you are.

SPINTHO *[gasping]* Thats it: strangle me. Kick me. Beat
me. Revile me. Our Lord was beaten and reviled. Thats my
way to heaven. Every martyr goes to heaven, no matter what
he's done. That is so, isnt it, brother?

CENTURION. Well, if youre going to heaven, *I* dont want
to go there. I wouldnt be seen with you.

LENTULUS. Haw! Good! *[Indicating the kneeling Ferro-
vius].* Is this one of the turn-the-other-cheek gentlemen,
Centurion?

CENTURION. Yes, sir. Lucky for you too, sir, if you want
to take any liberties with him.

LENTULUS *[to Ferrovius]* You turn the other cheek when
youre struck, I'm told.

FERROVIUS *[slowly turning his great eyes on him]* Yes, by
the grace of God, I do, now.

LENTULUS. Not that youre a coward, of course; but out
of pure piety.

FERROVIUS. I fear God more than man; at least I try to.

LENTULUS. Lets see. *[He strikes him on the cheek. Androcles
makes a wild movement to rise and interfere; but Lavinia holds* ·

him down, watching Ferrovius intently. Ferrovius, without flinching, turns the other cheek. Lentulus, rather out of countenance, titters foolishly, and strikes him again feebly]. You know, I should feel ashamed if I let myself be struck like that, and took it lying down. But then I'm not a Christian: I'm a man. *[Ferrovius rises impressively and towers over him. Lentulus becomes white with terror; and a shade of green flickers in his cheek for a moment].*

FERROVIUS *[with the calm of a steam hammer]* I have not always been faithful. The first man who struck me as you have just struck me was a stronger man than you: he hit me harder than I expected. I was tempted and fell; and it was then that I first tasted bitter shame. I never had a happy moment after that until I had knelt and asked his forgiveness by his bedside in the hospital. *[Putting his hands on Lentulus's shoulders with paternal weight].* But now I have learnt to resist with a strength that is not my own. I am not ashamed now, nor angry.

LENTULUS *[uneasily]* Er—good evening. *[He tries to move away].*

FERROVIUS *[gripping his shoulders]* Oh, do not harden your heart, young man. Come: try for yourself whether our way is not better than yours. I will now strike you on one cheek; and you will turn the other and learn how much better you will feel than if you gave way to the promptings of anger.*[He holds him with one hand and clenches the other fist].*

LENTULUS. Centurion: I call on you to protect me.

CENTURION. You asked for it, sir. It's no business of ours. Youve had two whacks at him. Better pay him a trifle and square it that way.

LENTULUS. Yes, of course. *[To Ferrovius]* It was only a bit of fun, I assure you: I meant no harm. Here. *[He proffers a gold coin].*

FERROVIUS *[taking it and throwing it to the old beggar, who snatches it up eagerly, and hobbles off to spend it]* Give all thou hast to the poor. Come, friend: courage! I may hurt your body for a moment; but your soul will rejoice in the victory of the spirit over the flesh. [*He prepares to strike*].

ANDROCLES. Easy, Ferrovius, easy: you broke the last man's jaw.

Lentulus, with a moan of terror, attempts to fly; but Ferrovius holds him ruthlessly.

FERROVIUS. Yes; but I saved his soul. What matters a broken jaw?

LENTULUS. Dont touch me, do you hear? The law—

FERROVIUS. The law will throw me to the lions tomorrow: what worse could it do were I to slay you? Pray for strength; and it shall be given to you.

LENTULUS. Let me go. Your religion forbids you to strike me.

FERROVIUS. On the contrary, it commands me to strike you. How can you turn the other cheek, if you are not first struck on the one cheek?

LENTULUS [*almost in tears*] But I'm convinced already that what you said is quite right. I apologize for striking you.

FERROVIUS [*greatly pleased*] My son: have I softened your heart? Has the good seed fallen in a fruitful place? Are your feet turning towards a better path?

LENTULUS [*abjectly*] Yes, yes. Theres a great deal in what you say.

FERROVIUS [*radiant*] Join us. Come to the lions. Come to suffering and death.

LENTULUS [*falling on his knees and bursting into tears*] Oh, help me. Mother! mother!

FERROVIUS. These tears will water your soul and make it bring forth good fruit, my son. God has greatly blessed my efforts at conversion. Shall I tell you a miracle—yes, a miracle—wrought by me in Cappadocia? A young man— just such a one as you, with golden hair like yours—scoffed at and struck me as you scoffed at and struck me. I sat up all night with that youth wrestling for his soul; and in the morning not only was he a Christian, but his hair was as white as snow. [*Lentulus falls in a dead faint*]. There, there:

867

take him away. The spirit has overwrought him, poor lad. Carry him gently to his house; and leave the rest to heaven.

CENTURION. Take him home. [*The servants, intimidated, hastily carry him out. Metellus is about to follow when Ferrovius lays his hand on his shoulder*].

FERROVIUS. You are his friend, young man. You will see that he is taken safely home.

METELLUS [*with awestruck civility*] Certainly, sir. I shall do whatever you think best. Most happy to have made your acquaintance, I'm sure. You may depend on me. Good evening, sir.

FERROVIUS [*with unction*] The blessing of heaven upon you and him.

Metellus follows Lentulus. The Centurion returns to his seat to resume his interrupted nap. The deepest awe has settled on the spectators. Ferrovius, with a long sigh of happiness, goes to Lavinia, and offers her his hand.

LAVINIA [*taking it*] So that is how you convert people, Ferrovius.

FERROVIUS. Yes: there has been a blessing on my work in spite of my unworthiness and my backslidings—all through my wicked, devilish temper. This man—

ANDROCLES [*hastily*] Dont slap me on the back, brother. She knows you mean me.

FERROVIUS. How I wish I were weak like our brother here! for then I should perhaps be meek and gentle like him. And yet there seems to be a special providence that makes my trials less than his. I hear tales of the crowd scoffing and casting stones and reviling the brethren; but when I come, all this stops: my influence calms the passions of the mob: they listen to me in silence; and infidels are often converted by a straight heart-to-heart talk with me. Every day I feel happier, more confident. Every day lightens the load of the great terror.

LAVINIA. The great terror? What is that?

Ferrovius shakes his head and does not answer. He sits down beside her on her left, and buries his face in his hands in gloomy meditation.

ANDROCLES. Well, you see, sister, he's never quite sure of himself. Suppose at the last moment in the arena, with the gladiators there to fight him, one of them was to say anything to annoy him, he might forget himself and lay that gladiator out.

LAVINIA. That would be splendid.

FERROVIUS [*springing up in horror*] What!

ANDROCLES. Oh, sister!

FERROVIUS. Splendid to betray my master, like Peter! Splendid to act like any common blackguard in the day of my proving! Woman: you are no Christian. [*He moves away from her to the middle of the square, as if her neighborhood contaminated him*].

LAVINIA [*laughing*] You know, Ferrovius, I am not always a Christian. I dont think anybody is. There are moments when I forget all about it, and something comes out quite naturally, as it did then.

SPINTHO. What does it matter? If you die in the arena, youll be a martyr; and all martyrs go to heaven, no matter what they have done. Thats so, isnt it, Ferrovius?

FERROVIUS. Yes: that is so, if we are faithful to the end.

LAVINIA. I'm not so sure.

SPINTHO. Dont say that. Thats blasphemy. Dont say that, I tell you. We shall be saved, no matter WHAT we do.

LAVINIA. Perhaps you men will all go into heaven bravely and in triumph, with your heads erect and golden trumpets sounding for you. But I am sure I shall only be allowed to squeeze myself in through a little crack in the gate after a great deal of begging. I am not good always: I have moments only.

SPINTHO. Youre talking nonsense, woman. I tell you, martyrdom pays all scores.

ANDROCLES. Well, let us hope so, brother, for your sake. Youve had a gay time, havnt you? with your raids on the temples. I cant help thinking that heaven will be very dull for a man of your temperament. [*Spintho snarls*]. Dont be

869

angry: I say it only to console you in case you should die in your bed tonight in the natural way. Theres a lot of plague about.

SPINTHO [*rising and running about in abject terror*] I never thought of that. Oh Lord, spare me to be martyred. Oh, what a thought to put into the mind of a brother! Oh, let me be martyred today, now. I shall die in the night and go to hell. Youre a sorcerer: youve put death into my mind. Oh, curse you, curse you! [*He tries to seize Androcles by the throat*].

FERROVIUS [*holding him in a grasp of iron*] Whats this, brother? Anger! Violence! Raising your hand to a brother Christian!

SPINTHO. It's easy for you. Youre strong. Your nerves are all right. But I'm full of disease. [*Ferrovius takes his hand from him with instinctive disgust*]. Ive drunk all my nerves away. I shall have the horrors all night.

ANDROCLES [*sympathetic*] Oh, dont take on so, brother. We're all sinners.

SPINTHO [*snivelling, trying to feel consoled*] Yes: I daresay if the truth were known, youre all as bad as I am.

LAVINIA [*contemptuously*] Does that comfort you ?

FERROVIUS [*sternly*] Pray, man, pray.

SPINTHO. Whats the good of praying? If we're martyred we shall go to heaven, shant we, whether we pray or not?

FERROVIUS. Whats that? Not pray! [*Seizing him again*] Pray this instant, you dog, you rotten hound, you slimy snake, you beastly goat, or—

SPINTHO. Yes: beat me: kick me. I forgive you: mind that.

FERROVIUS [*spurning him with loathing*] Yah! [*Spintho reels away and falls in front of Ferrovius*].

ANDROCLES [*reaching out and catching the skirt of Ferrovius's tunic*] Dear brother: if you wouldnt mind—just for my sake—

FERROVIUS. Well?

ANDROCLES. Dont call him by the names of the animals. Weve no right to. Ive had such friends in dogs. A pet snake

870

is the best of company. I was nursed on goat's milk. Is it fair to them to call the like of him a dog or a snake or a goat?

FERROVIUS. I only meant that they have no souls.

ANDROCLES [*anxiously protesting*] Oh, believe me, they have. Just the same as you and me. I really dont think I could consent to go to heaven if I thought there were to be no animals there. Think of what they suffer here.

FERROVIUS. Thats true. Yes: that is just. They will have their share in heaven.

SPINTHO [*who has picked himself up and is sneaking past Ferrovius on his left, sneers derisively*]!!

FERROVIUS [*turning on him fiercely*] Whats that you say?

SPINTHO [*cowering*] Nothing.

FERROVIUS [*clenching his fist*] Do animals go to heaven or not?

SPINTHO. I never said they didnt.

FERROVIUS [*implacable*] Do they or do they not?

SPINTHO. They do: they do. [*Scrambling out of Ferrovius's reach*]. Oh, curse you for frightening me!

A bugle call is heard.

CENTURION [*waking up*] Tention! Form as before. Now then, prisoners: up with you and trot along spry. [*The soldiers fall in. The Christians rise*].

A man with an ox goad comes running through the central arch.

THE OX DRIVER. Here, you soldiers! clear out of the way for the Emperor.

THE CENTURION. Emperor! Wheres the Emperor? You aint the Emperor, are you?

THE OX DRIVER. It's the menagerie service. My team of oxen is drawing the new lion to the Coliseum. You clear the road.

CENTURION. What! Go in after you in your dust, with half the town at the heels of you and your lion! Not likely. We go first.

THE OX DRIVER. The menagerie service is the Emperor's personal retinue. You clear out, I tell you.

ANDROCLES AND THE LION

CENTURION. You tell me, do you? Well, I'll tell you something. If the lion is menagerie service, the lion's dinner is menagerie service too. This [*pointing to the Christians*] is the lion's dinner. So back with you to your bullocks double quick; and learn your place. March. [*The soldiers start*]. Now then, you Christians: step out there.

LAVINIA [*marching*] Come along, the rest of the dinner. I shall be the olives and anchovies.

ANOTHER CHRISTIAN [*laughing*] I shall be the soup.

ANOTHER. I shall be the fish.

ANOTHER. Ferrovius shall be the roast boar.

FERROVIUS [*heavily*] I see the joke. Yes, yes: I shall be the roast boar. Ha! ha! [*He laughs conscientiously and marches out with them*].

ANDROCLES [*following*] I shall be the mince pie. [*Each announcement is received with a louder laugh by all the rest as the joke catches on*].

CENTURION [*scandalized*] Silence! Have some sense of your situation. Is this the way for martyrs to behave? [*To Spintho, who is quaking and loitering*] I know what youll be at that dinner. Youll be the emetic. [*He shoves him rudely along*].

SPINTHO. It's too dreadful: I'm not fit to die.

CENTURION. Fitter than you are to live, you swine.

They pass from the square westward. The oxen, drawing a waggon with a great wooden cage and the lion in it, arrive through the central arch.

ACT II

BEHIND *the Emperor's box at the Coliseum, where the performers assemble before entering the arena. In the middle a wide passage leading to the arena descends from the floor level under the imperial box. On both sides of this passage steps ascend to a landing at the back entrance to the box. The landing forms a bridge across the passage. At the entrance to the passage are two bronze mirrors, one on each side.*

On the west side of this passage, on the right hand of anyone coming from the box and standing on the bridge, the martyrs are sitting on the steps. Lavinia is seated half-way up, thoughtful, trying to look death in the face. On her left Androcles consoles himself by nursing a cat. Ferrovius stands behind them, his eyes blazing, his figure stiff with intense resolution. At the foot of the steps crouches Spintho, with his head clutched in his hands, full of horror at the approach of martyrdom.

On the east side of the passage the gladiators are standing and sitting at ease, waiting, like the Christians, for their turn in the arena. One (Retiarius) is a nearly naked man with a net and a trident. Another (Secutor) is in armor with a sword. He carries a helmet with a barred visor. The editor of the gladiators sits on a chair a little apart from them.

The Call Boy enters from the passage.

THE CALL BOY. Number six. Retiarius versus Secutor.

The gladiator with the net picks it up. The gladiator with the helmet puts it on; and the two go into the arena, the net thrower taking out a little brush and arranging his hair as he goes, the other tightening his straps and shaking his shoulders loose. Both look at themselves in the mirrors before they enter the passage.

LAVINIA. Will they really kill one another?

SPINTHO. Yes, if the people turn down their thumbs.

THE EDITOR. You know nothing about it. The people indeed! Do you suppose we would kill a man worth perhaps fifty talents to please the riffraff? I should like to catch any of my men at it.

SPINTHO. I thought—

873

ANDROCLES AND THE LION

THE EDITOR [*contemptuously*] You thought! Who cares what you think? Youll be killed all right enough.

SPINTHO [*groans and again hides his face*]!!!

LAVINIA. Then is nobody ever killed except us poor Christians?

THE EDITOR. If the vestal virgins turn down their thumbs, thats another matter. Theyre ladies of rank.

LAVINIA. Does the Emperor ever interfere?

THE EDITOR. Oh, yes: he turns his thumb up fast enough if the vestal virgins want to have one of his pet fighting men killed.

ANDROCLES. But dont they ever just only pretend to kill one another? Why shouldnt you pretend to die, and get dragged out as if you were dead; and then get up and go home, like an actor?

THE EDITOR. See here: you want to know too much. There will be no pretending about the new lion: let that be enough for you. He's hungry.

SPINTHO [*groaning with horror*] Oh, Lord! cant you stop talking about it? Isnt it bad enough for us without that?

ANDROCLES. I'm glad he's hungry. Not that I want him to suffer, poor chap! but then he'll enjoy eating me so much more. Theres a cheerful side to everything.

THE EDITOR [*rising and striding over to Androcles*] Here: dont you be obstinate. Come with me and drop the pinch of incense on the altar. Thats all you need do to be let off.

ANDROCLES. No: thank you very much indeed; but I really mustnt.

THE EDITOR. What! Not to save your life?

ANDROCLES. I'd rather not. I couldnt sacrifice to Diana: she's a huntress, you know, and kills things.

THE EDITOR. That dont matter. You can choose your own altar. Sacrifice to Jupiter: he likes animals: he turns himself into an animal when he goes off duty.

ANDROCLES. No: it's very kind of you; but I feel I cant save myself that way.

THE EDITOR. But I dont ask you to do it to save yourself:

I ask you to do it to oblige me personally.

ANDROCLES [*scrambling up in the greatest agitation*] Oh, please dont say that. This is dreadful. You mean so kindly by me that it seems quite horrible to disoblige you. If you could arrange for me to sacrifice when theres nobody looking, I shouldnt mind. But I must go into the arena with the rest. My honor, you know.

THE EDITOR. Honor! The honor of a tailor?

ANDROCLES [*apologetically*] Well, perhaps honor is too strong an expression. Still, you know, I couldnt allow the tailors to get a bad name through me.

THE EDITOR. How much will you remember of all that when you smell the beast's breath and see his jaws opening to tear out your throat?

SPINTHO [*rising with a yell of terror*] I cant bear it. Wheres the altar? I'll sacrifice.

FERROVIUS. Dog of an apostate. Iscariot!

SPINTHO. I'll repent afterwards. I fully mean to die in the arena: I'll die a martyr and go to heaven; but not this time, not now, not until my nerves are better. Besides, I'm too young: I want to have just one more good time. [*The gladiators laugh at him*]. Oh, will no one tell me where the altar is? [*He dashes into the passage and vanishes*].

ANDROCLES [*to the Editor, pointing after Spintho*] Brother: I cant do that, not even to oblige you. Dont ask me.

THE EDITOR. Well, if youre determined to die, I cant help you. But I wouldnt be put off by a swine like that.

FERROVIUS. Peace, peace: tempt him not. Get thee behind him, Satan.

THE EDITOR [*flushing with rage*] For two pins I'd take a turn in the arena myself today, and pay you out for daring to talk to me like that.

Ferrovius springs forward.

LAVINIA [*rising quickly and interposing*] Brother, brother: you forget.

FERROVIUS [*curbing himself by a mighty effort*] Oh, my temper, my wicked temper! [*To the Editor, as Lavinia sits down again, reassured*] Forgive me, brother. My heart was full of wrath: I should have been thinking of your dear precious soul.

THE EDITOR. Yah! [*He turns his back on Ferrovius contemptuously, and goes back to his seat*].

FERROVIUS [*continuing*] And I forgot it all: I thought of nothing but offering to fight you with one hand tied behind me.

THE EDITOR [*turning pugnaciously*] What!

FERROVIUS [*on the border line between zeal and ferocity*] Oh, dont give way to pride and wrath, brother. I could do it so easily. I could—

They are separated by the Menagerie Keeper, who rushes in from the passage, furious.

THE KEEPER. Heres a nice business! Who let that Christian out of here down to the dens when we were changing the lion into the cage next the arena?

THE EDITOR. Nobody let him. He let himself.

THE KEEPER. Well, the lion's ate him.

Consternation. The Christians rise, greatly agitated. The gladiators sit callously, but are highly amused. All speak or cry out or laugh at once. Tumult.

LAVINIA. Oh, poor wretch! FERROVIUS. The apostate has perished. Praise be to God's justice! ANDROCLES. The poor beast was starving. It couldnt help itself. THE CHRISTIANS. What! Ate him! How frightful! How terrible! Without a moment to repent! God be merciful to him, a sinner! Oh, I cant bear to think of it! In the midst of his sin! Horrible, horrible! THE EDITOR. Serve the rotter right! THE GLADIATORS. Just walked into it, he did. He's martyred all right enough. Good old lion! Old Jock doesnt like that: look at his face. Devil a better! The Emperor will laugh when he hears of it. I cant help smiling. Ha ha ha!!!!!

THE KEEPER. Now his appetite's taken off, he wont as much as look at another Christian for a week.

ANDROCLES. Couldnt you have saved him, brother?

THE KEEPER. Saved him! Saved him from a lion that I'd

ANDROCLES AND THE LION

just got mad with hunger! a wild one that came out of the forest not four weeks ago! He bolted him before you could say Balbus.

LAVINIA [*sitting down again*] Poor Spintho! And it wont even count as martyrdom!

THE KEEPER. Serve him right! What call had he to walk down the throat of one of my lions before he was asked?

ANDROCLES. Perhaps the lion wont eat me now.

THE KEEPER. Yes: thats just like a Christian: think only of yourself! What am *I* to do? What am I to say to the Emperor when he sees one of my lions coming into the arena half asleep?

THE EDITOR. Say nothing. Give your old lion some bitters and a morsel of fried fish to wake up his appetite. [*Laughter*].

THE KEEPER. Yes: it's easy for you to talk; but—

THE EDITOR [*scrambling to his feet*] Sh! Attention there! The Emperor. [*The Keeper bolts precipitately into the passage. The gladiators rise smartly and form into line*].

The Emperor enters on the Christians' side, conversing with Metellus, and followed by his suite.

THE GLADIATORS. Hail, Caesar! those about to die salute thee.

CAESAR. Good morrow, friends.

Metellus shakes hands with the Editor, who accepts his condescension with bluff respect.

LAVINIA. Blessing, Caesar, and forgiveness!

CAESAR [*turning in some surprise at the salutation*] There is no forgiveness for Christianity.

LAVINIA. I did not mean that, Caesar. I mean that we forgive you.

METELLUS. An inconceivable liberty! Do you not know, woman, that the Emperor can do no wrong and therefore cannot be forgiven?

LAVINIA. I expect the Emperor knows better. Anyhow, we forgive him.

THE CHRISTIANS. Amen!

CAESAR. Metellus: you see now the disadvantage of too

877

much severity. These people have no hope; therefore they have nothing to restrain them from saying what they like to me. They are almost as impertinent as the gladiators. Which is the Greek sorcerer?

ANDROCLES [*humbly touching his forelock*] Me, your Worship.

CAESAR. My Worship! Good! A new title. Well: what miracles can you perform?

ANDROCLES. I can cure warts by rubbing them with my tailor's chalk; and I can live with my wife without beating her.

CAESAR. Is that all?

ANDROCLES. You dont know her, Caesar, or you wouldnt say that.

CAESAR. Ah, well, my friend, we shall no doubt contrive a happy release for you. Which is Ferrovius?

FERROVIUS. I am he.

CAESAR. They tell me you can fight.

FERROVIUS. It is easy to fight. *I* can die, Caesar.

CAESAR. That is still easier, is it not?

FERROVIUS. Not to me, Caesar. Death comes hard to my flesh; and fighting comes very easily to my spirit [*beating his breast and lamenting*] Oh, sinner that I am! [*He throws himself down on the steps, deeply discouraged*].

CAESAR. Metellus: I should like to have this man in the Pretorian Guard.

METELLUS. *I* should not, Caesar. He looks a spoilsport. There are men in whose presence it is impossible to have any fun: men who are a sort of walking conscience. He would make us all uncomfortable.

CAESAR. For that reason, perhaps, it might be well to have him. An Emperor can hardly have too many consciences. [*To Ferrovius*] Listen, Ferrovius. [*Ferrovius shakes his head and will not look up*]. You and your friends shall not be outnumbered today in the arena. You shall have arms; and there will be no more than one gladiator to each Christian. If you come out of the arena alive, I will consider favorably any request of yours, and give you a place in the Pretorian Guard. Even if the request be that no questions be asked about your faith I shall perhaps not refuse it.

FERROVIUS. I will not fight. I will die. Better stand with the archangels than with the Pretorian Guard.

CAESAR. I cannot believe that the archangels—whoever they may be—would not prefer to be recruited from the Pretorian Guard. However, as you please. Come: let us see the show.

As the Court ascends the steps, Secutor and Retiarius return from the arena through the passage: Secutor covered with dust and very angry: Retiarius grinning.

SECUTOR. Ha, the Emperor. Now we shall see. Caesar: I ask you whether it is fair for the Retiarius, instead of making a fair throw of his net at me, to swish it along the ground and throw the dust in my eyes, and then catch me when I'm blinded. If the vestals had not turned up their thumbs I should have been a dead man.

CAESAR [*halting on the stair*] There is nothing in the rules against it.

SECUTOR [*indignantly*] Caesar: is it a dirty trick or is it not?

CAESAR. It is a dusty one, my friend. [*Obsequious laughter*]. Be on your guard next time.

SECUTOR. Let him be on his guard. Next time I'll throw my sword at his heels and strangle him with his own net before he can hop off. [*To the Retiarius*] You see if I dont. [*He goes out past the gladiators, sulky and furious*].

CAESAR [*to the chuckling Retiarius*]. These tricks are not wise, my friend. The audience likes to see a dead man in all his beauty and splendor. If you smudge his face and spoil his armor they will shew their displeasure by not letting you kill him. And when your turn comes, they will remember it against you and turn their thumbs down.

THE RETIARIUS. Perhaps that is why I did it, Caesar. He bet me ten sesterces that he would vanquish me. If I had had to kill him I should not have had the money.

879

ANDROCLES AND THE LION

CAESAR [*indulgent, laughing*] You rogues: there is no end to your tricks. I'll dismiss you all and have elephants to fight. They fight fairly. [*He goes up to his box, and knocks at it. It is opened from within by the Captain, who stands as on parade to let him pass*].

The Call Boy comes from the passage, followed by three attendants carrying respectively a bundle of swords, some helmets, and some breastplates and pieces of armor which they throw down in a heap.

THE CALL BOY. By your leave, Caesar. Number eleven! Gladiators and Christians!

Ferrovius springs up, ready for martyrdom. The other Christians take the summons as best they can, some joyful and brave, some patient and dignified, some tearful and helpless, some embracing one another with emotion. The Call Boy goes back into the passage.

CAESAR [*turning at the door of the box*] The hour has come, Ferrovius. I shall go into my box and see you killed, since you scorn the Pretorian Guard. [*He goes into the box. The Captain shuts the door, remaining inside with the Emperor. Metellus and the rest of the suite disperse to their seats. The Christians, led by Ferrovius, move towards the passage*].

LAVINIA [*to Ferrovius*] Farewell.

THE EDITOR. Steady there. You Christians have got to fight. Here! arm yourselves.

FERROVIUS [*picking up a sword*] I'll die sword in hand to shew people that I could fight if it were my Master's will, and that I could kill the man who kills me if I chose.

THE EDITOR. Put on that armor.

FERROVIUS. No armor.

THE EDITOR [*bullying him*] Do what youre told. Put on that armor.

FERROVIUS [*gripping the sword and looking dangerous*] I said, No armor.

THE EDITOR. And what am I to say when I am accused of sending a naked man in to fight my men in armor?

FERROVIUS. Say your prayers, brother; and have no fear

880

of the princes of this world.

THE EDITOR. Tsha! You obstinate fool! [*He bites his lips irresolutely, not knowing exactly what to do*].

ANDROCLES [*to Ferrovius*] Farewell, brother, till we meet in the sweet by-and-by.

THE EDITOR [*to Androcles*] You are going too. Take a sword there; and put on any armor you can find to fit you.

ANDROCLES. No, really: I cant fight: I never could: I cant bring myself to dislike anyone enough. I'm to be thrown to the lions with the lady.

THE EDITOR. Then get out of the way and hold your noise. [*Androcles steps aside with cheerful docility*]. Now then! Are you all ready there?

A trumpet is heard from the arena.

FERROVIUS [*starting convulsively*] Heaven give me strength!

THE EDITOR. Aha! That frightens you, does it?

FERROVIUS. Man: there is no terror like the terror of that sound to me. When I hear a trumpet or a drum or the clash of steel or the hum of the catapult as the great stone flies, fire runs through my veins: I feel my blood surge up hot behind my eyes: I must charge: I must strike: I must conquer: Caesar himself will not be safe in his imperial seat if once that spirit gets loose in me. Oh, brothers, pray! exhort me! remind me that if I raise my sword my honor falls and my Master is crucified afresh.

ANDROCLES. Just keep thinking how cruelly you might hurt the poor gladiators.

FERROVIUS. It does not hurt a man to kill him.

LAVINIA. Nothing but faith can save you.

FERROVIUS. Faith! Which faith? There are two faiths. There is our faith. And there is the warrior's faith, the faith in fighting, the faith that sees God in the sword. How if that faith should overwhelm me?

LAVINIA. You will find your real faith in the hour of trial.

FERROVIUS. That is what I fear. I know that I am a fighter. How can I feel sure that I am a Christian?

ANDROCLES AND THE LION

ANDROCLES. Throw away the sword, brother.

FERROVIUS. I cannot. It cleaves to my hand. I could as easily throw a woman I loved from my arms. [*Starting*] Who spoke that blasphemy? Not I.

LAVINIA. I cant help you, friend. I cant tell you not to save your own life. Something wilful in me wants to see you fight your way into heaven.

FERROVIUS. Ha!

ANDROCLES. But if you are going to give up our faith, brother, why not do it without hurting anybody? Dont fight them. Burn the incense.

FERROVIUS. Burn the incense! Never.

LAVINIA. This is only pride, Ferrovius.

FERROVIUS. Only pride! What is nobler than pride? [*Conscience stricken*] Oh, I'm steeped in sin. I'm proud of my pride.

LAVINIA. They say we Christians are the proudest devils on earth—that only the weak are meek. Oh, I am worse than you. I ought to send you to death; and I am tempting you.

ANDROCLES. Brother, brother: let them rage and kill: let us be brave and suffer. You must go as a lamb to the slaughter.

FERROVIUS. Aye, aye: that is right. Not as a lamb is slain by the butcher; but as a butcher might let himself be slain by a [*looking at the Editor*] by a silly ram whose head he could fetch off in one twist.

Before the Editor can retort, the Call Boy rushes up through the passage, and the Captain comes from the Emperor's box and descends the steps.

THE CALL BOY. In with you: into the arena. The stage is waiting.

THE CAPTAIN. The Emperor is waiting. [*To the Editor*] What are you dreaming of, man? Send your men in at once.

THE EDITOR. Yes, sir: it's these Christians hanging back.

FERROVIUS [*in a voice of thunder*] Liar!

THE EDITOR [*not heeding him*] March. [*The gladiators told off to fight with the Christians march down the passage*] Follow

882

ANDROCLES AND THE LION

up there, you.

THE CHRISTIAN MEN AND WOMEN [*as they part*] Be steadfast, brother. Farewell. Hold up the faith, brother. Farewell. Go to glory, dearest. Farewell. Remember: we are praying for you. Farewell. Be strong, brother. Farewell. Dont forget that the divine love and our love surround you. Farewell. Nothing can hurt you: remember that, brother. Farewell. Eternal glory, dearest. Farewell.

THE EDITOR [*out of patience*] Shove them in, there.

The remaining gladiators and the Call Boy make a movement towards them.

FERROVIUS [*interposing*] Touch them, dogs; and we die here, and cheat the heathen of their spectacle. [*To his fellow Christians*] Brothers: the great moment has come. That passage is your hill to Calvary. Mount it bravely, but meekly; and remember! not a word of reproach, not a blow nor a struggle. Go. [*They go out through the passage. He turns to Lavinia*] Farewell.

LAVINIA. You forget: I must follow before you are cold.

FERROVIUS. It is true. Do not envy me because I pass before you to glory. [*He goes through the passage*].

THE EDITOR [*to the Call Boy*] Sickening work, this. Why cant they all be thrown to the lions? It's not a man's job. [*He throws himself moodily into his chair*].

The remaining gladiators go back to their former places indifferently. The Call Boy shrugs his shoulders and squats down at the entrance to the passage, near the Editor.

Lavinia and the Christian women sit down again, wrung with grief, some weeping silently, some praying, some calm and steadfast. Androcles sits down at Lavinia's feet. The Captain stands on the stairs, watching her curiously

ANDROCLES. I'm glad I havnt to fight. That would really be an awful martyrdom. I am lucky.

LAVINIA [*looking at him with a pang of remorse*] Androcles: burn the incense: youll be forgiven. Let my death atone for both. I feel as if I were killing you.

ANDROCLES. Dont think of me, sister. Think of yourself.

That will keep your heart up.

The Captain laughs sardonically.

LAVINIA [*startled: she had forgotten his presence*] Are you there, handsome Captain? Have you come to see me die?

THE CAPTAIN [*coming to her side*] I am on duty with the Emperor, Lavinia.

LAVINIA. Is it part of your duty to laugh at us?

THE CAPTAIN. No: that is part of my private pleasure. Your friend here is a humorist. I laughed at his telling you to think of yourself to keep up your heart. *I* say, think of yourself and burn the incense.

LAVINIA. He is not a humorist: he was right. You ought to know that, Captain: you have been face to face with death.

THE CAPTAIN. Not with certain death, Lavinia. Only death in battle, which spares more men than death in bed. What you are facing is certain death. You have nothing left now but your faith in this craze of yours: this Christianity. Are your Christian fairy stories any truer than our stories about Jupiter and Diana, in which, I may tell you, I believe no more than the Emperor does, or any educated man in Rome?

LAVINIA. Captain: all that seems nothing to me now. I'll not say that death is a terrible thing; but I will say that it is so real a thing that when it comes close, all the imaginary things—all the stories, as you call them—fade into mere dreams beside that inexorable reality. I know now that I am not dying for stories or dreams. Did you hear of the dreadful thing that happened here while we were waiting?

THE CAPTAIN. I heard that one of your fellows bolted, and ran right into the jaws of the lion. I laughed. I still laugh.

LAVINIA. Then you dont understand what that meant?

THE CAPTAIN. It meant that the lion had a cur for his breakfast.

LAVINIA. It meant more than that, Captain. It meant that a man cannot die for a story and a dream. None of us believed the stories and the dreams more devoutly than poor Spintho; but he could not face the great reality. What he

884

would have called my faith has been oozing away minute by minute whilst Ive been sitting here, with death coming nearer and nearer, with reality become realler and realler, with stories and dreams fading away into nothing.

THE CAPTAIN. Are you then going to die for nothing?

LAVINIA. Yes: that is the wonderful thing. It is since all the stories and dreams have gone that I have now no doubt at all that I must die for something greater than dreams or stories.

THE CAPTAIN. But for what?

LAVINIA. I dont know. If it were for anything small enough to know, it would be too small to die for. I think I'm going to die for God. Nothing else is real enough to die for.

THE CAPTAIN. What is God?

LAVINIA. When we know that, Captain, we shall be gods ourselves.

THE CAPTAIN. Lavinia: come down to earth. Burn the incense and marry me.

LAVINIA. Handsome Captain: would you marry me if I hauled down the flag in the day of battle and burnt the incense? Sons take after their mothers, you know. Do you want your son to be a coward?

THE CAPTAIN [*strongly moved*] By great Diana, I think I would strangle you if you gave in now.

LAVINIA [*putting her hand on the head of Androcles*] The hand of God is on us three, Captain.

THE CAPTAIN. What nonsense it all is! And what a monstrous thing that you should die for such nonsense, and that I should look on helplessly when my whole soul cries out against it! Die then if you must; but at least I can cut the Emperor's throat and then my own when I see your blood.

The Emperor throws open the door of his box angrily, and appears in wrath on the threshold. The Editor, the Call Boy, and the gladiators spring to their feet.

THE EMPEROR. The Christians will not fight; and your curs cannot get their blood up to attack them. It's all that fellow with the blazing eyes. Send for the whip. [*The Call*

ANDROCLES AND THE LION

Boy rushes out on the east side for the whip]. If that will not move them, bring the hot irons. The man is like a mountain. [*He returns angrily into the box and slams the door*].

The Call Boy returns with a man in a hideous Etruscan mask, carrying a whip. They both rush down the passage into the arena.

LAVINIA [*rising*] Oh, that is unworthy. Can they not kill him without dishonoring him?

ANDROCLES [*scrambling to his feet and running into the middle of the space between the staircases*] It's dreadful. Now *I* want to fight. I cant bear the sight of a whip. The only time I ever hit a man was when he lashed an old horse with a whip. It was terrible: I danced on his face when he was on the ground. He mustnt strike Ferrovius: I'll go into the arena and kill him first. [*He makes a wild dash into the passage. As he does so a great clamor is heard from the arena, ending in wild applause. The gladiators listen and look inquiringly at one another*].

THE EDITOR. Whats up now?

LAVINIA [*to the Captain*] What has happened, do you think?

THE CAPTAIN. What can happen? They are killing them, I suppose.

ANDROCLES [*running in through the passage, screaming with horror and hiding his eyes*]!!!

LAVINIA. Androcles, Androcles: whats the matter?

ANDROCLES. Oh dont ask me, dont ask me. Something too dreadful. Oh! [*He crouches by her and hides his face in her robe, sobbing*].

THE CALL BOY [*rushing through from the passage as before*] Ropes and hooks there! Ropes and hooks!

THE EDITOR. Well, need you excite yourself about it? [*Another burst of applause*].

Two slaves in Etruscan masks, with ropes and drag hooks, hurry in.

ONE OF THE SLAVES. How many dead?

THE CALL BOY. Six. [*The slave blows a whistle twice; and four more masked slaves rush through into the arena with the same apparatus*] And the basket. Bring the baskets [*The slave whistles three times, and runs through the passage with his*
886

ANDROCLES AND THE LION

companion].

THE CAPTAIN. Who are the baskets for?

THE CALL BOY. For the whip. He's in pieces. Theyre all in pieces, more or less. [*Lavinia hides her face*].

Two more masked slaves come in with a basket and follow the others into the arena, as the Call Boy turns to the gladiators and exclaims, exhausted] Boys: he's killed the lot.

THE EMPEROR [*again bursting from his box, this time in an ecstasy of delight*] Where is he? Magnificent! He shall have a laurel crown.

Ferrovius, madly waving his bloodstained sword, rushes through the passage in despair, followed by his co-religionists, and by the menagerie keeper, who goes to the gladiators. The gladiators draw their swords nervously].

FERROVIUS. Lost! lost for ever! I have betrayed my Master. Cut off this right hand: it has offended. Ye have swords, my brethren: strike.

LAVINIA. No, no. What have you done, Ferrovius?

FERROVIUS. I know not; but there was blood behind my eyes; and theres blood on my sword. What does that mean?

THE EMPEROR [*enthusiastically, on the landing outside his box*] What does it mean? It means that you are the greatest man in Rome. It means that you shall have a laurel crown of gold. Superb fighter: I could almost yield you my throne. It is a record for my reign: I shall live in history. Once, in Domitian's time, a Gaul slew three men in the arena and gained his freedom. But when before has one naked man slain six armed men of the bravest and best? The persecution shall cease: if Christians can fight like this, I shall have none but Christians to fight for me. [*To the Gladiators*] You are ordered to become Christians, you there: do you hear?

RETIARIUS. It is all one to us, Caesar. Had I been there with my net, the story would have been different.

THE CAPTAIN [*suddenly seizing Lavinia by the wrist and dragging her up the steps to the Emperor*] Caesar: this woman is the sister of Ferrovius. If she is thrown to the lions he will fret. He will lose weight; get out of condition—

887

ANDROCLES AND THE LION

THE EMPEROR. The lions? Nonsense! [*To Lavinia*] Madam: I am proud to have the honor of making your acquaintance. Your brother is the glory of Rome.

LAVINIA. But my friends here. Must they die?

THE EMPEROR. Die! Certainly not. There has never been the slightest idea of harming them. Ladies and gentlemen: you are all free. Pray go into the front of the house and enjoy the spectacle to which your brother has so splendidly contributed. Captain: oblige me by conducting them to the seats reserved for my personal friends.

THE MENAGERIE KEEPER. Caesar: I must have one Christian for the lion. The people have been promised it; and they will tear the decorations to bits if they are disappointed.

THE EMPEROR. True, true: we must have somebody for the new lion.

FERROVIUS. Throw me to him. Let the apostate perish.

THE EMPEROR. No, no: you would tear him in pieces, my friend; and we cannot afford to throw away lions as if they were mere slaves. But we must have somebody. This is really extremely awkward.

THE MENAGERIE KEEPER. Why not that little Greek chap? He's not a Christian: he's a sorcerer.

THE EMPEROR. The very thing: he will do very well.

THE CALL BOY [*issuing from the passage*] Number twelve. The Christian for the new lion.

ANDROCLES [*rising, and pulling himself sadly together*] Well, it was to be, after all.

LAVINIA. I'll go in his place, Caesar. Ask the Captain whether they do not like best to see a woman torn to pieces. He told me so yesterday.

THE EMPEROR. There is something in that: there is certainly something in that—if only I could feel sure that your brother would not fret.

ANDROCLES. No: I should never have another happy hour. No: on the faith of a Christian and the honor of a tailor, I accept the lot that has fallen on me. If my wife turns up, give her my love and say that my wish was that she should be

888

happy with her next, poor fellow! Caesar: go to your box
and see how a tailor can die. Make way for number twelve
there. [*He marches out along the passage*].

*The vast audience in the amphitheatre now sees the Emperor
re-enter his box and take his place as Androcles, desperately
frightened, but still marching with piteous devotion, emerges
from the other end of the passage, and finds himself at the focus of
thousands of eager eyes. The lion's cage, with a heavy portcullis
grating, is on his left. The Emperor gives a signal. A gong sounds.
Androcles shivers at the sound; then falls on his knees and prays.
The grating rises with a clash. The lion bounds into the arena.
He rushes round frisking in his freedom. He sees Androcles. He
stops; rises stiffly by straightening his legs; stretches out his nose
forward and his tail in a horizontal line behind, like a pointer,
and utters an appalling roar. Androcles crouches and hides his
face in his hands. The lion gathers himself for a spring, swishing
his tail to and fro through the dust in an ecstasy of anticipation.
Androcles throws up his hands in supplication to heaven. The
lion checks at the sight of Androcles's face. He then steals towards
him; smells him; arches his back; purrs like a motor car; finally
rubs himself against Androcles, knocking him over. Androcles,
supporting himself on his wrist, looks affrightedly at the lion. The
lion limps on three paws, holding up the other as if it was wounded.
A flash of recognition lights up the face of Androcles. He flaps his
hand as if it had a thorn in it, and pretends to pull the thorn out
and to hurt himself. The lion nods repeatedly. Androcles holds
out his hands to the lion, who gives him both paws, which he
shakes with enthusiasm. They embrace rapturously, finally waltz
round the arena amid a sudden burst of deafening applause,
and out through the passage, the Emperor watching them in
breathless astonishment until they disappear, when he rushes
from his box and descends the steps in frantic excitement.*

THE EMPEROR. My friends, an incredible! an amazing
thing! has happened. I can no longer doubt the truth of
Christianity. [*The Christians press to him joyfully*]. This Christian sorcerer—[*with a yell, he breaks off as he sees Androcles
and the lion emerge from the passage, waltzing. He bolts wildly*

up the steps into his box, and slams the door. All, Christians and gladiators alike, fly for their lives, the gladiators bolting into the arena, the others in all directions. The place is emptied with magical suddenness].

ANDROCLES [*naïvely*] Now I wonder why they all run away from us like that. [*The lion, combining a series of yawns, purrs, and roars, achieves something very like a laugh.*]

THE EMPEROR [*standing on a chair inside his box and looking over the wall*] Sorcerer: I command you to put that lion to death instantly. It is guilty of high treason. Your conduct is most disgra—[*the lion charges at him up the stairs*] Help! [*He disappears. The lion rears against the box; looks over the partition at him; and roars. The Emperor darts out through the door and down to Androcles, pursued by the lion.*]

ANDROCLES. Dont run away, sir: he cant help springing if you run. [*He seizes the Emperor and gets between him and the lion, who stops at once*]. Dont be afraid of him.

THE EMPEROR. I am n o t afraid of him. [*The lion crouches, growling. The Emperor clutches Androcles*]. Keep between us.

ANDROCLES. Never be afraid of animals, your worship: thats the great secret. He'll be as gentle as a lamb when he knows that you are his friend. Stand quite still; and smile; and let him smell you all over just to reassure him; for, you see, he's afraid of you; and he must examine you thoroughly before he gives you his confidence. [*To the lion*] Come now, Tommy; and speak nicely to the Emperor, the great good Emperor who has power to have all our heads cut off if we dont behave very very respectfully to him.

The lion utters a fearful roar. The Emperor dashes madly up the steps, across the landing, and down again on the other side, with the lion in hot pursuit. Androcles rushes after the lion; overtakes him as he is descending; and throws himself on his back, trying to use his toes as a brake. Before he can stop him the lion gets hold of the trailing end of the Emperor's robe.

ANDROCLES. Oh bad wicked Tommy, to chase the Emperor like that! Let go the Emperor's robe at once, sir: wheres your manners? [*The lion growls and worries the robe*].

ANDROCLES AND THE LION

Dont pull it away from him, your worship. He's only play.. ing. Now I shall be really angry with you, Tommy, if you dont let go. [*The lion growls again*]. I'll tell you what it is, sir: he thinks you and I are not friends.

THE EMPEROR [*trying to undo the clasp of his brooch*] Friends! You infernal scoundrel [*the lion growls*]—dont let him go. Curse this brooch! I cant get it loose.

ANDROCLES. We mustnt let him lash himself into a rage. You must shew him that you are my particular friend—if you will have the condescension. [*He seizes the Emperor's hands and shakes them cordially*]. Look, Tommy: the nice Emperor is the dearest friend Andy Wandy has in the whole world: he loves him like a brother.

THE EMPEROR. You little brute, you damned filthy little dog of a Greek tailor: I'll have you burnt alive for daring to touch the divine person of the Emperor. [*The lion growls*].

ANDROCLES. Oh dont talk like that, sir. He understands every word you say: all animals do: they take it from the tone of your voice. [*The lion growls and lashes his tail*]. I think he's going to spring at your worship. If you wouldnt mind saying something affectionate. [*The lion roars*].

THE EMPEROR [*shaking Androcles's hands frantically*] My dearest Mr Androcles, my sweetest friend, my long lost brother, come to my arms. [*He embraces Androcles*]. Oh, what an abominable smell of garlic!

The lion lets go the robe and rolls over on his back, clasping his forepaws over one another coquettishly above his nose.

ANDROCLES. There! You see, your worship, a child might play with him now. See! [*He tickles the lion's belly. The lion wriggles ecstatically*]. Come and pet him.

THE EMPEROR. I must conquer these unkingly terrors. Mind you dont go away from him, though. [*He pats the lion's chest*].

ANDROCLES. Oh, sir, how few men would have the courage to do that!

THE EMPEROR. Yes: it takes a bit of nerve. Let us have the Court in and frighten them. Is he safe, do you think?

891

ANDROCLES AND THE LION

ANDROCLES. Quite safe now, sir.

THE EMPEROR [*majestically*] What ho, there! All who are within hearing, return without fear. Caesar has tamed the lion. [*All the fugitives steal cautiously in. The menagerie keeper comes from the passage with other keepers armed with iron bars and tridents*]. Take those things away. I have subdued the beast. [*He places his foot on it*].

FERROVIUS [*timidly approaching the Emperor and looking down with awe on the lion*] It is strange that I, who fear no man, should fear a lion.

THE CAPTAIN. Every man fears something, Ferrovius.

THE EMPEROR. How about the Pretorian Guard now?

FERROVIUS. In my youth I worshipped Mars, the God of War. I turned from him to serve the Christian god; but to-day the Christian god forsook me; and Mars overcame me and took back his own. The Christian god is not yet. He will come when Mars and I are dust; but meanwhile I must serve the gods that are, not the God that will be. Until then I accept service in the Guard, Caesar.

THE EMPEROR. Very wisely said. All really sensible men agree that the prudent course is to be neither bigoted in our attachment to the old nor rash and unpractical in keeping an open mind for the new, but to make the best of both dispensations.

THE CAPTAIN. What do you say, Lavinia? Will you too be prudent?

LAVINIA [*on the stairs*] No: I'll strive for the coming of the God who is not yet.

THE CAPTAIN. May I come and argue with you occasionally?

LAVINIA. Yes, handsome Captain: you may. [*He kisses her hand*].

THE EMPEROR. And now, my friends, though I do not, as you see, fear this lion, yet the strain of his presence is considerable; for none of us can feel quite sure what he will do next.

THE MENAGERIE KEEPER. Caesar: give us this Greek sorcerer to be a slave in the menagerie. He has a way with the beasts.

ANDROCLES [*distressed*] Not if they are in cages. They should not be kept in cages. They must be all let out.

THE EMPEROR. I give this sorcerer to be a slave to the first man who lays hands on him. [*The menagerie keepers and the gladiators rush for Androcles. The lion starts up and faces them. They surge back*]. You see how magnanimous we Romans are, Androcles. We suffer you to go in peace.

ANDROCLES. I thank your worship. I thank you all, ladies and gentlemen. Come, Tommy. Whilst we stand together, no cage for you: no slavery for me. [*He goes out with the lion, everybody crowding away to give him as wide a berth as possible*].

* * * * * *

In this play I have presented one of the Roman persecutions of the early Christians, not as the conflict of a false theology with a true, but as what all such persecutions essentially are: an attempt to suppress a propaganda that seemed to threaten the interests involved in the established law and order, organized and maintained in the name of religion and justice by politicians who are pure opportunist Have-and-Holders. People who are shewn by their inner light the possibility of a better world based on the demand of the spirit for a nobler and more abundant life, not for themselves at the expense of others, but for everybody, are naturally dreaded and therefore hated by the Have-and-Holders, who keep always in reserve two sure weapons against them. The first is a persecution effected by the provocation, organization, and arming of that herd instinct which makes men abhor all departures from custom, and, by the most cruel punishments and the wildest calumnies, force eccentric people to behave and profess exactly as other people do. The second is by leading the herd to war, which immediately and infallibly makes them forget everything, even their most cherished and hard won public liberties and private interests, in the irresistible surge of their pugnacity and the tense preoccupation of their terror.

There is no reason to believe that there was anything more in the Roman persecutions than this. The attitude of the Roman Emperor and the officers of his staff towards the opinions at issue were much the same as those of a modern British Home Secretary towards members of the lower middle classes when some pious policeman charges them with Bad Taste, technically called blasphemy: Bad Taste being a violation of Good Taste, which in such matters practically means Hypocrisy. The Home Secretary and the judges who try the case are usually far more sceptical and blasphemous than the poor men whom they persecute; and their professions of horror at the blunt utterance of their own opinions are revolting to those behind the scenes who have any genuine religious sensibility; but the thing is done because the governing classes, provided only the law against blasphemy is not applied to themselves, strongly approve of such persecution because it enables them to represent their own privileges as part of the religion of the country.

Therefore my martyrs are the martyrs of all time, and my persecutors the persecutors of all time. My Emperor, who has no sense of the value of common people's lives, and amuses himself with killing as carelessly as with sparing, is the sort of monster you can make of any silly-clever gentleman by idolizing him. We are still so easily imposed on by such idols that one of the leading pastors of the Free Churches in London denounced my play on the ground that my persecuting Emperor is a very fine fellow, and the persecuted Christians ridiculous. From which I conclude that a popular pulpit may be as perilous to a man's soul as an imperial throne.

All my articulate Christians, the reader will notice, have different enthusiasms, which they accept as the same religion only because it involves them in a common opposition to the official religion and consequently in a common doom. Androcles is a humanitarian naturalist, whose views surprise everybody. Lavinia, a clever and fearless freethinker, shocks the Pauline Ferrovius, who is comparatively stupid and

894

conscience ridden. Spintho, the blackguardly debauchee, is presented as one of the typical Christians of that period on the authority of St Augustine, who seems to have come to the conclusion at one period of his development that most Christians were what we call wrong uns. No doubt he was to some extent right: I have had occasion often to point out that revolutionary movements attract those who are not good enough for established institutions as well as those who are too good for them.

But the most striking aspect of the play at this moment is the terrible topicality given it by the war. We were at peace when I pointed out, by the mouth of Ferrovius, the path of an honest man who finds out, when the trumpet sounds, that he cannot follow Jesus. Many years earlier, in The Devil's Disciple, I touched the same theme even more definitely, and shewed the minister throwing off his black coat for ever when he discovered, amid the thunder of the captains and the shouting, that he was a born fighter. Great numbers of our clergy have found themselves of late in the position of Ferrovius and Anthony Anderson. They have discovered that they hate not only their enemies but everyone who does not share their hatred, and that they want to fight and to force other people to fight. They have turned their churches into recruiting stations and their vestries into munition workshops. But it has never occurred to them to take off their black coats and say quite simply, "I find in the hour of trial that the Sermon on the Mount is tosh, and that I am not a Christian. I apologize for all the unpatriotic nonsense I have been preaching all these years. Have the goodness to give me a revolver and a commission in a regiment which has for its chaplain a priest of the god Mars: *my* God." Not a bit of it. They have stuck to their livings and served Mars in the name of Christ, to the scandal of all religious mankind. When the Archbishop of York behaved like a gentleman and the Head Master of Eton preached a Christian sermon, and were reviled by the rabble, the Martian parsons encouraged the rabble. For this they made no apo-

Iogies or excuses, good or bad. They simply indulged their passions, just as they had always indulged their class prejudices and commercial interests, without troubling themselves for a moment as to whether they were Christians or not. They did not protest even when a body calling itself the Anti-German League (not having noticed, apparently, that it had been anticipated by the British Empire, the French Republic, and the Kingdoms of Italy, Japan, and Serbia) actually succeeded in closing a church at Forest Hill in which God was worshiped in the German language. One would have supposed that this grotesque outrage on the commonest decencies of religion would have provoked a remonstrance from even the worldliest bench of bishops. But no: apparently it seemed to the bishops as natural that the House of God should be looted when He allowed German to be spoken in it as that a baker's shop with a German name over the door should be pillaged. Their verdict was, in effect, "Serve God right, for creating the Germans!" The incident would have been impossible in a country where the Church was as powerful as the Church of England, had it had at the same time a spark of catholic as distinguished from tribal religion in it. As it is, the thing occurred; and as far as I have observed, the only people who gasped were the Freethinkers.

Thus we see that even among men who make a profession of religion the great majority are as Martian as the majority of their congregations. The average clergyman is an official who makes his living by christening babies, marrying adults, conducting a ritual, and making the best he can (when he has any conscience about it) of a certain routine of school superintendence, district visiting, and organization of almsgiving, which does not necessarily touch Christianity at any point except the point of the tongue. The exceptional or religious clergyman may be an ardent Pauline salvationist, in which case his more cultivated parishioners dislike him, and say that he ought to have joined the Methodists. Or he may be an artist expressing religious emotion without intellectual definition by means of poetry, music, vestments, and architecture, also producing religious ecstasy by physical expedients, such as fasts and vigils, in which case he is denounced as a Ritualist. Or he may be either a Unitarian Deist like Voltaire or Tom Paine, or the more modern sort of Anglican Theosophist to whom the Holy Ghost is the Élan Vital of Bergson, and the Father and Son are an expression of the fact that our functions and aspects are manifold, and that we are all sons and all either potential or actual parents, in which case he is strongly suspected by the straiter Salvationists of being little better than an Atheist. All these varieties, you see, excite remark. They may be very popular with their congregations; but they are regarded by the average man as the freaks of the Church. The Church, like the society of which it is an organ, is balanced and steadied by the great central Philistine mass above whom theology looms as a highly spoken of and doubtless most important thing, like Greek Tragedy, or classical music, or the higher mathematics, but who are very glad when church is over and they can go home to lunch or dinner, having in fact, for all practical purposes, no reasoned convictions at all, and being equally ready to persecute a poor Freethinker for saying that St James was not infallible, and to send one of the Peculiar People to prison for being so very peculiar as to take St James seriously.

In short, a Christian martyr was thrown to the lions not because he was a Christian, but because he was a crank: that is, an unusual sort of person. And multitudes of people, quite as civilized and amiable as we, crowded to see the lions eat him just as they now crowd the lion-house in the Zoo at feeding-time, not because they really cared twopence about Diana or Christ, or could have given you any intelligent or correct account of the things Diana and Christ stood against one another for, but simply because they wanted to see a curious and exciting spectacle. You, dear reader, have probably run to see a fire; and if somebody came in now and told you that a lion was chasing a man down the street you would rush to

897

the window. And if anyone were to say that you were as cruel as the people who let the lion loose on the man, you would be justly indignant. Now that we may no longer see a man hanged, we assemble outside the jail to see the black flag run up. That is our duller method of enjoying ourselves in the old Roman spirit. And if the Government decided to throw persons of unpopular or eccentric views to the lions in the Albert Hall or the Earl's Court stadium tomorrow, can you doubt that all the seats would be crammed, mostly by people who could not give you the most superficial account of the views in question. Much less unlikely things have happened. It is true that if such a revival does take place soon, the martyrs will not be members of heretical religious sects: they will be Peculiars, Anti-Vivisectionists, Flat-Earth men, scoffers at the laboratories, or infidels who refuse to kneel down when a procession of doctors goes by. But the lions will hurt them just as much, and the spectators will enjoy themselves just as much, as the Roman lions and spectators used to do.

It was currently reported in the Berlin newspapers that when Androcles was first performed in Berlin, the Crown Prince rose and left the house, unable to endure the (I hope) very clear and fair exposition of autocratic Imperialism given by the Roman captain to his Christian prisoners. No English Imperialist was intelligent and earnest enough to do the same in London. If the report is correct, I confirm the logic of the Crown Prince, and am glad to find myself so well understood. But I can assure him that the Empire which served for my model when I wrote Androcles was, as he is now finding to his cost, much nearer my home than the German one.